Arguing About Knowledge

Arguing About Knowledge is a fresh and engaging introduction to the core questions in the theory of knowledge. This comprehensive and imaginative selection of readings examines the subject in an unorthodox and entertaining manner whilst covering the fundamentals of epistemology. It includes classic and contemporary pieces from the most influential philosophers from Descartes, Russell, Quine and G. E. Moore to Richard Feldman, Edward Craig, Gilbert Harman and Roderick Chisholm. In addition students will find fascinating alternative pieces from literary and popular work such as Lewis Caroll and Jorge Luis Borges.

The volume breaks down the subject into ten key questions, helping the new student to get to grips with the central issues in epistemology, including:

- What is knowledge?
- What is the value of knowledge?
- What evidence do we have?
- What are the sources of knowledge?
- What can we know?

Each article selected is clear, interesting and free from unnecessary jargon. The editors provide lucid introductions to each section in which they give an overview of the debate and outline the arguments of the papers. *Arguing About Knowledge* is an inventive and stimulating reader for students new to the theory of knowledge.

Ram Neta is Associate Professor of Philosophy at the University of North Carolina at Chapel Hill, USA.

Duncan Pritchard is Professor of Philosophy at the University of Edinburgh, UK. He is the author of *What Is This Thing Called Knowledge?* (Routledge, 2006).

Arguing About Philosophy

This exciting and lively series introduces key subjects in philosophy with the help of a vibrant set of readings. In contrast to many standard anthologies which often reprint the same technical and remote extracts, each volume in the *Arguing About Philosophy* series is built around essential but fresher philosophical readings, designed to attract the curiosity of students coming to the subject for the first time. A key feature of the series is the inclusion of well-known yet often neglected readings from related fields, such as popular science, film and fiction. Each volume is edited by leading figures in their chosen field and each section carefully introduced and set in context, making the series an exciting starting point for those looking to get to grips with philosophy.

Arguing About Knowledge
Edited by Ram Neta and Duncan Pritchard

Arguing About Law
Edited by John Oberdiek and Aileen Kanvanagh

Arguing About Metaethics
Edited by Andrew Fisher and Simon Kirchin

Arguing About the Mind
Edited by Brie Gertler and Lawrence Shapiro

Arguing About Art 3rd Edition
Edited by Alex Neill and Aaron Ridley

Forthcoming titles:
Arguing About Language
Edited by Darragh Byrne and Max Kolbel

Arguing About Metaphysics
Edited by Michael Rea

Arguing About Political Philosophy
Edited by Matt Zwolinski

Arguing About Religion
Edited by Kevin Timpe

Arguing About Knowledge

Edited by

Ram Neta and Duncan Pritchard

Routledge
Taylor & Francis Group

LONDON AND NEW YORK

First published 2009
by Routledge
2 Park Square, Milton Park, Abingdon, Oxon OX14 4RN

Simultaneously published in the USA and Canada
by Routledge
711 Third Avenue, New York, NY 10017, USA

Routledge is an imprint of the Taylor & Francis Group, an informa business

Typeset in Joanna and Bell Gothic by
RefineCatch Limited, Bungay, Suffolk

British Library Cataloguing in Publication Data
A catalogue record for this book is available from the British Library

Library of Congress Cataloging-in-Publication Data
Arguing about knowledge / edited by Duncan Pritchard and Ram Neta.
     p. cm. – (Arguing about philosophy)
  Includes bibliographical references and index.
  1. Knowledge, Theory of.   I. Pritchard, Duncan.   II. Neta, Ram.
  BD161.A64 2008
  121 – dc22

2008036299

ISBN 10: 0–415–44838–7 (hbk)
ISBN 10: 0–415–44839–5 (pbk)

ISBN 13: 978–0–415–44838–3 (hbk)
ISBN 13: 978–0–415–44839–0 (pbk)

Contents

Acknowledgements

The following were reproduced with kind permission. Any omissions brought to our attention will be remedied in future editions.

Part one: What is knowledge?

A. J. Ayer, *The Problem of Knowledge*, 31–5, London: Macmillan, 1956.

Edmund Gettier, 'Is Justified True Belief Knowledge?', *Analysis* 23, 121–3 (1963).

Keith Lehrer, 'Knowledge, Truth and Evidence', *Analysis* 25, 168–75 (1965).

'Knowledge' reprinted by permission of the publisher from *Philosophical Explanations* by Robert Nozick, pp.167–96, Cambridge, MA.: The Belknap Press of Harvard University Press, Copyright © 1981 by Robert Nozick.

Part two: What is the value of knowledge?

Protagoras and Meno by Plato, translated by W. K. C. Guthrie (Penguin Classics, 1956). Copyright © W. K. C. Guthrie, 1956. Reproduced by permission of Penguin Books Ltd.

Jonathan Kvanvig, chapter 1, *The Value of Knowledge and the Pursuit of Understanding*, 2003, © Jonathan L. Kvanvig, published by Cambridge University Press, reproduced with permission.

Linda Zagzebski, 'The Search for the Source of Epistemic Good', *Metaphilosophy* 34, 12–28 (2003); and reprinted in D. H. Pritchard and M. S. Brady (eds) *Moral and Epistemic Virtues*, Oxford: Blackwell, 2003. Reproduced with permission of Wiley-Blackwell Publishing Ltd.

John Greco, 'The Value Problem', in *Epistemic Value*, eds A. Haddock, A. Millar and D. H. Pritchard, Oxford: Oxford University Press, forthcoming.

Part three: What evidence do we have?

Roderick Chisholm, '"Appear," "Take," and "Evident"', *Journal of Philosophy* 53(23), 722–31 (1956). Reprinted with permission.

Roderick Firth, 'Ultimate Evidence', *Journal of Philosophy* 53(23), 732–9 (1956). Reprinted with permission.

'Posits and Reality' reprinted by permission of the publisher from *The Ways of Paradox and Other Essays* by W. V. Quine, pp.246–54, Cambridge, MA.: Harvard University Press, Copyright © 1966, 1976 by the President and Fellows of Harvard College.

Richard Feldman, 'Having Evidence', in E. Conee and R. Feldman, *Evidentialism*, chapter 9, 219–41, Oxford: Oxford University Press, 2004.

Part four: How should we distribute our confidence?

Mark Kaplan, *Decision Theory as Philosophy*, 1–23, 1996/1998, © Cambridge University Press, reproduced with permission.

Adam Elga, 'Self-Locating Belief and the Sleeping Beauty Problem', *Analysis* 60(2), 143–7 (2000).

Paul Hoffman, *The Man Who Loved Numbers*, 233–6, London: Fourth Estate, 1998.

Part five: What is it to be justified in believing something?

Springer/Reidel, *Justification and Knowledge*, 1979, ed. George Pappas, 'What is Justified Belief?', 1–23, Alvin Goldman, copyright 1979, D. Reidel Publishing Company, with kind permission from Springer Science Business Media.

Springer, *Philosophical Studies* 48, 1985, 'Evidentialism', 15–34, Earl Conee & Richard Feldman. Reproduced with kind permission from Springer Science Business Media.

Springer, *Synthese* 74, 1988, 'An Internalist Externalism', 265–83, William Alston, copyright 1988 by Kluwer Academic Publishers. Reprinted by permission of Kluwer Academic Publishers, with kind permission from Springer Science Business Media.

Lewis Carroll, 'What the Tortoise Said to Achilles', *Mind* 4, 278–80 (1895).

Part six: What is the structure of justification and knowledge?

Laurence BonJour, 'Can Empirical Knowledge Have a Foundation?' *American Philosophical Quarterly* 15(1), 1–13 (1978). Reprinted with permission.

Laurence BonJour, 'Toward a Defense of Empirical Foundationalism', in *Resurrecting Old-Fashioned Foundationalism*, ed. M. DePaul, 21–38, Lanham, NJ: Rowman and Littlefield. Reprinted with permission.

Peter Klein, 'Human Knowledge and the Infinite Regress of Reasons', *Philosophical Perspectives* 13, 297–325 (1999). Reproduced with permission of Wiley-Blackwell Publishing Ltd.

Ernest Sosa, 'The Raft and the Pyramid: Coherence versus Foundations in the Theory of Knowledge', in *Midwest Studies in Philosophy*, Volume V: *Studies in Epistemology*, ed. P. A. French, T. E. Uehling Jr and H. K. Wettstein, Minneapolis, MN: University of Minnesota Press, 1980. Reprinted with permission.

Part seven: What is the nature of the epistemic 'ought'?

W. K. Clifford, 'The Ethics of Belief', *Contemporary Review* (1877).

William James, 'The Will to Believe', from his *The Will to Believe and Other Essays in Popular Philosophy*, New York: Dover Publications, 1956.

Reprinted 'Epistemic terms', from Roderick Chisholm; *Perceiving: A Philosophical Study*, 3–21. Copyright © 1957 Cornell University. Renewed copyright © 1985 by Roderick Chisholm. Used by permission of the publisher, Cornell University Press.

'The Deontological Conception of Epistemic Justification' by William Alston, appeared in *Philosophical Perspectives*, 2, *Epistemology*, 1988, 115–52, edited by James E. Tomberline (copyright by Ridgeview Publishing Co., Atascadero, CA). Reprinted by permission of Ridgeview Publishing Company.

Richard Fumerton, 'Epistemic Justification and Normativity', in *Knowledge, Truth, and Duty*, 49–60, ed. M. Steup, Oxford: Oxford University Press, 2001.

Edward Craig, *Knowledge and the State of Nature*, chapters 1–2, 1–17, Oxford: Clarendon Press, 1990.

Part eight: What are the sources of knowledge?

Bertrand Russell, 'On Induction', from his *The Problems of Philosophy*, 93–108, London: Williams and Norgate, 1912.

Robert Audi, 'The Place of Testimony in the Fabric of Knowledge and Justification', *American Philosophical Quarterly* 34(4), 405–22 (1997). Reprinted with permission.

Roderick Chisholm, 'The A Priori', chapter 4 of *Theory of Knowledge*, Third Edition, 26–38, Englewood Cliffs, NJ: Prentice Hall, 1989.

William Alston, 'Perceptual Knowledge', *Epistemology*, ed. J. Greco and E. Sosa, 223–42, Oxford: Blackwell, 1999.

Part nine: What can we know?

Jorge Luis Borges, 'The Circular Ruins', in *Collected Fictions*, tr. A. Hurley, London: Penguin, 1998.

'The Circular Ruins', from *Collected Fictions* by Jorge Luis Borges, translated by Andrew Hurley, copyright © 1988 by Maria Kodama; translation copyright © 1998 by Penguin Putnam Inc. Used by permission of Viking Penguin, a division of Penguin Group (USA) Inc.

The Problem of the Criterion by Roderick M. Chisholm. First published by Marquette University Press, Milwaukee, Wisconsin, USA. Copyright © 1973 by Marquette University Press. Reprinted with permission.

René Descartes, 'Meditation One', *Meditations on First Philosophy*, tr. Cottingham, Stoothoff and Murdoch, 1984, © Cambridge University Press, reproduced with permission.

O. K. Bouwsma, 'Descartes' Evil Genius', in *The Philosophical Review*, Volume 58, no. 2, pp. 141–51. Copyright, 1949, Cornell University Press. All rights reserved. Used by permission of the current publisher, Duke University Press.

'Certainty', G. E. Moore, reprinted in his *Philosophical Papers*, 223–46, Copyright © 1959 London: Allen & Unwin. Reproduced by permission of Taylor & Francis Books UK.

Peter Unger, 'An Argument for Skepticism', *Philosophical Exchange* 1, 1–10 (1974). Reprinted with permission.

David Lewis, 'Elusive Knowledge', *Australasian Journal of Philosophy* 74, 549–67 (1996), Taylor & Francis Ltd (http://www.informaworld.com, reprinted by permission of the publisher).

Part ten: Is knowledge in the eye of the beholder?

Luigi Pirandello, 'Right You Are (If You Think You Are)', tr. Stanley Appelbaum, London: Dover, 1997.

Peter Winch, 'Understanding a Primitive Society', *American Philosophical Quarterly* 1(4), 307–24 (1964). Reprinted with permission.

Paul Boghossian, 'What the Sokal Hoax Ought to Teach Us', *Times Literary Supplement* (13 December, 1996, 14–15).

Michael Williams, 'Why (Wittgensteinian) Contextualism is Not Relativism', *Episteme: A Journal of Social Epistemology* 4(1), 93–114 (2007) reprinted by permission of Edinburgh University Press, www.eup.ed.ac.uk.

GENERAL INTRODUCTION

Ram Neta and Duncan Pritchard*

THE THEORY OF KNOWLEDGE – otherwise known as *epistemology* – has been a central part of philosophy since the birth of the subject in ancient Greece. A starting-point in philosophical discussion of knowledge has always been its tremendous importance to us; as Aristotle famously declares in the opening sentence of his *Metaphysics,* 'all men by nature desire to know'. This starting-point gives the theory of knowledge its point and also directly leads to a number of other questions. The most immediate is why knowledge is so important to us; whether we are right to accord it such a status. In order to answer this question, it would help to know what knowledge is; what it is to possess knowledge. But a number of plausible thoughts about what knowledge is may lead us to raise the sceptical question of whether we really have any of this (putatively) valuable commodity. Could it be that our wide-spread conviction that we possess a great deal of knowledge is simply an illusion?

The readings in this collection address all of these questions, and many other related ones. For example, presumably whether one has knowledge is closely related to the quality and quantity of the evidence that one has. But what is it for one to *have evidence*? Again, whether one has knowledge that something is the case is closely related to whether it is rational for one to be confident that it is the case. But under what conditions is it rational for one to be confident that something is the case? Questions about the nature of knowledge thus immediately raise further epistemo-logical questions: about evidence, about rational confidence, about the justification of belief, about what one ought to believe, and so on. These questions are, of course, all interconnected. For example, on certain views of what knowledge is, it will be some-thing that is very difficult to acquire. On these views, then, one will find the sceptical challenge of demonstrating that we have lots of knowledge particularly pressing.

This volume has been structured around ten epistemological questions, with a selection of readings for each question and an introductory section which is intended to provide the stage-setting for the readings that follow. What we have tried to do here is not to supply a comprehensive list of readings for all the epistemological questions that one might reasonably ask, but rather to pick out some of the central questions along with a selection of additional questions that we think are very important but not sufficiently well addressed in other current introductions to epistemology. Through-out, we have chosen readings with a mind to both the classic papers in that specific field of epistemology and also some more popular writings that, we hope, will offer a vivid sense of how questions within that field can arise even outside professional philosophy. We hope that the resulting anthology can help students with little or no background in epistemology want to learn more about the subject.

---

* The running order of the editors' names here and elsewhere in the book is purely alphabetical.

PART ONE

What is knowledge?

INTRODUCTION TO PART ONE

Ram Neta and Duncan Pritchard

CLEARLY, THE ISSUE OF WHAT KNOWLEDGE IS – i.e. how best to define this notion – is central to the theory of knowledge (epistemology). Until relatively recently, it was generally thought that knowledge could be 'decomposed' into three conditions (this is why the classical account of knowledge was known as the 'tripartite' account of knowledge).

The first condition is the *truth condition* and it demands that if you know a proposition then that proposition must be true. This condition captures the key element of knowledge that knowledge involves being *right*. Of course, one might think that one knows a proposition and yet that proposition turns out to be false – i.e. one turned out to be wrong after all – but this just shows that one didn't *really* know that proposition at all.

The second condition is the *belief condition* and it demands that if you know a proposition then you believe that proposition. This condition captures a second key element of knowledge, which is that it is *you* who is getting things right – it is, after all, you who is believing a true proposition.

These first two conditions are relatively straightforward, and most epistemologists even today agree that knowledge has these conditions. By themselves, however, they are insufficient for knowledge. After all, one could come to believe a true proposition purely by luck. Imagine, for example, that you form a belief that you will win the lottery in this week's draw purely on the basis of wishful thinking. Suppose, further, that this belief turns out to be true, such that you do indeed win the lottery. Did you *know* that you were going to win? Surely not, since it was just a matter of luck that your belief was true. In contrast, suppose you form the belief that you are going to win the lottery in this week's draw on the basis that you have fixed the lottery to ensure that you win. In such a case you surely did know that you were going to win. What, then, is it that marks the difference between the two cases?

According to the tripartite account of knowledge, the difference is that in the second case, but not the first, your true belief is *justified*. There are various different accounts of what such justification might involve, but the general idea is that when one is justified in believing a proposition this is because one is able to offer good grounds in favour of what one believes. This, then, is the third condition – known as the *justification condition* – that the tripartite account lays down for knowledge.

We include an example of a tripartite account of knowledge in the readings for this section, due to A. J. Ayer (1910–89) (Chapter 1), to give you a flavour of the view. Rather than talk of belief in the target proposition, he talks of 'being sure' that the proposition is true, and rather than talk of having a justification for one's belief in the target proposition, he talks of 'having a right to be sure' that the proposition is true. The basic point is the same, however, in that what is required for knowledge on this view is that one has a true belief and that one is in addition able to offer adequate grounds in favour of what one believes (i.e. what one is sure of).

By incorporating the justification condition, the tripartite account of knowledge is able to deal with the cases just mentioned. In the first case, for example – where one's belief is based on wishful thinking – one clearly lacks good reason for what one believes, since one cannot acquire such reasons in this way. One thus lacks justification and hence it is no surprise on this view that one also lacks knowledge. In contrast, in the second case one clearly does have good grounds in favour of one's belief – one knows that one has fixed the lottery draw in one's favour after all – and hence one's belief is justified and thus, since it is also true, it is a case of knowledge. There is therefore good reason to suppose that knowledge just is justified true belief, just as the tripartite account of knowledge predicts.

In an extremely short and seminal article, however – which is reprinted in this section – Edmund Gettier (1927–) (Chapter 2) conclusively demonstrated that the tripartite account of knowledge, despite its strong *prima facie* plausibility, was completely unsustainable, at least in its current form. What Gettier noticed was that it is part and parcel of the tripartite account of justification to allow that one's belief can be justified even if one's belief is false. This is entirely in accordance with intuition, since one might well have good reason to believe a proposition even if that proposition is false (as when one is deceived by a temporary trick of the light, for example). Given this feature of justification, however, Gettier realised that it was relatively easy to construct counterexamples to the tripartite account of knowledge.

These examples have a general two-part structure. First, you take a belief which, while justified in the relevant sense (i.e. supported by good reasons), would ordinarily be such that it would, in those circumstances, have been false. Second, you add a twist to the case such that the belief is true anyway, though for reasons that are completely unconnected with the agent's justification.

Consider the following example that Gettier offers. Suppose that our hero, Smith, has applied for a job but has good grounds for believing that another candidate, Jones, will get the job (perhaps the head of the appointing panel intimated this to him). Since Smith also has good grounds for supposing that Jones has ten coins in his pocket, he infers that the person who will get the job has ten coins in his pocket. Given how Smith has arrived at this belief, it is certainly justified. As it happens, it is also true, in that the person who gets the job does indeed have ten coins in his pocket. Crucially, however, it is not Jones who gets the job but Smith, and the reason why the belief that Smith inferred is nonetheless true is that, unbeknownst to him, it so happens that Smith has ten coins in his pocket. Smith thus has a justified true belief. Nevertheless, it is surely not knowledge, since it is merely a matter of luck that his belief is true in this case (after all, he has no inkling that he has ten coins in his pocket, still less that he will get the job). The tripartite account of knowledge is thus in serious trouble.

As this case illustrates, the examples that Gettier offers are quite complicated. They needn't be, though. Here is a different case to the ones that Gettier himself offers in his article, but which illustrates the same point.[1] Suppose that our protagonist comes down one morning and forms her belief about what the time is by looking at what the reliable grandfather clock in the hall says. Suppose further that our hero has excellent grounds in support of this belief. For example, she knows first-hand that this clock is very reliable at telling the time, and that the time is roughly as the clock says that it is. Her belief is thus justified. Crucially, however, she is in fact forming her belief in a way that would have ordinarily led to a false belief, because the clock is broken. However, as it so happens, our hero is looking at the clock at the one time in the day when it is 'telling' the right time. Clearly, however, one cannot come to know what the time is by looking at a stopped clock. Our agent thus has a justified true belief which is not knowledge, and hence the tripartite account of knowledge is unsustainable.

Various sorts of responses were offered to Gettier's counterexamples to the tripartite account of knowledge in the ensuing literature. Many of them proceeded by trying to find an additional clause that one could add to the tripartite account in order to avoid the problem. A good example of this tendency can be found in the article by Keith Lehrer (1936–) reprinted in this section (Chapter 3). What Lehrer adds to the tripartite account is, very roughly, a clause to the effect that the agent in question should not form his belief on the basis of any false proposition.[2] For example, in the 'Smith and Jones' example given above, one could argue that the problem lies in the fact that Smith is basing his belief that the person who will get the job has ten coins in his pocket on the false proposition that Jones will get the job. Notice, however, that it isn't so clear how a strategy like this will work in Gettier-style cases where there is no obvious inference, such as the 'stopped clock' case.

Assuming that Lehrer's proposal does not work, where do we go from here? What is interesting about Lehrer's proposal is that, as noted above, it works on the assumption that the tripartite account of knowledge is at least roughly correct. A more radical way of responding to the problem that Gettier raised, however, would be to conclude that the tripartite account of knowledge was incorrect in a more fundamental way.

For example, some have argued that we should drop the justification condition altogether and opt for a different sort of epistemic condition. For instance, one kind of proposal contends that all there is to knowledge is a true belief that is formed in a *reliable* way – i.e. formed in such a way that it regularly leads you to the truth. Notice that what is different about this approach when compared with the tripartite account is that one's true belief could be reliably formed in the relevant sense – and hence amount to knowledge – even though one is unable to offer any grounds in favour of that belief. The move towards a reliability condition on knowledge rather than a justification condition is thus a radical move indeed.

The problem facing so-called 'reliabilist' accounts of knowledge is to give a compelling specification of what such reliability consists in. It is in this regard that Robert Nozick's (1938–2002) account of knowledge – extracts from which are reprinted in Chapter 4 – is so significant. Nozick argues that the sense of reliability that is in question is one which ensures that our belief appropriately 'tracks' the truth. That is, what we want when an agent knows is for that agent not just to have a true belief, but also to have a belief which tracks the truth in the sense that had what the agent believed been false (or true, but in a slightly different way), then her belief would have altered accordingly.

An example will help illustrate this. Consider again the Gettier-style case considered above involving the stopped clock. That the agent in question happens to form a true belief obviously doesn't suffice for knowledge, as we noted above, but what in addition is required? Nozick's account of knowledge offers a neat explanation, for in this case had what the agent believed been false – had, for example, the time been slightly different but everything else remained the same – then she would have formed a false belief (because the time on the stopped clock would remain the same). The problem with her belief is thus that although it happens to be true, it is not *sensitive* to the truth (i.e. it doesn't track it).

This is not to suggest that Nozick has resolved the problem of how to define knowledge, since objections have since emerged even to this account. The significance of the view, however (and the reason why it is collected here), is that it offers a clear statement of one influential position which is radically different from the sort of proposals that were common before, and in the immediate aftermath of, Gettier's famous paper. It thus should offer you a sense of the sort of theories of knowledge that are currently 'live' in the contemporary literature.

Study questions

1   Why does knowledge of a proposition entail having a true belief in that proposition? Why isn't this enough for knowledge?
2   What is the general structure of Gettier-style cases? Construct a Gettier-style example of your own.
3   Do Gettier-style examples essentially involve the agent basing her belief on a false assumption? Try to formulate a Gettier-style example of your own where the agent is not basing her belief on a false assumption.
4   What does Nozick mean when he says that in order for a belief to qualify as knowledge it must 'track' the truth? Explain how Nozick's proposal is meant to deal with the Gettier-style cases.
5   Is justification necessary for knowledge, do you think?

Further reading

A good place to start when it comes to learning more about this topic is Pritchard (2006: chapters 1–4), which offers an accessible introduction to some of the central issues that are relevant here. See also Steup (2005) for an excellent and readable overview of the contemporary literature on the different definitions of knowledge. For an in-depth study of the various responses to Gettier-style problems that have been offered in the literature, see Shope (1983). For a more accessible overview of the problem posed by Gettier cases and its impact on the contemporary epistemological literature, see Hetherington (2005). All of these sources contain lists of useful further readings.

Notes

1   This example is actually due to Russell (1948: 170–1), though he did not advance it as a Gettier-style case himself.
2   The actual formulation of this clause is much more complicated, for reasons that Lehrer discusses in the article.

References

Hetherington, S. (2005). 'Gettier Problems', *Internet Encyclopaedia of Philosophy*, ed. J. Fieser and B. Dowden, http://www.iep.utm.edu/g/gettier.htm.

Pritchard, D. H. (2006). *What Is this Thing Called Knowledge?*, London: Routledge.

Russell, B. (1948). *Human Knowledge: Its Scope and Its Limits*, London: George Allen & Unwin.

Shope, R. K. (1983). *The Analysis of Knowing: A Decade of Research*, Princeton, NJ: Princeton University Press.

Steup, M. (2005). 'The Analysis of Knowledge', *Stanford Encyclopaedia of Philosophy*, ed. E. Zalta, http://plato.stanford.edu/entries/knowledge-analysis/.

Chapter 1

A. J. Ayer

THE RIGHT TO BE SURE

The answers which we have found for the questions we have so far been discussing have not yet put us in a position to give a complete account of what it is to know that something is the case. The first requirement is that what is known should be true, but this is not sufficient; not even if we add to it the further condition that one must be completely sure of what one knows. For it is possible to be completely sure of something which is in fact true, but yet not to know it. The circumstances may be such that one is not entitled to be sure. For instance, a superstitious person who had inadvertently walked under a ladder might be convinced as a result that he was about to suffer some misfortune; and he might in fact be right. But it would not be correct to say that he knew that this was going to be so. He arrived at his belief by a process of reasoning which would not be generally reliable; so, although his prediction came true, it was not a case of knowledge. Again, if someone were fully persuaded of a mathematical proposition by a proof which could be shown to be invalid, he would not, without further evidence, be said to know the proposition, even though it was true. But while it is not hard to find examples of true and fully confident beliefs which in some ways fail to meet the standards required for knowledge, it is not at all easy to determine exactly what these standards are.

One way of trying to discover them would be to consider what would count as satisfactory answers to the question 'How do you know?' Thus people may be credited with knowing truths of mathematics or logic if they are able to give a valid proof of them, or even if, without themselves being able to set out such a proof, they have obtained this information from someone who can. Claims to know empirical statements may be upheld by a reference to perception, or to memory, or to testimony, or to historical records, or to scientific laws. But such backing is not always strong enough for knowledge. Whether it is so or not depends upon the circumstances of the particular case. If I were asked how I knew that a physical object of a certain sort was in such and such a place, it would, in general, be a sufficient answer for me to say that I could see it; but if my eyesight were bad and the light were dim, this answer might not be sufficient. Even though I was right, it might still be said that I did not really know that the object was there. If I have a poor memory and the event which I claim to remember is remote, my memory of it may still not amount to knowledge, even though in this instance it does not fail me. If a witness is unreliable, his unsupported evidence may not enable us to know that what he says is true, even in a case where we completely trust him and he is not in fact deceiving us. In a given instance it is possible to decide whether the backing is strong enough to justify a claim to knowledge. But to say in general how strong it has to be would require our drawing up a list of the conditions under which perception, or memory, or testimony, or other forms of evidence are reliable. And this would be a very complicated matter, if indeed it could be done at all.

Moreover, we cannot assume that, even in particular instances, an answer to the question 'How do you know?' will always be forthcoming. There may very well be cases in which one knows that something is so without its being possible to say how one knows it. I am not so much thinking now of claims to know facts of immediate experience, statements like 'I know that I feel pain', which raise problems of their own into which we shall enter later on. In cases of this sort it may be argued that the question how one knows does not arise. But even when it clearly does arise, it may not find an answer. Suppose that someone were consistently successful in predicting events of a certain kind, events, let us say, which are not ordinarily thought to be predictable, like the results of a lottery. If his run of successes were sufficiently impressive, we might very well come to say that he knew which number would win, even though he did not reach this conclusion by any rational method, or indeed by any method at all. We might say that he knew it by intuition, but this would be to assert no more than that he did know it but that we could not say how. In the same way, if someone were consistently successful in reading the minds of others without having any of the usual sort of evidence, we might say that he knew these things telepathically. But in default of any further explanation this would come down to saying merely that he did know them, but not by any ordinary means. Words like 'intuition' and 'telepathy' are brought in just to disguise the fact that no explanation has been found.

But if we allow this sort of knowledge to be even theoretically possible, what becomes of the distinction between knowledge and true belief? How does our man who knows what the results of the lottery will be differ from one who only

makes a series of lucky guesses? The answer is that, so far as the man himself is concerned, there need not be any difference. His procedure and his state of mind, when he is said to know what will happen, may be exactly the same as when it is said that he is only guessing. The difference is that to say that he knows is to concede to him the right to be sure, while to say that he is only guessing is to withhold it. Whether we make this concession will depend upon the view which we take of his performance. Normally we do not say that people know things unless they have followed one of the accredited routes to knowledge. If someone reaches a true conclusion without appearing to have any adequate basis for it, we are likely to say that he does not really know it. But if he were repeatedly successful in a given domain, we might very well come to say that he knew the facts in question, even though we could not explain how he knew them. We should grant him the right to be sure, simply on the basis of his success. This is, indeed, a point on which people's views might be expected to differ. Not everyone would regard a successful run of predictions, however long sustained, as being by itself a sufficient backing for a claim to knowledge. And here there can be no question of proving that this attitude is mistaken. Where there are recognized criteria for deciding when one has the right to be sure, anyone who insists that their being satisfied is still not enough for knowledge may be accused, for what the charge is worth, of misusing the verb 'to know'. But it is possible to find, or at any rate to devise, examples which are not covered in this respect by any established rule of usage. Whether they are to count as instances of knowledge is then a question which we are left free to decide.

It does not, however, matter very greatly which decision we take. The main problem is to state and assess the grounds on which these claims to knowledge are made, to settle, as it were, the candidate's marks. It is a relatively unimportant question what titles we then bestow upon them. So long as we agree about the marking, it is of no great consequence where we draw the line between pass and failure, or between the different levels of distinction. If we choose to set a very high standard, we may find ourselves committed to saying that some of what ordinarily passes for knowledge ought rather to be described as probable opinion. And some critics will then take us to task for flouting ordinary usage. But the question is purely one of terminology. It is to be decided, if at all, on grounds of practical convenience.

One must not confuse this case, where the markings are agreed upon, and what is in dispute is only the bestowal of honours, with the case where it is the markings themselves that are put in question. For this second case is philosophically important, in a way in which the other is not. The sceptic who asserts that we do not know all that we think we know, or even perhaps that we do not strictly know anything at all, is not suggesting that we are mistaken when we conclude that the recognized criteria for knowing have been satisfied. Nor is he primarily concerned with getting us to revise our usage of the verb 'to know', any more than one who challenges our standards of value is trying to make us revise our usage of the word 'good'. The disagreement is about the application of the word, rather than its meaning. What the sceptic contends is that our markings are too high; that the grounds on which we are normally ready to concede the right to be sure are worth less than we think; he may even go so far as to say that they are not worth anything at all. The attack is directed, not against the way in which we apply our standards of proof, but against these standards themselves. It has, as we shall see, to be taken seriously because of the arguments by which it is supported.

I conclude then that the necessary and sufficient conditions for knowing that something is the case are first that what one is said to know be true, secondly that one be sure of it, and thirdly that one should have the right to be sure. This right may be earned in various ways; but even if one could give a complete description of them it would be a mistake to try to build it into the definition of knowledge, just as it would be a mistake to try to incorporate our actual standards of goodness into a definition of good. And this being so, it turns out that the questions which philosophers raise about the possibility of knowledge are not all to be settled by discovering what knowledge is. . . .

Chapter 2

Edmund Gettier

IS JUSTIFIED TRUE BELIEF KNOWLEDGE?

Various attempts have been made in recent years to state necessary and sufficient conditions for someone's knowing a given proposition. The attempts have often been such that they can be stated in a form similar to the following:[1]

a.   S knows that P IFF
     i.   P is true,
     ii. S believes that P, and
     iii. S is justified in believing that P.

For example, Chisholm has held that the following gives the necessary and sufficient conditions for knowledge:[2]

b.   S knows that P IFF
     i.   S accepts P,
     ii. S has adequate evidence for P, and
     iii. P is true.

Ayer has stated the necessary and sufficient conditions for knowledge as follows:[3]

c.   S knows that P IFF
     i.   P is true,
     ii. S is sure that P is true, and
     iii. S has the right to be sure that P is true.

I shall argue that (a) is false in that the conditions stated therein do not constitute a sufficient condition for the truth of the proposition that S knows that P. The same argument will show that (b) and (c) fail if 'has adequate evidence for' or 'has the right to be sure that' is substituted for 'is justified in believing that' throughout.

I shall begin by noting two points. First, in that sense of 'justified' in which S's being justified in believing P is a necessary condition of S's knowing that P, it is possible for a person to be justified in believing a proposition that is in fact false. Secondly, for any proposition P, if S is justified in believing P, and P entails Q, and S deduces Q from P and accepts Q as a result of this deduction, then S is justified in believing Q. Keeping these two points in mind, I shall now present two cases in which the conditions stated in (a) are true for some proposition, though it is at the same time false that the person in question knows that proposition.

Case I

Suppose that Smith and Jones have applied for a certain job. And suppose that Smith has strong evidence for the following conjunctive proposition:

d.   Jones is the man who will get the job, and Jones has ten coins in his pocket.

Smith's evidence for (d) might be that the president of the company assured him that Jones would in the end be selected, and that he, Smith, had counted the coins in Jones's pocket ten minutes ago. Proposition (d) entails:

e. The man who will get the job has ten coins in his pocket.

Let us suppose that Smith sees the entailment from (d) to (e), and accepts (e) on the grounds of (d), for which he has strong evidence. In this case, Smith is clearly justified in believing that (e) is true.

But imagine, further, that, unknown to Smith, he himself, not Jones, will get the job. And, also, unknown to Smith, he himself has ten coins in his pocket. Proposition (e) is then true, though proposition (d), from which Smith inferred (e), is false. In our example, then, all of the following are true: (i) (e) is true, (ii) Smith believes that (e) is true, and (iii) Smith is justified in believing that (e) is true. But it is equally clear that Smith does not *know* that (e) is true; for (e) is true in virtue of the number of coins in Smith's pocket, while Smith does not know how many coins are in Smith's pocket, and bases his belief in (e) on a count of the coins in Jones's pocket, whom he falsely believes to be the man who will get the job.

Case II

Let us suppose that Smith has strong evidence for the following proposition:

f. Jones owns a Ford.

Smith's evidence might be that Jones has at all times in the past within Smith's memory owned a car, and always a Ford, and that Jones has just offered Smith a ride while driving a Ford. Let us imagine, now, that Smith has another friend, Brown, of whose whereabouts he is totally ignorant. Smith selects three place names quite at random and constructs the following three propositions:

g. Either Jones owns a Ford, or Brown is in Boston.

h. Either Jones owns a Ford, or Brown is in Barcelona.

i. Either Jones owns a Ford, or Brown is in Brest-Litovsk.

Each of these propositions is entailed by (f). Imagine that Smith realizes the entailment of each of these propositions he has constructed by (f), and proceeds to accept (g), (h), and (i) on the basis of (f). Smith has correctly inferred (g), (h), and (i) from a proposition for which he has strong evidence. Smith is therefore completely justified in believing each of these three propositions. Smith, of course, has no idea where Brown is.

But imagine now that two further conditions hold. First Jones does not own a Ford, but is at present driving a rented car. And secondly, by the sheerest coincidence, and entirely unknown to Smith, the place mentioned in proposition (h) happens really to be the place where Brown is. If these two conditions hold, then Smith does not know that (h) is true, even though (i) (h) is true, (ii) Smith does believe that (h) is true, and (iii) Smith is justified in believing that (h) is true.

These two examples show that definition (a) does not state a *sufficient* condition for someone's knowing a given proposition. The same cases, with appropriate changes, will suffice to show that neither definition (b) nor definition (c) does so either.

Notes

1 Plato seems to be considering some such definition at *Theaetetus* 201, and perhaps accepting one at *Meno* 98.

2 Roderick M. Chisholm, *Perceiving: A Philosophical Study* (Ithaca, New York: Cornell University Press, 1957), p. 16.

3 A. J. Ayer, *The Problem of Knowledge* (London: Macmillan, 1956), p. 34.

Chapter 3

Keith Lehrer

KNOWLEDGE, TRUTH AND EVIDENCE

If a man is not completely justified in believing something, then he does not know it. On the other hand, if what he believes is true and he is completely justified in believing it, then it would seem that he knows it. This suggests that we may analyze the statement

S knows h

as the conjunction of

(i)   h is true
(ii) S believes h and
(iii) S is completely justified in believing h.

Professor Gettier has recently shown this analysis to be defective.[1] To meet the kind of counter-example he has formulated, it is necessary to add some fourth condition to the proposed analysis.

The primary concern of my paper will be to solve the problem that Professor Gettier has raised. However, before turning to that problem I wish to make a few remarks concerning the third condition to avoid misunderstanding. Firstly, a person may be completely justified in believing something which is in fact false. We shall consider examples of this shortly.

Secondly, though there may be some cases in which a person is completely justified in believing something in the absence of any evidence to justify his belief, for the most part a person must have evidence to be completely justified in believing what he does. There are a number of ways in which a person who has evidence for what he believes may nevertheless fail to be completely justified in believing what he does. A person may, for example, fail to be completely justified simply because the evidence that he has is not adequate to completely justify his belief.

Moreover, if a person has evidence adequate to completely justify his belief, he may still fail to be completely justified in believing what he does because his belief is not *based on* that evidence. What I mean by saying that a person's belief is not based on certain evidence is that he would not appeal to that evidence to justify his belief. For example, a detective who rejects the truthful testimony of a reliable eye-witness to a crime, but accepts the lying testimony of an ignorant meddler, when both tell him that Brentano committed the crime, would fail to be completely justified in believing this. For his belief is not based on the adequate evidence supplied by the truthful eye-witness but is instead based on the inadequate evidence supplied by an ignorant man.

Again, even if a person has evidence adequate to completely justify his belief and his belief is based on that evidence, he may still fail to be completely justified in believing what he does. For he may be unable to provide any plausible line of reasoning to show how one could reach the conclusion he believes from the evidence that he has. For example, a detective who has a complicated mass of evidence that is conclusive evidence for the conclusion that Little Nelson is the leader of the gang might reach that conclusion from his evidence by what is nothing more than a lucky guess. Imagine that the only line of reasoning he can supply to show how he reached his conclusion is entirely fallacious or that he can supply none. In that case the detective would not be completely justified in believing what he does.

Having noted these ways in which the third condition may fail to be satisfied, let us now turn to the problem of amending the proposed analysis of knowledge to meet the counter-example Professor Gettier has presented against it.

Gettier argues that if a person is completely justified in believing P and he deduces H from P, and believes H on the basis of P, then he is completely justified in believing H. Given this principle we can construct a counter-example to the proposed analysis. Imagine the following. I see two men enter my office whom I know to be Mr. Nogot and Mr. Havit. I have just seen Mr. Nogot depart from a Ford, and he tells me that he has just purchased the car. Indeed, he shows me a certificate that states that he owns the Ford. Moreover, Mr. Nogot is a friend of mine whom I know to be honest and reliable. On the basis of this evidence, I would be completely justified in believing.

P1: Mr. Nogot, who is in my office, owns a Ford.

I might deduce from this that

H: Someone in my office owns a Ford.

I would then be completely justified in believing H. However, imagine that, contrary to my evidence, Mr. Nogot has deceived me and that he does not own a Ford. Moreover, imagine that Mr. Havit, the only other man I see in my room, does own a Ford, though I have no evidence that he

(or I) owns a Ford. In this case, which I shall hereafter refer to as *case one*, though H is true, and I am completely justified in my belief that it is true, I do not know that it is true.[2] For, the reason that H is true is that Mr. Havit owns a Ford, and I have no evidence that this is so.

We have said that a person is completely justified in believing a statement only if he has adequate evidence to completely justify his belief and his belief is based on that evidence. It might seem that since

P1: Mr. Nogot, who is in my office, owns a Ford

is false, it is also false that I have evidence adequate to completely justify my belief that

H: Someone in my office owns a Ford.

But this is incorrect. Leaving P1 aside, I have adequate evidence for H that consists entirely of *true* statements. The evidence is that which I have for P1, namely, that I see Mr. Nogot in my office, have just seen him get out of a Ford, etc. All these things are true and provide evidence adequate to completely justify my believing H. Moreover, my belief that H is true is based on that evidence, though it is also based on P1.

Nevertheless, it might seem reasonable to add to the proposed analysis of knowledge a fourth condition to the effect that if a person knows something, then his belief is not based on any false statements. Thus in addition to the previous three conditions, we would add the condition

(iv) It is not the case that S believes h on the basis of any false statement.

But this condition is much too strong. Imagine that case one is modified so that in addition to the evidence that I have for believing that Mr. Nogot owns a Ford, I have equally strong evidence for believing that Mr. Havit owns a Ford. Moreover, imagine that my belief that someone in my office owns a Ford is based both on the false statement

P1: Mr. Nogot, who is in my office, owns a Ford

and on the true statement

P2: Mr. Havit, who is in my office, owns a Ford.

In this case, which I shall refer to as *case two*, it would be correct to say that I know

H: Someone in my office owns a Ford.

But condition (iv) is not satisfied, and therefore must be rejected.[3]

I know H in case two, because in addition to the evidence that I have for the false statement P1 which entails (but is not entailed by) H, I also have evidence for the true statement P2 which entails H, and this additional evidence is adequate to completely justify my believing H. This suggests that the following condition might be more satisfactory than the one we have just considered:

> (iv a)   If S is completely justified in believing any false statement *p* which entails (but is not entailed by) *h*, then S has evidence adequate to completely justify his believing *h* in addition to the evidence he has for *p*.

This condition is not satisfied in case one. In that case I do not have evidence adequate to completely justify my believing

H: Someone in my office owns a Ford

in addition to the evidence I have for the false statement

P1: Mr. Nogot, who is in my office, owns a Ford

which entails H. Thus, condition (iv a) will yield the correct result that I do not know H in case one. So far so good, but now let us consider case two.

In case two, I know

H: Someone in my office owns a Ford

because I have adequate evidence for the true statement

P2: Mr. Havit, who is in my office, owns a Ford.

However, in this case I also have adequate evidence for the false statement

P3: Mr. Nogot and Mr. Havit, who are in my office, own Fords

and, consequently, I would be completely justified in believing P3. But P3 entails H, and, unfortunately, I have no evidence for H in addition to the evidence that I have for P3. The only evidence that I have for H is precisely the evidence that I have for the false statement P3 which entails H. Thus, condition (iv a) would yield the incorrect result that I do not know H in case two, and, consequently, this condition must also be rejected.

To avoid this difficulty, we could formulate a condition to the effect that if a person is completely justified in believing a false statement which entails a true one, then some part of his evidence must be adequate to completely justify his believing the true statement but not adequate to completely justify his believing the false statement. In case two, the evidence that I have for

P2: Mr. Havit, who is in my office, owns a Ford

is adequate to completely justify my believing the true statement

H: Someone in my office owns a Ford

but not adequate to completely justify my believing the false statements

P1: Mr. Nogot, who is in my office, owns a Ford

or

P3: Mr. Nogot and Mr. Havit, who are in my office, own Fords.

The fourth condition would read as follows:

> (iv b) If S is completely justified in believing any false statement *p* which entails (but is not entailed by) *h*, then S has some evidence adequate to completely justify his believing *h* but not adequate to completely justify his believing *p*.

This condition will not be satisfied in case one, because in that case I do not have any evidence that would be adequate to completely justify my believing

H: Someone in my office owns a Ford

that would not completely justify my believing

P1: Mr. Nogot, who is in my office, owns a Ford.

This is a desired result, because I do not know H in that case. But this condition must also be rejected.

The reason is that there are statements which a person might be completely justified in believing in the absence of any evidence to support them. I shall defend the claim that there are such statements presently, but let us assume for the moment that R is such a statement.[4] Moreover, assume that R is false. Now, imagine the following. I have adequate evidence to completely justify my believing

P2: Mr. Havit, who is in my office, owns a Ford

but do not have any evidence for P1, and again P2 is true. In this case, which I shall refer to as *case three*, we may suppose that the evidence I have for P2 is irrelevant to R and that I am completely

justified in believing the conjunction of P2 and R. However, this conjunction is a false statement, because R is false, and it entails

H: Someone in my office owns a Ford.

Thus I have no evidence adequate to completely justify my believing H that is not also adequate to completely justify my believing the false statement which is the conjunction of P2 and R and which entails H. So, condition (iv b) would not be satisfied in this case, even though I know that H is true.[5]

The proof that there are statements which a person is completely justified in believing in the absence of any evidence to support them is this. Assume that evidence *e* is adequate to completely justify my believing *h*. In that case, the statement that *e* materially implies *h* is one that I am completely justified in believing in the absence of any evidence to support it or its denial.

To solve the problem it is essential to notice what would result were I to suppose in the cases we have considered that those statements are false which are in fact false and which entail H. For example, if I were to suppose in case one that

P1: Mr. Nogot, who is in my office, owns a Ford

is false, I would not in that case be justified in appealing to the evidence that I have for P1 to justify my believing H. Consequently, I would not be completely justified in believing H in case one if I were to suppose that P1 is false.

On the other hand, if I were to suppose in case two that P1 is false, we would not obtain the same result. For in that case I have adequate evidence for P2 as well as P1, and, consequently, I would still be justified in believing H on the basis of the evidence I have for P2. Moreover, even if I were to suppose that the conjunction of P1 and P2 is false in case two, I would still be completely justified in believing H. For I could reason as follows. To suppose that the conjunction of P1 and P2 is false, I need only suppose that one of the conjuncts is false. If P1 is false, then I would be completely justified in believing H on the basis of the evidence that I have for P2. If P2 is false, then I would be completely justified in believing H on the basis of the evidence that I have for P1. Therefore, even if I were to suppose that the conjunction is false, since I am not thereby committed to supposing that both conjuncts are false, I would still be completely justified in believing H.

Similarly, in case three I would be completely justified in believing H even if I were to suppose the conjunction of P2 and R is false. For I could reason that to suppose the conjunction is false does not commit me to supposing that both conjuncts are false, and, consequently, I may suppose that R is false and P2 is true. I would then be completely justified in believing H on the basis of the evidence I have for P2.[6]

We now have the following results. In case one I would not be completely justified in believing H if I were to suppose that P1 is false, but in case two I would be completely justified in believing H even if I were to suppose that P1 is false or if I were to suppose that the conjunction of P1 and P2 is false, and in case three I would be completely justified in believing H even if I were to suppose that the conjunction of R and P2 is false. Since I know H to be true in case two and three but not in case one, I propose the following as a fourth condition in the analysis of knowledge:

(iv c) If S is completely justified in believing any false statement p which entails (but is not entailed by) h, then S would be completely justified in believing h even if S were to suppose that p is false.[7]

This condition, as we have seen, is satisfied in case two and three but not in case one. Consequently, by adding it to our analysis of knowledge, we gain the result that our analysis is satisfied in just those cases in which we have knowledge and not otherwise.

In connection with these remarks, it is important to notice certain facts about the role of supposition in justification. In the first place, a man need not believe what he supposes to be true. I may suppose that something is true (perhaps to comply with the wishes of another) and examine the consequence of such a supposition without believing what I suppose. I may suppose that P1 is false and examine the consequences of that supposition without believing what I suppose. Secondly, a man need not count as evidence all that he supposes. I may suppose that the conjunction of P1 and P2 is false without counting that as evidence that I have. For my supposition might be entirely unjustified. Thirdly, suppositions which are neither believed nor counted as evidence may still have the role of preventing a person from appealing to certain evidence that he has to justify his beliefs. Thus, were I to suppose in case one that P1 is false, I would not believe this nor would I count it as evidence that I have, but that supposition would prevent me from appealing to the evidence I have for P1 to justify my believing H.

With these qualifications, I propose the conjunction of conditions (i), (ii), (iii) and (iv c) as an analysis of knowledge.

Notes

1   Edmund L. Gettier, 'Is Justified True Belief Knowledge?', *Analysis*, Vol. 23, pp. 121–123. Mr. Michael Clark, 'Knowledge and Grounds: A Comment on Mr. Gettier's Paper', *Analysis*, Vol. 24, pp. 46–47, suggests that S's belief must be fully grounded. Defects in Mr. Clark's suggestion have been pointed out by John Turk Saunders and Narayan Champawat, 'Mr. Clark's Definition of "Knowledge"', *Analysis*, Vol. 25, pp. 8–9, and Ernest Sosa, 'The Analysis of "Knowledge that P"', *Analysis*, Vol. 25, pp. 1–3. Saunders and Champawat conclude that it is a mistake to believe that some set of conditions are individually necessary and jointly sufficient for knowledge. Unless there is some error in the

analysis of knowledge I propose at the end of this paper, I will have shown that there is no reason to accept their conclusion. Sosa also proposes an analysis of knowledge in his paper to meet the difficulty Gettier has raised. But I believe this analysis is defective and fails to solve the problem. For my reasons, see note 3 below. I have been fortunate enough to discuss this problem with a number of philosophers, and I am indebted to many for the ideas contained in this paper. I am especially indebted to Professors Roderick Chisholm, Gilbert Harman, David Kaplan and Edmund Gettier for their refutations of my mistakes.

2   My examples differ slightly from Gettier's.

3   Mr. Sosa, *op. cit.*, pp. 4–8, attempts to meet the difficulty that Gettier has raised, by adding the following condition to the analysis of knowledge: if S's belief is based substantially on the report that h or e_i (e_i is part of the evidence S has for h), then the reporter knows that h or e_i. This condition will fail to be satisfied in a slightly modified version of case two. Imagine that my belief that H is true is based on the report by Mr. Nogot that he owns a Ford, that this report is in fact true, but that this is not something that Mr. Nogot knows to be true. Mr. Nogot thinks that he does not own a Ford, but he has, unknown to himself, become a Ford owner. On the other hand, Mr. Havit reports knowingly that he, Havit, owns a Ford. In this case, my belief that H is true is based substantially on the unknowing report of Mr. Nogot. For, my belief that H is true is based as much on P1 as it is on P2. Thus, Mr. Sosa's condition is too strong, because it would not be satisfied in this case even though I do know that H is true. Moreover, the condition is also too weak. Imagine that in case one the evidence that I have for P1 does not involve the report of anyone and that P1 is false. For example, imagine that I have seen Mr. Nogot drive a Ford on many occasions and that I now see him drive away in it. Moreover, imagine that he leaves his wallet at my house and that I, being curious, examine its contents. Therein I discover a certificate asserting that Mr. Nogot owns the Ford I have just seen him drive away. This would supply me with evidence, consisting of true statements, which would completely justify my believing P1, and, therefore, H. But now imagine that, as in case one, P1 is false (due to some legal technicality) and P2 is true, though I have no evidence for P2. In this case, I do not know H, but all of Mr. Sosa's requirements for knowledge might well be met. Therefore, the analysis is too weak.

4   An example of R, that is, a statement a person might be completely justified in believing in the absence of any evidence to support it or its denial, is the following R: if I place twelve marbles into an urn on my desk (without observing their colour), draw out eleven at random which I observe to be black, replace the eleven marbles in the urn and repeat this procedure thirty times with the same results, then all of the marbles in the urn are black. The evidence that I have for P2 is irrelevant to R, R might be false, and I would be completely justified in believing the conjunction of P2 and R if I were completely justified in believing each conjunct.

5   This argument was suggested to me by David Kaplan.

6   I am assuming in both cases two and three that, though I suppose that certain statements are false, which are false, and which entail H, I do not suppose anything else (not entailed by the former suppositions) which would be adverse to justifying my belief that H is true.

7   The subjunctive character of this condition allows for some ambiguity concerning what S is to suppose other than the falsity of p and how his beliefs might be altered when the antecedent of this condition is satisfied. We can eliminate some of this ambiguity by stipulating that the expression 'if S were to suppose that p is false' is short for 'if S were to suppose that p is false but neither suppose anything else (except what is entailed by the supposition that p is false) which is adverse to justifying his belief that h is true, nor alter his beliefs in any way which is adverse to such justification'.

Chapter 4

Robert Nozick

KNOWLEDGE AND WHAT WE WOULD BELIEVE

[. . .]

Conditions for knowledge

Our task is to formulate conditions to go alongside

(1) p is true
(2) S believes that p.

We would like each condition to be necessary for knowledge, so any case that fails to satisfy it will not be an instance of knowledge. Furthermore, we would like the conditions to be jointly sufficient for knowledge, so any case that satisfies all of them will be an instance of knowledge. We first shall formulate conditions that seem to handle ordinary cases correctly, classifying as knowledge cases which are knowledge, and as non-knowledge cases which are not; then we shall check to see how these conditions handle some difficult cases discussed in the literature. [. . .]

One plausible suggestion is causal, something like: the fact that p (partially) causes S to believe that p, that is, (2) because (1). But this provides an inhospitable environment for mathematical and ethical knowledge; also there are well-known difficulties in specifying the type of causal connection. If someone floating in a tank oblivious to everything around him is given (by direct electrical and chemical stimulation of the brain) the belief that he is floating in a tank with his brain being stimulated, then even though that fact is part of the cause of his belief, still he does not know that it is true.

Let us consider a different third condition:

(3) If p were not true, S would not believe that p.

Throughout this work, let us write the subjunctive "if-then" by an arrow, and the negation of a sentence by prefacing "not-" to it. The above condition thus is rewritten as:

(3) not-p → not-(S believes that p).

This subjunctive condition is not unrelated to the causal condition. Often when the fact that p (partially) causes someone to believe that p, the fact also will be causally necessary for his having the belief—without the cause, the effect would not occur. In that case, the subjunctive condition (3) also will be satisfied. Yet this condition is not equivalent to the causal condition. For the causal condition will be satisfied in cases of causal overdetermination, where either two sufficient causes of the effect actually operate, or a back-up cause (of the same effect) would operate if the first one didn't; whereas the subjunctive condition need not hold for these cases.[1] When the two conditions do agree, causality indicates knowledge because it acts in a manner that makes the subjunctive (3) true.

The subjunctive condition (3) serves to exclude cases of the sort first described by Edmund Gettier, such as the following. Two other people are in my office and I am justified on the basis of much evidence in believing the first owns a Ford car; though he (now) does not, the second person (a stranger to me) owns one. I believe truly and justifiably that someone (or other) in my office owns a Ford car, but I do not know someone does. Concluded Gettier, knowledge is not simply justified true belief.

The following subjunctive, which specifies condition (3) for this Gettier case, is not satisfied: if no one in my office owned a Ford car, I wouldn't believe that someone did. The situation that would obtain if no one in my office owned a Ford is one where the stranger does not (or where he is not in the office); and in that situation I still would believe, as before, that someone in my office does own a Ford, namely, the first person. So the subjunctive condition (3) excludes this Gettier case as a case of knowledge.

The subjunctive condition is powerful and intuitive, not so easy to satisfy, yet not so powerful as to rule out everything as an instance of knowledge. A subjunctive conditional "if p were true, q would be true," $p \rightarrow q$, does not say that p entails q or that it is logically impossible that p yet not-q. It says that in the situation that would obtain if p were true, q also would be true. This point is brought out especially clearly in recent "possible-worlds" accounts of subjunctives: the subjunctive is true when (roughly) in all those worlds in which p holds true that are closest to the actual world, q also is true. (Examine those worlds in which p holds true closest to the actual world, and see if q holds true in all these.) Whether or not q is true in p worlds that are still farther away from the actual world is irrelevant to the truth of the subjunctive. I do not mean to endorse any particular possible-worlds account of subjunctives, nor am I committed to this type of account.[2] I sometimes shall use it, though,

when it illustrates points in an especially clear way. [. . .]

The subjunctive condition (3) also handles nicely cases that cause difficulties for the view that you know that p when you can rule out the relevant alternatives to p in the context. For, as Gail Stine writes,

what makes an alternative relevant in one context and not another? . . . if on the basis of visual appearances obtained under optimum conditions while driving through the countryside Henry identifies an object as a barn, normally we say that Henry knows that it is a barn. Let us suppose, however, that unknown to Henry, the region is full of expertly made papier-mâché facsimiles of barns. In that case, we would not say that Henry knows that the object is a barn, unless he has evidence against it being a papier-mâché facsimile, which is now a relevant alternative. So much is clear, but what if no such facsimiles exist in Henry's surroundings, although they once did? Are either of these circumstances sufficient to make the hypothesis (that it's a papier-mâché object) relevant? Probably not, but the situation is not so clear.[3]

Let p be the statement that the object in the field is a (real) barn, and q the one that the object in the field is a papier-mâché barn. When papier-mâché barns are scattered through the area, if p were false, q would be true or might be. Since in this case (we are supposing) the person still would believe p, the subjunctive

(3) not-$p \rightarrow$ not-(S believes that p)

is not satisfied, and so he doesn't know that p. However, when papier-mâché barns are or were scattered around another country, even if p were false q wouldn't be true, and so (for all we have been told) the person may well know that p. A hypothesis q contrary to p clearly is relevant when if p weren't true, q would be true; when not-p → q. It clearly is irrelevant when if p weren't true, q also would not be true; when not-p → not-q. The remaining possibility is that neither of these opposed subjunctives holds; q might (or might not) be true if p weren't true. In this case, q also will be relevant, according to an account of knowledge incorporating condition (3) and treating subjunctives along the lines sketched above. Thus, condition (3) handles cases that befuddle the "relevant alternatives" account; though that account can adopt the above subjunctive criterion for when an alternative is relevant, it then becomes merely an alternate and longer way of stating condition (3).[4]

Despite the power and intuitive force of the condition that if p weren't true the person would not believe it, this condition does not (in conjunction with the first two conditions) rule out every problem case. There remains, for example, the case of the person in the tank who is brought to believe, by direct electrical and chemical stimulation of his brain, that he is in the tank and is being brought to believe things in this way; he does not know this is true. However, the subjunctive condition is satisfied: if he weren't floating in the tank, he wouldn't believe he was.

The person in the tank does not know he is there, because his belief is not sensitive to the truth. Although it is caused by the fact that is its content, it is not sensitive to that fact. The operators of the tank could have produced any belief, including the false belief that he wasn't in the tank; if they had, he would have believed that. Perfect sensitivity would involve beliefs and facts varying together. We already have one portion of that variation, subjunctively at least: if p were false he wouldn't believe it. This sensitivity as specified by a subjunctive does not have the belief vary with the truth or falsity of p in all possible situations, merely in the ones that would or might obtain if p were false.

The subjunctive condition

(3) not-p → not-(S believes that p)

tells us only half the story about how his belief is sensitive to the truth-value of p. It tells us how his belief state is sensitive to p's falsity, but not how it is sensitive to p's truth; it tells us what his belief state would be if p were false, but not what it would be if it were true.

To be sure, conditions (1) and (2) tell us that p is true and he does believe it, but it does not follow that his believing p is sensitive to p's being true. This additional sensitivity is given to us by a further subjunctive: if p were true, he would believe it.

(4) p → S believes that p.

Not only is p true and S believes it, but if it were true he would believe it. Compare: not only was the photon emitted and did it go to the left, but (it was then true that): if it were emitted it would go to the left. The truth of antecedent and consequent is not alone sufficient for the truth of a subjunctive; (4) says more than (1) and (2).[5] Thus, we presuppose some (or another) suitable account of subjunctives. According to the suggestion tentatively made above, (4) holds true if not only does he actually truly believe p, but in the 'close' worlds where p is true, he also believes it. He believes that p for some distance out in the p neighborhood of the actual world; similarly, condition (3) speaks not of the whole not-p neighborhood of the actual world, but only of the first portion of it. (If, as is likely, these explanations do not help, please use your own intuitive understanding of the subjunctives (3) and (4).)

The person in the tank does not satisfy the subjunctive condition (4). Imagine as actual a world in which he is in the tank and is stimulated to believe he is, and consider what subjunctives are true in that world. It is not true of him there that if he were in the tank he would believe it; for in the close world (or situation) to his own where he is in the tank but they don't give him the belief that he is (much less instill the belief that he isn't) he doesn't believe he is in the tank.

Of the person actually in the tank and believing it, it is not true to make the further statement that if he were in the tank [. . .] he would believe it—so he does not know he is in the tank.

The subjunctive condition (4) also handles a case presented by Gilbert Harman.[6] The dictator of a country is killed; in their first edition, newspapers print the story, but later all the country's newspapers and other media deny the story, falsely. Everyone who encounters the denial believes it (or does not know what to believe and so suspends judgment). Only one person in the country fails to hear any denial and he continues to believe the truth. He satisfies conditions (1)–(3) (and the causal condition about belief) yet we are reluctant to say he knows the truth. The reason is that if he had heard the denials, he too would have believed them, just like everyone else. His belief is not sensitively tuned to the truth, he doesn't satisfy the condition that if it were true he would believe it. Condition (4) is not satisfied.[7]

There is a pleasing symmetry about how this account of knowledge relates conditions (3) and (4), and connects them to the first two conditions. The account has the following form.

(1)
(2)
(3) not-1 $\rightarrow$ not-2
(4) 1 $\rightarrow$ 2

I am not inclined, however, to make too much of this symmetry, for I found also that with other conditions experimented with as a possible fourth condition there was some way to construe the resulting third and fourth conditions as symmetrical answers to some symmetrical looking questions, so that they appeared to arise in parallel fashion from similar questions about the components of true belief.

Symmetry, it seems, is a feature of a mode of presentation, not of the contents presented. A uniform transformation of symmetrical statements can leave the results non-symmetrical. But if symmetry attaches to mode of presentation, how can it possibly be a deep feature of, for instance, laws of nature that they exhibit symmetry? (One of my favorite examples of symmetry is due to Groucho Marx. On his radio programme he spoofed a commercial, and ended, "And if you are not completely satisfied, return the unused portion of our product and we will return the unused portion of your money.") Still, to present our subject symmetrically makes the connection of knowledge to true belief especially perspicuous. It seems to me that a symmetrical formulation is a sign of our understanding, rather than a mark of truth. If we cannot understand an asymmetry as arising from an underlying symmetry through the operation of a particular factor, we will not understand why that asymmetry exists in that direction. (But do we also need to understand why the underlying asymmetrical factor holds instead of its opposite?)

A person knows that p when he not only does truly believe it, but also would truly believe it and wouldn't falsely believe it. He not only actually has a true belief, he subjunctively has one. It is true that p and he believes it; if it weren't true he wouldn't believe it, and if it were true he would believe it. To know that p is to be someone who would believe it if it were true, and who wouldn't believe it if it were false.

It will be useful to have a term for this situation when a person's belief is thus subjunctively connected to the fact. Let us say of a person who believes that p, which is true, that when (3) and (4) hold, his belief *tracks* the truth that p. To know is to have a belief that tracks the truth. Knowledge is a particular way of being connected to the world, having a specific real factual connection to the world tracking it.

One refinement is needed in condition (4). It may be possible for someone to have contradictory beliefs, to believe p and also believe not-p. We do not mean such a person to easily satisfy (4), and in any case we want his belief-state, sensitive to the truth of p, to focus upon p. So let us rewrite our fourth condition as:

(4) p → S believes that p and not-(S believes that not-p).

As you might have expected, this account of knowledge as tracking requires some refinements and epicycles. [. . .]

Ways and methods

The fourth condition says that if p were true the person would believe it. Suppose the person only happened to see a certain event or simply chanced on a book describing it. He knows it occurred. Yet if he did not happen to glance that way or encounter the book, he would not believe it, even though it occurred. As written, the fourth condition would exclude this case as one where he actually knows the event occurred. It also would exclude the following case. Suppose some person who truly believes that p would or might arrive at a belief about it in some other close situation where it holds true, in a way or by a method different from the one he (actually) used in arriving at his belief that p, and so thereby come to believe that not-p. In that (close) situation, he would believe not-p even though still p holds true. Yet, all this does not show he actually doesn't know that p, for actually he has not used this alternative method in arriving at his belief. Surely he can know that p, even though condition (4), as written, is not satisfied.

Similarly, suppose he believes that p by one method or way of arriving at belief, yet if p were false he wouldn't use this method but would use another one instead, whose application would lead him mistakenly to believe p (even though it is false). This person does not satisfy condition (3) as written; it is not true of him that if p were false he wouldn't believe it. Still, the fact that he would use another method of arriving at belief if p were false does not show he didn't know that p when he used this method. A grandmother

sees her grandson is well when he comes to visit; but if he were sick or dead, others would tell her he was well to spare her upset. Yet this does not mean she doesn't know he is well (or at least ambulatory) when she sees him. Clearly, we must restate our conditions to take explicit account of the ways and methods of arriving at belief.

Let us define a technical locution, S knows, via method (or way of believing) M, that p:

(1) p is true.
(2) S believes, via method or way of coming to believe M, that p.
(3) If p weren't true and S were to use M to arrive at a belief whether (or not) p, then S wouldn't believe, via M, that p.
(4) If p were true and S were to use M to arrive at a belief whether (or not) p, then S would believe, via M, that p.

[. . .]

Notes

1 [. . .] I should note here that I assume bivalence throughout this chapter, and consider only statements that are true if and only if their negations are false.
2 See Robert Stalnaker, "A Theory of Conditionals," in N. Rescher, ed., *Studies in Logical Theory* (Oxford 1968); David Lewis, *Counterfactuals* (Cambridge 1973); and Jonathan Bennett's critical review of Lewis, "Counterfactuals and Possible Worlds," *Canadian Journal of Philosophy*, 4 (1974), pp. 381–402. Our purposes require, for the most part, no more than an intuitive understanding of subjunctives. [. . .]
3 G. C. Stine, "Scepticism, Relevant Alternatives and Deductive Closure," *Philosophical Studies*, 29 (1976), p. 252, who attributes the example to Carl Ginet.
4 This last remark is a bit too brisk, for that account might use a subjunctive criterion for when an alternative q to p is relevant (namely, when if p were not to hold, q would or might), and utilize some further notion of what it is to rule out relevant alternatives (for example, have evidence against them), so that it

did not turn out to be equivalent to the account we offer.

5 More accurately, since the truth of antecedent and consequent is not necessary for the truth of the subjunctive either, (4) says something different from (1) and (2).

6 Gilbert Harman, *Thought* (Princeton 1973), ch. 9.

7 What if the situation or world where he too hears the later false denials is not so close, so easily occurring? Should we say that everything that prevents his hearing the denial easily could have not happened, and does not in some close world?

PART TWO

What is the value of knowledge?

INTRODUCTION TO PART TWO
Ram Neta and Duncan Pritchard

IT IS A GUIDING ASSUMPTION of epistemology that knowledge is valuable; that it is something that is worth caring about. Knowledge is, after all, the central notion of epistemology, the notion that is the principal focus of that enterprise. But although it might seem obvious that knowledge is valuable, on closer inspection it is in fact far from obvious. This problem was first noticed back in antiquity by Plato (429–347 BC), and the relevant reading from the *Theatetus* is collected here (Chapter 5). Through the mouthpiece of Socrates, Plato notes that it is not at all clear that knowledge is more valuable even than mere true belief, let alone any other epistemic standing that falls short of knowledge (such as justified true belief). As he puts the point in the extract that is contained here, suppose one wants to go to the town of Larissa. The problem is that a true belief about the correct way to Larissa seems just as good as knowledge of the correct way to go – after all, they both get you where you want to go. Why then should we prefer knowledge to true belief?

Plato's own solution to the problem was to say that the difference between knowledge and true belief – that feature of knowledge that makes it distinctively valuable – is that knowledge has a 'stability' that mere true belief lacks, in the sense that mere true belief, unlike knowledge, is easily lost. He offered an analogy to illustrate this. In ancient times there was a sculptor called Daedalus who carved statues that were so life-like that it was said that if you did not tether them down they would run away. As Plato puts the point, it would be far more valuable to own a 'tethered' statue of Deadalus than an untethered one, since only the former would remain with you rather than run away. Plato argues that knowledge is like the tethered statues of Deadalus in the sense that knowledge, unlike mere true belief, would not 'run away' from the knower.

We can illustrate what Plato means by this by returning to the example of the road to Larissa. Suppose that you merely have a true belief about which way is the right way to go. This belief may well get you where you want to go, but the problem with a mere true belief of this sort is that it is easily lost. Suppose, for example, that the road takes an unexpected direction, so that it seems to be heading the wrong way. If you formed your belief by, say, simply trusting a hunch – and so have a mere true belief in this regard – then upon encountering this unexpected turn you would in all likelihood no longer believe that this was the right road (even though, in fact, and unbeknownst to you, it is the right road). In contrast, if you *knew* the way to go – if you formed your belief by looking at a reliable map, say – then you would not be so perturbed by the unexpected turn in the road, and would in all likelihood retain your true belief that this was the right road. There is thus a practical advantage to having knowledge, in that knowledge, unlike mere true belief, is not easily lost, just as one is less likely to lose a statue of Daedalus if it is tied down than if it isn't.

Plato thus offers us some reason to think that it is better to have knowledge rather than mere true belief. Plato's argument, along with the more general question of whether the value of knowledge can be accounted for in terms of things that are external to it (such as its practical benefits), is explored in Jonathan Kvanvig's (1954–) contribution to this part (Chapter 6). Kvanvig's conclusion is that it isn't possible to account for our intuition that knowledge is valuable merely by appeal to things that are external to knowledge. In particular, he argues that two recent attempts to account for the value of knowledge in this way – due to Timothy Williamson (1955–) – are unpersuasive.

In her contribution to this part (Chapter 7), Linda Zagzebski (1946–) argues that the problem of accounting for why knowledge is more valuable than mere true belief is particularly salient for certain views of what knowledge is. Zagzebski's principal targets here are reliabilist accounts of knowledge, accounts which claim that the difference between knowledge and mere true belief is that knowledge is acquired in a way that normally tends to produce true beliefs. As Zagzebski points out, the value of forming one's belief in a reliable fashion seems to derive solely from the value of true belief – i.e. we care about forming our beliefs in a reliable fashion because we care about having true beliefs. The problem, however, as Zagzebski makes vivid in this article, is that, ordinarily at least, that something valuable is produced in a reliable fashion does not add any additional value. If this is right, then reliabilists cannot explain why knowledge is more valuable than mere true belief after all.

The example that Zagzebski offers to illustrate this point concerns two great cups of coffee which are identical in every relevant way – i.e. they look the same, taste the same, smell the same, etc. – except that one of the cups of coffee was produced by a coffee-making machine which generally produces good cups of coffee (i.e. it is a *reliable* coffee-making machine) while the other cup of coffee was produced by a coffee-making machine that generally produces bad cups of coffee (i.e. it is an *unreliable* coffee-making machine). Clearly, we value reliable coffee-making machines over unreliable coffee-making machines, and the reason for this is that we value good coffee. Notice, however, that once we have the two identical cups of coffee before us, it makes no difference which of them was produced by the reliable coffee-making machine. All we care about is how good the coffee is; how it was produced is irrelevant to its value.

Zagzebski appeals to this analogy in order to argue that true belief, as far as the reliabilist is concerned at any rate, is just like good coffee. We care that our beliefs are formed in a reliable fashion precisely because reliable belief-forming mechanisms are good ways of gaining something else that we value – i.e. true belief. But, if reliabilism is right, then so long as the true belief that we desire is present – as with the case of good cups of coffee – we don't care whether it was produced in a reliable fashion or not. Reliabilism is thus unable, argues Zagzebski, to explain why knowledge is more valuable than mere true belief.

If Zagzebski is right about this, then notice that the point is not confined simply to reliabilist accounts of knowledge. Indeed, any account of knowledge which argues that what turns mere true belief into knowledge is some property which is only itself valuable as a means to true belief will succumb to the same problem, since it will have to admit that the value of knowledge cannot be any greater than the value of a corresponding mere true belief. This is thus a serious problem indeed, and one that has important implications for contemporary thinking about knowledge.

Various responses to this problem have been proposed in the literature. One of the most dominant ways of responding to this problem has involved appeal to a virtue-theoretic account of knowledge. These are theories of knowledge which essentially define knowledge in terms of true belief that is formed via the exercise of stable and reliable cognitive traits – or epistemic *virtues* – on the part of the agent. Zagzebski herself offers one response to the problem that runs along these lines. A second virtue-theoretic response to the problem is offered by John Greco (1961–) in the paper contained in this part (Chapter 8). While there are subtle differences between these two proposals, since there is also considerable common ground we will here focus on outlining the solution that Greco proposes.

Greco begins with the observation that, in general, we value successes that are due to our own agency in a very different way than we value successes that are not due to our own agency (but which are, for example, due to luck). This seems exactly right. Suppose, for example, you are an archer in an archery competition. All other things being equal, wouldn't you prefer to hit the bull's-eye because of your archery abilities rather than because of luck (because of a freak but fortuitous gust of wind, say)? If this is right, however, then a virtue epistemologist like Greco has a very straightforward answer available to him as to why knowledge is more valuable than mere true belief (indeed, more valuable than any epistemic standing that falls short of knowledge). For, on his view, knowledge just is true belief that is the product of one's epistemic agency (one's epistemic virtue), and so what goes for success that is due to agency more generally straightforwardly applies to the specific case of epistemic success (i.e. true belief) that is due to epistemic agency (i.e. epistemic virtue).

This is a very elegant response to the problem, but note that even if one grants that this proposal works, it is only as compelling as the virtue-theoretic account of knowledge that it presupposes. If one does not accept this account – and many contemporary epistemologists don't – then one won't find this response to the problem of epistemic value very plausible either. Still, provided that one does find the virtue-theoretic account of knowledge plausible, then that it seems to be able to straightforwardly respond to the problem of epistemic value in this way is a pretty considerable point in its favour.

Study questions

1   In your own words, explain the 'road to Larissa' example that Plato offers and the challenge that it poses to the value of knowledge.

2   What does Plato mean when he compares the value of knowledge to the value of the 'tethered' statues of Daedalus? Do you find what Plato says on this score persuasive?

3   In your own words, explain the 'coffee cup' example that Zagzebski offers. Why does Zagzebski think that this example poses a problem for reliabilism? Is she right?

4   What solution does Zagzebski offer to the problem of epistemic value? In what
     sense is this proposal a *virtue-theoretic* response to the problem?
5   What is Greco's solution to the problem of epistemic value? How, if at all, does
     it differ from Zagzebski's solution? Is it persuasive, do you think?

Further reading

Pritchard (2006: chapter 2) offers an accessible introduction to some of the issues
related to the value of knowledge and his text also contains a list of useful further
readings. The *locus classicus* for contemporary discussions of the value of knowledge
is Kvanvig (2003). To learn more about Zagzebski's account of knowledge, see
Zagzebski (1996). To learn more about virtue epistemology more generally (the view
that both Zagzebski and Greco endorse, in different forms), see Greco (2004) and
Baehr (2006), both of which contain a list of useful further readings. For a collection
of contemporary papers dealing with this topic which also includes a symposium on
Kvanvig's book, see Haddock, Millar and Pritchard (2008). For a survey of recent
work on this topic, see Pritchard (2007), a slightly adapted version of which
(Pritchard 2008) is freely available online.

References

Baehr, J. (2006). 'Virtue Epistemology', *Internet Encyclopaedia of Philosophy*, ed. J.
     Fieser and B. Dowden, http://www.iep.utm.edu/v/VirtueEp.htm.
Greco, J. (2004). 'Virtue Epistemology', *Stanford Encyclopaedia of Philosophy*, ed.
     E. Zalta, http://plato.stanford.edu/entries/epistemology-virtue/.
Haddock, A., Millar, A. and Pritchard, D. H. (eds) (2009). *Epistemic Value*, Oxford:
     Oxford University Press.
Kvanvig, J. (2003). *The Value of Knowledge and the Pursuit of Understanding*,
     Cambridge: Cambridge University Press.
Pritchard, D. H. (2006). *What Is this Thing Called Knowledge?*, London: Routledge.
—— (2007). 'Recent Work on Epistemic Value', *American Philosophical Quarterly*
     44: 85–110.
—— (2008). 'The Value of Knowledge', *Stanford Encyclopaedia of Philosophy*, ed.
     E. Zalta, http://plato.stanford.edu/entries/knowledge-value/.
Zagzebski, L. (1996). *Virtues of the Mind: An Inquiry into the Nature of Virtue and
     the Ethical Foundations of Knowledge*, Cambridge: Cambridge University
     Press.

Chapter 5

Plato

THE MENO

[...]

SOCRATES: If a man knew the way to Larissa, or anywhere else, and went to the place and led others thither, would he not be a right and good guide?

MENO: Certainly.

SOCRATES: And a person who had a right opinion about the way, but had never been and did not know, might be a good guide also, might he not?

MENO: Certainly.

SOCRATES: And while he has true opinion about that which the other knows, he will be just as good a guide if he thinks the truth, as he who knows the truth?

MENO: Exactly.

SOCRATES: Then true opinion is as good a guide to correct action as knowledge; and that was the point which we omitted in our speculation about the nature of virtue, when we said that knowledge only is the guide of right action; whereas there is also right opinion.

MENO: True.

SOCRATES: Then right opinion is not less useful than knowledge?

MENO: The difference, Socrates, is only that he who has knowledge will always be right; but he who has right opinion will sometimes be right, and sometimes not.

SOCRATES: What do you mean? Can he be wrong who has right opinion, so long as he has right opinion?

MENO: I admit the cogency of your argument, and therefore, Socrates, I wonder that knowledge should be preferred to right opinion — or why they should ever differ.

SOCRATES: And shall I explain this wonder to you?

MENO: Do tell me.

SOCRATES: You would not wonder if you had ever observed the images of Daedalus; but perhaps you have not got them in your country?

MENO: What have they to do with the question?

SOCRATES: Because they require to be fastened in order to keep them, and if they are not fastened they will play truant and run away.

MENO: Well, what of that?

SOCRATES: I mean to say that they are not very valuable possessions if they are at liberty, for they will walk off like runaway slaves; but when fastened, they are of great value, for they are really beautiful works of art. Now this is an illustration of the nature of true opinions: while they abide with us they are beautiful and fruitful, but they run away out of the human soul, and do not remain long, and therefore they are not of much value until they are fastened by the tie of the cause; and this fastening of them, friend Meno, is recollection, as you and I have agreed to call it. But when they are bound, in the first place, they have the nature of knowledge; and, in the second place, they are abiding. And this is why knowledge is more honourable and excellent than true opinion, because fastened by a chain.

MENO: What you are saying, Socrates, seems to be very like the truth.

SOCRATES: I too speak rather in ignorance; I only conjecture. And yet that knowledge differs from true opinion is no matter of conjecture with me. There are not many things which I profess to know, but this is most certainly one of them.

Chapter 6

Jonathan Kvanvig

THE VALUE OF KNOWLEDGE IS EXTERNAL TO IT

With the scientific sophistication of the local news, I polled some folk (my son and daughter) about the value of knowledge. They apparently think of knowledge as Quine thinks of induction: Those eschewing it tend to fall off cliffs. Knowledge is good, the survey says, because you can make more money with it, get into a better college, get a better job, live a better life.

These answers are examples of finding the value of knowledge in its connection to practical affairs of life. Instead of tracing the value of knowledge to the value of its constituents or some intrinsic value that it has, these accounts claim that knowledge is valuable because it is useful.

The most obvious alternative to this account of the value of knowledge is the view that knowledge has value intrinsically. Academics often lament the pragmatism of undergraduates who prize knowledge only indirectly, in terms of what it can get for them in terms of money, prestige, power, and the like. Academics like to insist, instead, that knowledge is valuable for its own sake and not (just) because it helps you get a good job or get rich.

These two theories provide paradigm examples of the kinds of theories of the value of knowledge I want to explore, but they are only paradigms and not exhaustive of available approaches. The pragmatic theory is paradigmatic of theories that locate the value of knowledge in things logically distinct from knowledge itself, and the intrinsic value theory is paradigmatic of theories that locate the value of knowledge in things logically tied to knowledge itself. In this chapter, I will explore views that explain the value of knowledge in terms of things external to it, starting with the most obvious such theory, the theory that locates the value of knowledge in its usefulness.

The pragmatic theory

There is much to be said on behalf of this account. First, we often explain things not going well in terms of a lack of knowledge. Parents often lament not doing a better job raising their children with the phrase "if we'd only known better." And sometimes, at least, the lack of knowledge provides insulation from moral responsibility. Many of our military were told, on assignment in Nagasaki after World War II, that the dangers of radiation exposure could be eliminated by taking a good shower every day. Perhaps the advisors knew better, but if they didn't, they have an excuse for the damage they caused. We often unwittingly hurt the feelings of those we care about and offer as an excuse that we didn't know what effect our actions would have. Medical personnel are exonerated in court-room proceedings for damaging treatment because they simply didn't know and couldn't be held responsible for not knowing.

On the positive side, we often seek knowledge in order to obtain certain benefits. Those who invest in the stock market often spend enormous amounts of time in knowledge acquisition before making investment decisions, convinced that the additional knowledge will improve their likelihood of success. Good parents reward the search for knowledge in their children, viewing it as an indicator of success in life, and the most common defense given for spending time pursuing a college degree is that one's earning power will be greatly enhanced by the acquisition of knowledge that is required for the degree.

In a similar vein, it is often also said that knowledge is power. This slogan should not be taken literally, but it signals a perceived connection between what we know and the capacity for getting what we want.

It would be one-sided to ignore at this point the negative effects of knowledge as well, however. Knowing what causes pain helps torturers ply their trade; knowing that smallpox was deadly to native populations aided North American immigrants in destroying those populations.

So it is false to say that knowledge produces only good effects. The pragmatic theory of the value of knowledge need make no such claim, however. Instead of claiming that knowledge can only produce good effects, the pragmatic theory bids us to hold certain factors fixed in assessing the value of knowledge. Knowledge is valuable, on this account, because, in the hands of good and honest people, it opens up possibilities of good effects that wouldn't be available without knowledge.

It is in this special way that knowledge is associated with good things and the lack of knowledge with bad things in our ordinary patterns of activity and in our conception of such. It is somewhat of a shock to this way of thinking, then, to find that the earliest philosophical investigations of the value of knowledge begin by challenging this association. In Plato's *Meno*, Socrates challenges Meno on this very question.[1] In particular, Socrates wants to know what makes knowledge more valuable than true opinion, and he points out that true opinions have all the practical benefits of knowledge. His example concerns traveling "to Larissa, or anywhere else you like" (97a). The man who merely judges correctly how to get to Larissa will nonetheless be every bit as successful in his journey as the man who knows the way. So Socrates rejects the idea that knowledge is more valuable than true opinion because of its practical benefits. As he puts it, "Therefore true opinion is as good a guide as knowledge for the purpose of acting rightly" (97b), and "right opinion is something no less useful than knowledge" (97c).

Notice, however, that the question shifts here from the one with which we began. We began wanting to know whether knowledge is valuable, and if so, why. If we infer a negative answer to the first question on the basis of Socrates' discussion, we may be accused of the following mistake. Suppose we want to know whether gold is valuable, and we try to answer that question by asking whether it is more valuable than platinum. Upon learning that it is not more valuable than platinum, we infer that gold is not valuable.

Of course, this analogy is not perfect if we assume that true opinion is among the constituents of knowledge. For once we acknowledge the relationship of constitution, other analogies become more appropriate. If we claim that a diamond ring is valuable, we might be corrected by someone who knows that the diamond taken from its setting would be just as valuable. Or, again, if a hero-worshipping Little Leaguer claims that his Ken Griffey, Jr., autographed baseball bat hits better because of the autograph, he would be wrong. The bat without the signature would be just as good (once we control for the placebo effect of the signature, of course).

We could escape Socrates' counterexample, however, if we were willing to claim that knowledge is valuable but no more valuable than true opinion. Yet, part of the challenge of explaining the value of knowledge is in explaining how it has more value than other things, one of these other things being true opinion—as Meno claims after acquiescing to Socrates' point that true belief is every bit as useful as knowledge. "In that case, I wonder why knowledge should be so much more prized than right opinion" (97c–d). Meno expresses here a common presupposition about knowledge, one that is widely, if not universally, shared. Given this presupposition, an account of the value of knowledge must explain more than how knowledge is valuable. It must also explain why the value of knowledge is superior to the value of true opinion.

Socrates' claims are therefore telling against the pragmatic account of the value of knowledge. Knowledge is valuable because it is useful, but an account of the value of knowledge cannot be complete without something further. For true opinion, one of the constituents of knowledge, is equally useful, and yet knowledge is more valuable than true opinion. Hence the value of knowledge must be explained in terms beyond its pragmatic usefulness.

This conclusion holds so long as we refuse to identify knowledge with true opinion, an identification with which Meno toys ("I wonder . . . indeed how there is any difference between them" (97c–d)). Socrates uses an "analogy" (98b) to illustrate both the difference between them and the superiority of the value of knowledge over that of true belief, an analogy we shall look at carefully a bit later, and concludes:

> But it is not, I am sure, a mere guess to say that right opinion and knowledge are different. There are few things that I should claim to know, but that at least is among them, whatever else is.
>
> (98b)

Socrates does not tell us how knowledge is different from right opinion, but he is convinced

that there is a difference. So Socrates is convinced that he knows that the account of knowledge that Meno suggests is false. That fact is interesting in its own right, coming from a philosopher who conceived of his own wisdom in terms of an understanding of the limitations on what he knows, but equally interesting in the present context is the way in which Meno's theory is prompted. Meno's toying with the identification of knowledge and correct opinion is a result of having his proposed theory of the value of knowledge undermined, indicating an interplay in his mind between accounts of the nature of knowledge and accounts of the value of knowledge. For Meno, counterexamples to his suggestion about the value of knowledge tempt him to endorse an account of the nature of knowledge that blocks the counterexamples. Socrates' response is that even to one who knows (nearly) nothing, Meno's suggestion regarding the nature of knowledge is known to be false. This interplay between accounts of the nature and value of knowledge is no mistake on Meno's part. It would be a strange dialectic to find a theoretician completely satisfied with an account of the nature of knowledge known to be incompatible with any value for knowledge. Coherence might be restored by some further explanation, and the point to note is the need for such further explanation to address the cognitive dissonance present in such a strange conjunction of epistemological views. The interplay between the nature and value of knowledge present in Meno's thinking exists because there is a presumption in favor of holding an epistemological theory responsible to two criteria. A correct account of the nature of knowledge must resist counterexample, but it also ought to be amenable to an account of the value of knowledge. Meno's inclination to abandon an account of the nature of knowledge should still arise, even if that account is able to resist counterexample, provided that the account fails to allow an explanation of the value of knowledge.

Note what I am not claiming here: I am not

claiming that an adequate account of the nature of knowledge must contain an explanation of the value of knowledge. Nor am I claiming that an adequate account of the nature of knowledge must appeal to elements of knowledge that are themselves valuable. I am not even claiming that knowledge is valuable. I am, instead, claiming a presumption in favor of the view that knowledge is valuable, and more valuable than subsets of its constituents, and that failed attempts to account for the value of knowledge legitimately prompt questioning of one's assumed theory of the nature of knowledge. The presumption in favor of the value of knowledge is strong enough that it gives reason to abandon even a counter-example-free account of the nature of knowledge if that account leaves no way open for defending the value of knowledge.

It is important to note here a further thing that I am not saying. When I say that there is a presumption in favor of the value of knowledge, I am not saying that the only way an account of the nature of knowledge can be adequate is to be capable of being supplemented by some adequate account of the value of knowledge. I leave open the conclusion at which I aim in this work, namely, that we are mistaken to attach such significance to knowledge, that the valuable accomplishments of cognition are to be found in the general area inhabited by knowledge but do not require knowledge itself. That is, when knowledge is valuable, its value is to be explained in ways that do not require the presence of knowledge for that value to obtain. Coming to such a conclusion should change our conception of the tasks for epistemology, and I will indicate some of the differences such a conclusion will make.

But where I will end up is not where I begin, for there is a strong presumption in favor of the view that knowledge is valuable. So we ought to begin by seeking an explanation of the value of knowledge, and my discussion of Plato's *Meno* is meant to highlight dual presumptive conditions of adequacy for a theory of knowledge. First, an adequate theory of knowledge must contain an account of the nature of knowledge that is, at a minimum, counterexample-free. (I ignore for present purposes other theoretical virtues that the account will need to possess to be preferable to other counterexample-free accounts.) Second, the theory must be amenable to an account of the value of knowledge. What do I mean by "amenable to"? At the very least, the theory must be logically consistent with an account of the value of knowledge, but perhaps something stronger is required. Perhaps the two accounts should fit well together or cohere in some way beyond being merely consistent with each other; but we shall start with the minimal requirement of logical consistency.

Given these twin desiderata, Socrates' counterexample to Meno's account of the value of knowledge shows that Meno's account cannot be adequate so long as knowledge is anything more than true belief. Meno's reaction is to consider the possibility that knowledge is nothing more than true belief, but Socrates immediately rejects this idea, and this reaction is nearly universally shared among epistemologists. But only nearly universally shared; recently, Crispin Sartwell has tried to resurrect Meno's theory,[2] seriously defending Meno's first shot from the hip when confronted with the problem of the value of knowledge. It is very hard, however, not to side with Socrates against Sartwell. Socrates provides an interesting analogy to display the difference between knowledge and true belief, as well as the more straightforward route in terms of a counterexample.

Such counterexamples can be multiplied. For example, one need only look at the voluminous body of literature on the Gettier problem to find counterexample after counterexample to the claim that knowledge is true belief. One can even find an unanswered counterexample in Sartwell's own work. He says:

On the other hand, and this is where the present account runs into difficulties, we may be pressing the question of the source of belief. For example, if we find out that the claimant in this case has recently emerged from a mental hospital, and regards the voices in her head as reliable sources of information, we may well ask how she knows that $2 + 2 = 4$. If she now replies that one of these voices told her, we may say (though with some strain to common sense) that she didn't know it after all.[3]

Sartwell notes immediately that his account "obliges me to deny this claim,"[4] but all we get by way of argument for such a denial is a remark that "it *is* natural in a case such as this one to say that we *all* know that $2 + 2 = 4$; it is 'common knowledge'; in a typical case it would be perverse to ask of any one person *how* she knows it."[5] None of these claims is a sufficient reply to the counterexample, however. It may be natural to say that everyone knows simple arithmetical truths, but it is false. It is natural to say it because the counterexamples are so rare, not because they do not exist. Second, simple arithmetical truths are among the items of common knowledge, as Sartwell points out, but not everyone knows all of these items. Finally, though it is clearly not perverse to ask someone how he or she knows such simple truths, it is certainly unusual. But many of the questions therapists need to ask mental patients in order to ascertain their degree of sanity are similarly unusual.

Hence, Sartwell has no good response to his own counterexample. In light of this and the multitude of other counterexamples, how could Sartwell maintain the view that knowledge is only true belief? The answer lies in the argument that persuades him to maintain this uncommon and implausible thesis.

Sartwell's argument[6] focuses on the question of the goal, or *telos*, of inquiry with regard to particular propositions, which he maintains is knowledge.[7] He argues that an adequate theory of justification will be teleological, a means to the goal of truth. The argument is, he thinks, simple—that justification is not necessary for knowledge:

> If we describe justification as of merely instrumental value with regard to arriving at truth, as BonJour does explicitly, we can no longer maintain both that knowledge is the *telos* of inquiry and that justification is a necessary condition of knowledge. It is incoherent to build a specification of something regarded *merely* as a means of achieving some goal into the description of the goal itself; in such circumstances, the goal can be described independently of the means. So, if justification is demanded because it is instrumental to true belief, it cannot also be maintained that knowledge is justified true belief.[8]

Before commenting on the argument directly, I want to forestall one misunderstanding of Sartwell's conclusion. Because those familiar with the Gettier literature will balk at the claim that knowledge is justified true belief, it might seem that Sartwell's conclusion can be avoided just by holding that knowledge is more than justified true belief. But, as Sartwell makes clear, that would miss the point of the argument. Better put, Sartwell's conclusion is that if justification is of merely instrumental value, then knowledge is not even *at least* justified true belief. The instrumental value of justification is supposed to force us to take justification as only a criterion for knowledge, a mark we look for when we are trying to answer the question of whether someone knows, rather than a necessary condition for knowledge.[9]

The central stated premise of the argument for this claim is that "it is incoherent to build a specification of something regarded *merely* as a means of achieving some goal into the description of the goal itself." It is not obvious how to get from this claim to Sartwell's conclusion, but I think he is reasoning as follows:

1   Knowledge is the goal of inquiry.
2   Nothing that is merely a means to a goal is a necessary component of that goal.
3   Justification is merely a means to the goal of inquiry.
4   Therefore, justification is not a necessary component of the goal of inquiry.
5   Therefore, justification is not a necessary component of knowledge.

Premise 1, Sartwell admits, is undefended.[10] But that is not the primary defect of the argument. The primary defect is that this assumption simply will not be granted in the presence of premise 3, the claim that justification is a means to the goal of inquiry. Sartwell cites a long list of epistemologists who conceive of justification in instrumental terms, but they do not conceive of it as a means to the goal of inquiry except insofar as that goal is clarified in terms of getting to the truth and avoiding error. They do not conceive of justification as of instrumental value for knowledge, but rather for truth over error. So Sartwell cannot appeal to the views of epistemologists to establish the third premise of this argument unless he first abandons the first premise and clarifies the goal of inquiry in terms of truth.

Of course, if one already holds the view that knowledge is true belief, then one can easily accept both of these premises and even see the claims of epistemologists who endorse the view that justification is instrumentally valuable in the search for truth as supporting one's affirmations. But that is because one has already rejected the necessity of justification for knowledge. It appears, then, that the argument would only be accepted by those who already accept its conclusion.

What of the first premise, though? Is knowledge the goal of inquiry? I do not think that is the correct way to think of inquiry. When we engage in inquiry, we are trying to get to the truth about the subject matter in question. Inquiry ceases when we take ourselves to have

found the truth. That is, human beings do not typically conceive of inquiry in terms of knowledge, but rather, to use a common phrase, as "the search for truth." Inquirers describe the task in these terms, and the object of their intentions, when inquiry is accompanied by such, involves the concept of truth. Of course, it can also involve knowledge, but it needn't. So no argument will be forthcoming from reflective descriptions of human beings or from the contents of their intentions that knowledge must be the goal of inquiry. Inquiry is not "directed at" knowledge in either of these senses by its very nature, but instead can be, and often is (perhaps usually is), "directed at" finding the truth and avoiding error.

The best that might be true is that successful inquiry yields knowledge, and so that knowledge is a product of inquiry successfully conducted and hence the, or a, *telos* of inquiry in that sense. This is a claim that, if true, will not rescue Sartwell's argument. If knowledge is the result of successful inquiry in this sense, it is possible for justification to be both a means to it and a constituent of it as well. If becoming elected a senator is the result of a successful campaign, then running a successful campaign can be both a means to this goal and a constituent as well. The tension Sartwell cites between constituents of and means to some item arises at most in the intentional realm, but need not arise once we leave that realm. Indeed, if we consider the general concept of a means to a goal, some compelling examples are where the means are sufficient to produce the effect. So Sartwell's premise implies that no means sufficient to produce X can itself be necessary for X. This claim, however, is obviously false; some means toward a goal are both necessary and sufficient for achieving that goal.

Most means to a goal are not sufficient for the achievement of the goal to which they are directed, so Sartwell might restrict the premise to talk only of such insufficient means. This alteration is still false, however. A means toward the goal of getting a million dollars is getting half a million, or getting nine hundred thousand, or getting the first dollar (a journey of a thousand miles begins with the first step). Yet, each of these means is also a necessary constituent of the goal in question, so the alteration won't work either.

So Sartwell's argument is defective on several fronts, leaving his position that knowledge is true belief without adequate argumentative support. The proper conclusion to draw is that there is no reason to satisfy Meno's temptation by adopting the view that knowledge is true belief and many reasons against it in the form of counterexamples.

If knowledge is not true belief, then Socrates' counterexample shows that knowledge is no more practically useful than is true belief. So abandoning the claim that knowledge is true belief forces us to abandon the idea that the value of knowledge is to be accounted for by its practical significance in the lives of those who have it.

This conclusion is compatible with the claim that knowledge gives practical advantage to those who have it. It is just that the advantage they gain would have been achieved even if they had only gained true belief and not knowledge. So it is not their knowledge that explains their advantage but rather the fact that when one knows something, one has a true belief about it. Consider cases from the theory of explanation to make this point clear. A white, crystalline substance is immersed in water, and we want to know why it dissolves. Joe says it is because it is salt, but Billy disagrees. He says it is because it is *hexed* salt that it dissolves. If it is somehow useful to have a substance dissolved in our sample of water, we cannot claim that it is hexed salt that is valuable for that purpose. It does accomplish the goal we have in mind, but not because it is hexed salt; instead, it accomplishes the goal because all hexed salt is salt and salt dissolves in water. So hexed salt will be useful to us, but not because it is hexed salt. Instead, it will be useful to us

because it is salt. Just so, knowledge is useful to us, but not because it is knowledge. Instead, it is useful because it involves true belief. Hence, pragmatic usefulness does not explain why knowledge is valuable; in particular, it does not explain why knowledge is more valuable than true belief.

A natural response at this point might be skepticism concerning the value we seek to explain. We began by noting the value of knowledge and have found a sense in which it is valuable and a sense in which it may not be as valuable as we initially thought. Knowledge is valuable because of the practical benefits it provides. The only shadow of a problem is that it is not superior to true belief on this score. But, the skeptic might query, isn't that enough? We now have an account on which knowledge is valuable, and that is what we were looking for. What more do we seek?

The answer is that when we seek the value of knowledge, the description of the search is intended to be completely accurate. That is, it is *knowledge*'s value that we aim to understand, not the value of some of its constituents or the value of something in the logical neighborhood. It may be, in the end, that we will have to claim that what we seek cannot be found, but for the present, finding that true belief is valuable is not sufficient to end the search. What we have found is that when we have knowledge, we have something that is (often) practically useful to have, but it is not in virtue of being knowledge that it is practically useful. Instead, it is in virtue of being true belief. So if we are to succeed in giving an account of the value of knowledge, we will have to go further. In particular, we will have to address Socrates' concern in the *Meno* about what makes knowledge more valuable than true belief.

This skeptical inclination is useful, however, even if it should be resisted at this point. It is easy to mistake questions about the value of knowledge for comparative questions about its value relative to the value of its constituents or other cognitive states in the general conceptual neighborhood of knowledge. Thus, when we claim that knowledge is not more useful from a practical point of view than is true belief, we seem to threaten the view that knowledge is valuable. No such threat exists from this quarter, however. Instead, what is threatened is a further view about the nature and extent of the value of knowledge, a view that requires not only that knowledge is valuable, but that its value exceed that of its conceptual constituents and neighbors. I agree with those who hold that this view is an initially attractive one and that epistemological theorizing should take this attractiveness into account; that was my point in defending the twin desiderata on a theory of knowledge. Still, the twin desiderata are not *indefeasible*, for we might discover that we were mistaken in our assumptions about the value of knowledge. The previous skeptical response helps us to hold this possibility in our minds, for it might be that knowledge is valuable, but not as valuable or not possessing the kind of value that we initially thought. So even though we should reject the skeptical response that maintains that knowledge has no more value than true belief, keeping this response in mind will help us avoid confusing the question we will pursue with the quite different question of whether or not knowledge has any value at all.

[. . .]

The conclusion we must draw at this point is that we will not be able to account for the value of knowledge in terms of its practical significance. At first glance, this conclusion would seem to be sufficient to end our search for a value for knowledge that is external to it. For the obvious candidate for knowledge to help us achieve is well-being or happiness—more generally, whatever has practical utility. With the failure of that account, it might seem that we must look to the internal structure of knowledge to find its value, but moving to that position would be premature at this point, for there are two other approaches deserving attention before

we abandon the idea that the value of knowledge is found in things external to it. The first tries to find a defensible proposal in Socrates' analogy about the statues of Daedalus, and the second looks for an account in terms of the connection between knowledge and appropriate action. I turn first to Socrates' analogy.

Plato and the tethering of true belief

Return for a moment to the passage in the Meno with which we began. In that passage, Socrates first shows that knowledge is no more useful than true belief, leading Meno to wonder whether the two differ at all. Socrates answers by suggesting that the reason for Meno's wonderment is that Meno must not be familiar with the statues of Daedalus:

SOCRATES: It is because you have not observed the statues of Daedalus. Perhaps you don't have them in your country.
MENO: What makes you say that?
SOCRATES: They too, if no one ties them down, run away and escape. If tied, they stay where they are put.
MENO: What of it?
SOCRATES: If you have one of his works untethered, it is not worth much; it gives you the slip like a runaway slave. But a tethered specimen is very valuable, for they are magnificent creations. And that, I may say, has a bearing on the matter of true opinions. True opinions are a fine thing and do all sorts of good so long as they stay in their place, but they will not stay long. They run away from a man's mind; so they are not worth much until you tether them by working out the reason. That process, my dear Meno, is recollection, as we agreed earlier. Once they are tied down, they become knowledge, and are stable. That is why knowledge is something more valuable than right opinion. What distinguishes one from the other is the tether.[11]

Immediately following this passage, Socrates points out that his discussion is at the level of mere analogy, denying that it provides a theoretical basis for explaining the difference between knowledge and true belief. At first glance, Socrates is right to denigrate the theoretical sophistication of the analogy, for the analogy seems to suggest that knowledge is more valuable than true belief because knowledge does not get up and wander off, as do the statues of Daedalus when untethered. Yet, it is clear that knowledge does get up and wander off. Nothing beyond the most casual acquaintance with human forgetfulness and the graceful, and sometimes not so graceful, degradation of our cognitive equipment over time shows that knowledge has no such permanence to it. In short, knowledge, no less than true belief, can be lost. So no simple account of the implications of present knowledge in terms of what the future will hold can be adequate.

Still, there may be more to Socrates' suggestion than this initial glance reveals. At least Timothy Williamson thinks so. He says:

> Present knowledge is less vulnerable than mere present true belief to *rational* undermining by future evidence. . . . If your cognitive faculties are in good order, the probability of your believing p tomorrow is greater conditional on your knowing p today than on your merely believing p truly today. . . . Consequently, the probability of your believing p tomorrow is greater conditional on your knowing p today than on your believing p truly today.[12]

Williamson here takes the cross-temporal feature of Plato's analogy seriously, interpreting the value of knowledge in terms of the persistence of known beliefs as opposed to true beliefs. He holds that the likelihood that a belief will be held tomorrow is greater, given that it is known as opposed to merely believed truly, and he also holds that knowledge is less susceptible to

rational undermining by future evidence than is true belief.

So there are some who find more of substance in Socrates' analogy than Socrates himself thought he could find. Immediately upon giving the analogy, Socrates says, "Well of course, I have only been using an analogy myself, not knowledge. But it is not, I am sure, a mere guess to say that right opinion and knowledge are different."[13] Socrates used the analogy only to make the point that knowledge and true opinion are distinct, but he doubted that his analogy arose from any secure knowledge concerning the proper explanation of the difference between true belief and knowledge. Williamson thinks Socrates is on to something more. He thinks not only that the analogy points to a crucial difference between knowledge and true belief, but also that this difference is an important one for any attempt to explain the value of knowledge. In commenting on the argument previously cited, Williamson says, "[T]he present argument concerns only delayed impact, not action at the 'next' instant. We do not value knowledge more than true belief for instant gratification."[14] Williamson thus holds that cross-temporal differences are at the heart of the difference between the value of true belief and that of knowledge.

Williamson makes two points in the earlier quotation cited. The first claim is that knowledge is more immune from rational undermining by further evidence than is true belief. The second appears to be an attempt to make precise this first idea by employing the language of probability. According to it, "If your cognitive faculties are in good order, the probability of your believing p tomorrow is greater conditional on your knowing p today than on your merely believing p truly today."[15] Williamson notes that this probabilistic inequality is undermined if the true beliefs are thoroughly dogmatic ones, but claims that in such a case the cognitive faculties are not in good order.[16]

One flaw in Williamson's proposal is that it

does not attend sufficiently to the pragmatic dimension of the fixation of belief. It is true that discovery of evidence is a primary way in which fixation of belief occurs, but it is also well known that the importance of belief for survival and well-being depends on other factors for belief formation as well. For example, hasty generalizations are often important beliefs for survival, and false positives, even a high percentage of them, can be produced by cognitive systems for predators that are in good working order and have survival value. In general, our cognitive systems serve a variety of purposes besides truth and are in good working order because of their contribution to these other important goals.

So, in order to assess Williamson's claim, we should divide the class of true beliefs into those whose fixation depends on evidence and those whose fixation depends on nonevidential factors. Among the latter are not only beliefs that result from a cognitive system that is not in good working order, but also beliefs produced by cognitive systems in good working order aimed at some goal other than truth.

If we consider beliefs fixed by mechanisms having survival value, it would not be surprising to find such beliefs very difficult to unseat, perhaps even more difficult to unseat than knowledge would be. Knowledge can cease to exist in a number of ways, from simple forgetting to injury-induced trauma through the deterioration of cognitive abilities, but one would expect beliefs fixed by survival mechanisms to be among the most resistant beliefs one has.

Of equal importance for assessing Williamson's probabilistic inequality is that not all, and perhaps not even a majority of, beliefs fixed by evidence count as knowledge. It is essential that one exist in a cooperative environment for such beliefs to be known to be true, and it is implausible to discount true beliefs fixed by evidence in hostile environments as the product of cognitive equipment not in good working order.

When we compare knowledge with true beliefs fixed by evidence that do not count as knowledge, we find no obvious pattern favoring the retention of the former over the latter. Williamson is correct that the latter beliefs can be undermined by finding information of which one was unaware at the time of belief formation, whereas knowledge is incompatible with the presence of such undermining yet unknown information. This feature does not tell the whole story, however, for there are other ways in which knowledge can be undermined but true belief remains unaffected. In particular, knowledge can be undermined at a later time by future changes of which one is unaware, where true belief is retained. For example, my mathematical knowledge might be undermined tomorrow by the sincere testimony of a renowned mathematician to the effect that what I believe is false. Until such testimony is rendered, I have such knowledge, but I lose it when the defeating testimony is given, even though I am unaware that such testimony has occurred. I thereby lose my knowledge but not my true belief (I am assuming that the renowned mathematician has made an honest mistake, one that will take considerable effort and time to uncover, for even other important mathematicians will be taken in by his remarks). Or, again, consider the similar effect radical changes in nature can have on knowledge. Much of our common knowledge about the patterns in nature can be undercut by events of which we are unaware. The eruption of Mt. St. Helens, for example, caused noticeable shifts in weather patterns, and even more radical changes are imaginable. In such cases, the evidentiary basis for our knowledge of weather patterns can be undercut, even if some particular aspects of our views of such patterns are nonetheless true. In such cases, even before we become aware of the volcanic eruption, its occurrence introduces a defeater regarding our knowledge of weather patterns, but it does not undermine our beliefs (because we are not yet aware of the catastrophic event). So even though there is one respect in which true belief is capable of being undermined in a way in which knowledge is not, there are other respects in which knowledge is capable of being undermined in which true belief is not.

Perhaps a specific example would help in understanding my point. Suppose Joe is building a sand castle on a Japanese beach and wishes to show it to his children, who will arrive tomorrow. Joe thus uses his knowledge of high and low tides to find a location that will not be overrun before his children arrive. In fact, over a month ago he picked an especially safe location, planning the event carefully to ensure success. His knowledge of low and high tides serves as a basis for his knowledge that if he builds a castle at a certain location, the ocean won't ruin it before his children arrive.

His knowledge disappears before he builds the castle in the following way. Two weeks after he decides where to build the castle, an earthquake occurs that causes a *tsunami* headed for the Japanese coast that will arrive the night before his children arrive. He is unaware of these events, however, and so blissfully goes about constructing the castle. He has lost his knowledge but not his true belief (the *tsunami* improbably fails to damage his particular beach).

A defender of Williamson might turn skeptical about claims to knowledge in such cases, holding that we never have knowledge of the future, as this example maintains. Such skepticism would be overdone, however, for its basis would have to be that we can never have knowledge based on patterns of nature if those patterns are not completely exceptionless. I will not press this point here, however, for we already have presented other examples of cases where knowledge is undermined but true belief remains.

It is time to bring these strands of discussion to bear on Williamson's probabilistic inequality, which requires that the likelihood of a belief persisting until tomorrow is greater, given that it is known today as opposed to merely believed

truly. The previous information shows, I submit, that whether this claim is true is highly contingent. In some worlds, environments may be very cooperative and pragmatic matters less significant in the process of belief fixation. In such worlds, Williamson's inequality may well be true. The vast majority of beliefs will be fixed by evidence, and the vast majority of beliefs fixed by evidence will be both true and known. Moreover, pragmatic features may be relatively insignificant, implying that beliefs fixed by such factors need not be especially resistant to abandonment. In such worlds, one may be more likely to continue to know tomorrow what one knows today than to believe truly tomorrow what one believes truly today. In other worlds, the pragmatic dimensions may be more dominant, implying the falsity of Williamson's inequality. In such worlds, most of the true beliefs may be fixed by quite strong pragmatic mechanisms, with any other true beliefs having considerable fragility. In such cases, beliefs known today to be true will be much more susceptible to abandonment than will true beliefs fixed by nonevidentiary factors. And even if we restrict our attention to evidentially induced beliefs, there will be worlds in which known beliefs are more susceptible to cessation than are mere true beliefs. Such susceptibility would occur when (i) the unpossessed information that undermines knowledge for some true beliefs is resistant to discovery, while (ii) the universe conspires to generate future defeaters for a large percentage of what is known. So whether Williamson's inequality is true or not depends on what kind of world we live in and is thus a contingent truth at best.

Furthermore, even if we agree with Williamson about which kind of world we inhabit, the contingent truth of his inequality will be of little use in the present context, for the value of knowledge does not covary with the truth value of Williamson's inequality. It is simply false that knowledge loses its value in worlds where the environment is less cooperative and where pragmatics play a more significant role in belief fixation. So this inequality yields no adequate explanation of the value of knowledge.

It might appear that my objections to Williamson's inequality depend too much on a frequency conception of probability, but that is not so. If probability claims are contingent, then no matter which semantics for probability claims we adopt, Williamson's inequality will be true in some worlds and false in others. The only way to prevent this result in the face of the objections I raise is to insist on an interpretation of probability in which probabilistic claims are necessarily true if true at all. If we adopt such an interpretation, then my objections should be recast to argue that the probability involved here is simply inscrutable, for none of us is in a position to measure the proportion of worlds that have friendly or hostile environments or require truth for pragmatically effective belief. So whether probability claims are contingent or necessary, we have sufficient grounds for refusing to endorse Williamson's inequality as a sound explanation of the value of knowledge over that of true belief.

My argument has focused on Williamson's technical formulation in terms of the language of probability, as opposed to the more intuitive initial formulation in terms of rational undermining by future evidence. I don't think that resorting to the more intuitive formulation is helpful, however, for it, too, ignores the roles of pragmatic factors in belief fixation and co-operative environments for the existence of knowledge. It is possible for pragmatically useful beliefs to be highly resistant to being undermined by future evidence, and it is possible for beliefs known to be true to be highly fragile. Williamson could appeal to the qualifier of *rational* undermining and insist that pragmatically useful beliefs would be abandoned were the cognizers in question more rational, but such a response is weak. First, one need not be irrational to hold pragmatically significant beliefs in the face of contrary evidence. The most

one could defend is that it would be irrational *from an epistemic point of view* to do so.

What happens if we reformulate Williamson's intuitive idea along these lines? We get something like the following: True belief is more susceptible than is knowledge to being abandoned in the face of contrary evidence for cognizers who are rational from an epistemic point of view. Why is that so? Because, according to Williamson, knowledge is incompatible with the existence of such contrary evidence, whereas true belief is not.

The question we should ask, however, is why this result is significant. We should have no doubt that there is some respect in which knowledge is immune from loss in which true belief is not. They are, after all, logically distinct. When we compare the different ways in which one of the two can survive while the other is lost, the particular immunity from loss that knowledge possesses yields no immediate and direct advantage to it over the kinds of immunity from loss possessed by true belief.

We can thus draw together the variety of points in the preceding discussion of Williamson's proposal in the following way. We have seen some possible ways in which knowledge is more susceptible to loss than is true belief and other possible ways in which true belief can be more susceptible to loss than is knowledge. In the face of this variety, merely identifying one set of conditions that favor the persistence of knowledge will not explain the value of knowledge over that of true belief. For the existence of such conditions is compatible with the existence of other conditions under which true belief would survive and knowledge would not. What is needed is some reason to think that one of these considerations trumps the other, and Williamson gives no such reason. Moreover, it is exceedingly difficult to imagine what such a reason might be. That is, even if one agrees that we want an account of the value of knowledge that shows it to be more valuable than true belief, we have no reason to think that we will find such an account by looking for a reason to prefer persistence factors favoring knowledge as opposed to persistence factors favoring true belief. Williamson may be right that we do not value knowledge for instant gratification, but we can enjoy such a pleasantly pithy remark without being misled into searching among persistence conditions for an account of the importance of knowledge over that of true belief.

Given the infallibilist assumption about the nature of knowledge that dominates the history of epistemology, it is not difficult to be tempted to look in such a direction. For if knowledge is infallible in the sense of requiring the possession of evidence or information guaranteeing the truth of what one believes, no amount of further learning could threaten it. Furthermore, it could be just such an assumption that underlies Socrates' analogy about the statues of Daedalus, yielding as a conclusion that an account of the value of knowledge in terms of persistence conditions is much more attractive given this mistaken assumption about knowledge. We must not forget, however, the depth of the mistake here. Knowledge is fragile in a variety of ways, susceptible to being undermined by future events, by learning of such events, and by learning of present and past events that are misleading in their evidentiary force.

For those familiar with the Gettier literature in epistemology,[17] these last remarks will be akin to epistemological platitudes. [. . . Nevertheless] general remarks may prove helpful here. First, consider the following example:

Suppose Joe has strong evidence that his friend Fred has a silver dollar in his pocket. Fred is deceiving Joe, but Joe is unaware of this fact. Joe infers from the claim that Fred has a silver dollar in his pocket the claim that someone in this room has a silver dollar in his pocket, for the person at the podium in this room has just said, "Does someone here have a silver dollar in their pocket?" and Joe stands and says, "Yes, Fred does." So Joe believes two

things: Fred has a silver dollar in his pocket, and someone here has a silver dollar in his pocket. Joe is wrong about the first claim, however, for Fred is deceiving him, but it turns out by happenstance that Joe is right about the second claim, for the speaker has a silver dollar in his pocket. So Joe's belief in the second claim is true and is held for good reasons because it is correctly inferred from another belief of Joe's that he has good reasons for holding. But it is not knowledge, since his reasons in this case bear no connection with what makes the belief true.

Notice that examples like this one require that one be a fallibilist about good reasons. If one thought that one could never have good reasons for a belief unless those reasons guaranteed the truth of one's belief, cases like this one could not arise. The difficulty with such infallibilist assumptions about good reasons is that such assumptions imply that we almost never have good reasons for anything we think, contrary to what we know to be true. Even if our reasons don't guarantee the truth of what we believe, they are nonetheless often good reasons for those beliefs. If so, however, we can't identify true belief accompanied by good reasons with knowledge.

Furthermore, once we see the possibility of knowledge even when our reasons for belief are defeasible, the fragility of knowledge becomes apparent. The very same constellation of evidence can be present in cases of knowledge and in cases where knowledge is lacking. Moreover, while the adoption of a fallibilist account of knowledge leaves open the possibility of statistical knowledge, this openness signals further the fragility of knowledge, for such knowledge is compatible with the existence of pockets of misleading information of which one is unaware. For example, a carefully controlled collection of data can yield knowledge that most members of the entire population have a certain characteristic, and it is compatible with this knowledge that there are enough members of the population lacking the characteristic that, if added to one's data, one would no longer have sufficient evidence to confirm the claim in question. It is this fragility of knowledge arising from such fallibilism that undermines the attempt to account for the value of knowledge in terms of its persistence. The conclusion we must draw, therefore, is that Williamson's efforts to find in Socrates' analogy a cross-temporal explanation of the value of knowledge are unsuccessful.

Knowledge and action

The final proposal I want to examine for defending the value of knowledge on the basis of things extrinsic to it has to do with its relationship to things that we do, that is, to human actions. Perhaps some of our actions will be inadequate or unacceptable or deficient in some other way if they are not based on knowledge. We have already seen that they cannot be judged unacceptable by their fruits, for knowledge is not required in order for our actions to turn out well. But perhaps there is something more internal to the action itself that calls for a negative judgment when the action is not based on knowledge.

One might suggest, for example, that there is something immoral or blameworthy in performing an action that is not based on knowledge. Such a suggestion faces the same difficulty encountered by the practical usefulness theory presented earlier, for if actions are based on true beliefs, then it is hard to see how the actions could be immoral in virtue of the cognitive dimension of the act. The action could still be immoral because the desires that led to it are bad desires, but replacing true beliefs with knowledge will not correct this problem. For example, if after hurting a friend's feelings one desires to make amends and believes that sending flowers with an apology will do so, it is hard to see why it would matter whether one knows that sending flowers with an apology will make amends or merely believes this correctly.

In either case, sending the flowers with an apology is a good thing to do, and in the absence of some better approach to the situation, it may be the right thing to do as well.

One might still hold that in such a situation, one can be legitimately blamed for sending the flowers, even if it is the right thing to do, if one lacked good reasons for thinking that this action is the right thing to do. If one is doing the right thing only in virtue of what one learned from a fortune cookie, for example, we might still show legitimate disapproval even though we grant that the action was the right one. So we might require not only true belief about what to do, but true belief based on good reasons. Still, though, true belief based on good reasons is not knowledge.

Perhaps we might think of strengthening the cognitive requirement for blameless action so that knowledge of the beliefs the action is based on must be known to be true in order for the action to be blameless. Such a requirement is too strong, however. Consider the hurt feelings case again. Suppose one has good reasons for thinking that flowers and an apology would solve the problem because another friend is playing a practical joke. That friend tells you that sending flowers is the right thing to do (perhaps he claims he's been in the same situation several times with the hurt friend, and flowers plus an apology have always been effective, in fact singularly effective, because nothing else has ever worked). He's attempting to deceive you, relying on substantial experience that the hurt friend hates flowers, but the hurt friend has just acquired a love of fresh bouquets. So you have a true belief based on testimony that is ordinarily reliable, but you do not have knowledge. Your lack of knowledge, however, does not make your action blameworthy in any way. The only blame deserved applies to your deceitful friend.

So we might be able to defend the view that actions need to be based on true beliefs plus good reasons, but we cannot defend the view that actions need to be based on knowledge. Perhaps, though, there is a special kind of action that needs such a basis even though actions in general do not. Williamson has proposed such a theory for the special action of assertion, according to which assertion must be based on knowledge if the assertion is to be free of wrongdoing.[18] This view that knowledge is the norm of assertion can be used to account for the singular importance of knowledge, because, on it, knowledge is a necessary condition for legitimate assertion.

Thus, even though it cannot be defended that actions in general must be based on knowledge in order to be legitimate, the proposal here is that there is a special kind of act for which this claim is true, namely, a speech act. The speech act theory of the value of knowledge posits conditions under which acts of speech—assertions in particular—are legitimate. We can call these conditions "assertibility conditions." One way to discover such conditions is to investigate how we go about getting persons to take back an assertion. Sometimes we do so by claiming that they don't believe what they are saying. For example, a student, after failing a test, might discouragingly claim, "I never do well on multiple-choice tests." We can get the student to recant by reminding the student that the remark is the result of discouragement and not honest conviction: He really doesn't believe that he never does well; he's merely exaggerating because of discouragement. Such reminders often prompt retractions. He might say, "Yes, you're right, I shouldn't have said that."

Retractions are also appropriate when the remark is false. If I said a month ago that the Yankees wouldn't make the playoffs, you can come to me now and require a retraction from me because what I claimed is false. So among assertibility conditions seem to be both truth and belief: An assertion is illegitimate unless it is true and is believed to be so by the assertor.

Just as in the case of action generally, we might also have reason to insist on good reasons for belief in addition to truth and belief. Fundamentalist Christians often claim that there have

been more earthquakes in the twentieth century than in prior centuries. There is empirical evidence for this claim, but many make the claim unaware of the evidence. They say what they do because it fits their eschatological views, and I will assume here that this fit is insufficient in itself to warrant their assertion. If challenged by pointing out that they have no empirical evidence, they may recant. And even when they won't, their sheepishness and embarrassment often indicate that they should. So, even if they believe the claim, they shouldn't have said it without adequate evidence.

If we think of the Gettier problem as teaching the lesson that knowledge is justified true belief plus some condition aimed at handling the Gettier problem, then we may be tempted to say that retractions are in order when the Gettier condition is violated as well. In the preceding case used to show that knowledge is something more than true belief plus good reasons, we could get Joe to take back his claim that someone in the room has a silver dollar in his pocket by showing him that Fred's pockets are empty.

Given this procedural test of what we can use to get people to take back what they say, there is some plausibility to the view that knowledge is required for legitimate assertion; or, as Williamson puts it, knowledge is the norm, or rule, of assertion.[19] I want to argue, however, that this conclusion is mistaken and that the test of retraction employed earlier is a bit misleading. First, I'll engage in a bit of border skirmishing to the effect that the connections between legitimate assertion and knowledge are weaker than the preceding suggests. Afterward, I'll get to the main reason the proposal fails.

Let's begin by being precise about the proposal. First, it claims a logical relationship between the assertibility of p and knowing p: p's being assertible by S entails S's knowing p, where p's being assertible is understood to mean that it is permissible for S to assert p. This claim is false. Consider someone wishing to be a theist who takes Pascal's advice of going to Mass and hoping for the best; in line with such advice, a person may sincerely avow that God exists even though that person does not (yet) believe it. Furthermore, no one in such a condition need be moved to retract the assertion upon the complaint that the assertion is not backed by belief. All that would be required is an explanation and a defense of Pascal's advice and how the assertion fits with that advice. Again, consider someone who, moved by William James's pragmatic arguments,[20] comes to believe that God exists and asserts it, all the while knowing that there is insufficient evidence to confirm this claim. Such a person need not retract the claim when the absence of evidence is noted; all that is needed is a defense and an explanation of James's viewpoint and of how the assertion is supported by that argument. For a third case, imagine Churchland or Stich asserting, "I believe nothing that I assert," something their writings imply.[21] On the speech act proposal, no such sentence is assertible, but it is easy to see that neither would be guilty of any impropriety in asserting their position, even if it should turn out that they are philosophically mistaken in claiming that there are no beliefs. This latter case is a special instance of skeptical and Pyrrhonian assertion.[22] Skeptics are quite comfortable asserting that knowledge is not possible, and Pyrrhonian skeptics assert not only that knowledge is not possible but also that it is best not to hold any beliefs at all (though the interpretation of their belief–appearance distinction is controversial, a point to be pursued later). In each of these cases, assertion is legitimate even though the question of whether it is backed by knowledge is left open.

So it would appear that the most that can be claimed is that knowing p is *ordinarily* a requirement for legitimately asserting p. What, precisely, does such a claim mean, however? It is, of course, confused to say that one claim ordinarily entails another. Perhaps the notion of a requirement should be understood differently. Instead of thinking of requirement in terms of

entailment, perhaps we should think of it as a defeasible relation, so that x can require y even though x&z does not require y. If we understand the notion of requirement in this way, we might still be able to claim that the assertibility of p requires knowing p even though in the unusual cases described previously, additional factors come into play so that the assertibility of p in those circumstances does not require knowledge.

Even such retrenchment cannot save the proposal, however. Recall the way in which the proposal began. We look for ways in which we can require a person to take back an assertion, and it turns out that the conditions for knowledge are among those ways. There are, however, two quite different things a person might be doing in taking back an assertion. The person might be taking back only *what is said*, or she might be taking back *the saying of it*. So, for example, if Joe says, "I don't know why I keep trying to be friendly; nobody likes me at all," and Mary says, "Joe, you don't really believe that; you're just upset," Joe might apologize for saying what he knows is false. Such cases support the view that belief is ordinarily a requirement on assertion because the retraction involves taking back the saying itself. Moreover, when people assert things with no good reason whatsoever, we reprove such utterances, realizing that even though what is said might be true, *those individuals* have no business saying so. So once again, it is the saying itself that is at fault. But when new information is presented that undermines an assertion, only a retraction of what is said is in order. In the case of Joe and the silver dollar given earlier, pointing out that Fred's pockets are empty should lead Joe to retract his claim that someone in the room has a silver dollar in his pocket. It would be quite bizarre, however, to hear Joe apologizing for having made the claim at all. It is what was said that was mistaken, not the saying of it. Again, if I assert what is false and you show me that it is false, I'll retract my statement. But I wouldn't say that my uttering of it was out of order.

This distinction thus suggests that there is a better account of assertibility conditions than the speech act proposal developed by Williamson. Instead of conditions of knowledge being assertibility conditions, only belief and justification are among such conditions. The appeal to knowledge is superfluous, for all the explanatory work can be done by the concept of justified belief. When *the saying itself* is inappropriate, that is so in the ordinary case where standards of assertion and standards of belief converge because justified belief was not present when the assertion was made. When *what was said* must be retracted, as occurs when one learns that one has been gettiered or that one's statement is false, that is so because justification for belief is no longer present. That is all the explanation that is needed, and no appeal to [the] concept of knowledge is involved in it.

There is, however, still a smidgen of a difficulty. For when you find out that you've been gettiered, there is some residual embarrassment or regret for your assertions. If Joe says that someone has a silver dollar in his pocket because he believes that Fred has one and then is shown that Fred does not have one, he might not only retract his statement, but also experience some embarrassment or regret for the assertion. Does he thereby show the inappropriateness of assertion in the absence of knowledge? No. He shows only the common human inclination against being duped, and one can be duped because of truths that undermine knowledge and because of truths that do not undermine knowledge. You'd experience the same embarrassment or regret if the defeater mentioned were a misleading one. A classic case involving misleading defeaters is the case of Tom stealing a book from the library.[23] You see Tom steal the book and have a justified true belief that he stole it. But his mother, an inveterate liar, tells the police that it was his twin brother, Tim, who stole it. The police know the story is

concocted; they know she is an inveterate liar and will say anything to protect Tom. They also know Tom has no twin. But you don't know all this, and if you were told what the mother said, you'd be every bit as inclined to take back the assertion that Tom stole the book and to experience some embarrassment or regret for having confidently claimed it. But the defeater is a misleading one; without having been told it, it does not undermine your knowledge, because it is so obviously farcical. Yet, even misleading defeaters, when discovered, undermine knowledge; that is what makes them defeaters in the first place.

The lesson, then, is that your embarrassment, shame, or regret is not an indicator that knowledge is a prerequisite of appropriate assertion. Instead, it is only a sign that none of us is comfortable with the existence of information of which we are not aware that would undermine the justification of our beliefs. To have justifications immune from defeat is, of course, a valuable characteristic of a belief (provided that justification itself is). To conclude, however, that one should never say anything for which one lacks immunity from defeat is, to paraphrase William James, to show a preoccupation with not being duped.[24]

I suspect there are logically possible alternative explanations of the value of knowledge in terms of things external to it that I have not considered here. Still, I think the proper conclusion to draw is that there is good reason to doubt that the value of knowledge will be accounted for adequately in these terms. The theories I have considered here include the most obvious and most defended of such accounts, and though we lack any proof that no such account can be adequate, canvassing these available possibilities and seeing their faults gives us adequate reason to think that this approach to the value of knowledge will not be successful. [. . .]

Notes

1 Plato, *Meno*; all quotes are from the W. K. C. Guthrie translation in *The Collected Dialogues of Plato*, Edith Hamilton and Huntington Cairns, eds. (Princeton, NJ: Princeton University Press, 1963), pp. 353–84.

2 Crispin Sartwell, "Knowledge Is True Belief," *American Philosophical Quarterly*, 28, 2 (1991): 157–65.

3 Ibid., p. 162.

4 Ibid.

5 Ibid., p. 163.

6 Crispin Sartwell, "Why Knowledge Is Merely True Belief," *Journal of Philosophy*, 89, 4 (1992): 167–80.

7 Ibid., p. 173.

8 Ibid., p. 174.

9 Ibid.

10 Ibid. In fairness to Sartwell, he does claim in footnote 11 that "I hope to establish this claim on completely independent grounds." I am unaware of any place where he tries to so establish the claim.

11 Plato, *Meno*, pp. 97d–98a.

12 Timothy Williamson, *Knowledge and Its Limits* (Oxford: Oxford University Press, 2000), p. 79.

13 Plato, *Meno*, p. 98b.

14 Williamson, *Knowledge*.

15 Ibid., p. 79.

16 Ibid.

17 Edmund Gettier, "Is Justified True Belief Knowledge?" *Analysis*, 23 (1963): 121–3.

18 Timothy Williamson, "Knowing and Asserting," *The Philosophical Review*, 105, 4 (1996): 489–523.

19 Ibid., p. 519.

20 In "The Will to Believe," in *The Will to Believe and Other Essays in Popular Philosophy* (New York: Habnev, 1897).

21 See Stephen Stich, *From Folk Psychology to Cognitive Science: The Case Against Belief* (Cambridge, MA: MIT Press, 1983); Paul Churchland, *Scientific Realism and the Plasticity of Mind* (Cambridge: Cambridge University Press, 1979).

22 As an aside, such possibilities of appropriate assertion show that Moore's paradox, the paradox that arises from a person's asserting that a certain proposition is true but that he or she doesn't believe it, is not always paradoxical; it is paradoxical only given certain assumptions about how standards for belief and standards for assertion are correlated.

23 From Keith Lehrer and Thomas D. Paxson, Jr., "Knowledge: Undefeated Justified True Belief," *Journal of Philosophy*, 66, 8 (1969): 225–37.

24 The actual quote is: "He who says 'Better go without belief forever than believe a lie!' merely shows his own preponderant private horror of becoming a dupe." William James, *Essays in Pragmatism* (New York: Hafner, 1948), p. 100.

Chapter 7

Linda Zagzebski

THE SEARCH FOR THE SOURCE OF EPISTEMIC GOOD

Philosophers have traditionally regarded knowledge as a highly valuable epistemic state, perhaps even one of the great goods of life. At a minimum, it is thought to be more valuable than true belief. Contemporary proposals on the nature of knowledge, however, make it difficult to understand why knowledge is good enough to have received so much attention in the history of philosophy. Some of the most common theories cannot even explain why knowledge is better than true belief. I propose that the search for the source of epistemic value reveals some constraints on the way knowledge can be defined. I believe it will also show that the common view that epistemic good is independent of moral good is largely an illusion.

1 What makes knowledge better than true belief?

It is almost always taken for granted that knowledge is good, better than true belief *simpliciter*, but it is remarkably difficult to explain what it is about knowledge that makes it better. I call this 'the value problem'.[1] I have previously argued that most forms of reliabilism have a particularly hard time handling the value problem.[2] According to standard reliabilist models, knowledge is true belief that is the output of reliable belief-forming processes or faculties. But the reliability of the source of a belief cannot explain the difference in value between knowledge and

true belief. One reason it cannot do so is that reliability per se has no value or disvalue. A reliable espresso maker is good because espresso is good. A reliable water-dripping faucet is not good because dripping water is not good. The good of the product makes the reliability of the source that produces it good, but the reliability of the source does not then give the product an additional boost of value. The liquid in this cup is not improved by the fact that it comes from a reliable espresso maker. If the espresso tastes good, it makes no difference if it comes from an unreliable machine. If the flower garden is beautiful, it makes no difference if it was planted by an unreliable gardener. If the book is fascinating, it makes no difference if it was written by an unreliable author. If the belief is true, it makes no difference if it comes from an unreliable belief-producing source.

This point applies to any source of a belief, whether it be a process, faculty, virtue, skill – any cause of belief whose value is thought to confer value on the true belief that is its product, and which is thought to confer value because of its reliability. If knowledge is true belief arising out of the exercise of good traits and skills, it cannot be the reliability of the agent's traits and skills that adds the value. Those traits or skills must be good for some reason that does not wholly derive from the good of the product they produce: true belief. As reliabilism has matured, the location of reliability has shifted from processes to faculties to agents.[3] There are advantages in this progression, but if the good-making feature of a belief-forming process or faculty or agent is only its reliability, then these versions of reliabilism all share the same problem; being the product of a reliable faculty or agent does not add value to the product.[4] Hence, if knowledge arises from something like intellectual virtue or intellectually virtuous acts, what makes an intellectual trait good, and hence a virtue, cannot be simply that it reliably leads to true belief. This, then, is the first moral of the value problem: *Truth plus a reliable source of truth cannot explain the value of knowledge.*

It follows that there must be a value in the cause of a true belief that is independent of reliability or truth conduciveness, whether we call it virtue or something else. Suppose we succeed in identifying such a value. Is that sufficient to solve the value problem? Unfortunately, it is not, so long as we think of knowledge as the external product of a good cause. A cup of espresso is not made better by the fact that the machine that produces it is valuable, even when that value is independent of the value of good-tasting espresso. What the espresso analogy shows is not only that a reliable cause does not confer value on its effect but also that there is a general problem in attributing value to an effect because of its causes, even if the value of the cause is independent of the value of the effect. I am not suggesting that a cause can never confer value on its effect. Sometimes cause and effect have an internal connection, such as that between motive and act, which I shall discuss in a moment. My point is just that the value of a cause does not transfer to its effect automatically, and certainly not on the model of an effect as the output of the cause. So even if the cause of true belief has an independent value, that still does not tell us what makes knowledge better than true belief if knowledge is true belief that is good in some way other than its truth. The second moral of the value problem, then, is this: *Truth plus an independently valuable source cannot explain the value of knowledge.*

It follows from the second moral that to solve the value problem it is not enough to find another value in the course of analysing knowledge; one needs to find another value in the right place. Consider Alvin Plantinga's theory of warrant as proper function. A properly functioning machine does not confer value on its product any more than a reliable one does. The problem is not that proper function is not a good thing but that it is not a value in the knowing state itself. The first two morals of the value problem, then, reveal a deeper problem. We cannot explain what makes knowledge more valuable than true belief if we persist in using the machine-product model of belief that is so common in epistemological discourse.[5] Knowledge cannot be identified with the state of true belief that is the output of a valuable cause, whether or not the cause has a value independent of the value of true belief.[6]

In other work I have proposed that in a state of knowledge the agent gets to the truth because of the virtuous features of her belief-forming activity.[7] Wayne Riggs and John Greco's response to the value problem is that the extra value of knowing in addition to true belief is the state of affairs of the epistemic agent's getting credit for the truth that is acquired.[8] Ernest Sosa's response to the value problem is similar. He says that in a state of knowing, the truth is attributable to the agent as his or her own doing.[9] These approaches clearly are similar, but they solve the value problem only if we reject the machine-product model of knowledge.[10] For the same reason that the espresso in a cup is not made better by the fact that it is produced by a reliable espresso maker or a properly functioning espresso maker, it does not get any better if the machine gets credit for producing the espresso. That is to say, the coffee in the cup does not taste any better.

The conclusion is that true belief arising from cognitive activity cannot be like espresso coming out of an espresso maker. Not only is the reliability of the machine insufficient to make the coffee in the cup any better; nothing about the machine makes the product any better. So if knowledge is true belief that is made better by something, knowledge cannot be the external product of the believer the way the cup of espresso is the external product of the machine.

Let us look at the idea that knowing has something to do with the agent getting credit for the truth, that she gets to the truth because of something about her as a knowing agent – her virtues or virtuous acts. There are theoretical motives for this idea that have nothing to do with the value problem, such as the proposal that it avoids Gettier problems,[11] so it is supported by other constraints on the account of knowledge. But my concern in this article is the way this move can solve the value problem. If I am right that knowing is not an output of the agent, it must be a state of the agent. I am not suggesting that this is the only alternative to the machine-product model,[12] but if we think of a belief as part of the agent, the belief can get evaluative properties from features of the agent in the same way that acts get evaluative properties from the agent. In fact, the idea that in a state of knowing the agent gets credit for getting the truth suggests that her epistemic state is attached to her in the same way her acts are attached to her. An act is not a product of an agent but is a part of the agent, and the agent gets credit or discredit for an act because of features of the agent. In particular, an agent gets credit for certain good features of an act, for example, its good consequences or the fact that it follows a moral principle – because of features of the act that derive directly from the agent – for example, its intention or its motive. If believing is like acting, we have a model for the way the agent can get credit for the truth of a belief because of features of the belief that derive from the agent. I propose, then, that this is the third moral of the value problem: *Knowing is related to the knower not as product to machine but as act to agent.*[13]

The value problem arises for a group of theories wider than those that are reliabilist or even externalist. Internalists generally do not think of a true belief as the product of what justifies it, and so they accept the first part of the third moral. Nonetheless, some of them are vulnerable to the first moral of the value problem because they analyse justification in such a way that its value is explained by its truth conduciveness. Laurence BonJour does this explicitly in the following passage:

> The basic role of justification is that of a *means* to truth, a more directly attainable mediating link between our subjective starting point and our objective goal. . . . If epistemic justification were not conducive to truth in this way, if finding epistemically justified beliefs did not substantially increase the likelihood of finding true ones, then epistemic justification would be irrelevant to our main cognitive goal and of dubious worth. It is only if we have some reason for thinking that epistemic justification constitutes a path to truth that we as cognitive beings have any motive for preferring epistemically justified beliefs to epistemically unjustified ones. Epistemic justification is therefore in the final analysis only an instrumental value, not an intrinsic one.
>
> (BonJour 1985, 7–8)[14]

Notice that in this passage BonJour understands the value of justification the same way the reliabilist does, as something that is good because it is truth conducive. The internality of justification has nothing to do with its value on BonJour's account. But as we have seen, if the feature that converts true belief into knowledge is good just because of its conduciveness to truth, we are left without an explanation of why knowing *p* is better than merely truly believing *p*. And this is the case whether or not that feature is accessible to the consciousness of the believer. BonJour does not appeal to the machine-product model, and so the problem in his case is more subtle than it is for the reliabilist. Nonetheless, the problem is there, because a true belief does not gain any additional good property from justification. In contrast, the traditional account of knowledge as justified true belief does not have the value problem, because the justifying beliefs do not or do not simply produce the belief that is a candidate for knowledge. Instead, they give it a property, justifiedness. They make it justified. The conclusion is that if knowing p is better than truly believing p, there must be something other than the truth of p that *makes believing p better*. My proposal is that if believing is like acting, it can be made better by certain properties of the agent.

Consider a few of the ways an act acquires properties because of features of the agent. The class of acts subject to moral evaluation has traditionally been called the voluntary. A voluntary act is an act for which the agent gets credit or blame. The voluntary includes some acts that are intentional and some that are non-intentional. Acts that are voluntary but non-intentional can be motivated, and perhaps always are. My position is that acts of believing are generally in the category of acts that are voluntary but non-intentional, although for the purposes of this article it is not necessary that this position be accepted. What is important is just the idea that beliefs can be and perhaps typically are motivated, and that the motive can affect the evaluation of the belief in a way that is analogous to the way the motive can affect the evaluation of an overt act.

What I mean by a motive is an affective state that initiates and directs action. In my theory of emotion, a motive is an emotion that is operating to produce action. The appreciation for a value is an emotion that can initiate and direct action. When it does, it is a motive in the sense I mean. Acts motivated by appreciation of a value may not be intentional even when they are voluntary. My thesis is that, other things being equal, acts motivated by love of some value are highly valuable.[15]

As I analyse virtue, a motive disposition is a component of a virtue. A virtuous act is an act motivated by the motive of some virtue V and is characteristic of acts motivated by V in the circumstances in question.[16] An act can be compassionate, courageous, or generous, or unfair, cruel, and so on. The name of the virtue or vice out of which an act is done is typically given by the name of the motive out of which it is done, and the motive is a feature of the agent who performs the act. If believing is like acting, it can be virtuous or vicious. The properties of true believing that make it better than mere true believing are properties that it obtains from the agent in the same way good acts obtain evaluative properties from the agent. In particular, a belief can acquire value from its motive, in addition to the value it may have in being true.

The idea that to know is to act is not very common these days, although it has a lot of precedent in philosophical history.[17] Sometimes the word *judge* is used to distinguish that which can be converted into knowledge from belief, which is commonly understood as a disposition or a passive state rather than as an act. I shall continue to use the word *believe* to refer to an act since I think it is an acceptable use of the term, but some readers might find the substitution of the word *judge* in what follows clearer.

What motives of the agent could make believing better? I have previously argued that it is motives that are forms of the basic motive of love of truth.[18] The motivational components of the individual intellectual virtues such as open-mindedness or intellectual fairness or intellectual thoroughness or caution differ, but they are all based on a general love or valuing of truth or a disvaluing of falsehood.[19] The motivational components of the intellectual virtues are probably more complex than this since, for example, intellectual fairness may consist in part in respect for others as well as in respect or love of truth.[20] But love of truth is plausibly the primary motive underlying a wide range of intellectual virtues.[21] If love of truth is a good motive, it would add value to the intellectual acts it motivates.

What sort of value does love of truth have? Assuming that if something is valuable it is also valuable to appreciate or love it, then love of true belief has value because true belief has value. But the motive of love of truth also derives value from distinctively moral motives. That is because moral permissibility, praise and blame rest on epistemic permissibility, praise and blame.[22]

Let me propose a condition for impermissibility. When something of moral importance is at stake when someone performs an act S, then if S is a case of acting on a belief B, it is morally important that B be true. It is, therefore, impermissible for the agent to believe in a way that fails to respect the importance of the truth of B. That implies that the agent must believe out of certain motives. In particular, I suggest that the agent's motives must be such that they include a valuing of truth or, at a minimum, that they do not involve a disvaluing or neglect of truth.[23]

If moral blameworthiness rests on epistemic blameworthiness, then the same reasoning leads to the conclusion that moral praiseworthiness or credit rests on epistemic praiseworthiness or credit.[24] Suppose now that an act S is a case of acting on a belief B and that act S is an instance of an act type that is morally praiseworthy in the right conditions. I propose that act S is credited to the agent only if the truth of belief B is credited to the agent. So if knowing B is something like truly believing when the truth of B is credited to the agent, it follows that the agent gets moral credit for an act S based on belief B only if S knows B.[25]

Suppose also that I am right that there is a motivational requirement for getting credit for the truth that involves love of truth. It follows that the motive of love of truth is a requirement for love of moral goods, or at least is a requirement for love of those moral goods for which one gets praise or blame in one's acts. The praiseworthiness of love of truth is a condition for moral praiseworthiness. There is, therefore, a moral motive to have knowledge. The value that converts true believing into knowing is a con-

dition for the moral value of acts that depend upon the belief.

In spite of the moral importance of having true beliefs, we usually think that true belief is good in itself. The value of true belief is a distinctively epistemic value that allegedly permits epistemologists to treat the domain of belief and knowledge as something independent of acts subject to moral evaluation. This brings us to the deeper value problem of knowledge: in what sense, if any, is true belief good? If true believing is not good, we have a much more serious problem than that of finding the value that makes knowing better than true believing.

2 The value of true belief

I have been treating knowledge as something the knower earns. It is a state in which the prize of truth is credited to her; perhaps she is even deserving of praise for it. But why should we think that? I have already mentioned that this idea was developed because it avoids Gettier problems, but that objective is surely only a small part of the task of defining knowledge. Knowledge is worth discussing because it is worth having. But the fact that knowledge is valuable does not force us to think of it as something we earn or get credit for or are responsible for or praised for, although that way of looking at it follows from the sports analogies used in discussions of the value problem by Sosa, Greco, and Riggs, and from the analogy of winning a battle used by Michael DePaul.[26] They all treat knowledge as an achievement or points earned in a game rather than the blessings of good fortune. I think they are right about that, but it is worth mentioning that the fact that knowing is a valuable state does not force us to think of it in that way. Some goods are just as good if we do not have to work for them – for example good health and a safe environment – and some may even be better if we do not have to work for them – for example love and friendship. Good health, safety, love and friendship are all good in the sense of the desirable. The sense of good that we earn or get credit for is the sense of good as the admirable. I have argued that if we think of knowing as being like acting, it is the sort of thing that can be virtuous or vicious, which is to say, admirable or reprehensible. Knowledge is admirable. But surely knowledge is also desirable because its primary component, true belief, is thought to be desirable. That is to say, we think that true belief is good for us.

True belief may be desirable, but it is certainly not admirable. It is not something for which we get credit or praise. That is, true belief by itself does not carry credit with it, although I have said that in cases of knowing we get credit for the truth because of other features of the belief. The kind of value that makes knowing better than true believing is the admirable, whereas the kind of value true believing has is the desirable. But now we encounter a problem, because surely not all true beliefs are desirable. For one thing, many people have pointed out that some truths are trivial. This is a problem for the value of knowledge, because even if knowing a trivial truth is better than merely truly believing it, how much better can it be? There is only so much good that knowing a trivial truth can have. If it is fundamentally valueless to have a true belief about the number of times the word *the* is used in a McDonald's commercial, it is also valueless to know it. So even if trivial truths are believed in the most highly virtuous, skilful, rational or justified way, the triviality of the truth makes the knowing of such truths trivial as well. The unavoidable conclusion is that some knowledge is not good for us. Some might even be bad for us. It can be bad for the agent and it can be bad for others – for example, knowing exactly what the surgeon is doing to my leg when he is removing a skin cancer; knowing the neighbour's private life. It follows that either not all knowledge is desirable or some true beliefs cannot be converted into knowledge.

A common response to this problem is to say that truth is conditionally valuable. It is not true belief per se that is valuable but having the answer to our questions. Our interests determine the difference between valuable true beliefs and nonvaluable or disvaluable ones. Sosa gives the example of counting grains of sand on the beach. He says that we do not think that believing the outcome of such a count has value, because it does not serve any of our interests.[27] But, of course, somebody *might* be interested in the number of grains of sand on the beach, yet it seems to me that knowing the count does not get any better if he is. If a truth is trivial, believing it is not improved by the fact that the epistemic agent has peculiar or perverse interests. In fact, the interests may even make it worse, because we add the perversity of the interests to the triviality of the truth.[28]

Perhaps we can appeal to the idea of importance to save the intuition that our interests and goals have something to do with the truths that are valuable to us, by making the value more significant.[29] Maybe some things are just important *simpliciter*, where that means there are truths whose importance is not reducible to what is important to so-and-so. Perhaps there are degrees of distance from the individual in the concept of importance, where some things are important to people in a certain role or in a certain society, and some are important to everybody. But I don't think this move will help us. There are no important 'truths' if a truth is a true proposition, since propositions are not important in themselves, and if truth is a property of propositions, truth is not what is important. Instead, it is the state of truly believing the proposition that is important. So when we say that some truths are important and others are not, what we really mean is that some true *beliefs* are important and others are not. And then to say this means no more than that the value of true beliefs varies. But we already knew that. What we want to know is what makes them vary. The idea of important true beliefs is just another way of posing the problem. It is not a solution to the problem.

Another form of conditional value is instrumental value. It has been argued that satisfaction of our desires or reaching our goals is what reason aims at. True belief is surely a means to reaching our ends, most of which are non-epistemic. A good example of this position is that of Richard Foley, who argues that the epistemic goal of truth is instrumentally valuable as a means to other goals, whose value is left undetermined.[30] Clearly, many true beliefs have instrumental value, but instrumental value is a form of conditional value, since the condition for the value of the means is the value of the end. If the end is disvaluable, so is the means.[31] Conditional value is like a suspected terrorist: someone who is a suspected terrorist may not be a terrorist, and a belief that has conditional value may not have value. No form of conditional value possessed by true belief has the consequence that all true beliefs are valuable.

There is still the possibility that true belief has intrinsic value. Perhaps every true belief has some intrinsic value simply in virtue of being true, whether or not it is good for us. That may well be the case, but I do not see that it will have the consequence that every true belief is valuable on balance, because intrinsicality is unrelated to degree. Intrinsicality pertains to the source of a belief, not to its amount. So even if every true belief has some intrinsic value, it is unlikely that the intrinsic value of every true belief is great enough to outweigh the undesirability or other negative value some true beliefs have from other sources.

The inescapable conclusion is that not every true belief is good, all things considered. Whether we are considering admirability or desirability, or an intrinsic or extrinsic source of value, on balance it is likely that there are some true beliefs that have no value and probably some that have negative value.

Now consider what follows for the value of knowing. In the first section I concluded that knowing is better than true believing only if it is true believing in which the agent gets credit for

getting the truth. But if a given true belief is not valuable, how can the agent get credit for it if the truth in that case is not such that it is something someone should be given credit for? So long as some true beliefs are disvaluable, it makes just as much sense to say she is blamed for the truth as that she is praised for it. Assuming that every true belief is intrinsically good, it is good that the agent gets credited with the truth because of what is admirable about the agent's epistemic behaviour – her intellectually virtuous motives and acts. But the truth credited to her may not be much of a prize.

Consider also what happens to my proposal that knowledge is better than true belief because it is a case in which the truth is reached by intellectually virtuous motives and acts, the value of which can be traced back to the value of the motive of valuing truth. But if the truth in some cases is not valuable on balance, why should we be motivated to value it? Of course, we are assuming that true belief has some intrinsic value, and we can also assume that true belief is usually good for us, in which case it is reasonable to think that it is good to value it *as* something with some intrinsic value, however slight, as well as something that is usually good for us. But if we are looking for a value that has the potential to be a significant good, we still have not found it.

What is more, so long as some true beliefs are not desirable, the agent's getting the truth can be credited to her even though the agent's getting a *desirable* truth is not credited to her. And even when the truth *is* desirable, it may be a matter of luck that she got a desirable truth rather than an undesirable one. I think this leads us into a problem parallel to the Gettier problem. Gettier cases arise when there is an accidental connection between the admirability of a belief and its truth. Similarly, it is possible that there is an accidental connection between the admirability of a belief and its desirability. I think it is too strong to deny such cases the label of knowledge; nonetheless, they are not as good as they can be. They are not the best instances of knowledge, not the ones that are great goods. The solution to Gettier cases is to close the gap between the admirability of a belief and its truth. The solution to the new value problem is to close the gap between the admirability of a true belief and its desirability. To get a truly interesting value in knowledge, therefore, it should turn out that in some cases of knowing, not only is the truth of the belief credited to the agent but the desirability of the true belief is also credited to the agent. This is a general formula that can be filled out in different ways, just as the formula for the definition of knowledge can be filled out in different ways, depending upon the theorist's conception of credit, and that in turn depends upon a general theory of agent evaluation. In the next section I shall outline the contours of a virtue-theoretic account of knowledge that satisfies the constraints identified in the first two sections of the essay.

3   Knowledge, motives and *eudaimonia*

I have claimed that good motives add value to the acts they motivate, and this includes epistemic acts. Motives are complex, and I have not investigated them very far in this essay, but a feature of motives that is relevant to our present concern is that they themselves are often motivated by higher-order motives. Higher-order motives are important because they keep our motivational structure compact and aid us in making first-order motives consistent. If good motives can confer value on the acts they motivate, it follows that higher-order motives can confer value on the lower-order motives they motivate the agent to acquire. As we are looking for an additional source of value in some cases of knowledge, it is reasonable to look at the source of the value of the motive of true believing in the particular cases of knowing that are more valuable than ordinary knowing.

We have already seen at least two ways in which the valuing of truth in particular cases is required by other things we value. That is, we have a motive to have the motive for truth because of other good motives. First, if something of moral importance is at stake when we perform an act and that act depends upon the truth of a certain belief, then it is morally important that the belief be true. The motive for true belief in such cases is motivated by the higher-order motive to be moral or to live a good life. Second, since true belief is a means to most practical ends, the motive to value truth in some domain is motivated by the motive of valuing those ends, which is in turn motivated by the desire to have a good life. I propose that the higher-order motive to have a good life includes the motive to have certain other motives, including the motive to value truth in certain domains. The higher-order motive motivates the agent to have the motives that are constituents of the moral and intellectual virtues, and in this way it connects the moral and intellectual virtues together. If knowledge is true belief credited to the agent because of its place in her motivational structure, it gets value not only from the truth motive but also from the higher-order motive that motivates the agent to value truth in some domain or on some occasion. And that motive has nothing to do with epistemic value in particular; it is a component of the motive to live a good life.

My proposal, then, is this. An epistemic agent gets credit for getting a true belief when she arrives at a true belief because of her virtuous intellectual acts motivated by a love of truth. She gets credit for getting a desirable true belief when she arrives at a desirable true belief because of acts motivated by love of true beliefs that are components of a good life. The motive for desirable true beliefs is not the full explanation for the agent's getting credit for acquiring a desirable true belief, for the same reason that the motive for true belief is not the full explanation for the agent's getting credit for acquiring a true belief, but my position is that motives are primary causes of the other valuable features of cognitive activity. When the agent succeeds in getting a desirable true belief because of her admirable intellectual motives, there is a non-accidental connection between the admirability of a belief and its desirability. That connection avoids the parallel to Gettier problems that I mentioned above, and it results in some instances of knowledge being a great good.

Let me review the various ways a belief can be good.

1   All true beliefs probably have some intrinsic value simply in virtue of being true whether or not they are good for us. When the truth is credited to the agent, the belief is also admirable. That is knowledge.

2   Some true beliefs are good for us; they are desirable. They can be desirable whether or not they are admirable. But some true beliefs are undesirable. It is also possible that some false beliefs are desirable, but I have not discussed those cases in this essay.

3   Admirable beliefs are those that are virtuous. Admirable beliefs can be false.

4   Some true beliefs are both desirable and admirable. The most interesting cases are those in which there is a connection between their admirability and their desirability. A belief is admirable, and given its admirability, it is no accident that the agent has a desirable true belief. These are the most highly valuable instances of knowledge.

The problems we have encountered with the value of true belief indicate, I think, that the standard approach to identifying the value of knowledge is the wrong way round. The issue should be not what is added to true belief to make it valuable enough to be knowledge but what is added to virtuous believing to make it knowledge. And, of course, the answer to that question is obvious: it must be true. When we approach the value problem in this way, the harder question is answered first and the easier

one second. That is not the usual order, but I think it is the right one. If we begin in the usual way, by starting with true belief, we are starting with something that may have no value of any kind, neither admirability nor desirability. Furthermore, by starting with the value of virtuous believing we can explain why even false virtuously motivated belief is admirable.

Let me conclude by briefly considering what makes virtue in general a good thing. Suppose that Aristotle is right in thinking of virtuous acts as components of *eudaimonia*, a life of flourishing. If I am also right that believing is a form of acting, it follows that virtuous believings are components of *eudaimonia*. *Eudaimonia* is a challenging concept to elucidate for many reasons, but one aspect that contemporary commentators find particularly troublesome is Aristotle's apparent idea that *eudaimonia* fuses the admirable with the desirable. Nobody disputes the conception of *eudaimonia* as a desirable life; in fact, *eudaimonia* is generally defined as a desirable life. It then has to be argued that virtuous – that is, admirable – activity is a component of the desirable life. And that, of course, is hotly disputed. The same problem arises over the value of knowing. Nobody is likely to dispute the claim that some true beliefs are desirable. What can be disputed is whether beliefs that are intellectually virtuous, either in the way I have described or in some other, are also components of a desirable life. The question 'Why should we want to have admirable beliefs?' is really no different from the question 'Why should we want to do admirable acts?' If virtuous acts are desirable, it is because it is more desirable to act in an admirable way. Similarly, if knowing a proposition is more desirable than truly believing it, it is because it is more desirable to believe in an admirable way. But I can see no way to defend that without a general account of *eudaimonia*, or a good life. That means that the debates currently going on in virtue ethics on the relation between virtuous activity and the good life are relevant to an understanding of an intellectually good life as well as to an understanding of a life that is good *simpliciter*.

4 Conclusion

The question 'What is knowledge?' is not independent of the question 'Why do we value knowledge?' For those who consider the former question prior, compare the pair of questions 'What is knowledge?' and 'Can we get it?' It is common for anti-sceptic naturalistic epistemologists to say that whatever knowledge is, it has to be defined as something we have. We are not interested in a non-existent phenomenon. I say that knowledge has to be defined as something we value. We are not interested in a phenomenon with little or no value. It is possible that no phenomenon roughly coinciding with what has traditionally been called knowledge has the value I have been looking for in this essay. If so, we would have to move to an Error theory like that of J. L. Mackie in ethics. But I do not yet see that this will be necessary, since it is possible to give an account of knowledge that both satisfies the usual contemporary constraints and identifies a phenomenon with interesting value. I also think we should conclude that if knowledge is a state worthy of the sustained attention it has received throughout the history of philosophy, it is because its value goes well beyond the epistemic value of truth and what conduces to true belief. Knowledge is important because it is intimately connected to moral value and the wider values of a good life. It is very unlikely that epistemic value in any interesting sense is autonomous.

Acknowledgements

I thank Philip Percival, my commentator at the conference at the University of Stirling, for his interesting and helpful comments. Earlier versions of this article were presented at the University of California, Riverside, Tulane University, the University of Oklahoma, and the Eastern Division Meetings of the American Philosophical Association, December 2001. I thank the audiences at those presentations. Particular thanks go to my commentator at the APA session, Michael DePaul, for his help in improving the article.

Notes

1 For an exception to the almost universal view that knowledge is a better state than true belief, see Sartwell 1992. This move displaces the problem to that of identifying the value of true belief, which will be addressed in the second section.

2 I mention the value problem briefly in Zagzebski 1996 and discuss it in some detail in Zagzebski 2000. Another version of the value problem is proposed in DePaul 2001.

3 Sosa's earlier theory is what I call faculty reliabilism. Greco has a theory he calls agent reliabilism. In Greco 1999, he uses the term *agent reliabilism* for a class of theories beyond his own, including Sosa's, Plantinga's and my early theory.

4 On the other hand, reliabilists usually have particular faculties and properties of agents in mind, properties they call virtues, e.g. a good memory, keen eyesight, and well-developed powers of reasoning. The goodness of these virtues is not limited to their reliability, and so long as that is recognised, the theory has a way out of the value problem. But for the same reason, it is misleading to call these theories forms of reliabilism.

5 The machine-product model has been used by Alston, Plantinga, Sosa, Goldman and others. The word *output* is frequently used, and some of them illustrate their discussion with analogies of machines and their products.

6 My colleague Wayne Riggs has thought of the location issue as a way out of the value problem. See Riggs 2002.

7 Zagzebski 1996, part 3.

8 See Riggs (1998) and Greco (2003).

9 See Sosa (2003).

10 So far as I can tell, Greco and Riggs reject the machine-product model, but Sosa uses it repeatedly, including in Sosa 2003, the article in which he proposes his way out of the value problem.

11 I argued this in Zagzebski 1996. See also Riggs

(1998) and Greco (2003). DePaul 2001, note 7, argues that Gettier cases produce another form of the value problem, because we think that the value of the agent's epistemic state in Gettier cases is not as valuable as the state of knowledge.

12 Another alternative is that knowledge is identified with the entire process culminating in the belief, and it gets value from the value in the process as well as the truth of the end product of the process. I have proposed that it would serve the purposes of Sosa's account of epistemic value to think of knowledge as an organic unity in the sense used by Franz Brantano and G. E. Moore. That would permit the value of the whole to exceed the value of the sum of the parts. See Zagzebski (forthcoming). DePaul (2001, section 6) also discusses the possibility that knowledge is an organic unity.

13 I explore the requirement of agency in knowledge in Zagzebski 2001.

14 DePaul (1993, chap. 2) insightfully discusses the problem of BonJour and others in explaining the value of knowledge. I thank DePaul for bringing this passage to my attention.

15 I also think that acts motivated by love of some value are more valuable than those that *aim* at the same value but without the motive of love or appreciation for the value. So some non-intentional acts have moral value because they arise from a good motive. In contrast, some intentional acts may aim at a good end but have less value because they do not arise from a good motive. I discuss this in more detail in Zagzebski 2003.

16 In Zagzebski 1996 I distinguish a virtuous act from an act of virtue. Unlike the latter, a virtuous act need not be successful in its aim. I use *act of virtue* as a term of art to identify an act good in every respect. It is an act that arises out of a virtuous motive, is an act a virtuous person would characteristically do in the circumstances, is successful in reaching the aim of the virtuous motive, and does so because of the other virtuous features of the act.

17 Aquinas and other medieval philosophers seem to have thought of knowing as involving an act of intellect. There may be passages in Plato that suggest this also. See Benson 2000, chap. 9.

18 I argue this in Zagzebski 1996, part 2, and in more detail in Zagzebski 2003.

19 I have argued in Zagzebski 2003 that loving truth is not the same as hating falsehood, but I do not think the difference makes a difference to the point of this article.

20 Respect, love, and appreciation in most contexts are quite different, but I do not think the differences make much of a difference in the context of an emotional attitude towards truth. Since most epistemologists do not think *any* emotional attitude towards truth makes any difference to epistemic status, it is quite enough to try to show that one of these attitudes makes a difference.

21 Some intellectual virtues may aim at understanding rather than truth. I argue that epistemologists have generally neglected the value of understanding in Zagzebski 2001b. See also Riggs 2003.

22 The *locus classicus* for discussion of the connection between the moral permissibility of acts and the permissibility of beliefs is Clifford's article, 'The Ethics of Belief'. W. K. Clifford concludes that an unjustified belief is morally impermissible. See also Montmarquet 1993 for a good discussion of the relation between the permissibility of acts and beliefs.

23 The issue of what is involved in epistemic permissibility is a difficult one, because of the 'ought implies can' rule. But unless we are willing to say that no belief is impermissible, there must be some things we ought and ought not to believe, so the 'ought implies can' rule does not prohibit us from speaking of epistemic permissibility. I am not going to discuss the extent to which we can control each of our beliefs. My point is just that so long as we do think there are acts of belief that are impermissible, it follows that either we have whatever power over believing is intended in the 'ought implies can' rule or else the 'ought implies can' rule does not apply to these beliefs. In other words, I think the intuition that impermissibility applies in the realm of belief is stronger than the 'ought implies can' rule.

24 Praiseworthiness differs somewhat from credit in most people's vocabulary, in that deserving praise is a stronger commendation than deserving credit. I think the difference is only one of degree and do not believe that much hangs on the difference.

25 There is no doubt a variety of qualifications to be made here. For example, the agent generally gets

credit of some kind for S even when B is false so long as her intellectual motive sufficiently respects the importance of the truth of B, she does what intellectually virtuous persons characteristically do in her circumstances, and her belief is only false because of her bad luck.

26 DePaul 2001, 179. DePaul also uses the example of a commercial for a financial institution in which a pompous gentleman announces, 'We make money the old-fashioned way: we earn it.' The implication is that it is better to get money by working for it rather than by luck or inheritance. As DePaul points out, that implies that there is something valuable in addition to the money itself.

27 See Sosa 2001.

28 In addition to Sosa, Christopher Stephens uses our interests as a way to resolve the problem of the two values – getting truth and avoiding falsehood. Goldman 2001 identifies interest as a value that unifies the epistemic virtues.

29 This idea of briefly discussed by Riggs (2003).

30 See Foley 2001. Foley seems to be content with allowing the value of the goal to be set by the agent.

31 A given means could serve more than one end. I would think that the value of a means in a particular case is determined by its end in that case. This is compatible with a means of that type having value when it serves some other end that is good.

References

Benson, Hugh. 2000. Socratic Wisdom. Oxford: Oxford University Press.

BonJour, Laurence. 1985. The Structure of Empirical Knowledge. Cambridge, Mass.: Harvard University Press.

DePaul, Michael. 1993. Balance and Refinement. New York: Routledge.

——. 2001. 'Value Monism in Epistemology'. In Knowledge, Truth, and Duty, edited by Matthias Steup. Oxford: Oxford University Press.

Foley, Richard. 2001. 'The Foundational Role of Epistemology in a General Theory of Rationality'. In Virtue Epistemology: Essays on Epistemic Virtue and Responsibility, edited by Abrol Fairweather and Linda Zagzebski. Oxford: Oxford University Press.

Goldman, Alvin. 2001. 'The Unity of the Epistemic Virtues'. In Virtue Epistemology: Essays on Epistemic Virtue

and Responsibility, edited by Abrol Fairweather and Linda Zagzebski. Oxford: Oxford University Press.

Greco, John. 1999. 'Agent Reliabilism'. Philosophical Perspectives 13: 273–96.

——. 2003. 'Knowledge as Credit for True Belief'. In Intellectual Virtue: Perspectives from Ethics and Epistemology, edited by Michael DePaul and Linda Zagzebski. Oxford: Oxford University Press.

Montmarquet, James. 1993. Epistemic Virtue and Doxastic Responsibility. Lanham, Md.: Rowman and Littlefield.

Riggs, Wayne. 1998. 'What Are the "Chances" of Being Justified?' Monist 81: 452–72.

——. 2002. 'Reliability and the Value of Knowledge'. Philosophy and Phenomenological Research 64, no. 1 (January): 79–96.

——. 2003. 'Understanding Virtue and the Virtue of Understanding'. In Intellectual Virtue: Perspectives from Ethics and Epistemology, edited by Michael DePaul and Linda Zagzebski. Oxford: Oxford University Press.

Sartwell, Crispin. 1992. 'Knowledge Is Merely True Belief'. American Philosophical Quarterly 28: 157–65.

Sosa, Ernest. 2001. 'For the Love of Truth?' In Virtue Epistemology: Essays on Epistemic Virtue and Responsibility, edited by Abrol Fairweather and Linda Zagzebski. Oxford: Oxford University Press.

——. 2003. 'The Place of Truth in Epistemology'. In Intellectual Virtue: Perspectives from Ethics and Epistemology, edited by Michael DePaul and Linda Zagzebski. Oxford: Oxford University Press.

Zagzebski, Linda. 1996. Virtues of the Mind: An Inquiry into the Nature of Virtue and the Ethical Foundations of Knowledge. Cambridge, UK: Cambridge University Press.

——. 2000. 'From Reliabilism to Virtue Epistemology'. In Knowledge, Belief, and Character, edited by Guy Axtell. Lanham, Md.: Rowman and Littlefield.

——. 2001a. 'Must Knowers Be Agents?' In Virtue Epistemology: Essays on Epistemic Virtue and Responsibility, edited by Abrol Fairweather and Linda Zagzebski. Oxford: Oxford University Press.

——. 2001b. 'Recovering Understanding'. In Knowledge, Truth, and Obligation, edited by Matthias Steup. Oxford: Oxford University Press.

——. 2003. 'Intellectual Motivation and the Good of Truth'. In Intellectual Virtue: Perspectives from Ethics and Epistemology, edited by Michael DePaul and Linda Zagzebski. Oxford: Oxford University Press.

——. Forthcoming. 'Epistemic Value Monism'. In Sosa and His Critics, edited by John Greco. Oxford: Basil Blackwell.

Chapter 8

John Greco

THE VALUE PROBLEM

In Plato's *Meno*, Socrates raises a question about the value of knowledge. Why is knowledge valuable? Or perhaps better, what is it that makes knowledge valuable? Jonathan Kvanvig (2003) argues that this question is as important to epistemology as Socrates's question about the nature of knowledge, or what knowledge is. Any adequate epistemology must answer both the nature question and the value question. In fact, Kvanvig argues, the two questions interact: if a theory of knowledge does a poor job answering the value question, then that counts against its answer to the nature question. Likewise, if a theory does a good job explaining the value of knowledge, that counts in favour of its answer to the nature question. This seems exactly right. Put another way, the value question is at the heart of the project of explanation. The task of explaining what knowledge is involves the task of explaining why knowledge is valuable.

Before looking more closely at Plato's question in the *Meno*, however, we should distinguish it from a different question: why is the *concept* of knowledge valuable? A plausible answer to that question is that the concept plays valuable roles in the lives of information-using, information-sharing beings such as ourselves.[1] The human form of life demands good information and the reliable flow of that information. The concept of knowledge, along with related concepts, serves those needs. That is not yet to say, however, why

knowledge is valuable. We may put things this way: the concept of knowledge is valuable because it allows us to identify and share reliable information. But why is *knowledge* valuable? That question remains to be answered.

1 Why is there a problem?

We have seen that Socrates raises a question, but why is answering the question a problem? Why can't we say, for example, that knowledge is a kind of information, and that knowledge is valuable because information is valuable? Here I am understanding the concept of information to be 'factive': to be information is to be true information. The present suggestion, then, is that knowledge is valuable because true information is valuable. For example, true information has practical value – it helps us to get things that we want.

Socrates rejects this kind of answer because we think that knowledge is more valuable than *mere* true information, or true information that is not knowledge. In an often cited passage from the *Meno*, Socrates points out that mere true belief seems to have the same practical value as knowledge – the man who truly believes that the road leads to Larissa is as well served as the man who knows that it does. The problem then is this: we think that knowledge has value over and above its practical value as useful information. How do we explain that extra value? This is something that a good theory of knowledge should do.

2 A special problem for reliabilism?

The value question is ancient, and as we have described it, it is a problem for any theory of knowledge whatsoever. Recently, however, Linda Zagzebski has argued that the problem is especially difficult for reliabilism.[2] In her terminology, reliabilism can't explain the added value that knowledge has over true belief. This is because reliabilists conceive the difference between true belief that is knowledge and true belief that falls short of knowledge as a difference in the reliability of the source. But the reliability of a source, Zagzebski argues, cannot add value to its product. To make the point she draws an analogy to good espresso. The value of a good cup of espresso is not increased by the fact that it was made by a reliable espresso machine. Good espresso is valuable, and reliable espresso machines are valuable. But the value of the espresso is not increased by the value of its source. Consider: a cup of espresso with the same intrinsic qualities, but made by an unreliable machine, would have exactly the same value. The conclusion that Zagzebski draws is that simple reliabilism cannot solve the value problem for knowledge. If knowledge is more valuable than mere true belief, its value must be explained in some other way.

3 A problem for everyone

Kvanvig, however, argues that the value problem is even more intractable. According to Kvanvig, 'We are left . . . with no decent answer to the question of the value of knowledge. . . . [T]here is no good answer to the problem of the *Meno*.' (Kvanvig 2003, p. 184) Kvanvig's conclusion, it should be noted, depends on particular ways in which he conceives the problem. We have already seen that the question of the value of knowledge has a tendency to shift. For example,

it shifts in Plato's discussion from 'Why is knowledge valuable?' to 'Why is knowledge more valuable than mere true belief?' We will see that the question shifts again, and a number of times, in Kvanvig's discussion as well. For example, at times Kvanvig wants an explanation of why knowledge is more valuable than any of it proper parts. Even more strongly, he sometimes asks why knowledge is more valuable than the sum of its parts. Clearly, each question in this series requires an increasingly demanding solution to the value problem.

I will defend two theses. The first is that some of Kvanvig's formulations of the value problem are too demanding. That is, we should not expect an answer to each of his questions, since we should not expect that knowledge really is valuable in the ways that his questions suppose. For example, and most obviously, there is no pre-theoretic reason for thinking that knowledge is more valuable than the sum of its parts. The second thesis I will defend is that, nevertheless, a virtue-theoretic account of knowledge answers all of Kvanvig's questions. In other words, a virtue-theoretic approach solves each of his formulations of the value problem. Putting these two theses together, we get the following result: a virtue theory gives us a better answer to the value problem than anyone should expect!

4 Shifting questions

Consider again Kvanvig's two criteria for an adequate theory of knowledge: any such theory, he says, ought to give an account both of the nature of knowledge and the value of knowledge. Suppose that the question about the value of knowledge is the very general one: why is knowledge valuable? The idea that a theory of knowledge ought to answer this question seems right, and precisely because we are confident that knowledge is indeed valuable. It is a reasonable criterion of success, therefore, that a theory preserves this pre-theoretical data and explains it.

As Kvanvig notes, however, Socrates's question soon shifts to a more specific one: why is knowledge more valuable than true opinion? But once again, the demand for an answer seems appropriate. And once again, this is because we are pre-theoretically confident that knowledge has such a value. As Kvanvig writes,

> part of the challenge of explaining the value of knowledge is in explaining how it has more value than other things, one of these other things being true opinion – as Meno claims after acquiescing to Socrates' point that true belief is every bit as useful as knowledge.... Meno expresses here a common presupposition about knowledge, one that is widely, if not universally, shared. Given this presupposition, an account of the value of knowledge must explain more than how knowledge is valuable. It must also explain why the value of knowledge is superior to the value of true opinion.
>
> (Kvanvig 2003, pp. 3–4)

But now consider a second shift in Kvanvig's question about the value of knowledge. At another point in the book Kvanvig writes,

> To explain the value of knowledge in a way that satisfies the constraints of the *Meno* requires showing that knowledge is more valuable than any proper subset of its constituents.
>
> (Kvanvig 2003, p. 107)

This new and stronger demand is illustrated by what Kvanvig says about a widespread position in epistemology – that knowledge is composed of justified true belief, plus some further condition to handle Gettier cases.

> An adequate account of the value of knowledge must explain why it is more valuable than any subset of its constituents. If we assume that there is some property like justification that distinguishes knowledge from true belief, then an adequate explanation of the value of knowledge could be achieved by giving an adequate account of the value of justification. Because knowledge is more than justified true belief, such an explanation is only one part of a complete explanation. In addition, what is needed is an explanation of why knowledge is more valuable than justified true belief.
>
> (Kvanvig 2003, p. 112)

Finally, consider one more passage along the same lines:

> The conclusion to which our investigation seems to be pointing is that ordinary thinking about knowledge is mistaken, that knowledge does not have the kind of value it is ordinarily thought to have. In particular, we seem to be heading for the conclusion that knowledge does not have a value that exceeds that of subsets of its constituents.
>
> (Kvanvig 2003, p. 157)

Is it true what Kvanvig is implying here? In other words, is it true that 'ordinary thinking' assumes that knowledge is more valuable than any subset of its constituents? That is far from clear. To illustrate, suppose that some JTB+ account of knowledge is correct – that knowledge is justified true belief plus something further to handle Gettier problems. Suppose also that the 'plus' part amounts to some minor, technical adjustment to the traditional idea that knowledge is justified true belief, and that this further condition adds no further value to knowledge over justified true belief. Would these suppositions conflict with ordinary thought? Would this show 'that knowledge does not have the kind of value it is ordinarily thought to have'? It is hard to see how that could be the case. Most people are not at all aware of Gettier problems, and we can suppose that almost no one was before 1963. But then how could ordinary thought include the idea that knowledge is more valuable than justified true belief?

Kvanvig might reply that ordinary thinking does include the idea implicitly. For once ordinary thinkers are exposed to Gettier problems, they quickly agree that knowledge is not equivalent to justified true belief. But that reply does not address the issue at hand, which is whether ordinary thinkers assume that knowledge is more *valuable* than justified true belief. Put more generally, the issue is whether ordinary thinkers assume that knowledge is more valuable than any subset of its constituents, whether this is understood in terms of the JTB+ account or in terms of some other account. And this is what I am saying is dubious. Ordinary thinking, I am suggesting, contains no convictions about that issue.

And now the point is this: if there is no pre-theoretical conviction that knowledge is more valuable than any subset of its constituents, then Kvanvig has placed an inappropriate demand on a solution to the value problem. The original demand to explain the value of knowledge was grounded in an ordinary and widespread conviction that knowledge is indeed valuable. That is why we accepted it as an appropriate criterion for an adequate account of knowledge. When the question about value shifts in the way that it has by this point in Kvanvig's discussion, the stronger demand on an explanation that emerges is not so grounded.

To sum up, there is no pre-theoretical conviction that knowledge is more valuable than any subset of its constituents, and therefore it is not appropriate to require that a theory of knowledge explain why knowledge has that sort of value. Kvanvig's criterion for an adequate solution to the value problem is too strong.

That being said, in some places Kvanvig seems to place even stronger demands on a solution to the value problem. Specifically, he seems to demand that a solution explain how the value of knowledge exceeds the value *of all its parts together*. Consider the following passages:

[A] satisfactory answer to the question of the value of knowledge will need to explain why knowledge is, by its very nature, more valuable than its parts.

(Kvanvig 2003, p. xiv)

Thus, I will be arguing that knowledge is valuable, but that it fails to have a value exceeding that of its parts, thereby leaving us with no adequate answer to the problem of the value of knowledge first posed by Plato in the *Meno*.

(Kvanvig 2003, pp. xv–xvi)

On the assumption we have been making in the past several chapters (that the value of knowledge is in some way a function of the value of its parts), the need to account for both the nature and value of knowledge requires that we identify a fourth condition that not only yields a counterexample-free account of knowledge but also provides some basis for explaining the value of knowledge over the value of its constituents.

(Kvanvig 2003, p. 116)

There are aspects of Kvanvig's discussion that suggest that these latest passages are slips – that his considered position is to require only an explanation of why knowledge is more valuable than its *proper* parts. Nevertheless, it will be useful to explore the cogency of this newest demand on a solution to the value problem.

Someone might think that the demand is not even coherent. Consider, for example, an account of bachelorhood. Let us say that a bachelor is an unmarried male who is eligible for marriage. Now suppose we wanted a solution to 'the value problem for bachelorhood'. That is, suppose we want an account of why bachelorhood is valuable. Is it appropriate to demand that such an account explain why the value of bachelorhood exceeds the value of all its parts together? It can seem that this demand is not even coherent, for being a bachelor just *is* being an unmarried male who is eligible for marriage. But then how could the value of the former exceed the value of the latter?

We can take the question another way, however. For we can ask whether the value of being a bachelor exceeds the sum of the value of the parts. That is, we can ask whether the value of bachelorhood exceeds the value of being unmarried plus the value of being male plus the value of being eligible for marriage. We might answer in the negative, but the question is at least coherent. That is, at least sometimes the whole is worth more than the parts taken separately.

That is the way that we should understand the latest formulation of the value problem. It asks whether the value of knowledge exceeds the value of each of its parts taken alone. This might be the case if knowledge were some sort of organic whole, in the sense that its parts are organized in a particular way. Perhaps some relation among the parts adds value beyond that which the parts have of themselves.

The question is coherent, I take it, but there is no pre-theoretical reason for thinking that it should get a positive answer. And as such, it would be inappropriate to place such a demand on a solution to the value problem. Put another way, there is no pre-theoretical reason to think that knowledge is more valuable than its parts taken separately, and therefore no reason to expect that a solution to the value problem will explain why it is.

5 A solution to the value problem

There is no reason to expect such an explanation. However, I want to argue, a virtue-theoretic approach to the value problem gives us one. In this section I will articulate a solution to the value problem that is consistent with an account of knowledge that I have defended elsewhere.[3] In fact, we will see, the solution falls out of the account straightforwardly. In the next section I will argue that the account satisfies all of

Kvanvig's demands for an adequate solution – even the ones that are unreasonable.

According to the account I have in mind, knowledge is a kind of success through virtue. Put another way, knowledge is a kind of success through virtuous agency. The intellectual virtues that give rise to knowledge are best understood as intellectual abilities, and therefore knowledge is a kind of success through one's own abilities. This sort of success can be juxtaposed to mere lucky success: when S has knowledge, S gets things right as the result of her own abilities, as opposed to getting things right as the result of blind chance or dumb luck, or something else. Put yet another way, in a case of knowledge S gets things right *because* she is intellectually able and because she has exercised her abilities.

But now an answer to the value problem falls out of this account straightaway. In the *Nicomachean Ethics* Aristotle makes a distinction between (a) achieving some end by luck or accident, and (b) achieving the end through the exercise of one's abilities (or virtues). It is only the latter kind of action, Aristotle argues, that is both intrinsically valuable and constitutive of human flourishing. 'Human good', he writes, 'turns out to be activity of soul exhibiting excellence' (*Nicomachean Ethics*, §1.7). In this discussion Aristotle is clearly concerned with intellectual virtue as well as moral virtue: his position is that the successful exercise of one's intellectual virtues is both intrinsically good and constitutive of human flourishing.

If this is correct, then there is a clear difference in value between knowledge and mere true belief. In cases of knowledge, we achieve the truth through the exercise of our own intellectual abilities, which are a kind of intellectual virtue. Moreover, we can extend the point to include other kinds of intellectual virtue as well. It is plausible, for example, that the successful exercise of intellectual courage is also intrinsically good, and also constitutive of the best intellectual life. And of course there is a long tradition that says the same about wisdom and the same about understanding. On the view that results, there is a plurality of intellectual virtues, and their successful exercise gives rise to a plurality of epistemic goods. The best intellectual life – intellectual flourishing, so to speak – is rich with all of these.

6 Kvanvig's demands

We saw that Kvanvig places a series of increasing demands on an adequate solution to the value problem. These demands can be understood in terms of the series of questions articulated above. In effect, each demand is a requirement that one of the following questions be answered:

A   Why is knowledge valuable?
B   Why is knowledge more valuable than true belief?
C   Why is knowledge more valuable than any subset of its constituents?
D   Why is knowledge more valuable than the value of all its parts taken separately?

Finally, we may note that each question in the series, and each requirement that the question be answered, involves a supposition: that knowledge is valuable in the way to be explained.

We may now see that the solution proposed respects all the suppositions and answers all the questions. The answer to questions A and B is straightforward: knowledge is a kind of success through virtue, and in general success through virtue is both intrinsically valuable and constitutive of human flourishing, which is also intrinsically valuable. Therefore, knowledge has value over and above the practical value of true belief.

The proposed solution answers question C as well. Knowledge is a kind of success through virtue. And in general, success through virtue is more valuable than either success without virtue or virtue without success. In particular, virtuously produced true belief is more valuable than both true belief that is not virtuous and virtuous belief that is not true. Neither subset is

intrinsically valuable, or constitutive of what is intrinsically valuable, in just the way that knowledge is.

Finally, the proposed solution answers even question D, respecting the supposition that knowledge is more valuable than all of its parts taken together. This is because success through virtue is more valuable than an act that is both successful and virtuous, but not successful because virtuous. Suppose, for example, that an athlete runs a race in a way that is clearly an exercise of her athletic excellence. Suppose also that she wins, but only because the other runners, some of who are equally excellent, get sick before the race. Or suppose that she wins, but only because the other runners were bribed. Clearly, neither sort of win is as valuable as it could be. What one really values as an athlete is to win as the result of ability.

Likewise in the case of intellectual virtue. One's belief can be virtuously formed and true, but not true because virtuously formed. This is just the structure of Gettier cases, where true and virtuous belief falls short of knowledge.

It is apparent, then, that a virtue-theoretic approach to the value problem meets all the demands that Kvanvig requires of an adequate solution. So why is Kvanvig dissatisfied with this kind of answer? I can only speculate that it is because he misses the force of the proposal. For example, when he first introduces the virtue-theoretic approach he writes,

> Recently, several epistemologists have proposed such an idea, to the effect that credit accrues to the agent who has intellectually virtuous beliefs. . . .
>
> All three share a common theme about the value of the virtues, for they think of this value in term of some kind of credit due to the agent whose belief is virtue-based.
>
> (Kvanvig 2003, p. 81)

Just as actions that result from virtues yield credit for the actor, beliefs resulting from faculties that count as virtues generate credit for the believer.

(Kvanvig 2003, p. 82)

Notice that there is no mention here of *success* through virtue. The central idea of the proposal, which is that knowledge is valuable because it is a kind of success through ability or virtue, is entirely absent.

Even when Kvanvig talks about true virtuous belief, he seems to miss the distinction between (a) a belief's being true and virtuously formed, and (b) a belief's being true because virtuously formed. At places Kvanvig does seem aware of the distinction. For example, he quotes Ernest Sosa (2003) as follows:

> The grasping of the truth central to truth-connected reliabilist epistemology is not just the truth that may be visited upon our beliefs by happenstance or external agency. We desire rather truth gained through our own performances, and this seems a reflectively defensible desire for a good preferable not just extrinsically but intrinsically. What we prefer is the deed of true believing, where not only the believing but also its truth is attributable to the agent as his or her own doing.
>
> (Kvanvig 2003, p. 95)

But when Kvanvig describes the view in question, he says this:

> The basic idea of a virtue approach to the value of knowledge over that of its subparts is that there is a special value for beliefs that arise out of intellectual virtue. When true belief is a product of the virtues, the claim is that there is epistemic credit due to the agent in question and hence that virtuous true belief is more valuable than true belief.
>
> (Kvanvig 2003, p. 106)

In the first sentence he refers to the special value of 'beliefs that arise out of intellectual virtue', whereas in the second sentence he says that credit is due when 'true belief is a product of the virtues'. It isn't clear that he sees the importance of the distinction, and so it isn't clear whether the phrase 'virtuous true belief' in the second sentence means (a) belief that is both true and virtuous, or (b) belief that is true because virtuous.

In the following passage, however, it seems clear that Kvanvig is missing the distinction:

> It is equally true, however, that knowledge is more than intellectually true virtuous belief. Goldman's fake barn case discussed earlier is a well-known example that reveals a difference between knowledge and such virtuous belief, for impressive perceptual abilities count as intellectual virtues and could be displayed in the fake barn case. The reason the display of such virtues falls short of knowledge is that perception can be an impressive ability and still be unable to distinguish real barns from well-designed fake ones, and so a true belief could result that still was only accidentally true.
>
> (Kvanvig 2003, p. 107)

Kvanvig's claim in the last sentence is problematic for independent reasons. Specifically, it is unclear how perception can count as an ability relative to S's environment and yet be unable to distinguish real barns from fake ones. But suppose we agree for the sake of argument that S's belief is not only true but also formed from a virtue. Still, the belief is not true *because* it is formed from a virtue. Put more carefully, the belief's being so formed does not explain why S has a true belief rather than a false belief. On the contrary, S believes the truth because she happens (luckily) to be looking at the one real barn in the area. If she had been looking anywhere else nearby, excellent perception or no, she would have a false belief.

The fake barn case looks to be a counter-example, then, only if we ignore the distinction between (a) belief that is true and virtuous, and (b) belief that is true because virtuous. But as we have seen, it is just this distinction that is crucial to the proposed solution.

Notes

1 This is the answer defended by Craig (1999).
2 See Zagzebski (1996, 2000).
3 For example, in Greco (2003). See also, Sosa (1988, 1991, 2003, 2007), Zagzebski (1996, 1999) and Riggs (2002).

References

Craig, Edward (1999). *Knowledge and the State of Nature: An Essay in Conceptual Synthesis*. Clarendon Press, New York.

Greco, John (2003). 'Knowledge as Credit for True Belief'. In Michael DePaul and Linda Zagzebski (eds), *Intellectual Virtue: Perspectives from Ethics and Epistemology*, Oxford University Press, Oxford.

Kvanvig, Jonathan (2003). *The Value of Knowledge and the Pursuit of Understanding*. Cambridge University Press, Cambridge.

Riggs, Wayne (2002). 'Reliability and the Value of Knowledge'. *Philosophy and Phenomenological Research*, 64: 79–96.

Sosa, Ernest (1988). 'Beyond Skepticism, to the Best of Our Knowledge'. *Mind* 97: 153–89.

—— (1991). *Knowledge in Perspective*. Cambridge University Press, Cambridge.

—— (2003). 'The Place of Truth in Epistemology'. In Michael DePaul and Linda Zagzebski (eds), *Intellectual Virtue: Perspective from Ethics and Epistemology*, Oxford University Press, Oxford.

—— (2007). *Apt Belief and Reflective Knowledge*. Oxford University Press, Oxford.

Linda Zagzebski (1996). *Virtues of the Mind*. Cambridge University Press, Cambridge.

—— (1999). 'What Is Knowledge?' In John Greco and Ernest Sosa (eds), *The Blackwell Guide to Epistemology*, Blackwell, Oxford.

—— (2000). 'From Reliabilism to Virtue Epistemology'. In Guy Axtell (ed.), *Knowledge, Belief and Character*, Rowman and Littlefield Publishers, Lanham, MD.

PART THREE

What evidence do we have?

INTRODUCTION TO PART THREE
Ram Neta and Duncan Pritchard

YOU HAVE A CHOICE OF PURCHASING either one of two health insurance plans. Plan A is less expensive, but plan B provides more generous reimbursement of your medical expenses. Which plan should you purchase? That depends, at least in large part, on the likelihood of your having high medical expenses: the less likely you are to have high medical expenses, the more prudent it is for you to choose plan A over plan B. So, in order to make a rational choice between purchasing plan A and purchasing plan B, you need to form some rational estimate of how likely you are to have high medical expenses. How ought you to go about forming such an estimate? Clearly, you ought to do so by appeal to your evidence. But what is *your evidence*? What is it for you to *have* some evidence? And how can you tell what evidence you have? How can you tell whether your evidence is *adequate* to justify a particular belief or decision? These questions are all among the central concerns of epistemology, and in this part we consider some of the answers that epistemologists have offered to them.

Since you ought to estimate the likelihood of various types of events by appeal to your evidence, the question of what evidence you have is a substantive, normative question: it is a question the answer to which will have implications for how you ought to conduct yourself intellectually. But because it has such implications, we cannot try to answer the question by mere stipulation. To try to answer the question in this way, i.e. stipulating that such-and-such sorts of things count as your evidence, would be merely to stipulate that you are to conduct yourself intellectually in such-and-such a way – and of course no mere stipulation can settle general questions concerning how to conduct yourself intellectually.

So the issue of what evidence you have is connected to the issue of how you should estimate the likelihood of various types of events. Precisely how are these issues connected? That itself is a matter of some controversy. But one point that many philosophers can agree with is this: when estimating the likelihood of a certain type of event, you should base your estimation of that likelihood on *all* of your evidence, not just on a portion of your evidence. This is sometimes called 'the requirement of total evidence'.

But, even if we agree that, in estimating the likelihood of a certain kind of event, you should base your estimation on *all* of your evidence, we may wonder whether you should allow anything *other than* your evidence to figure in your estimation of that likelihood. Ordinary examples might seem to show that you should do so. Consider, say, a murder investigation. Evidence is gathered: a particular knife contains traces of the victim's blood, its handle has the culprit's fingerprints, the victim's autopsy revealed death by stabbing, the culprit had a clear motive, and so on. On the basis of all this evidence (at least), we form an estimation of the likelihood that the perpetrator is, say, the butler. Should we form this estimation on the basis of anything *over and above* our evidence? It may seem that we should also attend to our *background information*, e.g. that the victim was once a living human being, that knives do not simply spring into existence replete with people's fingerprints on them, and so on.

But our description of this case leaves open the issue of *what background information is yours*. And on this issue a philosopher might offer the following suggestion: background information is yours (i.e. is admissible as helping particular bits of your evidence to determine your rational degrees of confidence in hypotheses) only if that information is itself sufficiently well supported by your *total* evidence. Thus, when we conduct the murder investigation, we can estimate the likelihood of the perpetrator having been one or another person in light of our total evidence, and against the background of such information as that the victim was once a living human being, knives do not simply spring into existence replete with people's fingerprints on them, etc. But such background information helps us to estimate likelihoods only because that background information is itself sufficiently well supported by our total evidence (including a great deal of evidence that we did not collect in the course of this particular murder investigation, but that we possessed long before this murder investigation began). If our total evidence does not sufficiently support the proposition that, say, the victim was once a living human being, then, according to the present suggestion, we would not be able to use evidence in estimating the likelihood of various hypotheses against a background that includes the proposition that the victim was once a living human being. If this line of reasoning is correct, then we can draw a conclusion that's even stronger than the requirement of total evidence: in estimating the likelihood of various types of events, one should form that estimation on the basis of one's *total* evidence, and on the basis of *nothing other* than one's evidence.

Whether or not this stronger conclusion is correct, it is clear that how we ought to go about estimating the likelihood of various types of events depends substantially on what evidence we have. So, in general, what evidence does one possess at a given time? And how can we tell what evidence we have? Different philosophers have addressed these questions in different ways, and we display some of that variety in the readings contained in this part.

In the first reading (Chapter 9), Roderick Chisholm (1916–99) is concerned to identify those marks by means of which we can tell that we have adequate evidence for believing a proposition. He says that such marks must satisfy three conditions. First, such marks must be identifiable by us in non-epistemic terms. Second, they must be such that we do not believe them to obtain when they do not obtain, or vice versa. And third, they must be such that, whenever they obtain, we have adequate evidence that they obtain. Chisholm claims that many of the things that philosophers have regarded as marks of adequate evidence fail to satisfy all three of these conditions, and so they cannot be marks of adequate evidence. But then what, if anything, satisfies all three of these conditions? Chisholm identifies two sorts of things that do so: first, when it perceptually appears to you a certain way, then, Chisholm says, you have adequate evidence for believing that it does appear to you in that very way. For instance, when it looks to you as if there is something orange in front of you, then you have adequate evidence for believing that it does look to you as if there is something orange in front of you. And second, when you take something to have a certain property on the grounds that it appears to you in a certain way, then again, Chisholm says, you have adequate evidence that the thing in question has that property. For instance, when you take the object in front of you to be an orange tabby cat on the grounds that it appears to you in a certain way (i.e. it presents a visual appearance just like that presented by orange tabbies), then again, Chisholm says, you have adequate evidence that the thing in front of you is an orange tabby cat. On the basis of these two sorts of marks of evidence, Chisholm claims, we can know ourselves to have adequate evidence for believing a great many claims about the world around us.

In the second reading (Chapter 10), Roderick Firth (1917–87) raises a number of questions about Chisholm's views. First, Firth wonders whether our marks of evidence must indeed possess all three of the characteristics that Chisholm insists on and, second, Firth argues that our marks of evidence may, at least in some cases, be restricted to just the first of Chisholm's two categories: the ways in which things perceptually appear to us. If our marks of evidence are so restricted, is it possible for us to be justified in believing anything about the world around us, or to know that we are so justified? Firth insists that the answer to both of these questions is 'yes'. For Firth, it is a task of inductive logic to figure out those principles of rational inference that lead us from premises concerning how things perceptually appear to us to reasonable conclusions concerning the features of the world around us. Just as we begin our philosophising about moral questions with an antecedent sense of which actions are right and which are wrong, so, too, according to Firth, do we begin our philosophising about epistemological questions with an antecedent sense of which beliefs about the world around us are reasonable and which are not. And just as the moral theorist can treat our antecedent views about which actions are right and which are wrong as constraining our theory of right and wrong, so, too, the epistemologist can treat our antecedent views about which beliefs are reasonable and which are not as constraining our inductive logic.

In one very important respect, the view that W. V. Quine (1908–2000) advances in his essay 'Posits and Reality' (Chapter 11) resembles the view that I have just attributed to Firth: we start by granting that the evidence of our senses is all that we have to go on in forming our views about the world around us, and then by thinking about what conclusions it is reasonable to form about the world around us, we figure out what are the principles according to which it is reasonable for people who have such-and-such experiences to form such-and-such a view of the world around them. But Quine addresses some important worries that have arisen about this point. For instance, some philosophers have worried that the evidence of our senses *cannot* be all that we have to go on in forming our views about the world around us, and that is because we typically cannot so much as describe or conceive of the content of our sensory evidence except in terms of physical objects. For instance, I see something that looks like an orange tabby cat. How can I describe my visual experience without using the term 'cat', or any other term denoting physical objects? Maybe some extraordinarily articulate and perceptive people can offer such a description, but I cannot. Does this show that the evidence of our senses cannot be all that we have to go on in forming our views about the world around us? No, Quine says, the evidence of our senses is all that we have to go on in forming our views about the world around us, even if, once we've formed those views, those same views enable us to describe and to conceive of the content of our sensory evidence, and thereby to acquire other views.

Chisholm and Firth are both primarily interested in the question of how you can tell that you have evidence that is adequate for you to believe a proposition. In contrast, both Quine and Richard Feldman (1948–) are primarily interested in the distinct, but closely related, question of what evidence you have. For Quine, your evidence consists of all and only *your sensory evidence*. But according to Feldman (Chapter 12), your evidence at any given time consists of all and only the states of your consciousness at that time – whether that consciousness is sensory or not.

Now, this theory seems to raise a number of worries, such as the following: suppose that you are currently conscious of some considerations that provide a compelling reason to believe a particular proposition, but there are also overwhelming reasons against believing that proposition – reasons of which you are not currently conscious, but of which you could very easily become conscious. Under these circumstances, is it reasonable for you to regard the proposition in question as very likely to be true? It may seem that it is not reasonable for you to do so, and yet Feldman's theory predicts that it is reasonable for you to do so. Does this show that Feldman's theory is wrong? Not necessarily. Feldman distinguishes what he calls 'current-state epistemic rationality' from 'methodological epistemic rationality', and claims that your total evidence, i.e. your total states of consciousness at a particular time, determines only the former, not the latter.

Recently, a number of epistemologists have revisited questions about evidence, and arrived at some fascinating conclusions. But we leave it to the interested reader to pursue this recent work (e.g. Williamson 2000; Hyman 2006; Neta 2008).

Study questions

1   Suppose that you see an orange tabby cat in front of you, under normal circumstances. According to both Chisholm and Firth, you then have adequate evidence for believing that there is an orange tabby cat in front of you. But Chisholm and Firth disagree about what gives you adequate evidence for believing this. Explain their differing views on this issue.

2   If, under normal circumstances, you see an orange tabby cat in front of you, then, according to W. V. Quine, the evidence of your senses makes it reasonable for you to believe that there is an orange tabby cat in front of you. But what sort of thing does Quine mean to be talking about when he uses a phrase like 'the evidence of your senses'? And what reason does Quine have for thinking that this 'evidence' makes it reasonable for you to believe anything at all?

3   Explain Richard Feldman's distinction between 'current-state epistemic rationality' and 'methodological epistemic rationality'. Why does Feldman draw this distinction? Does it serve the purpose for which he intends it?

Further reading

While many philosophers have addressed the question of what it is for one thing to be evidence for a particular hypothesis, and while some philosophers have addressed the question of what kinds of things (e.g. facts, beliefs, experiences) are evidence, until recently not many philosophers have addressed the question of what it is for someone to *have* a particular piece of evidence. This question has only recently become a topic of widespread interest, in the wake of Timothy Williamson's enormously influential discussion of evidence in chapter 9 of Williamson (2000). For some accessible and non-technical responses to Williamson, see Hyman (2006) and Neta (2008).

References

Hyman, John. 2006. 'Knowledge and Evidence', *Mind* 115: 891–916.

Neta, Ram. 2008. 'What Evidence Do You Have?', *British Journal for the Philosophy of Science* 59(1): 89–119.

Williamson, Timothy. 2000. *Knowledge and Its Limits*, Oxford: Oxford University Press.

Chapter 9

Roderick Chisholm

"APPEAR," "TAKE," AND "EVIDENT"

1. If a man looks toward the roof and *sees* that his cat is there, he is not likely to *say*, "I take that to be a cat" or "I have adequate evidence for the proposition or hypothesis that that is a cat." But, I suggest, if he does see that his cat is there, he does take it to be his cat and he does have adequate evidence for the hypothesis that what he sees is his cat. And I would suggest, more generally, that the locution "There is something such that S *perceives that* it is f" may be defined as meaning: first, there is something which S takes to be f; secondly, S has adequate evidence for the proposition or hypothesis that the thing is f; and, lastly, the thing *is* f. By adding qualifications about sense organs we may formulate similar definitions of one of the more important senses of "see" and of "hear."

Such definitions will not be interesting or significant unless we can say what is meant by "take" and by "adequate evidence" without using "see," "hear," or "perceive." Let us begin, then, with the concept of *adequate evidence*.

2. "Adequate evidence" is an *epistemic* term—a term we use in appraising the epistemic, or cognitive, worth of statements, hypotheses, and beliefs. Making use of the locution "S ought to place more confidence in h than in i," where "S" may be replaced by the name of a person and "h" and "i" by the names of propositions, beliefs, statements, or hypotheses, we may explicate some of our more important epistemic terms in the following way. "It would be *unreason-*

able for S to accept *h*" means that S ought to place more confidence in non-*h* than in *h*; "*h* is *acceptable* for S" means that it would not be unreasonable for S to accept *h*; "*h* is (epistemically) *indifferent* for S" means that both *h* and non-*h* are acceptable for S; and "S has *adequate evidence* for *h*" means that non-*h* is unreasonable for S, or, in other words, that S ought to place more confidence in *h* than in non-*h*. By making use of the additional locution "S accepts *h*," we may define one important use of "know" and one important use of "certain." The locution "S *knows that* *h* is true" could be said to mean, first, that S accepts *h*, secondly that S has adequate evidence for *h*, and, thirdly, that *h* is true. And "S is *certain* that *h* is true" could be said to mean, first, that S knows that *h* is true, and, secondly, that there is no proposition or hypothesis *i* such that S ought to place more confidence in *i* than in *h*.[1]

Our present problem is this: How are we to decide which propositions are evident? Or, more exactly: By means of what principles could our subject S *apply* the locution "S has adequate evidence for *h*"?

In setting this problem for ourselves—the problem of "the criterion"[2]—we do not presuppose, nor should we presuppose, that there are certain principles which people actually think about, or refer to, in order to *decide* whether they have adequate evidence for their beliefs. The grammarian, similarly, may try to describe the conditions under which, say, people use the imperfect tense rather than the past perfect; but, in so doing, he does not mean to imply that, before using this tense, people think about these conditions or try to decide whether or not they apply.

It is important to note that we cannot answer our question by reference solely to the logic of induction and the theory of probability. For the principles of induction and probability will not tell a man which propositions are evident unless he applies them to *premises* which are evident.[3]

In the present paper, I wish to describe and to illustrate one approach to this philosophical problem.

3. I suggest that we consider the analogue of our problem in *moral philosophy*.

What do we regard as the proper way of applying our *moral* terms? To answer this question, let us ask further: How would we go about *defending* a particular application of some moral terms—say, some particular application of the term "right"?

If we say, of some particular act, that that act is *right* and if we are prepared to defend our statement, then we are prepared to appeal to some characteristic *in virtue of which* that act is right. Possibly we are prepared to show that the act is an instance of courage, or of forgiveness, or that it is motivated by a wish to decrease the amount of pain in the world. This characteristic, whatever it may be, is one such that *every* act to which it applies is an act which is right, or which "tends to be right." But it is not a characteristic which we need to describe or identify in distinctly *moral*, or *ethical*, terms. If we wish to point out that someone is motivated by the wish to decrease the amount of pain in the world, or that he is acting courageously, we can convey what we want to convey without using "right" or "good" or "ought" or any other ethical term. Let us say, following Professor Broad, that the characteristic to which we appeal is one which is "right-making."[4]

There are three important points to be made about "right-making" characteristics. (1) A

"right-making" characteristic is one which can be described and identified in ethically neutral language—without the use of ethical terms. (2) When we find out, or when we show, that a particular act is right, we find out, or show, that the act has some "right-making" characteristic. And (3) every act which is right is right *in virtue of* some "right-making" characteristic of the act— some characteristic such that every act which has that characteristic is right, or "tends to be right." Similar points may be made, *mutatis mutandis*, of such ethical terms as "wrong," "good," and "bad."

Among the traditional tasks of moral philosophy is that of describing characteristics which are "right-making," "wrong-making," "good-making," and the like. In listing such characteristics, the moral philosopher is not providing *definitions* of the ethical terms concerned. We may say, following one ancient usage, that he is providing *criteria* for applying these terms.

Our problem—the "problem of the criterion"—is that of finding similar criteria for applying our epistemic vocabulary.

4. Hobbes said, "The inn of evidence has no sign-board." But I suggest that, whenever a man has adequate evidence for some proposition or hypothesis, he is in a state which constitutes a *mark of evidence* for that proposition or hypothesis.

What, then, would be a "mark of evidence" for a proposition or hypothesis h? In asking this question, we are asking: What would be a *criterion* by means of which a particular subject S might apply our locution "S has adequate evidence for h"?

Just as there were three points to be made about "right-making" characteristics, there are three points to be made about marks of evidence—about "evidence-bearing" characteristics:

(1) A mark or criterion, for any subject S, that S has adequate evidence for a given proposition or hypothesis h, would be

some state or condition of S which could be described without using "know," or "perceive," or "evident," or any other epistemic term. That is to say, it would be a state or condition of S which would be described in language which is "epistemically neutral."

(2) It is tempting to say that a mark for S, that S has adequate evidence for a given proposition or hypothesis h, would be some state or condition to which S appeals when he wishes to *show* that he has evidence for h—or some state or condition which he *discovers* to hold when he discovers he has adequate evidence for h. But the words "discover" and "show," in this present use, are themselves epistemic terms. To *discover* that some condition holds is, among other things, to acquire adequate evidence for believing that it does; and to *show* some other person that some condition holds is, among other things, to enable him to have adequate evidence for believing that it holds. If we are to formulate our second requirement in "epistemically neutral" language, I believe we must say something like this: A mark or criterion, for any subject S, that S has adequate evidence for a given proposition or hypothesis h would be some state or condition of S which is such that S could not make any mistake at any time about his *being* in that state or condition at that time. That is to say, S could never believe falsely at any time either that he is in that state at that time or that he is not in that state at that time.

(3) Finally, a mark or criterion, for any subject S, that S has adequate evidence for a given proposition or hypothesis h would be a state or condition such that, whenever S is in that state or condition, S has adequate evidence for h.[5]

5. Philosophers have proposed various criteria, or marks, of evidence, but in most cases their proposals fail to meet one or more of the three conditions we have formulated.

We cannot be content to say, as apparently some philosophers would be, that a man has adequate evidence for any proposition which he *knows*, or *remembers*, or *sees*, or *perceives* to be true. For "see," "know," "remember," and "perceive," as here used, are epistemic terms—terms we have defined by means of our locution "S ought to place more confidence in h than in i." Such criteria, therefore, do not meet the first of our conditions.

It has been suggested that we have adequate evidence for any proposition which is accepted by "the scientists of our culture circle." It has also been suggested that we have adequate evidence for any proposition "revealed to us by God." Possibly the words "scientist" and "revealed," in these criteria, fail to conform to our first condition. In any case, both criteria fail to meet the second condition. We are all quite capable of believing falsely at any time that a given proposition is accepted by the scientists of our culture circle at that time or has been revealed to us by God at that time.

According to Descartes, we have adequate evidence for those propositions "we conceive very clearly and very distinctly." This criterion does not seem to meet our third condition. For we can conceive very clearly and very distinctly what is expressed by many statements we know to be false.

Are there *any* states or conditions which provide us with marks of evidence? I shall try to describe two such states.

6. The locution "x appears so-and-so to S," in one of its many senses, is used to describe one mark of evidence.

Possibly the sense of "appear" I have in mind will be suggested by the following example. Let us consider the statement "Things which are red usually appear red (look red) in ordinary light." Among the uses of "appear red" ("look red") is one such that, in that use, the statement "Things which are red usually appear red in ordinary light" is analytic. For, in this use, "appears red" may be taken to mean the same as "appears in the way that things which are red usually appear in ordinary light." But there is another use of "appears red" which is such that, in that use, the statement "Things which are red usually appear red in ordinary light" is synthetic. Using "appears red" in this second way, we could say: "There is a certain way of appearing—appearing red—which, as it happens, we have found to be the way in which red things usually appear." (The word "appear" is also intended in this second way in such statements as the following, which are to be found in the writings of empirical philosophers: "We can never know that such things as apples are red unless we first know either that they sometimes appear red or that they resemble, in important respects, things which do appear red.")

In the first of these two uses, the locution "appears so-and-so" functions essentially as a *comparative* locution. When we say of anything that it "appears so-and-so," in this sense, we mean to draw a comparison between the thing and things that *are* so-and-so. We mean to say something like this: "The thing appears the way you would normally expect things that are so-and-so to appear under conditions like these (or under conditions of such-and-such a sort)." But when we use "appears so-and-so" in the second of the two ways I have tried to describe, our statements are not in the same sense comparative statements; "x appears so-and-so," in this use, does not entail any such statement as "x appears the way things that are so-and-so might normally be expected to appear." Let us say that, in this second use, the locution "x appears so-and-so" is used *non-comparatively*.

According to my suggestion, then, the locution "x appears so-and-so to S," when used *non-comparatively*, describes a condition which provides S with a mark of evidence for the proposition that x appears so-and-so to S. If something appears blue to S (in the non-comparative sense of "appears blue"), then, in being thus "appeared to," S is in a state which provides him with a mark of evidence for the proposition that something appears blue to S.[6] Let us see whether this criterion of evidence fulfills our three conditions.

First, the ways of being "appeared to" in question can be described without using "know," or "perceive," or "evidence," or any other epistemic term. And since they can be described in "epistemically neutral" language, they meet the first of our conditions.

Secondly, if a subject S is "appeared to" in one of the ways in question, then, surely, he could not believe at that time that he is not being thus "appeared to." Nor could he believe that he was being thus "appeared to" at a time when he was not being thus "appeared to." Is it possible for something to appear blue to me while I believe that nothing does, or for me to believe that something appears blue to me at a time when nothing does? (If "appears blue" were meant in its comparative sense, then we should have to say that these things are quite possible. But it is here meant in its non-comparative sense.) We could say: There are ways of appearing which are such that, for any subject S, whenever S is appeared to in one of those ways, it is false that S believes he is *not* being appeared to in that particular way; and whenever S is not being appeared to in one of those ways, it is false that S believes he *is* being appeared to in that particular way. Hence *appearing* may be said to satisfy the second of the conditions we have proposed for a mark of evidence.

And surely *appearing* satisfies the third of our conditions. Whenever anything appears in such-and-such a way to a subject S (or, better, whenever S is appeared to in such-and-such a way), then S has adequate evidence for the proposition that something is appearing to him (or, better, that he is being appeared to) in that particular way.

To be sure, no one is ever likely to *say*, "I have adequate evidence for the proposition that something is appearing blue to me." But a man who is thus appeared to may use this proposition as a premise in the application of probability and induction. For example, if he happens to have adequate evidence for the proposition "Most of the things that appear blue in this light are blue," if something now appears blue to him, and if he has adequate evidence for no other proposition bearing upon the probability of "This is blue," then he has adequate evidence for the proposition "This is blue." It is in this sense that he may be said to have adequate evidence for "Something appears blue to me."

7. *Empiricism*, as an epistemological thesis, may now be defined by reference to this "appearing" criterion of evidence and to the logic of probability, or confirmation.[7] According to empiricism in its most extreme form, the "appearing" criterion, when supplemented by the logic of probability, affords us our *only* criterion of evidence. If a subject S has adequate evidence for some statement h, then, according to this form of empiricism, either (a) h describes one of the ways S is being appeared to, in the non-comparative sense of "appear," or (b) h is a statement which is probable in relation to such non-comparative appear statements.

I think that the philosophers who have accepted this empirical thesis, or some modification of it, have been influenced by certain facts concerning the way in which we defend, or try to justify, our beliefs. But I will not discuss these facts here. Rather, I will note what seems to be one of the limitations of empiricism, as defined, and I will try to formulate an alternative thesis.

The limitation of empiricism, as defined, is that it would seem to lead us to what Hume called "scepticism with regard to the senses." For it is very difficult to think of any proposition about the "external world" which is probable—more probable than not—in relation to any set of propositions about the way in which one is appeared to. That is to say, it is very difficult to think of a set of statements of this sort: one of them is a synthetic statement, attributing some

property to a material thing; the others are statements of the form "I am appeared to in such-and-such a way," where the expression "appeared to in such-and-such a way" has what I have called its non-comparative use; and, finally, the statement about the material thing is probable—more probable than not—in relation to the statements about appearing. If there are no such sets of statements and if the empirical thesis is true, then any synthetic proposition about a material thing would be one which, for each of us, is epistemically *indifferent*—no more worthy of our confidence than is its contradictory. And if all of this were true, we might well conclude, with Hume, that "it is in vain to ask, whether there be body or not?"[8]

I suggest, however, that there are other marks of evidence. One of them is described by the word "take" which occurs in our definition of "perceive." (And therefore reference to "adequate evidence" in our definition is, in a certain sense, redundant.) I shall restrict myself, in what follows, to certain comments on this additional mark of evidence.

8. What is it for a man to *take* something to have a certain characteristic—to take something to be a cat? First of all, of course, he *believes* that the thing is a cat. Secondly, the thing is appearing to him in a certain way. Thirdly, he believes (or assumes, or "takes it for granted") with respect to one of the ways he is being appeared to, that he would not now be appeared to in just that way if the thing were not a cat. (And undoubtedly he also believes, with respect to certain ways in which he might act, that if he were now to act in those ways he would be appeared to in still other cat-like ways—i.e. in ways he would not be appeared to if the thing were not a cat.) And, finally, these beliefs or assumptions were not arrived at as the result of reflection, deliberation, or inference; the man didn't weigh alternatives and then *infer* that the thing was a cat.

More generally, the locution "There is something x such that S *takes* x to be f" may be said to mean this: there is something x such that x appears in some way to S; S believes that x is f; S also believes, with respect to one of the ways he is appeared to, that he would not be appeared to in that way, under the conditions which now obtain, if x were not f; and S did not arrive at these beliefs as a result of deliberation, reflection, or inference.

If a man *takes* something to be a cat, then, as I have noted, he is not likely to *say*, "I take that to be a cat." He is more likely to say, "I *see* that that is a cat."[9] But the fact that he wouldn't *say*, "I take that to be a cat," doesn't imply that it's false that he takes the thing to be a cat. When the King dies, his subjects do not *say*, "Some public official has passed away." But the fact that they do not say it does not imply it's false that some public official has passed away.

If taking, as thus conceived, is a mark of evidence, then it must satisfy our three conditions. And I believe that it does. For (1) we have been able to say what *taking* is without using any epistemic terms; our description, or definition, does not make use of "know," "evident," "see," "perceive," or any other epistemic term. (2) No one can ever be said to believe falsely, or mistakenly, either that he is, or that he is not, taking something to be a cat. Of course a man may take something falsely to be a cat; i.e. he may *mistake* something for a cat. And a man may believe falsely today that yesterday he took something to be a cat. But no one can believe falsely now, with respect to himself, that he is now taking something to be a cat, or that he is not now taking something to be a cat. (Instead of saying, "No one can believe falsely that . . .," we may say, if we prefer, "It makes no sense to say of anyone that he believes falsely that . . .") And I suggest (3) that if a man takes something to be a cat he thereby has adequate evidence for the proposition or hypothesis that the thing *is* a cat.[10]

This theory of evidence has a kind of "internal" justification. For the hypotheses and propositions for which most of us *have* adequate evidence, if this theory is correct, indicate that most of our "takings" are true—that most of our "takings" are *perceivings*. These hypotheses and propositions indicate, as Peirce pointed out, that human beings have a tendency to make correct guesses and that the human mind is "strongly adapted to the comprehension of the world."[11]

Some of our "takings" are false. And therefore, if what I have been saying is true, there are times when we ought to place more confidence in a false proposition than in its true contradictory. The apparent paradox involved in saying that our false "takings"—our mistakes—are a mark of evidence has its analogue in moral philosophy. It is difficult to avoid saying that occasionally the *right* choice—or at least the choice that is *praiseworthy*—leads to consequences which are worse than those which the *wrong*—or *blameworthy*—choice would have led to.

And theories of evidence ("So-and-so, but not such-and-such, is a mark of evidence") are, generally, very much like theories of morals ("So-and-so, but not such-and-such, is invariably *right*"). If there is any good reason to think that statements expressing theories of morals are neither true nor false, then, I feel certain, there is also a good reason to think that statements expressing theories of evidence are neither true nor false.

Notes

1 If we wish to avoid the word "true" we may replace the locution "S accepts h" by "S accepts the hypothesis that x is f" or "S accepts the hypothesis that . . ."; then, instead of saying "h is true," we may say "x is f" or ". . . ." I have discussed the above concepts in more detail in "Epistemic Statements and the Ethics of Belief," *Philosophy and Phenomenological Research*, Vol. XVI (1956), pp. 447–460.

2 See Sextus Empiricus, *Outlines of Pyrrhonism*, Books I and II. Cardinal Mercier described the attempts to deal with this problem as works of "criteriology"; see D. J. Mercier, *Critériologie générale*.

3 Indeed, the principes of probability and induction will not tell S whether or not S has adequate

evidence for a certain hypothesis h unless two epistemic conditions are fulfilled: (i) S must apply the principles to premises for which he has adequate evidence; and (ii), in so doing, S must not leave out any relevant evidence—i.e. of those hypotheses for which he has adequate evidence, his premises should include all which have a probability relation to h. Carnap refers to this second requirement, which had been formulated by Bernoulli, as the "requirement of total evidence." See Carnap's *Logical Foundations of Probability*, pp. 211 ff., 494.

4 "Moral characteristics are always dependent upon certain other characteristics which can be described in purely neutral non-moral terms. Let us call those non-moral characteristics whose presence in anything confers rightness or goodness on it *right-making* and *wrong-making* characteristics. And let us define *good-making* and *bad-making* characteristics in a similar way." C. D. Broad, "Some of the Main Problems of Ethics," *Philosophy*, Vol. 21 (1946), p. 103. Compare *Butler's Moral Philosophy*, by A. E. Duncan-Jones, Chapter Eight, Sections 1 and 2; and R. M. Hare, *The Language of Morals*, pp. 80 ff.

5 Cardinal Mercier formulated three requirements—those of being "internal," "objective," and "immediate"—which would be met by any adequate theory of "certitude." The first and third of his requirements, I think, may be intended to serve the purpose of the second one I have listed above. His second requirement serves the purpose of the third condition I have listed above. It may be interpreted as also ruling out the philosophical view that statements expressing theories of evidence are neither true nor false. Although Mercier was sensitive to the charge of circularity, he did not formulate a requirement comparable to the first one I have listed above. And the criterion of "certitude" which he proposed does not seem to meet the first of my requirements. He said that we have certitude when the subjects and predicates of our judgments *express* or *manifest* reality; but I believe that the terms "express" and "manifest," as he intended them, are epistemic terms, the meanings of which can be conveyed only by such

terms as "know," "evident," or "perceive." See D. J. Mercier, *Critériologie générale*, eighth edition (Louvain, 1923), Sections 150–153, and *Manual of Modern Scholastic Philosophy*, Vol. I, p. 369.

6 Strictly speaking, a mark of evidence is described, not by "x appears so-and-so to S," but by "S is appeared to so-and-so, i.e. in such-and-such a way." The victim of delirium tremens, who says of an hallucinatory elephant or lizard, "That appears pink," may be right in using "pink" and wrong in thinking that *something* appears pink. But he couldn't go far wrong if he said only, "I'm appeared pink to"—or, in more philosophical language, "I sense pink."

7 I use "empiricism" in one of its traditional senses. The word has many other meanings, of course, in recent philosophy.

8 *Treatise of Human Nature*, Book I, Part IV, Section ii ("Of Scepticism with Regard to the Senses"). Thomas Reid wrote as follows, with respect to the empirical thesis and its apparent skeptical consequence: "A traveler of good judgment may mistake his way, and be unawares led into a wrong track; and while the road is fair before him, he may go on without suspicion and be followed by others; but when it ends in a coal-pit, it requires no great judgment to know that he hath gone wrong, nor perhaps to find out what misled him" (*An Inquiry into the Human Mind*, Chapter One, Section 8). The empiricist may be tempted at this point to accept "phenomenalism"—the view that statements about material things may be translated into statements about "appearances"—in the hope that phenomenalism provides a way out of the coal-pit. But we cannot be sure that phenomenalism would provide such a way out, for no one has ever been able to make the required translations. And therefore we have no map to examine.

9 If a second man is not sure that our perceiver sees that the thing is a cat, the second man will say "He *takes* it to be a cat" or—what comes to the same thing—"He *thinks he sees* that it's a cat."

10 H. H. Price suggests a similar view in *Perception*, p. 185.

11 C. S. Peirce, *Collected Papers*, 6.417.

Chapter 10

Roderick Firth

ULTIMATE EVIDENCE

1. Chisholm's paper deals with two topics of fundamental importance for theory of knowledge. In the first part of his paper (Sections 1 to 4), he explains what he means by "the problem of the criterion." He maintains that one of the tasks of the epistemologist is to find and formulate criteria for the application of epistemic terms such as "evidence" and "knowledge," just as the moral philosopher must try to discover right-making characteristics, wrong-making characteristics, good-making characteristics, etc., which are criteria for the application of ethical terms. In both cases, he asserts (Section 3), the problem of the criterion is to be distinguished from the problem of analyzing concepts or providing definitions for the terms in question: thus the definitions of epistemic terms which Chisholm offers at the beginning of his paper, if they are satisfactory, must not logically entail any particular answer to the issues considered in the second part of the paper. In this second part (Sections 5 to 8) Chisholm weighs the merits of two quite different criteria of evidence. He formulates a criterion of "appearing" which seems to be characteristic of empiricism in one of its traditional forms, and then argues that this criterion must be supplemented by a criterion of perceptual "taking." I think that I disagree with Chisholm's views on each of the two central topics of his paper; and it is possible, because of the admirable precision and clarity

with which Chisholm has stated the issues, that I can explain the grounds of my disagreement in a useful way. I shall be primarily concerned to defend the traditional empiricist theory of knowledge against the charge that the empiricist criterion of evidence is inadequate; but since the case might be prejudiced against the empiricist theory by Chisholm's treatment of criteria in general, I shall first say something about this.

2. To avoid some important questions which are too general to discuss here, I shall assume with Chisholm that we can draw a meaningful distinction, at least in many cases, between the meaning or definition of a given term and those characteristics which are the non-definitive conditions for the application of that term; and, following Chisholm, I shall henceforth refer to the latter, but not to the former, as *criteria* for the application of the term. With respect to Chisholm's ethical analogy, I can agree that there are characteristics of certain actions (e.g. their tendency to promote happiness) which are, in Broad's terminology, "right-making," and which are properly described as *criteria* (at least in the absence of wrong-making characteristics) for the application of the term "right." Thus even if there is an analyzable property of rightness, as naturalistic ethicists commonly maintain, it would be a mistake to identify this property, either in whole or in part, with any of the right-making characteristics. But in the case of epistemic terms like "evidence," "perception,"

and "knowledge," it seems doubtful to me that the characteristics (or "marks") which Chisholm is seeking are properly described as criteria. In any event, I see no reason for thinking that the "empiricist criterion," as Chisholm describes it, is really nothing but a criterion, or that it would be so considered by most empiricists. For an empiricist might well maintain that this "empiricist criterion" actually follows from the very definition of epistemic terms and is therefore no criterion at all. A statement of the form "S perceives that x is f," when used in an epistemic sense, logically entails the statement "S has adequate evidence that x is f"; and an empiricist might maintain that this in turn *logically entails* that S has certain sense experiences which support the statement "x is f" via certain principles of induction. (Let us call this, for present purposes, "the strong empiricist thesis" in contrast to the "weak empiricist thesis," which is the one formulated by Chisholm as a thesis about criteria.) The validity of this strong empiricist thesis could be tested only by logical analysis of such terms as "perceive" and "adequate evidence": it implies, if we use Chisholm's terminology of appearing to talk about sense experience, that the inductive relationship between the statement that I am being appeared to in a certain way, and the statement that I perceive something to be of such and such a kind, is an essential part of our concepts of "perception" and "adequate evidence," and must be mentioned in any satisfactory definition of these epistemic terms.

Now in view of this fact, it is a matter of crucial importance to determine the status of the definitions which Chisholm offers in the opening paragraphs of his paper. For these are proposed as definitions of epistemic terms such as "perception," "knowledge," and "adequate evidence," and yet they do *not* refer to the inductive relationship which enables us to draw inferences from sense experiences. The basic locutions, in terms of which all the epistemic terms are defined, are the locutions "S ought to place more confidence in h than in i" and "S accepts h"; and there seems to be no reason to suppose that either of these locutions is itself analyzable by reference to the logic of induction from sense experiences. Thus the strong empiricist thesis is ruled out *a priori* if we accept these definitions and interpret the basic locutions in anything like the ordinary way. These definitions have the effect of making epistemic statements into statements about what we ought or ought not to believe, so that anything further which an empiricist might say about the conditions of knowledge and adequate evidence is restricted to a thesis about criteria (the weak empiricist thesis). We must ask, therefore, whether there is any good reason for accepting such an "ethical interpretation" of epistemic terms.

3. It is a familiar fact that ordinary language, in addition to typically ethical words like "ought," "wrong," and "good," which are commonly used to make statements which might be called "purely ethical," also contains a wide variety of terms which are more commonly used to make statements which are only "derivatively ethical." Most of the words which designate human virtues and vices are derivatively ethical in the sense I have in mind. Thus if we say that Socrates is courageous, our statement would normally be taken as a favorable ethical evaluation of Socrates (however we may interpret "favorable evaluation"); but it would also describe Socrates by attributing to him a trait of character (viz., courage) which is understood to be the ground of the favorable evaluation. The distinction between these two functions of the statement—the evaluative and the ground-descriptive—can be exhibited by comparing "Socrates is courageous" with an analogous statement such as "Socrates is wise," which might express an equally favorable evaluation, but which describes Socrates in a very different way. And it should also be noted that the evaluative implications of words like "courageous" and "wise" can be removed for certain purposes.

In a suitable context it is possible to ask, without absurdity, whether it is in any respect good that Socrates should be courageous, and even whether courage in general is a virtue. It makes no difference whether we do or do not regard such questions as odd and uncolloquial: the significant point is that words like "courageous" do have a non-evaluative function which permits them to be used in this special way.

But so, it seems to me, do epistemic words like "adequate evidence," "perception," and "knowledge." If I assert that S has adequate evidence for h, my assertion might normally be understood to imply the ethical judgment that S ought to place more confidence in h than in non-h (Chisholm's definition). But surely it implies more than this: it also indicates the *ground* for saying that S ought to place more confidence in h than in non-h—the fact, namely, that S has evidence of a certain kind. The distinction between these two functions of the assertion—the ethical and the ground-descriptive—can be exhibited by showing that there are other, quite different, grounds on which we might meaningfully say that S ought to place more confidence in h than in non-h—the fact, for example, that S will be happier if he believes h, or the fact that God wants us all to believe h. In a suitable context, moreover, it is possible to use epistemic terms without their usual ethical implications. In discussing some of the doctrines of pragmatism, for example, or the roles of faith and reason in religion, it is meaningful to ask whether S ought not sometimes to believe h even though he has much stronger evidence of non-h, whether S ought not sometimes to accept on faith doctrines which he cannot be said to know, etc. These facts indicate that epistemic words, like those which designate human virtues and vices, have a ground-descriptive as well as an ethical function. And if this much is granted the strong empiricist thesis cannot be ruled out a priori. A philosopher who wishes to defend this thesis can admit that statements of the form "S perceives that x is f" and "S has adequate evidence for h" are normally

understood to entail a judgment about what S ought to believe; but he will maintain that these epistemic statements also entail a proposition which indicates the ground of the ethical judgment. And this latter proposition, he will argue, can ultimately be analyzed only by reference to sense experience and the inductive principles which enable us to draw inferences from sense experience.

4. Let us now turn to the second part of Chisholm's paper. Even if we conclude, for the reasons I have given, that Chisholm's ethical interpretation of epistemic terms is incorrect, this second part of his paper (Section 5 to end) can still be construed as a forceful argument against the strong empiricist thesis. To do this it is only necessary to read "empiricist analysis of 'evidence'" for "empiricist criterion of evidence" in the appropriate places. Chisholm's reasons for denying that the criterion of appearing is adequate would be equally good reasons for denying the strong empiricist thesis; and his reasons for preferring the criterion of perceptual taking might even be reasons for holding that the concept of "adequate evidence" cannot be analyzed except in terms of "taking." In order to evaluate these arguments, let us consider how the issues might be construed in more traditional terms, without employing the term "criterion."

Throughout the history of modern philosophy, most empiricists have maintained that our knowledge of the external world can be justified by appealing to perception, together with beliefs based on past perceptions, and that our perceptual judgments can in their turn be justified by appealing to the evidence of the senses. Thus my belief that the garden gate is ajar is justified by the fact that I see a dog digging up the peonies; and my belief that I see a *dog* (rather than a cat, for example) is justified by the character of my sense experience—by the look of the thing, or, in Chisholm's terminology, by the way I am "appeared to." But most empiricists have gone further than this: they have thought that the latter mode of justification (i.e. justification by appeal to sense experience) is evidentially ultimate. It is not, of course, the only way to justify perceptual beliefs. My belief that I see a dog is justified by the fact that I see an animal larger than a cat, that I see an animal digging in the manner characteristic of a dog, etc.; and it is facts of this sort about what I see, rather than facts about my sense experience, which I should probably mention if I were asked, "What makes you think you see a *dog*?" But regardless of what I might or might not say when questioned, it has seemed undeniable to most empiricists that the character of my sense experience provides me with evidence (and usually very good evidence) for thinking that I do (or that I do not) see such and such a thing. Thus the justification of one perceptual judgment (e.g. "I see a dog") by reference to another perceptual judgment (e.g. "I see an animal digging like a dog") is never ultimate: the latter can in turn always be supported by appealing to the evidence of the senses ("It has the look of an animal digging like a dog"). It has been generally agreed, on the other hand, that our judgments about present sense experience cannot in their turn be supported by further evidence: if I assert that something has the look of a dog to me, it does not make sense, unless the words are being used in an extraordinary way, to ask, "What reason have you for thinking that it has the look of a dog to you?" This traditional doctrine about the nature of empirical evidence, as I have so far described it, can be summed up in two propositions: (1) Sense experiences are evidence for perceptual judgments, and (2) Sense experiences are evidentially ultimate.

Now it seems to me that Chisholm does not intend to deny either of these two propositions. He specifically asserts that the fact that something appears blue to me may be evidence, under certain conditions, for the statement "This is blue" (Section 6). And the second proposition— that sense experiences are evidentially ultimate—is implied, I think, by Chisholm's stronger

(and, I think, more dubious) thesis that we cannot make mistakes in judging that we are appeared to in a certain way (Section 6). Chisholm does point out, however, that sense experiences are not the only things which are evidentially ultimate—that perceptual takings, in particular, are ultimate in exactly the same sense. This would not be denied, to be sure, by philosophers of the empiricist tradition: they would hold, I think, that sense experiences are epistemologically ultimate because they are *experiences*, and that any experiences, whether memory experiences, feelings of emotion, or perceptual takings, are evidentially ultimate for the same reason. But Chisholm's argument does have the effect of challenging the empiricist to justify the preferred epistemological status which has traditionally been given to sense experiences as opposed to perceptual takings. Let us consider how this challenge might be met.

5. In order to do justice to the traditional empiricist theory of evidence, I think that we must consider some further facts about the evidential relationship between sense experiences and perceptual judgments. As we commonly use the term "adequate evidence" it is quite possible for a person S to have adequate evidence for a true proposition p even when he does not happen to believe p (and, indeed, even when he believes not-p). We might explain S's condition in such cases by saying that he has failed to take certain evidence into account, has failed to draw rational inferences, etc. If we are to preserve this usage when speaking about the evidence for perceptual judgments, we must define our terms so that it is meaningful to make statements like the following: "S sees a dog and he has adequate evidence that he sees a dog, but he cannot decide whether he sees a dog or a cat," "S sees a dog and he has adequate evidence that he sees a dog, but he thinks he sees a cat," and "S sees a pink rat and he has adequate evidence that he sees a pink rat, but he thinks he's having an hallucination." And there is, of course, a familiar sense of "see" which does permit us to make

these statements. It is not, however, the (equally important) sense of "see" which Chisholm defines in his opening paragraph, for the idiom there introduced—"S perceives (sees) that something is f"—entails that there is something which S takes to be f; and this in turn entails that there is something which S *believes* to be f (Section 8). If we were to talk about perception only in terms of this idiom, therefore, we should have to draw our examples of adequate evidence only from cases in which we actually believe the proposition for which the evidence is said to be adequate. And this would prejudice the issue against the traditional empiricist theory of evidence, for it would prevent us from appealing to those crucial cases in which there is no state of perceptual taking which could possibly serve as evidence for our perceptual statement.

Let us suppose, for example, that I look down from a window at dusk and see an animal in the garden, but I am in doubt whether I see a cat or a small dog. So long as I remain in a state of doubt, I can correctly be said to take something to be an animal; but I do not take something to be a cat and I do not take something to be a dog. In such a case my doubt cannot be resolved by appealing to a perceptual taking, even if we grant that perceptual takings are usually valid. The only ultimate evidence to which I can possibly appeal—assuming that I do not acquire new evidence by going down, for example, into the garden—is the evidence of my visual sense experience. Let us suppose, furthermore, that I am soon able to decide, on reflection, that the look of the thing is characteristic of a black cocker spaniel, so that I no longer have any doubt that I am seeing a dog. In such a case it would surely not be plausible to maintain that I acquired adequate evidence only when I ceased to doubt. If my visual sense experience did not change in any appreciable way, it would be true to say that I had adequate evidence for the statement "I see a dog" even when I did not think that I was seeing a dog. And this is enough

to show that there are *some* cases in which sense experience provides adequate evidence for a perceptual statement and perceptual takings do not. It cannot be shown, on the other hand, by analogous methods, that there are any cases in which the contrary is true—cases in which perceptual takings provide adequate evidence for a perceptual statement and sense experience does not. The reason for this is suggested by Chisholm's definition of "S takes x to be f" (Section 8); for this definition recognizes the fact that whenever we take x to be f, we always have sense experiences which we believe to be good evidence that x is f. I think, therefore, that the epistemologist who is looking for ultimate criteria of adequate evidence for perceptual statements, or who wishes to analyze the concept of adequate evidence, is justified in concluding that sense experiences are essential and perceptual takings are not. This does not mean, of course, that perceptual takings are not good evidence for perceptual statements. They are good evidence, however, only in virtue of the truth of the general proposition that most of our "takings" are true. And this general proposition can be justified without circularity, once we admit that perceptual takings are not essential evidence in the justification of perceptual statements.

6. In conclusion I shall comment very briefly on an important methodological question which is raised by Chisholm's rejection of the traditional empiricist theory of evidence on the ground that it leads to skepticism about our knowledge of the external world (Section 7). It seems to me that the epistemologist who wants to formulate a schema for the justification of our knowledge of the external world, is faced with two quite different tasks. He must first select his premises. And in order to restrict these to a minimum, he must select them from among the statements which are evidentially ultimate: they must be statements about sense experiences, for example, and memory experiences—statements which cannot themselves be justified by infer-

ence from other statements. At this stage he can be guided only by our actual practice in justifying our beliefs, and there can be no question about the rationality of our actual practice in general. If we do in fact treat sense experiences as evidence for our perceptual statements, then they *are* evidence for our perceptual statements; and if, as I have maintained, we do not treat perceptual takings as essential to an adequate justification, then it is not necessary to include statements about perceptual takings among our premises.

Once our premises have been chosen, however, the character of the enterprise changes. It now becomes in part the purely logical task of exhibiting the principles of inference which are implicit in our treating of (say) sense experiences and memory experiences as adequate evidence; and, since the nature of these principles will depend on the meaning of the

statements we are trying to justify, it becomes in part the task of choosing among rival ontological theories like phenomenalism and causal realism. It seems clear to me, however, that under no circumstances could these tasks justifiably lead us to a skeptical conclusion, for at this second stage we are merely exhibiting the logic of an evidential relationship which has already been established by the only methods possible. If we reject phenomenalism we may be surprised or shocked at the principles of inference which are needed to get from our premises to our conclusion; but this is no ground for skepticism, nor even, I think, for supposing that we have started from the wrong premises. Thus it seems to me that the principal issues which Chisholm and I have been discussing must be settled (to use Reid's analogy, as quoted by Chisholm) at the beginning of the road, in full confidence that it cannot end in a coal pit.

Chapter 11

W. V. Quine

POSITS AND REALITY

I Subvisible particles

According to physics my desk is, for all its seeming fixity and solidity, a swarm of vibrating molecules. The desk as we sense it is comparable to a distant haystack in which we cannot distinguish the individual stalks; comparable also to a wheel in which, because of its rapid rotation, we cannot distinguish the individual spokes. Comparable, but with a difference. By approaching the haystack we can distinguish the stalks, and by retarding the wheel we can distinguish the spokes. On the other hand no glimpse is to be had of the separate molecules of the desk; they are, we are told, too small.

Lacking such experience, what evidence can the physicist muster for his doctrine of molecules? His answer is that there is a convergence of indirect evidence, drawn from such varied phenomena as expansion, heat conduction, capillary attraction, and surface tension. The point is that these miscellaneous phenomena can, if we assume the molecular theory, be marshaled under the familiar laws of motion. The fancifulness of thus assuming a substructure of moving particles of imperceptible size is offset by a gain in naturalness and scope on the part of the aggregate laws of physics. The molecular theory is felt, moreover, to gain corroboration progressively as the physicist's predictions of future observations turn out to be fulfilled, and

as the theory proves to invite extensions covering additional classes of phenomena.

The benefits thus credited to the molecular doctrine may be divided into five. One is simplicity: empirical laws concerning seemingly dissimilar phenomena are integrated into a compact and unitary theory. Another is familiarity of principle: the already familiar laws of motion are made to serve where independent laws would otherwise have been needed. A third is scope: the resulting unitary theory implies a wider array of testable consequences than any likely accumulation of separate laws would have implied. A fourth is fecundity: successful further extensions of theory are expedited. The fifth goes without saying: such testable consequences of the theory as have been tested have turned out well, aside from such sparse exceptions as may in good conscience be chalked up to unexplained interferences.

Simplicity, the first of the listed benefits, is a vague business. We may be fairly sure of this much: theories are more or less simple, more or less unitary, only relative to one or another given vocabulary or conceptual apparatus. Simplicity is, if not quite subjective, at any rate parochial. Yet simplicity contributes to scope, as follows. An empirical theory, typically, generalizes or extrapolates from sample data, and thus covers more phenomena than have been checked. Simplicity, by our lights, is what guides our extrapolation. Hence the simpler the theory, on the whole, the wider this unchecked coverage.

As for the fourth benefit, fecundity, obviously it is a consequence of the first two, simplicity and familiarity, for these two traits are the best conditions for effective thinking.

Not all the listed benefits are generally attributable to accepted scientific theories, though all are to be prized when available. Thus the benefit of familiarity of principle may, as in quantum theory and relativity theory, be renounced, its loss being regretted but outweighed.

But to get back. In its manifest content the molecular doctrine bears directly on unobservable reality, affirming a structure of minute swarming particles. On the other hand any defense of it has to do rather with its indirect bearing on observable reality. The doctrine has this indirect bearing by being the core of an integrated physical theory which implies truths about expansion, conduction, and so on. The benefits which we have been surveying are benefits which the molecular doctrine, as core, brings to the physics of these latter observable phenomena.

Suppose now we were to excise that core but retain the surrounding ring of derivative laws, thus not disturbing the observable consequences. The retained laws could be viewed thenceforward as autonomous empirical laws, innocent of any molecular commitment. Granted, this combination of empirical laws would never have been achieved without the unifying aid of a molecular doctrine at the center; note the recent remarks on scope. But we might still delete the molecular doctrine once it has thus served its heuristic purpose.

This reflection strengthens a natural suspicion: that the benefits conferred by the molecular doctrine give the physicist good reason to prize it, but afford no evidence of its truth. Though the doctrine succeeds to perfection in its indirect bearing on observable reality, the question of its truth has to do rather with its direct claim on unobservable reality. Might the molecular doctrine not be ever so useful in organizing and extending our knowledge of the behavior of observable things, and yet be factually false?

One may question, on closer consideration, whether this is really an intelligible possibility. Let us reflect upon our words and how we learned them.

II Posits and analogies

Words are human artifacts, meaningless save as our associating them with experience endows them with meaning. The word "swarm" is initially meaningful to us through association with such experiences as that of a hovering swarm of gnats, or a swarm of dust motes in a shaft of sunlight. When we extend the word to desks and the like, we are engaged in drawing an analogy between swarms ordinarily so-called, on the one hand, and desks, etc., on the other. The word "molecule" is then given meaning derivatively: having conceived of desks analogically as swarms, we imagine molecules as the things the desks are swarms of.

The purported question of fact, the question whether the familiar objects around us are really swarms of subvisible particles in vibration, now begins to waver and dissolve. If the words involved here make sense only by analogy, then the only question of fact is the question how good an analogy there is between the behavior of a desk or the like and the behavior, e.g., of a swarm of gnats. What had seemed a direct bearing of the molecular doctrine upon reality has now dwindled to an analogy.

Even this analogical content, moreover, is incidental, variable, and at length dispensable. In particular the analogy between the swarming of the molecules of a solid and the swarming of gnats is only moderately faithful; a supplementary aid to appreciating the dynamics of the molecules of a solid is found in the analogy of a stack of bedsprings. In another and more recondite part of physics, the theory of light, the tenuousness of analogy is notorious: the analogy of particles is useful up to a point and the analogy of waves is useful up to a point, but neither suffices to the exclusion of the other. Faithful analogies are an aid to the physicist's early progress in an unaccustomed medium, but, like water-wings, they are an aid which he learns to get along without.

In §I we contrasted a direct and an indirect bearing of the molecular doctrine upon reality. But the direct bearing has not withstood scrutiny. Where there had at first seemed to be an undecidable question of unobservable fact, we now find mere analogy at most and not necessarily that. So the only way in which we now find the molecular doctrine genuinely to bear upon reality is the indirect way, via implications in observable phenomena.

The effect of this conclusion upon the status of molecules is that they lose even the dignity of inferred or hypothetical entities which may or may not really be there. The very sentences which seem to propound them and treat of them are gibberish by themselves, and indirectly significant only as contributory clauses of an inclusive system which does also treat of the real. The molecular physicist is, like all of us, concerned with commonplace reality, and merely finds that he can simplify his laws by positing an esoteric supplement to the exoteric universe. He can devise simpler laws for this enriched universe, this "sesquiverse" of his own decree, than he has been able to devise for its real or original portion alone.

In §I we imagined deleting the molecular doctrine from the midst of the derivative body of physical theory. From our present vantage point, however, we see that operation as insignificant; there is no substantive doctrine of molecules to delete. The sentences which seem to propound molecules are just devices for organizing the significant sentences of physical theory. No matter if physics makes molecules or other insensible particles seem more fundamental than the objects of common sense; the particles are posited for the sake of a simple physics.

The tendency of our own reflections has been, conversely, to belittle molecules and their ilk, leaving common-sense bodies supreme. Still, it may now be protested, this invidious contrast is unwarranted. What are given in sensation are variformed and varicolored visual patches, varitextured and varitemperatured tactual feels, and an assortment of tones, tastes, smells, and other odds and ends; desks are no more to be found among these data than molecules. If we have evidence for the existence of the bodies of common sense, we have it only in the way in which we may be said to have evidence for the existence of molecules. The positing of either sort of body is good science insofar merely as it helps us formulate our laws—laws whose ultimate evidence lies in the sense data of the past, and whose ultimate vindication lies in anticipation of sense data of the future. The positing of molecules differs from the positing of the bodies of common sense mainly in degree of sophistication. In whatever sense the molecules in my desk are unreal and a figment of the imagination of the scientist, in that sense the desk itself is unreal and a figment of the imagination of the race.

This double verdict of unreality leaves us nothing, evidently, but the raw sense data themselves. It leaves each of us, indeed, nothing but his own sense data; for the assumption of there being other persons has no better support than has the assumption of there being any other sorts of external objects. It leaves each of us in the position of solipsism, according to which there is nobody else in the world, nor indeed any world but the pageant of one's own sense data.

III Restitution

Surely now we have been caught up in a wrong line of reasoning. Not only is the conclusion bizarre; it vitiates the very considerations that lead to it. We cannot properly represent man as inventing a myth of physical objects to fit past and present sense data, for past ones are lost except to memory; and memory, far from being a straightforward register of past sense data, usually depends on past posits of physical objects. The positing of physical objects must be seen not as an *ex post facto* systematization of data, but as a move prior to which no appreciable data would be available to systematize.

Something went wrong with our standard of reality. We became doubtful of the reality of molecules because the physicist's statement that there are molecules took on the aspect of a mere technical convenience in smoothing the laws of physics. Next we noted that common-sense bodies are epistemologically much on a par with the molecules, and inferred the unreality of the common-sense bodies themselves. Here our bemusement becomes visible. Unless we change meanings in midstream, the familiar bodies around us are as real as can be; and it smacks of a contradiction in terms to conclude otherwise. Having noted that man has no evidence for the existence of bodies beyond the fact that their assumption helps him organize experience, we should have done well, instead of disclaiming evidence for the existence of bodies, to conclude: such, then, at bottom, is what evidence is, both for ordinary bodies and for molecules.

This point about evidence does not upset the evidential priority of sense data. On the contrary, the point about evidence is precisely that the testimony of the senses *does* (contrary to Berkeley's notion) count as evidence for bodies, such being (as Samuel Johnson perceived) just the sort of thing that evidence is. We can continue to recognize, as in §II, that molecules and even the gross bodies of common sense are simply posited in the course of organizing our responses to stimulation; but a moral to draw from our reconsideration of the terms "reality" and "evidence" is that posits are not *ipso facto* unreal. The benefits of the molecular doctrine which so impressed us in §I, and the manifest benefits of the aboriginal posit of ordinary bodies, are the best evidence of reality we can ask (pending, of course, evidence of the same sort for some alternative ontology).

Sense data are posits too. They are posits of psychological theory, but not, on that account, unreal. The sense datum may be construed as a hypothetical component of subjective experience standing in closest possible correspondence to the experimentally measurable conditions of physical stimulation of the end organs. In seeking to isolate sense data we engage in empirical psychology, associating physical stimuli with human resources. I shall not guess how useful the positing of sense data may be for psychological theory, or more specifically for a psychologically grounded theory of evidence, nor what detailed traits may profitably be postulated concerning them. In our flight from the fictitious to the real, in any event, we have come full circle.

Sense data, if they are to be posited at all, are fundamental in one respect; the small particles of physics are fundamental in a second respect, and common-sense bodies in a third. Sense data are *evidentially* fundamental: every man is beholden to his senses for every hint of bodies. The physical particles are *naturally* fundamental, in this kind of way: laws of behavior of those particles afford, so far as we know, the simplest formulation of a general theory of what happens. Common-sense bodies, finally, are *conceptually* fundamental: it is by reference to them that the very notions of reality and evidence are acquired, and that the concepts which have to do with physical particles or even with sense data tend to be framed and phrased. But these three types of priority must not be viewed as somehow determining three competing, self-sufficient conceptual schemes. Our one serious conceptual scheme is the inclusive, evolving one of science, which we inherit and, in our several small ways, help to improve.

IV Working from within

It is by thinking within this unitary conceptual scheme itself, thinking about the processes of the physical world, that we come to appreciate that the world can be evidenced only through stimulation of our senses. It is by thinking within the same conceptual scheme that we come to appreciate that language, being a social art, is learned primarily with reference to intersubjectively conspicuous objects, and hence that such objects are bound to be central conceptually. Both of these *aperçus* are part of the scientific understanding of the scientific enterprise; not prior to it. Insofar as they help the scientist to proceed more knowingly about his business, science is using its findings to improve its own techniques. Epistemology, on this view, is not logically prior somehow to common sense or to the refined common sense which is science; it is part rather of the overall scientific enterprise, an enterprise which Neurath has likened to that of rebuilding a ship while staying afloat in it.

Epistemology, so conceived, continues to probe the sensory evidence for discourse about the world; but it no longer seeks to relate such discourse somehow to an imaginary and impossible sense-datum language. Rather it faces the fact that society teaches us our physicalistic language by training us to associate various physicalistic sentences directly, in multifarious ways, with irritations of our sensory surfaces, and by training us also to associate various such sentences with one another.

The complex totality of such associations is a fluctuating field of force. Some sentences about bodies are, for one person or for many, firmly conditioned one by one to sensory stimulation of specifiable sorts. Roughly specifiable sequences of nerve hits can confirm us in statements about having had breakfast, or there being a brick house on Elm Street, beyond the power of secondary associations with other sentences to add or detract. But there is in this respect a grading-off from one example to another. Many sentences even about common-sense bodies rest wholly on indirect evidence; witness the statement that one of the pennies now in my pocket was in my pocket last week. Conversely, sentences even about electrons are sometimes directly conditioned to sensory stimulation, e.g., via the cloud chamber. The status of a given sentence, in point of direct or indirect connection with the senses, can change as one's experience accumulates; thus a man's first confrontation with a cloud chamber may forge a direct sensory link to some sentences which hitherto bore, for him, only the most indirect sensory relevance. Moreover the sensory relevance of sentences will differ widely from person to person; uniformity comes only where the pressure for communication comes.

Statements about bodies, common-sense or recondite, thus commonly make little or no empirical sense except as bits of a collectively significant containing system. Various statements can surely be supplanted by their negations, without conflict with any possible sensory contingency, provided that we revise other portions of our science in compensatory ways. Science is empirically underdetermined: there is slack. What can be said about the hypothetical particles of physics is underdetermined by what can be said about sensible bodies, and what can be said about these is underdetermined by the stimulation of our surfaces. An inkling of this circumstance has doubtless fostered the tendency to look upon the hypothetical particles of physics as more of a fiction than sensible bodies, and these as more of a fiction than sense data. But the tendency is a perverse one, for it ascribes full reality only to a domain of objects for which there is no autonomous system of discourse at all.

Better simply to explore, realistically, the less-than-rigid connections that obtain between sensory stimulus and physical doctrine, without viewing this want of rigidity as impugning the physical doctrine. Benefits of the sort recounted in §I are what count for the molecular doctrine or any, and we can hope for no surer touchstone of reality. We can hope to improve our physics by seeking the same sorts of benefits in fuller measure, and we may even facilitate such endeavors by better understanding the degrees of freedom that prevail between stimulatory evidence and physical doctrine. But as a medium for such epistemological inquiry we can choose no better than the selfsame world theory which we are trying to improve, this being the best available at the time.

Chapter 12

Richard Feldman

HAVING EVIDENCE

Although theories about epistemic rational-ity and justification often appeal to the notion of the evidence a person has at a time, little has been written about what the conditions are under which a person "has" something as evidence. Philosophers seem to have failed to notice that the implications of their epistemo-logical theories are largely dependent upon how this concept is interpreted. In this paper I will attempt to correct this deficiency. In the first part I will show, by means of several examples, that it is not at all obvious what it is to have something as evidence. I will then show that a wide variety of epistemological theories impli-citly or explicitly appeal to an (uninterpreted) concept of evidence possessed. I will then con-sider a series of possible accounts of evidence possessed and defend a restrictive account that limits the evidence a person has at a time to the things the person is thinking of or aware of at that time.

1

That there is some question about what evidence a person has at a time can be brought out by consideration of some examples. A good example for our purposes is one used by Alvin Goldman in his defense of a causal theory of knowledge.[1] Goldman says that he knows that Abraham Lincoln was born in 1809, but he has forgotten where he learned this and he no longer has any "explicit evidence" for this proposition. Goldman took this, when he wrote this essay, to show that knowledge did not require justifica-tion. His assumption, then, was that justification does require having evidence, but the unrecalled facts about the source of one's beliefs do not count as evidence possessed. Thus, he regarded this as a case of knowledge without justification. However, the assumption that he no longer has evidence for his belief about Lincoln is at least questionable. It might be that with some prompting Goldman could bring back to mind information about where he first learned this fact. Perhaps such retrievable information counts as part of the evidence he has now, even if he is not thinking of it now.

More generally, people often consciously entertain beliefs that were initially formed on the basis of evidence that they do not, and perhaps cannot, recall. It is unclear whether such evi-dence counts as part of the evidence they have. Possibly, whether it counts depends upon if, or how easily, it can be recalled. Whether the initial evidence still counts as evidence possessed may well affect the epistemic status of the belief. Unless other currently possessed information makes the belief justified, it seems that the belief is justified only if the currently unconsidered evidence still is evidence possessed by the believer. Of course, one might also hold (con-trary to Goldman) that if a belief is originally justified and the belief is retained, then it remains justified even if the evidence is forgotten.

Similar issues arise with respect to perceptual beliefs. Suppose, for example, that an expert bird-watcher sees a bird that she immediately identifies as a scarlet tanager. We can imagine that she does not consciously think of the field marks of these birds when she forms the belief that she sees one. She just looks at the bird and classifies it. Do the stored beliefs she has about the distinguishing features of scarlet tanagers count as part of her current evidence? Does it matter now difficult it would be for her to articulate these facts or call them to mind? Obviously, similar questions arise in the case of nearly any perceptual belief in which one attributes to an object some property that is not "directly perceptible." We might put the question this way: when, if ever, do stored background beliefs count as part of the evidence one has at a time?

Again, there are plausible accounts of justification that make the epistemic status of perceptual beliefs depend upon the answers to these questions about evidence possessed. Any account of justification that implies that the expert must currently have as evidence the facts about the field marks makes these questions about evidence possessed immediately relevant to epistemic evaluations. Once again, it is possible to make the questions somewhat less pressing by holding that other things she is currently aware of, or her knowledge that she is an expert, or perhaps even her mere expertise (whatever she knows about it), make her belief justified.

Getting clear about what counts as evidence possessed seems essential to epistemic evaluations of cases in which stored information which does not come to mind counts against something that is supported by the evidence one does consider. Suppose my friend Jones tells me that the hike up to Precarious Peak is not terribly strenuous or dangerous, that it is the sort of thing I can do without undue difficulty. Assume

that Jones knows my abilities with respect to these sorts of things and that he seems to be an honest person. On the basis of his testimony, I believe that the hike is something I can do. It seems that it is rational for me to believe this proposition. But suppose I've failed to think about the time Jones told me that I could paddle my canoe down Rapid River, something he knew to be far beyond my abilities. He just gets a kick out of sending people off on grueling expeditions. If you were to say to me, "Remember when Jones lied about the canoe trip?" I'd say, "Yes! How could I have failed to think of that?" Once I was reminded of this episode, it would no longer be rational for me to believe that I can complete the hike, unless I had some additional information supporting the view that Jones was not lying this time. But are the facts about the past lie part of my evidence *before* you remind me of them? Whether my belief is justified depends upon the answer. If this stored information is part of my evidence, then my belief is not justified, but if it is not part of my evidence, then the belief is justified.

The general question about evidence possessed suggested by this example is this: when one believes some proposition on the basis of newly acquired evidence and one has stored in memory some counter-evidence that one fails to think of, when, if ever, does this counter-evidence count as part of the evidence one has at the time?

A final example is drawn from recent studies by psychologists that seem to show that people are systematically irrational. Some studies suggest that people regularly violate the conjunction rule of probability theory.[2] For example, when given a description of a person and asked to decide which of two categories the person is most likely in, people often select categories based on representative characteristics, overlooking probabilistic considerations that ought to be decisive. In one series of studies, people were given a description of a typical liberal and politically active woman. Most people, including people trained in statistics, judged that it is more likely that the woman is a feminist bank teller than a bank teller. In giving this response people are saying that her having a conjunctive property—being a bank teller and a feminist—is more probable than her having one of the conjuncts—being a bank teller. This response violates the conjunction rule, which says that the probability of a conjunction cannot exceed the probability of one of its conjuncts. It is not implausible to think that beliefs formed in violation of such a fundamental rule are irrational.[3]

The claim that beliefs that violate the conjunction rule, or other basic rules of logic or probability, are irrational rests on assumptions about what evidence people have in these cases and what that evidence supports. Perhaps many people, and surely experts, have stored in memory some evidence that supports the conjunction rule and shows that the evidence they're given about the woman does not support the conclusion most people make. However, just as in the cases described above, since this evidence does not come to mind, it is not clear that it is part of the body of evidence people have *at the time* they form their beliefs.

Moreover, it may be that the evidence people generally do have supports the beliefs they form. It is commonly suggested[4] that people use in these cases a "representativeness heuristic," according to which it is more probable that something has property A than B if it is more like the typical, or representative, A than it is like the representative B. In the case at hand, the woman described is more like the typical feminist bank teller than she is like the typical bank teller. Hence, people (mistakenly) judge that she is more probably a feminist bank teller than a bank teller.

What complicates our assessment of the rationality of these beliefs is that people may well have evidence supporting the heuristic they use. After all, in a wide variety of cases, using it has probably yielded correct results that were subsequently corroborated. Moreover, the heuristic has considerable intuitive plausibility and may have been given testimonial support for many people. On the other hand, many people have learned the rules of probability or could easily be made to see, on the basis of things they already believe, that the rule leads them astray in cases such as this one. Thus, the rationality of their beliefs apparently depends in part upon exactly what evidence they have, and what the status is of stored but unconsidered facts about probability. If such information is not part of their evidence, then their beliefs may well be rational.

All of these examples are designed to show that in a wide variety of cases there is some question about what evidence a person has at a time and that assessments of rationality or justification depend upon their answers. The general question is when, if ever, a person has as evidence information that is, in some sense, stored in memory but not recalled at the time.

2

In the previous section I argued that there are difficult questions about exactly what counts as the evidence a person has at a given time and that how these questions are properly answered often has significant implications for which beliefs are rational or justified. My arguments for that second conclusion rested on the assumption that a correct theory about rationality and justification makes these epistemic properties of beliefs a function of the relation the beliefs have to the evidence possessed by the believer. Not all theories about epistemic justification and rationality explicitly refer to evidence possessed, but, as I will show in this section, similar questions arise for nearly any theory about rationality and justification.

The puzzles about evidence possessed arise most clearly for theories that explicitly analyze rationality in terms of evidence possessed. According to one such view, evidentialism, believing p is rational for a person provided believing p (as opposed to disbelieving p or withholding judgment about p) fits the evidence the person has.[5] (I'll say that believing a proposition is rational for a person whenever believing that proposition is epistemically better than disbelieving or suspending judgment about it. Believing something can be rational, then, but less than fully justified, in the sense that is an important necessary condition for knowledge.) Obviously, what counts as the evidence a believer has drastically affects the implications of this view. In the example about the hike, if I have as evidence the fact that Jones has lied about this sort of thing in the past, then believing that the hike is feasible is not rational. But if that is not part of my evidence, then the belief is rational.

What counts as the evidence one has significantly affects the implications of theories that analyze justification in terms of *prima facie* reasons and defeaters.[6] Theories of this sort imply that believing something is rational (or justified) for a person provided the person has good reasons to believe that thing and those reasons are not defeated by other evidence the person has. The relevance of our question about evidence possessed to these theories is obvious.

Similar questions also arise with respect to the theories of justification that Roderick Chisholm defends.[7] It is not necessary here to go into the details of Chisholm's system of definitions. What is crucial to notice for present purposes is that Chisholm defines all the central epistemic concepts in terms of the primitive notion of epistemic preferability. This, Chisholm says, is "an expression that may be used to compare different beliefs with respect to reasonableness."[8] Thus, we may say that believing p is more reasonable for S than believing (or disbelieving or withholding) q. Chisholm attempts to clarify this primitive expression in his system by providing a paraphrase for it. He says that "(believing) p is more reasonable than (believ-

ing) q for S at t" provided "S is so situated at t that his intellectual requirement, his responsibility as an intellectual being, is better fulfilled by (believing) p than by (believing) q."[9] Without going into any details about intellectual requirements, we can see easily that our questions about evidence possessed carry over into Chisholm's system. How, exactly, is a person who has failed to think of some relevant information concerning a proposition he is now entertaining situated? Does this stored but unconsidered information enter into our evaluation of his situation and of how he can best fulfill his intellectual requirement? Thus, questions about evidence possessed arise in Chisholm's system as questions about what factors affect assessments of epistemic reasonability.

Similar considerations apply to coherence theories.[10] Coherence theories imply that a belief is justified provided it coheres with one's body of beliefs. But what counts as one's body of beliefs? A coherence theorist could restrict one's body of beliefs to what one is currently thinking of, one's *occurrent* beliefs. But a coherence theorist could also include in one's body of beliefs some or all of the things that are stored in one's mind, the things one believes *dispositionally*. Thus, for example, in the hiking case described above, one may construe my body of beliefs narrowly so that the unconsidered belief about my friend's past lie is excluded, or one may construe my body of beliefs more broadly and include that belief. Believing that I can complete the hike seems to cohere with the narrower body, but not with the broader one. Hence, the implications of coherence theories for this example, as well as many others, depend upon how the relevant body of beliefs is determined. Questions about evidence possessed arise in coherence theories as questions about what is included in the body of beliefs relative to which coherence, and thus justification, is measured.

It is important to realize that saying that the relevant evidence is limited to what one actually believes is of no help here. It is just as difficult to figure out whether the things stored, perhaps buried, in one's memory are among the things one believes as it is to tell whether they are part of one's evidence. Thus, I find it just as hard to decide whether the facts about the source of my belief about the year of Lincoln's birth, or facts about my friend's past lie, are among my beliefs as it is to decide whether they are included in my evidence.

A question about evidence possessed also arises in connection with at least some reliabilist views about justification. For example, Alvin Goldman claims that a belief is justified provided it is produced by a reliable belief-forming process and the believer has available no alternative reliable process such that, had he used it, he would not have formed the belief in question.[11] The point of introducing the second clause is to deal with defeaters—cases in which a person forms a belief as a result of a reliable process, but has reasons to think that the outputs of that process are not true. The example of the hike described above is just such a case. A question Goldman must face is whether it is *available* to me to infer from the past lie that my friend's testimony about the hike is not trustworthy. Which inferences from which stored but unconsidered beliefs are available at any given time? Thus, questions about evidence possessed arise for this reliability theory as questions about availability.

These considerations show that essentially the same questions about what evidence one has affect numerous theories of epistemic justification. This is just to point out a feature of the theories that needs development, not to say that any of these theories is incorrect. In fact, it will generally be difficult to determine what implications a theory has, and thus difficult to evaluate it, until these questions about evidence possessed are answered. Proposed objections may well rest in part on debatable assumptions about what counts as the evidence a person has at a time.

3

In this section I will make a few terminological and other preliminary points before, in the following sections, formulating and evaluating several accounts of what it is for a person to have something as evidence at a time.

In what follows I will sometimes refer to pieces of evidence as beliefs, but I do not wish to rule out the possibility that experiences or perceptual states can count as evidence as well. I will also speak of the implications of various views about evidence possessed for what is justified, or rational, for a person at a time. As I will use these terms, it can be rational for a person to believe a proposition even though the person does not actually believe it. Similarly, a person can be justified in believing some proposition without believing it. I assume that, roughly, it is justified or rational for a person to believe a proposition when the evidence he has supports that proposition. Whether the person does believe the proposition does not affect this evaluation. There are, of course, senses of these or related terms that apply only to existent beliefs. For example, we say such things as "Jones justifiably believes p" and this does imply "Jones believes p." But these senses of epistemic terms are not the senses under discussion here.

It will be useful to introduce some terminology for the discussion that follows. Let us say that the *total possible evidence* a person has at a time includes all and only the information the person has "stored in his mind" at the time. This is intended to be a very broad notion. It includes *everything* that one has actively believed and could recall with some prompting. It thus includes past beliefs that were adopted for no good reason. It includes things that could be recalled only with great difficulty. In each of the examples discussed earlier in this paper, all of the items whose evidential status was said to be questionable were clearly part of the total possible evidence.

There are some things that are excluded from one's total possible evidence that are worth mentioning here. Things that one has never learned about, even if they are known by others, are excluded. Things that one once knew but could not recall with any amount of prompting are also excluded. And, finally, things that one does not yet believe, but would first come to believe as a result of prompting, are excluded from the total possible evidence one has at a time. I exclude these items from consideration because the topic here is the evidence a person *has* at a time, and I assume that facts which are completely out of one's cognizance, as these things are, are plainly not part of the evidence one has.

The *total evidence* one has at a time is some part of the total possible evidence one has at that time. Something that is part of one's total possible evidence may fail to be part of one's total (actual) evidence for one (or both) of two reasons. It may fail to meet some psychological accessibility condition and it may fail to meet some epistemic acceptability condition. I will say that any part of one's total possible evidence which satisfies this psychological condition is part of the evidence one has *available*. Evidence which satisfies the epistemic condition will be said to be *acceptable*. That portion of one's total possible evidence which is both available and acceptable is the total evidence one has.

My concern here is primarily with the conditions under which evidence is available, but it will be useful to discuss briefly the conditions under which evidence is acceptable. It is possible to hold that the acceptability condition is vacuous and that if something is part of one's total possible evidence, then it is acceptable. Perhaps some coherence theorists hold this. They would then hold that anything which is available is part of the evidence one has. Some simple examples suggest that this view is incorrect. If I believe, for no good reason, that P and I infer (correctly) from this that Q, I don't think we want to say that I "have" P as evidence for Q.

Only things that I believe (or could believe) rationally, or perhaps with justification, count as part the evidence I have. It seems to me that this is a good reason to include an epistemic acceptability constraint on evidence possessed, but I will not pursue this point here.

There is an alternative way to set up the issue here. I have said that the evidence one has at a time is restricted to what is both available and acceptable. One might say instead that everything that is available is part of the evidence one has, but that what this body of evidence makes rational or justified depends upon the epistemic status of that evidence. On this view, acceptability determines not what counts as evidence possessed but rather what is made rational or justified by the evidence possessed. I think that matters can be spelled out in this second way and that any differences between the views discussed below and (versions of) this second view are purely terminological. Since nothing important turns on this matter, I will continue to assume that there is an epistemic condition on evidence possessed.

One final preliminary point concerns the conditions of adequacy for accounts of epistemic availability. Factors of two different sorts seem relevant. First, we do have some fairly clear intuitions about what evidence a person has at a time, and a theory must not violate those intuitions. It is clear, for example, that I don't have as evidence now facts I have never learned and have never thought about. Any theory that implies otherwise is mistaken. Things that I am consciously aware of now and explicitly use as the basis for some further belief are part of my available evidence, so no adequate account should rule them out. Second, an account of available evidence will contribute to an account of justification and knowledge. Thus, acceptable accounts of available evidence must not preclude our having knowledge or justification in cases in which we clearly do have them. As we will see in the following section, some initially plausible accounts of available evidence have some remarkably implausible implications.

4

I turn now to some views about the conditions under which something is available as evidence. I will begin with the most inclusive or liberal view:

> (1)   S has p available as evidence at t iff p is included in S's total possible evidence at t.

According to (1), everything one actively believes at a time and every belief that is retrievable from one's memory is part of one's available evidence at that time. (It is unclear whether there are any irretrievable propositions that are in any sense stored in one's memory, but I will not pursue that point here.)

Easily devised examples suggest that (1) is far too inclusive. Some such examples concern the evidential status of childhood memories that could only be recalled with extensive and highly directed prompting. Suppose, for example, that the house I lived in as a young child was painted yellow, but on my own I cannot remember the house and have no testimonial evidence concerning its color. If I were asked its color, I would report honestly that I couldn't remember. If we add to the story the fact that some complex set of prompts will trigger in me a clear memory of the house, and reveal its color, then (1) has the highly counter-intuitive result that I now, prior to the prompt, have as evidence this memory of the house. Coupled with standard theories of justification, (1) yields the implausible result that I am now justified (or at least highly rational) in believing that the house was yellow. In this situation it would be most unfair to claim that I am epistemically irresponsible or blameworthy for failing to make proper use of my evidence or for failing to believe that my house was yellow. Indeed, it seems clear that the

epistemically proper thing for me to do is to suspend judgment on most propositions concerning its color. (I may have inductive evidence, about people generally and my family in particular, that lends strong support to some propositions about the color, for example that it was not painted purple.)

There are variations on this example that add to the implausibility of (1). Suppose that I do have testimonial evidence supporting some false proposition about the color of my house. Suppose, for some reason, my generally honest family has consistently said that the house was white. I have no recollection of the house and dutifully believe that it was white. Again, a complex prompt could trigger a memory of the house and its color. If we couple (1) with plausible theories of justification and rationality, we get the result that I am not justified or rational in believing what my family tells me because I have this defeater available to me. But that result is surely wrong. I am clearly believing exactly what I should believe, given the situation in which I find myself.

One possible response to these objections to (1) is worth brief consideration. It might be claimed that deeply buried memories are part of one's psychologically available evidence, but that they are not part of one's epistemically adequate evidence. Thus, my claims about what's rational or justified in the examples just discussed are correct, but (1) does not conflict with them.

The view that deeply buried memories are psychologically available but not epistemically adequate is implausible. It is difficult to see how a plausible account of the epistemic adequacy condition could go that would rule these memories out. In the example about the color of my house, it may be that the relevant memory belief about the color of my house was completely justified when it was formed and that it would be justified once it was brought back to mind. So what epistemic adequacy condition could it be that it fails? The only plausible answer to this seems to be that it is not supported by other available evidence. However, without rejecting (1), that is an implausible claim. After all, as the example was described, psychologically associated with this memory were other memories that did support it. So it seems that if (1) is true, then all these other supporting beliefs are also available and thus my belief about the color of my house is adequate as well. So, this defense of (1) fails. I conclude, therefore, that (1) is too inclusive and turn now to a consideration of some more restrictive accounts of available evidence.

There are several ways in which a less inclusive account of available evidence might be developed. One approach begins with an account of the evidence one has for a particular proposition, and then defines one's total available evidence as the combination of all the evidence one has for anything. The following remark from BonJour is suggestive of one possibility along these lines:

> a person for whom a belief is inferentially justified need not have explicitly rehearsed the justificatory argument in question to others or even to himself. It is enough that the inference be available to him if the belief is called into question by others or by himself.[12]

Thus, we might propose:

> (2) S has p available as evidence relative to q iff S would mention p if S were asked what S's evidence concerning q is.

This proposal has close affinities to the view that a belief is justified just in case one is able to produce, and would produce on demand, an adequate defense of the belief.

(2) is a behavioristic proposal that has the defects often found in behavioristic analyses of psychological concepts. The most serious of these is that it excludes from evidence possessed things that should be included. When asked to state my evidence concerning some proposition,

I might get very nervous and not be able to state some of the things that I do think of. I might think that the truth wouldn't persuade the questioner, and choose not to state my best reasons. I might find it very embarrassing to reveal my evidence concerning some proposition, and so choose not to state it. Thus, there are many things that seem plainly to be part of a person's evidence concerning some proposition, but which the person might fail to mention if asked for evidence concerning that proposition.

The problem with (2) is its behavioristic character. A proposal similar in spirit to (2) but without the behavioristic element can be constructed. It specifies a condition for having evidence in terms of a disposition to go into other mental states, rather than in terms of a disposition to overt behavior. It can be formulated this way:

> (3) S has p available as evidence relative to q iff S would think of p if S were to think about what evidence he has that pertains to q.

This avoids the problems mentioned in connection with (2), but it succumbs to another objection. The proposed account has the weakness that it excludes from the evidence one has relative to a particular proposition other beliefs whose relevance one fails to appreciate. Suppose I consciously believe both p and d, but fail to recognize that d constitutes strong evidence against p. I'd therefore not mention d when asked about my evidence concerning p. Thus, this proposal excludes d from the evidence I possess concerning p and may lead to the result that I am justified in believing p when in fact I surely am not. The problem is that it restricts a person's available evidence concerning some proposition to those things whose relevance the person appreciates. However, it seems clear that there could be available evidence whose relevance is unappreciated by a particular believer.

A way around the problem just mentioned is to characterize one's total body of available evidence, rather than the evidence relative to some specific proposition. The idea is that one's total body of available evidence includes all those things one would think of as evidence for anything. Underlying this proposal is the assumption that everything one has available as evidence would be thought to be pertinent to something or other. Thus,

> (4) S has p available as evidence iff there is some proposition q such that S would think of p if S were asked to think about S's evidence relevant to q.

The sorts of cases that constituted problems for (2) and (3) are not problems for (4). It avoids the behavioristic implications of (2) and does not restrict available evidence to what is seen to be relevant in the way (3) does.

One correctable problem with (4) is that it includes as available evidence things that one has not yet thought of, but would think of for the first time if asked about evidence for some proposition q. The request might stimulate new thoughts, not just prompt the recollection of old ones. (4) is too inclusive for this reason. This problem can be corrected, however, by requiring that everything one has available as evidence at any time is part of one's total possible evidence at that time. Thus,

> (5) S has p available as evidence iff (i) p is part of S's total possible evidence and (ii) there is some proposition q such that S would think of p if S were asked to think about S's evidence relevant to q.

(5) seems to me to be the best formulation of this general sort of approach. It is, however, quite clearly unsatisfactory. The problem with (5) is not that it is too restrictive, but rather that it is implausibly inclusive. It is likely to include as

evidence possessed nearly every retrievable item in one's total possible evidence. The reason for this is that nearly everything in one's total possible evidence might be mentioned in response to a request for evidence concerning some (possibly very complex) proposition. Suppose Jones has long forgotten that her first grade teacher was named "Mrs. Potts." However, if she were asked what evidence she has concerning the proposition that her first grade teacher was named "Mrs. Potts," a whole set of relevant memories would be recalled. The current proposal implies, perversely, that all these memories were available as evidence prior to the prompt. One could imagine more extreme cases of this sort in which the proposition asked about is extremely long and complex. Indeed, it seems clear that some such request would bring to mind nearly every retrievable memory. This makes (5) just about as inclusive as (1).

The problem with (5) suggests that a better way to analyze available evidence is in terms of what is easily accessible or easily retrievable. The idea here is that some of the things that are included by the previous account are not easily retrievable and therefore are not part of the available evidence. But (5) allowed them in since it included everything that could be recalled in response to any request for evidence, including requests that might be highly suggestive and helpful. Such requests make one able to remember things that otherwise are not easily accessed. Thus, we might propose:

> (6) S has p available as evidence at t iff S is currently aware of p or S could easily access a memory of p.

One problem with this view is its vagueness. There seems to be no definite boundary between those memories that are easily accessible and those that are not. However, I don't think that this vagueness is as serious a problem as is a different sort of obscurity in the notion of easy accessibility. Whether a person will think of some fact depends largely upon how the person is prompted or stimulated. If I ask my childhood friend if he remembers the time we spray-painted my neighbor's dog, I may get an embarrassed "Yes." If I ask him if he remembers any of our childhood pranks, this one may fail to come to mind. Is the fact that we spray-painted the dog easily accessible? There seems to be no clear answer. If we say that something can be easily accessed if there is *some* prompt that will bring it rapidly to mind, then almost everything stored in memory is likely to be easily accessible and this view scarcely differs from (5).

I know of no plausible way to modify (6) to avoid the result just discussed. Introducing factors such as speed of recall hardly seems to help. How long it will take a person to recall something depends upon how he is prompted. If I ask the person described a few paragraphs back what the name of her first grade teacher is, I may get no answer or may get the correct answer only after a long time. But if I ask if her first grade teacher was named "Mrs. Potts," I may get an immediate affirmative response. There seems to be no straightforward notion of speed of recall useful in the present context.

In this section I have considered an extremely inclusive account of available evidence and some proposals designed to achieve a more moderate account. I have argued that all of these views are unsatisfactory. I turn next to the other extreme and a view that limits available evidence to what one is thinking of at the time.

5

A much more restrictive view about available evidence may be formulated as follows:

> (7) S has p available as evidence at t iff S is currently thinking of p.

This view obviously limits what one has available as evidence far more severely than does any of the previously considered proposals. I will

evaluate it by considering several objections intended to show that it is too restrictive.

The first objection goes as follows: sometimes a person has some evidence supporting a proposition and believes that proposition even though there is convincing counter-evidence to it that he could have thought about. If he fails to think about this counter-evidence because of inattentiveness, lack of concentration, or some other epistemic failing, then it is not rational for the person to believe that proposition. However, any theory that includes (7) will make it rational for him to believe this proposition since the theory will imply that his available evidence includes only the supporting evidence he does think of. This seems to be an incorrect result and the source of the error is the fact that (7) overly restricts the evidence a person has.

Versions of the example described above about the hike to Precarious Peak illustrate the point of this objection. In that example, I believe something on the basis of some plausible evidence, but I fail to think of some important counter-evidence which I could have thought of. In order to make the case more convincing, let us add that I am quite hasty in forming my opinion that I can complete the hike. I am not reflective and do not give the possibility that my friend is lying any consideration. Isn't it plain that my belief is irrational and thus that (7) overly restricts the evidence I have?

I believe that the answer to these questions is "No." In order to understand why, it is necessary to distinguish two senses of epistemic terms such as "rational." (Other epistemic terms have similar senses, but for simplicity I will consider only "rational" here.) One sort of epistemic appraisal concerns whether believing a particular proposition is rational for a person at a time given exactly the situation the person happens to be in at the time. We may say that this is an assessment of the *current-state epistemic rationality* of believing the proposition. (Analogously, in asking what a person morally ought to do, we look at the situation the person is in and evaluate the options open to him. How he's gotten himself into his current situation is not strictly relevant to the evaluation.)

A second possible epistemic evaluation of a belief has to do with the methods that led to it. We may call this *methodological epistemic rationality*. Beliefs are methodologically rational if and only if they are formed as the result of good epistemic methods. Good methods might include a consideration of all the evidence, careful reflection, and the like.

It is plausible to maintain that my belief that I can complete the hike is methodologically irrational. One might contend that I should think about the feasibility of the hike more carefully and reflect on the reliability of my friend. If I did that, I would remember his past lie, and then perhaps I would not believe that I could complete the hike. Because I didn't do these things, I did not follow rational methods in arriving at this belief, and my belief is methodologically irrational. On the other hand, it is quite reasonable to maintain that my belief is current-state rational. In the situation I am in, in which I have not thought about the counter-evidence, it would be quite irrational for me to believe anything else. The evidence I do have quite clearly supports my belief. Given the situation that I am in, holding the belief is exactly what I should (epistemically) do.

This distinction between methodological and current-state rationality provides the basis for an adequate response to the first objection to (7). The objection was that (7) overly restricted the evidence I had, leading to the incorrect result that my belief that I could complete the hike was rational. My response is that (7) only leads to the result that my belief is current-state rational, and that result is unobjectionable.

Consideration of a variation on the example about the hike provides support for my claims that (7) is not overly restrictive and that my belief is current-state rational. Suppose that the information about the falsity of my friend's claim about the hike is not stored in my memory

but rather is contained in a book—*A Pocket Guide to the Difficulty of Hikes in the Precarious Peak Area*—that I have in my pocket. Since I trust my friend, I don't bother to look up the difficulty of the proposed hike in the guidebook. My critics might say, "You should have looked it up. Your belief is irrational since you did not." They may well be right about its methodological rationality, but surely the fact that I could and should have looked it up does not show that my belief is current-state irrational. It does not show that my belief was not supported by the evidence I already had. In the relevant sense I did not yet possess the evidence in the guidebook. (I did physically possess a book from which I could obtain that evidence. There may be some derivative sense of "have the evidence" in which I did have the evidence in this case. But surely it is not the sense in which we are interested.) The difference between this example and the original one is that in one case the relevant counter-evidence is in a book in my pocket and in the other case it is "in my head." In each case I could have "looked it up" but I didn't. Perhaps my failure to do so constitutes methodological irrationality in each case, but it does not show current-state irrationality in either case. It does not show that I had psychologically available, in the relevant sense, the counter-evidence. (It is available only in the sense that I could have obtained it.) In the two versions of the example my belief is equally current-state rational, and there is no need, in order to account for our intuitive assessments of rationality, to say that the evidence I actually have in the two cases differs. Since it is clear that in the revised case I do not already have the counter-evidence provided by the book, there is no good reason to say that I have (in the relevant sense) the evidence I fail to think of in the original case. So (7) is not shown to be too restrictive by this example.

The intuitive distinction between current-state and methodological rationality can be further clarified by considering judgments about what I should do or believe, rather than judgments about what I did or should have believed. Even if it is true that I should look up the difficulty of the hike in my book, it does not follow that it is irrational for me to believe that I can complete the hike. It may be that the most reasonable thing for me to believe until I look it up is that I can complete the hike. After all, that is what my evidence supports. Moreover, my evidence suggests that the book will say that it is not a difficult hike. It would be a mistake to infer from the fact that I should acquire more evidence that it is most reasonable for me to suspend judgment until I do. It would also be a mistake to hold that the mere fact that I know that there is additional evidence about the hike somehow neutralizes the evidence I already have about its difficulty. So, the fact that I should look up this additional information just does not show that my belief is current-state irrational. Questions about what I should do, or what I should have done, with regard to evidence for a particular belief are independent of questions about the relation that belief has to the evidence I have at any given time.

The final step in my defense of (7) from this first objection is to emphasize that (7) is part of a theory about current-state rationality, not a theory of methodological rationality. Theories about the conditions under which beliefs are current-state rational are theories about the conditions under which beliefs are well supported by the evidence one has. (7), as well as the other proposals considered here, obviously fills out a crucial element of any such theory. On the other hand, (7) would play no central role in views about what methods one should follow in forming beliefs. Traditional theories of epistemic justification are best construed as theories about current-state justification (or rationality). That is, coherence theories and foundations theories of justification are theories about the relation of beliefs to evidence. They have nothing to say about the methods by which beliefs should be formed or how evidence should be acquired. Such theories do not give directives about what

one should think about or how one should go about gathering evidence.

It is unclear to me whether methodological epistemic rationality is an epistemologically central notion at all. Whether believing something is methodologically rational seems to depend largely on practical matters. For example, in the case of my hike to Precarious Peak, whether I should have thought about whether my friend lied in the past about such matters depends largely on a variety of practical issues: how bad would it be if I set off on a hike I couldn't complete? Are there other matters to which it is more important for me to direct my attention at the time? These are practical questions. No purely epistemic considerations yield answers to them. This seems to be the case generally. Questions about methodological rationality are practical questions that cannot be answered without information about the agent's goals and preferences. The central epistemological questions, as I understand them, do not concern such practical matters but rather are questions about the relation of beliefs to evidence. (7) forms an important part of an answer to such epistemological questions. Considerations about methodological rationality provide no good reason to reject (7).

I turn now to a second objection to (7). The objection is that if, as (7) implies, available evidence were restricted to what one is thinking of, then many things that surely are known, and therefore justified, would not be known or justified. For example, while listening to a philosophy lecture you still know, and are justified in believing, that Washington, D.C. is the capital of the United States. But (presumably) that wasn't supported by what you were thinking of during the lecture. Hence, (7) is too restrictive.

It surely is true that we attribute knowledge of propositions to people when they are not thinking of those propositions or of any evidence relevant to them. While this appears to conflict with (7), I believe that there is a distinction between occurrent and dispositional senses of epistemic terms and that our ordinary talk can be reconciled with (7) by appeal to this distinction.

It is uncontroversial that there is an occurrent sense of "believe" or of some closely related term. That is, there clearly are cases in which people think of or consider some proposition and mentally assent to it. We can define occurrent knowledge in terms of this notion of occurrent belief. In this sense of "know," while thinking about philosophy, one typically does not know that Washington, D.C. is the capital of the United States. We can, however, introduce a dispositional sense of "know" in which such things are known. That sense might be roughly characterized in terms of the occurrent sense: a person knows a thing dispositionally provided the person would know it occurrently if he thought of it. Since the thought that Washington is the capital would, presumably, be accompanied by an awareness of justifying evidence, this fact can be known dispositionally by most of us. Hence, the intuition that we know simple facts even when we are not thinking of them can be accommodated by the minimalist view of evidence possessed: they are known dispositionally but not occurrently.[13] This objection also fails to refute (7).[14]

The suggested account of dispositional knowledge is not exactly right, but I will not propose a more precise account here. The main trouble with it is that there are some things that, intuitively, are not known at all, but would be known if they were considered. That is, there may be some things that I do not know now, but if [I] were to think of them I would then come to believe them, and come to have evidence for them, for the first time. Such propositions satisfy the condition specified, but they are not even dispositionally known. The problem here, similar to those discussed in connection with (2)–(5), is that dispositional knowledge cannot be exactly characterized by means of the counterfactual proposed. I know of no entirely adequate replacement.

Another problem with this account of dispositional knowledge is that it apparently implies that things one could only bring to mind with helpful prompts (such as the color of my childhood house or my first grade teacher's name) are things that are known, because if they were thought of (an unlikely occurrence) they would be occurrently known. It seems, however, that in criticizing other accounts I said that such things were not known at all.

I don't think that these are decisive objections. The difficult and obscure dispositional elements enter this theory at a less central and less crucial stage, whereas in (2)–(5) the troublesome dispositional and counterfactual concepts play a crucial role in the definitions of the primary epistemic notions. On my view, in the most fundamental sense, one does not know things such as that Washington is the capital when one is not thinking of them. As a concession to those with the contrary intuition, I admit that there is a less clear dispositional conception of knowledge in which one does know such things. It may be that my view also implies that one also knows, in this same sense, things that one is only likely to recall with suggestive and helpful prompts. I don't believe that that is an intolerable consequence. Indeed, it captures the point expressed when one says, after being reminded of one of these facts, "I knew that."

The difficulty involved in spelling out the dispositional epistemic notions would be troublesome for my view if some central problem in epistemology or philosophy of mind turned on specifying those conceptions precisely. I don't see that any problem does turn on that. Hence, I don't see that this unclarity in my account is a serious defect.

One claim made in the response to the second objection to (7) may suggest a third objection. In responding to the objection I said that, typically, if a person who we are inclined to say knows that Washington, D.C. is the capital of the United States were to think about that proposition, he would also think of evidence that supports it. But that claim may not seem clearly true. He may just think of that proposition, but not of other supporting propositions, such as testimony of teachers, friends, or newspaper reporters. We are still inclined to say that he has occurrent knowledge when he does think about this proposition, even though he does not think of supporting evidence. Thus, it seems that (7) is still too restrictive.

This example is similar to the example about Lincoln's birthday mentioned in section 1. I think that the proper reply makes use of the fact, mentioned earlier, that evidence can include things other than beliefs. The fact that one feels a certain way, or that things look a certain way, can also count as evidence. A significant fact about a typical adult who thinks about the propositions in these examples is that the thought is accompanied by a strong feeling of certainty or conviction. It is plausible to think that these feelings carry evidential weight. Indeed, if I have forgotten my initial evidence but still am rational in thinking that Lincoln was born in 1809, or that Washington is the capital, it seems reasonable to suppose that the source of my current rationality is my current conviction or feeling of certainty that accompanies those beliefs. I suggest, therefore, that "thinking of" in (7) be interpreted in a sufficiently broad way so that it is true that I am thinking of these sorts of facts when I consider propositions. This is not meant to suggest that I am consciously mulling over or saying to myself that I feel certain that Lincoln was born in 1809. It's just that the feeling of certainty is something of which I am conscious. Thus, with "thinking of" interpreted in this way, I believe that this objection to (7) can be rejected.[15]

I turn now to a final objection to (7). It is based on the claim that (7) underplays the role of background knowledge in determining current-state rationality. Consider again the case of the expert bird-watcher. Upon seeing a bird, the belief that it is a scarlet tanager just comes to mind. She may be conscious of nothing other

than the look of the bird and her thought about the kind of bird it is. Of course, she could recite upon request the field marks of that kind of bird, but she need not consciously think of them at the time. What the expert is conscious of may be quite similar to what a novice bird-watcher is conscious of upon seeing the same bird. The novice, however, may not know the field marks and may believe the bird is a scarlet tanager because that's the only bird of approximately that color that he knows of. (He may admit, if asked, that it is likely that other birds have similar markings and that he couldn't distinguish them.) It's implausible to hold that their beliefs are of the same epistemic status. It seems reasonable to say that the expert's operative background beliefs make her belief rational, whereas the novice's belief is not rational. However, the extreme view now in question apparently evaluates their beliefs similarly, since they are conscious of the same evidence—the look of the bird—at the time.

There is, I think, very little plausibility to the reply that believing that the bird is a scarlet tanager is not justified for the expert unless she consciously considers the field marks that enabled her to identify it. The argument for this is simple. Suppose that while becoming an expert bird-watcher the subject had consciously gone through the process of identifying the field marks of the bird in view and recalling the list of distinguishing features in the field guide. At that time, the resulting beliefs about the kinds of birds she saw were justified. She no longer needs to go through that process consciously. She can just look at the birds and classify them. It is plainly mistaken to say that her beliefs were rational and justified previously, but no longer are now that she has automated the identification process.

There are, however, two plausible replies to the objection. First, the expert may have feelings of certainty about her identification that help justify her belief in much the way similar feelings help justify memory beliefs. If she lacks the feeling of certainty and her belief seems to her to be just a guess or a hunch, then it is far from clear that the belief is current-state justified.

A second possible response requires interpreting (7) to allow as available evidence more than we have so far acknowledged. The idea is that "operative" background beliefs, beliefs that are playing an active role in sustaining one's current state, are also being thought of (nonconsciously) and thus are available. Some support for this view can be derived from the following considerations. In the case of the bird-watcher, at some earlier time she would not have formed the belief that she was seeing a scarlet tanager when she had a visual presentation of the sort in question. She then learned that birds that looked that way were scarlet tanagers. When first learning to identify birds, she had to repeat consciously the identifying characteristics to herself. That conscious process is no longer necessary for her. It is plausible to think, however, that she is making use of these beliefs when she "automatically" identifies the bird. The process that previously occurred consciously still occurs, but not consciously. If (7) is interpreted to imply that this additional evidence is available, then (7) does not conflict with our intuitive judgment that the expert's belief is justified.

There are, then, two ways in which this final objection to (7) can be met. Admittedly, the second response introduces additional complexity to the theory. Nevertheless, the availability of these two responses shows that a restrictive account of available evidence can be defended from this final objection. My conclusion is that (7), interpreted to include among one's available evidence everything one is thinking of, consciously and perhaps nonconsciously, as well as non-belief states of which one is aware, is an adequate view about the evidence available to a person at a time. As far as I can tell, this view is compatible with all the theories of current-state epistemic justification and rationality mentioned in section 2. It also seems to conform to the intuitions that underlie our judgments about rationality and justification in the examples discussed.

The restrictive view about evidence possessed may also have the implication that we are not quite as irrational as Stich[16] and other interpreters of the psychological studies mentioned earlier suggest. One of the facts about those studies, such as the ones about the conjunction rule, is that people fail to consider stored evidence that may be relevant to the beliefs they form. But if questions about rationality are, in their primary sense, questions about how well people's beliefs are supported by the evidence they do have, then it is far from clear that their beliefs are regularly irrational. It may well be that the incomplete and unsystematic evidence that people do have in mind when they form those beliefs supports the beliefs they do form. So, their beliefs may be current-state rational.

Possibly, many of the beliefs discussed in these studies are methodologically irrational because people "should" think about additional evidence in these cases. Whether this charge of irrationality is appropriate is, as suggested earlier, difficult to assess. Whether people should think more about these matters, and search their memories for evidence against the heuristic they naturally use, depends largely upon their goals and purposes at the time.

This is not to say, however, that people never have beliefs that are current-state irrational, that what they believe is always supported by the evidence they have. In other words, I am not concurring with the view defended by Daniel Dennett that "[i]t is at least *not obvious* that there are any cases of systematically irrational behavior or thinking" or that alleged cases of irrationality "defy description in ordinary terms of belief and desire."[17] It is compatible with my view, and with common sense, that people sometimes believe things because it is comforting or reassuring to do so. That is, they sometimes engage in wishful thinking. Typically, though not always, when they do this their beliefs are not well supported by their evidence and are current-state irrational. So, the view I have defended here is not so charitable as to make all beliefs rational. That, too, I think, is a virtue of the view.[18]

Afterword

A point mentioned near the end of section 2 of "Having Evidence" warrants emphasis. The point is that questions similar to those raised there are likely to arise for any plausible version of any epistemological theory. I will provide two brief illustrations of this here.

Alvin Plantinga defends the view that a belief is warranted provided it results from the proper function of the believer's cognitive system.[19] Presumably, when a cognitive system functions properly, it evaluates newly obtained information in the light of some range of its stored information. But the question of what stored information matters is a close analogue of the problem of evidence possessed. To take one other example, for a causal theory to be plausible, it must include some sort of "no defeater" condition. Thus, it will say that a belief is justified only if it is caused in the right sort of way and is not defeated by other information the believer has. (This is similar to the requirement, mentioned in the paper, that Goldman adds to his reliabilist theory.) Determining what counts as the potentially defeating evidence a believer has is similar to determining what evidence a person has. Thus, these two theories face a problem similar to the problem discussed in this paper.

While the fact that other theories face a similar problem neither vindicates evidentialism nor relieves evidentialists of the burden of providing a solution, it does show that the existence of this problem does not undermine evidentialism. Opponents of evidentialism who find the solutions proposed here unsatisfactory might consider how their preferred theory would deal with comparable issues.

Notes

1 Alvin Goldman, "A Causal Theory of Knowing," in G. Pappas and M. Swain (eds.), *Essays on Knowledge and Justification* (Ithaca, NY: Cornell University Press, 1978), 83.

2 These studies are reported in Amos Tversky and Daniel Kahneman, "Judgments of and by Representativeness," in D. Kahneman, P. Slovic, and A. Tversky (eds.), *Judgement under Uncertainty: Heuristics and Biases* (Cambridge: Cambridge University Press, 1982), 84–98. For discussion of this and other examples of apparent irrationality, see Richard Nisbett and Lee Ross, *Human Inference: Strategies and Shortcomings of Social Judgment* (Englewood Cliffs, NJ: Prentice-Hall, 1980).

3 The view that these and other cases reveal widespread irrationality is defended by Stephen Stich in "Could Man be an Irrational Animal? Some Notes on the Epistemology of Rationality," *Synthese*, 64 (1985), 115–35.

4 See Tversky and Kahneman, "Judgments of and by Representativeness."

5 This sort of view is defended in Richard Feldman and Earl Conee, "Evidentialism," *Philosophical Studies*, 48 (1985), 15–34.

6 A view of this sort is defended in John Pollock, *Knowledge and Justification* (Princeton: Princeton University Press, 1974).

7 See, for example, Roderick Chisholm, *Theory of Knowledge* (Englewood Cliffs, NJ: Prentice-Hall, 1977).

8 Ibid., 6.

9 Ibid., 14.

10 For defenses of the coherence theory, see Laurence BonJour, *The Structure of Empirical Knowledge* (Cambridge, Mass., and London: Harvard University Press, 1985), and Keith Lehrer, *Knowledge* (Oxford: Oxford University Press, 1974).

11 See Alvin Goldman, "What is Justified Belief?," in G. Pappas (ed.), *Justification and Knowledge* (Dordrecht: Reidel, 1979), 20.

12 Laurence BonJour, "Can Empirical Knowledge Have a Foundation?," *American Philosophical Quarterly*, 15 (1978), 2.

13 (7) can also be reconciled with the view that there is one ordinary sense of the word "know" and that simple facts are known in that sense whether they

are thought of or not. One can define this ordinary sense as the disjunction of the occurrent and dispositional senses just described. Interpreting "know" in this way does not require abandoning (7).

14 An attractive feature of the view just described is that it enables us to deal with some puzzling cases in which believing each of two incompatible propositions seems to be rational for a person. It may be that each proposition is such that the evidence the person would think of in connection with it is evidence that does support the proposition. The two bodies of evidence may be unconnected in the believer's mind, so that each proposition is considered only in the light of supporting evidence. The proposed view allows us to say that believing each proposition is (dispositionally) rational. Presumably, however, believing their conjunction would not be rational, since, in considering the conjunction, the conflicting evidence would all be brought to mind at once.

15 My claim here is that the feeling of certainty accompanying a belief may count as available evidence supporting the belief. This does not imply that all such feelings are epistemically adequate or that every belief accompanied by such a feeling is rational.

16 Stich, "Could Man be an Irrational Animal?"

17 Daniel Dennett, "Making Sense of Ourselves," in J. I. Biro and R. W. Shahan (eds.), *Mind, Brain, and Function* (Norman, Okla.: University of Oklahoma Press, 1982), 66–7.

18 I am grateful to Earl Conee, John Heil, Peter Markie, and Paul Weirich for helpful comments on earlier drafts of this paper.

19 This statement of Plantinga's theory ignores many of the details Plantinga provides. Those details do not affect the point made here. For a full statement of Plantinga's theory, see his *Warrant and Proper Function* (Oxford: Oxford University Press, 1993).

PART FOUR

How should we distribute our confidence?

INTRODUCTION TO PART FOUR

Ram Neta and Duncan Pritchard

JACKSON HAS BEEN WORKING HARD in his statistics course all term, and he's extremely confident that he's going to get an 'A' in the course. But he's also extremely confident that his friend Ophelia will get an 'A': she's clearly been doing better in the course than he has. Furthermore, Jackson has heard the teacher announce that only one 'A' will be given in the course, and so, at the same time that he's extremely confident that he's going to get an 'A', and extremely confident that Ophelia is going to get an 'A', Jackson is also extremely confident that there will be only one 'A' in the course. Is Jackson being irrational?

It may seem that Jackson is being irrational, but why? What is irrational about Jackson's being simultaneously extremely confident of each of the following things:

(a)   he will get an 'A', and
(b)   Ophelia will get an 'A', and
(c)   there will be only one 'A'.

You might think that what is irrational about this is that, obviously, (a) and (b) and (c) cannot all be true. Somehow, you might think, the fact that they obviously cannot all be true makes Jackson's extreme confidence in each of them irrational.

But why should the fact that (a) and (b) and (c) obviously cannot all be true make Jackson's extreme confidence in each of them irrational? Consider a lottery which I know to have 1000 tickets and only one winner. Now suppose I am simultaneously extremely confident of each of the following things:

(t1)   ticket #1 will lose, and
(t2)   ticket #2 will lose, and
(t3)   ticket #3 will lose, and

. . .

(t1001) one of the 1000 tickets will win.

It seems that there is nothing irrational about my being simultaneously extremely confident in each of (t1) through (t1001). And yet obviously (t1) through (t1001) cannot all be true: if one ticket will win, then it cannot be true of each ticket that it will lose. So there is nothing irrational about my being simultaneously extremely confident in each one of a number of propositions that obviously cannot all be true. But that shows that what makes Jackson irrational cannot be the fact that (a) and (b) and (c) obviously cannot all be true. So, if Jackson is being irrational, it must be for some other reason. But what is this other reason? In general, which distributions of confidence are rational or irrational, and why are they rational or irrational?

Many epistemologists have attempted to answer these questions. They have attempted to state and explain the constraints that rationality imposes upon how we distribute our confidence. Unlike the work done on most other topics in epistemology, much of the work that has been done on this particular topic has been very mathematically sophisticated. But why is this? Many topics in epistemology do not seem to be susceptible to mathematical treatment: for instance, it is not clear how we could use mathematical tools to help us understand the nature of knowledge, or the nature of epistemic justification. So why is it that, when epistemologists study the constraints that rationality imposes upon our distribution of confidence, they usually end up employing sophisticated mathematics?

One reason for this is that, in his enormously influential article 'Truth and Probability',[1] Frank Ramsey argued that rationality requires that your degrees of confidence at any particular time are *probabilistically coherent*. What does this mean? It means that rationality requires that your degrees of confidence have a certain overall structure, and the overall structure that they are required to have is precisely the same as the overall structure that probabilities have. Let's call Ramsey's idea 'probabilism'. A probabilist, then, is someone who thinks that, in order for your degrees of confidence to be rational, they must have the same structure that probabilities have. The structure of probabilities was described by, among others, the Russian mathematician Andrey Nikolaevich Kolmogorov, in his study in the foundations of probability theory.[2] According to Kolmogorov, all of probability theory can be derived from just three axioms. Although the axioms themselves are few and simple, the mathematics needed to derive everything else in probability theory from just those three axioms is intricate. Consequently, if rational degrees of confidence have the same structure that probabilities have, then, just as we can learn more and more about probabilities by means of intricate mathematical arguments from three simple axioms, so too we can learn more and more about rational degrees of confidence by means of intricate mathematical arguments from three simple axioms.

More specifically, if rational degrees of confidence have the same structure that probabilities have, then they can be mapped onto the real numbers between 0 and 1, such that, for any two propositions p and q:

> your degree of confidence in p is equal to or greater than 0,
> if p is a tautology, then your degree of confidence in p is equal to 1, and
> if p and q entails a contradiction, then your degree of confidence in the disjunction
>> of p and q is equal to your degree of confidence in p added to your degree of confidence in q.

If probabilism is true, then everything else about our rational degrees of confidence follows, sometimes by means of intricate mathematical argument, from the three simple claims listed here. Therefore, if probabilism is true, intricate mathematical argument can teach us a great deal about the constraints that rationality imposes upon our degrees of confidence. It is the widespread acceptance of probabilism that explains (at least in large part) why it is that, in this particular region of epistemology, we sometimes find mathematically intricate arguments.

Even if probabilism is true, however, we still want to understand *why* it is true, i.e. why rationality requires our degrees of confidence at a particular time to have the same structure that probabilities have. Mathematical arguments alone will not provide us with this understanding: in addition to the mathematical arguments, we also need to do some philosophy, and in particular we need to think about why rationality would require certain things of us. Such thinking will inevitably involve a non-mathematical component, and that component will be subject to philosophical scrutiny and controversy.

For instance, when Ramsey argued for probabilism, his argument went very roughly like this: if an agent's degrees of confidence at a particular time are not probabilistically coherent, then the agent is, at that time, willing to place a set of bets such that, no matter what happens, the agent is guaranteed to lose money. (A set of bets with this feature is called a 'Dutch Book'.) It is irrational to be willing to place a set of bets like this, and so it is irrational for an agent's degrees of confidence at a particular time to be probabilistically incoherent. Now, this argument – which is commonly known as the 'Dutch Book Argument' – assumes that what bets an agent is willing to place at a particular time is completely fixed by her degrees of confidence at that time. But this assumption may very well be false. What bets an agent is willing to place is at least partly fixed by her degrees of confidence, but why think that what bets an agent is willing to place is *completely* fixed by her degrees of confidence? Might not other factors, besides her degrees of confidence, influence her willingness to place various bets? In general, our willingness to perform any action – whether it is the action of placing a bet, or any other action – is a function not simply of our degrees of confidence, but also of other factors (e.g. our whims, resolutions, appetites, fatigue, and so on) that may vary independently of our degrees of confidence.

Considerations like this have led a number of philosophers to reject the Dutch Book Argument, and have led other philosophers to attempt to offer new and improved versions of it. An enormous literature has grown around this debate, but that literature is, for the most part, very mathematically sophisticated, and so we will not include it in this volume. (There is also another literature generated by the attempt of David Lewis (1941–2001)[3] to offer a diachronic version of the Dutch Book Argument, in order to argue that our degrees of confidence at any one time must bear certain mathematical relations to our degrees of confidence at any other time, given the stretch of evidence that we've received between those two times. We will not examine the many complex issues surrounding the diachronic Dutch Book Argument.)

Nonetheless, the selections that we do include in this part – in particular, the selection from Mark Kaplan's (1951–) book *Decision Theory as Philosophy* (Chapter 13) – require a firm handle on high-school algebra, and an ability to follow long rigorous stretches of argument. Kaplan offers an intricate argument for probabilism, but his argument is not a version of the Dutch Book Argument, and it makes no appeal to the contentious premise that our willingness to place bets is completely fixed by our degrees of confidence. For Kaplan, what is fixed by our degrees of confidence is not our *willingness to place bets*, but rather our *commitment to the fairness of certain bets.* Kaplan attempts to argue for probabilism not by showing that, if our degrees of confidence are probabilistically incoherent, then we are *willing to do something* that is guaranteed to make us worse off, but rather that, if our degrees of confidence are probabilistically incoherent, then we are *committed to the fairness of a set of bets* that is guaranteed to make us worse off.

So has Kaplan shown that probabilism is true? This is not yet clear. Many philosophers have pointed out that probabilism appears to have a number of counter-intuitive consequences.

For instance, probabilism, as standardly understood, implies that it is irrational for us to have anything less than maximal confidence in the truth of any tautology. But some tautologies are so extraordinarily long and complicated that it is impossible for any human being to understand them in the course of a human lifetime. Does rationality nonetheless demand of us that we be maximally confident in their truth, despite not being able to understand them? Perhaps the probabilist will say that an *agent* can be rational even if her *degrees of confidence* are not rational. But then how are we to understand this distinction?

The selections that follow the Kaplan reading in this part indirectly raise other problems for probabilism. Adam Elga (1974–) describes the so-called 'Sleeping Beauty' problem (Chapter 14), which goes like this: Sleeping Beauty is told on Sunday that she is going to go to sleep for the next two days, and she will be woken up either once or twice. A fair coin is tossed, and if it lands on 'heads' she will be woken up on both Monday and Tuesday, but if it lands on 'tails' she'll be woken up only on Tuesday. If she is woken up Monday, she is put back to sleep with a drug that makes her forget that she was woken up on Monday. Now, Sleeping Beauty knows all of this. When she wakes up for the first time, how confident should she be that the coin landed on 'heads'? Elga argues for an answer to this question that is compatible with probabilism (namely, the answer that Sleeping Beauty should have a degree of confidence equal to 1/3). Although Elga does not challenge probabilism, his exposition of the problem shows how counterintuitive all of the probabilist's options are for solving the Sleeping Beauty problem. If all of the probabilist's options for solving the problem are counterintuitive, then that may seem to constitute a problem for the probabilist.

The selection from Paul Hoffman's biography of the Turkish mathematician Erdosh (Chapter 15) describes a problem famously known as the 'Monty Hall' problem. The problem goes like this: you are a contestant on the game show 'Let's Make a Deal', and you know that the grand prize is behind one of the three doors in front of you. You guess that it is behind door #1. Then, without telling you whether or not your guess is correct, the game show host (Monty Hall) shows you that the prize is *not* behind door #3. Should this make it rational for you to increase your confidence that the prize is behind door #2? Common sense seems to tell us that the answer to this question is 'no'. But, as is detailed in the reading, if probabilism is true, then it seems that the answer to this question is 'yes'. Does this pose a problem for the probabilist?

Study questions

1   What is probabilism? Can you think of any obvious objections to probabilism?

2   Can you explain the steps of Mark Kaplan's argument in favour of probabilism? Do you see any flaws in Kaplan's reasoning?

3   When Sleeping Beauty wakes up for the first time, how confident should she be that the coin landed on 'heads'? Why does Elga think that she should be twice as confident that it landed on 'tails' than that it landed on 'heads'? Can you find any problem in Elga's reasoning?

4   If you are the contestant on 'Let's Make a Deal', and you guess that the prize is behind door #1 and then Monty Hall shows you that it's not behind door #3, should you switch your guess? Why, or why not?

5   If you don't know on which side a six-sided die will land, how confident should you be that it will land on one, two or three? If you don't know what a man's name is, how confident should you be that his name is 'Lopez', 'Talbot' or 'Johnson'? If you answered the last two questions differently, explain why there is a difference.

Further reading

Although most of the work that has been done on the issue addressed in this section is highly mathematical, there is at least one recent exception: Christensen (2004) is a highly accessible and non-technical recent work on the issue of how to distribute our confidence over propositions.

Notes

1   Ramsey (1926)
2   Kolmogorov (1933).
3   Lewis (1976).

References

Christensen, David. (2004). *Putting Logic in its Place*, Oxford: Oxford University Press.

Kolmogorov, Andrey Nikolaevich. (1933/1956). *Foundations of the Theory of Probability*, ed. Nathan Morrison, New York: Chelsea Publishing Co.

Lewis, David. (1976). 'Probabilities of Conditionals and Conditional Probabilities', *Philosophical Review* 85: 297–315.

Ramsey, F. P. (1926). 'Truth and Probability', *The Foundations of Mathematics and Other Logical Essays*, ed. R. B. Braithwaite. London: Kegan, Paul, Trench, Trubner, and Co., 1931.

Chapter 13

Mark Kaplan

CONFIDENCE AND PROBABILITY

I A decision problem

You know precious little about the election. It is being held rather far away and it has little national importance. But what you *have* heard—and you haven't heard much—is that the incumbent is ahead of her lone opponent. As a consequence, you find yourself more confident that the incumbent will win. That is, where h is the hypothesis that the incumbent will win, you are more confident that h than you are that ~h.

Not so for g. There is an urn containing exactly 50 black balls and 50 white, all of the same composition and size. The contents of the urn have been thoroughly mixed. One ball has been drawn, but not yet examined. g is the hypothesis that the ball drawn is black. With good reason, you are just as confident that g as you are that ~g.

Suppose I confront you with the following decision problem. Suppose I offer you a choice between

(i) a ticket which entitles you to $1 if h is true and $0 if h is false; and
(ii) a coupon which entitles you to $1 if g is true and $0 if g is false.

Suppose further that, for the purpose of solving your problem, money is all you intrinsically value and you value every dollar gained or lost equally, no matter what the size of your fortune.

You may, if you like, imagine that you have undertaken an obligation to manage the fortune of someone who has these values. In either case, your (her, his) monetary fortune will be to you as pleasure is to a utilitarian. Like pleasure to a utilitarian, it is something measurable, it is something to be maximized, and its quantity in no way affects the value of losing (gaining) one unit of it.

What should you do?

It is not obvious. On the one hand, you are more confident than not that the incumbent will win and you are not more confident than not that the ball drawn is black. This would seem to speak in favor of taking the ticket, of letting the $1 prize ride on h rather than on g. On the other hand, given how little you know about the election (the evidence you have about its outcome is quite meager) and how much you know about the drawing from the urn (you know enough to know the precise odds that the ball drawn is black), it may seem that, even though you do invest more confidence in h than in ~h, you have reason to invest more still in g and in ~g. If so, it would seem that you should take the coupon—you should let the $1 prize ride on g.

In fact, you should take the ticket. The nominal purpose of this chapter is to say why, but its more substantial purpose lies elsewhere. As the considerations rehearsed above suggest, what lies at the heart of the decision problem is the question: in which (if either) of h and g are you warranted in investing more confidence? You will want the $1 to ride on the hypothesis in which you invest more confidence. But, as the considerations rehearsed above also reveal, our epistemic intuitions seem to give us no sure grasp on how that question is to be answered. The purpose of this chapter is to show how, by focusing instead on principles governing rational preference, we can do better. The purpose of this chapter is to provide a first glimpse of how decision theory can constitute a piece of epistemology.

As you can imagine, the reason I mean to offer you for taking the ticket has nothing to do with the physical properties of the ticket or the coupon or the bundles of cash set aside to supply prizes. It has nothing to do with the particular time or location in which the entitlement promised by each option will be conferred, the prize delivered. Rather, it has to do with the state of affairs each option will realize if you choose it. Take the ticket and you will realize the state of affairs in which you increase your fortune by $1 if h and by $0 if ~h—you will realize ($1 if h, $0 if ~h). Take the coupon and you will realize the state of affairs in which you increase your fortune by $1 if g and by $0 if ~g—you will realize ($1 if g, $0 if ~g). You should take the ticket because you should prefer ($1 if h, $0 if ~h) to ($1 if g, $0 if ~g).

To convince you of as much, I will devote section II to introducing and defending a set of general principles that purport to describe ways in which the values we are imagining you harbor, together with the demands of reason, would constrain your preferences. In section III, I will show that, on pain of violating these principles, you must prefer ($1 if h, $0 if ~h) to ($1 if g, $0 if ~g). In section IV, I will exhibit how the principles to which I have appealed entail a general (and recognizably Bayesian) theory of rational decision and, with it, an epistemological doctrine I will call "Modest Probabilism." [. . .]

But before I begin, some preliminary remarks are in order.

First, I ask you to imagine throughout that my description of your decision problem is faithful and accurate. That is, I ask you to imagine that there is nothing auspicious about your two options other than what I have explicitly described: the truth-values of the hypotheses involved, g, ~g, h and ~h, are not auspicious for you in any way other than the way stated and the truth-values of these hypotheses will not be affected by what option you take or by any of your attitudes. And I ask you to imagine that all my subsequent descriptions of decision problems and states of affairs are faithful and accurate in this way.[1]

Second, I will be assuming, as I talk about decision problems and their elements, that it is tolerably clear what counts as a hypothesis—it is something that is either true or false and not both—and what (by virtue of its vagueness or some other failing) does not count as a hypothesis. People will differ on cases—on what is too vague or unclear to have a truth-value. But I will be happy for my purposes to leave the decision to you. All I will require is that, if P and Q are members of what, as far as you are concerned, is the set of all hypotheses, then so are all their truth-functional combinations.

Third, I should note at the outset that the particular decision theory I will be placing before you is rather modest in scope. It is concerned only with how you should want to constrain your preferences among *well-mannered states of affairs*.

Definition. *A* is a *well-mannered state of affairs* just in case, for some set of mutually exclusive and jointly exhaustive hypotheses, $\{P_1, \ldots, P_n\}$, and some set of real numbers, $\{a_1, \ldots, a_n\}$, *A* is identical to (a_1 if $P_1, \ldots,$ a_n if P_n).

[Where all the a_i are equal to the same sum a, we will say that *A* is *identical to* a. Thus, for example, we will regard the state of affairs in which you increase your fortune by $1—a state of affairs we will refer to simply as "$1"—as identical to ($1 if P_1, . . ., $1 if P_n) where {P_1, . . ., P_n} is any set of mutually exclusive and jointly exhaustive hypotheses.] Moreover, the decision theory is applicable only in contexts in which you have the peculiar values we are assuming you have— i.e. in contexts in which you value only money and every dollar as much as every other no matter what your fortune.

These restrictions (that monetary prizes be in dollars, that the prizes be finite in size, that each state of affairs of interest has but a finite number of possible outcomes, that you care for dollars in the way a utilitarian cares for utility) are designed to make the theory more accessible. Fortunately [. . .] these restrictions will not undermine the generality of the epistemological results whose morals I am concerned to draw. Nor will they in any way hamper my attempt to say how you should solve the decision problem with which we began. We have already supposed that, for the purpose of the problem, you *do* care for dollars the way a utilitarian cares for utility. And, as I have already noted, it is by persuading you that you should prefer the well-mannered state of affairs ($1 if *h*, $0 if ~*h*) to the well-mannered state of affairs ($1 if *g*, $0 if ~*g*) that I mean to persuade you that you should take the ticket.

II The five principles

Pick any two well-mannered states of affairs, *A* and *B*, and the following will be true: either you prefer *A* to *B*, you prefer *B* to *A*, you are indifferent between *A* and *B*, or you are undecided between *A* and *B*. Each of these four states of preference excludes the others. This is particularly important to appreciate in the case of the last two. Both when you are indifferent between *A* and *B* and when you are undecided between *A* and *B* you can be said not to prefer either state of affairs to the other. Nonetheless, indifference and indecision are distinct. When you are indifferent between *A* and *B*, your failure to prefer one to the

other is born of a determination that they are equally preferable. When you are undecided, your failure to prefer one to the other is born of no such determination.

Another way to distinguish indifference from indecision is to notice how differently they behave in the context of decision-making. After all, reason subjects your preferences and indifferences to substantive constraint. For example, where *A*, *B*, and *C* are any states of affairs, reason holds your preferences and indifferences open to criticism if you are indifferent between *A* and *B* and indifferent between *B* and *C* but you fail to be indifferent between *A* and *C*.[2]

But rational indecision resists such neat treatment. Suppose you find yourself unable to gauge *B*'s worth to you. Suppose that, as a consequence, you are undecided between *A* and *B* and undecided between *B* and *C*. Notice that the fact that you are undecided between *A* and *B* and between *B* and *C* in no way constrains what attitude you may adopt toward *A* and *C*. All your options—preference, indifference, indecision— are still completely open.

This assumes, of course, that there *is* such a thing as rational indecision. Orthodox Bayesians will demur. They hold that any indecision you may suffer opens your attitudes to criticism— that indecision constitutes a (perhaps excusable, but nonetheless real) failure fully to heed the demands of reason. But, for reasons I will explain in section V, Bayesian orthodoxy is in error. It is an error which condemns orthodox Bayesianism to a false precision that the theory under construction here is designed to avoid.

There is, however, nothing unorthodox in the next three principles. To say that you should want to conform to the first of these principles, is just to spell out in complete generality the moral about rational preference and indifference we have already acknowledged.

1.1 Ordering. Where *A*, *B*, and *C* are any well-mannered states of affairs between no pair of which you are undecided,

(i)   you do not prefer A to A; and

(ii)   if you do not prefer A to B and you do not prefer B to C, then you do not prefer A to C.[3]

Now for the second principle. Suppose I had presented you with a somewhat different decision problem than the one which actually confronts you. Suppose I had offered you a choice between $1 and a stub entitling you to $2 if h is true and $1.50 if h is false. Notice how straightforward the solution would have been. The following argument would have been available to you: "Either h is true or h is false. If h is true and I take the stub I will receive $2 and will be $1 better off than I would have been had I taken the $1. If h is false and I take the stub, I will receive $1.50 and be $0.50 better off than I would have been had I taken the $1. So, no matter whether h is true or false, my net fortune will be greater if I take the stub. I should prefer taking the stub."

On the other hand, suppose I had offered you a choice between the stub—it gives you $2 if h is true and $1.50 if h is false—and a coupon which also gives you $2 if h is true and $1.50 if h is false. Again, the solution of your decision problem would have been straightforward. The argument is compelling: "Either h is true or h is false. If h is true, I will be up $2 no matter whether I take the stub or the coupon. If h is false, I will be up $1.50 no matter whether I take the stub or the coupon. So, no matter whether h is true or false, I will do equally well with the stub as I will with the coupon. I should be indifferent between them."

To say that you should want to conform to the next principle is just to generalize these two arguments.

1.2 Dominance. Where A is the well-mannered state of affairs (a_1 if P_1, . . ., a_n if P_n) and B is the well-mannered state of affairs (b_1 if P_1, . . ., b_n if P_n),

(i)   if $a_i > b_i$ for every i, then you prefer A to B; and

(ii)   if $a_i = b_i$ for every i, then you are indifferent between A and B.

But now suppose I had begun this chapter with yet a different decision problem. Suppose I had offered you a choice between the ticket and a claim check which entitles you to $1 if ~h and $0 if h. The problem would have been easy to solve. You would have had available to you the following argument. "The choice between the ticket, ($1 if h, $0 if ~ h), and the claim check, ($1 if ~h, $0 if h), is just a choice between having $1 ride on h or having $1 ride on ~h— i.e. between identical bets on h and on ~h. But given that I have good reason to be more confident that h is true, I have good reason to be more confident that I will win the bet on h. I should take the ticket."

Furthermore, had I placed before you the choice between the ticket and the claim check without giving you any information about the state of your opinion about h and ~h, and had I promised to offer you a reason why you should take the ticket, you would know that I was promising you a reason why you should be more confident that h. For you could reason as follows: "I have a reason to take the ticket only if I have a reason to prefer having $1 ride on the truth of h rather than on its falsehood—i.e. only if I have a reason to find a bet on h preferable to an identical bet on ~h. And I have a reason to find a bet on h preferable to an identical bet on ~h only if I have a reason to be more confident that h is true."

The moral is that the following relation ought to hold between your states of opinion and your preferences: you find the ticket preferable to the claim check if and only if you are more confident that h than you are that ~h. This moral can be generalized, by saying that you should want to conform to the following principle.

1.3 Confidence. For any hypotheses P and Q, you are more confident that P than you are that Q if *and only if* you prefer ($1 if P, $0 if ~P) to ($1 if Q, $0 if ~Q).

But you may worry about this generalization and, in particular, about the necessary condition it would impose on your investing more confidence in P than in Q. Suppose I have pulled a card from a well-shuffled complete deck of cards and placed it face down on the table. No one has seen what card it is. I then replace the card in the deck and incinerate the deck. Let p be "The card was the ace of spades." It would seem rational for you to invest more confidence in ~p than in p. According to Confidence, then, you should also prefer a bet on ~p to an identical bet on p. But you may wonder how this can be so. There *can be* no bet on either. There is no way to determine whether you win either bet since the evidence relevant to that determination has been destroyed. In general, betting on the truth of a hypothesis makes sense only if there is an acknowledged means, agreed upon by the parties to the bet, of determining whether the hypothesis is true or not.

Now this conclusion will not really block my argument that you should take the ticket. After all, the truth-values of h and g are both determinable. But the conclusion will, if left unchallenged, rob my argument of its generality and philosophical interest. It will place beyond the reach of Confidence a great many of the hypotheses, scientific and otherwise, that we find most interesting. In the case of many hypotheses and theories, there *is* no acknowledged means of determining whether they are true; no one is in a position to make a definitive determination.[4] Fortunately, it is not hard to see why this is a conclusion too hastily drawn.

There can be little doubt that, in the case described above, the preconditions for your actually placing a bet on p or on ~p are simply not met. But then, neither are the preconditions for my having spent the last five minutes on

Pinney's Beach in Nevis. I have, in fact, spent the last five minutes working in Milwaukee and there is nothing anyone can do to change that. Yet it still makes sense for me to prefer having spent the last five minutes on that idyllic Caribbean beach to having spent the time at work in Milwaukee. But if it ever makes sense to prefer that things were otherwise than they in fact were, we must reject the view that the preconditions for the realization of a state of affairs must be met for there to be sense in speaking of your preferring that state of affairs to some other. Once we reject that view, it is hard to see anything at all problematic in supposing—even as we concede that the preconditions for betting on p and for betting on ~p are not met—that you prefer having $1 ride on ~p to having $1 ride on p.

Obviously, Dominance and Confidence depend for their propriety on the assumption that you value only money. The next principle exploits, in addition, the assumption that you value every dollar as much as every other no matter what your fortune.

As should be clear by now, the well-mannered states of affairs over which the foregoing principles constrain your preferences are *types* of states of affairs of which their realizations are *tokens*.[5] As a type, the state of affairs in which you increase your fortune by $1 if h and by $0 if ~h is unique. Yet it admits of many tokens, each of which is a realization of that state of affairs at a particular time. (Your taking the ticket would constitute one such realization.) Now let us say that

Definition. A sequence of well-mannered states of affairs is *realized* just when each state of affairs that occurs in the sequence is realized as many times as it occurs in the sequence.

Thus, to realize the sequence

(1) ($1 if h, $0 if ~h), ($1 if h, $0 if ~h), ($1 if g, $0 ~g),

is to realize ($1 if h, $0 if ~h) twice and ($1 if g, $0 ~ g) once. Next, let us say that

Definition. A sequence of well-mannered states of affairs φ is a *decomposition of a well-mannered state of affairs A (A is composable from φ)* just in case φ is finite and it is logically impossible that the realization of φ will effect (*qua* realization)[6] a different net change in your fortune than the realization of A will.

Thus the sequence (1) constitutes a decomposition of

(2)   ($3 if h & g, $2 if h & ~g, $1 if ~h & g, $0 if ~h & ~g).

Finally, let us say that

Definition. You *place a monetary value of $a on A* just if you are indifferent between $a and A.

The fourth principle says the following:

1.4 Decomposition. If

(i)   A is a well-mannered state of affairs;
(ii) φ is a decomposition of A; and
(iii) you place a monetary value on A and on each of the terms of φ;

then the value you place on A is equal to the sum of the values you place on the terms of φ.

Thus Decomposition requires that the sum of the monetary values you place on the terms of (1) equal the monetary value you place on (2).

But why should you want to submit to this requirement? Suppose you were bound by a budgetary constraint (or an aversion to gambling) that forbids you to gamble more than $1. Why could you not then rationally place a monetary value of $0.60 on each of the first two terms of (1) and a value of $0.50 on the last yet be unwilling to place a monetary value equal to their sum, $1.70, on (2)?

It is because of the way we are supposing you value money. We are supposing that you value only money, and every dollar as much as every other no matter what your fortune. It is incompatible with that supposition that you should be averse to gambling, or averse to risk, or that the monetary value you place on a state of affairs should depend on how much money you have in play—i.e. on the disposition of your fortune. Given the way we are supposing you value money, you are committed to satisfying Decomposition.

How much of a commitment is it? Granted, Decomposition is a strong principle. Every well-mannered state of affairs admits of an infinite number of decompositions[7] and, for every finite sequence of well-mannered states of affairs, there is a well-mannered state of affairs of which that sequence is a decomposition. But you are constrained by Decomposition only insofar as you place monetary values on a state of affairs and each term of a sequence from which it is composable. In the absence of any requirement that you place a monetary value on every well-mannered state of affairs—a requirement that (as I will argue in section V) would commit you to false precision—it may not seem that Decomposition imposes a very important constraint at all. The point of the next principle is to show that it does, all the same.

Suppose you do not place a monetary value on every well-mannered state of affairs. Suppose (as is doubtless the case) there are plenty of states of affairs on which you find it difficult to place a precise monetary value—indeed, plenty of pairs of states of affairs between which you are quite undecided. Those preferences (indifferences) that you do harbor still rule out certain assignments of monetary values to all well-mannered states of affairs. Insofar as you are indifferent between A and B, you have ruled out any assignment of monetary values to all well-mannered states of affairs that does not place the same monetary value on A as it places on B. And, insofar as you prefer A to B, you have ruled out any assignment that places a greater monetary value on B and (at the very least) have not ruled out at least one assignment that places a greater monetary value on A.[8]

So, even if you do not place a monetary value on every well-mannered state of affairs, we can characterize your preferences and indifferences in terms of the assignments of monetary values to every well-mannered state of affairs you have not ruled out. We can characterize your preferences and indifferences by a set V of such assignments: you count as being indifferent between A and B just in case every member of V assigns A the same monetary value as it assigns B; and you count as preferring A to B just in case no member of V assigns B a greater monetary value than it assigns A and at least one member of V assigns A a greater value than it assigns B.

We can also say something substantive about what assignments V should contain. First, each member of V should satisfy the three relevant principles adumbrated so far. That is, you should rule out any assignment of monetary values to all well-mannered states of affairs whose adoption would require you to violate Ordering, Dominance or Decomposition. Second, V should not be empty. Even if such preferences and indifferences as you have do not violate any of the three principles, it would certainly seem that they are nonetheless open to criticism if your preferences and indifferences are not compatible with even one assignment of monetary values to all well-mannered states of affairs that satisfies the three principles.[9] That is, we can say that you should want to satisfy the following principle:

> **1.5 Modest Connectedness.** Your preferences are characterized by a non-empty set V; of assignments of monetary values to all well-mannered states of affairs where each assignment satisfies Ordering, Dominance and Decomposition, and where

(i) you are indifferent between A and B just in case every member of V assigns A the same monetary value as it assigns B; and

(ii) you prefer A to B just in case no member of V assigns B a greater monetary value than it assigns A and some member of V assigns A a greater value than it assigns B.

With Modest Connectedness, we have all we need to derive the crucial epistemological result on which your decision problem turns. What we will see in the next section is that, from Confidence, Modest Connectedness and the assumption that you are more confident that h than you are that ~h and the assumption that you are just as confident that g as you are that ~g, it follows that you are more confident that h than you are that g—thus that, short of violating Confidence or Modest Connectedness, you must invest more confidence in h than in g. Once this is established, so is the solution to your decision problem. For, so long as you satisfy Confidence, you cannot invest more confidence in h than in g without preferring ($1 if h, $0 if ~h) to ($1 if g, $0 if ~g)—without preferring the ticket to the coupon.

III Decision problem solved

One might reasonably wonder how we can possibly derive the epistemological result just advertised by appeal to Modest Connectedness, a principle whose only concern is to place a constraint on your preferences. The answer lies in the relation Confidence requires your preferences and states of confidence to bear to one another. Confidence requires that, for any hypotheses P and Q, you are more confident that P than that Q if and only if you prefer ($1 if P, $0 if ~P) to ($1 if Q, $0 if ~Q). This tells us that, insofar as you satisfy Confidence, questions about the propriety of the way in which you invest confidence in hypotheses mirror questions about the propriety of your preferences among bets. Thus, our question, "Given that you are more confident that h than you are that ~h and you are equally confident that g as you are that ~g, in which (if either) of h and g should you invest more confidence?" can equally well be posed by asking, "Given that you prefer ($1 if h, $0 if ~h) to ($1 if ~h, $0 if h) and you are indifferent between ($1 if g, $0 if ~g) and ($1 if ~g, $0 if g), which (if either) of ($1 if h, $0 if ~h) and ($1 if g, $0 if ~g), should you prefer?" The latter is just the sort of question that we might expect a principle like Modest Connectedness would help us answer.

And so it will. Insofar as you satisfy Confidence and Modest Connectedness, the fact that you prefer ($1 if h, $0 if ~h) to ($1 if ~h, $0 if h) and you are indifferent between ($1 if g, $0 if ~g) and ($1 if ~g, $0 if g) means that

(i)   you have ruled out every monetary assignment to all well-mannered states of affairs that fails to place the same value on ($1 if g, $0 if ~g) as it places on ($1 if ~g, $0 if g);

(ii) you have ruled out every assignment that places a greater value on ($1 if ~h, $0 if h) than it places on ($1 if h, $0 if ~h);

(iii) you have not ruled out at least one assignment that places a greater value on ($1 if h, $0 if ~h) than it places on ($1 if ~h, $0 if h); and

(iv) you have ruled out every assignment that does not satisfy Ordering, Dominance and Decomposition.[10]

What we will prove is that, among the assignments left (i.e. among the members of V), there is none that assigns ($1 if g, $0 if ~g) a greater value than it assigns ($1 if h, $0 if ~h) and there is at least one that assigns ($1 if h, $0 if ~h) a greater value than it assigns ($1 if g, $0 if ~g). That means that, on pain of violating Modest Connectedness, you must prefer ($1 if h, $0 if

~h) to ($1 if g, $0 if ~g), and that, by Confidence, you must invest more confidence in h than you do in g.

To that end, the following definitions will be very helpful. Let us say that (where P is any hypothesis)

Definition. $con(P) = r$ just if you place a monetary value equal to $r on ($1 if P, $0 if ~P).

It follows from this definition that, if you place a monetary value on ($1 if P, $0 if ~P), then that value is equal to $con(P) \times \$1$, or (as we will express it) $con(P)\$1$. Next, let us say that

Definition. $con(P) = r$ *on an assignment of monetary values to all well-mannered states of affairs* just if that assignment assigns ($1 if P, $0 if ~P) the monetary value, $r.

We can then recast (i)–(iv) as follows:

(i')   you have ruled out every monetary assignment to all well-mannered states of affairs on which $con(g) \neq con(\sim g)$;

(ii') you have ruled out every assignment on which $con(\sim h) > con(h)$;

(iii') you have not ruled out at least one assignment on which $con(h) > con(\sim h)$; and

(iv') you have ruled out every assignment that does not satisfy Ordering, Dominance and Decomposition.

We can recast our objective as well. It is to show that, among the monetary assignments to all well-mannered states of affairs that are left, there is none on which $con(g) > con(h)$ and there is at least one on which $con(h) > con(g)$.

The key to realizing that objective clearly lies in finding out what (iv) says about the way the assignments that are left give values to $con(-)$. The following principle tells us what we want know.

1.6 Probabilism. Any assignment of monetary values to all well-mannered states of affairs that satisfies Ordering, Dominance and Decomposition assigns a real number to con(P) for every hypothesis P and does so in such a way that con(-) satisfies the Kolmogorov axioms of probability; that is, in such a way that, for any hypotheses P and Q,

(i) $con(P) \geq 0$;

(ii) if P is a tautology, then $con(P) = 1$; and

(iii) if P and Q are mutually exclusive,[11] then $con(P \vee Q) = con(P) + con(Q)$.

That any monetary assignment to all well-mannered states of affairs will assign a real number to every hypothesis follows directly from the definitions of con(-) and *well-mannered state of affairs*.[12] But the rest of Probabilism requires a bit more proof.

For the purpose of that proof, let us suppose that you adopt an assignment of monetary values to each well-mannered state of affairs, and that this assignment satisfies Ordering, Dominance, and Decomposition. We will prove that, in so doing, you assign values to con(-) that satisfy the three clauses in Probabilism.

To see why this is true in the case of the first clause, consider the following three states of affairs, where P is any hypothesis:

(3) con(P)$1

(4) (con(P)$1 if P, con(P)$1 if ~P)

(5) ($1 if P, $0 if ~P).

Since (3) is identical to (4) and (3) is the monetary value you place on (5), Ordering requires you to be indifferent between (4) and (5). But unless $con(P) \geq 0$, this will require violating Dominance. For, unless $con(P) \geq 0$ (and thus con(P)$1 $\geq$ $0), Dominance requires you to prefer (5) to (4). Thus, so long as you satisfy Ordering and Dominance, $con(P) \geq 0$ for every hypothesis P.

Let us turn, then, to clause (ii). Suppose that P is a tautology. Consider

(6) con(P)$1

(7) ($1 if P, $0 if ~P)

(8) $1.

Since P is a tautology, the sequence (7) is a decomposition of (8)—it is logically impossible that ~P and thus logically impossible that the lone term of (7) effect (*qua* realization) a different net change in your fortune than the realization of (8) will: they will both net you $1. So, since (6) is the monetary value you place on the lone term of (7), Decomposition requires that (6) be the monetary value you place on (8). Since both (6) and (8) are sums of money, Dominance requires that they be equal sums:

$con(P) = 1$.

We come, finally, to clause (iii). Suppose that P and Q are any mutually exclusive hypotheses. Now consider the following:

(9) con(P)$1 + con(Q)$1 + con(~(P v Q))$1

(10) ($1 if P, $0 if ~P), ($1 if Q, $0 if ~Q), ($1 if ~(P v Q), $0 if P v Q)

(11) $1

Since (10) is a decomposition of (11)—it is logically impossible that the realization of the sequence (10) effect (*qua* realization) a different net change in your fortune than the realization of (11) will[13]—and since (9) is the sum of the monetary values you place on the terms of (10), Decomposition requires that (9) be the monetary value you place on (11). Since both (9) and (11) are sums of money, Dominance requires that they be equal sums; i.e. (dropping superfluous 1s and dollar signs), that

$con(P) + con(Q) + con(\sim(P \vee Q)) = 1$.

Now consider

(12) $con(P \vee Q)\$1 + con(\sim(P \vee Q))\$1$

(13) ($1 if P v Q, $0 if $\sim(P \vee Q)$), ($1 if $\sim$P v Q), $0 if P v Q)

(14) $1

Since (13) is a decomposition of (14) and (12) is the sum of the monetary values you place on the terms of (13), Decomposition requires that (12) be the monetary value you place on (14)— by Dominance, that (12) and (14) be equal sums: i.e. that

$$con(P \vee Q) + con(\sim(P \vee Q)) = 1.$$

From these two equations, we get

$$con(P) + con(Q) + con(\sim(P \vee Q)) = con(P \vee Q) \\ + con(\sim(P \vee Q)).$$

Subtracting $con(\sim(P \vee Q))$ from each side:

$$con(P) + con(Q) = con(P \vee Q).$$

With the proof of Probabilism, our epistemological result is at hand. Recall that you invest more confidence in h than in ~h, the same amount of confidence in g as in ~g—and all with good reason. The question is, "In which (if either) of h and g should you then invest more confidence?" We know this much: insofar as you satisfy Modest Connectedness,

(i′) you have ruled out every monetary assignment to all well-mannered states of affairs on which $con(g) \neq con(\sim g)$;

(ii′) you have ruled out every assignment on which $con(\sim h) > con(h)$;

(iii′) you have not ruled out at least one assignment on which $con(h) > con(\sim h)$; and

(to update (iv) in the light of our derivation of Probabilism)

(iv′) you have ruled out every assignment

on which $con(-)$ does not satisfy the Kolmogorov axioms of probability (i.e. on which $con(-)$ does not satisfy the three clauses of Probabilism).

And we know that, if we can show that, among the assignments left, there is none on which $con(g) > con(h)$ and at least one on which $con(h) > con(g)$, we will have shown that (on pain of violating Confidence or Modest Connectedness) you must invest more confidence in h than in g.

What do (i′)–(iv′) tell us about the assignments that are left? (iv′) tells us, by the first clause of Probabilism, that on each of these assignments

$$con(g) \geq 0 \ ' \ con(\sim g)$$

and, by the second and third clauses of Probabilism,

$$con(g) + con(\sim g) = con(g \vee \sim g) = 1.$$

(i′) tells us that, on each of these assignments,

$$con(g) = con(\sim g).$$

From this it follows that, on each of the assignments that you have not ruled out,

$$con(g) = 0.5.$$

(iv′) likewise tells us that, on each of these assignments,

$$con(h) \geq 0 \ ' \ con(\sim h)$$

and

$$con(h) + con(\sim h) = 1.$$

Given this, it follows from (ii′) that there is no assignment left on which

$$0.5 > con(h),$$

and thus none on which

$$con(g) > con(h).$$

Finally, (iii′) tells us that at least one assignment is left on which

$$con(h) > 0.5,$$

and thus at least one on which

$$con(h) > con(g).$$

So it follows from (i′)–(iv′) that there is no assignment left on which $con(g) > con(h)$ and at least one left on which $con(h) > con(g)$. On pain of violating Modest Connectedness, you must prefer (\$1 if h, \$0 if ~h) to (\$1 if g, \$0 if ~g). By Confidence, this means you must invest more confidence in h than in g. In the decision problem with which I began this chapter, you must take the ticket.

IV Modest probabilism

So far, we have exploited Modest Connectedness in a narrow way. We have drawn from it just those of its consequences that bear directly on the solution of the decision problem with which this chapter began. But that problem is now solved. It is time to take a broader view. It is time to see what general morals, epistemological and decision-theoretic, Modest Connectedness holds for us.

We already know all we need to know to see the general epistemological moral. We know, from Probabilism, that every assignment of monetary values to all well-mannered states of affairs contains, as a proper part, an assignment of values of con(-) to all hypotheses, a *con-assignment*.

We know, from Confidence, that you are equally confident that P as you are that Q iff you are indifferent between (\$1 if P, \$0 if ~P) and (\$1 if Q, \$0 if ~Q); iff (by Modest Connected-

ness) you have ruled out every assignment of monetary values to all well-mannered states of affairs which fails to place the same monetary value on the two states of affairs; iff (by the definition of con(-)) you have ruled out every assignment of monetary values to all well-mannered states of affairs on which $con(P) \neq con(Q)$; iff you have ruled out every con-assignment on which $con(P) \neq con(Q)$.

We know, from Confidence, that you are more confident that P than you are that Q iff you prefer (\$1 if P, \$0 if ~P) to (\$1 if Q, \$0 if ~Q); iff (by Modest Connectedness) you have ruled out every assignment of monetary values to all well-mannered states of affairs which places a greater monetary value on the latter state of affairs and you have not ruled out every assignment that places a greater value on the former; iff (by the definition of con(-)) you have ruled out every assignment of monetary values to all well-mannered states of affairs on which $con(Q) > con(P)$ and not every assignment on which $con(P) > con(Q)$; iff you have ruled out every con-assignment on which $con(Q) > con(P)$ and not every con-assignment on which $con(P) > con(Q)$.

Finally, we know from Modest Connectedness that you have ruled out every assignment of monetary values to all well-mannered states of affairs that does not satisfy Ordering, Dominance, and Decomposition; thus (by the definition of con(-) and Probabilism) every con-assignment that does not satisfy the Kolmogorov axioms of probability.

From all this, it follows that

1.7 Modest Probabilism. Your state of opinion is characterized by a non-empty set W of con-assignments where each of the assignments satisfies the Kolmogorov axioms of probability, and where

(i)   you are just as confident that P as you are that Q just in case, on every member of W, $con(P) = con(Q)$; and

(ii)   you are more confident that P than that Q just in case, on no member of W, $con(Q) > con(P)$ and, on at least one member of W, $con(P) > con(Q)$.

To satisfy Confidence and Modest Connectedness, you must satisfy Modest Probabilism.

The decision-theoretic moral that Modest Connectedness holds in store is a bit further from the surface. The reason, in large part, is that the decision problem with which I began this chapter was so simple and convenient: it follows from Confidence that, if I could convince you that you should invest more confidence in h than g, I would have convinced you that you should prefer the ticket to the coupon. There was no need to find out in any generality what constraint Modest Connectedness imposes on your preferences. What we will see now is that, insofar as you satisfy Modest Connectedness, *all* your preferences and indifferences among all well-mannered states of affairs will be just as completely determined by your state of opinion as your preference for the ticket over the coupon was.

It is pretty easy to see that, if you nominate a precise value for $con(h)$ (and satisfy Ordering, Dominance, and Decomposition) you will do more than just place a monetary value on ($1 if h, $0 if ~h). Consider, for example,

(15) $con(h)$3

(16)   ($1 if h, $0 if ~h), ($1 if h, $0 if ~h), ($1 if h, $0 if ~h)

(17)   ($3 if h, $0 if ~h).

Since the sequence (16) is a decomposition of (17), and since (15) is the sum of the monetary values $(con(h)$1 + con(h)$1 + con(h)$1)$ you place on the terms of (16), Decomposition requires that you place the monetary value (15) on (17)—i.e. that $con(h)$3 be the monetary value you place on ($3 if h, $0 if ~h). Thus, if you nominate a value for $con(h)$ [place a monetary value on ($1 if h, $0 if ~h)], you

have placed a monetary value on ($3 if h, $0 if ~h) as well. The conclusion is entirely generalizable:

1.8 If an assignment of monetary values to all well-mannered states of affairs satisfies Ordering, Dominance, and Decomposition, then for any real number a and hypothesis P, it assigns the value $con(P)$a$ to ($a if P, $0 if ~P).

Given this much, we can show that, so long as it satisfies Ordering, Dominance, and Decomposition, an assignment of monetary values to all well-mannered states of affairs is entirely determined by its *con*-assignment:

1.9 Expectation. Where $\{a_1, \ldots, a_n\}$ and $\{b_1, \ldots, b_m\}$ are any sets of rational numbers and $\{P_1, \ldots, P_n\}$ and $\{Q_1, \ldots, Q_m\}$ any sets of mutually exclusive and jointly exhaustive hypotheses, an assignment of monetary values to all well-mannered states of affairs that satisfies Ordering, Dominance, and Decomposition places a greater monetary value on ($a_1 if P_1, \ldots,$ $a_n if P_n) than it places on ($b_1 if Q_1, \ldots,$ $b_m if Q_m) if and only if it assigns the former greater *subjectively expected monetary value*: that is, if and only if the assignment is one on which $(con(P_1)\ \$a_1 + \ldots + con(P_n)\$a_n) > (con(Q_1)\$b_1 + \ldots + con(Q_m)\ \$b_m)$.

And with this, the decision-theoretic moral Modest Connectedness has for us is clear: insofar as you satisfy Modest Connectedness, you must satisfy the following principle.

1.10 Modest Expectation. Your preferences are characterized by a non-empty set V of assignments of monetary values to all well-mannered states of affairs that satisfy Ordering, Dominance, and Decomposition, where

(i) you are indifferent between A and B just in case every member of V assigns A the same subjectively expected monetary value as it assigns B; and

(ii) you prefer A to B just in case no member of V assigns B a greater subjectively expected monetary value than it assigns A and some member of V assigns A a greater subjectively expected monetary value than it assigns B.

V The sin of false precision

It is important to bear in mind that, despite the fact that Confidence and Modest Connectedness proved decisive in solving the decision problem with which I began this chapter, it is *not* a consequence of these principles that your confidence rankings will invariably provide solutions to your decision problems.

For example, suppose I were to alter the decision problem by replacing the option of taking the coupon with the option of taking $0.75. Your choice now is between ($1 if h, $0 if ~h) and $0.75. It is still the case that you invest more confidence in h than you do in ~h. So, by Modest Probabilism, you are still bound to rule out any con-assignment on which $0.5 > con(h)$, and not to rule out at least one on which $con(h) > 0.5$. That is, you are bound to rule out any assignment of monetary values to all well-mannered states of affairs which places a value less than $0.50 on ($1 if h, $0 if ~h), and not to rule out at least one that nominates a value greater than $0.50. But that leaves you with some assignments which place a value greater than $0.75 on ($1 if h, $0 if ~h) and some that nominate a value that is less than $0.75. The fact that you invest more confidence in h than you do in ~h and you satisfy Confidence and Modest Connectedness provides you with no solution to your decision problem. It leaves you undecided.

Notes

1 Thus, for example, I will be assuming that, if j is the hypothesis that you will receive $5 from your uncle, then ($100 if j, $0 if ~j) includes that $5 in the $100 prize you win if j.

2 The demand that your indifferences be transitive is sometimes expressed "if you are indifferent between A and B and indifferent between B and C, then you should be indifferent between A and C." But this is a mistake. Once you harbor the first two indifferences, there are two ways to avoid opening your preferences and indifferences to criticism, not one: you can either be indifferent between A and C or abandon at least one of the first two indifferences. Similar remarks apply to the second clause of Ordering, which I introduce below.

3 Given that you are undecided between no two of A, B, and C, this second clause says that if you either prefer B to A or are indifferent between them and you either prefer C to B or are indifferent between them, then you either prefer C to A or are indifferent between them.

To see how the transitivity of your indifference and preference follows from Ordering, suppose that A, B, and C are any well-mannered states of affairs between no pair of which you are undecided. Let "A ~ B" signify that you are indifferent between A and B, "A > B" that you prefer A to B. Then A > B, B > A, and A ~ B are mutually exclusive and they exhaust the preferential attitudes you may have toward the pair A and B; in particular, A ~ B iff A ⊁ B and B ⊁ A.

First, the transitivity of your indifference. Suppose A ~ B and B ~ C. Then A ⊁ B and B ⊁ C and so, by Ordering, A ⊁ C. Likewise, C ⊁ B and B ⊁ A and so, by Ordering, C ⊁ A. But, if A ⊁ C and C ⊁ A, A ~ C. Thus, if A ~ B and B ~ C, A ~ C.

Now the transitivity of your preference. Suppose A > B and B > C. Suppose, for reductio that A ⊁ C. From A ⊁ C and the supposition that B > C—and hence that C ⊁ B—it follows by Ordering that A ⊁ B, which contradicts the assumption that A > B. So, if A > B and B > C, A > C.

Some other consequences of Ordering: where A, B, C, and D are any well-mannered states of affairs between no pair of which you are undecided, if $A > B$ and $B \sim C$, then $A > C$; if $A \sim B$ and $B > C$, then $A > C$; if $A > B$, $B \sim C$, and $C > D$, then $A > D$.

4 This consideration leads Hilary Putnam (Putnam 1967) to argue that principles linking confidence and betting are incapable of illuminating scientific inquiry.

5 For example, Dominance says, "Where A is the well-mannered state of affairs, (a_1 if P_1, . . ., a_n if P_n) . . ." not "Where A is *a* well-mannered state of affairs, (a_1 if P_1, . . ., a_n if P_n). . . ."

6 That is, apart from what other consequences the realization of the sequence might have.

7 Consider, for example, ($1 if h, $0 if $\sim h$). For every positive natural number n, there is a distinct decomposition of ($1 if h, $0 if $\sim h$), consisting of a sequence of n terms each of which is identical to ($1/n$ if h, $0 if $\sim h$).

8 It might be thought that you do something stronger when you prefer A to B: you rule out any assignment that does not place a greater monetary value on A. But this is surely wrong. For suppose that (as far as you are concerned) the monetary value of A is at least as great as that of B and possibly greater. You haven't ruled out every assignment of monetary values to all states of affairs that places the same value on A as on B—you are still open to the possibility that A is no more valuable than B. But, having closed the possibility that B is more valuable than A and having not done likewise to the possibility A is more valuable than B, you will surely prefer A to B all the same. [. . .]

9 This non-emptiness condition has also been put forward in Ellis 1979, pp. 15–6; Skyrms 1984, pp. 28–9; Jeffrey 1983, pp. 139–41; Maher 1993, p. 20—although the first three writers appear more sympathetic to the stronger principle, Immodest Connectedness, than I am (see section V below). I should note that there are two distinct considerations that lie behind the condition. The first is the intuition that, even if the preferences and indifferences you harbor do not corporately violate Ordering, Dominance, or Decomposition in any way, they are still subject to criticism if they so tie your hands that there is no way you could decide all the matters about which you are now undecided without either violating at least one of the three principles or abandoning some of your current preferences or indifferences. The second is an archimedean assumption (so called for its affinity to Euclid's archimedean axiom—see Krantz *et al.* 1971, pp. 25–6): that the only way you are permitted to decide all those matters is by placing a monetary value on each well-mannered state of affairs.

Although the intuition is (in my view) quite compelling, the archimedean assumption is not. You could decide all matters about which you are undecided without placing a monetary value on each well-mannered state of affairs. Suppose for some well-mannered state of affairs A, you preferred A to every sum of money less than or equal to a and preferred every sum of money greater than a to A. You would suffer no indecision between sums of money and A but you would also fail to place a monetary value on A: for every sum of money a, you would either prefer A to a or prefer a to A.

On the other hand, apart from blocking this way of deciding matters, the archimedean assumption is completely unrestrictive—it imposes no further constraint on your preferences at all. And herein lies its innocence. Although reason cannot be said to demand that you satisfy the archimedean assumption, there also seems no reason why you would want *not* to satisfy it.

10 By virtue of (iii), there is no need to add that there is at least one assignment you have not ruled out.

11 That is, if their conjunction entails a contradiction.

12 For any hypothesis P, $con(P) = r$ iff you place a monetary value equal to $r on ($1 if P, $0 if P)— that is, iff you are indifferent between $r and ($1 if P, $0 if $\sim$P) where both are well-mannered states of affairs. And, by definition, $r is a well-mannered state of affairs only if r is a real number.

13 Notice that, were it logically possible that P & Q, (10) would *not* count as a decomposition of (11): in the event that P & Q, the realization of (10) would increase your fortune by $2. But since, by assumption, P and Q are mutually exclusive, P & Q is not logically possible and, thus, it is logically impossible that the realization of (10) increases your fortune by $2. When it is not the case that P & Q, the realization of (10) will increase your fortune by $1.

References

Ellis, Brian. 1979. *Rational Belief Systems*. Oxford: Basil Blackwell.

Jeffrey, Richard. 1983. "Bayesianism with a Human Face," in John Earman (ed.) *Testing Scientific Theories*. Minneapolis: University of Minnesota Press.

Krantz, David H., R. Duncan Luce, Patrick Suppes, and Amos Tversky. 1971. *Foundations of Measurement*, vol. 1. New York: Academic Press.

Maher, Patrick. 1993. *Betting on Theories*. Cambridge: Cambridge University Press.

Putnam, Hilary. 1967. "Probability and Confirmation," in Sidney Morgenbesser (ed.) *Philosophy of Science Today*. New York: Basic Books, pp. 100–14.

Skyrms, Brian. 1984. *Pragmatics and Empiricism*. New Haven, CT: Yale University Press.

Chapter 14

Adam Elga

SELF-LOCATING BELIEF AND THE SLEEPING BEAUTY PROBLEM

In addition to being uncertain about what the world is like, one can also be uncertain about one's own spatial or temporal location in the world. My aim is to pose a problem arising from the interaction between these two sorts of uncertainty, solve the problem, and draw two lessons from the solution.

1

The Sleeping Beauty problem:[1] Some researchers are going to put you to sleep. During the two days that your sleep will last, they will briefly wake you up either once or twice, depending on the toss of a fair coin (Heads: once; Tails: twice). After each waking, they will put you to back to sleep with a drug that makes you forget that waking.[2] When you are first awakened, to what degree ought you believe that the outcome of the coin toss is Heads?

First answer: 1/2, of course! Initially you were certain that the coin was fair, and so initially your credence in the coin's landing Heads was 1/2. Upon being awakened, you receive no new information (you knew all along that you would be awakened). So your credence in the coin's landing Heads ought to remain 1/2.

Second answer: 1/3, of course! Imagine the experiment repeated many times. Then in the long run, about 1/3 of the wakings would be *Heads-wakings*—wakings that happen on trials in which the coin lands Heads. So on any particular waking, you should have credence 1/3 that that waking is a Heads-waking, and hence have credence 1/3 in the coin's landing Heads on that trial. This consideration remains in force in the present circumstance, in which the experiment is performed just once.

I will argue that the correct answer is 1/3.

2

Suppose that the first waking happens on Monday, and that the second waking (if there is one) happens on Tuesday. Then when you wake up, you're certain that you're in one of three "predicaments":

H_1 HEADS and it is Monday.
T_1 TAILS and it is Monday.
T_2 TAILS and it is Tuesday.

Notice that the difference between your being in T_1 and your being in T_2 is not a difference in which possible world is actual, but rather a difference in your temporal location within the world. (In a more technical treatment we might adopt a framework similar to the one suggested in Lewis 1983, according to which the elementary alternatives over which your credence is divided are not possible worlds, but rather *centered possible worlds*: possible worlds each of which is equipped with a designated individual and time. In such a framework, H_1, T_1, and T_2 would be represented by appropriate sets of centered worlds.)

Let P be the credence function you ought to have upon first awakening. Upon first awakening, you are certain of the following: you are in predicament H_1 if and only if the outcome of the coin toss is Heads. Therefore, calculating $P(H_1)$ is sufficient to solve the Sleeping Beauty problem. I will argue first that $P(T_1) = P(T_2)$, and then that $P(H_1) = P(T_1)$.

If (upon first awakening) you were to learn that the toss outcome is Tails, that would amount to your learning that you are in either T_1 or T_2. Since being in T_1 is subjectively just like being in T_2, and since exactly the same propositions are true whether you are in T_1 or T_2, even a highly restricted principle of indifference yields that you ought then to have equal credence in each. But your credence that you are in T_1, after learning that the toss outcome is Tails, ought to be the same as the conditional credence $P(T_1 | T_1$ or $T_2)$, and likewise for T_2. So $P(T_1 | T_1$ or $T_2) = P(T_2 | T_1$ or $T_2)$, and hence $P(T_1) = P(T_2)$.

The researchers have the task of using a fair coin to determine whether to awaken you once or twice. They might accomplish their task by either

1 first tossing the coin and then waking you up either once or twice depending on the outcome; or

2 first waking you up once, and *then* tossing the coin to determine whether to wake you up a second time.

Your credence (upon awakening) in the coin's landing Heads ought to be the same regardless of whether the researchers use method 1 or 2. So without loss of generality suppose that they use—and you know that they use—method 2.

Now: if (upon awakening) you were to learn that it is Monday, that would amount to your learning that you are in either H_1 or T_1. Your credence that you are in H_1 would then be your credence that a fair coin, soon to be tossed,

will land Heads. It is irrelevant that you will be awakened on the following day if and only if the coin lands Tails—in this circumstance, your credence that the coin will land Heads ought to be 1/2. But your credence that the coin will land Heads (after learning that it is Monday) ought to be the same as the conditional credence $P(H_1 | H_1$ or $T_1)$. So $P(H_1 | H_1$ or $T_1) = 1/2$, and hence $P(H_1) = P(T_1)$.

Combining results, we have that $P(H_1) = P(T_1) = P(T_2)$. Since these credences sum to 1, $P(H_1) = 1/3$.

3

Let H be the proposition that the outcome of the coin toss is Heads. Before being put to sleep, your credence in H was 1/2. I've just argued that when you are awakened on Monday, that credence ought to change to 1/3. This belief change is unusual. It is not the result of your receiving new information—you were already certain that you would be awakened on Monday.[3] (We may even suppose that you knew at the start of the experiment exactly what sensory experiences you would have upon being awakened on Monday.) Neither is this belief change the result of your suffering any cognitive mishaps during the intervening time—recall that the forgetting drug isn't administered until well *after* you are first awakened. So what justifies it?

The answer is that you have gone from a situation in which you count your own temporal location as *irrelevant* to the truth of H, to one in which you count your own temporal location as *relevant* to the truth of H.[4] Suppose, for example, that at the start of the experiment, you weren't sure whether it was 1:01 or 1:02. At that time, you counted your temporal location as irrelevant to the truth of H: your credence in H, conditional on its being 1:01, was 1/2, and your credence in H, conditional on its being 1:02, was *also* 1/2.

In contrast (assuming that you update your beliefs rationally), when you are awakened on Monday, you count your current temporal location as *relevant* to the truth of H: your credence in H, conditional on its being Monday, is 1/2, but your credence in H, conditional on its being Tuesday, is 0. On Monday, your unconditional credence in H differs from 1/2 because it is a weighted average of these two conditional credences—that is, a weighted average of 1/2 and 0.

It is no surprise that the manner in which an agent counts her own temporal location as relevant to the truth of some proposition can change over time. What is surprising—and this is the first lesson—is that this sort of change can happen to a perfectly rational agent during a period in which that agent neither receives new information nor suffers a cognitive mishap.

At the start of the experiment, you had credence 1/2 in H. But you were also certain that upon being awakened on Monday you would have credence 1/3 in H—even though you were certain that you would receive no new information and suffer no cognitive mishaps during the intervening time. Thus the Sleeping Beauty example provides a new variety of counter-example to Bas van Fraassen's 'Reflection Principle' (1984: 244, 1995: 19), even an extremely qualified version of which entails the following:

> Any agent who is certain that she will tomorrow have credence *x* in proposition R (though she will neither receive new information nor suffer any cognitive mishaps in the intervening time) ought *now* to have credence *x* in R.[5]

David Lewis once asked, "what happens to decision theory if we [replace the space of possible worlds by the space of centered possible worlds]?" and answered, "Not much." (Lewis 1983: 149). A second lesson of the Sleeping Beauty problem is that something *does* happen. Namely: at least one new question arises about how a rational agent ought to update her beliefs over time.[6]

Notes

1 So named by Robert Stalnaker (who first learned of examples of this kind in unpublished work by Arnold Zuboff). This problem appears as Example 5 of Piccione and Rubenstein, which motivates two distinct answers but suspends judgment as to which answer is correct (1997: 12–14). Aumann *et al.* 1997 uses a fair lottery approach to analyze a similar problem. Adapted to the Sleeping Beauty problem, that analysis yields the same answer as the one I will defend in section 2. However, unlike the argument in Aumann *et al.* 1997, my argument does not depend on betting considerations.

2 The precise effect of the drug is to reset your belief-state to what it was just before you were put to sleep at the beginning of the experiment. If the existence of such a drug seems fanciful, note that it is possible to pose the problem without it—all that matters is that the person put to sleep *believes* that the setup is as I have described it.

3 To say that an agent receives new information (as I shall use that expression) is to say that the agent receives evidence that rules out possible worlds not already ruled out by her previous evidence. Put another way, an agent receives new information when she learns the truth of a proposition express-ible by an eternal sentence (Quine 1960: 191) of some appropriately rich language.

4 To say that an agent counts her temporal location as relevant to the truth of a certain proposition is to say that there is a time t such that the agent's beliefs are compatible with her being located at t, and her credence in the proposition, conditional on her being located at t, differs from her unconditional credence in the proposition.

5 I am indebted to Ned Hall for pointing out that an answer of 1/3 conflicts with the Reflection Principle.

6 Many thanks to Jamie Dreier, Gary Gates, Ned Hall, Vann McGee, Robert Stalnaker, Roger White, Sarah Wright, the participants in a 1999 conference at Brown University (at which an earlier version of this paper was presented), and an anonymous referee.

References

Aumann, R. J., S. Hart, and M. Perry. 1997. The forgetful passenger. *Games and Economic Behavior* 20: 117–120.

Lewis, D. 1983. Attitudes de dicto and de se. In his *Philosophical Papers, Volume I*, 133–159. New York: Oxford University Press.

Piccione, M. and A. Rubenstein. 1997. On the interpretation of decision problems with imperfect recall. *Games and Economic Behavior* 20: 3–24.

Quine, W. V. 1960. *Word and Object*. Cambridge, Mass.: The MIT Press.

van Fraassen, B. C. 1984. Belief and the will. *Journal of Philosophy* 81: 235–256.

——. B. C. 1995. Belief and the problem of Ulysses and the Sirens. *Philosophical Studies* 77: 7–37.

Chapter 15

Paul Hoffman

GETTING THE GOAT

My only advice is, if you can get me to offer you $5,000 not to open the door, take the money and go home.

(Monty Hall)

Although numbers were Erdős's intimate friends, he did occasionally misjudge them. Good as he was, his intuition was not always perfect. Indeed, the last time he visited Vázsonyi, at his retirement home in California's wine country, he tripped up on a tricky brain teaser posed in "Ask Marilyn," Marilyn vos Savant's column in *Parade* magazine. Flashy and confident, vos Savant is someone professional mathematicians love to hate. She bills herself as the person with the "Highest IQ" ever recorded, a whopping 228, according to *The Guinness Book of World Records*. She sports a wedding ring of pyrolytic carbon, a special material used in the Jarvik artificial heart, which was invented by her husband, Robert Jarvik. Her reputation in the mathematics community was not helped by her book *The World's Most Famous Math Problem* (1993), in which she questions Wiles's proof of Fermat's Last Theorem and Einstein's theory of relativity. "Ask Marilyn" has been described as a kind of "Hints from Heloise" for the mind, with lots of mathematics thrown in. Some of the dislike for her stems from puzzle envy: Her *Parade* column is read by millions every Sunday, and the accompanying books and speaking engagements have earned her a good living. Many professional mathematicians, on the other hand, have not earned a cent from their books.

In her column for September 9, 1990, vos Savant answered a well-known brain teaser submitted by one of her readers. You're on a game show and you're given the choice of three doors. Behind one door is a car, behind the other two are goats. You choose, say, door 1, and the host, who knows where the car is, opens another door, behind which is a goat. He now gives you the choice of sticking with door 1 or switching to the other door? What should you do?

This was the so-called Monty Hall dilemma faced by guests on Monty Hall's classic TV game show *Let's Make a Deal*, only the consolation prizes weren't goats. Vos Savant advised her correspondent to switch doors. Sticking with the first choice gives a one-third chance of winning, she said, but switching doubles the odds to two-thirds. To convince her readers, she asked them to imagine a million doors. "You pick door No. 1," she said. "Then the host, who knows what's behind the doors and will always avoid the one with the prize, opens them all except door No. 777,777. You'd switch to the door pretty fast, wouldn't you?"

Evidently not. No sooner had her column appeared than she was besieged by mail from readers who disagreed, including many mathematicians. They maintained the odds were only fifty-fifty, not two-thirds, in favor of switching.

In her December 2, 1990, column vos Savant ran some of the letters:

As a professional mathematician, I'm very concerned with the general public's lack of mathematical skills. Please help by confessing your error.

(Robert Sachs, Ph.D., George Mason University)

You blew it, and you blew it big! I'll explain: After the host reveals a goat, you now have a one-in-two chance of being correct. Whether you change your answer or not, the odds are the same. There is enough mathematical illiteracy in this country, and we don't need the world's highest IQ propagating more. Shame!

(Scott Smith, Ph.D., University of Florida)

This time, to drive her analysis home, vos Savant made a table that exhaustively listed the six possible outcomes:

Door 1	Door 2	Door 3	Outcome
(choose No. 1 and stick with No. 1)			
Car	Goat	Goat	Win
Goat	Car	Goat	Lose
Goat	Goat	Car	Lose

Door 1	Door 2	Door 3	Outcome
(choose No. 1 and switch)			
Car	Goat	Goat	Lose
Goat	Car	Goat	Win
Goat	Goat	Car	Win

The table demonstrates, she wrote, that "when you switch, you win two out of three times and lose one time in three; but when you don't switch, you only win one in three times."

But the table did not silence her critics. In a third column on the subject (February 17, 1991), she said the thousands of letters she received were running nine to one against her and included rebukes from a statistician at the National Institutes of Health and the deputy director of the Center for Defense Information. The letters had gotten shrill, with suggestions that she was the goat and that women look at mathematical problems differently from men. "You are utterly incorrect about the game-show question," wrote E. Ray Bobo, a Ph.D. at Georgetown, "and I hope this controversy will call some public attention to the serious national crisis in mathematical education. If you can admit your error, you will have contributed constructively toward the solution to a deplorable situation. How many irate mathematicians are needed to get you to change your mind?"

"When reality clashes so violently with intuition," vos Savant responded in her column, "people are shaken." This time she tried another tack. Imagine, she said, that just after the host opens the door, revealing a goat, a UFO lands on the game-show stage, and a little green woman emerges. Without knowing what door you originally chose, she is asked to choose one of the two unopened doors. The odds that she'll randomly choose the car are fifty-fifty. "But that's because she lacks the advantage the original contestant had—the help of the host. . . . If the prize is behind No. 2, the host shows you No. 3; and if the prize is behind No. 3, the host shows you No. 2. So when you switch, you win if the prize is behind No. 2 or No. 3. *YOU WIN EITHER WAY!* But if you *don't* switch, you win only if the prize is behind door No. 1." Vos Savant was completely correct, as mathematicians with egg on their faces ultimately had to admit.

PART FIVE

What is it to be justified in believing something?

INTRODUCTION TO PART FIVE

Ram Neta and Duncan Pritchard

I T IS ONE THING TO BE *very confident* that it will rain tonight. It is another thing to *believe* that it will rain tonight. If I believe that it will rain tonight, and then it turns out not to rain, it follows that I was wrong. But if I am very confident that it will rain tonight, and then it turns out not to rain, it doesn't follow that I was wrong. When you believe that p, you make it the case that, if p is not true, then you are wrong. But you don't make this the case just by being very confident that p is true. *Believing*, in contrast to *being confident*, involves rendering yourself vulnerable to being wrong. But why would it ever be a good idea to render yourself vulnerable to being wrong? Why not simply protect yourself from such vulnerability, by not believing anything, but simply being more or less confident of various things? Why bother sticking your neck out by *believing* things?

Of course, in some cases there is a very simple answer to such questions. For example, if I know that my boss will promote me if and only if I behave competently, and furthermore I know that I will behave competently if and only if I believe that I am competent, then it is clearly in my interest to believe that I am competent: even if I thereby render myself vulnerable to the risk of being wrong, I reap rewards that more than compensate me for those risks, viz. I enjoy a promotion. In cases such as this, it is clearly in my interest to hold a particular belief.

But is there anything *else* – independently of the practical costs or benefits of holding a belief – that could make it a good idea for me to believe something, and thereby render myself vulnerable to being wrong? Or, to ask this question in a slightly different way, what makes me *justified* in believing something? This is one of the central questions of epistemology.

Before surveying different proposed answers to this question, it will help us to understand the question a little better. What do we mean when we speak of being *justified*? What do epistemologists mean by the term 'justification'? There is no single answer to this question, because epistemologists use the term 'justification' to mean a number of things that differ from each other along different dimensions.

Sometimes, the term 'justification' is used to denote a property of beliefs (what is sometimes called 'doxastic justification'), whereas other times it is used to denote a property of persons (what is sometimes called 'propositional justification'). A belief is justified (i.e. doxastically justified) when the belief is held *in the right way*. Different theories of doxastic justification will give different accounts of what this 'right way' of holding a belief is (we'll mention some of those different accounts on p. 152). But they all agree on this, that whether your belief is justified depends upon the way in which that belief is held. That is not relevant, however, to the issue of whether a person is justified in holding a belief. A person may be justified (i.e. propositionally justified) in holding a belief no matter how, or even whether, she holds that belief. Thus, propositional justification is not the same as doxastic justification. The former might be necessary for the latter, but it is certainly not sufficient.

Now, no matter whether the term 'justification' is used to denote a property of beliefs or a property of persons, either way it may be used to denote a *quantity* (i.e. something of which there can be more or less), or else it may be used to denote a *modal property* (e.g. the status of being permissible – something that is not such that you ought not to believe it). In the first case, we may say that one belief is *more* justified than another belief, or that one person is *more* justified in believing a certain proposition than another person is, or that a person is *less* justified in believing one proposition than another. In the second case, when 'justification' is used to denote a modal status such as permissibility, we cannot say that one thing is more or less justified than another: permissibility is not a matter of more or less. It is an open question how, or whether, the modal notion of justification is related to the quantitative notion. Could belief *x* be more justified than belief *y* just in case belief *x* is closer to being (modally) justified than belief *y*? Or might there be some other relation between quantitative justification and modal justification? We will not attempt to address these questions here.

The two distinctions just mentioned give rise to four different kinds of 'justification' that epistemologists might try to understand, as shown in Figure 1. Some theories of justification are theories of only one of the four kinds of thing represented in Figure 1. Most of the readings gathered together in this part represent different accounts of *doxastic modal justification*: we have chosen these readings because they are relatively accessible, and they continue to be very influential in epistemology. Nonetheless, the reader should be aware that not all theories of justification are theories of doxastic modal justification.

	Propositional Justification	Doxastic Justification
Quantitative Justification		
Modal Justification		

Figure 1 Four varieties of epistemic justification

Now, with regard to each of the kinds of justification mentioned in Figure 1, epistemologists have divided into two schools of thought. Some epistemologists – let us call them 'internalists' – think that the only things that can confer justification (of whatever kind) are, in some sense, *intrinsic* features of your own mind, that is to say, they are features of your mind that are, in some sense, independent of how the extra-mental world is. Thus, according to the internalist about propositional modal justification, whether it is rationally permissible for you to believe something is determined solely by intrinsic features of your own mind. And similarly, according to the internalist about doxastic quantitative justification, the extent to which a particular belief of yours is justified is determined completely by intrinsic features of your own mind. Let's use the label 'externalist' to denote those philosophers who deny 'internalism' about one or another kind of justification. So, with respect to each variety of justification, a philosopher may be an internalist or an externalist about that variety of justification. And, of course, we can understand the distinction between internalism and externalism in as many different ways as we can understand the notion of something being 'intrinsic' to your own mind. For instance, we can understand the notion of something being intrinsic to your own mind in terms of its being epistemically accessible to you in some special way. Alternatively, we can understand the notion of something being intrinsic to your own mind in terms of its being completely determined by how things appear to you. We can also understand the notion of something being intrinsic to your own mind in various other ways. And so the distinction between internalism and externalism in the theory of justification can be drawn in different ways, and can apply to different topics (e.g. doxastic quantitative justification, propositional modal justification, etc.).

However we draw that distinction, the theory of justification that Alvin Goldman (1938–) advances in his article 'What Is Justified Belief?' (Chapter 16) will clearly count as an *externalist* theory of doxastic modal justification. Goldman is interested in the question of what it is for a particular belief, formed in a particular way, to be rationally permissible. Roughly the first half of Goldman's paper is devoted to criticising various internalist answers to this question. Goldman's own 'historical reliabilist' answer, to a first approximation, is this: for a belief to be rationally permissible is for the belief to be caused, or causally sustained, by a process that tends to produce true beliefs. Since it is generally thought that the fact that one's belief-forming process tends to produce true beliefs is not an intrinsic feature of one's own mind, it is also thought that Goldman's theory of doxastic modal justification is an externalist theory.

In contrast, Richard Feldman (1948–) and Earl Conee's (1951–) article 'Evidentialism' (Chapter 17) offers an internalist theory of doxastic modal justification (a theory they call 'evidentialism'), and also an internalist theory of doxastic modal justification (or what they call 'well-foundedness'). For Feldman and Conee, what determines whether a person is doxastically modally justified in holding a belief is simply that person's total evidence. Feldman and Conee devote most of their article to addressing the various objections (from Goldman and others) that have been levelled against this thesis.

William Alston (1921–) attempts to develop an account of doxastic modal justification that combines the strengths of reliabilism and the strengths of evidentialism in his article 'An Internalist Externalism' (Chapter 18). The internalistic feature of Alston's account is this: for Alston, whether a particular belief is justified is determined completely by features of the believer's perspective. But the externalistic feature of Alston's account is this: for Alston, a particular feature of a believer's perspective contributes to justifying a particular belief only if there is a high objective conditional probability of the belief being true, given that the believer has that feature in her perspective. Although this objective conditional probability is not, in any sense, an intrinsic feature of the believer's mind, it helps to determine whether a particular intrinsic feature of the believer's mind can make the believer's belief justified.

Epistemologists sometimes use the term 'justification' in a way that is not represented in Figure 1. For instance, I might be said to have a 'justification' for the proposition that *p* if I can offer a seemingly cogent argument in support of *p*. But from the fact that I have such a justification (i.e. from the fact that I can offer such an argument), it does not immediately follow that I am propositionally justified in believing that *p*, nor does it follow that my belief that *p* is doxastically justified. If, say, I fail to notice that I possess a compelling reason to think that the seemingly cogent argument that I can offer on behalf of *p* is not really a cogent argument, then, even if I have a justification for *p*, I am still not justified in believing that *p*, and my belief that *p* is not justified. So having a justification for *p* is not the same as being justified in believing that *p*, nor is it the same as justifiably believing that *p*.

Under what conditions does someone have a justification for a proposition *p*? This general question is raised, but not explicitly answered, by Lewis Carroll's (1832–98) story 'What the Tortoise Said to Achilles' (Chapter 19). Carroll's story contains two fictional characters, the Tortoise and Achilles. The latter is trying to persuade the former of a particular conclusion by arguing to that conclusion from two premises that the former accepts. But when Achilles sets out an argument, the Tortoise objects that the argument does not constitute a justification of its conclusion: it constitutes a justification of nothing stronger than the conditional that *if* the two other premises are true, *then* the conclusion is true. When Achilles proposes to add this conditional to the set of premises, the Tortoise objects that the newly supplemented set of three premises constitutes a justification of nothing other than the conditional that if the three premises are true, then the conclusion is true. When Achilles proposes to add this conditional to the set of premises, the Tortoise objects that the newly supplemented set of four premises constitutes a justification of nothing other than the conditional that if the four premises are true, then the conclusion is true. And so there arises a regress, and so, it may seem, either it is never possible to have a justification for any conclusion, or else having a justification for a conclusion will involve relying on some rules of inference that are not premises in the justification.

Study questions

1   How does Goldman argue against internalist theories of justification? How would Feldman and Conee reply to Goldman's argument?

2   Goldman offers a theory of modal doxastic justification. Can you try to extend his theory to account for quantitative doxastic justification? How about for modal propositional justification?

3   Feldman and Conee offer a theory of modal doxastic justification. Can you try to extend their theory to account for quantitative doxastic justification? How about for modal propositional justification?

4   On what points, if any, would Alston disagree with Feldman and Conee's evidentialism? On what points, if any, would he disagree with Goldman's reliabilism?

5   What is the difference between being justified in believing something and having a justification to believe it?

6   Is Lewis Carroll's dialogue 'What the Tortoise said to Achilles' supposed to suggest to its reader an argument for some conclusion? If so, then what is the argument, and what is its conclusion?

Further reading

Students interested in thinking more about the topic addressed in this part should read the essays in Alston (1989) and Audi (1993): many of the issues that come up in the course of thinking about what makes one justified in believing something are explicitly and carefully discussed in those essays. Swinburne (2001) is an excellent and accessible monograph on the topic of epistemic justification. Finally, BonJour and Sosa (2003) is a very clearly presented book-length exchange between Laurence BonJour and Ernest Sosa on the question of what makes us justified in belief. The exchange provides an unusual opportunity for students to witness a philosophical exchange between two of the most important living researchers in this field.

References

Alston, William. 1989. *Epistemic Justification: Essays in the Theory of Knowledge*, Ithaca, NY and London: Cornell University Press.

Audi, Robert. 1993. *The Structure of Justification*, Cambridge: Cambridge University Press.

BonJour, Laurence and Sosa, Ernest. 2003. *Epistemic Justification: Internalism vs. Externalism, Foundations vs. Virtues*, London and Malden, MA: Blackwell.

Swinburne, Richard. 2001. *Epistemic Justification*, Oxford: Clarendon Press.

Chapter 16

Alvin Goldman

RELIABILISM: WHAT IS JUSTIFIED BELIEF?

The aim of this essay is to sketch a theory of justified belief. What I have in mind is an explanatory theory, one that explains in a general way why certain beliefs are counted as justified and others as unjustified. Unlike some traditional approaches, I do not try to prescribe standards for justification that differ from, or improve upon, our ordinary standards. I merely try to explicate the ordinary standards, which are, I believe, quite different from those of many classical, e.g. "Cartesian," accounts.

Many epistemologists have been interested in justification because of its presumed close relationship to knowledge. This relationship is intended to be preserved in the conception of justified belief presented here. In previous papers on knowledge,[1] I have denied that justification is necessary for knowing, but there I had in mind "Cartesian" accounts of justification. On the account of justified belief suggested here, it is necessary for knowing, and closely related to it.

The term "justified," I presume, is an evaluative term, a term of appraisal. Any correct definition or synonym of it would also feature evaluative terms. I assume that such definitions or synonyms might be given, but I am not interested in them. I want a set of *substantive* conditions that specify when a belief is justified. Compare the normal term "right." This might be defined in other ethical terms or phrases, a task appropriate to meta-ethics. The task of normative ethics, by contrast, is to state substantive conditions for the rightness of actions. Normative ethics tries to specify non-ethical conditions that determine when an action is right. A familiar example is act-utilitarianism, which says an action is right if and only if it produces, or would produce, at least as much net happiness as any alternative open to the agent. These necessary and sufficient conditions clearly involve no ethical notions. Analogously, I want a theory of justified belief to specify in non-epistemic terms when a belief is justified. This is not the only kind of theory of justifiedness one might seek, but it is one important kind of theory and the kind sought here.

In order to avoid epistemic terms in our theory, we must know which terms are epistemic. Obviously, an exhaustive list cannot be given, but here are some examples: "justified," "warranted," "has (good) grounds," "has reason (to believe)," "knows that," "sees that," "apprehends that," "is probable" (in an epistemic or inductive sense), "shows that," "establishes that," and "ascertains that." By contrast, here are some sample non-epistemic expressions: "believe that," "is true," "causes," "it is necessary that," "implies," "is deducible from," and "is probable" (either in the frequency sense or the propensity sense). In general, (purely) doxastic, metaphysical, modal, semantic, or syntactic expressions are not epistemic.

There is another constraint I wish to place on a theory of justified belief, in addition to the constraint that it be couched in non-epistemic language. Since I seek an explanatory theory, i.e. one that clarifies the underlying source of justificational status, it is not enough for a theory to state "correct" necessary and sufficient conditions. Its conditions must also be appropriately deep or revelatory. Suppose, for example, that the following sufficient condition of justified belief is offered: "If S senses redly at t and S believes at t that he is sensing redly, then S's belief at t that he is sensing redly is justified." This is not the kind of principle I seek; for, even if it is correct, it leaves unexplained *why* a person who senses redly and believes that he does, believes this justifiably. Not every state is such that if one is in it and believes one is in it, this belief is justified. What is distinctive about the state of sensing redly, or "phenomenal" states in general? A theory of justified belief of the kind I seek must answer this question, and hence it must be couched at a suitably deep, general, or abstract level.

A few introductory words about my *explicandum* are appropriate at this juncture. It is often assumed that whenever a person has a justified belief, he knows that it is justified and knows what the justification is. It is further assumed that the person can state or explain what his justification is. On this view, a justification is an argument, defense, or set of reasons that can be given in support of a belief. Thus, one studies the nature of justified belief by considering what a person might *say* if asked to defend, or justify, his belief. I make none of these sorts of assumptions here. I leave it an open question whether, when a belief *is* justified, the believer *knows* it is justified. I also leave it an open question whether, when a belief is justified, the believer can *state* or *give* a justification for it. I do not even assume that when a belief is justified there is something "possessed" by the believer which can be called a "justification." I do assume that a justified belief gets its status of being justified from some processes or properties that make it justified. In short, there must be some justification-conferring processes or properties. But this does not imply that there must be an argument, or reason, or anything else, "possessed" at the time of belief by the believer.

I

A theory of justified belief will be a set of principles that specify truth-conditions for the schema [S's belief in p at time t is justified], i.e. conditions for the satisfaction of this schema in all possible cases. It will be convenient to formulate candidate theories in a recursive or inductive format, which would include (A) one or more base clauses, (B) a set of recursive clauses (possibly null), and (C) a closure clause. In such a format, it is permissible for the predicate "is a justified belief" to appear in recursive clauses. But neither this predicate, nor any other epistemic predicate, may appear in (the antecedent of) any base-clause.[2]

Before turning to my own theory, I want to survey some other possible approaches to justified belief. Identification of problems associated with other attempts will provide some motivation for the theory I shall offer. Obviously, I cannot examine all, or even very many, alternative attempts. But a few sample attempts will be instructive.

Let us concentrate on the attempt to formulate one or more adequate base-clause principles.[3] Here is a classical candidate:

(1) If S believes p at t, and p is indubitable for S (at t), then S's belief in p at t is justified.

To evaluate this principle, we need to know what "indubitable" means. It can be understood in at least two ways. First, "p is indubitable for S" might mean: "S has no *grounds* for doubting p." Since "ground" is an epistemic term, however, principle (1) would be inadmissible in this reading, for epistemic terms may not legitimately appear in the antecedent of a base-clause. A second interpretation would avoid this difficulty. One might interpret "*p* is indubitable for *S*" psychologically, i.e. as meaning "*S* is psychologically incapable of doubting *p*." This would make principle (1) admissible, but would it be correct? Surely not. A religious fanatic may be psychologically incapable of doubting the tenets of his faith, but that doesn't make his belief in them justified. Similarly, during the Watergate affair, someone may have been so blinded by the aura of the presidency that even after the most damaging evidence against Nixon had emerged he was still incapable of doubting Nixon's veracity. It doesn't follow that his belief in Nixon's veracity was justified.

A second candidate base-clause principle is this:

> (2) If *S* believes *p* at *t* and *p* is self-evident, then *S*'s belief in *p* at *t* is justified.

To evaluate this principle, we again need an interpretation of its crucial term, in this case "self-evident." On one standard reading, "evident" is a synonym for "justified." "*Self-evident*" would therefore mean something like "directly justified," "intuitively justified," or "non-derivatively justified." On this reading "self-evident" is an epistemic phrase, and principle (2) would be disqualified as a base-clause principle.

However, there are other possible readings of "*p* is self-evident" on which it isn't an epistemic phrase. One such reading is: "It is impossible to understand *p* without believing it."[4] According to this interpretation, trivial analytic and logical truths might turn out to be self-evident. Hence, any belief in such a truth would be a justified belief, according to (2).

What does "it is *impossible* to understand *p* without believing it" mean? Does it mean "*humanly* impossible"? That reading would probably make (2) an unacceptable principle. There may well be propositions which humans have an innate and irrepressible disposition to believe, e.g. "Some events have causes." But it seems unlikely that people's inability to refrain from believing such a proposition makes every belief in it justified.

Should we then understand "impossible" to mean "impossible in principle," or "logically impossible"? If that is the reading given, I suspect that (2) is a vacuous principle. I doubt that even trivial logical or analytic truths will satisfy this definition of "self-evident." Any proposition, we may assume, has two or more components that are somehow organized or juxtaposed. To understand the proposition one must "grasp" the components and their juxtaposition. Now in the case of *complex* logical truths, there are (human) psychological operations that suffice to grasp the components and their juxtaposition but do not suffice to produce a belief that the proposition is true. But can't we at least *conceive* of an analogous set of psychological operations even for simple logical truths, operations which perhaps are not in the repertoire of human cognizers but which might be in the repertoire of some conceivable beings? That is, can't we conceive of psychological operations that would suffice to grasp the components and componential-juxtaposition of these simple propositions but do not suffice to produce *belief* in the propositions? I think we can conceive of such operations. Hence, for any proposition you choose, it will be possible for it to be understood without being believed.

Finally, even if we set these two objections aside, we must note that self-evidence can at best confer justificational status on relatively few beliefs, and the only plausible group are beliefs in necessary truths. Thus, other base-clause principles will be needed to explain the justificational status of beliefs in contingent propositions.

The notion of a base-clause principle is naturally associated with the idea of "direct" justifiedness, and in the realm of contingent propositions first-person-current-mental-state propositions have often been assigned this role.

In Chisholm's terminology, this conception is expressed by the notion of a *"self-presenting"* state or proposition. The sentence "I am thinking," for example, expresses a self-presenting proposition. (At least I shall *call* this sort of content a "proposition," though it only has a truth value given some assignment of a subject who utters or entertains the content and a time of entertaining.) When such a proposition is true for person S at time t, S is justified in believing it at t: in Chisholm's terminology, the proposition is "evident" for S at t. This suggests the following base-clause principle:

(3) If p is a self-presenting proposition, and p is true for S at t, and S believes p at t, then S's belief in p at t is justified.

What, exactly, does "self-presenting" mean? In the second edition of *Theory of Knowledge*, Chisholm offers this definition: "h is self-presenting for S at t = df. h is true at t; and necessarily, if h is true at t, then h is evident for S at t."[5] Unfortunately, since "evident" is an epistemic term, "self-presenting" also becomes an epistemic term on this definition, thereby disqualifying (3) as a legitimate base-clause. Some other definition of self-presentingness must be offered if (3) is to be a suitable base-clause principle.

Another definition of self-presentation readily comes to mind. "Self-presentation" is an approximate synonym of "self-intimation," and a proposition may be said to be self-intimating if and only if whenever it is true of a person that person believes it. More precisely, we may give the following definition:

(SP) Proposition p is self-presenting if and only if: necessarily, for any S and any t, if p is true for S at t, then S believes p at t.

On this definition, "self-presenting" is clearly not an epistemic predicate, so (3) would be an admissible principle. Moreover, there is initial plausibility in the suggestion that it is this feature of first-person-current-mental-state propositions—viz., their truth guarantees their being believed—that makes beliefs in them justified.

Employing this definition of self-presentation, is principle (3) correct? This cannot be decided until we define self-presentation more precisely. Since the operator "necessarily" can be read in different ways, there are different forms of self-presentation and correspondingly different versions of principle (3). Let us focus on two of these readings: a *"nomological"* reading and a *"logical"* reading. Consider first the nomological reading. On this definition a proposition is self-presenting just in case it is nomologically necessary that if p is true for S at t, then S believes p at t.[6]

Is the nomological version of principle (3)—call it "(3_N)"—correct? Not at all. We can imagine cases in which the antecedent of (3_N) is satisfied, but we would not say that the belief is justified. Suppose, for example, that p is the proposition expressed by the sentence "I am in brain-state B," where "B" is shorthand for a certain highly specific neural state description. Further suppose it is a nomological truth that anyone in brain-state B will ipso facto *believe* he is in brain-state B. In other words, imagine that an occurrent belief with the content "I am in brain-state B" is realized whenever one is in brain-state B.[7] According to (3_N), any such belief is justified. But that is clearly false. We can readily imagine circumstances in which a person goes into brain-state B and therefore has the belief in question, though this belief is by no means justified. For example, we can imagine that a brain-surgeon operating on S artificially induced brain-state B. This results, phenomenologically, in S's suddenly believing—out of the blue—that he is in brain-state B, without any relevant antecedent beliefs. We would hardly say, in such a case, that S's belief that he is in brain-state B is justified.

Let us turn next to the logical version of (3)—call it "(3_L)"—in which a proposition is defined as self-presenting just in case it is logically necessary that if *p* is true for S at t, then S believes *p* at t. This stronger version of principle (3) might seem more promising. In fact, however, it is no more successful than (3_N). Let *p* be the proposition "I am awake" and assume that it is logically necessary that if this proposition is true for some person S and time t, then S believes *p* at t. This assumption is consistent with the further assumption that S frequently believes *p* when it is false, e.g. when he is dreaming. Under these circumstances, we would hardly accept the contention that S's belief in this proposition is always justified. Nor should we accept the contention that the belief is justified when it is *true*. The truth of the proposition logically guarantees that the belief is *held*, but why should it guarantee that the belief is *justified*?

The foregoing criticism suggests that we have things backwards. The idea of self-presentation is that truth guarantees belief. This fails to confer justification because it is compatible with there being belief without truth. So what seems necessary—or at least sufficient—for justification is that belief should guarantee truth. Such a notion has usually gone under the label of "*infallibility*" or "*incorrigibility.*" It may be defined as follows:

(INC) Proposition *p* is incorrigible if and only if: necessarily, for any S and any t, if S believes *p* at t, then *p* is true for S at t.

Using the notion of incorrigibility, we may propose principle (4).

(4) If *p* is an incorrigible proposition, and S believes *p* at t, then S's belief in *p* at t is justified.

As was true of self-presentation, there are different varieties of incorrigibility, corresponding to different interpretations of "necessarily." Accordingly, we have different versions of principle (4). Once again, let us concentrate on a nomological and a logical version, (4_N) and (4_L) respectively.

We can easily construct a counterexample to (4_N) along the lines of the belief-state/brain-state counterexample that refuted (3_N). Suppose it is nomologically necessary that if anyone believes he is in brain-state B then it is true that he is in brain-state B, for the only way this belief-state is realized is through brain-state B itself. It follows that "I am in brain-state B" is a nomologically incorrigible proposition. Therefore, according to (4_N), whenever anyone believes this proposition at any time, that belief is justified. But we may again construct a brain-surgeon example in which someone comes to have such a belief but the belief isn't justified.

Apart from this counterexample, the general point is this. Why should the fact that S's believing *p* guarantees the truth of *p* imply that S's belief is justified? The nature of the guarantee might be wholly fortuitous, as the belief-state/brain-state example is intended to illustrate. To appreciate the point, consider the following related possibility. A person's mental structure might be such that whenever he believes that *p* will be true (of him) a split second later, then *p* is true (of him) a split second later. This is because, we may suppose, his believing it brings it about. But surely we would not be compelled in such a circumstance to say that a belief of this sort is justified. So why should the fact that S's believing *p* guarantees the truth of *p precisely at the time of belief* imply that the belief is justified? There is no intuitive plausibility in this supposition.

The notion of *logical* incorrigibility has a more honored place in the history of conceptions of justification. But even principle (4_L), I believe, suffers from defects similar to those of (4_N). The mere fact that belief in *p* logically guarantees its truth does not confer justificational status on such a belief.

The first difficulty with (4_L) arises from logical or mathematical truths. Any true proposition of logic or mathematics is logically necessary. Hence, any such proposition *p* is logically incorrigible, since it is logically necessary that, for any S and any t, if S believes p at t then p is true (for S at t). Now assume that Nelson believes a certain very complex mathematical truth at time t. Since such a proposition is logically incorrigible, (4_L) implies that Nelson's belief in this truth at t is justified. But we may easily suppose that this belief of Nelson is not at all the result of proper mathematical reasoning, or even the result of appeal to trustworthy authority. Perhaps Nelson believes this complex truth because of utterly confused reasoning, or because of hasty and ill-founded conjecture. Then his belief is not justified, contrary to what (4_L) implies.

The case of logical or mathematical truths is admittedly peculiar, since the truth of these propositions is assured independently of any beliefs. It might seem, therefore, that we can better capture the idea of "belief logically guaranteeing truth" in cases where the propositions in question are *contingent*. With this in mind, we might restrict (4_L) to *contingent* incorrigible propositions. Even this amendment cannot save (4_L), however, since there are counterexamples to it involving purely contingent propositions.

Suppose that Humperdink has been studying logic—or, rather, pseudo-logic—from Elmer Fraud, whom Humperdink has no reason to trust as a logician. Fraud has enunciated the principle that any disjunctive proposition consisting of at least 40 distinct disjuncts is very probably true. Humperdink now encounters the proposition p, a contingent proposition with 40 disjuncts, the 7th disjunct being "I exist." Although Humperdink grasps the proposition fully, he doesn't notice that it is entailed by "I exist." Rather, he is struck by the fact that it falls under the disjunction rule Fraud has enunciated (a rule I assume Humperdink is not *justified* in believing). Bearing this in mind, Humperdink forms a belief in p. Now notice that p is logically incorrigible. It is logically necessary that if anyone believes p, then p is true (of him at that time). This simply follows from the fact that,

first, a person's believing anything entails that he exists, and second, "I exist" entails p. Since p is logically incorrigible, principle (4_L) implies that Humperdink's belief in p is justified. But surely, given our example, that conclusion is false. Humperdink's belief in p is not at all justified.

One thing that goes wrong in this example is that while Humperdink's belief in p logically implies its truth, Humperdink doesn't *recognize* that his believing it implies its truth. This might move a theorist to revise (4_L) by adding the requirement that S "recognize" that p is logically incorrigible. But this, of course, won't do. The term "recognize" is obviously an epistemic term, so the suggested revision of (4_L) would result in an inadmissible base-clause.

II

Let us try to diagnose what has gone wrong with these attempts to produce an acceptable base-clause principle. Notice that each of the foregoing attempts confers the status of "justified" on a belief without restriction on *why* the belief is held, i.e. on what *causally initiates* the belief or *causally sustains* it. The logical versions of principles (3) and (4), for example, clearly place no restriction on causes of belief. The same is true of the nomological versions of (3) and (4), since nomological requirements can be satisfied by simultaneity or cross-sectional laws, as illustrated by our brain-state/belief-state examples. I suggest that the absence of causal requirements accounts for the failure of the foregoing principles. Many of our counterexamples are ones in which the belief is caused in some strange or unacceptable way, e.g. by the accidental movement of a brain-surgeon's hand, by reliance on an illicit, pseudo-logical principle, or by the blinding aura of the presidency. In general, a strategy for defeating a noncausal principle of justifiedness is to find a case in which the principle's antecedent is satisfied but the belief is caused by some faulty belief-forming process. The faultiness of the belief-forming process will incline us, intuitively, to regard the belief as unjustified. Thus, correct principles of justified belief must be principles that make causal requirements, where "cause" is construed broadly to include sustainers as well as initiators of belief (i.e. processes that determine, or help to overdetermine, a belief's continuing to be held).[8]

The need for causal requirements is not restricted to base-clause principles. Recursive principles will also need a causal component. One might initially suppose that the following is a good recursive principle: "If S justifiably believes q at t, and q entails p, and S believes p at t, then S's belief in p at t is justified." But this principle is unacceptable. S's belief in p doesn't receive justificational status simply from the fact that p is entailed by q and S justifiably believes q. If what causes S to believe p at t is entirely different, S's belief in p may well not be justified. Nor can the situation be remedied by adding to the antecedent the condition that S justifiably believes that q entails p. Even if he believes this, and believes q as well, he might not put these beliefs together. He might believe p as a result of some other wholly extraneous considerations. So once again, conditions that fail to require appropriate causes of a belief don't guarantee justifiedness.

Granted that principles of justified belief must make reference to causes of belief, what kinds of causes confer justifiedness? We can gain insight into this problem by reviewing some faulty processes of belief-formation, i.e. processes whose belief-outputs would be classed as unjustified. Here are some examples: confused reasoning, wishful thinking, reliance on emotional attachment, mere hunch or guesswork, and hasty generalization. What do these faulty processes have in common? They share the feature of *unreliability*: they tend to produce *error* a large proportion of the time. By contrast, which species of belief-forming (or belief-sustaining) processes are intuitively justification-conferring? They include standard perceptual processes,

remembering, good reasoning, and introspection. What these processes seem to have in common is *reliability*: the beliefs they produce are generally true. My positive proposal, then, is this. The justificational status of a belief is a function of the reliability of the process or processes that cause it, where (as a first approximation) reliability consists in the tendency of a process to produce beliefs that are true rather than false.

To test this thesis further, notice that justifiedness is not a purely categorical concept, although I treat it here as categorical in the interest of simplicity. We can and do regard certain beliefs as more justified than others. Furthermore, our intuitions of comparative justifiedness go along with our beliefs about the comparative reliability of the belief-causing processes.

Consider perceptual beliefs. Suppose Jones believes he has just seen a mountain-goat. Our assessment of the belief's justifiedness is determined by whether he caught a brief glimpse of the creature at a great distance, or whether he had a good look at the thing only 30 yards away. His belief in the latter sort of case is (*ceteris paribus*) more justified than in the former sort of case. And, if his belief is true, we are more prepared to say he *knows* in the latter case than in the former. The difference between the two cases seems to be this. Visual beliefs formed from brief and hasty scanning, or where the perceptual object is a long distance off, tend to be wrong more often than visual beliefs formed from detailed and leisurely scanning, or where the object is in reasonable proximity. In short, the visual processes in the former category are less reliable than those in the latter category. A similar point holds for memory beliefs. A belief that results from a hazy and indistinct memory impression is counted as less justified than a belief that arises from a distinct memory impression, and our inclination to classify those beliefs as "*knowledge*" varies in the same way. Again, the reason is associated with the comparative reliability of the processes. Hazy and indistinct memory impressions are generally less reliable indicators of what actually happened, so beliefs formed from such impressions are less likely to be true than beliefs formed from distinct impressions. Further, consider beliefs based on inference from observed samples. A belief about a population that is based on random sampling, or on instances that exhibit great variety, is intuitively more justified than a belief based on biased sampling, or on instances from a narrow sector of the population. Again, the degree of justifiedness seems to be a function of reliability. Inferences based on random or varied samples will tend to produce less error or inaccuracy than inferences based on non-random or non-varied samples.

Returning to a categorical concept of justifiedness, we might ask just *how* reliable a belief-forming process must be in order that its resultant beliefs be justified. A precise answer to this question should not be expected. Our conception of justification is *vague* in this respect. It does seem clear, however, that *perfect* reliability isn't required. Belief-forming processes that *sometimes* produce error still confer justification. It follows that there can be justified beliefs that are false.

I have characterized justification-conferring processes as ones that have a "tendency" to produce beliefs that are true rather than false. The term "tendency" could refer either to *actual* long-run frequency, or to a "propensity," i.e. outcomes that would occur in merely *possible* realizations of the process. Which of these is intended? Unfortunately, I think our ordinary conception of justifiedness is vague on this dimension too. For the most part, we simply assume that the "observed" frequency of truth versus error would be approximately replicated in the actual long-run, and also in relevant counterfactual situations, i.e. ones that are highly "realistic" or conform closely to the circumstances of the actual world. Since we ordinarily assume these frequencies to be roughly the same, we make no concerted effort to distinguish them. Since the purpose of my

present theorizing is to capture our ordinary conception of justifiedness, and since our ordinary conception is vague on this matter, it is appropriate to leave the theory vague in the same respect.

We need to say more about the notion of a belief-forming "*process*." Let us mean by a "process" a *functional operation* or procedure, i.e. something that generates a *mapping* from certain states —"inputs"—into other states—"outputs." The outputs in the present case are states of believing this or that proposition at a given moment. On this interpretation, a process is a *type* as opposed to a *token*. This is fully appropriate, since it is only types that have statistical properties such as producing truth 80 percent of the time; and it is precisely such statistical properties that determine the reliability of a process. Of course, we also want to speak of a process as *causing* a belief, and it looks as if types are incapable of being causes. But when we say that a belief is caused by a given process, understood as a functional procedure, we may interpret this to mean that it is caused by the particular *inputs* to the process (and by the intervening events "through which" the functional procedure carries the inputs into the output) on the occasion in question.

What are some examples of belief-forming "processes" construed as functional operations? One example is reasoning processes, where the inputs include antecedent beliefs and entertained hypotheses. Another example is functional procedures whose inputs include desires, hopes, or emotional states of various sorts (together with antecedent beliefs). A third example is a memory process, which takes as input beliefs or experiences at an earlier time and generates as output beliefs at a later time. For example, a memory process might take as input a belief *at* t_1 that Lincoln was born in 1809 and generate as output a belief *at* t_n that Lincoln was born in 1809. A fourth example is perceptual processes. Here it isn't clear whether inputs should include states of the environment, such as the distance of the stimulus from the cognizer, or only events within or on the surface of the organism, e.g. receptor stimulations. I shall return to this point in a moment.

A critical problem concerning our analysis is the degree of generality of the process-types in question. Input–output relations can be specified very broadly or very narrowly, and the degree of generality will partly determine the degree of reliability. A process-type might be selected so narrowly that only one instance of it ever occurs, and hence the type is either completely reliable or completely unreliable. (This assumes that reliability is a function of *actual* frequency only.) If such narrow process-types were selected, beliefs that are intuitively unjustified might be said to result from perfectly reliable processes, and beliefs that are intuitively justified might be said to result from perfectly unreliable processes.

It is clear that our ordinary thought about process-types slices them broadly, but I cannot at present give a precise explication of our intuitive principles. One plausible suggestion, though, is that the relevant processes are *content-neutral*. It might be argued, for example, that the process of *inferring p whenever the Pope asserts p* could pose problems for our theory. If the Pope is infallible, this process will be perfectly reliable; yet we would not regard the belief-outputs of this process as justified. The content-neutral restriction would avert this difficulty. If relevant processes are required to admit as input beliefs (or other states) with *any* content, the aforementioned process will not count, for its input beliefs have a restricted propositional content, viz., "*the Pope asserts p.*"

In addition to the problem of "generality" or "abstractness" there is the previously mentioned problem of the "*extent*" of belief-forming processes. Clearly, the causal ancestry of beliefs often includes events outside the organism. Are such events to be included among the "inputs" of belief-forming processes? Or should we restrict the extent of belief-forming processes to "*cognitive*" events, i.e. events within the

organism's nervous system? I shall choose the latter course, though with some hesitation. My general grounds for this decision are roughly as follows. Justifiedness seems to be a function of how a cognizer deals with his environmental input, i.e. with the goodness or badness of the operations that register and transform the stimulation that reaches him. ("Deal with," of course, does not mean *purposeful* action, nor is it restricted to *conscious* activity). A justified belief is, roughly speaking, one that results from cognitive operations that are, generally speaking, good or successful. But "*cognitive*" operations are most plausibly construed as operations of the cognitive faculties, i.e. "information-processing" equipment *internal* to the organism.

With these points in mind, we may now advance the following base-clause principle for justified belief.

(5) If S's believing p at t results from a reliable cognitive belief-forming process (or set of processes), then S's belief in p at t is justified.

Since "reliable belief-forming process" has been defined in terms of such notions as belief, truth, statistical frequency, and the like, it is not an epistemic term. Hence, (5) is an admissible base-clause.

It might seem as if (5) promises to be not only a successful base-clause, but the only principle needed whatever, apart from a closure clause. In other words, it might seem as if it is a necessary as well as a sufficient condition of justifiedness that a belief be produced by reliable cognitive belief-forming processes. But this is not quite correct, given our provisional definition of "reliability."

Our provisional definition implies that a reasoning process is reliable only if it generally produces beliefs that are true, and similarly, that a memory process is reliable only if it generally yields beliefs that are true. But these requirements are too strong. A reasoning procedure cannot be expected to produce true belief if it is applied to false premises. And memory cannot be expected to yield a true belief if the original belief it attempts to retain is false. What we need for reasoning and memory, then, is a notion of *"conditional reliability."* A process is conditionally reliable when a sufficient proportion of its output-beliefs are true *given that its input-beliefs are true.*

With this point in mind, let us distinguish *belief-dependent* and *belief-independent* cognitive processes. The former are processes *some* of whose inputs are belief-states.[9] The latter are processes *none* of whose inputs are belief-states. We may then replace principle (5) with the following two principles, the first a base-clause principle and the second a recursive-clause principle.

(6_A) If S's belief in p at t results ("immediately") from a belief-independent process that is (unconditionally) reliable, then S's belief in p at t is justified.

(6_B) If S's belief in p at t results ("immediately") from a belief-independent process that is (at least) conditionally reliable, and if the beliefs (if any) on which this process operates in producing S's belief in p at t are themselves justified, then S's belief in p at t is justified.[10]

If we add to (6_A) and (6_B) the standard closure clause, we have a complete theory of justified belief. The theory says, in effect, that a belief is justified if and only if it is *"well-formed,"* i.e. it has an ancestry of reliable and/or conditionally reliable cognitive operations. (Since a dated belief may be over-determined, it may have a number of distinct ancestral trees. These need not all be full of reliable or conditionally reliable processes. But at least one ancestral tree must have reliable or conditionally reliable processes throughout.)

The theory of justified belief proposed here, then, is an *Historical* or *Genetic* theory. It contrasts with the dominant approach to justified belief, an approach that generates what we may call (borrowing a phrase from Robert Nozick) *"Current Time-Slice"* theories. A Current Time-Slice theory makes the justificational status of a belief wholly a function of what is true of the cognizer *at the time of belief*. An Historical theory makes the justificational status of a belief depend on its prior history. Since my Historical theory emphasizes the reliability of the belief-generating processes, it may be called *"Historical Reliabilism."*

The most obvious examples of Current Time-Slice theories are "Cartesian" Foundationalist theories, which trace all justificational status (at least of contingent propositions) to current mental states. The usual varieties of Coherence theories, however, are equally Current Time-Slice views, since they too make the justificational status of a belief wholly a function of *current* states of affairs. For Coherence theories, however, these current states include all other beliefs of the cognizer, which would not be considered relevant by Cartesian Foundationalism. Have there been other Historical theories of justified belief? Among contemporary writers, Quine and Popper have Historical epistemologies, though the notion of "justification" is not their avowed *explicandum*. Among historical writers, it might seem that Locke and Hume had Genetic theories of sorts. But I think that their Genetic theories were only theories of ideas, not of knowledge or justification. Plato's theory of recollection, however, is a good example of a Genetic theory of knowing.[11] And it might be argued that Hegel and Dewey had Genetic epistemologies (if Hegel can be said to have had a clear epistemology at all).

The theory articulated by (6_A) and (6_B) might be viewed as a kind of "Foundationalism" because of its recursive structure. I have no objection to this label, as long as one keeps in mind how different this "diachronic" form of

Foundationalism is from Cartesian, or other "synchronic" varieties of, Foundationalism.

Current Time-Slice theories characteristically assume that the justificational status of a belief is something which the cognizer is able to know or determine at the time of belief. This is made explicit, for example, by Chisholm.[12] The Historical theory I endorse makes no such assumption. There are many facts about a cognizer to which he lacks "privileged access," and I regard the justificational status of his beliefs as one of those things. This is not to say that a cognizer is necessarily ignorant, at any given moment, of the justificational status of his current beliefs. It is only to deny that he necessarily has, or can get, knowledge or true belief about this status. Just as a person can know without knowing that he knows, so he can have justified belief without knowing that it is justified (or believing justifiably that it is justified).

A characteristic case in which a belief is justified though the cognizer doesn't know that it's justified is where the original evidence for the belief has long since been forgotten. If the original evidence was compelling, the cognizer's original belief may have been justified, and this justificational status may have been preserved through memory. But since the cognizer no longer remembers how or why he came to believe, he may not know that the belief is justified. If asked now to justify his belief, he may be at a loss. Still, the belief is justified, though the cognizer can't demonstrate or establish this.

The Historical theory of justified belief I advocate is connected in spirit with the causal theory of knowing I have presented elsewhere.[13] I had this in mind when I remarked near the outset of the essay that my theory of justified belief makes justifiedness come out closely related to knowledge. Justified beliefs, like pieces of knowledge, have appropriate histories; but they may fail to be knowledge either because they are false or because they founder on some other requirement for knowing of the kind discussed in the post-Gettier knowledge-trade.

There is a variant of the Historical conception of justified belief that is worth mentioning in this context. It may be introduced as follows. Suppose S has a set B of beliefs at time t_0, and some of these beliefs are unjustified. Between t_0 and t_1 he reasons from the entire set B to the conclusion p which he then accepts at t_1. The reasoning procedure he uses is a very sound one, i.e. one that is conditionally reliable. There is a sense or respect in which we are tempted to say that S's belief in p at t_1 is "justified." At any rate, it is tempting to say that the *person* is justified in believing p at t. Relative to his antecedent cognitive state, he did as well as could be expected: the *transition* from his cognitive state at t_0 to his cognitive state at t_1 was entirely sound. Although we may acknowledge this brand of justifiedness—it might be called *"Terminal-Phase Reliabilism"*—it is not a kind of justifiedness so closely related to knowing. For a person to know proposition p, it is not enough that the *final phase* of the process that leads to his belief in p be sound. It is also necessary that some entire history of the process be sound (i.e. reliable or conditionally reliable).

Let us return now to the Historical theory. In the next section, I shall adduce reasons for strengthening it a bit. Before looking at these reasons, however, I wish to review two quite different objections to the theory.

First, a critic might argue that *some* justified beliefs do not derive their justificational status from their causal ancestry. In particular, it might be argued that beliefs about one's current phenomenal states and intuitive beliefs about elementary logical or conceptual relationships do not derive their justificational status in this way. I am not persuaded by either of these examples. Introspection, I believe, should be regarded as a form of retrospection. Thus, a justified belief that I am "now" in pain gets its justificational status from a relevant, though brief, causal history.[14] The apprehension of logical or conceptual relationships is also a cognitive process that occupies time. The psychological process of "seeing" or "intuiting" a simple logical truth is very fast, and we cannot introspectively dissect it into constituent parts. Nonetheless, there are mental operations going on, just as there are mental operations that occur in *idiots savants*, who are unable to report the computational processes they in fact employ.

A second objection to Historical Reliabilism focuses on the reliability element rather than the causal or historical element. Since the theory is intended to cover all possible cases, it seems to imply that for any cognitive process C, if C is reliable in possible world W, then any belief in W that results from C is justified. But doesn't this permit easy counterexamples? Surely we can imagine a possible world in which wishful thinking is reliable. We can imagine a possible world where a benevolent demon so arranges things that beliefs formed by wishful thinking usually come true. This would make wishful thinking a reliable process in that possible world, but surely we don't want to regard beliefs that result from wishful thinking as justified.

There are several possible ways to respond to this case, and I am unsure which response is best, partly because my own intuitions (and those of other people I have consulted) are not entirely clear. One possibility is to say that in the possible world imagined, beliefs that result from wishful thinking *are* justified. In other words, we reject the claim that wishful thinking could never, intuitively, confer justifiedness.[15]

However, for those who feel that wishful thinking couldn't confer justifiedness even in the world imagined, there are two ways out. First, it may be suggested that the proper criterion of justifiedness is the propensity of a process to generate beliefs that are true *in a non-manipulated environment*, i.e. an environment in which there is no purposeful arrangement of the world either to accord or conflict with the beliefs that are formed. In other words, the suitability of a belief-forming process is only a function of its success in "*natural*" situations, not situations of the sort involving benevolent or malevolent demons or any other such manipulative creatures. If we reformulate the theory to include this qualification, the counterexample in question will be averted.

Alternatively, we may reformulate our theory, or reinterpret it, as follows. Instead of construing the theory as saying that a belief in possible world W is justified if and only if it results from a cognitive process that is reliable in W, we may construe it as saying that a belief in possible world W is justified if and only if it results from a cognitive process that is reliable in *our world*. In short, our conception of justifiedness is derived as follows. We note certain cognitive processes in the actual world, and form beliefs about which of these are reliable. The ones we believe to be reliable are then regarded as justification-conferring processes. In reflecting on hypothetical beliefs, we deem them justified if and only if they result from processes already picked out as justification-conferring, or processes very similar to those. Since wishful thinking is not among these processes, a belief formed in a possible world W by wishful thinking would not be deemed justified, even if wishful thinking is reliable *in W*. I am not sure that this is a correct reconstruction of our intuitive conceptual scheme, but it would accommodate the benevolent demon case, at least if the proper thing to say in that case is that the wishful-thinking-caused beliefs are unjustified.

Even if we adopt this strategy, however, a problem still remains. Suppose that wishful thinking turns out to be reliable *in the actual world!*[16] This might be because, unbeknownst to us at present, there is a benevolent demon who, lazy until now, will shortly start arranging things so that our wishes come true. The long-run performance of wishful thinking will be very good, and hence even the new construal of the theory will imply that beliefs resulting from wishful thinking (in *our* world) are justified. Yet this surely contravenes our intuitive judgment on the matter.

Perhaps the moral of the case is that the standard format of a "conceptual analysis" has its shortcomings. Let me depart from that format and try to give a better rendering of our aim and the theory that tries to achieve that aim. What we really want is an *explanation* of why we count, or would count, certain beliefs as justified and others as unjustified. Such an explanation must refer to our *beliefs* about reliability, not to the actual *facts*. The reason we *count* beliefs as justified is that they are formed by what we *believe* to be reliable belief-forming processes. Our beliefs about which belief-forming processes are reliable may be erroneous, but that does not affect the adequacy of the explanation. Since we *believe* that wishful thinking is an unreliable belief-forming process, we regard beliefs formed by wishful thinking as unjustified. What matters, then, is what we *believe* about wishful thinking, not what is *true* (in the long run) about wishful thinking. I am not sure how to express this point in the standard format of conceptual analysis, but it identifies an important point in understanding our theory.

III

Let us return, however, to the standard format of conceptual analysis, and let us consider a new objection that will require some revisions in the theory advanced until now. According to our theory, a belief is justified in case it is caused by a process that is in fact reliable, or by one we generally believe to be reliable. But suppose that although one of S's beliefs satisfies this condition, S has no reason to believe that it does. Worse yet, suppose S has reason to believe that his belief is caused by an *unreliable* process (although *in fact* its causal ancestry is fully reliable). Wouldn't we deny in such circumstances that S's belief is justified? This seems to show that our analysis, as presently formulated, is mistaken.

Suppose that Jones is told on fully reliable authority that a certain class of his memory beliefs are almost all mistaken. His parents fabricate a wholly false story that Jones suffered from amnesia when he was seven but later developed *pseudo*-memories of that period. Though Jones listens to what his parents say and has excellent reason to trust them, he persists in believing the ostensible memories from his seven-year-old past. Are these memory beliefs justified? Intuitively, they are not justified. But since these beliefs result from genuine memory and original perceptions, which are adequately reliable processes, our theory says that these beliefs are justified.

Can the theory be revised to meet this difficulty? One natural suggestion is that the actual reliability of a belief's ancestry is not enough for justifiedness; in addition, the cognizer must be *justified in believing* that the ancestry of his belief is reliable. Thus one might think of replacing (6_A), for example, with (7). (For simplicity, I neglect some of the details of the earlier analysis.)

> (7) If S's belief in p at t is caused by a reliable cognitive process, and S justifiably believes at t that his p-belief is so caused, then S's belief in p at t is justified.

It is evident, however, that (7) will not do as a base-clause, for it contains the epistemic term "justifiably" in its antecedent.

A slightly weaker revision, without this problematic feature, might next be suggested, viz.,

> (8) If S's belief in p at t is caused by a reliable cognitive process, and S believes at t that his p-belief is so caused, then S's belief in p at t is justified.

But this won't do the job. Suppose that Jones believes that his memory beliefs are reliably caused despite all the (trustworthy) contrary testimony of his parents. Principle (8) would be satisfied, yet we wouldn't say that these beliefs are justified.

Next, we might try (9), which is stronger than (8) and, unlike (7), formally admissible as a base-clause.

(9)   If S's belief in p at t is caused by a reliable cognitive process, and S believes at t that his p-belief is so caused, and this meta-belief is caused by a reliable cognitive process, then S's belief in p at t is justified.

A first objection to (9) is that it wrongly precludes unreflective creatures—creatures like animals or young children, who have no beliefs about the genesis of their beliefs—from having justified beliefs. If one shares my view that justified belief is, at least roughly, *well-formed* belief, surely animals and young children can have justified beliefs.

A second problem with (9) concerns its underlying rationale. Since (9) is proposed as a substitute for (6$_A$), it is implied that the reliability of a belief's own cognitive ancestry does not make it justified. But, the suggestion seems to be, the reliability of a *meta-belief's* ancestry confers justifiedness on the first-order belief. Why should that be so? Perhaps one is attracted by the idea of a "trickle-down" effect: if an n + 1-level belief is justified, its justification trickles down to an n-level belief. But even if the trickle-down theory is correct, it doesn't help here. There is no assurance from the satisfaction of (9)'s antecedent that the meta-belief itself is *justified*.

To obtain a better revision of our theory, let us re-examine the Jones case. Jones has strong evidence against certain propositions concerning his past. He doesn't *use* this evidence, but if he *were* to use it properly, he would stop believing these propositions. Now the proper use of evidence would be an instance of a (conditionally) reliable process. So what we can say about Jones is that he *fails* to use a certain (conditionally) reliable process that he could and should have used. Admittedly, had he used this process, he

would have "worsened" his doxastic states: he would have replaced some true beliefs with suspension of judgment. Still, he couldn't have known this in the case in question. So he failed to do something which, epistemically, he should have done. This diagnosis suggests a fundamental change in our theory. The justificational status of a belief is not only a function of the cognitive process *actually* employed in producing it, it is also a function of processes that could and should be employed.

With these points in mind, we may tentatively propose the following revision of our theory, where we again focus on a base-clause principle but omit certain details in the interest of clarity.

(10)   If S's belief in p at t results from a reliable cognitive process, and there is no reliable or conditionally reliable process available to S which, had it been used by S in addition to the process actually used, would have resulted in S's not believing p at t, then S's belief in p at t is justified.

There are several problems with this proposal. First, there is a technical problem. One cannot use an additional belief-forming (or doxastic-state-forming) process *as well as* the original process if the additional one would result in a different doxastic state. One wouldn't be using the original process at all. So we need a slightly different formulation of the relevant counterfactual. Since the basic idea is reasonably clear, however, I won't try to improve on the formulation here. A second problem concerns the notion of "*available*" belief-forming (or doxastic-state-forming) processes. What is it for a process to be "available" to a cognizer? Were scientific procedures "available" to people who lived in pre-scientific ages? Furthermore, it seems implausible to say that all "available" processes ought to be used, at least if we include such processes as gathering *new* evidence. Surely a belief can sometimes be justified even if additional evidence-gathering would yield a different doxastic attitude. What I think we should have in mind here are such additional processes as calling previously acquired evidence to mind, assessing the implications of that evidence, etc. This is admittedly somewhat vague, but here again our ordinary notion of justifiedness is vague, so it is appropriate for our analysans to display the same sort of vagueness.

This completes the sketch of my account of justified belief. Before concluding, however, it is essential to point out that there is an important use of "justified" which is not captured by this account but can be captured by a closely related one.

There is a use of "justified" in which it is not implied or presupposed that there is a *belief* that is justified. For example, if S is trying to decide whether to believe p and asks our advice, we may tell him that he is "justified" in believing it. We do not thereby imply that he *has* a justified *belief*, since we know he is still suspending judgment. What we mean, roughly, is that he *would* or *could* be justified if he were to believe p. The justificational status we ascribe here cannot be a function of the causes of S's believing p, for there is no belief by S in p. Thus, the account of justifiedness we have given thus far cannot explicate *this* use of "justified." (It doesn't follow that this use of "justified" has no connection with causal ancestries. Its proper use may depend on the causal ancestry of the cognizer's cognitive state, though not on the causal ancestry of his believing p.)

Let us distinguish two uses of "justified": an *ex post* use and an *ex ante* use. The *ex post* use occurs when there exists a belief, and we say of *that belief* that it is (or isn't) justified. The *ex ante* use occurs when no such belief exists, or when we wish to ignore the question of whether such a belief exists. Here we say of the *person*, independent of his doxastic state vis-à-vis p, that p is (or isn't) suitable for him to believe.[17]

Since we have given an account of *ex post* justi-

fiedness, it will suffice if we can analyze *ex ante* justifiedness in terms of it. Such an analysis, I believe, is ready at hand. S is *ex ante* justified in believing p at t just in case his total cognitive state at t is such that from that state he could come to believe p in such a way that this belief would be *ex post* justified. More precisely, he is *ex ante* justified in believing p at t just in case a reliable belief-forming operation is available to him such that the application of that operation to his total cognitive state at t would result, more or less immediately, in his believing p and this belief would be *ex post* justified. Stated formally, we have the following:

(11) Person S is *ex ante* justified in believing p at t if and only if there is a reliable belief-forming operation available to S which is such that if S applied that operation to this total cognitive state at t, S would believe p at t-plus-delta (for a suitably small delta) and that belief would be *ex post* justified.

For the analysans of (11) to be satisfied, the total cognitive state at t must have a suitable causal ancestry. Hence, (11) is implicitly an Historical account of *ex ante* justifiedness.

As indicated, the bulk of this essay was addressed to *ex post* justifiedness. This is the appropriate analysandum if one is interested in the connection between justifiedness and knowledge, since what is crucial to whether a person knows a proposition is whether he has an actual *belief* in the proposition that is justified. However, since many epistemologists are interested in *ex ante* justifiedness, it is proper for a general theory of justification to try to provide an account of that concept as well. Our theory does this quite naturally, for the account of *ex ante* justifiedness falls out directly from our account of *ex post* justifiedness.[18]

Notes

1 "A Causal Theory of Knowing"; "Innate Knowledge," in S. P. Stich, ed., *Innate Ideas* (Berkeley: University of California Press, 1975); and "Discrimination and Perceptual Knowledge."

2 Notice that the choice of a recursive format does not prejudice the case for or against any particular theory. A recursive format is perfectly general. Specifically, an explicit set of necessary and sufficient conditions is just a special case of a recursive format, i.e. one in which there is no recursive clause.

3 Many of the attempts I shall consider are suggested by material in William P. Alston, "Varieties of Privileged Access."

4 Such a definition (though without the modal term) is given, for example, by W. V. Quine and J. S. Ullian in *The Web of Belief*, p. 21. Statements are said to be self-evident just in case "to understand them is to believe them."

5 Page 22.

6 I assume, of course, that "nomologically necessary" is *de re* with respect to "S" and "t" in this construction. I shall not focus on problems that may arise in this regard, since my primary concerns are with different issues.

7 This assumption violates the thesis that Davidson calls "The Anomalism of the Mental." Cf. "Mental Events" in L. Foster and J. W. Swanson, eds., *Experience and Theory* (Amherst: University of Massachusetts Press, 1970). But it is unclear that this thesis is a necessary truth. Thus, it seems fair to assume its falsity in order to produce a counter-example. The example neither entails nor precludes the mental–physical identity theory.

8 Keith Lehrer's example of the gypsy lawyer is intended to show the inappropriateness of a causal requirement. (See *Knowledge*, pp. 124–25.) But I find this example unconvincing. To the extent that I clearly imagine that the lawyer fixes his belief solely as a result of the cards, it seems intuitively wrong to say that he *knows*—or has a *justified belief*—that his client is innocent.

9 This definition is not exactly what we need for the purposes at hand. As Ernest Sosa points out, introspection will turn out to be a belief-dependent process, since sometimes the input into the process will be a belief (when the introspected content is a belief). Intuitively, however, introspection is not the sort of process which may be merely conditionally reliable. I do not know how to refine the definition so as to avoid this difficulty, but it is a small and isolated point.

10 It may be objected that principles (6_A) and (6_B) are jointly open to analogues of the lottery paradox. A series of processes composed of reliable but less-than-perfectly-reliable processes may be extremely unreliable. Yet applications of (6_A) and (6_B) would confer justifiedness on a belief that is caused by such a series. In reply to this objection, we might simply indicate that the theory is intended to capture our ordinary notion of justifiedness, and this ordinary notion has been formed without recognition of this kind of problem. The theory is not wrong *as* a theory of the ordinary (naive) conception of justifiedness. On the other hand, if we want a theory to do more than capture the ordinary conception of justifiedness, it might be possible to strengthen the principles to avoid lottery-paradox analogues.

11 I am indebted to Mark Pastin for this point.

12 Cf. *Theory of Knowledge*, 2nd edn, pp. 17, 114–16.

13 Cf. "A Causal Theory of Knowing." The reliability aspect of my theory also has its precursors in earlier papers of mine on knowing: "Innate Knowledge" and "Discrimination and Perceptual Knowledge."

14 The view that introspection is retrospection was taken by Ryle, and before him (as Charles Hartshorne points out to me) by Hobbes, Whitehead, and possibly Husserl.

15 Of course, if people in world *W* learn *inductively* that wishful thinking is reliable, and regularly base their beliefs on this inductive inference, it is quite unproblematic and straightforward that their beliefs are justified. The only interesting case is where their beliefs are formed *purely* by wishful thinking, without using inductive inference. The suggestion contemplated in this paragraph of the text is that, in the world imagined, even pure wishful thinking would confer justifiedness.

16 I am indebted here to Mark Kaplan.

17 The distinction between *ex post* and *ex ante* justifiedness is similar to Roderick Firth's distinction between *doxastic* and *propositional* warrant. See his "Are Epistemic Concepts Reducible to Ethical Concepts?" in Alvin I. Goldman and Jaegwon Kim,

eds., *Values and Morals, Essays in Honor of William Frankena, Charles Stevenson, and Richard Brandt* (Dordrecht: D. Reidel, 1978).

18 Research on this essay was begun while the author was a fellow of the John Simon Guggenheim Memorial Foundation and of the Center for Advanced Study in the Behavioral Sciences. I am grateful for their support. I have received helpful comments and criticism from Holly S. Goldman, Mark Kaplan, Fred Schmitt, Stephen P. Stich, and many others at several universities where earlier drafts of the paper were read.

Chapter 17

Richard Feldman and Earl Conee

EVIDENTIALISM

I

We advocate evidentialism in epistemology. What we call evidentialism is the view that the epistemic justification of a belief is determined by the quality of the believer's evidence for the belief. Disbelief and suspension of judgment also can be epistemically justified. The doxastic attitude that a person is justified in having is the one that fits the person's evidence. More precisely:

EJ   Doxastic attitude D toward proposition p is epistemically justified for S at t if and only if having D toward p fits the evidence S has at t.[1]

We do not offer EJ as an analysis. Rather it serves to indicate the kind of notion of justification that we take to be characteristically epistemic—a notion that makes justification turn entirely on evidence. Here are three examples that illustrate the application of this notion of justification. First, when a physiologically normal person under ordinary circumstances looks at a plush green lawn that is directly in front of him in broad daylight, believing that there is something green before him is the attitude toward this proposition that fits his evidence. That is why the belief is epistemically justified. Second, suspension of judgment is the fitting attitude for each of us toward the proposition that an even number of ducks exists, since our evidence makes it equally likely that the number is odd. Neither belief nor disbelief is epistemically justified when our evidence is equally balanced. And third, when it comes to the proposition that sugar is sour, our gustatory experience makes disbelief the fitting attitude. Such experiential evidence epistemically justifies disbelief.[2]

EJ is not intended to be surprising or innovative. We take it to be the view about the nature of epistemic justification with the most initial plausibility. A defense of EJ is now appropriate because several theses about justification that seem to cast doubt on it have been prominent in recent literature on epistemology. Broadly speaking, these theses imply that epistemic justification depends upon the cognitive capacities of people, or upon the cognitive processes or information-gathering practices that led to the attitude. In contrast, EJ asserts that the epistemic justification of an attitude depends only on evidence.

We believe that EJ identifies the basic concept of epistemic justification. We find no adequate grounds for accepting the recently discussed theses about justification that seem to cast doubt on EJ. In the remainder of this paper we defend evidentialism. Our purpose is to show that it continues to be the best view of epistemic justification.

II

In this section we consider two objections to EJ. Each is based on a claim about human limits and a claim about the conditions under which an attitude can be justified. One objection depends on the claim that an attitude can be justified only if it is voluntarily adopted, the other depends on the claim that an attitude toward a proposition or propositions can be justified for a person only if the ability to have that attitude toward the proposition or those propositions is within normal human limits.

Doxastic voluntarism

EJ says that a doxastic attitude is justified for a person when that attitude fits the person's evidence. It is clear that there are cases in which a certain attitude toward a proposition fits a person's evidence, yet the person has no control over whether he forms that attitude toward that proposition. So some involuntarily adopted attitudes are justified according to EJ. John Heil finds this feature of the evidentialist position questionable. He says that the fact that we "speak of a person's beliefs as being warranted, justified, or rational . . . makes it appear that . . . believing something can, at least sometimes, be under the voluntary control of the believer."[3] Hilary Kornblith claims that it seems "unfair" to evaluate beliefs if they "are not subject" to direct voluntary control.[4] Both Heil and Kornblith conclude that although beliefs are not under direct voluntary control, it is still appropriate to evaluate them because "they are not entirely out of our control either."[5] "One does have a say in the procedures one undertakes that lead to" the formation of beliefs.[6]

Doxastic attitudes need not be under any sort of voluntary control for them to be suitable for epistemic evaluation. Examples confirm that beliefs may be both involuntary and subject to epistemic evaluation. Suppose that a person spontaneously and involuntarily believes that the lights are on in the room, as a result of the familiar sort of completely convincing perceptual evidence. This belief is clearly justified, whether or not the person cannot voluntarily acquire, lose, or modify the cognitive process that led to the belief. Unjustified beliefs can also be involuntary. A paranoid man might believe without any supporting evidence that he is being spied on. This belief might be a result of an uncontrollable desire to be a recipient of special attention. In such a case the belief is clearly epistemically unjustified even if the belief is involuntary and the person cannot alter the process leading to it.

The contrary view that only voluntary beliefs are justified or unjustified may seem plausible if one confuses the topic of EJ with an assessment of the *person*.[7] A person deserves praise or blame for being in a doxastic state only if that state is under the person's control.[8] The person who involuntarily believes in the presence of overwhelming evidence that the lights are on does not deserve praise for this belief. The belief is nevertheless justified. The person who believes that he is being spied on as a result of an uncontrollable desire does not deserve to be blamed for that belief. But there is a fact about the belief's epistemic merit. It is epistemically defective—it is held in the presence of insufficient evidence and is therefore unjustified.

Doxastic limits

Apart from the questions about doxastic voluntarism, it is sometimes claimed that it is inappropriate to set epistemic standards that are beyond normal human limits. Alvin Goldman recommends that epistemologists seek epistemic principles that can serve as practical guides to belief formation. Such principles, he contends, must take into account the limited cognitive capacities of people. Thus, he is led to deny a principle instructing people to believe all the logical consequences of their beliefs, since they are unable to have the infinite number of beliefs that following such a principle would require.[9] Goldman's view does not conflict with EJ, since EJ does not instruct anyone to believe anything. It simply states a necessary and sufficient condition for epistemic justification. Nor does Goldman think this view conflicts with EJ, since he makes it clear that the principles he is discussing are guides to action and not principles that apply the traditional concept of epistemic justification.

Although Goldman does not use facts about normal cognitive limits to argue against EJ, such an argument has been suggested by Kornblith and by Paul Thagard. Kornblith cites Goldman's work as an inspiration for his view that "having justified beliefs is simply doing the best one can in the light of the innate endowment one starts from . . ."[10] Thagard contends that rational or justified principles of inference "should not demand of a reasoner inferential performance which exceeds the general psychological abilities of human beings."[11] Neither Thagard nor Kornblith argues against EJ, but it is easy to see how such an argument would go: A doxastic attitude toward a proposition is justified for a person only if having that attitude toward that proposition is within the normal doxastic capabilities of people. Some doxastic attitudes that fit a person's evidence are not within those capabilities. Yet EJ classifies them as justified. Hence, EJ is false.[12]

We see no good reason here to deny EJ. The argument has as a premise the claim that some attitudes beyond normal limits do fit someone's evidence. The fact that we are limited to a finite number of beliefs is used to support this claim. But this fact does not establish the premise. There is no reason to think that an infinite number of beliefs fit any body of evidence that anyone ever has. The evidence that people have under ordinary circumstances never makes it evident, concerning every one of an infinite number of logical consequences of that evidence, that it is a consequence. Thus, believing each consequence will not fit any ordinary evidence. Furthermore, even if there are circumstances in which more beliefs fit a person's evidence than he is able to have, all that follows is that he cannot have at one time all the beliefs that fit. It does not follow that there is any particular fitting belief which is unattainable. Hence, the premise of the argument that says that EJ classifies as justified some normally unattainable beliefs is not established by means of this example. There does not seem to be any sort of plausible evidence that would establish this premise. While some empirical evidence may show that people typically do not form fitting attitudes in certain contexts, or that some fitting attitudes are beyond some individual's abilities, such evidence fails to show that any fitting attitudes are beyond normal limits.

There is a more fundamental objection to this argument against EJ. There is no basis for the premise that what is epistemically justified must be restricted to feasible doxastic alternatives. It can be a worthwhile thing to help people to choose among the epistemic alternatives open to them. But suppose that there were occasions when forming the attitude that best fits a person's evidence was beyond normal cognitive limits. This would still be the attitude *justified* by the person's evidence. If the person had normal abilities, then he would be in the unfortunate position of being unable to do what is justified according to the standard for justification asserted by EJ. This is not a flaw in the account of justification. Some standards are met only by going beyond normal human limits. Standards that some teachers set for an "A" in a course are unattainable for most students. There are standards of artistic excellence that no one can meet, or at least standards that normal people cannot meet in any available circumstance. Similarly, epistemic justification might have been normally unattainable.

We conclude that considerations neither of doxastic voluntarism nor of doxastic limits provide any good reason to abandon EJ as an account of epistemic justification.

III

EJ sets an epistemic standard for evaluating doxastic conduct. In any case of a standard for conduct, whether it is voluntary or not, it is appropriate to speak of "requirements" or "obligations" that the standard imposes. The person who has overwhelming perceptual evidence for the proposition that the lights are on, epistemically ought to believe that proposition. The paranoid person epistemically ought not to believe that he is being spied upon when he has no evidence supporting this belief. We hold the general view that one epistemically ought to have the doxastic attitudes that fit one's evidence. We think that being epistemically obligatory is equivalent to being epistemically justified.

There are in the literature two other sorts of view about epistemic obligations. What is epistemically obligatory, according to these other views, does not always fit one's evidence. Thus, each of these views of epistemic obligation, when combined with our further thesis that being epistemically obligatory is equivalent to being epistemically justified, yields results incompatible with evidentialism. We shall now consider how these proposals affect EJ.

Justification and the obligation to believe truths

Roderick Chisholm holds that one has an "intellectual requirement" to try one's best to bring it about that, of the propositions one considers, one believes all and only the truths.[13] This theory of what our epistemic obligations are, in conjunction with our view that the justified attitudes are the ones we have an epistemic obligation to hold, implies the following principle:

CJ Doxastic attitude D toward proposition p is justified for person S at time t if and only if S considers p at t and S's having D toward p at t would result from S's trying his best to bring it about that S believe p at t iff p is true.

Evaluation of CJ is complicated by an ambiguity in "trying one's best." It might mean "trying in that way which will in fact have the best results." Since the goal is to believe all and only the truths one considers, the best results would be obtained by believing each truth one considers and disbelieving each falsehood one considers. On this interpretation, CJ implies that believing each truth and disbelieving each falsehood one considers is justified whenever believing and disbelieving in these ways would result from something one could try to do.

On this interpretation CJ is plainly false. We are not justified in believing every proposition we consider that happens to be true and which we could believe by trying for the truth. It is possible to believe some unsubstantiated proposition in a reckless endeavor to believe a truth, and happen to be right. This would not be an epistemically justified belief.[14]

It might be contended that trying one's best to believe truths and disbelieve falsehoods really amounts to trying to believe and disbelieve in accordance with one's evidence. We agree that gaining the doxastic attitudes that fit one's evidence is the epistemically best way to use one's evidence in trying to believe all and only the truths one considers. This interpretation of CJ makes it nearly equivalent to EJ. There are two relevant differences. First, CJ implies that one can have justified attitudes only toward propositions one actually considers. EJ does not have this implication. CJ is also unlike EJ in implying that an attitude is justified if it would result from trying to form the attitude that fits one's evidence. The attitude that is justified according to EJ is the one that as a matter of fact does fit one's evidence. This seems more plausible. What would happen if one tried to have a fitting attitude seems irrelevant—one might try but fail to form the fitting attitude.

We conclude that the doxastic attitudes that would result from carrying out the intellectual requirement that Chisholm identifies are not the epistemically justified attitudes.

Justification and epistemically responsible action

Another view about epistemic obligations, proposed by Hilary Kornblith, is that we are obligated to seek the truth and gather evidence in a responsible way. Kornblith also maintains that the justification of a belief depends on how responsibly one carried out the inquiry that led to the belief.[15] We shall now examine how the considerations leading to this view affect EJ.

Kornblith describes a case of what he regards as "epistemically culpable ignorance." It is an example in which a person's belief seems to fit his evidence, and thus it seems to be justified according to evidentialism. Kornblith contends that the belief is unjustified because it results from epistemically irresponsible behavior. His example concerns a headstrong young physicist who is unable to tolerate criticism. After presenting a paper to his colleagues, the physicist pays no attention to the devastating objection of a senior colleague. The physicist, obsessed with his own success, fails even to hear the objection, which consequently has no impact on his beliefs. Kornblith says that after this the physicist's belief in his own theory is unjustified. He suggests that evidentialist theories cannot account for this fact.

Crucial details of this example are left unspecified, but in no case does it provide a refutation of evidentialism. If the young physicist is aware of the fact that his senior colleague is making an objection, then this fact is evidence he has against his theory, although it is unclear from just this much detail how decisive it would be. So, believing his theory may no longer be justified for him according to a purely evidentialist view. On the other hand, perhaps he remains entirely ignorant of the fact that a senior colleague is objecting to his theory. He might be "lost in thought"—privately engrossed in proud admiration of the paper he has just given—and fail to understand what is going on in the audience. If this happens, and his evidence supporting his theory is just as it was prior to his presentation of the paper, then believing the

theory does remain justified for him (assuming that it was justified previously). There is no reason to doubt EJ in the light of this example. It may be true that the young physicist is an unpleasant fellow, and that he lacks intellectual integrity. This is an evaluation of the character of the physicist. It is supported by the fact that in this case he is not engaged in an impartial quest for the truth. But the physicist's character has nothing to do with the epistemic status of his belief in his theory.

Responsible evidence-gathering obviously has some epistemic significance. One serious epistemological question is that of how to engage in a thorough-going rational pursuit of the truth. Such a pursuit may require gathering evidence in responsible ways. It may also be necessary to be open to new ideas, to think about a variety of important issues, and to consider a variety of opinions about such issues. Perhaps it requires, as BonJour suggests, that one "reflect critically upon one's beliefs."[16] But everyone has some justified beliefs, even though virtually no one is fully engaged in a rational pursuit of the truth. EJ has no implication about the actions one must take in a rational pursuit of the truth. It is about the epistemic evaluation of attitudes given the evidence one does have, however one came to possess that evidence.

Examples like that of the headstrong physicist show no defect in the evidentialist view. Justified beliefs can result from epistemically irresponsible actions.

Other sorts of obligation

Having acknowledged at the beginning of this section that justified attitudes are in a sense obligatory, we wish to forestall confusions involving other notions of obligations. It is not the case that there is always a *moral* obligation to believe in accordance with one's evidence. Having a fitting attitude can bring about disastrous personal or social consequences. Vicious beliefs that lead to vicious acts can be epistemically justified. This rules out any moral obligation to have the epistemically justified attitude.[17]

It is also false that there is always a *prudential* obligation to have each epistemically justified attitude. John Heil discusses the following example.[18] Sally has fairly good evidence that her husband Burt has been seeing another woman. Their marriage is in a precarious condition. It would be best for Sally if their marriage were preserved. Sally foresees that, were she to believe that Burt has been seeing another woman, her resulting behavior would lead to their divorce. Given these assumptions, EJ counts as justified at least some measure of belief by Sally in the proposition that Burt has been seeing another woman. But Sally would be better off if she did not have this belief, in light of the fact that she would be best served by their continued marriage. Heil raises the question of what Sally's prudential duty is in this case. Sally's *epistemic* obligation is to believe that her husband is unfaithful. But that gives no reason to deny what seems obvious here. Sally *prudentially* ought to refrain from believing her husband to be unfaithful. It can be prudent not to have a doxastic attitude that is correctly said by EJ to be justified, just as it can be moral not to have such an attitude.

More generally, the causal consequences of having an unjustified attitude can be more beneficial in *any* sort of way than the consequences of having its justified alternative. We have seen that it can be morally and prudentially best not to have attitudes justified according to EJ. Failing to have these attitudes can also have the best results for the sake of *epistemic* goals such as the acquisition of knowledge. Roderick Firth points out that a scientist's believing against his evidence that he will recover from an illness may help to effect a recovery and so contribute to the growth of knowledge by enabling the scientist to continue his research.[19] William James's case for exercising "the will to believe" suggests that some evidence concerning the existence of God

is available only after one believes in God in the absence of justifying evidence. EJ does not counsel against adopting such beliefs for the sake of these epistemic ends. EJ implies that the beliefs would be unjustified when adopted. This is not to say that the believing would do no epistemic good.

We acknowledge that it is appropriate to speak of epistemic obligations. But it is a mistake to think that what is epistemically obligatory, i.e. epistemically justified, is also morally or prudentially obligatory, or that it has the overall best epistemic consequences.

IV

Another argument that is intended to refute the evidentialist approach to justification concerns the ways in which a person can come to have an attitude that fits his evidence. Both Kornblith and Goldman propose examples designed to show that merely *having* good evidence for a proposition is not sufficient to make believing that proposition justified.[20] We shall work from Kornblith's formulation of the argument, since it is more detailed. Suppose Alfred is justified in believing p, and justified in believing if p then q. Alfred also believes q. EJ seems to imply that believing q is justified for Alfred, since that belief does seem to fit this evidence. Kornblith argues that Alfred's belief in q may still not be justified. It is not justified, according to Kornblith, if Alfred has a strong distrust of *modus ponens* and believes q because he likes the sound of the sentence expressing it rather than on the basis of the *modus ponens* argument. Similarly, Goldman says that a person's belief in q is not justified unless the belief is caused in some appropriate way.

Whether EJ implies that Alfred's belief in q is justified depends in part on an unspecified detail—Alfred's evidence concerning *modus ponens*. It is possible that Alfred has evidence against *modus ponens*. Perhaps he has just seen a version of the Liar paradox that seems to render *modus ponens* as suspect as the other rules and premises in the derivation. In the unlikely event that Alfred has such evidence, EJ implies that believing q is *not* justified for him. If rather, as we shall assume, his overall evidence supports *modus ponens* and q, then EJ does imply that believing q is justified for him.

When Alfred has strong evidence for q, his believing q is epistemically justified. This is the sense of "justified" captured by EJ. However, if Alfred's basis for believing q is not his evidence for it, but rather the sound of the sentence expressing q, then it seems equally clear that there is some sense in which this state of believing is epistemically "defective"—he did not arrive at the belief in the right way. The term "well-founded" is sometimes used to characterize an attitude that is epistemically both well-supported and properly arrived at. Well-foundedness is a second evidentialist notion used to evaluate doxastic states. It is an evidentialist notion because its application depends on two matters of evidence—the evidence one *has*, and the evidence one *uses* in forming the attitude. More precisely:

> WF   S's doxastic attitude D at t toward proposition p is well-founded if and only if
>
> (i)   having D toward p is justified for S at t; and
>
> (ii) S has D toward p on the basis of some body of evidence e, such that
>
> > (a)   S has e as evidence at t;
> > (b)   having D toward p fits e; and
> > (c)   there is no more inclusive body of evidence e' had by S at t such that having D toward p does not fit e'.[21]

Since the evidentialist can appeal to this notion of well-foundedness, cases in which a person has but does not use justifying evidence do not refute evidentialism. Kornblith and Goldman's intuitions about such cases can be accommodated. A person in Alfred's position *is* in an epistemically defective state—his belief in q is not well-founded. Having said this, it is reasonable also to affirm the other evidentialist judgment that Alfred's belief in q is in another sense epistemically right—it is justified.[22]

V

The theory of epistemic justification that has received the most attention recently is reliabilism. Roughly speaking, this is the view that epistemically justified beliefs are the ones that result from belief-forming processes that reliably lead to true beliefs.[23] In this section we consider whether reliabilism casts doubt on evidentialism.

Although reliabilists generally formulate their view as an account of epistemic justification, it is clear that in its simplest forms it is better regarded as an account of well-foundedness. In order for a belief to be favorably evaluated by the simple sort of reliabilism sketched above, the belief must actually be held, as is the case with WF. And just as with WF, the belief must be "grounded" in the proper way. Where reliabilism appears to differ from WF is over the conditions under which a belief is properly grounded. According to WF, this occurs when the belief is based on fitting evidence. According to reliabilism, a belief is properly grounded if it results from a belief-forming process that reliably leads to true beliefs. These certainly are *conceptually* different accounts of the grounds of well-founded beliefs.

In spite of this conceptual difference, reliabilism and WF may be extensionally equivalent. The question of equivalence depends on the resolution of two unclarities in reliabilism. One pertains to the notion of a belief-forming process, and the other to the notion of reliability.

An unclarity about belief-forming processes arises because every belief is caused by a sequence of particular events which is an instance of many types of causal processes. Suppose that one evening Jones looks out of his window and sees a bright shining disk-shaped object. The object is in fact a luminous frisbee, and Jones clearly remembers having given one of these to his daughter. But Jones is attracted to the idea that extraterrestrials are visiting the Earth. He manages to believe that he is seeing a flying saucer. Is the process that caused this belief reliable? Since the sequence of events leading to his belief is an instance of many types of process, the answer depends upon which of these many types is the relevant one. The sequence falls into highly general categories such as perceptually based belief formation and visually based belief formation. It seems that if these are the relevant categories, then his belief is indeed reliably formed, since these are naturally regarded as "generally reliable" sorts of belief-forming processes. The sequence of events leading to Jones's belief also falls into many relatively specific categories such as night-vision-of-a-nearby-object and vision-in-Jones's-precise-environmental-circumstances. These are not clearly reliable types. The sequence is also an instance of this contrived kind: process-leading-from-obviously-defeated-evidence-to-the-belief-that-one-sees-a-flying-saucer. This, presumably, is an unreliable kind of process. Finally, there is the maximally specific process that occurs only when physiological events occur that are exactly like those that led to Jones's belief that he saw a flying saucer. In all likelihood this kind of process occurred only once. Processes of these types are of differing degrees of reliability, no matter how reliability is determined. The implications of reliabilism for the case are rendered definite only when the kind of process whose reliability is relevant is specified. Reliabilists have given little attention to this matter, and those that have specified relevant kinds have not done so in a way that gives their theory an intuitively acceptable extension.[24]

The second unclarity in reliabilism concerns the notion of reliability itself. Reliability is fundamentally a property of kinds of belief-forming processes, not of sequences of particular events. But we can say that a sequence is reliable provided its relevant type is reliable. The problem raised above concerns the specification of relevant types. The current problem is that of specifying the conditions under which a kind of process is *reliable*. Among possible accounts is one according to which a kind of process is reliable provided most instances of that kind until now have led to true beliefs. Alternative accounts measure the reliability of a kind of process by the frequency with which instances of it produce true beliefs in the future as well as the past, or by the frequency with which its instances produce true beliefs in possible worlds that are similar to the world of evaluation in some designated respect, or by the frequency with which its instances produce true beliefs in all possible worlds.[25]

Because there are such drastically different ways of filling in the details of reliabilism the application of the theory is far from clear. The possible versions of reliabilism seem to include one that is extensionally equivalent to WF. It might be held that all beliefs are formed by one of two relevant kinds of belief-forming process. One kind has as instances all and only those sequences of events leading to a belief that is based on fitting evidence; the other is a kind of process that has as instances all and only those sequences leading to a belief that is not based on fitting evidence. If a notion of reliability can be found on which the former sort of process is reliable and the latter is not, the resulting version of reliabilism would be very nearly equivalent to WF.[26] We do not claim that reliabilists would favor this version of reliabilism. Rather, our point is that the fact that this *is* a version shows that reliabilism may not even be a rival to WF.[27]

Evaluation of reliabilism is further complicated by the fact that reliabilists seem to differ about whether they *want* their theory to have approximately the same extension as WF in fact has. The credibility of reliabilism and its relevance to WF depend in part on the concept reliabilists are really attempting to analyze. An example first described by Laurence BonJour helps to bring out two alternatives.[28] BonJour's example is of a person who is clairvoyant. As a result of his clairvoyance he comes to believe that the President is in New York City. The person has no evidence showing that he is clairvoyant and no other evidence supporting his belief about the President. BonJour claims that the example is a counter-example to reliabilism, since the clairvoyant's belief is not justified (we would add: and therefore ill-founded), although the process that caused it is reliable—the person really is clairvoyant.

The general sort of response to this example that seems to be most commonly adopted by reliabilists is in effect to agree that such beliefs are not well-founded. They interpret or revise reliabilism with the aim of avoiding the counter-example.[29] An alternative response would be to argue that the reliability of clairvoyance shows that the belief *is* well-founded, and thus that the example does not refute reliabilism.[30]

We are tempted to respond to the second alternative—beliefs such as that of the clairvoyant in BonJour's example really are well-founded—that this is so clear an instance of an ill-founded belief that any proponent of that view must have in mind a different concept from the one we are discussing. The clairvoyant has no reason for holding his belief about the President. The fact that the belief was caused by a process of a reliable kind—clairvoyance—is a significant fact about it. Such a belief may merit some favorable term of epistemic appraisal, e.g. "objectively probable." But the belief is not well-founded.

There are, however, two lines of reasoning that could lead philosophers to think that we must reconcile ourselves to the clairvoyant's belief turning out to be well-founded. According to one of these arguments, examples such as that of Alfred (discussed in Section IV above) show

that the evidentialist account of epistemic merit is unsatisfactory and that epistemic merit must be understood in terms of the reliability of belief-forming processes.[31] Since the clairvoyant's belief is reliably formed, our initial inclination to regard it as ill-founded must be mistaken.

This argument is unsound. The most that the example about Alfred shows is that there is a concept of favorable epistemic appraisal other than justification, and that this other concept involves the notion of the *basis* of a belief. We believe that WF satisfactorily captures this other concept. There is no need to move to a reliabilist account, according to which some sort of causal reliability is *sufficient* for epistemic justification. The Alfred example does not establish that some version of reliabilism is correct. It does not establish that the clairvoyant's belief is well-founded.

The second argument for the conclusion that the clairvoyant's belief is well-founded makes use of the strong similarity between clairvoyance in BonJour's example and normal perception. We claim that BonJour's clairvoyant is not justified in his belief about the President because that belief does not fit his evidence. Simply having a spontaneous uninferred belief about the whereabouts of the President does not provide evidence for its truth. But, it might be asked, what better evidence is there for any ordinary perceptual belief, say, that one sees a book? If there is no relevant epistemological difference between ordinary perceptual beliefs and the clairvoyant's belief, then they should be evaluated similarly. The argument continues with the point that reliabilism provides an explanation of the crucial similarity between ordinary perceptual beliefs and the clairvoyant's belief—both perception and clairvoyance *work*, in the sense that both are reliable. So beliefs caused by each process are well-founded on a reliabilist account. The fact that reliabilism satisfactorily explains this is to the theory's credit. On the other hand, in advocating evidentialism we have claimed that perceptual beliefs are well-founded and that the clairvoyant's belief is not. But there appears to be no relevant evidential difference between these beliefs. Thus, if the evidentialist view of the matter cannot be defended, then reliabilism is the superior theory and we should accept its consequence—the clairvoyant's belief is well-founded.

One problem with this argument is that reliabilism has no satisfactory explanation of *anything* until the unclarities discussed above are removed in an acceptable way: What shows that perception and clairvoyance are relevant and reliable types of processes? In any event, there *is* an adequate evidentialist explanation of the difference between ordinary perceptual beliefs and the clairvoyant's belief. On one interpretation of clairvoyance, it is a process whereby one is caused to have beliefs about objects hidden from ordinary view without any conscious state having a role in the causal process. The clairvoyant does not have the conscious experience of, say, seeming to see the President in some characteristic New York City setting, and on that basis form the belief that he is in New York. In this respect, the current version of clairvoyance is unlike ordinary perception, which does include conscious perceptual states. Because of this difference, ordinary perceptual beliefs are based on evidence—the evidence of these sensory states—whereas the clairvoyant beliefs are not based on evidence. Since WF requires that well-founded beliefs be based on fitting evidence, and typical clairvoyant beliefs on the current interpretation are not based on any evidence at all, the clairvoyant beliefs do not satisfy WF.

Suppose instead that clairvoyance does include visual experiences, though of remote objects that cannot stimulate the visual system in any normal way. Even if there are such visual experiences that could serve as a basis for a clairvoyant's beliefs, still there is a relevant epistemological difference between beliefs based on normal perceptual experience and the clairvoyant's belief in BonJour's example. We have

collateral evidence to the effect that when we have perceptual experience of certain kinds, external conditions of the corresponding kinds normally obtain. For example, we have evidence supporting the proposition that when we have the usual sort of experience of seeming to see a book, we usually do in fact see a book. This includes evidence from the coherence of these beliefs with beliefs arising from other perceptual sources, and it also includes testimonial evidence. This latter point is easily overlooked. One reason that the belief that one sees a book fits even a child's evidence when she has a perceptual experience of seeing a book is that children are taught, when they have the normal sort of visual experiences, that they are seeing a physical object of the relevant kind. This testimony, typically from people whom the child has reason to trust, provides evidence for the child. And of course testimony from others during adult life also gives evidence for the veridicality of normal visual experience. On the other hand, as BonJour describes his example, the clairvoyant has no confirmation at all of his clairvoyant beliefs. Indeed, he has evidence against these beliefs, since the clairvoyant perceptual experiences do not cohere with his other experiences. We conclude, therefore, that evidentialists can satisfactorily explain why ordinary perceptual beliefs are typically well-founded and unconfirmed clairvoyant beliefs, even if reliably caused, are not. There is no good reason to abandon our initial intuition that the beliefs such as those of the clairvoyant in BonJour's example are not well-founded.

Again, reliabilists could respond to BonJour's example either by claiming that the clairvoyant's belief is in fact well-founded or by arguing that reliabilism does not imply that it is well-founded. We turn now to the second of these alternatives, the one most commonly adopted by reliabilists. This view can be defended by arguing either that reliabilism can be reformulated so that it lacks this implication, or that as currently formulated it lacks this implication. We pointed

184 Richard Feldman and Earl Conee

out above that as a general approach reliabilism is sufficiently indefinite to allow interpretations under which it does lack the implication in question. The only way to achieve this result that we know of that is otherwise satisfactory requires the introduction of evidentialist concepts. The technique is to specify the relevant types of belief-forming processes in evidentialist terms. It is possible to hold that the relevant types of belief-forming process are believing something on the basis of fitting evidence and believing not as a result of fitting evidence. This sort of "reliabilism" is a roundabout approximation of the straightforward evidentialist thesis, WF. We see no reason to couch the approximated evidentialist theory in reliabilist terms. Moreover, the reliabilist approximation is not exactly equivalent to WF, and where it differs it appears to go wrong. The difference is this: it seems possible for the process of believing on the basis of fitting evidence to be unreliable. Finding a suitable sort of reliability makes all the difference here. In various possible worlds where our evidence is mostly misleading, the frequency with which fitting evidence causes true belief is low. Thus, this type of belief-forming process is not "reliable" in such worlds in any straightforward way that depends on actual frequencies. Perhaps a notion of reliability that avoids this result can be found. We know of no such notion which does not create trouble elsewhere for the theory. So, the reliabilist view under consideration has the consequence that in such worlds beliefs based on fitting evidence are not well-founded. This is counterintuitive.[32]

In this section we have compared reliabilism and evidentialism. The vagueness of reliabilism makes it difficult to determine what implications the theory has and it is not entirely clear what implications reliabilists want their theory to have. If reliabilists want their theory to have approximately the same extension as WF, we see no better way to accomplish this than one which makes the theory an unnecessarily complex and relatively implausible approximation to evi-

dentialism. If, on the other hand, reliabilists want their theory to have an extension which is substantially different from that of WF, and yet some familiar notion of "a reliable kind of process" is to be decisive for their notion of well-foundedness, then it becomes clear that the concept they are attempting to analyze is not one evidentialists seek to characterize. This follows from the fact that on this alternative they count as well-founded attitudes that plainly do not exemplify the concept evidentialists are discussing. In neither case, then, does reliabilism pose a threat to evidentialism.

VI

Summary and conclusion

We have defended evidentialism. Some opposition to evidentialism rests on the view that a doxastic attitude can be justified for a person only if forming the attitude is an action under the person's voluntary control. EJ is incompatible with the conjunction of this sort of doxastic voluntarism and the plain fact that some doxastic states that fit a person's evidence are out of that person's control. We have argued that no good reason has been given for thinking that an attitude is epistemically justified only if having it is under voluntary control.

A second thesis contrary to EJ is that a doxastic attitude can be justified only if having that attitude is within the normal doxastic limits of humans. We have held that the attitudes that are epistemically justified according to EJ are within these limits, and that even if they were not, that fact would not suffice to refute EJ.

Some philosophers have contended that believing a proposition, p, is justified for S only when S has gone about gathering evidence about p in a responsible way, or has come to believe p as a result of seeking a meritorious epistemic goal such as the discovery of truth. This thesis conflicts with EJ, since believing p may fit one's evidence no matter how irresponsible one may have been in seeking evidence about p and no matter what were the goals that led to the belief. We agree that there is some epistemic merit in responsibly gathering evidence and in seeking the truth. But we see no reason to think that epistemic justification turns on such matters.

Another thesis conflicting with EJ is that merely having evidence is not sufficient to justify belief, since the believer might not make proper use of the evidence in forming the belief. Consideration of this claim led us to make use of a second evidentialist notion, well-foundedness. It does not, however, provide any good reason to think that EJ is false. Nor do we find reason to abandon evidentialism in favor of reliabilism. Evidentialism remains the most plausible view of epistemic justification.

Afterword

1 Our bedrock epistemic view is a supervenience thesis. Justification strongly supervenes on evidence. More precisely, a whole body of evidence entirely settles which doxastic attitudes toward which propositions are epistemically justified in any possible circumstance. That is,

> ES The epistemic justification of anyone's doxastic attitude toward any proposition at any time strongly supervenes on the evidence that the person has at the time.

The use of EJ to formulate evidentialism in our paper "Evidentialism" has its advantages. For one thing, ES says less than EJ. EJ implies that all and only "evidence-fitting" doxastic attitudes are justified, while ES does not say what relation to evidence justifies an attitude. But, on the other hand, "fit" in EJ is vague at best. This makes non-trivial trouble, as is illustrated by cases like this. Suppose that Smith receives apparently sincere testimonial evidence to the effect that Jones, a person whom Smith has long regarded as a close friend, has been spreading malicious gossip

about Smith. If the evidence from the testimony is strong enough, Smith's evidence may favor the conclusion that Jones has been maliciously gossiping about Smith. Yet it may be that the loyalty Smith owes to Jones morally requires him to resist such a conclusion until his evidence is more conclusive than the evidence that he currently has. What attitude toward the proposition that Jones has been maliciously gossiping about him then "fits" Smith's evidence? The answer is not clear. Perhaps belief is the attitude that "epistemically fits" Smith's evidence, and suspension of judgment is the attitude that "morally fits," and there is no summary notion of fit. Or perhaps moral considerations always override in conflicts of fit. If the latter is true, then EJ makes the mistake of counting Smith as not justified in believing that Jones has been maliciously gossiping about Smith.

This mistake would be an accident arising from our use of the term. We could have said, albeit more obscurely, that the justified attitude is the one that is "epistemically fitting." Also, there is something nearly equivalent to EJ that we could have expressed in a more cumbersome way. We could have said this:

> EC Believing is the justified attitude when the person's evidence on balance supports a proposition, disbelieving is the justified attitude when the person's evidence on balance supports the negation of a proposition, and suspension of judgment is the justified attitude when the person's evidence on balance supports neither a proposition nor its negation.

EC avoids "fit" altogether. But it closes some options that we would prefer that our general thesis leave open. One such option is that when someone's evidence on balance just barely supports a proposition, a suspension of judgment is justified. EJ leaves open the possibility that suspending judgment as well as believing "fits"

the evidence, and thus that each attitude is justified. It also leaves open the possibility that only
suspending judgment fits such meager evidence.
A second option worth leaving open is that no
doxastic attitude is justified when a person's
evidence supports a proposition that the person
does not understand. This problem could be
avoided by restricting EC to justification for
propositions that the person does understand.
But then EC leaves out some justified attitudes, if
understanding is not required. A third option
worth leaving open is that there are many more
doxastic attitudes than the three just mentioned,
because there are degrees of belief and disbelief.
A given strength of evidence would fit with a
corresponding degree of belief or disbelief.

The formulation in terms of "fit" or "epistemic fit" nicely avoids clear implications
about any of those options. In any event, as we
say, ES is bedrock evidentialism.

2 Jeremy Fantl and Matthew McGrath have
recently argued against what they call evidentialism.[33] Their target is this thesis:

> EK   For any two subjects, S and S',
> necessarily, if S and S' have the same
> evidence for/against p, then S is justi-
> fied in believing p iff S' is, too.[34]

Someone is "justified in believing p," as Fantl
and McGrath intend the phrase, just when the
person has evidence that is good enough to
know that p.[35] They argue that there is a pragmatic element in the justification needed for
knowledge. Roughly, this element is how
important the truth-value of the proposition is
to the person. Fantl and McGrath oppose EK by
arguing that there can be cases in which subjects
have the same evidence about a proposition,
while the pragmatic element differs, with the
result that in only one case is that evidence good
enough for knowledge of the proposition. Fantl
and McGrath cite the present work as a defense
of EK.[36] But our work is noncommittal with

regard to EK, given the way that Fantl and
McGrath interpret "justified." Our work is a
defense of EJ. EJ is subject to the misgivings
expressed above, and perhaps our view is
clarified by ES. As EJ and ES bear on belief, they
are about the epistemic justification that a person
may have for believing a proposition (or the
degree of belief that is justified). They hold that
this justification is entirely determined by the
evidence that the person has. They do not
imply anything about how justification relates to
knowledge. In particular, they do not imply that
the strength of justification that is needed for
knowledge is the same in all cases.

There would be a counter-example to EJ
and ES if there were a case in which two people
are unequally justified in some attitude while
possessing the same evidence. Fantl and McGrath
do not so much as seek to establish that this is
a possibility. In opposing what they call evidentialism, namely EK, they seek only to show
that the justification condition on knowledge of
a given proposition is not always met by someone who has the same evidence as a person
who does meet the justification condition on
knowledge of the proposition. Again, nothing in
our paper commits us to denying that. Fantl and
McGrath's topic is an epistemic classification of
a belief for which epistemologists often use the
term "justified" in a relatively technical way.
Someone's belief is thus "justified" when the
belief is well enough justified for the person to
know the proposition. EJ and ES are compatible
with this status *not* being entirely determined by
evidence. It is compatible with EJ and ES to hold
that whether or not someone's epistemic justification for believing a proposition is good
enough for knowledge is partly determined by
something other than how strongly justified the
proposition is for the person. EJ and ES are compatible with Fantl and McGrath's view that the
practical significance to the person of the truth-
value of the proposition makes a difference to
what strength of justification is sufficient for the
person to know the proposition.

This is not a suitable place for a full discussion of the relation of the strength of epistemic justification to knowledge. [. . .] Here we will respond very briefly to Fantl and McGrath's position. The practical significance to someone of a proposition's truth does not seem to us to contribute to when the person is well enough justified to know it. Rather, it seems to us that this practical factor may exert influence on how readily an attribution of knowledge is made, both by the knower and by others. We deny that knowing entails knowing that one knows, or even reasonably believing that one knows. One reason for this denial is that people can make reasonable mistakes about whether their justification is strong enough for knowledge. When the evidence is strong enough, generally there is nothing inescapably manifest about that fact. So even when it is strong enough, people can reasonably doubt that their evidence gives them knowledge, and when the truth matters enough to them, they can reasonably seek better evidence. [. . .] Lastly, a variety of factors can affect whether a person prudentially, morally, or in some other way *ought* to get additional evidence regarding a proposition. Possibly judgments about this affect our willingness to ascribe knowledge to someone, without affecting whether the person has knowledge.

3 The notion of a well-founded belief makes a cameo appearance in "Evidentialism." It serves only to accommodate the intuition that there is something epistemically defective about drawing justified conclusions for bad reasons. Such beliefs are ill-founded, in virtue of not being based on justifying evidence.

We think that WF is an acceptable evidentialist account of the pre-theoretical notion of a well-founded belief. This is a good place to state our view that the notion has at least two significant epistemic roles to play.

First, and most simply, one useful epistemic role for an account of a well-founded belief concerns theorizing about what it is to be reasonable. A reasonable person is, among other things, one who has an inclination to base her beliefs on undefeated justifying reasons. That is, a reasonable person must have an inclination toward well-founded beliefs. WF seems to us to impose the right requirements on reasonableness. And second, knowledge of P requires a well-founded belief in P. If a belief is justified and otherwise apt for knowledge, but not well-founded, then the belief is accidentally correct in a way that somewhat resembles what occurs in the classic Gettier cases. But, unlike in classic Gettier cases, there is nothing epistemically defective about the connection between the person's justification for P and a fact making P true. The belief itself is not held in light of the justification, though. It is held dogmatically, or from wishful thinking, or on some other epistemically faulty basis. Knowing a proposition to be true requires a well-founded belief in the proposition.

This necessary condition for knowledge requires a fairly broad notion of a basis for a belief. For example, in many cases of knowing by remembering, the person has forgotten her original basis for the belief. [. . .] In such cases, her current justification derives partly from background evidence she has that she sufficiently tends to acquire true beliefs on subject matters that are similar enough to that of the remembered proposition. This evidence in the background distinguishes knowledge by memory, when the original source is forgotten, from fortunately accurate recollective beliefs that are not thereby known. The need for a broad notion of basing arises because this sort of background contribution to the justification is almost never a conscious part of knowing by remembering. Yet it is an essential part of the evidence by which the belief is currently justified. So it must be part of the basis for the belief if the belief is to be well-founded and thereby known.

4 Stewart Cohen has raised an issue about how basic sources of knowledge provide evidence.[37]

Evidentialists seem required to say something implausible about what is justified. To illustrate the problem, we can suppose that simple perceptual experiences all by themselves provide justification for some simple corresponding beliefs about the external world. For example, one might hold the following principle:

> RED   If S seems to see something red (S is appeared-to-redly), then S is justified in believing that there is something red before S provided S has no defeaters for this proposition.[38]

Analogous principles might be defended for other simple sensory qualities. A corresponding principle might be advanced concerning memory. We will say that any property for which any such principle is true is a property that "directly justifies" belief in the relevant external world proposition.

If there are any properties that directly justify belief in the relevant external world propositions, then it seems that one can all too easily come to know facts about one's visual accuracy. Suppose that RED is true. And suppose one wonders whether one's visually formed beliefs that things are red are usually correct. That is, one wonders whether things really are red when one judges that there is something red on the basis of seeming to see something red. If RED is true, then one seems to be all set to construct a good inductive argument for the accuracy of one's judgments that things are red. The argument would have as premises such propositions as:

> Now (when I am seeming to see something red) I believe that something is red, and I am right.

Each such judgment is justified. The first conjunct is justified, we assume, because one knows what one visually experiences and what one believes. And, given RED, the second conjunct is justified as well. If one can combine enough such premises, one gets what looks like a good inductive argument for a general conclusion that affirms the accuracy of one's beliefs that something is red. Yet, one does this without needing any general information about one's perceptual abilities. Nothing more is needed than the truth of RED and one's realization that one is believing that something is red on the relevant experiential basis. This is an implausibly easy way to justify the conclusion that one is making uniformly true color judgments.

We believe that this argument helps to bring out challenging issues about how experiences justify beliefs. We do not think that the accuracy of one's color judgments can be so easily supported by inductive argument. In our view, RED is false, as are other principles of the same structure. It might be thought that if RED is false, then the nearest true principle is one according to which the experience of redness must be combined with a justified general principle about the reliability of one's perceptions of red in order to have justification for the belief that there is something red before one. It is difficult to see how one could acquire justification for the general principle without prior justification for specific beliefs. Cohen advocates a holist view according to which, at some point in intellectual development, both the individual belief and the general belief first become justified.[39]

One can reject RED without resorting to Cohen's holism. The experience of redness all by itself does not justify to any degree the corresponding external world belief. Perhaps very young children and newly sighted adults can have the experience of redness without being justified at all in believing that there is something red before them. They may even lack the requisite concepts. People learn to respond to particular kinds of experiences with the judgment that there is something red present. Exactly what it is in this learning that equips people for justified color judgments is not clear. One learns not to make the judgments in response to any and all episodes where one is appeared-to-redly. It is reasonable to think that one must learn something about distinguishing sufficiently apt environments for visual color judgments and perhaps also something about signs of perceptual abnormalities. Evidence acquired in this learning makes it true that people can be justified in believing that something red is present. If an account along these lines is correct, then what is learned need not be some general proposition about the reliability of one's redness judgments. This is supported by the fact that people can know that things are red without having the sophistication required for knowing any such generalization. Children who have learned their colors can know that there is a red object before them without having any such general knowledge.

Though we believe that the evidentialist approach to this matter that we have sketched is correct, the details must await another occasion.

Notes

1 EJ is compatible with the existence of varying strengths of belief and disbelief. If there is such variation, then the greater the preponderance of evidence, the stronger the doxastic attitude that fits the evidence.

2 There are difficult questions about the concept of fit, as well as about what it is for someone to *have* something as evidence, and of what kind of thing constitutes evidence. As a result, there are some cases in which it is difficult to apply EJ. For example, it is unclear whether a person has as evidence propositions he is not currently thinking of, but could recall with some prompting. As to what constitutes evidence, it seems clear that this includes both beliefs and sensory states such as feeling very warm and having the visual experience of seeing blue. Some philosophers seem to think that only beliefs can justify beliefs. (See, for example, Keith Lehrer, *Knowledge* (Oxford: Oxford University Press, 1974), pp. 187–8.) The application of EJ is clear enough to do the work that we intend here—a defense of the evidentialist position.

3 See [Heil] "Doxastic agency," *Philosophical Studies*, 43 (1983), pp. 355–64. The quotation is from p. 355.

4 See [Kornblith] "The psychological turn," *Australasian Journal of Philosophy*, 60 (1982), pp. 238–53. The quotation is from p. 252.

5 Kornblith, *op. cit.*, p. 253.

6 Heil, *op. cit.*, p. 363.

7 Kornblith may be guilty of this confusion. He writes, "if a person has an unjustified belief, that person is epistemically culpable," *op. cit.*, p. 243.

8 Nothing we say here should be taken to imply that any doxastic states are in fact voluntarily entered.

9 See "Epistemics: The regulative theory of cognition," *Journal of Philosophy*, 75 (1978), pp. 509–23, esp. p. 510 and p. 514.

10 "Justified belief and epistemically responsible action," *Philosophical Review*, 92 (1983), pp. 33–48. The quotation is from p. 46.

11 Paul Thagard, "From the descriptive to the normative in psychology and logic," *Philosophy of Science*, 49 (1982), pp. 24–42. The quotation is from p. 34.

12 Another version of this argument is that EJ is false because it classifies as justified for a person attitudes that are beyond *that person's* limits. This version is subject to similar criticisms.

13 See *Theory of Knowledge*, 2nd edn (Englewood Cliffs, NJ: Prentice-Hall, 1977), especially pp. 12–15.

14 Roderick Firth makes a similar point against a similar view in "Are epistemic concepts reducible to ethical concepts," in *Values and Morals*, edited by A. I. Goldman and J. Kim (D. Reidel, Dordrecht, 1978), pp. 215–29.

15 Kornblith defends this view in "Justified belief and epistemically responsible action." Some passages suggest that he intends to introduce a new notion of justification, one to be understood in terms of epistemically responsible action. But some passages, especially in section II, suggest that the traditional analysis of justification is being found to be objectionable and inferior to the one he proposes.

16 Laurence BonJour, "Externalist theories of empirical knowledge," *Midwest Studies of Philosophy*, 5 (1980), p. 63.

17 This is contrary to the view of Richard Gale, defended in "William James and the ethics of

belief," *American Philosophical Quarterly*, 17 (1980), pp. 1–14, and of W. K. Clifford, who said, "It is wrong always, everywhere, and for every one, to believe anything upon insufficient evidence" (quoted by William James in "The will to believe," reprinted in *Reason and Responsibility*, edited by J. Feinberg (Belmont, California, Wadsworth Publishing Co., 1981) p. 100).

18   See "Believing what one ought," *Journal of Philosophy*, 80 (1983), pp. 752–65. The quotation is from pp. 752 ff.

19   See "Epistemic merit, intrinsic and instrumental," *Proceedings and Addresses of the American Philosophical Association*, 55 (1981), pp. 5–6.

20   See Kornblith's "Beyond foundationalism and the coherence theory," *Journal of Philosophy*, 77 (1980), pp. 597–612, esp. pp. 601 f., and Goldman's "What is justified belief?" in *Justification and Knowledge*, George S. Pappas, ed. (D. Reidel, Dordrecht, 1979), pp. 1–24.

21   Clause (ii) of WF is intended to accommodate the fact that a well-founded attitude need not be based on a person's whole body of evidence. What seems required is that the person base a well-founded attitude on a justifying part of the person's evidence, and that he not ignore any evidence he has that defeats the justifying power of the evidence he does base his attitude on. It might be that his defeating evidence is itself defeated by a still wider body of his evidence. In such a case, the person's attitude is well-founded only if he takes the wider body into account.

     WF uses our last main primitive concept—that of *basing* an attitude on a body of evidence. This notion is reasonably clear, though an analysis would be useful. See note 22 below for one difficult question about what is entailed.

22   Goldman uses this sort of example only to show that there is a causal element in the concept of justification. We acknowledge that there is an epistemic concept—well-foundedness—that appeals to the notion of basing an attitude on evidence, and this may be a causal notion. What seems to confer epistemic merit on basing one's belief on the evidence is that in doing so one *appreciates* the evidence. It is unclear whether one can appreciate the evidence without being caused to have the belief by the evidence. But in any event we see no such causal requirement in the case of justification.

23   The clearest and most influential discussion of reliabilism is in Goldman's "What is justified belief?" One of the first statements of the theory appears in David Armstrong's *Belief, Truth and Knowledge* (Cambridge University Press, Cambridge, 1973). For extensive bibliographies on reliabilism, see Frederick Schmitt's "Reliability, objectivity, and the background of justification," *Australasian Journal of Philosophy*, 62 (1984), pp. 1–15, and Richard Feldman's "Reliability and justification," *The Monist*, 68 (1985), pp. 159–74.

24   For discussion of the problem of determining relevant kinds of belief-forming processes, see Goldman, "What is justified belief?," Schmitt, "Reliability, objectivity, and the background of justification," Feldman, "Reliability and justification," and Feldman, "Schmitt on reliability, objectivity, and justification," *Australasian Journal of Philosophy*, 63 (1985), pp. 354–60.

25   In "Reliability and justified belief," *Canadian Journal of Philosophy*, 14 (1984), pp. 103–14, John Pollock argues that there is no account of reliability suitable for reliabilists.

26   This version of reliabilism will not be exactly equivalent to WF because it ignores the factors introduced by clause (ii) of WF.

27   It is also possible that versions of reliabilism making use only of natural psychological kinds of belief-forming processes are extensionally equivalent to WF. Goldman seeks to avoid evaluative epistemic concepts in his theory of epistemic justification, so he would not find an account of justification satisfactory unless it appealed only to such natural kinds. See "What is justified belief?," p. 6.

28   See "Externalist theories of empirical knowledge," p. 62.

29   See Goldman, "What is justified belief?," pp. 18–20, Kornblith, "Beyond foundationalism and the coherence theory," pp. 609–11, and Frederick Schmitt, "Reliability, objectivity, and the background of justification."

30   We know of one who has explicitly taken this approach. It seems to fit most closely with the view defended by David Armstrong in *Belief, Truth and Knowledge*.

31   We know of no one who explicitly defends this inference. In "The psychological turn," pp. 241 f., Kornblith argues that these examples show that

justification depends upon "psychological connections" and "the workings of the appropriate belief forming process." But he clearly denies there that reliabilism is directly implied.

32 Stewart Cohen has made this point in "Justification and truth," *Philosophical Studies*, 46 (1984), pp. 279–95. Cohen makes the point in the course of developing a dilemma. He argues that reliabilism has the sort of flaw that we describe above when we appeal to worlds where evidence is mostly misleading. Cohen also contends that reliabilism has the virtue of providing a clear explanation of how the epistemic notion of justification is connected with the notion of truth. A theory that renders this truth connection inexplicable is caught on the second horn of Cohen's dilemma.

Although Cohen does not take up evidentialism as we characterize it, the second horn of his dilemma affects EJ and WF. They do not explain how having an epistemically justified or well-founded belief is connected to the truth of that belief. Evidentialists can safely say this much about the truth connection: evidence that makes believing p justified is evidence on which it is *epistemically* probable that p is true. Although there is this connection between justification and truth, we acknowledge that there may be no analysis of epistemic probability that makes the connection to truth as close, or as clear, as might have been hoped.

Cohen argues that there must be a truth connection. This shows no flaw in EJ or WF unless they are incompatible with there being such a connection. Cohen does not argue for this incompatibility and we know of no reason to believe that it exists. So at most Cohen's dilemma shows that evidentialists have work left to do.

33 "Evidence, Pragmatics, and Justification," *Philosophical Review*, 111 (2002), 67–94.

34 Ibid., 68.

35 Ibid., 67.

36 Ibid., 68.

37 See Stewart Cohen, "Basic Beliefs and the Problem of Easy Knowledge," *Philosophy and Phenomenological Research*, 65 (2002), 309–29.

38 Defeaters of the sort mentioned in RED are parts of one's overall evidence that defeat one's justification. They are "internal" defeaters. They differ from the external defeaters of justified true beliefs that disqualify the beliefs from being knowledge.

39 See Cohen, "Basic Beliefs and the Problem of Easy Knowledge," section VI.

Chapter 18

William Alston

AN INTERNALIST EXTERNALISM

In this essay I will explain, and at least begin to defend, the particular blend of internalism and externalism in my view of epistemic justification. So far as I know, this is my own private blend;[1] many, I'm afraid, will not take that as a recommendation. Be that as it may, it's mine, and it's what I will set forth in this paper. I will first have to present the general contours of the position, as a basis for specifying the points at which we have an internalism–externalism issue. I won't have time to defend the general position, or even to present more than a sketch. Such defense as will be offered will be directed to the internalist and externalist features.

In a word, my view is that to be justified in believing that p is for that belief *to be based on an adequate ground*. To explain what I mean by this I will have to say something about the correlative terms "based on" and "ground" and about the *adequacy* of grounds.

The ground of a belief is what it is based on. The notion of *based on* is a difficult one. I am not aware that anyone has succeeded in giving an adequate and illuminating general explanation of it. It seems clear that some kind of causal dependence is involved, whether the belief is based on other beliefs or on experience. If my belief that it rained last night is based on my belief that the streets are wet, then I hold the former belief *because* I hold the latter belief; my holding the latter belief *explains* my holding the former. Similarly, if my belief that the streets are

wet is based on their looking wet, I believe that they are wet *because* of the way they look, and their looking that way *explains* my believing that they are wet. And presumably these are relations of causal dependence. But, equally clearly, not just any kind of causal dependence will do. My belief that p is causally dependent on a certain physiological state of my brain, but the former is not based on the latter. How is *being based on* distinguished from other sorts of causal dependence? We have a clear answer to this question for cases of maximally explicit inference, where I come to believe that p because I see (or at least take it) that it is adequately supported by the fact that q (which I believe). And where the ground is experiential we can also come to believe that p because we take its truth to be adequately indicated by the experience from which it arises. In these cases the belief-forming process is *guided* by our belief in the adequate support relation, and this marks them out as cases of a belief's being based on a ground, rather than just causally depending on something.[2] A belief, however, may be based on other beliefs or on experiences, where no such guiding belief in support relations is in evidence.[3] My belief that you are upset may be based on various aspects of the way you look and act without my consciously believing that these features provide adequate support for that belief; in a typical case of this sort I have no such belief simply because I am not consciously aware of which features these are; I do not consciously discriminate them. And even where I am more explicitly aware of the ground, I may not consciously believe anything at all about support relations. It is very dubious that very small children, for example, ever have such support beliefs; and yet surely a small child's belief that the kitten is sick can be based on her belief that the kitten is not running around as usual. But then what feature is common to all cases of a belief's being *based on* something, and serves to distinguish this kind of causal dependence from other kinds? Here I will have to content myself with making a suggestion. Wherever it is clear that a belief is *based on* another belief or on an experience, the belief-forming "process" or "mechanism" is *taking account* of that ground or features thereof, being *guided* by it, even if this does not involve the conscious utilization of a belief in a support relation. To say that my belief that the streets are wet is based on the way they look is to say that in forming a belief about the condition of the streets I (or the belief-forming "mechanism") am differentially sensitive to the way the streets look; the mechanism is so constituted that the belief formed about the streets will be some, possibly very complex, function of the visual experience input. Even where an explicit belief in a support relation is absent, the belief formation is the result of a *taking account* of features of the experience and forming the belief *in the light of* them, rather than just involving some subcognitive transaction.[4] Much more could and should be said about this, but the foregoing will have to suffice for now. In any event, whether or not this suggestion is along the right line, I shall take it that we have an adequate working grasp of the notion of a belief's being based on something, and that this suffices for the concerns of this essay.

In the foregoing I was speaking of the ground of a belief as playing a role in its *formation*. That is not the whole story. It is often pointed out that a belief may acquire a new basis after its initial acquisition. However the role of post-origination bases in justification is a complex matter, one not at all adequately dealt with in the epistemological literature. To keep things manageable for this short conspectus of my view, I shall restrict myself to bases on which a belief is originally formed. That means, in effect, that the discussion will be limited to what it takes for a belief to be justified at the moment of its acquisition.

In taking the justification of a belief to be determined by what it is based on, I am reflecting the subject-relative character of justification. I may be justified in believing that p while you are not. Indeed, justification is time as well as subject relative; I may be justified in believing that p at one time but not at another.[5] Whether I am justified in believing that p is a matter of how I am situated vis-à-vis the content of that belief. In my view, that is cashed out in terms of what the subject was "going on" in supposing the proposition in question to be true, on what basis she supposed p to be the case.[6]

What sort of things do subjects go on in holding beliefs? The examples given above suggest that the prime candidates are the subject's other beliefs and experiences; and I shall consider grounds to be restricted to items of those two categories. Though I will offer no a priori or transcendental argument for this, I will adopt the plausible supposition that where the input to a belief-forming mechanism is properly thought of as *what the belief is based on*, it will be either a belief or an experience. But we must tread carefully here. Where a philosopher or a psychologist would say that S's belief that it rained last night is based on S's *belief* that the streets are wet, S would probably say, if he were aware of the basis of his belief, that his ground, basis, or reason for believing that it rained last night is the *fact* that the streets are wet. The ordinary way of talking about reasons specifies the (putative) fact believed as the reason rather than the belief.[7] I think we can set up the matter either way. I choose to use "ground" for the psychological input to the belief-forming mechanism, that is, the belief or experience, thus deviating from the most ordinary way of speaking of these matters.

I need to be more explicit about how grounds are specified in my account. I can best approach this by considering a difficulty raised by Marshall Swain in his comments on this essay at the Brown conference. Swain wrote as follows:

Suppose two subjects, Smith and Jones, who have the same evidence (grounds) for the belief that p, where the evidence consists of the proposition p V (p & q). Both subjects come to believe that p on this basis of the evidence (and no other evidence). In the case of Smith, the mechanism for generating the belief is an inference which instantiates a tendency to invalidly infer p from any sentence of the form "p V q". In the case of Jones, the mechanism is an inference which is based on an internalized valid inference schema (of which several are possible). It seems clear to me that only Jones has a justified belief that p, even though they have the same grounds.

Such cases can be proliferated indefinitely. For an example involving experiential grounds, consider two persons, A and B, who come to believe that a collie is in the room on the basis of qualitatively identical visual experiences. But A recognizes the dog as a collie on the basis of distinctively collie features, whereas B would take any largish dog to be a collie. Again, it would seem that A is justified in his belief while B is not, even though they have the same grounds for a belief with the same propositional content.[8] Swain takes it that such cases show that characteristics of the subject must be brought into the account in addition to what we have introduced.

However, I believe that unwanted applications like these can be excluded just by giving a sufficiently discriminating specification of grounds. As I am using the term, the "ground" for a belief is not what we might call the total concrete input to the belief-forming mechanism, but rather those features of that input that are actually taken

account of in forming the belief, in, so to say, "choosing" a propositional content for a belief. In Swain's case, the only feature of the belief input taken account of by Smith was that its propositional object was of the form "p V q." No further features of the input were playing a role in that belief formation; no further features were "guiding" the operation of the belief-forming mechanism. In Jones' case, however, the belief formation was guided by the fact that the input belief had a propositional content of the form "p V (p & q)." In Smith's case any input of the "p V q" form would have led to the same doxastic output, whereas for Jones many other inputs of that form would *not* have led to the formation of a belief that p. Thus, strictly speaking, the grounds were different. Similarly in the canine identification case, for A the ground was the object's visually presenting certain features that are in fact distinctively collie-like, whereas for B the ground was the object's visually presenting itself as a largish dog.

We may sum this up by saying that the ground of a belief is made up of those features of the input to the formation of that belief that were actually taken account of in the belief formation. (Again, remember that our discussion is restricted to the bases of beliefs when formed.)

Not every grounded belief will be justified, but only one that has an *adequate* ground. To get at the appropriate criterion of adequacy, let's note that a belief's *being justified* is a favorable status vis-à-vis the basic aim of believing or, more generally, of cognition, viz., to believe truly rather than falsely. For a ground to be favorable relative to this aim it must be "truth conducive"; it must be sufficiently indicative of the truth of the belief it grounds. In other terms, the ground must be such that the *probability* of the belief's being true, given that ground, is very high. It is an objective probability that is in question here. The world is such that, at least in the kinds of situations in which we typically find ourselves, the ground is a reliable indication of the fact believed. In this paper I will not attempt to spell out the kind of objective probability being appealed to. So far as I am aware, no adequate conception of this sort of probability (or perhaps of any other sort) has been developed. Suffice it to say that I am thinking in terms of some kind of "tendency" conception of probability, where the lawful structure of the world is such that one state of affairs renders another more or less probable.

The ambiguity noted earlier as to what constitutes a ground has to be dealt with here as well. Suppose that the ground of my belief that p is my belief that q. In order that the former belief be justified, is it required that the belief that q be a reliable indication of the truth of the belief that p, or is it required that the fact that q be a reliable indication? The latter is the ordinary way of thinking about the matter. If my belief that Jones is having a party is based on my belief that there are a lot of cars around his house, then just as I would ordinarily cite the *fact* that there are a lot of cars around his house as my reason for supposing that he is having a party, so I would think that my reason is an adequate one because the former *fact* is a reliable indication of the latter one. The adequacy requirement, however, could be set up in either way. To appreciate this let's first note that in either case the belief that p will be justified only if the grounding belief is justified (a stronger requirement would be that the grounding belief constitute knowledge, but I won't go that far). Even if the fact that q is a highly reliable indication that p, that won't render my belief that p justified by virtue of being based on a belief that q unless I am justified in believing that q. An unjustified belief cannot transfer justification to another belief via the basis relation. But if I am justified in believing that q and if q is a reliable indication of p, then my belief that q will also be a (perhaps slightly less) reliable indication that p, provided a belief cannot be justified unless its ground renders it likely to be true. For in that case my having a justified belief that q renders it likely that q, which in turn renders it likely that p. And so if q is

a strong indication of the truth of p, so is my belief that q (assuming that we don't lose too much of the strength of indication in the probabilistic relation between the justified belief that q and q). This being the case, I will simplify matters for purposes of this paper by taking the adequacy of a ground to depend on *its* being a sufficiently strong indication of the truth of the belief grounded.

II

Now we are in a position to say what is internalist and what is externalist about this position, and to make a start, at least, in defending our choices. The view is internalist most basically, and most minimally, by virtue of the requirement that there be a ground of the belief. As we have made explicit, the ground must be a psychological state of the subject and hence "internal" to the subject in an important sense. Facts that obtain independently of the subject's psyche, however favorable to the truth of the belief in question, cannot be *grounds* of the belief in the required sense.

But this is only a weak form of internalism, one that would hardly be deemed worthy of the name by those who flaunt the label. There are, in fact, several constraints on justification that have gone under this title. [. . .] I distinguish two main forms: Perspectival Internalism (PI), according to which only what is within the subject's perspective in the sense of being something the subject knows or justifiably believes can serve to justify; and Accessibility Internalism (AI), according to which only that to which the subject has cognitive access in some specially strong form can be a justifier. However, it is now clear to me that I should have added at least one more version, Consciousness Internalism (CI), according to which only those states of affairs of which the subject is actually conscious or aware can serve to justify.[9]

[. . .] I argue against PI, partly on the grounds that its only visible means of support is from an unacceptable deontological conception of justification that makes unrealistic assumptions about the voluntary control of belief, and partly on the grounds that it rules out the possibility of immediate justification by experience of such things as introspective and perceptual beliefs. CI has the crushing disability that one can never complete the formulation of a sufficient condition for justification. For suppose that we begin by taking condition C to be sufficient for the justification of S's belief that p. But then we must add that S must be aware of C (i.e. the satisfaction of condition C) in order to be justified. Call this enriched condition C_1. But then C_1 is not enough by itself either; S must be aware of C_1. So that must be added to yield a still richer condition, C_2. And so on ad infinitum. Any thesis that implies that it is in principle impossible to complete a statement of conditions sufficient for justification is surely unacceptable.[10]

I find AI to be much more promising. To be sure, many formulations are, I believe, much too strong to be defensible. Thus Carl Ginet's version is in terms of what he calls being "directly recognizable":

> Every one of every set of facts about S's position that minimally suffices to make S, at a given time, justified in being confident that p must be *directly recognizable* to S at that time. By "directly recognizable" I mean this: if a certain fact obtains, then it is directly recognizable to S at a given time if and only if, provided that S at that time has the concept of that sort of fact, S needs at that time only to reflect clear-headedly on the question of whether or not that fact obtains in order to know that it does.[11]

But there are very plausible conditions for justification that are not directly recognizable in this sense. Consider, for example, the familiar situation in which I recognize something or someone on the basis of subtle perceptual cues I am unable to specify, even on careful reflection.

Here it seems correct to say that my belief that the person before me is John Jones is justified, if it is, by virtue of being based on a visual experience with such-and-such features, where the experience's having those features is crucial for its providing justification. But those features are not "directly recognizable" by me. Or again consider the familiar situation of a belief, for example, that Republicans are unlikely to be tough on big business, that is based on a wide diversity of evidence, most of which I cannot specify even after careful reflection. Ginet's form of AI is too stringent to be suited to our condition.[12]

However, I believe that it is possible to support a more moderate version of AI. To determine just what sort of accessibility is required I had better make explicit what I see as the source of the requirement. I find widely shared and strong intuitions in favor of some kind of accessibility requirement for justification. We expect that if there is something that justifies my belief that p, I will be able to determine what it is. We find something incongruous, or conceptually impossible, in the notion of my being justified in believing that p while totally lacking any capacity to determine what is responsible for that justification. Thus when reliability theorists of justification maintain that any reliably formed belief is ipso facto justified, most of us balk. For since it is possible for a belief to be reliably formed without the subject's having any capacity to determine this, and, indeed, without there being anything accessible to the subject on which the belief is based—as when invariable correct beliefs about the future of the stock market seem to pop out of nowhere—it seems clear to many of us that reliable belief formation cannot be sufficient for justification.

Why these intuitions? Why is some kind of accessibility required for justification? Is this just a basic constituent of the concept? Or can it be derived from other more basic components? I myself do not see any way to argue from other "parts" of the concept to this one. Hence I will not attempt to *prove* that accessibility is required for justification. But I believe that we can get some understanding of the presence of this accessibility requirement by considering the larger context out of which the concept of epistemic justification has developed and which gives it its distinctive importance. Thus I will attempt to *explain* the presence of the requirement.

First I want to call attention to a view of justification I do not accept. Suppose, with pragmatists like Peirce and Dewey and other contextualists, we focus on the *activity of justifying* beliefs to the exclusion of the *state of being justified* in holding a belief. The whole topic of epistemic justification will then be confined to the question of what it takes to successfully carry out the activity of justifying a belief, *showing* it to be something one is entitled to believe, establishing its credentials, responding to challenges to its legitimacy, and so on. But then the only considerations that can have any bearing on justification (i.e. on the successful outcome of such an activity) are those that are cognitively accessible to the subject. For only those can be appealed to in order to justify the belief.

Now I have no temptation to restrict the topic of epistemic justification to the activity of justifying. Surely epistemology is concerned with the epistemic status of beliefs with respect to which no activity of justifying has been carried on. We want to know whether people are justified in holding normal perceptual beliefs, normal memory beliefs, beliefs in generalizations concerning how things generally go in the physical world, beliefs about the attitudes of other people, religious beliefs, and so on, even where, as is usually the case, such beliefs have not been subjected to an attempt to justify. It is quite arbitrary to ban such concerns from epistemology.

But though the activity of responding to challenges is not the whole story, I do believe that in a way it is fundamental to the concept of *being justified*. Why is it that we have this concept

of *being justified in holding a belief* and why is it important to us? I suggest that the concept was developed, and got its hold on us, because of the practice of critical reflection on our beliefs, of challenging their credentials and responding to such challenges—in short the practice of attempting to *justify* beliefs. Suppose there were no such practice; suppose that no one ever challenges the credentials of anyone's beliefs; suppose that no one ever critically reflects on the grounds or basis of one's own beliefs. In that case would we be interested in determining whether one or another belief is justified? I think not. It is only because we participate in such activities, only because we are alive to their importance, that the question of whether someone is in a state of *being justified* in holding a belief is of live interest to us. I am not suggesting that being justified is a matter of engaging in, or successfully engaging in, the activity of justifying. I am not even affirming the less obviously false thesis that being justified in believing that *p* is a matter of *being able* to successfully justify the belief. Many persons are justified in many beliefs without possessing the intellectual or verbal skills to exhibit what justifies those beliefs. Thus the *fact* of being justified is not dependent on any particular actual or possible activity of justifying. What I am suggesting is that those facts of justification would not have the interest and importance for us that they do have if we were not party to a social practice of demanding justification and responding to such demands.

Now for the bearing of this on AI. I want to further suggest that this social practice has strongly influenced the development of the *concept of being justified*. What has emerged from this development is the concept of *what would have to be specified to carry out a successful justification of the belief*. Our conception of what a belief needs in the way of a basis in order to *be justified* is the conception of that the specification of which in answer to a challenge would suffice to answer that challenge. But then it is quite understandable that the concept should include the requirement that the justifier be accessible to the subject. For only what the subject can ascertain can be cited by that subject in response to a challenge. This, I believe, provides the explanation for the presence of the AI constraint on justification.

Now that we have a rationale for an AI constraint, let's see just what form of the constraint is dictated by that rationale. There are at least two matters to be decided: (a) what is required to be accessible; (b) what degree of accessibility is to be required.

As for (a), the most important distinction is between (1) the "justifier," that is, the ground of the belief, and (2) its adequacy or justificatory efficacy: its "truth-conduciveness." I'm going to save adequacy for the next section and concentrate here on the justifier. But there are still choices. Should we say that in order for S's belief that p to be justified by being based on a ground, G, G itself, that very individual ground, must be accessible to S? Or is it enough that G is the sort of thing that is typically accessible to normal human subjects? The latter, weaker requirement would allow a justifying ground in a particular case to be a belief that is not in fact accessible to the subject's consciousness, because of repression, a cognitive overload, or whatever, provided beliefs are in general the sort of thing to which subjects have cognitive access. The rationale offered above for AI would not demand of every justifying ground that it itself be available for citation, but only that it be the *sort* of thing that is, in general, so available. We were not arguing that it is conceptually necessary, or even universally true, that a justifying ground can be cited in response to a challenge. We were only contending that the concept of being justified in believing that p (including the concept of a justifying ground for a belief) has been developed against the background of the practice of citing grounds in defense of assertions. This looser sort of relationship of justifying grounds to the activity of justifying supports at most the weaker requirement that a justifying ground is the sort of thing that, in general or when nothing

interferes, is available for citation by the subject. And it is just as well that only this weaker requirement is mandated, for, because of the considerations adduced in criticizing Ginet's form of AI, it seems that we must allow cases in which the basis of a belief is blocked from consciousness through some special features of that situation. Thus we are free to recognize cases of justification in which the complexity of the grounds or the rapidity of their appearance and disappearance renders the subject unable to store and retrieve them as she would have to in order to cite them in answer to a challenge.

Now for degree. Just *how* does a kind of state have to be generally accessible to its subject in order to be a candidate for a justifying ground? I have already argued that Ginet's version of AI is too demanding to be realistic. On the other hand, if we simply require that justifiers be the sorts of things that are knowable in principle by the subject, somehow or other, that is too weak. That would allow anything to count as a justifier that it is not *impossible* for the subject to come to know about. That would not even rule out neurophysiological states of the brain about which no one knows anything now. What is needed here is a concept of something like "fairly direct accessibility." In order that justifiers be generally available for presentation as the legitimizers of the belief, they must be fairly readily available to the subject through some mode of access much quicker than lengthy research, observation, or experimentation. It seems reasonable to follow Ginet's lead and suggest that to be a justifier an item must be the sort of thing that, in general, a subject can explicitly note the presence of just by sufficient reflection on his situation. However, the amount and depth of reflection needed for this will vary in different cases. I want to avoid the claim that justifiers can always be spotted right away, just by raising the question. I don't know how to make this notion of "fairly direct accessibility" precise, and I suspect that it may be impossible to do so. Perhaps our concept of justification is not itself precise enough to require a precise degree of ease or rapidity of access. Let's just say that to be a justifier of a belief, its ground must be the sort of thing whose instances are fairly directly accessible to their subject on reflection.

I am going to just mention in passing another internalist feature of this position. Being based on an adequate ground is sufficient only for prima facie justification, justification that can be nullified by sufficient overriding reasons from the subject's stock of knowledge and justified belief.[13] Reasons that override a given justification for a belief that p are of two sorts. First there are sufficient reasons for supposing p to be false; call them *rebutters*. Second, there are reasons such that the combination of them with the initial ground fails to be sufficiently indicative of the truth of p; call them *neutralizers*. Thus even if my current visual experience is, in itself, a strong indication that there is a tree in front of me, I will not be, all things considered, justified in believing that there is a tree in front of me provided I have even stronger reasons for supposing there to be no tree there (rebutter), or provided I have strong reasons for supposing my visual apparatus not to be working properly at the moment (neutralizer). The effect of the requirement (for unqualified justification) of no sufficient overriders is to make unqualified justification sensitive to the totality of what the subject knows and justifiably believes. I am unqualifiedly justified in believing that p only if the totality of my knowledge, justified belief, and experience constitutes an adequate ground for that belief. Since the fate of prima facie justification is determined by what is in the subject's perspective on the world, rather than by the way the world is, this is an additional internalist factor, though as the last note makes explicit, not of the AI sort.

III

So much for internalism. Now where is the externalism? To see where that comes in we must move from the existence of grounds to their adequacy. An internalist position on this point will make it a condition of justification that the adequacy of the ground be internal to the subject in some way or other. The externalism of my position will consist in the rejection of all such requirements. We can distinguish here between making the internality of adequacy a *necessary* condition of justification and making it sufficient for justification, along with the belief's being based on the ground in question. I shall consider these in turn.

Go back to the distinction between PI and AI. (We may ignore CI in this connection, since we are unlikely to find a plausible way of construing the notion of an "awareness" or "consciousness" of the *adequacy* of a ground.) A PI necessary condition in this area would presumably run as follows.

(I) One is justified in believing that p only if one knows or is justified in believing that the ground of that belief is an adequate one.

Let's focus on the justified belief alternative. This requirement labors under the very considerable disadvantage of requiring an infinite hierarchy of justified beliefs in order to be justified in any belief. For the requirement will also apply to the higher level belief that the ground of the belief that p is adequate. (Call the propositional content of this higher level belief "q.") To be justified in the belief that q one must be justified in believing that *its* ground is adequate. Call the propositional object of this still higher level belief "r." Then to be justified in believing that r one must be justified in the still higher level belief that the ground of one's belief that r is an adequate one. . . . Since it seems clear that no human being is capable of possessing all at once an infinite hierarchy of beliefs, it is equally clear that this requirement allows no one to have any justified beliefs. And that should be a sufficient basis for rejecting it.

The story with AI is somewhat different. First we have to decide on what is to count as "accessibility to the adequacy of the ground". The most obvious suggestion would be that accessibility consists in the capacity of the subject to come into the state required by the PI requirement, viz., being justified in believing that the ground of the target belief that p is adequate. We can then add the specification of the required degree and mode of accessibility. This will give us the following.

(II)   S is justified in believing that p only if S is capable, fairly readily on the basis of reflection, to acquire a justified belief that the ground of S's belief that p is an adequate one.

Clearly (II), unlike (I), does not imply that S has an infinite hierarchy of justified beliefs. For (II) does not require that S actually have a justified higher level belief for each belief in the hierarchy, but only that, for each justified belief she actually has, it is possible for her to acquire, by a certain route, an appropriately related justified higher level belief. To be sure, this does imply that S has, as we might say, an infinite hierarchy of possibilities for the acquisition of justified beliefs. But it is not at all clear that this is impossible, in the way it is clearly impossible for one of us to have an infinite hierarchy of actually justified beliefs. Thus I will have to find some other reason for rejecting (II).

That reason can be found by turning from possibility to actuality. Though it may well be within the limits of human capacity, it is by no means always the case that the subject of a justified belief is capable of determining the adequacy of his ground, just by careful reflection on the matter, or, indeed, in any other way. For one thing, many subjects are not at the level of conceptual sophistication to even raise the question of adequacy of ground, much less determine an answer by reflection. One thinks here of small children and, I fear, many adults as

well. The maximally unsophisticated human perceiver is surely often justified in believing that what he sees to be the case is the case, even though he is in no position to even raise a question about the adequacy of his grounds. But even if capable of raising the question, he may not be able to arrive at a justified answer. Our judgment on this will depend both on what we take to be required for adequacy and what we regard as necessary for the justification of a belief that certain grounds are adequate. The two are, of course, intimately connected. I have already made it explicit that I take a ground, G, of belief B to be adequate if and only if it is sufficiently indicative of the truth of B. And this being the case, it seems clear that for me to be justified in believing G to be an adequate basis for belief, B, I must have sufficient *reasons* for supposing that this truth-indication relation does hold. (And, on my view, the belief in adequacy must be based on those reasons.) And many, or most, subjects are just not up to this. Consider, for instance, all the things we believe on authority. If we have been trained properly, we generally recognize the marks of competence in an area, and when we believe the pronouncements of one who exhibits those marks, we are believing on adequate grounds, proceeding aright in our belief formation, and so epistemically justified. But how many of us can, on reflection, come up with adequate evidence on which to base the belief that a given putative authority is to be relied on? Very few of us. (II) would imply that we are rarely justified in believing on authority, even when we are utilizing what we have been trained to recognize as marks of authority, marks that are indeed reliable indications of expertise.

A weaker AI condition on adequacy of grounds would be the following.

(III)   S is justified in believing that p only if S has adequate grounds for a judgment that the grounds for S's belief that p are adequate.

This is weaker than (II) because it does not require that S actually be able to acquire a justified belief about adequacy, whether just on reflection or otherwise. It only requires that she "have" the grounds (evidence, experiences, or whatever) that would serve to justify such a belief if that belief were based on those grounds. A subject could conceivably satisfy (III) even if she lacked the conceptual equipment to formulate the issue of adequacy. Nevertheless, the considerations I have advanced make it dubious that even this condition is met by all or most justified believers. Do I have the evidence it would take to adequately support a belief that my present perceptual grounds for believing that there is a maple tree near my study window are adequate? I very much doubt it. Even if we can overcome problems of circularity (relying on other perceptual beliefs to support the claim that this perceptual ground is adequate), as I believe we can, it seems very dubious that we store enough observational evidence to constitute adequate evidence for the thesis that normal sensory experience is an adequate ground for our beliefs about the physical environment. No doubt our experience reinforces our tendency to believe this, but that is another matter. For these and other reasons, I very much doubt that all or most justified believers satisfy (III).

We must, of course, be alive to the point that our AI principles concerning the presence of the ground did not require that the ground be fairly directly accessible to the subject in each case, but only that it be the sort of thing that is typically so accessible. This suggests a weakening of (I)–(III) so that the requirement is not that so-and-so be true in each case, but only that it be generally or normally the case. But if the above contentions are sound, these weaker principles would be excluded also. For I have argued that it is not even generally or typically the case that, taking (II) as our example, one who has a justified belief that p is capable of arriving fairly readily at a justified belief that the ground of his belief that p is an adequate one.

What about an internalist *sufficient* condition of adequacy (sufficient along with the belief's being based on the ground in question)? Here again we will have both PI and AI versions. Let's say that the PI version takes it as sufficient for the justification of S's belief that p that:

> (IV) S's belief that p is based on an accessible ground that S is justified in supposing to be adequate.

The AI version can be construed as taking the condition to consist in the appropriate sort of possibility of S's satisfying (IV). More explicitly:

> (V) S's belief that p is based on an accessible ground such that S can fairly readily come to have a justified belief that this ground is an adequate one.

Since the PI condition is stronger, it will suffice to show that it is not strong enough.[14]

The crucial question here is whether (IV) ensures truth-conducivity, which we saw at the beginning of the paper to be an essential feature of epistemic justification. And this boils down to the question of whether S's being justified in supposing the ground of his belief in p to be adequate guarantees that the belief that p is likely to be true. This depends on both the concept of adequacy and the concept of justification used in (IV). If (IV) employs a non-truth-indicative concept of adequacy, the game is up right away. Suppose, for example, that an adequate ground for a belief that p is one on which a confident belief of this sort is customarily based. In that case likelihood of truth is not ensured even by the ground's *being* adequate, much less by S's being justified in supposing it to be adequate. Let's take it, then, that our PI internalist is using our concept of a ground's *being* adequate; his difference from us is simply that where we require for justification that the ground *be* adequate, he takes it as sufficient that S be justified in supposing it to be adequate. But then we must ask what concept of justification he is using. If he were using our concept of justification in (IV), the satisfaction of that condition would imply that p is likely to be true. For if S is justified in believing the ground to be adequate, on our concept of justification, then the belief that the ground is adequate is thereby likely to be true; and so, if there is not too much leakage in the double probabilification, the likelihood that the ground of the belief that p is adequate implies in turn that it is likely that p. But this would mean that our internalist opponent avoids our concept of justification (requiring actual adequacy of ground) at the first level only to embrace it at the second and, presumably, at all higher levels. The only effect of this is that the implication of truth-conducivity at the first level is somewhat weaker than on our view; since whereas we flat-out require adequacy at the first level, his view only requires the likelihood of adequacy. But this difference lacks motivation, and in any event it certainly doesn't give his view a distinctively *internalist* cast in contrast to ours, since he uses our concept of justification at all higher levels. Hence if our opponent is to be more than a paper internalist, he will have to be using some non-truth-conducive conception of justification at the higher levels;[15] and in that case the fact that S is justified in believing that the ground of his belief that p is adequate has no tendency to imply that the ground *is* adequate, and hence no tendency to imply that p is (likely to be) true. And therefore (IV) cannot be sufficient for epistemic justification.

Thus it would seem that internalist conditions concerning adequacy are neither necessary nor sufficient for justification. And so the view here being defended is resolutely and uncompromisingly externalist, so far as adequacy of grounds is concerned. In order for my belief that p, which is based on ground G, to be justified, it is quite sufficient, as well as necessary, that G be sufficiently indicative of the truth of p. It is in no way required that I know anything, or be justified in believing anything, about this

relationship. No doubt, we sometimes do have justified beliefs about the adequacy of our grounds, and that is certainly a good thing. But that is icing on the cake.

IV

In this essay I have proposed an account of the prima facie epistemic justification of beliefs according to which that amounts to a belief's having an adequate ground. The justification will be ultima facie provided there are not sufficient overriders from within the subject's knowledge and justified belief. I have given reasons for placing a (rather weak) AI constraint on something's being a ground that could justify a belief, but I have resisted attempts to put any internalist constraint on what constitutes the adequacy of a ground. There I have insisted that it is both necessary and sufficient that the world be such that the ground be "sufficiently indicative of the truth" of the belief, both necessary and sufficient that this actually be the case, and neither necessary nor sufficient that the subject have any cognitive grasp of this fact. Thus my position has definite affinities with reliabilism, especially with that variant thereof sometimes called a "reliable indication" view, as contrasted with a "reliable process" view.[16] But it differs from a pure reliabilism by holding that the justification of a belief requires that the belief be based on a "ground" that satisfies an AI constraint, as well as by letting the subject's perspective on the world determine whether overriding occurs.[17] Beliefs that, so far as the subject can tell, just pop into his head out of nowhere would not be counted as justified on this position. I do hold that mere reliable belief production, suitably construed, is sufficient for knowledge, but that is another story.

Notes

1 The position does, however, bear a marked family resemblance to that put forward in Marshall

Swain's *Reasons and Knowledge* (Ithaca: Cornell University Press, 1981).

2 For an elaborate development of this idea, along with much else relevant to the notion of believing for a reason, see Robert Audi's "Belief, Reason, and Inference," *Philosophical Topics*, 14, no. 1 (1986), 27–65.

3 Audi in the article referred to in the previous note alleges that there are such "connecting beliefs," as he calls them, in every case of "believing for a reason" (what I am calling beliefs based on other beliefs). However, I do not find his arguments compelling.

4 It may be contended that where such "taking account" is involved, this amounts to the subject's having and using a belief in a support relation. And perhaps this is right, for a minimal, low-level grade of belief possession and use. One could "have" and "use" the belief in this way, however, without the belief's being available for conscious entertainment, assertion, or use in inference.

5 For simplicity of exposition I shall omit temporal qualifiers from my formulations, but they are to be understood. Thus, a tacit "at t" qualifies "S is justified in believing that p."

6 Admittedly there are other ways of cashing out this general idea of subject-relativity, e.g. by making justification hang on what the subject "had to go on" by way of support, rather than on what the subject actually went on, but I won't have time to go into those alternatives.

7 With experiential grounds we do not have the same problem, for, at least as I am thinking of it, an experiential ground is not, qua experiential ground, a propositional attitude, or set thereof, like a belief, so that here there is no propositional or factive object to serve as a ground rather than the experience itself. One who does take experiences to be essentially propositional attitudes will find the same problem as with doxastic grounds.

8 This is similar to problem cases involving perceptual discrimination introduced in Alvin Goldman's "Discrimination and Perceptual Knowledge," *Journal of Philosophy*, 73 (1976), 771–91.

9 For an example of CI see Paul Moser, *Empirical Justification* (Dordrecht: D. Reidel, 1985), p. 174.

10 The proponent of CI might seek to avoid this consequence by construing the awareness requirement not as part of the condition for justification but as a constraint on what can be a sufficient condition for justification. Indeed this is the way Moser, ibid., formulates it on p. 174: "we should require that one have some kind of awareness of the justifying conditions of one's given-beliefs." The suggestion is that the awareness does not itself form part of the justifying conditions. But I take this to be a shuffling evasion. If the awareness of condition C is required for justification, then it is an essential part of a sufficient condition for justification, whatever the theorist chooses to call it.

11 Carl Ginet, *Knowledge, Perception, and Memory* (Dordrecht: D. Reidel, 1975), p. 34.

12 I might also add that AI is typically supported by inconclusive arguments from an unacceptable deontological conception of justification. [. . .]

13 More generally, the points made in this essay specifically concern prima facie justification. For example the accessibility constraint on grounds does not apply to the subject's perspective as a whole, from which overriders emerge. Or, to put the point more modestly, nothing I say in this essay gives any support to the idea that in order for something the subject knows or justifiably believes to override a prima facie justification that something has to be fairly readily accessible to the subject.

[. . .]

14 Note that if the condition is asserted only as sufficient and not also as necessary, no infinite hierarchy can be shown to follow even from the PI version. Since the claim is compatible with there being other sufficient conditions of justification, it does not imply that one can be justified in believing that p only if one has an infinite hierarchy of justified beliefs. But, of course, if other sufficient conditions are countenanced, the position loses its distinctively internalist clout.

15 We have not ruled out the possibility that our opponent is using, in (IV), some truth-conducive concept of justification other than ours, e.g. a straight reliability concept according to which it is sufficient for the justification of a belief that it have been acquired in some reliable way. But if that's what he's doing, he turns out to be even less internalist than if he had used our concept.

16 To be sure, in explaining early on in the essay the way in which I pick out grounds, I appealed to

features of the *process* of belief formation. (I am indebted to Hilary Kornblith and Alvin Goldman for calling this to my attention.) Nevertheless, reliability enters into my formulation of what is necessary and sufficient for justification by way of the truth indicativeness of the ground, rather than by way of the reliability of any belief-forming process.

17 I would suggest that much of the plausibility of some prominent attacks on externalism in general, and reliabilism in particular, stems from a failure to distinguish externalism with respect to the ground and externalism with respect to the adequacy of the ground. See, e.g., Laurence BonJour, *The Structure of Empirical Knowledge* (Cambridge: Harvard University Press, 1985), chap. 3; and Richard Foley, "What's Wrong with Reliabilism?," *The Monist,* 68 (1985), 188–202.

Chapter 19

Lewis Carroll

WHAT THE TORTOISE SAID TO ACHILLES

Achilles had overtaken the Tortoise, and had seated himself comfortably on its back.

"So you've got to the end of our race-course?" said the Tortoise. "Even though it *does* consist of an infinite series of distances? I thought some wiseacre or other had proved that the thing couldn't be done?"

"It *can* be done," said Achilles. "It *has* been done! *Solvitur ambulando.* You see the distances were constantly *diminishing:* and so—"

"But if they had been constantly *increasing?*" the Tortoise interrupted. "How then?"

"Then I shouldn't be *here*," Achilles modestly replied; "and *you* would have got several times round the world, by this time!"

"You flatter me—*flatten*, I mean," said the Tortoise; "for you *are* a heavy weight, and *no* mistake! Well now, would you like to hear of a race-course, that most people fancy they can get to the end of in two or three steps, while it *really* consists of an infinite number of distances, each one longer than the previous one?"

"Very much indeed!" said the Grecian warrior, as he drew from his helmet (few warriors possessed *pockets* in those days) an enormous note-book and a pencil. "Proceed! And speak *slowly*, please! *Short-hand* isn't invented yet!"

"That beautiful First Proposition of Euclid!" the Tortoise murmured dreamily. "You admire Euclid?"

"Passionately! So far, at least, as one *can* admire a treatise that won't be published for some centuries to come!"

"Well, now, let's take a little bit of the argument in that First Proposition—just *two* steps, and the conclusion drawn from them. Kindly enter them in your note-book. And, in order to refer to them conveniently, let's call them *A*, *B*, and *Z*:

(A) Things that are equal to the same are equal to each other.

(B) The two sides of the Triangle are things that are equal to the same.

(Z) The two sides of this Triangle are equal to each other.

"Readers of Euclid will grant, I suppose, that *Z* follows logically from *A* and *B*, so that anyone who accepts *A* and *B* is true, must accept *Z* as true?"

"Undoubtedly! The youngest child in a High School—as soon as High Schools are invented, which will not be till some two thousand years later—will grant *that*."

"And if some reader had *not* yet accepted *A* and *B* as true, he might still accept the *Sequence* as a *valid* one, I suppose?"

"No doubt such a reader might exist. He might say, 'I accept as true the Hypothetical Proposition that, if *A* and *B* be true, *Z* must be true; but I *don't* accept *A* and *B* as true.' Such a reader would do wisely in abandoning Euclid, and taking to football."

"And might there not *also* be some reader who would say, 'I accept *A* and *B* as true, but I *don't* accept the Hypothetical'?"

"Certainly there might. He, also, had better take to football."

"And *neither* of these readers," the Tortoise continued, "is *as yet* under any logical necessity to accept Z as true?"

"Quite so," Achilles assented.

"Well, now, I want you to consider *me* as a reader of the *second* kind, and to force me, logically, to accept Z as true."

"A tortoise playing football would be—" Achilles was beginning.

"—an anomaly, of course," the Tortoise hastily interrupted. "Don't wander from the point. Let's have Z first, and football afterwards!"

"I'm to force you to accept Z, am I?" Achilles said musingly. "And your present position is that you accept *A* and *B*, but you *don't* accept the Hypothetical—"

"Let's call it C," said the Tortoise.

"—but you don't accept:

(C)   If *A* and *B* are true, Z must be true."

"That is my present position," said the Tortoise.

"Then I must ask you to accept C."

"I'll do so," said the Tortoise, "as soon as you've entered it in that note-book of yours. What else have you got in it?"

"Only a few memoranda," said Achilles, nervously fluttering the leaves: "a few memoranda of—of the battles in which I have distinguished myself!"

"Plenty of blank leaves, I see!" the Tortoise cheerily remarked. "We shall need them *all*!" (Achilles shuddered.) "Now write as I dictate:

(*A*)   Things that are equal to the same are equal to each other.

(B)   The two sides of this triangle are things that are equal to the same.

(C)   If *A* and *B* are true, Z must be true.

(Z)   The two sides of this Triangle are equal to each other."

"You should call it D, not Z," said Achilles. "It comes *next* to the other three. If you accept *A* and *B* and C, you must accept Z."

"And why *must* I?"

"Because it follows *logically* from them. If *A* and *B* and C are true, Z must be true. You don't dispute *that*, I imagine?"

"If *A* and *B* and C are true, Z *must* be true," the Tortoise thoughtfully repeated. "That's *another* Hypothetical, isn't it? And, if I failed to see its truth, I might accept *A* and *B* and C, and *still* not accept Z, mightn't I?"

"You might," the candid hero admitted; "though such obtuseness would certainly be phenomenal. Still, the event is *possible*. So I must ask you to grant one more Hypothetical."

"Very good. I'm quite willing to grant it, as soon as you've written it down. We will call it

(D)   If *A* and *B* and C are true, Z must be true.

"Have you entered that in your note-book?"

"I *have*!" Achilles joyfully exclaimed, as he ran the pencil into its sheath. "And at last we've got to the end of this ideal race-course! Now that you accept *A* and *B* and C and D, *of course* you accept Z."

"Do I?" said the Tortoise innocently. "Let's make that quite clear. I accept *A* and *B* and C and D. Suppose I *still* refuse to accept Z?"

"Then Logic would take you by the throat, and *force* you to do it!" Achilles triumphantly replied. "Logic would tell you 'You can't help yourself. Now that you've accepted *A* and *B* and C and D, you *must* accept Z!' So you've no choice, you see."

"Whatever *Logic* is good enough to tell me is worth *writing down*," said the Tortoise. "So enter it in your book, please. We will call it

(E)   If *A* and B and C and D are true, Z must
        be true.

"Until I've granted *that*, of course, I needn't
grant Z. So it's quite a *necessary* step, you see?"

"I see," said Achilles; and there was a touch
of sadness in his tone.

Here the narrator, having pressing business at
the Bank, was obliged to leave the happy pair,
and did not again pass the spot until some
months afterwards. When he did so, Achilles was
still seated on the back of the much-enduring
Tortoise, and was writing in his note-book,
which appeared to be nearly full. The Tortoise
was saying "Have you got that last step written
down? Unless I've lost count, that makes a
thousand and one. There are several millions
more to come. And *would* you mind—a personal
favor—considering what a lot of instruction this
colloquy of ours will provide for the Logicians
of the Nineteenth Century—*would* you mind
adopting a pun that my cousin the Mock-Turtle
will then make, and allowing yourself to be
re-named Taught-Us?"

"As you please!" replied the weary warrior, in
the hollow tones of dispair, as he buried his face
in his hands. "Provided that *you*, for *your* part, will
adopt a pun the Mock-Turtle never made, and
allow yourself to be re-named A Kill-Ease!"

PART SIX

What is the structure of justification and knowledge?

INTRODUCTION TO PART SIX

Ram Neta and Duncan Pritchard

LISA KNOWS THAT THE electricity company has turned off the electricity supply to her house. How does she know that? Because the electricity company had threatened to do this a month ago, and she has not paid her bill since then, and now her lightbulbs do not illuminate when she flips the switch to turn them on. But how does Lisa know any of these last three things? For instance, how does she know that the electricity company had threatened to turn off the electricity supply to her house? They issued this threat in writing in her last month's electricity bill. How does she know that? She currently recalls reading the threat in her last month's electricity bill.

The preceding series of questions and answers is one example of what philosophers sometimes call a 'regress', which means roughly 'the act of going back'. In the example above, we began by claiming that Lisa knows some fact – call it f – and then we say that Lisa knows f by knowing some other facts f1, f2 and f3, each of which she knows by knowing some other facts. At each step, we 'go back' from Lisa's knowing one fact to her knowing it by knowing some other fact. We may visualise such regresses as tracing out the downward paths in Figure 2. Each downward path in this pyramidal diagram represents a single regress. The arrows that run from one piece of knowledge to a lower piece of knowledge should be understood as indicating that the higher piece of knowledge is something that Lisa knows *by knowing* the lower piece of knowledge. The figure may lead us to wonder: is there going to be a lowest stage in any of these regresses? In other words, is there some fact (f, or whatever) such that Lisa knows some other facts *by* knowing that fact, but Lisa does not know that fact *by* knowing any other fact? Or, to adopt the terminology employed by many epistemologists, does Lisa have any 'foundational knowledge'?

Just as there is a regress concerning knowledge, so too is there a regress concerning each of the various kinds of justification distinguished in the preceding part. And just as we may wonder whether Lisa has any *foundational knowledge*, so too, for each of the varieties of justification that we distinguished in part five (i.e. doxastic vs

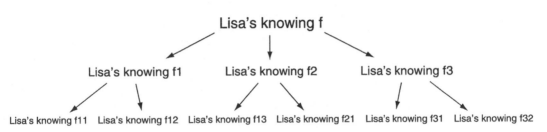

Figure 2 Lisa's knowledge

propositional justification, modal vs quantitative justification), we may wonder whether Lisa has any *foundational justification*. For instance, is there any proposition such that Lisa is (modally propositionally) justified in believing that proposition, but not by virtue of her being (modally propositionally) justified in believing any other proposition? Or, to take another example, is there any belief that Lisa holds that is highly doxastically justified, but not by virtue of being held on the basis of any other highly doxastically justified belief?

Finally, just as there is a regress concerning knowledge and the various kinds of justification, so too is there a regress concerning the reasons that *we can offer* in support of our beliefs, the reasons that *we possess* in support of our beliefs, and the reasons that *there are* in support of our beliefs. And just as we may wonder whether Lisa has any foundational knowledge or foundational justification, so too may we wonder whether there is any belief for which Lisa can offer a reason, which itself requires no further reason; or we may wonder whether there is any belief for which Lisa possesses a reason, which itself requires no further reason; or we may wonder whether there is any belief for which there is a reason, which itself requires no further reason.

An epistemologist who believes that we do have foundational knowledge is a 'foundationalist' about knowledge. An epistemologist who believes that we do have foundational justification (of one kind or another) is a 'foundationalist' about (that variety of) justification. And an epistemologist who believes that there are foundational reasons is a 'foundationalist' about reasons.

Historically, many epistemologists have been foundationalists of one or another of these kinds. But it is also true that many epistemologists think that at least one or another of these kinds of foundationalism suffers from serious problems, and cannot be true. Such philosophers have often protested that it is impossible for anything to play the role of a foundation for one or another regress. For instance, in his essay 'Can Empirical Knowledge Have a Foundation?' (Chapter 20), Laurence BonJour (1942–) argues that the regress of modal doxastic justification cannot have a foundation: the only things that can justify someone in holding a belief, says BonJour, are other justified beliefs.

Now, if one of these epistemological regresses does not terminate in a foundation, then the diagram that depicts that regress has no bottom layer. For instance, if BonJour is right that modal doxastic justification has no foundation, then the regress concerning the modal doxastic justification of Lisa's beliefs will look like Figure 3.

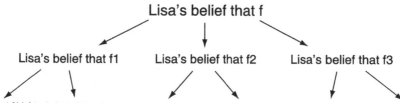

Figure 3 Lisa's beliefs

And so on, with no foundation. (Of course, if justification is a necessary condition of knowledge, and if it is possible for someone to have a justified false belief, then the pyramid in Figure 3 may contain more nodes than the pyramid of Lisa's knowledge in Figure 2, since Lisa may have a justified belief that p but fail to know that p.) How can there be no foundation? According to BonJour, what happens as we trace out paths of justification farther and farther is that, eventually, those paths loop back to justified beliefs that were already on those same paths.

Now recall that, in our original picture of Lisa's knowledge, we said that the arrows were to be understood as indicating that Lisa knows one fact by knowing another fact. By analogy, we might then think that we should understand the arrows in Figure 3 as indicating that Lisa's belief in one proposition is modally doxastically justified by Lisa's belief in some other proposition. But, in fact, this is not how BonJour proposes to understand the arrows. According to BonJour, particular beliefs are modally doxastically justified not *simply* by virtue of being held on the basis of some other modally doxastically justified beliefs. Rather, BonJour says, particular beliefs are modally doxastically justified by virtue of being part of *a coherent system of beliefs*. This is what makes BonJour a 'coherentist' about modal doxastic justification. Other philosophers have espoused coherentism about knowledge, about other forms of justification or about reasons. In general, coherentists say that what gives any particular item in a regress its epistemic credentials – that is to say, what makes that item a bit of knowledge, or what makes it have the relevant kind of justification, or what makes it a reason for belief – is its being part of a coherent system of other such items.

Many philosophers have defended a coherentist account of one or another of these things. But at least as many philosophers have claimed that coherentism, in one or another of these forms, cannot be specified in a form that stands any chance of being true. What, they demand to know, is coherence? If it is nothing more than logical consistency, then coherentism cannot be true, for there are countless many logically consistent systems of propositions, and not all of them can be known to be true, or can be justifiably believed, or what have you. But if it is more than mere logical consistency, then what is it? And, no matter how the coherentist attempts to answer this difficult question, there seems to be the following problem with her view:

> [C]onsider the Case of the Epistemically Inflexible Climber. Ric is climbing Guide's Wall, on Storm Point in the Grand Tetons; having just led the difficult next to last pitch, he is seated on a comfortable ledge, bringing his partner up. He believes that Cascade Canyon is down to his left, that the cliffs of Mount Owen are directly in front of him, that there is a hawk gliding in lazy circles 200 feet below him, that he is wearing his new *Fire* rock shoes, and so on. His beliefs, we may stipulate, are coherent. Now add that Ric is struck by a wayward burst of high-energy cosmic radiation. This induces a cognitive malfunction; his beliefs become fixed, no longer responsive to changes in experience. No matter what his experience, his beliefs remain the same. At the cost of considerable effort his partner gets him down and, in a desperate last-ditch attempt at therapy, takes him to the opera in nearby Jackson, where the New York Metropolitan Opera on tour is performing *La Traviata*. Ric is

appeared to in the same way as everyone else there; he is inundated by wave after wave of golden sound. Sadly enough, the effort at therapy fails; Ric's beliefs remain fixed and wholly unresponsive to his experience; he still believes that he is on the belay ledge at the top of the next to last pitch of Guide's Wall, that Cascade Canyon is down to his left, that there is a hawk sailing in lazy circles 200 feet below him, that he is wearing his new *Fire* rock shoes, and so on. Furthermore, since he believes the very same things he believed when seated on the ledge, his beliefs are coherent.

(Plantinga 1993: 82)

Although Ric's beliefs are, by hypothesis, coherent, it seems that he, or his beliefs, are, in various ways, epistemically badly off.

In his essay 'Toward a Defense of Empirical Foundationalism' (Chapter 21), Laurence BonJour recants his earlier defence of coherentism about modal doxastic justification, and espouses a form of foundationalism instead. It is a remarkable fact that, in the second half of the twentieth century, one of the most prominent defenders of coherentism turned into one of the most prominent defenders of foundationalism. It is no surprise that BonJour's defence of foundationalism displays a keen sense of precisely what objections the foundationalist must answer.

So, with respect to the regress of knowledge, or of justification, or of reasons, do foundationalism and coherentism exhaust the possible options? Not at all. As Peter Klein (1940–) argues in his essay 'Human Knowledge and the Infinite Regress of Reasons' (Chapter 22), a regress may simply go on interminably. This is precisely Klein's view of the regress of reasons: according to Klein, there is simply no end to this regress. For any reason *r* that you give for believing a proposition *p*, there will be another reason *r'* for believing that *r* is true, and there will be still another reason *r''* for believing that *r'* is true, and so on. Of course, it is impossible to present all of these reasons in a conversation – conversations cannot go on forever! But just because it is impossible to present all of these reasons in a conversation, or to draw them in a diagram, that does not show that those reasons do not exist. It is of course possible for there to be reasons that we never express, and of which we are not aware. So, Klein asks, why could there not be an infinite series of such reasons?

So far, we have considered three possibilities with respect to any particular one of the epistemological regresses: foundationalism, coherentism and infinitism. Are these three options mutually exclusive? Not according to Ernest Sosa (1940–). In his essay 'The Raft and the Pyramid', Sosa introduces a view that he calls 'virtue epistemology'. It is a view that has exerted a great deal of influence over recent thinking in epistemology. But one of the striking features of the view is that it combines elements of foundationalism with elements of coherentism. For Sosa, a reflective person's beliefs are knowledgeably held only if they are appropriately grounded in experience, and also coherent with each other. Thus, foundationalism and coherentism are each right about something, on Sosa's view.

Study questions

1   Present a valid regress argument in favour of foundationalism about propositional justification. Now present a valid regress argument in favour of foundationalism about knowledge. Could one of these arguments be sound even if the other wasn't sound?

2   Where might a coherentist lodge an objection against the regress arguments presented in response to question 1? How would BonJour, in his coherentist phase, have objected to them?

3   Where might an infinitist lodge an objection against the regress arguments presented in response to question 1? How might Klein object to them?

4   What is virtue epistemology? Precisely what does Ernest Sosa think that the foundationalist is right about? Precisely what does Ernest Sosa think that the coherentist is right about?

Further reading

For a comprehensive and accessible introduction to the various regress problems and their proposed solution, see Keith Lehrer's book *Theories of Knowledge* (1990). Since the publication of that book, there have been some genuinely new and important attempts to solve one or another of these regress problems. One recently influential attempt to do this is offered in Michael Williams' book *Unnatural Doubts* (1991). Another still more recent attempt to do this is offered in Adam Leite's 2005 article 'A Localist Solution to the Regress of Epistemic Justification'.

References

BonJour, Laurence. (1985). *The Structure of Empirical Knowledge*, Cambridge, MA: Harvard University Press.

Lehrer, Keith. (1990). *Theories of Knowledge*, Boulder, CO: Westview Press.

Leite, Adam. (2005). 'A Localist Solution to the Regress of Epistemic Justification', *Australasian Journal of Philosophy* 83: 395–421.

Plantinga, Alvin. (1993). *Warrant: The Current Debate*, Oxford: Oxford University Press.

Williams, Michael. (1991). *Unnatural Doubts*, Princeton, NJ: Princeton University Press.

Chapter 20

Laurence BonJour

CAN EMPIRICAL KNOWLEDGE HAVE A FOUNDATION?

The idea that empirical knowledge has, and must have, a *foundation* has been a common tenet of most major epistemologists, both past and present. There have been, as we shall see further below, many importantly different variants of this idea. But the common denominator among them, the central thesis of epistemological foundationism as I shall understand it here, is the claim that certain empirical beliefs possess a degree of epistemic justification or warrant which does not depend, inferentially or otherwise, on the justification of other empirical beliefs, but is instead somehow immediate or intrinsic. It is these non-inferentially justified beliefs, the unmoved (or self-moved) movers of the epistemic realm as Chisholm has called them,[1] that constitute the foundation upon which the rest of empirical knowledge is alleged to rest.

In recent years, the most familiar foundationist views have been subjected to severe and continuous attack. But this attack has rarely been aimed directly at the central foundationist thesis itself, and new versions of foundationism have been quick to emerge, often propounded by the erstwhile critics themselves. Thus foundationism has become a philosophical hydra, difficult to come to grips with and seemingly impossible to kill. The purposes of this paper are, first, to distinguish and clarify the main dialectical variants of foundationism, by viewing them as responses to one fundamental problem which is both the main motivation and the primary obstacle for foundationism; and second, as a result of this discussion to offer schematic reasons for doubting whether any version of foundationism is finally acceptable.

The main reason for the impressive durability of foundationism is not any overwhelming plausibility attaching to the main foundationist thesis in itself, but rather the existence of one apparently decisive argument which seems to rule out all non-skeptical alternatives to foundationism, thereby showing that *some* version of foundationism must be true (on the assumption that skepticism is false). In a recent statement by Quinton, this argument runs as follows:

> If any beliefs are to be justified at all, . . . there must be some terminal beliefs that do not owe their . . . credibility to others. For a belief to be justified it is not enough for it to be accepted, let alone merely entertained: there must also be good reason for accepting it. Furthermore, for an inferential belief to be justified the beliefs that support it must be justified themselves. There must, therefore, be a kind of belief that does not owe its justification to the support provided by others. Unless this were so no belief would be justified at all, for to justify any belief would require the antecedent justification of an infinite series of beliefs. The terminal . . . beliefs that are needed to bring the regress of

justification to a stop need not be strictly self-evident in the sense that they somehow justify themselves. All that is required is that they should not owe their justification to any other beliefs.[2]

I shall call this argument *the epistemic regress argument*, and the problem which generates it, *the epistemic regress problem*. Since it is this argument which provides the primary rationale and argumentative support for foundationism, a careful examination of it will also constitute an exploration of the foundationist position itself. The main dialectical variants of foundationism can best be understood as differing attempts to solve the regress problem, and the most basic objection to the foundationist approach is that it is doubtful that any of these attempts can succeed. (In this paper, I shall be concerned with the epistemic regress argument and the epistemic regress problem only as they apply to empirical knowledge. It is obvious that an analogous problem arises also for *a priori* knowledge, but there it seems likely that the argument would take a different course. In particular, a foundationist approach might be inescapable in an account of *a priori* knowledge.)

I

The epistemic regress problem arises directly out of the traditional conception of knowledge as *adequately justified true belief*[3]—whether this be taken as a fully adequate definition of knowledge or, in light of the apparent counter-examples discovered by Gettier,[4] as merely a necessary but not sufficient condition. (I shall assume throughout that the elements of the traditional conception are at least necessary for knowledge.) Now the most natural way to justify a belief is by producing a justificatory argument: belief *A* is justified by citing some other (perhaps conjunctive) belief *B*, from which *A* is inferable in some acceptable way and which is thus offered as a reason for accepting *A*.[5] Call this *inferential justifica-*

tion. It is clear, as Quinton points out in the passage quoted above, that for *A* to be genuinely justified by virtue of such a justificatory argument, *B* must itself be justified in some fashion; merely being inferable from an unsupported guess or hunch, e.g., would confer no genuine justification upon *A*.

Two further points about inferential justification, as understood here, must be briefly noted. First, the belief in question need not have been *arrived at* as the result of an inference in order to be inferentially justified. This is obvious, since a belief arrived at in some other way (e.g. as a result of wishful thinking) may later come to be maintained solely because it is now seen to be inferentially justifiable. Second, less obviously, a person for whom a belief is inferentially justified need not have explicitly rehearsed the justificatory argument in question to others or even to himself. It is enough that the inference be available to him if the belief is called into question by others or by himself (where such availability may itself be less than fully explicit) and that the availability of the inference be, in the final analysis, his reason for holding the belief.[6] It seems clear that many beliefs which are quite sufficiently justified to satisfy the justification criterion for knowledge depend for their justification on inferences which have not been explicitly formulated and indeed which could not be explicitly formulated without considerable reflective effort (e.g. my current belief that this is the same piece of paper upon which I was typing yesterday).[7]

Suppose then that belief *A* is (putatively) justified via inference, thus raising the question of how the justifying premise-belief *B* is justified. Here again the answer may be in inferential terms: *B* may be (putatively) justified in virtue of being inferable from some further belief *C*. But then the same question arises about the justification of *C*, and so on, threatening an infinite and apparently vicious regress of epistemic justification. Each belief is justified only if an epistemically prior belief is justified, and that epistemically prior belief is justified only if a still prior belief is justified, etc., with the apparent result that justification can never get started—and hence that there is no justification and no knowledge. The foundationist claim is that only through the adoption of some version of foundationism can this skeptical consequence be avoided.

Prima facie, there seem to be only four basic possibilities with regard to the eventual outcome of this potential regress of epistemic justification: (i) the regress might terminate with beliefs for which no justification of any kind is available, even though they were earlier offered as justifying premises; (ii) the regress might proceed infinitely backwards with ever more new premise beliefs being introduced and then themselves requiring justification; (iii) the regress might circle back upon itself, so that at some point beliefs which appeared earlier in the sequence of justifying arguments are appealed to again as premises; (iv) the regress might terminate because beliefs are reached which are justified—unlike those in alternative (i)—but whose justification does not depend inferentially on other empirical beliefs and thus does not raise any further issue of justification with respect to such beliefs.[8] The foundationist opts for the last alternative. His argument is that the other three lead inexorably to the skeptical result, and that the second and third have additional fatal defects as well, so that some version of the fourth, foundationist alternative must be correct (assuming that skepticism is false).

With respect to alternative (i), it seems apparent that the foundationist is correct. If this alternative were correct, empirical knowledge would rest ultimately on beliefs which were, from an epistemic standpoint at least, entirely arbitrary and hence incapable of conferring any genuine justification. What about the other two alternatives?

The argument that alternative (ii) leads to a skeptical outcome has in effect already been sketched in the original formulation of the problem. One who opted for this alternative could hope to avoid skepticism only by claiming that the regress, though infinite, is not vicious; but there seems to be no plausible way to defend such a claim. Moreover, a defense of an infinite regress view as an account of how empirical knowledge is actually justified—as opposed to how it might in principle be justified—would have to involve the seemingly dubious thesis that an ordinary knower holds a literally infinite number of distinct beliefs. Thus it is not surprising that no important philosopher, with the rather uncertain exception of Peirce,[9] seems to have advocated such a position.

Alternative (iii), the view that justification ultimately moves in a closed curve, has been historically more prominent, albeit often only as a dialectical foil for foundationism. At first glance, this alternative might seem even less attractive than the second. Although the problem of the knower having to have an infinite number of beliefs is no longer present, the regress itself, still infinite, now seems undeniably vicious. For the justification of each of the beliefs which figure in the circle seems now to presuppose *its own* epistemically prior justification: such a belief must, paradoxically, be justified before it can be justified. Advocates of views resembling alternative (iii) have generally tended to respond to this sort of objection by adopting a holistic conception of justification in which the justification of individual beliefs is subordinated to that of the closed systems of beliefs which such a view implies; the property of such systems usually appealed to as a basis for justification is internal *coherence*. Such coherence theories attempt to evade the regress problem by abandoning the view of justification as essentially involving a linear order of dependence (though a non-linear view of justification has never been worked out in detail).[10] Moreover, such a coherence theory of empirical knowledge is subject to a number of other familiar and seemingly decisive objections.[11] Thus alternative (iii) seems unacceptable, leaving only alternative (iv), the foundationist alternative, as apparently viable.

As thus formulated, the epistemic regress argument makes an undeniably persuasive case for foundationism. Like any argument by elimination, however, it cannot be conclusive until the surviving alternative has itself been carefully examined. The foundationist position may turn out to be subject to equally serious objections, thus forcing a re-examination of the other alternatives, a search for a further non-skeptical alternative, or conceivably the reluctant acceptance of the skeptical conclusion.[12] In particular, it is not clear on the basis of the argument thus far whether and how foundationism can itself solve the regress problem; and thus the possibility exists that the epistemic regress argument will prove to be a two-edged sword, as lethal to the foundationist as it is to his opponents.

II

The most straightforward interpretation of alternative (iv) leads directly to a view which I will here call *strong foundationism*. According to strong foundationism, the foundational beliefs which terminate the regress of justification possess sufficient epistemic warrant, independently of any appeal to inference from (or coherence with) other empirical beliefs, to satisfy the justification condition of knowledge and qualify as acceptable justifying premises for further beliefs. Since the justification of these *basic beliefs*, as they have come to be called, is thus allegedly not dependent on that of any other empirical belief, they are uniquely able to provide secure starting-points for the justification of empirical knowledge and stopping-points for the regress of justification.

The position just outlined is in fact a fairly modest version of strong foundationism. Strong foundationists have typically made considerably stronger claims on behalf of basic beliefs. Basic beliefs have been claimed not only to have sufficient non-inferential justification to qualify

as knowledge, but also to be *certain*, *infallible*, *indubitable*, or *incorrigible* (terms which are usually not very carefully distinguished).[13] And most of the major attacks on foundationism have focused on these stronger claims. Thus it is important to point out that nothing about the basic strong foundationist response to the regress problem demands that basic beliefs be more than adequately justified. There might of course be other reasons for requiring that basic beliefs have some more exalted epistemic status or for thinking that in fact they do. There might even be some sort of indirect argument to show that such a status is a consequence of the sorts of epistemic properties which are directly required to solve the regress problem. But until such an argument is given (and it is doubtful that it can be), the question of whether basic beliefs are or can be certain, infallible, etc., will remain a relatively unimportant side-issue.

Indeed, many recent foundationists have felt that even the relatively modest version of strong foundationism outlined above is still too strong. Their alternative, still within the general aegis of the foundationist position, is a view which may be called *weak foundationism*. Weak foundationism accepts the central idea of foundationism—viz. that certain empirical beliefs possess a degree of independent epistemic justification or warrant which does not derive from inference or coherence relations. But the weak foundationist holds that these foundational beliefs have only a quite low degree of warrant, much lower than that attributed to them by even modest strong foundationism and insufficient by itself to satisfy the justification condition for knowledge or to qualify them as acceptable justifying premises for other beliefs. Thus this independent warrant must somehow be augmented if knowledge is to be achieved, and the usual appeal here is to coherence with other such minimally warranted beliefs. By combining such beliefs into larger and larger coherent systems, it is held, their initial, minimal degree of warrant can gradually be enhanced until knowledge is finally achieved.

Thus weak foundationism, like the pure coherence theories mentioned above, abandons the linear conception of justification.[14]

Weak foundationism thus represents a kind of hybrid between strong foundationism and the coherence views discussed earlier, and it is often thought to embody the virtues of both and the vices of neither. Whether or not this is so in other respects, however, relative to the regress problem weak foundationism is finally open to the very same basic objection as strong foundationism, with essentially the same options available for meeting it. As we shall see, the key problem for any version of foundationism is whether it can itself solve the regress problem which motivates its very existence, without resorting to essentially *ad hoc* stipulation. The distinction between the two main ways of meeting this challenge both cuts across and is more basic than that between strong and weak foundationism. This being so, it will suffice to concentrate here on strong foundationism, leaving the application of the discussion to weak foundationism largely implicit.

The fundamental concept of strong foundationism is obviously the concept of a basic belief. It is by appeal to this concept that the threat of an infinite regress is to be avoided and empirical knowledge given a secure foundation. But how can there be any empirical beliefs which are thus basic? In fact, though this has not always been noticed, the very idea of an epistemically basic empirical belief is extremely paradoxical. For on what basis is such a belief to be justified, once appeal to further empirical beliefs is ruled out? Chisholm's theological analogy, cited earlier, is most appropriate: a basic belief is in effect an epistemological unmoved (or self-moved) mover. It is able to confer justification on other beliefs, but apparently has no need to have justification conferred on it. But is such a status any easier to understand in epistemology than it is in theology? How can a belief impart epistemic "motion" to other beliefs unless it is itself in "motion"? And, even more para-

doxically, how can a belief epistemically "move" itself?

This intuitive difficulty with the concept of a basic empirical belief may be elaborated and clarified by reflecting a bit on the concept of epistemic justification. The idea of justification is a generic one, admitting in principle of many specific varieties. Thus the acceptance of an empirical belief might be morally justified, i.e. justified as morally obligatory by reference to moral principles and standards; or pragmatically justified, i.e. justified by reference to the desirable practical consequences which will result from such acceptance; or religiously justified, i.e. justified by reference to specified religious texts or theological dogmas; etc. But none of these other varieties of justification can satisfy the justification condition for knowledge. Knowledge requires *epistemic* justification, and the distinguishing characteristic of this particular species of justification is, I submit, its essential or internal relationship to the cognitive goal of truth. Cognitive doings are epistemically justified, on this conception, only if and to the extent that they are aimed at this goal—which means roughly that one accepts all and only beliefs which one has good reason to think are true.[15] To accept a belief in the absence of such a reason, however appealing or even mandatory such acceptance might be from other standpoints, is to neglect the pursuit of truth; such acceptance is, one might say, *epistemically irresponsible*. My contention is that the idea of being epistemically responsible is the core of the concept of epistemic justification.[16]

A corollary of this conception of epistemic justification is that a satisfactory defense of a particular standard of epistemic justification must consist in showing it to be truth-conducive, i.e. in showing that accepting beliefs in accordance with its dictates is likely to lead to truth (and more likely than any proposed alternative). Without such a meta-justification, a proposed standard of epistemic justification lacks any underlying rationale. Why after all should an epistemically responsible inquirer prefer justified beliefs to unjustified ones, if not that the former are more likely to be true? To insist that a certain belief is epistemically justified, while confessing in the same breath that this fact about it provides no good reason to think that it is true, would be to render nugatory the whole concept of epistemic justification.

These general remarks about epistemic justification apply in full measure to any strong foundationist position and to its constituent account of basic beliefs. If basic beliefs are to provide a secure foundation for empirical knowledge, if inference from them is to be the sole basis for the justification of other empirical beliefs, then that feature, whatever it may be, in virtue of which a belief qualifies as basic must also constitute a good reason for thinking that the belief is true. If we let "φ" represent this feature, then for a belief B to qualify as basic in an acceptable foundationist account, the premises of the following justificatory argument must themselves be at least justified:[17]

(i)   Belief B has feature φ.
(ii) Beliefs having feature φ are highly likely to be true.

Therefore, B is highly likely to be true.

Notice further that while either premise taken separately might turn out to be justifiable on an *a priori* basis (depending on the particular choice of φ), it seems clear that they could not both be thus justifiable. For B is *ex hypothesi* an empirical belief, and it is hard to see how a particular empirical belief could be justified on a purely *a priori* basis.[18] And if we now assume, reasonably enough, that for B to be justified for a particular person (at a particular time) it is necessary, not merely that a justification for B exist in the abstract, but that the person in question be in cognitive possession of that justification, we get the result that B is not basic after all since its justification depends on that of at least one

other empirical belief. If this is correct, strong foundationism is untenable as a solution to the regress problem (and an analogous argument will show weak foundationism to be similarly untenable).

The foregoing argument is, no doubt, exceedingly obvious. But how is the strong foundationist to answer it? *Prima facie*, there seem to be only two general sorts of answer which are even remotely plausible, so long as the strong foundationist remains within the confines of the traditional conception of knowledge, avoids tacitly embracing skepticism, and does not attempt the heroic task of arguing that an empirical belief could be justified on a purely *a priori* basis. First, he might argue that although it is indeed necessary for a belief to be justified and *a fortiori* for it to be basic that a justifying argument of the sort schematized above be in principle available in the situation, it is *not* always necessary that the person for whom the belief is basic (or anyone else) know or even justifiably believe that it is available; instead, in the case of basic beliefs at least, it is sufficient that the premises for an argument of that general sort (or for some favored particular variety of such argument) merely be *true*, whether or not that person (or anyone else) justifiably believes that they are true. Second, he might grant that it is necessary both that such justification exist and that the person for whom the belief is basic be in cognitive possession of it, but insist that his cognitive grasp of the premises required for that justification does not involve further empirical beliefs which would then require justification, but instead involves cognitive states of a more rudimentary sort which do not themselves require justification: *intuitions* or *immediate apprehensions*. I will consider each of these alternatives in turn.

III

The philosopher who has come the closest to an explicit advocacy of the view that basic beliefs may be justified even though the person for whom they are basic is not in any way in cognitive possession of the appropriate justifying argument is D. M. Armstrong. In his recent book, *Belief, Truth and Knowledge*,[19] Armstrong presents a version of the epistemic regress problem (though one couched in terms of knowledge rather than justification) and defends what he calls an "Externalist" solution:

> According to 'Externalist' accounts of non-inferential knowledge, what makes a true non-inferential belief a case of *knowledge* is some natural relation which holds between the belief-state . . . and the situation which makes the belief true. It is a matter of a certain relation holding between the believer and the world.
>
> [157]

Armstrong's own candidate for this "natural relation" is "that there must be a *law-like connection* between the state of affairs *Bap* [i.e. *a*'s believing that *p*] and the state of affairs that makes '*p*' true such that, given *Bap*, it must be the case that *p*." [166] A similar view seems to be implicit in Dretske's account of perceptual knowledge in *Seeing and Knowing*, with the variation that Dretske requires for knowledge not only that the relation in question obtain, but also that the putative knower *believe* that it obtains—though *not* that this belief be justified.[20] In addition, it seems likely that various views of an ordinary-language stripe which appeal to facts about how language is learned either to justify basic belief or to support the claim that no justification is required would, if pushed, turn out to be positions of this general sort. Here I shall mainly confine myself to Armstrong, who is the only one of these philosophers who is explicitly concerned with the regress problem.

There is, however, some uncertainty as to how views of this sort in general and Armstrong's view in particular are properly to be interpreted. On the one hand, Armstrong might be taken as

offering an account of how basic beliefs (and perhaps others as well) satisfy the adequate-justification condition for knowledge; while on the other hand, he might be taken as simply repudiating the traditional conception of knowledge and the associated concept of epistemic justification, and offering a surrogate conception in its place—one which better accords with the "naturalistic" world-view which Armstrong prefers.[21] But it is only when understood in the former way that externalism (to adopt Armstrong's useful term) is of any immediate interest here, since it is only on that interpretation that it constitutes a version of foundationism and offers a direct response to the anti-foundationist argument set out above. Thus I shall mainly focus on this interpretation of externalism, remarking only briefly at the end of the present section on the alternative one.

Understood in this way, the externalist solution to the regress problem is quite simple: the person who has a basic belief need not be in possession of any justified reason for his belief and indeed, except in Dretske's version, need not even think that there is such a reason; the status of his belief as constituting knowledge (if true) depends solely on the external relation and not at all on his subjective view of the situation. Thus there are no further empirical beliefs in need of justification and no regress.

Now it is clear that such an externalist position succeeds in avoiding the regress problem and the anti-foundationist argument. What may well be doubted, however, is whether this avoidance deserves to be considered a *solution*, rather than an essentially *ad hoc* evasion, of the problem. Plainly the sort of "external" relation which Armstrong has in mind would, if known, provide a basis for a justifying argument along the lines sketched earlier, roughly as follows:

(i) Belief *B* is an instance of kind *K*.
(ii) Beliefs of kind *K* are connected in a law-like way with the sorts of states of

affairs which would make them true, and therefore are highly likely to be true.

Therefore, B is highly likely to be true.

But precisely what generates the regress problem in the first place is the requirement that for a belief B to be epistemically justified for a given person P, it is necessary, not just that there be justifiable or even true premises available in the situation which could in principle provide a basis for a justification of B, but that P himself know or at least justifiably believe some such set of premises and thus be in a position to employ the corresponding argument. The externalist position seems to amount merely to waiving this general requirement in cases where the justification takes a certain form, and the question is why this should be acceptable in these cases when it is not acceptable generally. (If it were acceptable generally, then it would seem that any true belief would be justified for any person, and the distinction between knowledge and true belief would collapse.) Such a move seems rather analogous to solving a regress of causes by simply stipulating that although most events must have a cause, events of a certain kind need not.

Whatever plausibility attaches to externalism seems to derive from the fact that if the external relation in question genuinely obtains, then P will not go wrong in accepting the belief, and it is, in a sense, not an accident that this is so. But it remains unclear how these facts are supposed to justify P's acceptance of B. It is clear, of course, that an external observer who knew both that P accepted B and that there was a law-like connection between such acceptance and the truth of B would be in a position to construct an argument to justify *his own* acceptance of B. P could thus serve as a useful epistemic instrument, a kind of cognitive thermometer, for such an external observer (and in fact the example of a thermometer is exactly the analogy which Armstrong employs to illustrate the relationship which is supposed to obtain between the person who has the belief and the external state of affairs [166ff.]). But P himself has no reason at all for thinking that B is likely to be true. From his perspective, it *is* an accident that the belief is true.[22] And thus his acceptance of B is no more rational or responsible from an epistemic standpoint than would be the acceptance of a subjectively similar belief for which the external relation in question failed to obtain.[23]

Nor does it seem to help matters to move from Armstrong's version of externalism, which requires only that the requisite relationship between the believer and the world obtain, to the superficially less radical version apparently held by Dretske, which requires that P also believe that the external relation obtains, but does not require that this latter belief be justified. This view may seem slightly less implausible, since it at least requires that the person have some idea, albeit unjustified, of why B is likely to be true. But this change is not enough to save externalism. One way to see this is to suppose that the person believes the requisite relation to obtain on some totally irrational and irrelevant basis, e.g. as a result of reading tea leaves or studying astrological charts. If B were an ordinary, non-basic belief, such a situation would surely preclude its being justified, and it is hard to see why the result should be any different for an allegedly basic belief.

Thus it finally seems possible to make sense of externalism only by construing the externalist as simply abandoning the traditional notion of epistemic justification and along with it anything resembling the traditional conception of knowledge. (As already remarked, this may be precisely what the proponents of externalism intend to be doing, though most of them are not very clear on this point.) Thus consider Armstrong's final summation of his conception of knowledge:

Knowledge of the truth of particular matters of fact is a belief which must be true, where the "must" is a matter of law-like necessity. Such knowledge is a reliable representation or "mapping" of reality.

[220]

Nothing is said here of reasons or justification or evidence or having the right to be sure. Indeed the whole idea, central to the western epistemological tradition, of knowledge as essentially the product of reflective, critical, and rational inquiry has seemingly vanished without a trace. It is possible of course that such an altered conception of knowledge may be inescapable or even in some way desirable, but it constitutes a solution to the regress problem or any problem arising out of the traditional conception of knowledge only in the radical and relatively uninteresting sense that to reject that conception is also to reject the problems arising out of it. In this paper, I shall confine myself to less radical solutions.

IV

The externalist solution just discussed represents a very recent approach to the justification of basic beliefs. The second view to be considered is, in contrast, so venerable that it deserves to be called the standard foundationist solution to the problem in question. I refer of course to the traditional doctrine of cognitive givenness, which has played a central role in epistemological discussion at least since Descartes. In recent years, however, the concept of the given, like foundationism itself, has come under serious attack. One upshot of the resulting discussion has been a realization that there are many different notions of givenness, related to each other in complicated ways, which almost certainly do not stand or fall together. Thus it will be well to begin by formulating the precise notion of givenness which is relevant in the present context and distinguishing it from some related conceptions.

In the context of the epistemic regress problem, givenness amounts to the idea that basic beliefs are justified by reference, not to further *beliefs*, but rather to states of affairs in the world which are "immediately apprehended" or "directly presented" or "intuited." This justification by reference to non-cognitive states of affairs thus allegedly avoids the need for any further justification and thereby stops the regress. In a way, the basic gambit of givenism (as I shall call positions of this sort) thus resembles that of the externalist positions considered above. In both cases the justificatory appeal to further beliefs which generates the regress problem is avoided for basic beliefs by an appeal directly to the non-cognitive world; the crucial difference is that for the givenist, unlike the externalist, the justifying state of affairs in the world is allegedly apprehended *in some way* by the believer.

The givenist position to be considered here is significantly weaker than more familiar versions of the doctrine of givenness in at least two different respects. In the first place, the present version does not claim that the given (or, better, the apprehension thereof) is certain or even incorrigible. As discussed above, these stronger claims are inessential to the strong foundationist solution to the regress problem. If they have any importance at all in this context it is only because, as we shall see, they might be thought to be entailed by the only very obvious intuitive picture of how the view is supposed to work. In the second place, givenism as understood here does not involve the usual stipulation that only one's private mental and sensory states can be given. There may or may not be other reasons for thinking that this is in fact the case, but such a restriction is not part of the position itself. Thus both positions like that of C. I. Lewis, for whom the given is restricted to private states apprehended with certainty, and positions like that of Quinton, for whom ordinary physical states of affairs are given with no claim of certainty or incorrigibility being involved, will count as versions of givenism.

As already noted, the idea of givenness has been roundly criticized in recent philosophical discussion and widely dismissed as a piece of philosophical mythology. But much at least of this criticism has to do with the claim of certainty on behalf of the given or with the restriction to private, subjective states. And some of it at least has been mainly concerned with issues in the philosophy of mind which are only distantly related to our present epistemological concerns. Thus even if the objections offered are cogent against other and stronger versions of givenness, it remains unclear whether and how they apply to the more modest version at issue here. The possibility suggests itself that modest givenness may not be a myth, even if more ambitious varieties are, a result which would give the epistemological foundationist all he really needs, even though he has usually, in a spirit of philosophical greed, sought considerably more. In what follows, however, I shall sketch a line of argument which, if correct, will show that even modest givenism is an untenable position.[24]

The argument to be developed depends on a problem within the givenist position which is surprisingly easy to overlook. I shall therefore proceed in the following way. I shall first state the problem in an initial way, then illustrate it by showing how it arises in one recent version of givenism, and finally consider whether any plausible solution is possible. (It will be useful for the purposes of this discussion to make two simplifying assumptions, without which the argument would be more complicated, but not essentially altered. First, I shall assume that the basic belief which is to be justified by reference to the given or immediately apprehended state of affairs is just the belief that this same state of affairs obtains. Second, I shall assume that the given or immediately apprehended state of affairs is not itself a belief or other cognitive state.)

Consider then an allegedly basic belief that-p which is supposed to be justified by reference to a given or immediately apprehended state of affairs that-p. Clearly what justifies the belief is not the state of affairs simpliciter, for to say that would be to return to a form of externalism. For the givenist, what justifies the belief is the *immediate apprehension* or *intuition* of the state of affairs. Thus we seem to have three items present in the situation: the belief, the state of affairs which is the object of the belief, and the intuition or immediate apprehension of that state of affairs. The problem to be raised revolves around the nature of the last of these items, the intuition or immediate apprehension (hereafter I will use mainly the former term). It *seems* to be a cognitive state, perhaps somehow of a more rudimentary sort than a belief, which involves the thesis or assertion that-p. Now if this is correct, it is easy enough to understand in a rough sort of way how an intuition can serve to justify a belief with this same assertive content. The problem is to understand why the intuition, involving as it does the cognitive thesis that-p, does not *itself* require justification. And if the answer is offered that the intuition is justified by reference to the state of affairs that-p, then the question will be why this would not require a second intuition or other apprehension of the state of affairs to justify the original one. For otherwise one and the same cognitive state must somehow constitute both an apprehension of the state of affairs and a justification of that very apprehension, thus pulling itself up by its own cognitive bootstraps. One is reminded here of Chisholm's claim that certain cognitive states justify themselves,[25] but that extremely paradoxical remark hardly constitutes an explanation of how this is possible.

If, on the other hand, an intuition is not a cognitive state and thus involves no cognitive grasp of the state of affairs in question, then the need for a justification for the intuition is obviated, but at the serious cost of making it difficult to see how the intuition is supposed to justify the belief. If the person in question has no cognitive grasp of that state of affairs (or of any other) by virtue of having such an intuition, then how does the intuition give him a *reason* for thinking that his belief is true or likely to be true? We seem again to be back to an externalist position, which it was the whole point of the category of intuition or givenness to avoid.

As an illustration of this problem, consider Quinton's version of givenism, as outlined in his book *The Nature of Things*.[26] As noted above, basic beliefs may, according to Quinton, concern ordinary perceptible states of affairs and need not be certain or incorrigible. (Quinton uses the phrase "intuitive belief" as I have been using "basic belief" and calls the linguistic expression of an intuitive belief a "basic statement"; he also seems to pay very little attention to the difference between beliefs and statements, shifting freely back and forth between them, and I will generally follow him in this.) Thus "this book is red" might, in an appropriate context, be a basic statement expressing a basic or intuitive belief. But how are such basic statements (or the correlative beliefs) supposed to be justified? Here Quinton's account, beyond the insistence that they are not justified by reference to further beliefs, is seriously unclear. He says rather vaguely that the person is "aware" [129] or "directly aware" [139] of the appropriate state of affairs, or that he has "direct knowledge" [126] of it, but he gives no real account of the nature or epistemological status of this state of "direct awareness" or "direct knowledge," though it seems clear that it is supposed to be a cognitive state of some kind. (In particular, it is not clear what "direct" means, over and above "non-inferential.")[27]

The difficulty with Quinton's account comes out most clearly in his discussion of its relation to the correspondence theory of truth:

The theory of basic statements is closely connected with the correspondence theory of truth. In its classical form that theory holds that to each true statement, whatever its form may be, a fact of the same form corresponds. The theory of basic statements indicates the

point at which correspondence is established, at which the system of beliefs makes its justifying contact with the world.

[139]

And further on he remarks that the truth of basic statements "is directly determined by their correspondence with fact" [143]. (It is clear that "determined" here means "epistemically determined.") Now it is a familiar but still forceful idealist objection to the correspondence theory of truth that if the theory were correct we could never know whether any of our beliefs were true, since we have no perspective outside our system of beliefs from which to see that they do or do not correspond. Quinton, however, seems to suppose rather blithely that intuition or direct awareness provides just such a perspective, from which we can in some cases apprehend both beliefs and world and judge whether or not they correspond. And he further supposes that the issue of justification somehow does not arise for apprehensions made from this perspective, though without giving any account of how or why this is so.

My suggestion here is that no such account can be given. As indicated above, the givenist is caught in a fundamental dilemma: if his intuitions or immediate apprehensions are construed as cognitive, then they will be both capable of giving justification and in need of it themselves; if they are non-cognitive, then they do not need justification but are also apparently incapable of providing it. This, at bottom, is why epistemological givenness is a myth.[28]

Once the problem is clearly realized, the only possible solution seems to be to split the difference by claiming that an intuition is a semi-cognitive or quasi-cognitive state,[29] which resembles a belief in its capacity to confer justification, while differing from a belief in not requiring justification itself. In fact, some such conception seems to be implicit in most if not all givenist positions. But when stated thus baldly, this "solution" to the problem seems hopelessly contrived and *ad hoc*. If such a move is accept-able, one is inclined to expostulate, then once again any sort of regress could be solved in similar fashion. Simply postulate a final term in the regress which is sufficiently similar to the previous terms to satisfy, with respect to the penultimate term, the sort of need or impetus which originally generated the regress; but which is different enough from previous terms so as not itself to require satisfaction by a further term. Thus we would have semi-events, which could cause but need not be caused; semi-explanatia, which could explain but need not be explained; and semi-beliefs, which could justify but need not be justified. The point is not that such a move is always incorrect (though I suspect that it is), but simply that the nature and possibility of such a convenient regress-stopper need at the very least to be clearly and con-vincingly established and explained before it can constitute a satisfactory solution to any regress problem.

The main account which has usually been offered by givenists of such semi-cognitive states is well suggested by the terms in which immedi-ate or intuitive apprehensions are described: "immediate," "direct," "presentation," etc. The underlying idea here is that of *confrontation*: in intuition, mind or consciousness is directly con-fronted with its object, without the intervention of any sort of intermediary. It is in this sense that the object is *given* to the mind. The root metaphor underlying this whole picture is vision: mind or consciousness is likened to an immaterial eye, and the object of intuitive awareness is that which is directly before the mental eye and open to its gaze. If this metaphor were to be taken seriously, it would become relatively simple to explain how there can be a cognitive state which can justify but does not require justification. (If the metaphor is to be taken seriously enough to do the foundationist any real good, it becomes plausible to hold that the intuitive cognitive states which result would after all have to be infallible. For if all need for justification is to

be precluded, the envisaged relation of con-frontation seemingly must be conceived as too intimate to allow any possibility of error. To the extent that this is so, the various arguments which have been offered against the notion of infallible cognitive states count also against this version of givenism.)

Unfortunately, however, it seems clear that the mental eye metaphor will not stand serious scrutiny. The mind, whatever else it may be, is not an eye or, so far as we know, anything like an eye. Ultimately the metaphor is just far too simple to be even minimally adequate to the complexity of mental phenomena and to the variety of conditions upon which such phenomena depend. This is not to deny that there is considerable intuitive appeal to the con-frontational model, especially as applied to per-ceptual consciousness, but only to insist that this appeal is far too vague in its import to adequately support the very specific sorts of epistemological results which the strong foundationist needs. In particular, even if empirical knowledge at some point involves some sort of confrontation or seeming confrontation, this by itself provides no clear reason for attributing epistemic justifi-cation or reliability, let alone certainty, to the cognitive states, whatever they may be called, which result.

Moreover, quite apart from the vicissitudes of the mental eye metaphor, there are powerful independent reasons for thinking that the attempt to defend givenism by appeal to the idea of a semi-cognitive or quasi-cognitive state is fundamentally misguided. The basic idea, after all, is to distinguish two aspects of a cognitive state, its capacity to justify other states and its own need for justification, and then try to find a state which possesses only the former aspect and not the latter. But it seems clear on reflection that these two aspects cannot be separated, that it is one and the same feature of a cognitive state, viz. its assertive content, which both enables it to confer justification on other states and also requires that it be justified itself. If this is right, then it does no good to introduce semi-cognitive states in an attempt to justify basic beliefs, since to whatever extent such a state is capable of conferring justification, it will to that very same extent require justification. Thus even if such states do exist, they are of no help to the givenist in attempting to answer the objection at issue here.[30]

Hence the givenist response to the anti-foundationist argument seems to fail. There seems to be no way to explain how a basic cognitive state, whether called a belief or an intuition, can be directly justified by the world without lapsing back into externalism—and from there into skepticism. I shall conclude with three further comments aimed at warding off certain likely sorts of misunderstanding. First, it is natural in this connection to attempt to justify basic beliefs by appealing to *experience*. But there is a familiar ambiguity in the term "experience," which in fact glosses over the crucial distinction upon which the foregoing argument rests. Thus "experience" may mean either an *experiencing* (i.e. a cognitive state) or something *experienced* (i.e. an object of cognition). And once this ambiguity is resolved, the concept of experience seems to be of no particular help to the givenist. Second, I have concentrated, for the sake of simplicity, on Quinton's version of givenism in which ordinary physical states of affairs are among the things which are given. But the logic of the argument would be essentially the same if it were applied to a more traditional version like Lewis's in which it is private experiences which are given, and I cannot see that the end result would be different—though it might be harder to discern, especially in cases where the allegedly basic belief is a belief about another cognitive state. Third, notice carefully that the problem raised here with respect to givenism is a logical problem (in a broad sense of "logical"). Thus it would be a mistake to think that it can be solved simply by indicating some sort of state which seems intuitively to have the appropriate sorts of characteristics; the problem is to understand

how it is *possible* for any state to have those characteristics. (The mistake would be analogous to one occasionally made in connection with the free-will problem: the mistake of attempting to solve the logical problem of how an action can be not determined but also not merely random by indicating a subjective act of effort or similar state, which seems intuitively to satisfy such a description.)

Thus foundationism appears to be doomed by its own internal momentum. No account seems to be available of how an empirical belief can be genuinely justified in an epistemic sense, while avoiding all reference to further empirical beliefs or cognitions which themselves would require justification. How then is the epistemic regress problem to be solved? The natural direction to look for an answer is to the coherence theory of empirical knowledge and the associated non-linear conception of justification which were briefly mentioned above.[31] But arguments by elimination are dangerous at best: there may be further alternatives which have not yet been formulated; and the possibility still threatens that the epistemic regress problem may in the end be of aid and comfort only to the skeptic.[32]

Notes

1 Roderick M. Chisholm, *Theory of Knowledge* (Englewood Cliffs, N.J., 1966), p. 30.

2 Anthony Quinton, *The Nature of Things* (London, 1973), p. 119. This is an extremely venerable argument, which has played a central role in epistemological discussion at least since Aristotle's statement of it in the *Posterior Analytics*, Book I, ch. 2–3. (Some have found an anticipation of the argument in the *Theaetetus* at 209E–210B, but Plato's worry in that passage appears to be that the proposed definition of knowledge is circular, not that it leads to an infinite regress of justification.)

3 "Adequately justified" because a belief could be justified to some degree without being sufficiently justified to qualify as knowledge (if true). But it is far from clear just how much justification

is needed for adequacy. Virtually all recent epistemologists agree that certainty is not required. But the lottery paradox shows that adequacy cannot be understood merely in terms of some specified level of probability. (For a useful account of the lottery paradox, see Robert Ackermann, *Knowledge and Belief* (Garden City, N.Y., 1972), pp. 39–50.) Armstrong, in *Belief, Truth and Knowledge* (London, 1973), argues that what is required is that one's reasons for the belief be "conclusive," but the precise meaning of this is less than clear. Ultimately, it may be that the concept of knowledge is simply too crude for refined epistemological discussion, so that it may be necessary to speak instead of degrees of belief and corresponding degrees of justification. I shall assume (perhaps controversially) that the proper solution to this problem will not affect the issues to be discussed here, and speak merely of the reasons or justification making the belief *highly likely* to be true, without trying to say exactly what this means.

4 See Edmund Gettier, "Is Justified True Belief Knowledge?" *Analysis*, vol. 23 (1963), pp. 121–123. Also Ackermann, *op. cit.*, ch. V, and the corresponding references.

5 For simplicity, I will speak of inference relations as obtaining between beliefs rather than, more accurately, between the propositions which are believed. "Inference" is to be understood here in a very broad sense; any relation between two beliefs which allows one, if accepted, to serve as a good reason for accepting the other will count as inferential.

6 It is difficult to give precise criteria for when a given reason is *the* reason for a person's holding a belief. G. Harman, in *Thought* (Princeton, 1973), argues that for a person to believe for a given reason is for that reason to *explain* why he holds that belief. But this suggestion, though heuristically useful, hardly yields a usable criterion.

7 Thus it is a mistake to conceive the regress as a *temporal* regress, as it would be if each justifying argument had to be explicitly given before the belief in question was justified.

8 Obviously these views could be combined, with different instances of the regress being handled in different ways. I will not consider such combined views here. In general, they would simply inherit all of the objections pertaining to the simpler views.

9 Peirce seems to suggest a virtuous regress view in "Questions concerning Certain Faculties Claimed for Man," *Collected Papers* V, pp. 135–155. But the view is presented metaphorically and it is hard to be sure exactly what it comes to or to what extent it bears on the present issue.

10 The original statement of the non-linear view was by Bernard Bosanquet in *Implication and Linear Inference* (London, 1920). For more recent discussions, see Gilbert Harman, *Thought* (Princeton, 1973); and Nicholas Rescher, "Foundationalism, Coherentism, and the Idea of Cognitive System-atization," *The Journal of Philosophy*, vol. 71 (1974), pp. 695–708.

11 I have attempted to show how a coherence view might be defended against the most standard of these objections in "The Coherence Theory of Empirical Knowledge," *Philosophical Studies*, vol. 30 (1976), pp. 281–312.

12 The presumption against a skeptical outcome is strong, but I think it is a mistake to treat it as absolute. If no non-skeptical theory can be found which is at least reasonably plausible in its own right, skepticism might become the only rational alternative.

13 For some useful distinctions among these terms, see William Alston, "Varieties of Privileged Access," *American Philosophical Quarterly*, vol. 8 (1971), pp. 223–241.

14 For discussions of weak foundationism, see Bertrand Russell, *Human Knowledge* (New York, 1949), part II, ch. 11, and part V, chs. 6 and 7; Nelson Goodman, "Sense and Certainty," *Philosophical Review*, vol. 61 (1952), pp. 160–167; Israel Scheffler, *Science and Subjectivity* (New York, 1967), chapter V; and Roderick Firth, "Coherence, Certainty, and Epistemic Priority," *The Journal of Philosophy*, vol. 61 (1964), pp. 545–557.

15 How good a reason must one have? Presumably some justification accrues from any reason which makes the belief even minimally more likely to be true than not, but considerably more than this would be required to make the justification adequate for knowledge. (See note 3, above.) (The James–Clifford controversy concerning the "will to believe" is also relevant here. I am agreeing with Clifford to the extent of saying that epistemic

justification requires some positive reason in favor of the belief and not just the absence of any reason against.)

16 For a similar use of the notion of epistemic irresponsibility, see Ernest Sosa, "How Do You Know?" *American Philosophical Quarterly*, vol. 11 (1974), p. 117.

17 In fact, the premises would probably have to be true as well, in order to avoid Gettier-type counter-examples. But I shall ignore this refinement here.

18 On a Carnap-style *a priori* theory of probability it could, of course, be the case that very general empirical propositions were more likely to be true than not, i.e. that the possible state-descriptions in which they are true outnumber those in which they are false. But clearly this would not make them likely to be true in a sense which would allow the detached assertion of the proposition in question (on pain of contradiction), and this fact seems to preclude such justification from being adequate for knowledge.

19 Armstrong, *op. cit.*, chapters 11–13. Bracketed page references in this section are to this book.

20 Fred I. Dretske, *Seeing and Knowing* (London, 1969), ch. III, especially pp. 126–139. It is difficult to be quite sure of Dretske's view, however, since he is not concerned in this book to offer a general account of knowledge. Views which are in some ways similar to those of Armstrong and Dretske have been offered by Goldman and by Unger. See Alvin Goldman, "A Causal Theory of Knowing," *The Journal of Philosophy*, vol. 64 (1967), pp. 357–372; and Peter Unger, "An Analysis of Factual Knowledge," *The Journal of Philosophy*, vol. 65 (1968), pp. 157–170. But both Goldman and Unger are explicitly concerned with the Gettier problem and not at all with the regress problem, so it is hard to be sure how their views relate to the sort of externalist view which is at issue here.

21 On the one hand, Armstrong seems to argue that it is *not* a requirement for knowledge that the believer have "sufficient evidence" for his belief, which sounds like a rejection of the adequate-justification condition. On the other hand, he seems to want to say that the presence of the external relation makes it rational for a person to accept a belief, and he seems (though this is not clear) to have *epistemic* rationality in mind; and there appears to be no substantial difference between saying that a belief is epistemically rational and saying that it is epistemically justified.

22 One way to put this point is to say that whether a belief is likely to be true or whether in contrast it is an accident that it is true depends significantly on how the belief is described. Thus it might be true of one and the same belief that it is "a belief connected in a law-like way with the state of affairs which it describes" and also that it is "a belief adopted on the basis of no apparent evidence"; and it might be likely to be true on the first description and unlikely to be true on the second. The claim here is that it is the believer's own conception which should be considered in deciding whether the belief is justified. (Something analogous seems to be true in ethics: the moral worth of a person's action is correctly to be judged only in terms of that person's subjective conception of what he is doing and not in light of what happens, willy-nilly, to result from it.)

23 Notice, however, that if beliefs standing in the proper external relation should happen to possess some subjectively distinctive feature (such as being spontaneous and highly compelling to the believer), and if the believer were to notice empirically, that beliefs having this feature were true a high proportion of the time, he would then be in a position to construct a justification for a new belief of that sort along the lines sketched at the end of section II. But of course a belief justified in that way would no longer be basic.

24 I suspect that something like the argument to be given here is lurking somewhere in Sellars' "Empiricism and the Philosophy of Mind" (reprinted in Sellars, *Science, Perception, and Reality* [London, 1963], pp. 127–196), but it is difficult to be sure. A more recent argument by Sellars which is considerably closer on the surface to the argument offered here is contained in "The Structure of Knowledge," his Machette Foundation Lectures given at the University of Texas in 1971, in Hector-Nerl Casteneda (ed.), *Action, Knowledge, and Reality: Critical Studies in Honor of Wilfrid Sellars* (Indianapolis, 1975), Lecture III, sections III–IV. A similar line of argument was also offered by Neurath and Hempel. See Otto Neurath, "Protocol Sentences," trans. in A. J. Ayer (ed.), *Logical Positivism* (New York, 1959), pp. 199–208; and Carl G.

Hempel, "On the Logical Positivists' Theory of Truth," *Analysis*, vol. 2 (1934–5), pp. 49–59. The Hempel paper is in part a reply to a foundationist critique of Neurath by Schlick in "The Foundation of Knowledge," also translated in *Logical Positivism*, *op. cit.*, pp. 209–227. Schlick replied to Hempel in "Facts and Propositions," and Hempel responded in "Some Remarks on 'Facts' and Propositions," both in *Analysis*, vol. 2 (1934–5), pp. 65–70 and 93–96, respectively. Though the Neurath–Hempel argument conflates issues having to do with truth and issues having to do with justification in a confused and confusing way, it does bring out the basic objection to givenism.

25   Chisholm, "Theory of Knowledge," in Chisholm *et al.*, Philosophy (Englewood Cliffs, N.J., 1964), pp. 270ff.

26   *Op. cit.* Bracketed page references in this section will be to this book.

27   Quinton does offer one small bit of clarification here, by appealing to the notion of ostensive definition and claiming in effect that the sort of awareness involved in the intuitive justification of a basic belief is the same as that involved in a situation of ostensive definition. But such a comparison is of little help, for at least two reasons. First, as Wittgenstein, Sellars, and others have argued, the notion of ostensive definition is itself seriously problematic. Indeed, an objection quite analogous to the present one against the notion of a basic belief could be raised against the notion of an ostensive definition; and this objection, if answerable at all, could only be answered by construing the awareness involved in ostension in such a way as to be of no help to the foundationist

in the present discussion. Second, more straight-forwardly, even if the notion of ostensive definition were entirely unobjectionable, there is no need for the sort of awareness involved to be *justified*. If all that is at issue is learning the meaning of a word (or acquiring a concept), then justification is irrelevant. Thus the existence of ostensive definitions would not show how there could be basic beliefs.

28   Notice, however, that to reject an epistemological given does not necessarily rule out other varieties of givenness which may have importance for other philosophical issues. In particular, there may still be viable versions of givenness which pose an obstacle to materialist views in the philosophy of mind. For useful distinctions among various versions of givenness and a discussion of their relevance to the philosophy of mind, see James W. Cornman, "Materialism and Some Myths about Some Givens," *The Monist*, vol. 56 (1972), pp. 215–233.

29   Compare the Husserlian notion of a "pre-predicative awareness."

30   It is interesting to note that Quinton seems to offer an analogous critique of givenness in an earlier paper, "The Problem of Perception," reprinted in Robert J. Swartz (ed.), *Perceiving, Sensing, and Knowing* (Garden City, N.Y., 1965), pp. 497–526; cf. especially p. 503.

31   For a discussion of such a coherence theory, see my paper cited in note 11, above.

32   I am grateful to my friends Jean Blumenfeld, David Blumenfeld, Hardy Jones, Jeff Pelletier, and Martin Perlmutter for extremely helpful comments on an earlier version of this paper.

Chapter 21

Laurence BonJour

TOWARD A DEFENSE OF EMPIRICAL FOUNDATIONALISM

My aim in this paper is to take some initial steps toward the development and defense of a quite traditional foundationalist view of the justification of empirical beliefs and in particular of beliefs about physical objects: the view that such justification depends ultimately on basic or foundational beliefs about the contents of sensory experience. I say "justification" rather than "knowledge," because I want to sidestep issues about whether justification is a requirement for knowledge and about the, to my mind, rather vexed concept of knowledge itself. My concern is thus with what reasons there are for thinking that our familiar beliefs about the physical world are true, where I have in mind reasons: (i) that do not in some way beg the question by presupposing the acceptability of other beliefs about physical objects; and (ii) that are in principle available through reflection and analysis to believers more or less like ourselves. (But I will not be very concerned with the question of whether the justification in question is actually in the minds of ordinary people.) It is to this question that I now think that a traditional foundationalism offers the only hope of a non-skeptical answer.

Until roughly forty years ago, such a foundationalist view was generally acknowledged as obviously correct and indeed as more or less the only serious epistemological alternative to a pervasive skepticism. In the intervening period, however, empirical foundationalism of this sort,

or indeed of any sort, has been subjected to incessant attack and has come to be widely regarded as an obviously untenable and even hopeless view. As a result, a very substantial proportion of the epistemological work in this period has been aimed at the delineation and development of nonskeptical alternatives to empirical foundationalism. This effort has spawned various widely discussed views, such as coherentism, contextualism, externalism, and a variety of others that are less easily labeled. (Though externalism can be regarded as a version of foundationalism, it rejects the internalist requirement, common to all traditional versions of foundationalism, that the justification for a belief must be cognitively accessible to the believer. My concern here is to defend a foundationalist view of the more traditional, internalist sort, and it is such a view that subsequent uses of the term "foundationalism" should be taken to refer to.)

I myself have played a role in these developments, offering some of the arguments against foundationalism and attempting to develop and defend the coherentist alternative in particular. But having labored long in the intriguing but ultimately barren labyrinths of coherentism, I have come to the conviction that the recent antifoundationalist trend is a serious mistake, one that is taking epistemological inquiry in largely the wrong direction and giving undeserved credibility to those who would reject epistemology altogether.

I have two main reasons for this conviction. One, which can only be briefly touched on here, is that none of the recent alternatives seem to me to succeed in providing a genuinely nonskeptical alternative to traditional foundationalism or to have any serious prospect of doing so. Of the main alternatives, contextualism and external-ism concede more or less openly that we do not in general have internally accessible, non-question-begging reasons for thinking that our beliefs about the world are true, a result that seems to me to constitute in itself a very deep and intuitively quite implausible version of skepticism. And coherentism, despite my efforts and those of others to avoid such a fate (efforts that in retrospect seem rather obviously des-perate), now seems to me to lead inexorably to the same dismal result—largely, as many have long argued, because of the problem of access to one's own system of beliefs.[1]

The second reason, elaborated below, is that I now think that I can see a way to develop a foundationalist position that avoids the objec-tions to such a view that seem to me most important. I should make clear at the outset, however, that I will be concerned here almost exclusively with objections that challenge the possibility or availability of the foundational beliefs themselves. There is, of course, a second main problem that any foundationalist must face: that of whether and how it is possible to infer in an adequately justified way from the foundational beliefs to nonfoundational beliefs and especially to beliefs about the physical world.[2] This problem, as discussion of the "problem of the external world" extending at least back to Descartes makes clear, is very serious. But it does not seem to me to provide in itself a clear basis for an objection to foundation-alism until and unless some alternative view does better in this respect—and does so without construing justification (or knowledge) in ways that amount to the tacit acceptance of serious versions of skepticism. For this reason, and also for lack of space and very likely, for the present at

least, of adequate wit, I will leave this second main problem largely untouched on the present occasion, saying only a little about it at the very end of the paper.

I Foundationalism and a central objection

I begin with a closer examination of the central concept of a basic or foundational belief. This will lead to one of the main objections to empirical foundationalism, in relation to which the specific account of the foundational beliefs to be offered here will be developed.

As reflected in the familiar epistemic regress argument for empirical foundationalism, which I will not take the time to rehearse here, a foundational or "basic" belief is supposed to be an empirical belief that (a) is adequately justified in the epistemic sense, but (b) whose epistemic justification does not depend on inference from further empirical beliefs that would in turn have to be somehow justified. The main problem is to understand how these two elements can be successfully combined. To say that such a foundational belief is epistemically justified is to say that there is some sort of reason or basis or warrant for thinking that it is true or at least likely to be true—one, I will assume here, that is available or accessible to the person in question. But this reason or basis or warrant is not supposed to take the form of a further empirical belief, for example a belief that the belief originally in question has some feature that can be independently shown to be indicative of truth.[3] What form then does it take?

It is sometimes suggested that the basic or foundational beliefs are either "self-justifying" or else "not in need of justification," but both of these formulations seem to me to render the epistemic status of such beliefs needlessly problematic and even paradoxical. A basic belief cannot literally be self-justifying unless the foundationalist accepts circular reasoning as a source of justification, a view that seems obviously unacceptable (and that would also undercut one main objection to coherentism). Nor can it be plausibly claimed that the foundational beliefs are self-evident in the sense that is sometimes claimed to apply to beliefs justified a priori: the content of an empirical, contingent belief cannot by itself provide a good reason for thinking that it is true.[4] And the only way that a belief that is to serve as a foundation for other beliefs can itself be "not in need of justification" is if it already possesses something tantamount to justification (whether or not that term is employed), in which case this status needs to be further explained.

Here the obvious and, I now believe, correct thing to say is that basic or foundational beliefs are justified by appeal to *experience*. But the difficulty, which turns out to be very formidable, is to give a clear and dialectically perspicuous picture of how this is supposed to work.

Foundationalists such as C. I. Lewis and Richard Fumerton,[5] among many others, have spoken at this point of the "direct apprehension" of or "direct acquaintance" with the relevant experiential content. Contrary to my own earlier arguments,[6] I now believe that there is a way to understand such formulations that leads to a defensible view. On the surface, however, this answer is seriously problematic in the following way. The picture it suggests is that in a situation of foundational belief there are two distinguishable elements, in addition to the relevant sensory experience itself. First, there is an allegedly basic or foundational belief whose content pertains to some aspect of that experience. Second, there is what appears to be a second, independent mental act, an act of direct apprehension of or direct acquaintance with the relevant experiential feature. And it is, of course, this second act that is supposed to supply the person's reason for thinking that the belief is true.

But the problem now is to understand the nature and epistemic status of this second mental act itself. If it is construed as cognitive and conceptual, having as its content something like the proposition or claim that the experience in question has the specific character indicated by the belief, then it is easy to see how this second mental act can, if it *is itself justified*, provide a reason for thinking that the belief is true, but hard to see why it does not itself require justification of some further sort, some reason for thinking that its propositional or assertive content is true or correct. And to say simply that acts of direct apprehension, unlike ordinary beliefs, somehow cannot by their very nature be mistaken is to stipulate that the problem does not exist without offering any clear explanation of how and why this is so.

If, on the other hand, the mental act of direct apprehension or direct acquaintance is construed as noncognitive and nonconceptual in character, as not involving any propositional claim about the character of the experience, then while no further issue of justification is apparently raised, it becomes difficult to see how such an act of direct apprehension can provide any reason or other basis for thinking that the original allegedly foundational belief is true. If one who is directly acquainted with an experience is not thereby propositionally aware that it has such-and-such features, in what way is his belief that he has an experience with those features justified by the act of direct acquaintance?

It is this dilemma[7] that has always seemed to me to be the most fundamental objection to empirical foundationalism, and the core of the present paper will be an account of how it can be answered. I will begin in the next two sections by considering the somewhat tangential but more easily accessible case of the justification of a metabelief about a conscious, occurrent first-order belief or assertive thought, and then turn in the following section to the main issue of the justification of beliefs about sensory experience.

II Foundational beliefs about one's own beliefs

As I work on this paper, I believe that I am having various occurrent beliefs or assertive thoughts about foundationalism and its problems. For example, I believe that I currently have the occurrent belief or thought that foundationalism is much more defensible than most philosophers think. What is my justification for this second-order metabelief (assuming that there is any)?

As already indicated, the natural answer to this question, which is also the one that I want to elaborate and defend here, is to appeal to the conscious *experience* involved in having the occurrent belief or thought in question. But it is crucial for present purposes that the nature and status of this experience be understood in the right way. My suggestion is that an intrinsic and essential aspect of having an occurrent belief is being consciously aware of the two correlative aspects of its content: first, its propositional content, in this case the proposition that foundationalism is much more defensible than most philosophers think; and, second, the assertory rather than, for example, questioning character of one's entertaining of that content. These two awarenesses (or rather two aspects of one awareness) are, I am suggesting, not apperceptive or reflective in character: they do not involve a second-order mental act with the propositional content that I have the belief in question. Instead, they are *constitutive* of the first-level state of belief itself in that they are what make it the very belief that it is, rather than some other belief or a different sort of conscious state altogether. The point here is simply that occurrent belief or thought is, after all, a *conscious* state, and that what one is primarily conscious of in having such a belief is precisely its propositional and assertive content; not to be consciously aware of that content would be not to have the conscious, occurrent belief at all.

It is this account of the experiential aspect of occurrent belief that seems to me to allow an escape between the horns of the antifoundationalist dilemma posed in the previous section. The crucial point is that the most fundamental experience involved in having an occurrent belief is *neither* a second-order apperceptive or reflective awareness that it has occurred nor a purely noncognitive awareness that fails to reflect the specific character of the belief and its content. Instead it is an intrinsic and constitutive awareness of the propositional and assertive content of the belief.[8]

Because of its nonapperceptive, constituent character, this "built-in" awareness of content, as it might be described, neither requires any justification itself, nor for that matter even admits of any. Indeed, as far as I can see, such a nonapperceptive, constituent awareness of content is strictly *infallible* in pretty much the way that foundationalist views have traditionally claimed, but which most have long since abandoned. Since it is in virtue of this constitutive or "built-in" awareness of content that the belief is the particular belief that it is with the specific content that it has, rather than some other belief or some other sort of state, there is apparently no way in which this awareness of content could be mistaken—simply because there is no independent fact or situation for it to be mistaken about.

It is by appeal to this intrinsic, constitutive awareness of propositional and assertive content that the metabelief that I have the first-level belief can, I suggest, be justified. Such a constitutive awareness of content seems obviously enough to constitute in and by itself, at least if other things are equal, a reason for thinking that the metabelief that I have an occurrent belief with that very content is true (or, perhaps more realistically, for thinking that a metabelief that gives a less detailed, more abstract description of the first-order content, but one that the actual, more specific content falls under, is true). The point here, elaborated further below, is that the metabelief is a *description* of the very content involved in the constitutive awareness of content, so that by consciously having that constitutive awareness, I am in an ideal position to judge whether or not this description is correct.

In this way, such a metabelief can have precisely the epistemic status required by foundationalism: it can be justified in the sense of there being a clear and internally accessible reason for thinking that it is true, but the reason in question can be such as to avoid any appeal to a further belief that would itself be in need of justification—though we now see that it is the first-level constitutive or "built-in" awareness of content, rather than the metabelief that it justifies, that turns out to be the ultimate source of justification.

The infallibility of the "built-in" awareness does not, of course, extend to the apperceptive metabelief: it would still be possible to apperceptively misapprehend one's own belief, that is, to have a second-level belief that does not accurately reflect the content contained in the constitutive or "built-in" awareness constitutive of the first-level belief. Such a mistake might be a case of mere inattention, or it might result from the complexity or obscurity of the belief content itself or from some further problem. But unless there is some special reason in a particular case to think that the chances of such a misapprehension are large, this possibility of error does not seem to prevent the second-level metabelief from being justifiable by appeal to the first-level constituent awareness. This is just to say that while such justification is defeasible in various ways, it is adequate until and unless it is defeated, rather than requiring an independent and prior showing of reliability.

The foregoing account of the foundational status of metabeliefs about one's own occurrent beliefs or thoughts seems to me to possess a good deal of intuitive plausibility, but this is hardly enough to show that it is correct. The best way to defend it further is to examine and defend the underlying view of the nature of consciousness upon which it rests. This will be the job of the next section.

III Two theories of consciousness

As just suggested, what underlies the foundationalist picture just offered is a view concerning the nature of consciousness itself: the view that a consciousness of the appropriate sort of content is an intrinsic, constitutive feature of a conscious mental state,[9] one that is a part of its own internal character and depends not at all on any further apperceptive state. Perhaps the best way to both clarify and defend this view is to contrast it with the only very clear alternative, a view that has become known as the "higher-order thought" theory of consciousness, first explicitly advanced and defended by David Rosenthal.[10] According to Rosenthal's view, consciousness is not an intrinsic property of any mental state. Instead, one mental state becomes conscious only by being the object of a *second* mental state, a higher-order thought that one is in the first mental state.

The issue between these two views of the nature of consciousness is obviously crucial for the defensibility of the version of foundationalism suggested in the previous section (and elaborated further below). If Rosenthal is right, the conscious dimension of my first-level belief or thought that foundationalism is much more defensible than most philosophers think depends on the existence of an appropriate second-order thought, namely, the thought that I have the occurrent belief that foundationalism is much more defensible than most philosophers think. In consequence (as he never quite says explicitly but seems clearly to intend), there would be no consciousness at all of the content of the first-level belief or thought, were that content not apprehended in a second-order thought. And if this were so, then conscious awareness of the first-level content would apparently occur only as a part of the content of the second-order thought, so that there would be no "built-in" or constitutive awareness of the content of the first-order belief or thought to appeal to for the justification of the metabelief discussed in the previous section. And since such a second-order thought appears to be just as much in need of justification as the original metabelief—indeed it might apparently just be that meta-belief in an occurrent form—appealing to its content also yields no foundational justification. Thus if the higher-order thought theory of consciousness is correct, the foundationalist view that I am trying to develop will not work.

Fortunately, however, there is a clear and decisive reason why the higher-order thought theory cannot be correct. (A second, somewhat less decisive but still weighty reason will emerge later.) This arises by first noticing that the higher-order thoughts whose occurrence supposedly confers consciousness on lower-order thoughts cannot themselves all be conscious. One such higher-order thought may of course be conscious by virtue of being the object of a still higher-order thought, but since it is reasonably clear that an infinite hierarchy of such higher-order thoughts does not and probably cannot exist, there must in any sequence of such thoughts, each having the previous one as its object, be a highest-order thought in that sequence that is not in turn the object of a still higher-order thought and thus, according to the higher-order thought theory, that is not itself conscious. All this Rosenthal accepts and indeed seems to advocate [467], though, if I am right, without fully appreciating its significance.

Now consider again my earlier example of my first-order conscious belief that foundationalism is much more defensible than most philosophers think. On Rosenthal's account, as we have seen, the status of this thought as conscious must result from a second-level thought that I have the first-level thought, rather than from a "built-in" or constitutive conscious awareness. And let us suppose, for the sake of simplicity, that the second-order thought is in this case not itself the object of any higher-order thought, and so, according to his account, is not itself conscious. Rosenthal seems to regard this as the most typical case [465–66], and considering more

complicated possibilities would yield the same ultimate result, albeit in a somewhat more convoluted way.

The problem is now to understand how and why according to this picture I am conscious of the content of my first-level belief or thought at all. I am not conscious of that content merely by virtue of having the first-order thought. And though the first-level content is reflected in the content of the second-level thought, *I am not conscious of that second-level content either*, on Rosenthal's view, since there is no higher-order thought about it. Thus it is entirely obscure where the consciousness of the first-level content is supposed to come from or to reside. If the first-order thought is not in itself conscious and the second-order thought is not in itself conscious, and if there are in this case no higher-order thoughts (which would yield only a longer sequence of nonconscious thoughts), then there seems to be no consciousness of the first-level content present at all—contrary to the initial stipulation that we are dealing with a first-level thought that is (somehow) conscious.

My diagnosis is that Rosenthal (along with many others including, perhaps, Descartes himself) has confused two subtly but crucially different things: first, the consciousness of the *content* of a conscious mental state, which is, I have suggested, intrinsic to the occurrence of that state itself; and, second, the reflective or apperceptive consciousness of that state itself, the consciousness *that* such a state has occurred, which I agree requires a second-level or apperceptive state. This confusion is plainly reflected in Rosenthal's statement that "conscious states are simply mental states we are conscious of being in" [462]. Conflating these two things leads quite inevitably to the view that a mental state could be intrinsically conscious only by somehow paradoxically having *both* its ordinary content and the further, self-referential content that it itself occurs. Rosenthal is surely right to reject such a view [469–70], but wrong that it is the only alternative to his higher-order thought theory.

One important point worth adding here is that if a particular mental state lacks such an intrinsic awareness of its own content (which I have not argued here to be impossible), one may still come in some way to have a higher-order thought that it (the lower-order state) exists. But such a higher-order thought, even if it is itself intrinsically conscious in the way indicated, would not, contrary to Rosenthal's claim, somehow transmute the state that is its object into a conscious state, even though the subject would be conscious of that state as an object. An important corollary of this point is that in such a situation, the subject would be conscious of the content of the lower-order state only indirectly and only as described or characterized in the content of the higher-order state—which description may of course be incomplete or less than fully accurate and will in any case be in conceptual terms. Especially where the state in question is a qualitative or sensory state with a content that is not itself conceptual (see further below), there is all the difference in the world between an external and conceptual awareness that it occurs and an actual conscious awareness of the qualitative or sensory content itself.

My conclusion here is that the higher-order thought theory is untenable and indeed obviously so, with the only apparent alternative being the view, advocated above, that an awareness of the appropriate sort of content is an intrinsic, constitutive feature of those mental states that are conscious—thus making it possible, as discussed above, to appeal to that awareness to justify a foundational belief.

IV Foundational beliefs about sensory experience

If I am right, the foregoing provides at least a sketch of how a certain specific sort of belief, namely, an apperceptive metabelief about an occurrent belief of one's own, can be basic in the sense of there being an internally available reason why it is likely to be true without that

reason depending on any further belief or other cognitive state that is itself in need of justification. Apart from possible objections based on externalist theories of belief content, which I find extremely implausible but have no time to go into here,[11] the account in question also seems extremely obvious, too obvious to warrant discussing, were it not that so many, my earlier self included, have managed to miss it.

Where does this leave us? Even this much of a foundationalist ingredient would be a valuable addition to erstwhile coherence theories like my own earlier view.[12] Though there would still be a serious problem of what to say about non-occurrent beliefs, to which the account sketched so far is not directly applicable, at least a good deal of the problem of access to one's own beliefs would be solved. It is doubtful, however, that foundational beliefs about my own beliefs, even if worries stemming from the occurrent-dispositional distinction are set aside, are enough by themselves to provide an adequate basis for justification of beliefs about the objective physical world.[13] And in any case, having shown how a foundational grasp of the content of one's own beliefs is possible, there is an analogous, albeit somewhat more complicated and problematic possibility with respect to the contents of other kinds of experience, especially sensory or perceptual experience, that needs to be considered.

Consider then a state of, for example, visual experience, such as the one that I am currently having as I look out over this room. Like an occurrent belief, such an experience is a conscious state. What this means, I suggest, is that, in a way that parallels the account of occurrent belief or thought offered above, it automatically involves a constitutive or "built-in," non-apperceptive awareness of its own distinctive sort of content, namely sensory or experiential content.[14] And, again in parallel fashion, such a constitutive awareness of sensory content is in no need of justification and is indeed infallible in the sense that there is no sort of mistake that is even relevant to it. Since it is this awareness of sensory content that gives my experiential state the specific content that it has and thus constitutes it as the specific experiential state that it is, there is no logical room for this awareness to be mistaken about the content in question. And thus such an awareness of sensory content is also apparently available to justify foundational beliefs.

Before we embrace this idea too eagerly, however, there is a recently popular objection that needs to be addressed. This objection, which is present with various degrees of explicitness in the thought of philosophers as different as Popper, Sellars, Davidson, and Rorty,[15] begins with the idea that the distinctive content of a sensory or perceptual experience, that content the awareness of which makes the experience the very experience that it is, is nonpropositional and nonconceptual in character—where what this means is at least that this most basic awareness of sensory content is not couched in general or classificatory terms, is not a propositional awareness that the experience falls under general categories or universals. And from this the conclusion is drawn that such an awareness cannot stand in any intelligible justificatory relation to a belief formulated in propositional and conceptual terms, and hence that the relation between the two must be merely causal. As Davidson puts it:

> The relation between a sensation and a belief cannot be logical, since sensations are not beliefs or other propositional attitudes. What then is the relation? The answer is, I think, obvious: the relation is causal. Sensations cause some beliefs and in this sense are the basis or ground of those beliefs. But a causal explanation of a belief does not show how or why the belief is justified.[16]

And if this were correct, what I have been calling the constitutive or "built-in" awareness of sensory content, even though it undeniably

exists, would be incapable of playing any justificatory role and thus would apparently have no real epistemological significance.

The premise of this objection, namely the claim that sensory experience is essentially nonconceptual in character, seems to me both true and important. At least part of the point is that the content of, for example, the visual experience that I am having as I look out over this room is far too specific, detailed, and variegated to be adequately captured in any conceptual or propositional formulation—or at least in any that I am currently able to formulate or even understand. Moreover, even if we imagine an ideally complete and fine-grained conceptual description, it seems clear that thinking in conceptual terms of, for example, very specific shades of color in some complicated pattern is not at all the same thing as actually experiencing the pattern of colors itself. (Here we see the second objection, alluded to above, to the higher-order thought theory of consciousness: a higher-order conceptual thought could not account for the distinctive sort of consciousness that a conscious sensory state involves.)

But although I confess to being one of those who has in the past been influenced by this objection, it now seems to me that its conclusion simply does not follow from its premise. For even if we grant and indeed insist that the specific content of the experience is itself nonpropositional and nonconceptual, it, like various other kinds of nonconceptual phenomena, can of course still be conceptually described with various degrees of detail and precision. The relation between the nonconceptual content and such a conceptual description thereof may not be *logical*, as Davidson uses the term, but it is also obviously not merely causal. Rather it is a *descriptive* relation. And where such a relation of description exists, the character of the nonconceptual object can obviously constitute a kind of reason or basis for thinking that the description is true or correct (or equally, of course, untrue or incorrect).

Such a reason is, of course, only available to one who has some sort of independent access to the character of the nonconceptual item, that is, an access that does not depend on the conceptual description itself. In the most usual sorts of cases, for example, where it is some physical object or situation that is being described, one could have an access that is independent of the description in question only by having a second conceptual state embodying a second, perhaps more specific description, and this second description would of course itself equally require justification, so that no foundational justification would result. But in the very special case we are concerned with, where the nonconceptual item being described is itself a conscious state, one can be aware of its character via the constitutive or "built-in" awareness of content without the need for a further conceptual description and thereby be in a position to recognize that a belief about that state is correct.

Thus where I have a conscious state of sensory experience, I am, as already argued, aware of the specific sensory content of that state simply by virtue of having that experience. And thus if an apperceptive belief that I entertain purports to describe or conceptually characterize that perceptual content, albeit no doubt incompletely, and if I understand the descriptive content of that belief, that is, understand what an experience would have to be like in order to satisfy the conceptual description, then I seem to be in a good, indeed an ideal, position to judge whether the conceptual description is accurate as far as it goes, and if so, to be thereby justified in accepting the belief. Here again there is no reason to think that mistake is impossible and thus no reason to think that such an apperceptive belief is infallible or indubitable. But as long as there is no special reason for suspecting that a mistake has occurred, the fact that such a belief seems to accurately characterize the conscious experience that it purports to describe seems to provide an entirely adequate basis for thinking that the

description is correct, and hence an adequate basis for justification.

Here indeed we seem to have exactly the sort of direct comparison or "confrontation" between a conceptual description and the nonconceptual chunk of reality that it purports to describe which seems intuitively to be essential if our conceptual descriptions are ever to make contact with reality in a verifiable way, but which many philosophers, myself again alas included, have rejected as impossible. Such a confrontation is only possible, to be sure, where the reality in question is itself a conscious state and where the description in question pertains to the conscious content of that very state, but in that very specific case it seems to be entirely unproblematic. Thus we can see that the given is, after all, not a myth!

I am inclined to suspect that it is this sort of nonapperceptive, intrinsic awareness of the content of a conscious state that epistemologists such as those mentioned earlier had at least primarily in mind in their use of the notion of "direct acquaintance" or "immediate awareness." But if this is right, then discussions of direct acquaintance were often needlessly obscure, suggesting as they did some sort of mysteriously authoritative or infallible apprehension of an independent cognitive object, rather than an awareness that is simply constitutive of a conscious state itself. Moreover, the claim of some proponents of direct acquaintance that one might possibly be directly acquainted with physical objects or their surfaces simply makes no sense on the present account of what direct acquaintance really amounts to, thus perhaps vindicating the frequent claim of other proponents of this concept that one can be directly acquainted only with one's own mental states.[17] I also believe that it is this sort of constitutive or "built-in" awareness of the content of a conscious state that Chisholm had in mind in speaking of states that are "self-presenting,"[18] a terminology that seems rather more appropriate to the phenomenon in question than "acquaintance." Alas, he did not succeed in making the idea sufficiently clear to philosophers like myself, though it now seems to me that at the very least a substantial part of the fault lies with those who failed to understand.

The foregoing discussion seems to me to establish that a potential foundation for empirical justification genuinely exists, consisting, more or less as traditional foundationalists thought, of beliefs about the content of sensory experience (and the content of other conscious states). But while such a result is necessary for the defense of a traditional foundationalism, it is obviously very far from sufficient, leaving a host of further questions and issues to be dealt with. In the final two sections, I will try to say a little about some of these, though the largest and most important one of all, namely, the problem of the external world itself, will have to remain largely untouched.

V The conceptual formulation of sensory content

Perhaps the most immediate question is what form the allegedly foundational beliefs about sensory content actually take and the related issue of whether it is plausible to suppose that ordinary people actually have any such beliefs.

Here I am assuming that for the content of sensory experience to play any justificatory role, it is necessary that such content be conceptually formulated in beliefs that are explicitly about it. Things would be far easier if it were plausible to hold, as some have,[19] that nonconceptual content could somehow directly justify beliefs that are not directly about it, for example that are directly about physical objects, without that content needing to be itself formulated in conceptual terms. It seems to me, however, that any such view is untenable, that Davidson and the others are right in thinking that there is no intelligible relation of justification between nonconceptual sensory content and conceptual beliefs in

general. I have argued that such a justificatory relation can exist in the specific case where the conceptual belief is a purported description of the conscious experiential content itself, but I think that this is the only sort of case where it makes clear and intelligible sense. Thus it is impossible, in my view, for a foundationalist to avoid the issues of what form such descriptions might actually take and of whether or not we actually have any.

These issues would be relatively simple to deal with if it were plausible to suppose that we are able to conceptually formulate the given content in phenomenological terms that are as close as possible to the apparent character of the given experience itself—in terms of something like the pure sense-datum language or concepts envisaged by various philosophers earlier in this century. The advocates of such views have usually assumed that the resulting description of, for example, visual experience would be in terms of patches of color arranged in a two-dimensional visual space, and I have no desire at present to quarrel with such a picture. The idea that such a purely phenomenological description could accurately capture the content of experience would nowadays be rejected by many as wrong-headed in principle,[20] but this now seems to me to be a mistake. I can see no reason why it would not be possible for us to have the conceptual resources to provide such a phenomenological description of experience to any level of precision and accuracy desired, even though it seems obvious that we would always fall short of an ideally complete description.

But even if an account of experience in phenomenological terms represents a theoretical possibility, the idea that our main conceptual grasp of the content of experience is in such terms faces two obvious difficulties of a more narrowly practical sort. First, we clearly do not in fact possess the needed conceptual resources, even if I am right that it would be possible in principle to possess them. It is important, however, not to exaggerate this point. Most people are capable of giving reasonably precise and accurate phenomenological or at least quasi-phenomenological descriptions of some aspects of their experience, and a person, such as an artist or a wine taster, who cultivates this ability can often do a good deal better. But it is doubtful whether even those whose abilities of this sort are the best developed are in a position to conceptually formulate a strictly phenomenological characterization of sense experience that is sufficiently detailed and precise to capture all or even most of its justificatory significance for claims about the physical world (assuming for the moment that it has such significance). And in any case, it is exceedingly clear that most of us do not even begin to approach such a capacity. Second, even if we did possess the needed conceptual resources, it seems abundantly clear that the time and effort required to formulate justificatorily adequate descriptions of experience in such terms, whether overtly in language or internally to oneself, would be prohibitive from a practical standpoint.

But if our conceptual formulations of the given content of sensory experience are not, at least for the most part, couched in purely phenomenological terms, the only very obvious alternative is that we conceptually grasp such content in terms of the physical objects and situations that we would be inclined on the basis of that experience, other things being equal, to think we are perceiving. Thus, for example, my primary conceptual grasp of my present visual experience characterizes it as the sort of experience that in the absence of countervailing considerations would lead me to think that I am perceiving a moderately large room of a specifiable shape, containing many chairs, a variety of people, and so forth, all of which could be spelled out at great length. The usual way of putting this is to say that what I am conceptually aware of is certain physical-object *appearances* or apparent physical objects—or, in a slightly more technical terminology, of ways of being "appeared to."[21] Where the appearance in

question is a visual appearance, we may say instead that it *looks* as though there are objects of the sorts indicated, and analogously for other sensory modalities.[22]

Many philosophers have questioned whether ordinary people in ordinary perceptual situations normally or standardly have beliefs about the nonconceptual content of their sensory experience, even ones that are couched in such appearance terms. I am not convinced that this issue has the importance that is often ascribed to it, because it does not seem to me in any clear way to be a requirement for an adequate philosophical account of empirical justification that ordinary beliefs will turn out to be fully and explicitly justified. But it nonetheless seems to me that an ordinary person who has, for example, a visual belief about a certain sort of physical object plausibly has something that is tantamount to a grasp of the character of his visual experience in physical-object appearance terms: such a person is after all surely aware that the perceptual claim in question is a result of vision, that is, that he sees the object; and this seems to amount to at least an implicit realization that his or her visual experience is such as to make it look as though an object of that sort is there. That an ordinary person would not couch matters in such explicitly philosophical terms must, of course, be granted, but this does not seem to me to show that they are not aware of what the philosophical account more explicitly formulates.

But while this seems to me to be the main answer to the question of how we grasp sensory content in conceptual terms, the potential for misunderstanding its significance is very serious, and many philosophers seem to me to have succumbed to this danger. In particular, it is crucially important to distinguish a description of experience that merely indicates what sort of physical objects and situations seem or appear, on the basis of that experience, to be present from one that embodies some further causal or relational claim about the connection between experience and the physical realm, one whose justification would clearly have to appeal to something beyond the experienced content itself.

A useful example of the sort of danger that I am warning against is provided by Susan Haack in her recent book on epistemology, in the course of which she attempts to give a specification of the evidential force of a state of perceptual experience. Her suggestion is that this can be captured by a set of propositions ascribing the perceptual states to the subject in question. Thus, for example, such an ascription might say that the subject "is in the sort of perceptual state a person would be in, in normal circumstances, when looking at a rabbit three feet away and in good light" or "is in the sort of perceptual state a normal subject would be in, in normal circumstances, when getting a brief glimpse of a fast-moving rabbit at dusk."[23] Haack's discussion of this point is perhaps not as clear or full as one might like, but the specific formulations offered make it reasonable to suppose that these characterizations are intended to describe the experience in terms of the physical situations that are *causally* or *lawfully* connected with it, rather than in terms of its intrinsic content. This, however, is precisely the sort of description that *cannot* be justified by appeal to the experienced content alone. My experience may be such as to incline me to think that a rabbit is present, but the experience cannot by itself reveal that it is actually of the sort that is normally caused by rabbits. A useful way of putting the point is to say that the claims about physical appearances or ways of being appeared to that constitute our primary conceptual formulations of sensory experience must be understood in something like what Chisholm has called the "descriptive, noncomparative" sense of the terms or concepts in question,[24] for only in that sense can the claim to be "appeared to" in a certain way be adequately justified simply by appeal to our constitutive, nonconceptual awareness of sensory content.

As already argued, it seems quite obvious that we have the ability to grasp or represent the character of our perceptual experience fairly accurately, albeit somewhat obliquely, in terms of such physical object appearances. But once illegitimate construals like Haack's are set aside, it is far from obvious exactly what such characterizations of experience really amount to. In giving them, we seem to be relying on a tacitly grasped and, we think, mutually understood correlation or association, perhaps learned or perhaps at least partially innate, between experiential features and the physical situations of which they are taken to be appearances, one that we are confidently guided by in the vast majority of cases, even though we are unable even to begin to formulate it explicitly.

To speak here of a "correlation" might suggest the idea that it is a mere correlation, that the experiential content and the corresponding propositional claim about physical objects are only externally coordinated, without being connected with each other in any more intimate way. This, however, is not the view that I mean to be advocating. On the contrary, as discussed a bit further in the final section, it seems intuitively pretty clear that the experiential content is in itself *somehow* strongly suggestive of or in some interesting way isomorphic to the correlated physical situation. But however this correlation ultimately works, the important issue is whether the beliefs about the physical world that we adopt on the basis of it are at least likely to be true, something that cannot be simply assumed.

VI The problem of the external world

This brings me then, finally and necessarily briefly, to the most important issue that arises for this sort of position: If the foregoing is at least approximately the right way to understand our primary conceptual representations of the given content of sensory experience, how, if at all, do such representations contribute to the justification of beliefs about the physical world? In particular, how does the fact that my given sensory experience can be correctly described, in light of the tacit correlation just mentioned, as the appearance of a certain sort of physical object or situation contribute to the *justification* of the claim that such an object or situation is actually present and being perceived? This is of course the ultimate question in this general area, one that would take far more time than is available here to deal with adequately. For the moment, I will therefore have to be content with a brief canvassing of what I take to be the main alternative possibilities for a nonskeptical solution.

First, perhaps the most historically standard solution is the reductive phenomenalist attempt to define physical object concepts in terms of sensory appearance concepts, thereby making the connection between claims about sensory appearances and claims about physical objects a matter of conceptual or analytic necessity. Though there are difficult issues of conceptual priority involved,[25] it seems to me that this approach is likely to succeed for the specific case of secondary qualities like color. But the problems afflicting a more global phenomenalist approach are both well known and, in my judgment, clearly fatal.

Second, a quite different solution is advocated by H. H. Price[26] and, in what seems to be a rather seriously qualified form, by Chisholm. The core idea of this view is that the mere occurrence of a physical appearance or state of being appeared to confers prima facie justification on the corresponding physical claim. Chisholm's own version of this solution, presented in the most recent edition of *Theory of Knowledge*,[27] appeals to a logical relation of "tending to make evident" that is alleged to exist between claims or beliefs about sensory appearances and the corresponding claims or beliefs about the actual perception of physical objects. Thus my belief that my present visual experience involves appearances of a distinctive group of people in a distinctive room, or my belief that I am being appeared to in the

corresponding ways, *tends to make evident* my belief that I am perceiving such people and such a room and that they really exist in the physical world. Such a tendency is capable of being defeated by countervailing evidence, but where no such defeater is present, the claim of genuine perception is justified.

My difficulty with this sort of view is that it seems to me very implausible to suppose that such a logical relation of "tending to make evident" or "tending to justify" genuinely exists between an individual belief about physical appearances and the corresponding belief about physical reality. To be sure, Chisholm's claim is not that any such relation is discernible a priori in itself, but only that it is an a priori consequence of the "general presupposition" or "faith," roughly, that epistemological success is possible.[28] The skeptical implications of ascribing no stronger epistemic status than that to the claim that such a connection between appearances and physical reality really exists seem pretty serious in themselves. But over and above that, my objection is that if the belief about appearance is construed, as I have argued that it must be construed, as merely a useful though oblique way of describing the nonconceptual content of sensory experience, then there is no apparent way that it could by itself have any direct or immediate bearing of this sort on the truth or likely truth of the corresponding physical claim, assuming that claim to be non-reductively understood—and thus no way that there could be any such logical relation of "tending to make evident" or "tending to justify," whether a priori knowable or not.

One way to argue this point is to notice that if descriptions of the given content of experience in terms of physical object appearances are understood in the way just indicated, rather than as embodying some further claim or inference for which additional justification would be required, then it would be a mistake to think that they have any epistemological, as opposed to practical, advantage over descriptions of such experience in purely phenomenological terms. The experiential content being described is the same in either case, and its justificatory capacity is not somehow enhanced by failing to conceptualize it in the terms that would be most explicitly descriptive of it. But there seems to me to be no plausibility at all to the idea that a purely phenomenological description of the same experience that is in fact conceptualized as a particular physical object appearance (or state of being appeared to) would by itself have any tendency to justify or render evident the corresponding claim about the physical world. At the very least, some more specific account would have to be given of why this is supposed to be so.

Third, my own fairly tentative suggestion would be that the basis for the needed inference from sensory appearance to physical reality is to be found in several fundamental facts about such appearances. Two of these were noticed by Locke and Berkeley, among others: first, the involuntary, spontaneous character of such appearances; and second, the fact that they fit together and reinforce each other in, dare I say, a *coherent* fashion, presenting a relatively seamless and immensely complicated (albeit also incomplete) picture of an ongoing world.[29] These two fundamental facts are, of course, the central ones appealed to by Locke in justifying his inference from sensory ideas to the external world; and by Berkeley, in justifying his inference to the God who is supposed to produce our ideas. In both cases, the underlying idea, rather more explicit in Berkeley, is that some *explanation* is needed for the combination of involuntariness and coherence, and that the conclusion advocated by the philosopher in question is thereby justified as the best explanation of the facts in question.[30]

I once believed that an inference on something like this basis, to Locke's conclusion rather than Berkeley's, was ultimately cogent, but this now seems to me mistaken. No doubt the combination of spontaneity and intricate coherence requires *some* explanation, which is just to say that it is unlikely to result from chance. But why an explanation in physical object terms, rather than any of the other possibilities (including Berkeley's) that so obviously exist? What makes the physical explanation so obviously salient is our ingrained inclination to describe the experiential content in physical terms (or, indeed, to leap directly to a physical claim with no explicit acknowledgment of the experiential premise). Since it is, however, this very correlation between experience and physical object claims whose justification is at issue, no appeal to that correlation can as such have any justificatory weight.

The obvious response at this point would appeal to the idea, briefly mentioned earlier, that the correlation between experiential content and physical objects is not a mere correlation, that is, that there are features of the experiential content itself that are strongly and systematically isomorphic or structurally similar to the correlated physical situations. It is only if something like this is so that there could be any reason to prefer the physical explanation of experience to the various others that might be given. I have already suggested that such a view seems to me intuitively plausible, and I think (perhaps somewhat optimistically) that it is ultimately correct. But an account of how this isomorphism and the inference to the physical world that, I have suggested, must be based on it would go in detail is a long story that I have neither the space here nor very likely, at present, the ability to recount.

Notes

1   For a much fuller discussion of coherentism and its problems, along with an earlier sketch of the foundationalist view presented here, see BonJour ([1998]).

2   There are, of course, versions of empirical foundationalism that hold that at least some perceptual beliefs about physical objects are themselves basic or foundational. See, for example, Quinton (1973). My reasons for rejecting such views can be

gleaned from the account of foundational beliefs offered below.

3 I will assume here without further discussion that an adequate reason for thinking that an empirical belief is true could not consist entirely of beliefs that are justified a priori.

4 For a defense of this conception of self-evidence in relation to a priori justification, see BonJour ([1998]).

5 See Lewis ([1946]) and Fumerton (1995).

6 In BonJour (1985): Chapter 4.

7 The original source of the dilemma is Wilfrid Sellars. See Sellars (1963), pp. 127–96, esp. pp. 131–32, and (1975), pp. 295–347. For my own previous development and elaboration of it, see BonJour (1985): Chapter 4.

8 I interpret this as "going between the horns of the dilemma," because I am construing the horns as embodying the development and elaboration indicated in the earlier discussion and just summarized in the text, according to which the conceptual horn involves a conceptual or propositional awareness that a state of the specified sort occurs. Though the constitutive awareness of the content of the belief of course involves the concepts that figure in that content, it is not a conceptual or propositional awareness *that* I have a belief with the content in question, and so, as explained further in the text, does not raise any issue of justification. But one could instead interpret the present argument as showing that the conceptual side of the conceptual/nonconceptual dichotomy is not necessarily incompatible with foundationalism after all, because it need not involve such a propositional awareness; this would amount to "grasping one of the horns of the dilemma" rather than going between them. (On this latter interpretation, the analogous possibility for sensory experience, discussed below, would show that the nonconceptual horn also includes a possibility that is compatible with foundationalism.) I am grateful to Matthias Steup for helping me to see this alternative way of viewing the relation of the constitutive awareness of content to the Sellarsian dilemma.

9 Though not necessarily of all mental states—that is a further issue.

10 Rosenthal ([1986/91]). Page references in the text are to this reprint.

11 For some relevant discussion, see BonJour (1991).

12 In BonJour (1985).

13 Some of the problems with coherentism discussed in the paper cited in note 1 are also relevant to this point.

14 Such content is not, as we will see, propositional or conceptual in character, and this may seem to some to make the very word "content" inappropriate. But while agreeing that there is a certain potential for confusion here, I know of no better term for what one is conscious of in having sensory or phenomenal states of consciousness, and so will continue to employ it, with the warning that the two sorts of content are importantly different and should not be conflated.

15 See Popper (1959): §§ 25–30; Sellars (1963); Davidson (1983); and Rorty (1979): Chapters 3 and 4. (As will be obvious, this objection is not unrelated to the Sellarsian dilemma discussed above, though still different enough in its explicit formulation to warrant separate treatment.)

16 Davidson (1983): 428.

17 I am limiting my attention here to claims of direct acquaintance with matters of concrete and contingent fact. The application of the idea of direct acquaintance to necessary truths and abstract entities generally raises issues that lie beyond the scope of the present paper.

18 See, for example, Chisholm (1989): 18–19.

19 See, for example, Moser (1989). Moser's view is that nonconceptual contents justify physical object claims in virtue of the fact that the latter explain the former, but he says almost nothing about how the explanatory relation in question is supposed to work.

20 See, for example, Strawson (1979).

21 As this last formulation suggests, I am inclined to favor an "adverbial" construal of sensory experience, as opposed to the "act-object" construal advocated by the sense-datum theory. But the ontological issue that separates these two sorts of views does not, in my judgment, make any difference at all to the epistemological issues that are the focus of the present paper.

22 Many philosophers have objected to the idea that, for example, ordinary "looks" statements can be construed as descriptions of nonconceptual sensory content. See, for example, Sellars (1963): §§ 10–23. I do not have space to enter into this

controversy here and must content myself with saying that the objections in question seem to me to show at most that there are other senses of "looks" besides the one that I want here (e.g. one that indicates a tentative or guarded opinion about what is actually there), but they have no serious tendency to show that the sense currently at issue does not exist. For further discussion of this issue, see Jackson (1977): Chapter 2.

23   Haack (1993): 80.

24   See, for example, Chisholm (1989): 23.

25   See, for example, the discussion of this issue in the first of Sellars' Carus lectures (1981).

26   See Price (1950): Chapter 7.

27   Chisholm (1989): 46–54, 64–68, 71–74.

28   Chisholm (1989): 4–6, 72–73.

29   See Locke (1975): Book IV, Chapter xi; and Berkeley (1965): §§ 28–30.

30   For a useful discussion and elaboration of Locke's argument, see Mackie (1976): Chapter 2. See also BonJour (1985): Chapter 8, for some of the ideas that I take to be relevant, even though they are couched there in terms of a coherence theory.

References

Berkeley, George. 1965. *Principles of Human Knowledge*.

BonJour, Laurence. 1985. *The Structure of Empirical Knowledge*. Cambridge, MA: Harvard University Press.

BonJour, Laurence. 1991. "Is Thought a Symbolic Process?," *Synthese* 89.

BonJour, Laurence. 1998. *In Defense of Pure Reason*. Cambridge: Cambridge University Press.

Chisholm, Roderick. 1989. *Theory of Knowledge*, 3rd edn. Englewood Cliffs, NJ: Prentice-Hall.

Davidson, Donald. 1983. "A Coherence Theory of Truth and Knowledge," in Dieter Heinrich (ed.) *Kant oder Hegel*. Stuttgart: Klett-Cotta.

Fumerton, Richard. 1995. *Metaepistemology and Skepticism*. Lanham, MD: Rowman and Littlefield.

Haack, Susan. 1993. *Evidence and Inquiry: Towards Reconstruction in Epistemology*. Oxford: Blackwell.

Jackson, Frank. 1977. *Perception: A Representative Theory*. Cambridge: Cambridge University Press.

Lewis, C. I. 1946. *An Analysis of Knowledge and Valuation*. La Salle, IL: Open Court.

Locke, John. 1975. *An Essay Concerning Human Understanding*, edited with an introduction by P. H. Nidditch. Oxford: Oxford University Press.

Mackie. J. L. 1976. *Problems from Locke*. Oxford: Oxford University Press.

Moser, Paul. 1989. *Knowledge and Evidence*. London: Cambridge University Press.

Popper, Karl. 1959. *The Logic of Scientific Discovery*. New York: Harper.

Price, H. H. 1950. *Perception*, 2nd edn. London: Methuen.

Quinton, Anthony. 1973. *The Nature of Things*. London: Routledge and Kegan Paul.

Rorty, Richard. 1979. *Philosophy and the Mirror of Nature*. Princeton, NJ: Princeton University Press.

Rosenthal, David. 1986/91. "Two Concepts of Consciousness," *Philosophical Studies* 94 (1986); reprinted in David Rosenthal (ed.) *The Nature of Mind*. New York: Oxford University Press, 1991.

Sellars, Wilfrid. 1963. *Science, Perception and Reality*. London: Routledge and Kegan Paul.

Sellars, Wilfrid. 1975. "The Structure of Knowledge," in Hector-Neri Castaneda (ed.) *Action, Knowledge and Reality: Critical Studies in Honor of Wilfrid Sellars*. Indianapolis: Bobbs-Merrill.

Sellars, Wilfrid. 1981. "The Lever of Archimedes," *The Monist* 64.

Strawson, P. F. 1979. "Perception and Its Object," in G. F. Macdonald (ed.) *Perception and Identity*. Ithaca, NY: Cornell University Press.

Chapter 22

Peter Klein

HUMAN KNOWLEDGE AND THE INFINITE REGRESS OF REASONS*

Introduction

The purpose of this paper is to ask you to consider an account of justification that has largely been ignored in epistemology. When it has been considered, it has usually been dismissed as so obviously wrong that arguments against it are not necessary. The view that I ask you to consider can be called "Infinitism."[1] Its central thesis is that the structure of justificatory reasons is infinite and non-repeating. My primary reason for recommending infinitism is that it can provide an acceptable account of *rational beliefs*, i.e. beliefs held on the basis of adequate reasons, while the two alternative views, foundationalism and coherentism, cannot provide such an account.

Typically, just the opposite viewpoint is expressed. Infinitism is usually mentioned as one of the logically possible forms that our reasoning can take; but it is dismissed without careful consideration because it appears initially to be so implausible.[2] Foundationalists often begin by somewhat cavalierly rejecting infinitism. Then they proceed by eliminating coherentism through a series of complex and carefully developed arguments. Coherentists often follow a similar general strategy by first rejecting infinitism without any careful examination of the view and then they provide well considered reasons for rejecting foundationalism. Of course, if there are no convincing reasons for rejecting

infinitism, then these typical defenses of foundationalism and of coherentism fail.

I will not rehearse the many arguments against foundationalism or coherentism in any detail here. But very briefly, foundationalism is unacceptable because it advocates accepting an arbitrary reason at the base, that is, a reason for which there are no further reasons making it even slightly better to accept than any of its contraries. Traditional coherentism is unacceptable because it advocates a not too thinly disguised form of begging the question; and seemingly more plausible forms of coherentism are just foundationalism in disguise.

Thus, if having rational beliefs is a necessary condition of some type of knowledge, both foundationalism and coherentism lead directly to the consequence that this type of knowledge is not possible because each view precludes the possibility of having beliefs based upon adequate reasons. On the other hand, infinitism makes such knowledge at least possible because it advocates a structure of justificatory reasons that satisfies the requirements of rational belief possession.

This paper has two main sections. In the first section I sketch infinitism in broad outline and argue that it is the only account of the structure of reasons that can satisfy two intuitively plausible constraints on good reasoning. In the second section I defend infinitism against the best objections to it.

A sketch of infinitism

Let me begin by pointing out some important similarities and dissimilarities between infinitism and the two alternative accounts of justification. Infinitism is *like* most forms of *traditional coherentism* in holding that only reasons can justify a belief.[3] Infinitism is *unlike* traditional coherentism because infinitism does not endorse question begging reasoning.[4] Indeed, this can be captured in what can be called the "Principle of Avoiding Circularity" (PAC).

> PAC: For all x, if a person, S, has a justification for x, then for all y, if y is in the evidential ancestry of x for S, then x is not in the evidential ancestry of y for S.

By "evidential ancestry" I am referring to the links in the chains of reasons, sometimes branching, that support beliefs.[5] For example, if r is a reason for p, and q is a reason for r, then r is in the evidential ancestry of p, and q is in the evidential ancestry of both p and r.[6] I will not defend PAC in this paper because it strikes me as an obvious presupposition of good reasoning. It is intended merely to make explicit the intuition behind the prohibition of circular reasoning.

Not all so-called "coherentists" would deny PAC. These "coherentists" are really closet foundationalists because it is not the propositions within a set of coherent propositions that serve as reasons for other beliefs in the set; rather *the* reason for every belief in the set is simply that it is a member of such a set.[7] Thus, these non-traditional coherentists avoid question begging reasoning by a two stage procedure. First, they define what it means for a set of propositions to be coherent (perhaps mutual probability enhancements plus some other conditions) and, then, they claim that the reason for accepting each proposition in the set is that it is a member of such a set of beliefs. That is consistent with endorsing PAC. But as we will see, this type of coherentism, like foundationalism, can offer no hope of blocking the regress of reasons.

Infinitism is *like* foundationalism in holding that there are features of the world, perhaps non-normative features, that make a belief a reason. Not just any old belief is a reason. Infinitism is *unlike* foundationalism because infinitism holds that there are no ultimate, foundational reasons. *Every* reason stands in need of another reason. This can be stated in a principle—the Principle of Avoiding Arbitrariness (PAA).

> PAA: For all x, if a person, S, has a justification for x, then there is some reason, r_1, available to S for x; and there is some reason, r_2, available to S for r_1; etc.

Note that there are two features of this principle. The first is that it is reasons (as opposed to something else like appropriate causal conditions responsible for a belief) that are required whenever there is a justification for a belief. The second is that the chain of reasons cannot end with an arbitrary reason—one for which there is no further reason. I conjoin these features in one principle because both are needed to capture the well-founded intuition that *arbitrary beliefs*, beliefs for which no reason is available, should be avoided. I will consider some objections to both aspects of PAA shortly.

Some foundationalists could accept PAA by claiming that the available reason, r, could just be x, itself. They could assert that some propositions are "self-justified." That is not ruled out by PAA; but coupled with PAC, that possibility is ruled out. Indeed, the combination of PAC and PAA entails that the evidential ancestry of a justified belief be infinite and non-repeating. Thus, someone wishing to avoid infinitism must reject either PAC or PAA (or both).[8] *It is the straightforward intuitive appeal of these principles that is the best reason for thinking that if any beliefs are justified, the structure of reasons must be infinite and non-repeating.*

PAA requires that the reason for a belief must be *available* to S. "Availability" is a key notion in my account of infinitism for, among other things, it has the potential for anchoring justification, as understood by the infinitist, in non-normative properties.[9] So, it would be well for us to dwell a bit on that notion.

There are two conditions that must be satisfied in order for a reason to be available to S. It must be both "objectively" and "subjectively" available. I will discuss each condition in turn.

There are many accounts of objective availability. Each specifies either some normative or non-normative property or, perhaps, a mixed property that is sufficient to convert a belief into a reason.[10] For example, one could say that a belief, r, is objectively available to S as a reason for p if (1) r has some sufficiently high probability and the conditional probability of p given r is sufficiently high; or (2) an impartial, informed observer would accept r as a reason for p; or (3) r would be accepted in the long run by an appropriately defined set of people; or (4) r is evident for S and r makes p evident for S;[11] or (5) r accords with S's deepest epistemic commitments;[12] or (6) r meets the appropriate conversational presuppositions;[13] or (7) an intellectually virtuous person would advance r as a reason for p.[14]

Infinitism, per se, is compatible with each of these depictions of objectively available reasons.[15] In addition, whether any of these mentioned accounts proves ultimately acceptable or whether another, unmentioned account is the best one is unimportant for the purposes of this paper. What is crucial to note at this point is that not just any proposition will function as a reason for other beliefs. If, for example, I offer as my reason for believing that *all fish have fins* my belief that *all fish wear army boots and anything wearing army boots has fins*, my offered-reason entails *that all fish have fins*, but on the accounts mentioned above it is not an objectively available reason. It has a low probability of being true; an impartial observer would not accept it; it would not be accepted in the long run by any appropriately defined set of people; there is no evident

proposition that makes it evident; accepting it does not accord with my deepest epistemic commitments; there is no actual context in which appealing to that proposition will persuade anyone that all fish have fins; and an intellectually virtuous person would not offer it. Contrast this case with another. My belief *that dark clouds are gathering over the mountains and it is mid-winter in Montana* could satisfy the objective availability constraints contained in all of the accounts mentioned above for functioning as a reason for the proposition *that a snowstorm is likely*.

There is second feature of "availability" to S that is subjective. There might be a good reason, r, that is *objectively* available for use by any person, but unless it is properly hooked up with S's own beliefs, r will not be *subjectively* available to S. In an appropriate sense to be discussed later, S must be able to call on r.

It is this subjective sense of "availability" that has provoked many of the objections to infinitism. For example: How can a "finite" human mind have an infinite number of beliefs?[16] I think that rhetorical question involves a deep misunderstanding of the infinitist's position that will be discussed in some detail when we consider the objections to infinitism, but let me now just state the obvious: Humans have many beliefs that are not occurrent. It is in the non-occurrent sense of "belief" that the members of an infinite series of reasons might be subjectively available to S. Roughly, but I hope good enough for the purposes of this paper, let us say that S believes p just in case S would affirm that p, or endorse p in another fashion—perhaps *sotto voce*—in some appropriately restricted circumstances. For example, S may not now be thinking that she is in Montana in mid-winter looking at dark clouds gathering, but if asked why she believes a snowstorm is imminent, she will consciously affirm that she is in Montana in mid-winter looking at dark clouds gathering. The point is that she has the belief even before she forms the conscious thought.[17]

Having briefly sketched the two ways in

which a belief must be available, let me return to the central motivation for infinitism—the two intuitive principles. As mentioned above, I think the only way to avoid infinitism is to reject either PAC or PAA. PAC seems completely safe to me. The old rejoinder that a large enough circle of reasons is acceptable, strikes me as just plain wrong. That a circle is larger might make it more difficult to detect the flaw in the reasoning, but large circles, nevertheless, involve question begging reasoning. An error in reasoning is still an error no matter how difficult it is to detect.

What probably is meant by invoking the "large circle" is that it has seemed plausible to argue that one has a better reason for accepting a proposition if, *ceteris paribus*, it is a member of a larger set of coherent propositions. There is greater "mutual support" in larger sets. This feature of a non-traditional coherentist account is offered as a way of maintaining a coherentist position while still accepting PAC.[18] Indeed, I think PAC, once understood, will be accepted in any context of discussion that presupposes a distinction between good and bad reasoning. Circular reasoning is just not acceptable.

But PAA might not seem so secure. Can't something other than reasons make a belief justified? For example, couldn't a belief be justified just in case it arose in some reliable fashion? Or couldn't there be a "meta-justification" available that (i) shows that some propositions are justified but that (ii) is not, itself, directly involved in the justification of the proposition? And, finally, couldn't it be epistemically rational to accept some propositions even when there is no reason for believing them? Perhaps arbitrariness isn't such a bad thing after all!

There are, no doubt, other objections to PAA, but the three just mentioned seem the most serious. First, the intuitive appeal of reliabilism needs to be reckoned with. Second, the move to a "meta-justification" seems initially plausible. Finally, there is an ingenious argument developed by Stephen Luper-Foy to the effect that it is rational to accept basic beliefs even

though they are not rational beliefs—that is, even though there is no reason that can be given to believe that they are true. Let us consider these objections in order.

Reliabilism?

Reliabilism, or at least the relevant form, holds either that *reasons* are not always required to justify a belief or that knowledge does not require justification, if "justification" is used in such a way as to entail that only rational beliefs are justified. A reliabilist could accept the claim that the structure of reasons is infinite and simply deny that reasons are required either for knowledge or for justification. A "moderate" form of reliabilism maintains that not all forms of knowledge or justification require reasoned belief. A "radical" form of reliabilism maintains that no form of knowledge requires reasoned belief. What are we to make of these claims? Does knowledge or justification require having reasons?

I maintain that being able to produce reasons for beliefs is a distinctive characteristic of adult human knowledge. Apparently, nothing else knows in this way. Of course, many things have knowledge that is not *rational* belief. Dogs scratch at doors knowing, in *some* sense, that they will be opened; but dogs do not have reasons. Even adult humans know (in *that* sense) when they do not have reasons. As Fred Dretske says, when adult humans are in Minnesota in mid-winter, they know that it is cold without having reasons.[19]

Nevertheless, even some reliabilists employ intuitions involving the having of adequate reasons in order to distinguish cases of justified belief from cases of unjustified beliefs. Alvin Goldman, one of the architects of reliabilism, considers a case in which a subject, S, believes "I am in brain-state B" just in case S is in brain-state B. The belief acquisition method is perfectly reliable, but "we can imagine that a brain surgeon operating on S artificially induces brain-state B. This results, phenomenologically, in S's suddenly believing—out of the blue—that he is in brain-state B, without any relevant antecedent beliefs. We would hardly say, in such a case, that S's belief that he is in brain-state B is justified."[20]

I think the best explanation for Goldman's intuition about this case is that some reliabilists still feel the bite of the evidentialist requirement that in some cases we—adult humans—must have reasons for our beliefs in order for them to count as knowledge.

More directly, I am convinced by examples like Keith Lehrer's Truetemp Case that there is a sense of "know" such that belief, though completely reliable, is not knowledge in the relevant sense. Recall that Mr. Truetemp has a thermometer-cum-temperature-belief-generator implanted in his head so that within certain ranges of temperatures he has perfectly reliable temperature beliefs. As Lehrer puts it:

> He accepts [beliefs about the temperature] unreflectively . . . Thus he thinks and accepts that the temperature is 104 degrees. It is. Does he know that it is? Surely not.[21]

Some reliabilists might maintain that Mr. Truetemp does, indeed, know. Now, as I see it, the issue is not whether Mr. Truetemp "knows" in *some* sense that the temperature is 104 degrees. He may very well have knowledge in some sense—the same sense in which a dog can "recognize" her owner's voice or in which a thermometer "knows" the room temperature. In the other sense of "know"—the sense that is only predicated of humans who have reached "the age of reason"—Mr. Truetemp lacks knowledge because he does not have a subjectively available reason for thinking that it is 104 degrees. There is nothing he could think of which is a reason for believing that it is 104 degrees. In other words, "knowledge" might not refer to a natural kind—there being only *one* fundamental type. Ernest Sosa makes this point persuasively when he writes:

The challenge of doxastic assent might well be thought a pseudo-challenge, however, since it would deny knowledge to infants and animals. Admittedly, there is a sense in which even a supermarket door "knows" when someone approaches, and in which a heating system "knows" when the temperature in a room rises above a certain setting. Such is "servo-mechanic" knowledge. And there is an immense variety of animal knowledge, instinctive or learned, which facilitates survival and flourishing in an astonishingly rich diversity of modes and environments. Human knowledge is on a higher plane of sophistication, however, precisely because of its enhanced coherence and comprehensiveness and its capacity to satisfy self-reflective curiosity. Pure reliabilism is questionable as an adequate epistemology for such knowledge.[22]

Thus, I believe that radical reliabilism—the view that claims that having reasons is never necessary for knowledge—fails to capture what is distinctive about adult human knowledge.

On the other hand, the intuitive appeal of moderate reliabilism can be adequately recognized without giving up PAA. For one can grant that in some senses of "know," rational beliefs are not required for knowledge. Where "knows that p" means roughly "possess the information that p" we can say of "servo-mechanic" objects that they possess knowledge that p. They do not need reasons. Nevertheless, there is another sense of "know" such that the mere possession of information is not adequate. The information must be supported by appropriate reasons. Beliefs that come "out of the blue" do not qualify as knowledge in this sense.

There is one further, relevant move available to the infinitist. It could even be granted that no form of knowledge requires having rational beliefs. That is, radical reliabilism could be accepted. But even granting that, the infinitist's claim remains significant if only because, if correct, it would delineate an important condition of rational beliefs, even if such beliefs were not required for knowledge. Foundationalism and coherentism would remain less attractive than infinitism as accounts of rational belief.

Meta-justifications?

Let us now turn to what Laurence BonJour calls "meta-justifications"—justifications designed to show that certain types of beliefs are acceptable even in the absence of another belief that serves as a reason. Such beliefs are acceptable, it is claimed, because they have some property, call it P, and beliefs having P are likely to be true.[23] Both non-traditional coherentism and foundationalism are alike in that they hold that there is some such property, P.

Let us turn directly to foundationalism. Can it avoid advocating the acceptance of arbitrary reasons by moving to meta-justifications? Suppose it is claimed that a foundational proposition is justified because it has a certain causal history (e.g. involving the proper use of our senses or memory) or that it is justified in virtue of its content (e.g. it is about a current mental state or it is about some necessary truth). Pick your favorite accounts of the property, P. I think, as does BonJour, that the old Pyrrhonian question is reasonable: Why is having P truth-conducive?[24] Now, either there is an answer available to that question or there isn't. (BonJour thinks there is.) If there is an answer, then the regress continues—at least one more step, and that is all that is needed here, because that shows that the offered reason that some belief has P or some set of beliefs has P does not stop the regress. If there isn't an answer, the assertion is arbitrary!

Now, let me be clear here in order to anticipate a possible objection. I am not claiming that in order for a belief to be justified or known, either we must *believe* that it is justified or we must be *justified in believing* that it is justified. As many have pointed out, that confuses p's being

justified with a belief about p's justificatory status.[25] I am not supposing that the foundationalist, or for that matter, the non-traditional coherentist thinks that what Alston has called "epistemic beliefs" (beliefs about the epistemic status of beliefs) must play a role in the justification of all beliefs.[26] Quite the contrary, I think the foundationalist typically advocates an explicit process of reasoning that ends with beliefs which have P rather than with epistemic beliefs about P. The meta-justification is invoked in order to avoid the appearance of arbitrariness for it is designed to show why the "final" beliefs are likely to be true. My point is merely that moving to the meta-level, that is, arguing that such beliefs are likely to be true because they possess a certain property, P, will not avoid the problem faced by foundationalism. Either the meta-justification provides a reason for thinking the base proposition is true (and hence, the regress does not end) or it does not (hence, accepting the base proposition is arbitrary). The Pyrrhonians were right.

The same is true of non-traditional coherentism. Claiming that a belief is justified because it is a member of a set of propositions that is coherent cannot stop the regress in any but an arbitrary way. The non-traditional coherentist must produce a meta-justification for the belief that propositions satisfying that requirement are likely to be true. As BonJour says:

> one crucial part of the task of an adequate epistemological theory is to show that there is an appropriate connection between its proposed account of epistemic justification and the cognitive goal of truth. That is, it must somehow be shown that justification as conceived by the theory is truth-conducive, that one who seeks justified beliefs is at least likely to find true ones.[27]

So the non-traditional coherentist, like the foundationalist, will move to a meta-level in an attempt to show why a belief that coheres with others is likely to be true.[28] But the same question will arise: Why is coherence truth-conducive?[29]

To generalize: Foundationalism and non-traditional coherentism cannot avoid the regress by appealing to a meta-claim that a belief having some property, P, is likely to be true. That claim itself requires an argument that appeals to reasons. Indeed, the appeal to such a meta-claim invokes just the kind of dialectical context involving what is distinctive about adult human knowledge. For surely a reason is required to justify the belief that propositions with property, P, are likely to be true; and whatever justifies that claim will require a reason; and—well, you get the point. Thus, the move to a meta-justification cannot stop the regress without violating either PAA or PAC.

Harmless arbitrariness?

One objection to PAA remains to be considered: Perhaps it is rational to accept arbitrary, non-rational, beliefs even though there are no reasons for thinking that they are true. If that were the case, it would presumably dampen the enthusiasm some epistemologists have for foundationalism, for they think that the foundational propositions are not arbitrary (they appeal to meta-justifications to show that). In addition, it would call into question a primary motivation for traditional coherentism, namely that it is irrational to accept a belief without a reason. But it would also undermine my argument for infinitism based in part on PAA because that principle is designed to capture the widely endorsed intuition that it is rational to accept a belief only if there is some reason for thinking the belief is true.

Stephen Luper-Foy has argued that it is rational to accept foundational beliefs even though they cannot be supported by reasons. Here is his argument (some of what follows is close paraphrase, some is direct quotation as indicated):

The epistemic goal is to acquire a complete and accurate picture of the world. Granted, at base our reasons are arbitrary but "an injunction against believing anything . . . would obviously make it impossible for us to achieve the goal of arriving at a complete and accurate understanding of what is the case . . . Indeed, given that our ultimate beliefs are arbitrary, it is rational to adopt management principles that allow us to retain these foundational yet arbitrary views, since the alternative is to simply give up on the attempt to achieve the epistemic goal."[30]

His point, I take it, is that since the goal of an epistemic agent is to acquire a complete and accurate picture of the world, accepting a basic, though arbitrary, reason is rational since if one did not accept it, there would be no possibility of attaining the goal. It is "rational to do and believe things without reason"[31] because if we did not, we could not attain our goal.

There are two responses. First, if I am right, we need not worry about reasons being arbitrary, since the regress does not stop. There are no arbitrary, ultimate reasons because there are no ultimate reasons. But more to the point at hand, if the regress did end with an arbitrary reason (as Luper-Foy is assuming at this point in his argument), I think his argument for making it rational to accept arbitrary reasons does not succeed.

Luper-Foy is using a prudential account of rationality such that we are prudentially rational just in case our chosen means to a goal are efficient in achieving that goal. But such an instrumental conception of rationality is acceptable only if the definition of rationality is understood to imply that it is rational to adopt a means to a given goal only if the means are more likely to achieve *that* goal rather than some incompatible and highly undesirable goal. Suppose, as Luper-Foy claims, that the epistemic goal is to gain a complete and accurate picture of the world, then believing x would be rational only if believing x furthered that goal instead of the incompatible and highly undesirable goal, let us say, of obtaining a complete and inaccurate picture of the world. But if my basic beliefs are arbitrary, that is, if there is no available reason for thinking that accepting them is more likely to contribute to obtaining an accurate picture than an inaccurate picture, then, for all I know, accepting the basic beliefs could equally well lead to obtaining a complete and inaccurate picture of the world. So, if at the base, reasons are arbitrary, it is not even prudentially rational to accept them since doing so is no more likely to satisfy rather than frustrate my epistemic goals.

Objections to infinitism

We have completed the examination of what I take to be the best reasons for rejecting PAA and found that they are inadequate. As mentioned earlier, I take PAC to be the *sine qua non* of good reasoning. Nevertheless, in spite of the fact that there appear to be no good grounds for rejecting PAA or PAC taken individually, the view that results from accepting both of them, namely infinitism, has never been advocated by anyone with the possible exception of Peirce.[32] The remainder of this paper will focus on the reasons that have been advanced against infinitism. Of course, if only for the sake of consistency, I cannot take it that this matter is finally settled. But I do think the proposed objections to the position fail.

So, what are the arguments designed to show that the structure of reasons could not be infinite and non-repeating? They can be divided into four types presented in the order in which I think they present deep issues for the infinitist— beginning with the least troubling and moving to the most troubling: (1) Varieties of the Finite Human Mind Objection; (2) the Aristotelian Objection that If Some Knowledge Is Inferential, Some Is Not Inferential; (3) the *Reductio* Argument Against the Possibility of an Infinite Regress Providing a Justification for Beliefs

(most clearly developed by John Post and I. T. Oakley); (4) the Specter of Skepticism Objection—namely that nothing is known unless reasoning somehow settles the matter.

Objection 1: The Finite Mind Objection

Very roughly, the intuition behind this objection is that the human mind is finite and if such a mind is to have reasons for beliefs (a requirement for the distinctive adult human kind of knowledge), it cannot be the case that such beliefs are justified only if there is an infinite chain of reasons. Here, for example, is what John Williams says:

> The [proposed] regress of justification of S's belief that p would certainly require that he holds an infinite number of beliefs. This is psychologically, if not logically, impossible. If a man can believe an infinite number of things, then there seems to be no reason why he cannot know an infinite number of things. Both possibilities contradict the common intuition that the human mind is finite. Only God could entertain an infinite number of beliefs. But surely God is not the only justified believer.[33]

As stated, it is a bit difficult to get a purchase on this objection. It cannot mean simply that we are finite beings—occupying a finite amount of space and lasting a finite duration of time—and consequently, we cannot be in an infinite number of states (in particular, belief states). A "finite" thing, say a one foot cube existing for only ten minutes, has its center at an infinite number of positions during the ten minutes it moves, say, from point $\{0,0,0\}$ in a three dimensional Cartesian coordinate system to, say, point $\{1,1,1\}$. So, a finitely extended thing can be in an infinite number of states in a finite amount of time.

But Williams does not leave matters at this fuzzy, intuitive level. What he means, I think, is that there is something about belief states or justified belief states in particular which is such that no finite human can be in an infinite number of them. The argument, as best as I can ferret it out, is this: It is impossible to consciously believe an infinite number of propositions (because to believe something takes some time) and it is impossible to "unconsciously believe" ("unconscious belief" is his term) an infinite number of propositions because the candidate beliefs are such that some of them "defeat human understanding."[34]

Granted, I cannot consciously assent to an infinite number of propositions in my lifetime. The infinitist is not claiming that in any finite period of time—the "threescore and ten" assigned to us, for example—we can consciously entertain an infinite number of thoughts. It is rather that there are an infinite number of propositions such that each one of them would be consciously thought were the appropriate circumstances to arise.

Williams is, indeed, right that the putative examples given thus far in the literature of infinite sets of propositions in which each member is subjectively available are not plausible because consciously thinking some of them is impossible. But, of course, it is a non-sequitur to claim that because some examples fail, they all will.

Richard Foley, for example, suggests that since I believe that I am within one hundred miles of Boston, I believe that I am within two hundred miles of Boston, and I believe that I am within 300 miles, etc.[35] Williams correctly points out that eventually a proposition in such a series will contain a "number so large that no one can consider it."[36] Robert Audi gives a similar argument against the possibility of a mind like ours having an infinite number of beliefs.[37]

It is easy to see the general reason why such examples fail.[38] They all presuppose a finite vocabulary for expressing beliefs. Hence, it would *seem* that any method of generating an infinite series of beliefs by some manipulation on the items in the vocabulary (e.g. conjoining them, disjoining them) will eventually produce a member in the set that is too "large" or too "long" for us to consider.

But even with a finite vocabulary, we do have another way of picking out objects and forming beliefs about them. We can use indexicals. We can point to an object and say "this." We can also say of an object that it has some shape, say a. Now, suppose that there were an infinite number of discernible objects with the shape a. I claim that there would be an infinite number of propositions each of the form "this is a-shaped" such that were we to discern the object referred to by "this" in each proposition, we would consciously think "this is a-shaped" under the appropriate circumstances. So, if there were an infinite number of a-shaped discernible objects, then there would be an infinite set of propositions such that each member would be consciously endorsed under the appropriate circumstances—i.e. when we discern the object and consider whether it is a-shaped. Of course, this is only a hypothetical claim. I do not know whether there is an infinite number of such discernible objects. But it does not matter for my point. My claim is merely that, in principle, nothing prevents so-called "finite minds" from being such that each proposition in an infinite set of propositions is subjectively available. There might not be an infinite number of such discernible objects, but we certainly have the capacity to think about each such object that we discern that it is a-shaped. Therefore, we have the capacity to believe each member of an infinite set of propositions. No member in the set gets too "large" or too "long" or too "complex" for us to grasp.

I mentioned earlier that I thought there was a deep misunderstanding of the infinitist's position underlying the infinite mind objection. Now is the time to consider it. I have already said that the infinitist is not claiming that during our lifetime we consciously entertain an infinite number of beliefs. But what might not be so obvious is that the infinitist is also not even claiming that we *have* an infinite number of what Williams calls "unconscious beliefs" if such beliefs are taken to be *already formed* dispositions. (We might, but that isn't necessary for infinitism.) Consider the following question: Do you believe that 366 + 71 is 437? I take it that for most of us answering that question brings into play some of our capacities in a way that answering the question "Do you believe that 2 + 2 = 4?" does not. For I simply remember that 2 + 2 = 4. I have already formed the belief that manifests itself when I consciously think that 2 + 2 = 4. By contrast, I had not already formed a similar disposition concerning the sum of 366 plus 71. We do not simply remember that 366 + 71 = 437. Rather, we do a bit of adding. We are *disposed to think* that 366 + 71 = 437 after a bit of adding given our belief that 6 + 1 = 7, that 7 + 6 = 13, etc. We have a second-order disposition—a disposition to form the disposition to think something. Thus, there is clearly a sense in which we believe that 366 + 71 = 437. The proposition that 366 + 71 = 437 is subjectively available to me because it is correctly hooked up to already formed beliefs.

We have many second-order dispositions that are counted as beliefs. For example, you believe that apples do not normally grow on pear trees even though you had never formed the disposition to consciously think that (at least up until just now!). *Infinitism requires that there be an infinite set of propositions such that each member is subjectively available to us. That requires that we have the capacity to form beliefs about each member. It does not require that we have already formed those beliefs.*

The distinction between already formed first-order beliefs and dispositions to form a first-order belief is important for another reason. Earlier I had argued that there was a way, in principle, to show that even with a finite vocabulary, we could have an infinite number of beliefs by employing indexicals. Nevertheless, that response will not be useful here since we cannot point to reasons (as we can point to objects) with "this" or "that" unless the reasons are already formed. The problem is to show that there can be an infinite number of reasons given a finite vocabulary each of which can be entertained by a human being.

The solution to this problem is ready-to-hand. Since we can appeal to second order dispositions, we can say that when our vocabulary and concepts fall short of being able to provide reasons, we can develop new concepts and ways of specifying them. That is, we can discover, develop or invent new concepts to provide a reason for our beliefs.

This seems to happen regularly. When we have no ready-to-hand explanation of events, we devise new concepts that can be employed in understanding those events. Consider the following: the development of the concept of unconscious mechanisms to account for our behavior, the development of the concept of quarks to provide for some unity in our understanding of sub-atomic particles and their interactions, and the development of evolutionary theory to account for the fossil record as well as the diversity and commonality among species. In each case there was a temporary stopping point reached in our ability to provide reasons for our beliefs. But we have the capacity to develop new concepts that can provide us with further reasons for our beliefs.

Let me sum up my response to this first reason for thinking that a finite mind cannot have an infinite number of justified beliefs. We have seen that the notion of "belief" is ambiguous. It can refer to already formed dispositions and it can refer to the disposition to form dispositions. It is in the second sense that the infinitist is committed to the claim that there is an infinite number of beliefs both subjectively and objectively available to us whenever (if ever) we have distinctively adult human knowledge.

There is a second argument that is sometimes given for supposing that the requirements of having an infinite number of *justified* beliefs cannot be satisfied. Both Richard Foley and Richard Fumerton suppose that in order for S to be justified in believing that p on the basis of e, S must (at least paradigmatically for Foley) *justifiably* believe that e justifies p. Fumerton puts it this way:

> To be justified in believing one proposition P on the basis of another E one must be 1) justified in believing E and 2) justified in believing that E makes probable P.[39]

It is easy to see that if this condition of inferential justification were coupled with infinitism, the consequence would be that any person having a justified belief must have a belief that gets "so complex" that no human could ever have it. Foley argues to the same conclusion by claiming that a condition like (2) is a feature of the "best justifications" and that any theory of justification will include a description of the best justifications.[40]

I agree that such a requirement would force the rejection of infinitism. But as I mentioned earlier, I can see no reason to agree to the premise that in order for S to be justified in believing that p on the basis of e, S must be *justified* in believing that e is a good reason for p. I think this simply confuses having a justified belief that p with having justified beliefs about p's justificatory status. This amounts to requiring that S not only be an epistemologist, but also that S have a well reasoned epistemology in order to be justified in believing, for example, that a thunderstorm is likely. Epistemology is important, but having a justified epistemology is not required in order to have justified beliefs! Thus, this argument provides no grounds for thinking that the chain of good reasons, even if infinite, includes beliefs that are too complex for us to grasp.[41]

Objection 2: The Aristotelian Objection that If Some Knowledge Is Inferential, Some Is Not Inferential

In the *Posterior Analytics* Aristotle claims that if some knowledge is the result of inference, some knowledge must not be the result of inference. I think that is correct. And I grant that some knowledge is the result of inference. So, some knowledge is not the result of inference. But, somewhat surprisingly, it does not follow that the structure of justificatory reasons is finite.

Assume, as I think it is evident that Aristotle does, that at some early time in the development of a human being, the being is completely ignorant. At some later point, the being has knowledge. It would not be possible to account for all of the being's knowledge on the basis of previously obtained knowledge, for that *could not* give us an account of the original, first, change from ignorance to knowledge. So, all knowledge could not be *produced* by inference from previous knowledge—not because the structure of justificatory reasons could not be infinite but because all knowledge could not arise from previous knowledge if at one time we are ignorant and at a later time we are knowledgeable. But nothing in this argument prevents the chain of justificatory reasons from being infinite. We could acquire most of our beliefs in ways that do not involve reasons as causes. My claim is merely that in order to have the distinctively adult human type of knowledge, there must be reasons of the appropriate sort available. Thus, it can be granted that we, humans, move from a state of complete ignorance to a state of having the distinctively adult human type of knowledge during our lifetimes and still maintain, as I do, that we make that transition only when there are reasons subjectively and objectively available for our beliefs.

Now, Aristotle may never have intended, at least in the *Posterior Analytics*, that the description of the role of experience in the acquisition of knowledge be used to show that there are beliefs for which there are no reasons.[42] Nevertheless, there is a passage in the *Metaphysics* that might be cited to show that Aristotle endorsed an argument against infinitism:

> There are, both among those who have these convictions [man is the measure of all things] and among those who merely profess these views, some who raise a difficulty by asking, who is to be the judge of the healthy man, and in general who is likely to judge rightly on each class of question. But such inquiries are like puzzling over the question whether we are now asleep or awake. And all such questions have the same meaning. These people demand that a reason shall be given for everything, for they seek a starting point and they seek to get this by demonstration, while it is obvious from their actions that they have no conviction. But their mistake is what we have stated it to be: they seek a reason for things for which no reason can be given; for the starting point of demonstration is not demonstration.[43]

Now, I grant that there are occasions when it is absurd to ask for reasons for a belief. Roughly, those are the occasions in which it is clear that the conversational presuppositions are not to be questioned. For example, when we are distinguishing features of waking states from features of dream states, it is absurd to ask whether we can tell the difference. But it does not follow that such questions are always inappropriate. Indeed, when the presuppositions of the conversational context are revealed, they can be questioned. Thus, one can grant what I think Aristotle is suggesting, namely that demonstration can take place only within a context of agreed upon presuppositions and that it is absurd to ask for reasons to justify those presuppositions within that kind of a context. He is right. But, of course, the contextual situation can change.

Objection 3: The Reductio Argument Against the Possibility of an Infinite Regress Providing a Justification for Beliefs

The gist of the argument is this: If there were an infinite regress of reasons, any arbitrarily chosen contingent proposition would be justified. That is absurd. So there can't be an infinite regress of justification.

The argument has two forms. Let me deal with them in the order of their ascending plausibility. I. T. Oakley's argument is this (what follows is a close and, I hope, fair paraphrase):

> Let us suppose that S is justified in believing p in the way envisaged by the regress theorist. That is, there is a regress from p to r, to s to t, etc. Now, conjoin with every member of the series a further belief of S's, say q. If the first set of beliefs {p, r, s, t, etc.} is justified, so is the new set of conjunctive beliefs {(p&q), (r&q), (s&q), (t&p), etc.}. And if (p&q) is justified, then q is justified.[44]

I think this argument rests on an assumed principle of justification, namely this: If e justifies p, then (e & q) justifies (p & q). If that assumed principle were true, and if (p & q) justifies p and justifies q, then I think this argument does constitute a *reductio* of infinitism. But the assumed principle of justification is false—or better, it is clear that it and the principle endorsing justification over simplification cannot both be true. For, jointly, they lead to the unwelcome consequence that any arbitrary proposition, q, is justified given *any* theory of justification.

To see that, suppose that there is some proposition, e, and any theory of justification such that e is justified and e justifies p. Then, by parallel reasoning, since e justifies p, then (e & q) justifies (p & q). And, by parallel reasoning, q is justified. So, there is a quick and dirty way of showing that every proposition would be justified given *any* theory of justification.

But surely what is wrong here is that the argument fails to note what is essential to infinitism. It is a consequence of the infinitist's constraints on constructing a non-question begging chain that the ancestors of x in the chain cannot "contain" x.[45] The assumed principle violates that constraint and is a clear violation of PAC because the only reason offered for (p & q) is (e & q). Indeed, *every* link in the proposed infinite chain is question begging, for q is contained in each. Thus, this objection fails because the type of infinite chain presupposed in this objection does not have the appropriate form.[46]

There is another *reductio* argument that has been advanced against infinitism that does not violate the proposed constraints on the form of the chain of reasons. Here is a close paraphrase of the argument as given by John Post:

Consider an example of an infinite regress that does not violate the appropriate constraints. Let p be contingent and use *modus ponens* as follows:

$$\ldots, r \,\&\, (r \to (q \,\&\, (q \to p))),\ q \,\&\, (q \to p),\ p$$

This sort of infinitely iterated application of *modus ponens* guarantees that for any contingent proposition, p, one can construct an instance of an infinite regress.[47]

Post takes that as a *reductio* of the infinitist's position. I agree that if on some view of justification every contingent proposition were justified, the view would be unacceptable.[48] But Post has assumed that the infinitist takes the mere existence of such a chain of propositions with the appropriate form (non-repeating and infinite) to be a sufficient condition for a belief's having a justification. However, as I emphasized at the outset, the existence of such a chain is necessary, but it is not sufficient. The beliefs in the chain must also be "available" to S as reasons. Thus, not all infinite chains having the required structural properties make beliefs justified.

In considering Post's objection, Ernest Sosa distinguishes between what he calls chains that provide potential justification and those that provide actual justification.[49] I think Sosa is right.[50] As I see it, there is a potential justification for every contingent proposition; that is, there is an infinite chain of propositions like the one Post describes for every proposition. But only some chains contain reasons. Hence, not every proposition will have a justification because a proposition has a justification only if each member of the chain is available as a reason in both the objective sense and subjective sense to serve as a reason.[51]

Objection 4: The Specter of Skepticism

This is the most difficult objection to answer because it is the most difficult to fully understand. It apparently goes to some deeply held intuitions that, perhaps, I do not fully appreciate. The objection rests upon a Cartesian-like view that the whole point of reasoning is to "settle" an issue. According to that view, ideally, reasoning should produce *a priori* demonstrations; but where that is not possible or feasible (for example with regard to empirical propositions), something approximating a demonstration is required in order for a proposition to be justified or known. Reasoning should settle what it is we are to believe. If it can't, then what's the point of employing it? Reasoning is valuable, at least in part, because it can produce a final guarantee that a proposition is more reasonable than its contraries. But if the reasoning process is infinite, there can be no such guarantee. Thus, one of the claimed virtues of infinitism, namely, that it makes the distinctively adult human type of knowledge possible, is an illusion because that type of knowledge obtains only if reasoning can settle matters.

Here is the way that Jonathan Dancy puts the objection:

Suppose that all justification is inferential. When we justify belief A by appeal to belief B and C, we have not yet shown A to be justified. We have only shown that it is justified if B and C are. Justification by inference is conditional justification only; A's justification is conditional upon the justification of B and C. But if all justification is conditional in this sense, then nothing can be shown to be actually non-conditionally justified.[52]

Now, there is an unfortunate conflation in the passage that should be avoided—namely, failing to distinguish between *showing* that a belief is justified and a belief's being justified. Nevertheless, that equivocation could be removed and the objection remains: if all justification is provisional, no belief becomes unprovisionally justified.[53]

This is an old objection. It is, I think, what the Pyrrhonists thought made the infinite regress unacceptable as a theory of rational belief. Sextus wrote:

The Mode [of reasoning] based upon the regress *ad infinitum* is that whereby we assert that the thing adduced as a proof of the matter proposed needs a further proof, and this again another, and so on *ad infinitum*, so that the consequence is suspension, as we possess no starting-point for our argument.[54]

I have endorsed the Pyrrhonian objections to foundationalism and coherentism. Why not accept their argument against the infinite regress?

The answer is simply that although every proposition is only provisionally justified, that is good enough if one does not insist that reasoning settle matters once and for all. Once that is recognized, surprisingly enough, the Pyrrhonian goal of avoiding dogmatism while continuing to inquire is obtainable.

I readily grant that the kind of final guarantee that Descartes and others have sought is not available if infinitism is correct. In general, as we have seen, the foundationalist's reliance upon a

meta-justification to locate a property shared by all "basic" propositions is not a viable strategy for avoiding the regress. In particular, why should Descartes' suggestion for a truth-conducive property, namely clarity-and-distinctness, be accepted without a reason being given? Indeed, Descartes, himself, thought that a reason was required for believing that clarity-and-distinctness is truth-conducive. He attempted to provide that reason by producing an argument demonstrating the existence of an epistemically benevolent god. But surely that is only a temporary stopping point in the regress of reasons because the premises in that argument need to be supported by further reasons in order to avoid arbitrariness.

But, let me take the objection more seriously. Is a proposition justified only when belief in it *results from a process of justification that has been concluded?* Richard Fumerton has argued against infinitism because "[f]inite minds cannot *complete* an infinitely long chain of reasoning, so, if all justification were inferential we would have no justification for believing anything [emphasis added]."[55]

This objection to infinitism implicitly appeals to a principle that we can call the *Completion Requirement*: In order for a belief to be justified for someone, that person must have actually completed the chain of reasoning that terminates in the belief in question. The infinitist cannot accept the Completion Requirement because it is clearly incompatible with infinitism. Justifications are never finished. More to the point, however, the Completion Requirement demands more than what is required to have a justified belief even on non-infinitist accounts of justified beliefs.

To see that, apply the Completion Requirement to a foundationalist conception of justification coupled with the dispositional account of belief mentioned above that includes second-order dispositions. The result would be that most, if not all, of our beliefs are not justified. I have thousands and thousands of beliefs—if not infinitely many. I have not carried out the process of reasoning to many (if any) of those beliefs from some foundational beliefs (even if there were foundational beliefs). In fact, I couldn't have explicitly entertained any significant number of the propositions I believe. There are just too many.

Nevertheless, Fumerton's claim that S's belief is not justified merely because there is a justification available to S seems correct. In discussing the requirements for a belief's being justified, he draws an important distinction between S's merely *having* a justification for P and S's belief that P being justified. He claims, correctly I believe, the former is necessary but not sufficient for the latter:

> The expression "S has a justification for believing P" will be used in such a way that it implies nothing about the causal role played by that justification in sustaining the belief. The expression "S's belief that P is justified" will be taken to imply both that S has justification and that S's justification is playing the appropriate causal role in sustaining the belief.[56]

I think that an infinitist must grant the distinction between S's merely *having* a justification for the belief P and the belief P *being* justified for S. PAC and PAA specified necessary conditions for S's having a justification; they did not specify what else is required in order for S's belief to be justified. The question, then, becomes this: Can the infinitist draw the distinction between S *having* a justification for P and S's belief P *being* justified?

Ernest Sosa and others have suggested that the infinitist will be hard pressed to distinguish between S's merely having available a justification for a proposition and the proposition's being justified for S. Return to the case discussed earlier in which S calculates the sum of two numbers by employing some "already formed" dispositions. Now suppose (Sosa would suggest)

that S had, instead, merely guessed that the sum of the two numbers is 437, and, also, that when exploring whether the guessed sum is actually correct, S does a bit of adding and sees that the sum that he had guessed was, in fact, the right answer.[57] Presumably we want to say that although S had a justification available (if S can add) prior to calculating the sum, the belief that the numbers summed to 437 was not even provisionally justified until S does a bit of adding. So, merely *having* a justification available will not suffice for a belief's *being* provisionally justified.

Here is the way Sosa states the point:[58]

> Someone who guesses the answer to a complex addition problem does not already know the answer just because, given a little time, he could do the sum in his head. If he had not done the sum, if he had just been guessing, then he *acquires* his knowledge, he does not know beforehand . . . We are not just interested in the weaker position of someone who *would* be able to defend the belief, but only because its exposure to reflection would lead the subject to new arguments and reasonings that had never occurred to him, and that in any case had played no role in his acquisition or retention of the target belief.[59]

Now one might respond by saying that arriving at the sum of two numbers is not appropriately analogous to coming to believe, for example, that I hear my neighbor's dog, Fido, barking. Summing two large numbers requires (at least for most of us) some conscious process; whereas coming to believe that it is Fido barking does not require having gone through a process of conscious reasoning. To repeat, the Completion Requirement is just too strong in many cases. I can be justified in believing that it is Fido barking even if I have not arrived at that belief through some conscious process of reasoning.

Nevertheless, a question still remains even about my belief that it is Fido barking: How is the infinitist to distinguish between (1) the case of a lucky guess that it is Fido barking when a justification is available and (2) the case in which the belief is actually justified?[60]

The crucial point to recall is that for the infinitist *all* justification is provisional. S *has* a provisional justification for a proposition, p, only if there is a reason, r_1, both subjectively and objectively available to S for p; whereas S's belief p *is* provisionally justified only if S's belief r_1 "is playing the appropriate causal role in sustaining" (to use Fumerton's expression) S's belief p. But what about the belief r_1? Doesn't it have to be provisionally justified in order for the belief p to be provisionally justified? No. There does have to be a reason, r_2, for r_1 that is subjectively and objectively available if S is to *have* a justification for p, but the belief r_2 does not have to be provisionally justified in order for the belief p to be provisionally justified. It is sufficient that the belief p is causally sustained by the belief r_1 for the belief p to be provisionally justified. Beliefs originating from wild guesses would not be provisionally justified. Thus, the infinitist can make the requisite distinction between the case of a lucky guess when a justification is available and the case in which the belief is justified.

Still, I suspect that there is a deep skeptical worry lurking here. Infinitism envisions the possibility that if we begin to provide the reasons available for our beliefs, we might eventually arrive at a reason for which there is no further reason that is both subjectively and objectively available. Perhaps, our capacities to form new dispositions and concepts will reach a limit. Perhaps, the objective requirements of availability will not be met. Those possibilities cannot be ruled out *a priori*. Thus, the possibility of skepticism is a serious one. It is not, as some have thought, only a philosopher's nightmare.[61] Here I side with Richard Foley, who writes:

The way to respond to skeptical doubts is not to legislate against them metaphysically, and it is not to dismiss them as meaningless, self-defeating, or even odd . . . It is to recognize what makes epistemology possible makes skeptical worries inevitable—namely, our ability to make our methods of inquiry themselves into an object of inquiry.[62]

Now, of course, I think there might be an infinite series of reasons available; and if so, our desire for a reason can be answered whenever it arises. Foley thinks that the lack of final guarantees implies that "the reality of our intellectual lives is that we are working without nets."[63] And I agree that there are no final guarantees. There is no final net of that sort.

Nevertheless, although I think the kind of "lifetime" guarantee that would settle things once and for all is not available, my view is that there are important, "limited" guarantees available; and there might be a limitless set of limited guarantees available. The limited guarantees are the reasons that we can find for our beliefs. We have a limited guarantee that p is true whenever we have a reason for p. Is this an airtight guarantee?

No. But, we do have limited guarantees. And, for all I know, there might be an infinite number of such limited guarantees. Thus, although no *a priori* argument is available whose conclusion is that there is an infinite regress of objectively and subjectively available reasons, as we have seen there is also no such argument for the claim that there is no such set of reasons available.

Thus, I would not characterize our epistemic predicament as one in which there are *no* nets. For there might be a net whenever we need one. Rather, I would characterize it as one in which it is possible, as Lewis Carroll would say, that there are nets all the way down.

Notes

*   There are many people to thank for their assistance in writing this paper. The first public airing of a distant ancestor of the current paper took place at an NEH Summer Institute at Berkeley in the

summer of 1993. Keith Lehrer and Nicholas Smith were the co-directors, so I have them to thank for the opportunity to present the paper. The experience at the Institute was the best professional one I have ever had. Virtually everyone at the Institute had important comments and criticisms of the paper. There were just too many participants to cite them all. However, in addition to the co-directors, those who helped me most were: Hugh Benson, Mylan Engel, Ann Forster, Richard Garrett, Anthony Graybosch, Andrew Norman, Mark Patterson, Glenn Ross, Michael Roth, Bruce Russell, Sharon Ryan, and James Sennett. Other people read various ancestors of the paper whose comments, criticisms, and suggestions were very helpful: William Alston, Richard Fumerton, Stephen Luper-Foy, Paul Moser, John Post, Ernest Sosa, and Linda Zagzebski. In addition, three of my colleagues at Rutgers—Richard Foley, Brian McLaughlin, and Vann McGee (now at MIT)—provided telling criticism of earlier drafts and, luckily for me, also helped me to see ways of revising the argument to meet those criticisms. Finally, students in my graduate seminars—especially Ted Warfield, Carl Gillett, Troy Cross, and Jeff Engel—were helpful to me in developing the arguments put forth in this paper. Indeed, so many people helped me with this paper, it is only in some extended sense of "my" that this is my paper. But (if only to keep the Preface Paradox going) the mistakes are my own.

1   The term "infinitism" is not original with me. To the best of my knowledge, the first use of a related term is in Paul Moser's paper "A Defense of Epistemic Intuitionism," *Metaphilosophy* (15.3), 1984, pp. 196–204, in which he speaks of "epistemic infinitism." Also, John Post in *The Faces of Existence* (Ithaca: Cornell University Press, 1987) refers to a position similar to the one I am defending as the "infinitist's claim" (p. 91). There is, however, an important difference between the view that Post correctly criticizes and my view that will become clear later when I discuss his objection to infinitism.

2   For example, Robert Audi in *The Structure of Justification* (New York: Cambridge University Press, 1993) uses the "regress problem in a way that brings out its role in motivating both foundationalism and coherentism" (p. 10). He specifically

eschews a "full-scale assessment" of the regress argument (p. 127). In addition, William Alston, in his *Epistemic Justification* (Ithaca: Cornell University Press, 1989) employs the regress argument to motivate a type of foundationalism. He, too, does not examine the argument in detail but says "I do not claim that this argument is conclusive; I believe it to be open to objection in ways I will not be able to go into here. But I do feel that it gives stronger support to foundationalism than any other regress argument" (p. 55). Finally, Laurence BonJour in his *The Structure of Empirical Knowledge* (Cambridge: Harvard University Press, 1985) says that the considerations surrounding the regress argument are "perhaps the most crucial in the entire theory of knowledge" (p. 18) but dismisses the infinite regress by alluding to the "finite mental capacity" of human beings. Indeed, he says "though it is difficult to state in a really airtight fashion, this argument [that humans have a finite mental capacity] seems to me an adequate reason for rejecting [the view that the structure of justificatory reasons is infinite]" (p. 24). We will, of course, consider the "finite mind" objection in due course. My point is that such a crucial issue in the theory of knowledge deserves careful consideration.

3   I might note in passing that Davidson's characterization of coherence theories—namely that "what distinguishes a coherence theory is simply the claim that nothing can count as a reason for holding a belief except another belief"—might distinguish it from foundationalist theories, but it does not distinguish it from infinitism. See "Coherence Theory of Truth and Knowledge" in *Truth and Interpretation*, Ernest Lepore, ed. (New York: Blackwell, 1986), pp. 307–319. Citation from p. 310.

4   I take *traditional coherentism* to be the view that the structure of justification is such that some proposition, say x, provides some warrant for another proposition, say y, and y also provides some warrant for x. It is to be distinguished from another view, discussed later, which holds that coherence is a property of sets of propositions and individual propositions in the set are warranted because they belong to such a set. In this *non-traditional coherentist* view, warrant attaches to beliefs because they are members of such a set.

Unlike traditional coherentism, warrant is not a property transferred from one proposition to another.

5   Throughout I will be using single-strand chains of reasons. Nothing depends upon that. I do so in order to make the contrast between foundationalism and coherentism more readily evident.

6   Note that stating PAC this way does not entail that "being a reason for" is transitive. This avoids a valid criticism of an argument for infinitism. (See John Post, "Infinite Regress Argument" in *Companion to Epistemology*, Jonathan Dancy and Ernest Sosa, eds. (New York: Blackwell, 1992), pp. 209–212. His criticism of infinitism depends upon my own argument against the transitivity of justification. See *Certainty* (Minneapolis: University of Minnesota Press, 1981), pp. 30–35. Those criticisms do not apply here because "being in the evidential ancestry of" is transitive.)

7   Laurence BonJour in *The Structure of Empirical Knowledge* and Keith Lehrer in *Theory of Knowledge* (Boulder: Westview Press, 1990) develop accounts of what I call "non-traditional coherentism."

8   There are other necessary conditions of justification, but they are not important for the discussion here. For example, there must not be another proposition, d, available to S that overrides r (unless there is an ultimately non-overridden overrider of d). See my *Certainty*, pp. 44–70.

9   This is important to note since as I understand Ernest Sosa's objection to infinitism it is its supposed incompatibility with the supervenience of the normative on the non-normative that makes it unacceptable. See his "The Raft and the Pyramid," *Midwest Studies in Philosophy*, vol 5 (Minneapolis: University of Minnesota Press, 1980), pp. 3–25, especially section 7. James Van Cleve makes a similar point in his "Semantic Supervenience and Referential Indeterminacy," *Journal of Philosophy*, LXXXIX, no. 7 (July 1992), pp. 344–361, especially pp. 350–1 and 356–7. Note that I am not asserting that the normative does, in fact, supervene on the non-normative. Indeed, I think the issue might be misconceived. Perhaps there are some properties—the so-called "normative" properties of knowledge and justification—that are hybrid properties, being neither normative nor non-normative. My claim is merely that, as

sketched in this paper, infinitism is compatible with the supervenience of the normative on the non-normative.

10   Thus, each one of these accounts of objective availability specifies a sufficient condition that entails that a belief is a reason. If the sufficient condition appeals only to non-normative properties, as some of them do, then what is unique to infinitism satisfies Van Cleve's requirement for epistemic supervenience. He says:

One of the tasks of epistemology is to articulate *epistemic principles*—principles of the form 'If—, then subject S is justified in believing proposition p'. Such principles divide into two classes. One class includes principles that warrant inference from already justified propositions to further propositions; the antecedents of such principles will specify that certain propositions already have some epistemic status for the subject. But not all epistemic principles can be like this. There must also be a class of epistemic principles that specify the non-epistemic conditions under which some beliefs come to have some epistemic status or other in the first place—the conditions, one might say, under which epistemic status is *generated* . . . [This] requirement is really just the requirement of epistemic supervenience—that there be some nonepistemic features that ultimately underlie the instantiation of any epistemic property.

(Van Cleve, *op. cit.*, p. 350)

If I am right that the sufficient conditions for both subjective and objective availability can be specified in nonepistemic terms, then there is no reason for thinking that infinitism is incompatible with epistemic supervenience. For the conditions are sufficient for making beliefs into the required sort of reasons.

There are other conditions besides those specified in PAC and PAA that a belief must satisfy in order to be justified (see note 8), but if those also supervene on the non-normative facts, then infinitism is compatible with epistemic supervenience. Those other features are not unique to infinitism. The combination of PAC and PAA is what distinguishes infinitism from coherentism and foundationalism. My point is that what distinguishes infinitism is compatible with epistemic supervenience.

11 This is a paraphrase of an account developed by Roderick Chisholm, *Theory of Knowledge* (Englewood Cliffs, NJ: Prentice-Hall Inc., 1966). See especially fn. 22, p. 23.

12 For a development of the individualistically relativistic account of objective availability, see Richard Foley, *The Theory of Epistemic Rationality* (Cambridge: Harvard University Press, 1987), especially pp. 68–154.

13 See, for example: David Lewis, "Scorekeeping in a Language Game," *Journal of Philosophical Logic*, VIII (1979), pp. 339–359; L. Wittgenstein, *On Certainty*, G.E.M. Anscombe and G.H. von Wright, eds. (New York: Harper and Row, 1972). There are also hints at such a view in Aristotle. (*Metaphysics*, 1006a–1011b.)

14 This position is advocated by Linda Zagzebski in *Virtues of the Mind* (Cambridge: Cambridge University Press, 1996).

15 One problem for some interpretations of objective availability needs to be avoided. Troy Cross has pointed out to me that if the probability of propositions diminishes as the chain of reasons lengthens, our beliefs might have such a low probability that they would not in any normal sense of "justified," in fact, be justified. There are four ways around that worry. The first is that there is an infinite number of probability gradations available given any required probability level of the putatively justified proposition. The second is that it is the proposition, itself, that is located in the chain rather than a proposition with a probability assigned. The third is to simply reject the reading of "objective probability" in frequency terms and treat "p is probable" as roughly synonymous with "p is acceptable and can be used to make other propositions acceptable." The fourth is simply to reject probability theory as providing an appropriate set of conditions for objective availability.

16 See, for example, the passage cited earlier in BonJour, *The Structure of Empirical Knowledge*. (See note 2.)

17 There is a deep problem with treating beliefs as dispositions to have thoughts *under the appropriately restricted circumstances*. For it appears that almost any proposition as well as its negation could count as believed under some range of "appropriately

restricted circumstances." I do not have a settled view regarding the way to restrict the range of circumstances to avoid that consequence. Obviously, this is a general, difficult problem for a dispositional account of belief. There just seem to be too many beliefs. But, as we will see, the problem for the infinitist is just the opposite. For infinitism seems to require more beliefs than we can or do have. It would be nice to have a satisfactory dispositional account of belief. A fully developed infinitist theory must address this issue. Nevertheless, since my purpose here is merely to make infinitism a view worth exploring, we can proceed without solving this general problem concerning a dispositional account of beliefs.

18 Ernest Sosa makes a similar point in "The Raft and the Pyramid." It is reprinted in his book *Knowledge in Perspective* (New York: Cambridge University Press, 1991), pp. 165–191, see especially p. 178.

19 Dretske, "Two Conceptions of Knowledge: Rational Belief vs. Reliable Belief," *Grazer Philosophische Studien*, 40 (1991), pp. 15–30, especially p. 18.

20 Alvin Goldman, "What Is Justified Belief?" in *On Knowing and the Known*, Kenneth G. Lucy, ed. (Amherst, New York: Prometheus Books, 1996), p. 190.

21 Keith Lehrer, *Theory of Knowledge*, p. 164.

22 Ernest Sosa, *Knowledge in Perspective*, p. 95.

23 Laurence BonJour, *The Structure of Empirical Knowledge*, especially pp. 9–14.

24 See, for example, *Outlines of Pyrrhonism*, PH I 114–117, 122–124.

25 See, for example, John Williams, "Justified Belief and the Infinite Regress Argument," *American Philosophical Quarterly*, XVIII, no 1 (1981), pp. 85–88, especially p. 86.

26 William Alston, "Two Types of Foundationalism," *Journal of Philosophy*, LXXIII (1976), pp. 165–85. The article also appears as Essay 1 in Alston's book *Epistemic Justification*, pp. 19–38.

27 Laurence BonJour, *The Structure of Empirical Knowledge*, pp. 108–9.

28 Donald Davidson also seems concerned to establish this sort of connection between coherence and truth:

What is needed to answer the skeptic is to show that someone with a (more or less) coherent set of beliefs has a reason to suppose that his beliefs are not mistaken in the main. What we have shown is that it is absurd to look for a justifying ground for the totality of beliefs, something outside the totality which we can use to test or compare with our beliefs. The answer to our problem must then be to find a *reason* for supposing most of our beliefs are true that is not a form of *evidence*.

(Davidson, "Coherence Theory of Truth and Knowledge," p. 314)

29 See Peter Klein and Ted Warfield, "What Price Coherence?", *Analysis*, 54.3, July 1994, pp. 129–32.

30 Steven Luper-Foy, "Arbitrary Reasons," in *Doubting: Contemporary Perspectives on Skepticism*, Michael Roth and Glenn Ross, eds. (Dordrecht: Kluwer Academic Publishers, 1990), pp. 39–55. Citation is from p. 45.

31 Luper-Foy, "Arbitrary Reasons," p. 40.

32 See "Questions Concerning Certain Faculties Claimed for Man" in the *Collected Papers of Charles Sanders Peirce*, Charles Hartshorne and Paul Weiss, eds. (Cambridge, Massachusetts: Belknap Press of Harvard University Press, 1965), vol. V, Bk. II, pp. 135–155, especially pp. 152–153. There he writes:

Question 7. *Whether there is any cognition not determined by a previous cognition.* 259. It would seem that there is or has been; for since we are in possession of cognitions, which are all determined by previous ones and these by cognitions earlier still, there must have been a first in this series or else our state of cognition at any time is completely determined according to logical laws, by our state at any previous time. But there are many facts against this last supposition, and therefore in favor of intuitive cognitions.

260. On the other hand, since it is impossible to know intuitively that a given cognition is not determined by a previous one, the only way in which this can be known is by hypothetic inference from observed facts. But to adduce the cognition by which a given cognition has been determined is to explain the determinations of that cognition. And it is a way of explaining them. For something entirely out of consciousness which may be supposed to determine it,

can, as such, only be known and only adduced in the determinate cognition in question. So, that to suppose that a cognition is determined solely by something absolutely external, is to suppose its determinations incapable of explanation. Now, this is a hypothesis which is warranted under no circumstances, inasmuch as the only possible justification for a hypothesis is that it explains that fact, and to say that they are explained and at the same time to suppose them inexplicable is self-contradictory.

Peirce may, indeed, be arguing that only beliefs (cognitions) can provide a basis for other beliefs—nothing "external" can do so. He also might be arguing that the "meta-argument" referred to earlier can not succeed because one can always ask of the supposed meta-justification what justifies it. But I am not certain that either is what he is claiming. Further, if he is merely claiming that cognitions are infinitely revisable given new experiences, then he is not advocating infinitism.

33 John Williams, "Justified Belief and the Infinite Regress Argument," p. 85.

34 Williams, p. 86.

35 Richard Foley, "Inferential Justification and the Infinite Regress," *American Philosophical Quarterly*, XV, no. 4 (1978), pp. 311–316; quotation from pages 311–312.

36 Williams, p. 86.

37 Robert Audi considers the set of beliefs: 2 is twice 1, 4 is twice 2, etc. Then, he says, "Surely, for a finite mind there will be some point or other at which the relevant proposition cannot be grasped." (See Audi's "Contemporary Foundationalism" in *The Theory of Knowledge: Classic and Contemporary Readings*, Louis Pojman, ed. (Belmont: Wadsworth, 1993), pp. 206–213. The quotation is from page 209.) The example is repeated in Audi's book *The Structure of Justification* (New York: Cambridge University Press, 1993), p. 127. My reply is that there are other examples of infinite series of beliefs (understood as dispositions) that do not involve increasingly difficult to grasp propositions (like the one about to be given in the main text).

38 I am indebted to Vann McGee for this point.

39 Richard Fumerton, "Metaepistemology and Skepticism," in *Doubting: Contemporary Perspectives on*

Skepticism, pp. 57–68, quotation from p. 60. The same account of justification is given in Fumerton's book *Metaepistemology and Skepticism* (Lanham, Maryland: Rowman & Littlefield Publishers, 1995), p. 36.

40 Richard Foley, "Inferential Justification and the Infinite Regress," especially pp. 314–315.

41 There is a related point which I do think might be telling against the relatively thin view of justification I am proposing; and it might appear that this would jeopardize infinitism. Although it is clear that the requirement that S have a justification about what constitutes good reasoning is too strong a requirement of having a justification *simpliciter* or of paradigmatic forms of having a justification *simpliciter* for the reason just given, it is plausible to suggest that S must *believe*, at least dispositionally, that e makes p probable (to use Fumerton's terminology) whenever S is justified *simpliciter* in believing that p and S's available reason for p is e. That is a somewhat thicker notion of justification than the one I am proposing. It is plausible because the intuitions that inform the Truetemp case can be employed to support this moderately thick view. Suppose Mr. Truetemp believes it is 104 degrees and he also believes that he has an accurate thermometer-cum-temperature-belief-generator implanted in his head. On my "thin" view, if S believes that he has an accurate thermometer-cum-temperature-belief-generator implanted in his head, then S has a justification for the belief that it is 104 degrees, if, *ceteris paribus*, he has a good enough, non-question begging reason for believing that he has an accurate thermometer-cum-temperature-belief-generator implanted in his head, and he has a reason for that reason, etc. But on my thin view, S might not believe that is his real reason. He might believe (dispositionally or occurrently) falsely, for example, that his reason is that it is Tuesday and that it is always 104 degrees on Tuesday. Of course, that is not a reason on my account because that belief, like the one offered in the Fish/Army Boots Case considered earlier, is not objectively available to Mr. Truetemp. I think such a case is best seen as one in which Mr. Truetemp does not know what his real reason is—but that he has a good enough reason available in both the objective and subjective sense. Thus, I think that, *ceteris paribus*, he has a

justification *simpliciter* and that, *ceteris paribus*, he does know that the temperature is 104 degrees, but he does not know *how* he knows that the temperature is 104 degrees or even *that* he knows that. Nevertheless, I acknowledge the intuitive tug in the opposite direction—namely that he is not justified *simpliciter*, and hence does not know, because he would offer the "wrong" reason for his belief that it is 104 degrees.

Let me make the distinction between the three views of justification absolutely clear. The "thin" view (the one I think is correct) holds that *S has a justification for p on the basis of r* entails that (a) *S believes r* and (b) *r is a reason for p*. It does not require that, in addition, either (1) S believes that r is a reason for p or (2) S is justified in believing that r is a reason for p. The "moderately thick view" (the one I think is plausible) adds (1) to the thin view. The "extremely thick" view (the one I think cannot be correct) adds (2), and presumably (1) as well, to the thin view.

What is crucial to note is that, without jeopardizing infinitism, I can grant that S must dispositionally believe that e makes p probable in order for p to be justified by e for S. Of course on such a view, S would, at the next link in the chain, have to believe that e^1 makes e probable, and at the next link believe that e^2 makes e^1 probable, etc. But note that granting that this thicker view of justification is correct would not force the infinitist into requiring that S have an implausibly complex belief. The beliefs at every step of the regress are no more complex than the one at the first step. So, the intuitive tug of this moderately thick view of justification can be allowed to modify the thin view without damaging my central claim. I resist the tug because I think it is the reasons available to S for p that determine whether S has a justification for p regardless of S's beliefs about those reasons.

42 There are some places in the *Posterior Analytics* where Aristotle *might* be claiming that it does follow from the fact that not all reasoning is the result of demonstration that the structure of reasons cannot be infinite:

> Our own doctrine is that not all knowledge is demonstrative: on the contrary, knowledge of the immediate premises is independent of

demonstration. (The necessity of this is obvious: for since we must know the prior premisses from which the demonstration is drawn, and since the regress must end in immediate truths, those truths must be indemonstrable.) [72b18–23]

(*Basic Works of Aristotle*, Richard McKeon, ed. (New York: Random House, 1941))

My point is that Aristotle's argument concerning the genesis of knowledge can be granted without granting that the structure of justification is finite. Demonstration cannot be required to bring about all knowledge. But it does not follow that reasons could not be given for all beliefs.

43 *Basic Works of Aristotle*, Richard McKeon, ed., 1011a1–14.

44 I. T. Oakley, "An Argument for Skepticism Concerning Justified Beliefs," *American Philosophical Quarterly*, XIII, no. 3 (1976), pp. 221–228, especially pp. 226–227.

45 We said, in PAC, that for all x and for all y, if x is contained in the ancestry of y, y cannot be contained in the ancestry of x. Let "xCy" stand for "x is contained in the ancestry of y".

1 $(x)(y)(xCy \rightarrow \sim(yCx))$ 1 Premiss (PAC)
2 $aCa \rightarrow \sim(aCa)$ 2 UI (twice), 1
3 aCa 3 Assume, for reductio
4 $\sim(aCa)$ 4 2,3 MP
5 $\sim(aCa)$ 5 CP (discharge), 3–4
6 $(x)\sim(xCx)$ 6 UG, 5

46 In order to foreclose a possible objection, it is important to note that my claim that if every link contains q, the chain would be question begging does not have the unacceptable consequence that if S is justified in believing (p & q), then S is not justified in believing that q. My claim is merely that it is not always the case that (p & q) is an acceptable (i.e. non-question begging) reason for q. What typically occurs is that the chain of reasons includes p and includes q before including (p & q). But, of course, if the chain is of that form, then S would be justified in believing p and justified in believing q when S is justified in believing (p & q) because the justification of (p & q) depends upon the prior justification of p and the prior justification of q.

I say "typically" in the preceding paragraph, because there do seem to be some chains of reasoning in which (p & q) precedes p and precedes q. Consider this one (where "xRy" stands for "x is a reason for y"):

Sally says "p & q" and whatever Sally says is true} **R** {(p & q)} **R** {q}

That chain does not appear to me to be question begging. The crucial point here is that my denial that (p & q) is always a reason for q (the presupposition of Oakley's argument) does not commit me to denying that justification distributes over conjunction.

47 I have condensed the argument a bit. In particular, there are other constraints besides the question begging one discussed by Post. But I believe that they are not relevant. See John Post, "Infinite Regress of Justification and of Explanation," *Philosophical Studies*, XXXVIII (1980), pp. 32–37, especially pp. 34–35. The argument, in a slightly revised form, appears in Post's book *The Faces of Existence* (Ithaca: Cornell University Press, 1987), pp. 84–92.

48 I might note in passing that if PAA and PAC are necessary requirements of justification, both foundationalism and coherentism lead to the result that no contingent proposition is justified, since they advocate reasoning that violates those principles. I think any theory of justification that automatically leads to the view that *no* proposition is justified ought to be rejected as readily as a view that has the consequence that *all* contingent propositions are justified.

49 Ernest Sosa, "The Raft and the Pyramid," *Midwest Studies in Philosophy*, Section 5.

50 Post claims in *The Faces of Existence* that his new formulation of the *reductio* argument meets the objection by Sosa (see his fn. 21, p. 91). As I construe Sosa's objection, namely that more is required for a belief to have a justification than the mere existence of a series of beliefs which under some circumstances would provide a justification, Post's reformulation does not meet Sosa's objection. Post says that in such a series "justification is supposed to accumulate for [the first item in the series] merely as a result of [the person's] being able endlessly to meet the demand for justification

simply by appealing to the next inferential justification in the [series]" (p. 90). My point is that there will not be such a series of available reasons for some beliefs.

51 The infinitist must be careful here not to fall into a trap laid by Paul Moser. He points out correctly that if the distinction between conditional (or potential) regresses and actual ones were that there is some external *information* that makes each step justified, then it could appear that the infinitist is committed to the view that the *reason* for believing any member of the chain is not merely the antecedent in the chain but the antecedent *plus* the "external" information. That is, the external information would become an additional reason for holding the belief. See Paul Moser, "Whither Infinite Regresses of Justification?" *The Southern Journal of Philosophy*, XXIII, no. 1 (1985), pp. 65–74, especially page 71.

But the infinitist need not fall into the trap. The infinitist holds that there are some facts in virtue of which a belief is a reason. These facts are not part of the chain of reasoning.

52 Jonathan Dancy, *Introduction to Contemporary Epistemology* (Oxford: Basil Blackwell, 1985), p. 55.

53 I use the term "provisional" justification rather than "conditional" justification (as used by Dancy) because the term "provisional" more clearly underscores the fact that the reasons in the chains are replaceable.

54 *Outlines of Pyrrhonism*, PH I, 166.

55 Richard Fumerton, *Metaepistemology and Skepticism*, p. 57. Some of what follows repeats my comments on Fumerton's book in "Foundationalism and the Infinite Regress of Reasons," *Philosophy and Phenomenological Research*, LVIII, no. 4 (1989), pp. 219–225.

56 Fumerton, p. 92.

57 A case similar to this one was discussed in a paper that Ernest Sosa presented at the Chapel Hill Philosophy Colloquium entitled "Two False Dichotomies: Foundationalism/Coherentism and Internalism/Externalism" on 10/17/97.

58 BonJour makes a similar point this way:

the fact that a clever person could invent an acceptable inferential justification on the spot when challenged to justify a hunch or arbitrary claim of some sort, so that the justification was in a sense available to him, would not mean that his belief was inferentially justified prior to that time.

(See BonJour, *The Structure of Empirical Knowledge*, p. 19)

59 Sosa, "Two False Dichotomies: Foundationalism/Coherentism and Internalism/Externalism," manuscript, p. 6.

60 It is crucial to note that I have been arguing that a necessary condition of S's being justified in believing that p is that S has an appropriate justification for p and having such a justification requires that there be an infinite number of non-repeating reasons available to S. I was not suggesting that was a sufficient condition for S's being justified or even having a justification (see note 8 above). So, Sosa's objection, even if valid, cannot be directed towards the main claim of this paper. Nevertheless, it is an important objection since the infinitist will at least have to show how it is possible for S to have a justified belief *according to the infinitist's account of justified belief*, if the distinctive type of adult human knowledge is to be shown to be possible. Nevertheless, let us grant for the sake of argument that somehow it could be shown—either through philosophic argument, or perhaps even by cognitive science, that our beliefs do not (or can not) have the requisite causal history as required by infinitism (or foundationalism or coherentism, for that matter). What would be the consequences to infinitism (foundationalism or coherentism)? I think that is very far from clear cut. The infinitist is claiming that a normatively acceptable set of reasons must be infinitely long and non-repeating if we are to avoid the pitfalls of foundationalism (arbitrariness) and coherentism (begging the question). If infinitism correctly specifies our current concept about what is required for a belief to have the appropriate normative pedigree and if it were to turn out that beliefs don't (or can't) have the requisite causal structure, then we have at least three choices: (1) We can revise our concept of the normative structure of good reasoning or (2) we can adopt a form of Pyrrhonism (withholding assent to any proposition requiring a justification) or (3) we can accept an antinomy. It would not follow that the normative constraints were incorrectly described—unless, perhaps, epistemic

oughts imply epistemic cans. But that seems highly dubious. Would it not be possible for it to be the case that the rules of inference that are most truth-conducive are such that we are not "wired" to employ them? If so, there is a perfectly good sense in which we ought to reason in some way that we can't.

61 See Michael Williams, *Unnatural Doubts* (Oxford, UK and Cambridge, Mass.: Blackwell, 1991).

62 Richard Foley, "Skepticism and Rationality," in *Doubting: Contemporary Perspectives on Skepticism*, cited earlier, pp. 69–81, quotation from p. 75.

63 Foley, "Skepticism and Rationality," p. 80. For a full development of the "no nets" view, see Richard Foley, *Working Without a Net: A Study of Egocentric Epistemology* (New York: Oxford University Press, 1993).

Chapter 23

Ernest Sosa

THE RAFT AND THE PYRAMID
Coherence versus foundations in the theory of knowledge

Contemporary epistemology must choose between the solid security of the ancient foundationalist pyramid and the risky adventure of the new coherentist raft. Our main objective will be to understand, as deeply as we can, the nature of the controversy and the reasons for and against each of the two options. But first of all we take note of two underlying assumptions.

Two assumptions

(A1) Not everything believed is known, but nothing can be known without being at least believed (or accepted, presumed, taken for granted, or the like) in some broad sense. What additional requirements must a belief fill in order to be knowledge? There are surely at least the following two: (a) it must be true, and (b) it must be justified (or warranted, reasonable, correct, or the like).

(A2) Let us assume, moreover, with respect to the second condition A1(b): first, that it involves a normative or evaluative property; and, second, that the relevant sort of justification is that which pertains to knowledge: epistemic (or theoretical) justification. Someone seriously ill may have two sorts of justification for believing he will recover: the practical justification that derives from the contribution such belief will make to his recovery and the theoretical justification provided by the lab results, the doctor's diagnosis and prognosis, and so on. Only the latter is relevant to the question whether he knows.

Knowledge and criteria (or canons, methods, or the like)

a. There are two key questions of the theory of knowledge:

(i) What do we know?
(ii) How do we know?

The answer to the first would be a list of bits of knowledge or at least of types of knowledge: of the self, of the external world, of other minds, and so on. An answer to the second would give us criteria (or canons, methods, principles, or the like) that would explain how we know whatever it is that we do know.

b. In developing a theory of knowledge, we can begin either with a(i) or with a(ii). Particularism would have us begin with an answer to a(i) and only then take up a(ii) on the basis of that answer. Quite to the contrary, methodism would reverse that order. The particularist thus tends to be antiskeptical on principle. But the methodist is as such equally receptive to skepticism and to the contrary. Hume, for example, was no less a methodist than Descartes. Each accepted, in effect, that only the obvious and what is proved deductively on its basis can possibly be known.

c. What, then, is the obvious? For Descartes it is what we know by intuition, what is clear and distinct, what is indubitable and credible with no fear of error. Thus for Descartes basic knowledge is always an infallible belief in an indubitable truth. All other knowledge must stand on that basis through deductive proof. Starting from such criteria (canons, methods, etc.), Descartes concluded that knowledge extended about as far as his contemporaries believed.[1] Starting from similar criteria, however, Hume concluded that both science and common sense made claims far beyond their rightful limits.

d. Philosophical posterity has rejected Descartes's theory for one main reason: that it admits too easily as obvious what is nothing of the sort. Descartes's reasoning is beautifully simple: God exists; no omnipotent perfectly good being would descend to deceit; but if our common sense beliefs were radically false, that would represent deceit on His part. Therefore, our common sense beliefs must be true or at least cannot be radically false. But in order to buttress this line of reasoning and fill in details, Descartes appeals to various principles that appear something less than indubitable.

e. For his part, Hume rejects all but a miniscule portion of our supposed common sense knowledge. He establishes first that there is no way to prove such supposed knowledge on the basis of what is obvious at any given moment through reason or experience. And he concludes, in keeping with this methodism, that in point of fact there really is no such knowledge.

Two metaphors: the raft and the pyramid

Both metaphors concern the body or system of knowledge in a given mind. But the mind is of course a more complex marvel than is sometimes supposed. Here I do not allude to the depths plumbed by Freud, nor even to Chomsky's. Nor need we recall the labyrinths inhabited by statesmen and diplomats, nor the rich patterns of some novels or theories. We need look no further than the most common, everyday beliefs. Take, for instance, the belief that driving tonight will be dangerous. Brief reflection should reveal that any of us with that belief will join to it several other closely related beliefs on which the given belief depends for its existence or (at least) its justification. Among such beliefs we could presumably find some or all of the following: that the road will be icy or snowy; that driving on ice or snow is dangerous; that it will rain or snow tonight; that the temperature will be below freezing; appropriate beliefs about the forecast and its reliability; and so on.

How must such beliefs be interrelated in order to help justify my belief about the danger of driving tonight? Here foundationalism and coherentism disagree, each offering its own metaphor. Let us have a closer look at this dispute, starting with foundationalism.

Both Descartes and Hume attribute to human knowledge an architectonic structure. There is a nonsymmetric relation of physical support such that any two floors of a building are tied by that relation: one of the two supports (or at least helps support) the other. And there is, moreover, a part with a special status: the foundation, which is supported by none of the floors while supporting them all.

With respect to a body of knowledge K (in someone's possession), foundationalism implies that K can be divided into parts $K_1, K_2, \ldots$, such that there is some nonsymmetric relation R (analogous to the relation of physical support) which orders those parts in such a way that there is one—call it F—that bears R to every other part while none of them bears R in turn to F.

According to foundationalism, each piece of knowledge lies on a pyramid such as [that in

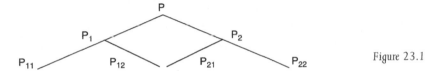

Figure 23.1

Figure 23.1]. The nodes of such a pyramid (for a proposition P relative to a subject S and a time t) must obey the following requirements:

a.   The set of all nodes that succeed (directly) any given node must serve jointly as a base that properly supports that node (for S at t).

b.   Each node must be a proposition that S is justified in believing at t.

c.   If a node is not self-evident (for S at t), it must have successors (that serve jointly as a base that properly supports that node).

d.   Each branch of an epistemic pyramid must terminate.

For the foundationalist Descartes, for instance, each terminating node must be an indubitable proposition that S believes at t with no possibility of error. As for the nonterminal nodes, each of them represents inferential knowledge, derived by deduction from more basic beliefs.

Such radical foundationalism suffers from a fatal weakness that is twofold:

(a)   there are not so many perfectly obvious truths as Descartes thought; and

(b)   once we restrict ourselves to what is truly obvious in any given context, very little of one's supposed common sense knowledge can be proved on that basis.

If we adhere to such radical foundationalism, therefore, we are just wrong in thinking we know so much.

Note that in citing such a "fatal weakness" of radical foundationalism, we favor particularism as against the methodism of Descartes and Hume. For we reject the methods or criteria of Descartes and Hume when we realize that they

plunge us in a deep skepticism. If such criteria are incompatible with our enjoyment of the rich body of knowledge that we commonly take for granted, then as good particularists we hold on to the knowledge and reject the criteria.

If we reject radical foundationalism, however, what are we to put in its place? Here epistemology faces a dilemma that different epistemologists resolve differently. Some reject radical foundationalism but retain some more moderate form of foundationalism. Others react more vigorously, however, by rejecting all forms of foundationalism in favor of a radically different coherentism. Coherentism is associated with idealism—of both the German and the British variety—and has recently acquired new vigor and interest.

The coherentists reject the metaphor of the pyramid in favor of one that they owe to the positivist Neurath, according to whom our body of knowledge is a raft that floats free of any anchor or tie. Repairs must be made afloat, and though no part is untouchable, we must stand on some in order to replace or repair others. Not every part can go at once.

According to the new metaphor, what justifies a belief is not that it be an infallible belief with an indubitable object, nor that it have been proved deductively on such a basis, but that it cohere with a comprehensive system of beliefs.

A coherentist critique of foundationalism

What reasons do coherentists offer for their total rejection of foundationalism? The argument that follows below summarizes much of what is alleged against foundationalism. But first we must distinguish between subjective states that incorporate a propositional attitude and those that do not. A propositional attitude is a mental state of someone with a proposition for its object: beliefs, hopes, and fears provide examples. By way of contrast, a headache does not incorporate any such attitude. One can of course be conscious of a headache, but the headache itself does not constitute or incorporate any attitude with a proposition for its object. With this distinction in the background, here is the antifoundationalist argument, which has two lemmas—a(iv) and b(iii)—and a principal conclusion.

a. (i) If a mental state incorporates a propositional attitude, then it does not give us direct contact with reality, e.g., with pure experience, unfiltered by concepts or beliefs.

   (ii) If a mental state does not give us direct contact with reality, then it provides no guarantee against error.

   (iii) If a mental state provides no guarantee against error, then it cannot serve as a foundation for knowledge.

   (iv) Therefore, if a mental state incorporates a propositional attitude, then it cannot serve as a foundation for knowledge.

b. (i) If a mental state does not incorporate a propositional attitude, then it is an enigma how such a state can provide support for any hypothesis, raising its credibility selectively by contrast with its alternatives. (If the mental state has no conceptual or propositional content, then what logical relation can it possibly bear to any hypothesis? Belief in a hypothesis would be a propositional attitude with the hypothesis itself as object. How can one depend logically for such a belief on an experience with no propositional content?)

   (ii) If a mental state has no propositional content and cannot provide logical support for any hypothesis, then it cannot serve as a foundation for knowledge.

   (iii) Therefore, if a mental state does not incorporate a propositional attitude, then it cannot serve as a foundation for knowledge.

c. Every mental state either does or does not incorporate a propositional attitude.

d. Therefore, no mental state can serve as a foundation for knowledge. (From a(iv), b(iii), and c.)

According to the coherentist critic, foundationalism is run through by this dilemma. Let us take a closer look.[2]

In the first place, what reason is there to think, in accordance with premise b(i), that only propositional attitudes can give support to their own kind? Consider practices—e.g. broad policies or customs. Could not some person or group be justified in a practice because of its consequences: that is, could not the consequences of a practice make it a good practice? But among the consequences of a practice may surely be found, for example, a more just distribution of goods and less suffering than there would be under its alternatives. And neither the more just distribution nor the lower degree of suffering is a propositional attitude. This provides an example in which propositional attitudes (the intentions that sustain the practice) are justified by consequences that are not propositional attitudes. That being so, is it not conceivable that the justification of belief that matters for knowledge be analogous to the objective justification by consequences that we find in ethics?

Is it not possible, for instance, that a belief that there is something red before one be justified in part because it has its origin in one's visual experience of red when one looks at an apple in daylight? If we accept such examples, they show us a source of justification that serves as such without incorporating a propositional attitude.

As for premise a(iii), it is already under suspicion from our earlier exploration of premise b(i). A mental state M can be nonpropositional and hence not a candidate for so much as truth, much less infallibility, while it serves, in spite of that, as a foundation of knowledge. Leaving that aside, let us suppose that the relevant mental state is indeed propositional. Must it then be infallible in order to serve as a foundation of justification and knowledge? That is so far from being obvious that it seems more likely false when compared with an analogue in ethics. With respect to beliefs, we may distinguish between their being true and their being justified. Analogously, with respect to actions, we may distinguish between their being optimal (best of all alternatives, all things considered) and their being (subjectively) justified. In practical deliberation on alternatives for action, is it inconceivable that the most *eligible* alternative *not* be objectively the best, all things considered? Can there not be another alternative—perhaps a most repugnant one worth little if any consideration—that in point of fact would have a much better total set of consequences and would thus be better, all things considered? Take the physician attending to Frau Hitler at the birth of little Adolf. Is it not possible that if he had acted less morally, that would have proved better in the fullness of time? And if that is so in ethics, may not its likeness hold good in epistemology? Might there not be justified (reasonable, warranted) beliefs that are not even true, much less infallible? That seems to me not just a conceivable possibility, but indeed a familiar fact of everyday life, where observational beliefs too often prove illusory but no less reasonable for being false.

If the foregoing is on the right track, then the antifoundationalist is far astray. What has led him there?

As a diagnosis of the antifoundationalist argument before us, and more particularly of its second lemma I would suggest that it rests on an Intellectualist Model of Justification.

According to such a model, the justification of belief (and psychological states generally) is parasitical on certain logical relations among propositions. For example, my belief (i) that the streets are wet, is justified by my pair of beliefs (ii) that it is raining, and (iii) that if it is raining, the streets are wet. Thus we have a structure such as this:

B(Q) is justified by the fact that B(Q) is grounded on (B(P), B(P⊃Q)).

And according to an Intellectualist Model, this is parastical on the fact that

P and (P⊃Q) together logically imply Q.

Concerning this attack on foundationalism I will argue (a) that it is useless to the coherentist, since if the antifoundationalist dilemma impales the foundationalist, a form of it can be turned against the coherentist to the same effect; (b) that the dilemma would be lethal not only to foundationalism and coherentism but also to the very possibility of substantive epistemology; and (c) that a form of it would have the same effect on normative ethics.

(a) According to coherentism, what justifies a belief is its membership in a coherent and comprehensive set of beliefs. But whereas being grounded on B(P) and (B(P⊃Q) is a property of a belief B(Q) that yields immediately the logical implication of Q and P and (P⊃Q) as the logical source of that property's justificatory power, the property of being a member of a coherent set is not one that immediately yields any such implication.

It may be argued, nevertheless, (i) that the property of being a member of a coherent set would supervene in any actual instance on the property of being a member of a particular set *a* that is in fact coherent, and (ii) that this would enable us to preserve our Intellectualist Model, since (iii) the justification of the member belief B(Q) by its membership in *a* would then be parasitical on the logical relations among the beliefs in *a* which constitute the coherence of that set of beliefs, and (iv) the justification of B(Q) by the fact that it is part of a coherent set would then be *indirectly* parasitical on logical relations among propositions after all.

But if such an indirect form of parasitism is allowed, then the experience of pain may perhaps be said to justify belief in its existence parasticially on the fact that P logically implies P! The Intellectualist Model seems either so trivial as to be dull, or else sharp enough to cut equally against both foundationalism and coherentism.

(b) If (i) only propositional attitudes can justify such propositional attitudes as belief, and if (ii) to do so they must in turn be justified by yet other propositional attitudes, it seems clear that (iii) there is no hope of contructing a complete epistemology, one which would give us, in theory, an account of what the justification of any justified belief would supervene on. For (i) and (ii) would rule out the possibility of a finite regress of justification.

(c) If only propositional attitudes can justify propositional attitudes, and if to do so they must in turn be justified by yet other propositional attitudes, it seems clear that there is no hope of constructing a complete normative ethics, one which would give us, in theory, an account of what the justification of any possible justified action would supervene upon. For the justification of an action presumably depends on the intentions it embeds and the justification of these, and here we are already within the net of propositional attitudes

from which, for the Intellectualist, there is no escape.

It seems fair to conclude that our coherentist takes his antifoundationalist zeal too far. His antifoundationalist argument helps expose some valuable insights but falls short of its malicious intent. The foundationalist emerges showing no serious damage. Indeed, he now demands equal time for a positive brief in defense of his position.

The regress argument

a. The regress argument in epistemology concludes that we must countenance beliefs that are justified in the absence of justification by other beliefs. But it reaches that conclusion only by rejecting the possibility in principle of an infinite regress of justification. It thus opts for foundational beliefs justified in some non-inferential way by ruling out a chain or pyramid of justification that has justifiers, and justifiers of justifiers, and so on *without end*. One may well find this too short a route to foundationalism, however, and demand more compelling reasons for thus rejecting an infinite regress as vicious. We shall find indeed that it is not easy to meet this demand.

b. We have seen how even the most ordinary of everyday beliefs is the tip of an iceberg. A closer look below the surface reveals a complex structure that ramifies with no end in sight. Take again my belief that driving will be dangerous tonight, at the tip of an iceberg, (I), that looks like [Figure 23.2]. The immediate cause of my belief that driving will be hazardous tonight is the sound of raindrops on the windowpane. All but one or two members of the underlying iceberg are as far as they can be from my thoughts at the time. In what sense, then, do they form an iceberg whose tip breaks the calm surface of my consciousness?

Here I will assume that the members of (I) are beliefs of the subject, even if unconscious or

(I)

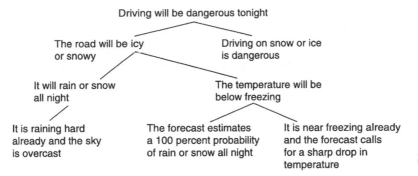

Figure 23.2

subconscious, that causally buttress and thus justify his prediction about the driving conditions.

Can the iceberg extend without end? It may appear obvious that it cannot do so, and one may jump to the conclusion that any piece of knowledge must be ultimately founded on beliefs that are *not* (inferentially) justified or warranted by other beliefs. This is a doctrine of *epistemic foundationalism*.

Let us focus not so much on the *giving* of justification as on the *having* of it. Can there be a belief that is justified in part by other beliefs, some of which are in turn justified by yet other beliefs, and so on without end? Can there be an endless regress of justification?

c. There are several familiar objections to such a regress:

(i) *Objection:* "It is incompatible with human limitations. No human subject could harbor the required infinity of beliefs." *Reply:* It is mere presumption to fathom with such assurance the depths of the mind, and especially its unconscious and dispositional depths. Besides, our object here is the nature of epistemic justification in itself and not only that of such justification as is accessible to humans. Our question is not whether humans could harbor an infinite iceberg of justification. Our question is rather whether *any* mind,

no matter how deep, could do so. Or is it ruled out in *principle* by the very nature of justification?

(ii) *Objection:* "An infinite regress is indeed ruled out in principle, for if justification were thus infinite how could it possibly end?" *Reply:* (i) If the end mentioned is *temporal*, then why must there be such an end? In the first place, the subject may be eternal. Even if he is not eternal, moreover, why must belief acquisition and justification occur seriatim? What precludes an infinite body of beliefs acquired at a single stroke? Human limitations may rule this out for humans, but we have yet to be shown that it is precluded in principle, by the very nature of justification. (ii) If the end mentioned is justificatory, on the other hand, then to ask how justification could possibly end is just to beg the question.

(iii) *Objection:* "Let us make two assumptions: first, that S's belief of q justifies his belief of p only if it works together with a justified belief on his part that q provides good evidence for p; and, second, that if S is to be justified in believing p on the basis of his belief of q and is to be justified in believing q on the basis of his belief of r, then S must be justified in believing that r provides good evidence for p via q. These assumptions imply that an actual regress of justification requires belief in an infinite proposition. Since no one (or at least no human) can believe an infinite proposition, no one (no human) can be a subject of such an actual regress."[3]

Reply: Neither of the two assumptions is beyond question, but even granting them both, it may still be doubted that the conclusion follows. It is true that each finitely complex belief of the form "r provides good evidence for p via $q_1, \ldots, q_n$" will *omit* how some members of the full infinite regress are epistemically tied to belief of p. But that seems irrelevant given the fact that for each member r of the regress, such that r is tied epistemically to belief of p, there *is* a finite belief of the required sort ("r provides good evidence for p via $q_1, \ldots, q_n$") that ties the two together. Consequently, there is no apparent reason to suppose—even granted the two assumptions—that an infinite regress will require a single belief in an infinite proposition, and not just an infinity of beliefs in increasingly complex finite propositions.

(iv) *Objection:* "But if it is allowed that justification extend infinitely, then it is too easy to justify any belief at all or too many beliefs altogether. Take, for instance, the belief that there are perfect numbers greater than 100. And suppose a mind powerful enough to believe every member of the following sequence:

$(\sigma 1)$ There is at least one
              perfect number > 100
     There are at least two
              perfect numbers >100
     There are at least three
              perfect numbers >100

If such a believer has no other belief about perfect numbers save the belief that a perfect number is a whole number equal to the sum of its whole factors, then surely he is *not* justified in believing that there

are perfect numbers greater than 100. He is quite unjustified in believing any of the members of sequence $(\sigma 1)$, in spite of the fact that a challenge to any can be met easily by appeal to its successor. Thus it cannot be allowed after all that justification extend infinitely, and an infinite regress is ruled out."

Reply: We must distinguish between regresses of justification that are actual and those that are merely potential. The difference is *not* simply that an actual regress is composed of actual beliefs. For even if all members of the regress are actual beliefs, the regress may still be *merely potential* in the following sense: while it is true that if any member *were* justified then its predecessors *would* be, still none is in fact justified. Anyone with our series of beliefs about perfect numbers in the absence of any further relevant information on such numbers would presumably be the subject of such a merely potential justificatory regress.

(v) *Objection:* "But defenders of infinite justificatory regresses cannot distinguish thus between actual regresses and those that are merely potential. There is no real distinction to be drawn between the two. For if any regress ever justifies the belief at its head, then every regress must always do so. But obviously not every regress does so (as we have seen by examples), and hence no regress can do so."[4]

Reply: One can in fact distinguish between actual justificatory regresses and merely potential ones, and one can do so both abstractly and by examples.

What an actual regress has that a merely potential regress lacks is the property of containing only justified beliefs as members. What they both share is the property of containing no member without successors that would jointly justify it.

Recall our regress about perfect numbers greater than 100: i.e. there is at least one; there are at least two; there are at least three; and so on. Each member has a successor that would justify it, but no member is justified (in the absence of further information external to the regress). That is therefore a merely potential infinite regress. As for an actual regress, I see no compelling reason why someone (if not a human, then some more powerful mind) could not hold an infinite series of actually justified beliefs as follows:

(σ2)   There is at least one even number
There are at least two even numbers
,,   three   ,,   ,,

It may be that no one could be the subject of such a series of justified beliefs unless he had a proof that there is a denumerable infinity of even numbers. But even if that should be so, it would not take away the fact of the infinite regress of potential justifiers, each of which is actually justified, and hence it would not take away the fact of the actual endless regress of justification.

The objection under discussion is confused, moreover, on the nature of the issue before us. Our question is *not* whether there can be an infinite potential regress, each member of which would be justified by its successors, such that the belief at its head is justified in virtue of its position there, at the head of such a regress. The existence and even the possibility of a single such regress with a belief at its head that was *not* justified in virtue of its position there would of course settle that question in the negative. Our question is, rather, whether there can be an actual infinite regress of justification, and the fact that a belief at the head of a potential regress might still fail to be justified despite its position does *not* settle this question. For even if there can be a merely potential regress with an unjustified belief

at its head, that leaves open the possibility of an infinite regress, each member of which is justified by its immediate successors working jointly, where every member of the regress is in addition actually justified.

The relation of justification and foundationalist strategy

The foregoing discussion is predicated on a simple conception of justification such that a set of beliefs β conditionally justifies (*would justify*) a belief X iff, necessarily, if all members of β are justified then X is also justified (if it exists). The fact that on such a conception of justification actual endless regresses—such as (σ2)—seem quite possible blocks a straightforward regress argument in favor of foundations. For it shows that an actual infinite regress cannot be dismissed out of hand.

Perhaps the foundationalist could introduce some relation of justification—presumably more complex and yet to be explicated—with respect to which it could be argued more plausibly that an actual endless regress is out of the question.

There is, however, a more straightforward strategy open to the foundationalist. For he *need not* object to the possibility of an endless regress of justification. His essential creed is the more positive belief that every justified belief must be at the head of a terminating regress. Fortunately, to affirm the universal necessity of a terminating regress is *not* to deny the bare possibility of a nonterminating regress. For a single belief can trail at once regresses of both sorts: one terminating and one not. Thus the proof of the denumerably infinite cardinality of the set of evens may provide for a powerful enough intellect a *terminating* regress for each member of the *endless* series of justified beliefs:

(σ2)   There is at least one even number
There are at least two even numbers
,,   three   ,,   ,,

At the same time, it is obvious that each member of (σ2) lies at the head of an actual endless regress of justification, on the assumption that each member is conditionally justified by its successor, which is in turn actually justified.

"Thank you so much," the foundationalist may sneer, "but I really do not need that kind of help. Nor do I need to be reminded of my essential creed, which I know as well as anyone. Indeed my rejection of endless regresses of justification is only a means of supporting my view that every justified belief must rest ultimately on foundations, on a terminating regress. You reject that strategy much too casually, in my view, but I will not object here. So we put that strategy aside. And now, my helpful friend, just what do we put in its place?"

Fair enough. How then could one show the need for foundations if an endless regress is not ruled out?

Two levels of foundationalism

a. We need to distinguish, first, between two forms of foundationalism: one *formal*, the other *substantive*. A type of *formal foundationalism* with respect to a normative or evaluative property φ is the view that the conditions (actual and possible) within which φ would apply can be specified in general, perhaps recursively. *Substantive foundationalism* is only a particular way of doing so, and coherentism is another.

Simpleminded hedonism is the view that:

(i)   every instance of pleasure is good,
(ii) everything that causes something good is itself good, and
(iii) everything that is good is so in virtue of (i) or (ii) above.

Simpleminded hedonism is a type of formal foundationalism with respect to the good.

Classical foundationalism in epistemology is the view that:

(i)   every infallible, indubitable belief is justified,

(ii) every belief deductively inferred from justified beliefs is itself justified, and
(iii) every belief that is justified is so in virtue of (i) or (ii) above.

Classical foundationalism is a type of formal foundationalism with respect to epistemic justification.

Both of the foregoing theories—simpleminded hedonism in ethics, and classical foundationalism in epistemology—are of course flawed. But they both remain examples of formal foundationalist theories.

b. One way of arguing in favor of formal foundationalism in epistemology is to formulate a convincing formal foundationalist theory of justification. But classical foundationalism in epistemology no longer has for many the attraction that it had for Descartes, nor has any other form of epistemic foundationalism won general acceptance. Indeed epistemic foundationalism has been generally abandoned and its advocates have been put on the defensive by the writings of Wittgenstein, Quine, Sellars, Rescher, Aune, Harman, Lehrer, and others. It is lamentable that in our headlong rush away from foundationalism we have lost sight of the different types of foundationalism (formal vs. substantive) and of the different grades of each type. Too many of us now see it as a blur to be decried and avoided. Thus our present attempt to bring it all into better focus.

c. If we cannot argue from a generally accepted foundationalist theory, what reason is there to accept formal foundationalism? There is no reason to think that the conditions (actual and possible) within which an object is spherical are generally specifiable in nongeometric terms. Why should we think that the conditions (actual and possible) within which a belief is epistemically justified are generally specifiable in nonepistemic terms?

So far as I can see, the main reason for accepting formal foundationalism in the absence of an actual, convincing formal foundationalist theory is the very plausible idea that epistemic justification is subject to the supervenience that characterizes normative and evaluative properties generally. Thus, if a car is a good car, then any physical replica of that car must be just as good. If it is a good car in virtue of such properties as being economical, little prone to break down, etc., then surely any exact replica would share all such properties and would thus be equally good. Similarly, if a belief is epistemically justified, it is presumably so in virtue of its character and its basis in perception, memory, or inference (if any). Thus any belief exactly like it in its character and its basis must be equally well justified. Epistemic justification is supervenient. The justification of a belief supervenes on such properties of it as its content and its basis (if any) in perception, memory, or inference. Such a doctrine of supervenience may itself be considered, with considerable justice, a grade of foundationalism. For it entails that every instance of justified belief is founded on a number of its nonepistemic properties, such as its having a certain basis in perception, memory, and inference, or the like.

But there are higher grades of foundationalism as well. There is, for instance, the doctrine that the conditions (actual and possible) within which a belief would be epistemically justified *can be specified* in general, perhaps recursively (and by reference to such notions as perception, memory, and inference).

A higher grade yet of formal foundationalism requires not only that the conditions for justified belief be specifiable, in general, but that they be specifiable by a simple, comprehensive theory.

d. Simpleminded hedonism is a formal foundationalist theory of the highest grade. If it is true, then in every possible world goodness supervenes on pleasure and causation in a way that is recursively specifiable by means of a very simple theory.

Classical foundationalism in epistemology is also a formal foundationalist theory of the highest grade. If it is true, then in every possible world epistemic justification supervenes on infallibility cum indubitability and deductive inference in a way that is recursively specifiable by means of a very simple theory.

Surprisingly enough, coherentism may also turn out to be formal foundationalism of the highest grade, provided only that the concept of coherence is itself both simple enough and free of any normative or evaluative admixture. Given these provisos, coherentism explains how epistemic justification supervenes on the nonepistemic in a theory of remarkable simplicity: a belief is justified iff it has a place within a system of beliefs that is coherent and comprehensive.

It is a goal of ethics to explain how the ethical rightness of an action supervenes on what is not ethically evaluative or normative. Similarly, it is a goal of epistemology to explain how the epistemic justification of a belief supervenes on what is not epistemically evaluative or normative. If coherentism aims at this goal, that imposes restrictions on the notion of coherence, which must now be conceived innocent of epistemically evaluative or normative admixture. Its substance must therefore consist of such concepts as explanation, probability, and logical implication—with these conceived, in turn, innocent of normative or evaluative content.

e. We have found a surprising kinship between coherentism and substantive foundationalism, both of which turn out to be varieties of a deeper foundationalism. This deeper foundationalism is applicable to any normative or evaluative property φ, and it comes in three grades. The first or lowest is simply the supervenience of φ: the idea that whenever something has φ its having it is founded on certain others of its properties which fall into certain restricted sorts. The *second* is the explicable supervenience of φ: the idea that there are formulable principles that explain in quite general terms the conditions (actual and possible) within which φ applies. The third and highest is the easily explicable supervenience of φ: the idea that there is a *simple* theory that explains the conditions within which φ applies. We have found the coherentist and the substantive foundationalist sharing a primary goal: the development of a formal foundationalist theory of the highest grade. For they both want a simple theory that explains precisely how epistemic justification supervenes, in general, on the nonepistemic. This insight gives us an unusual viewpoint on some recent attacks against foundationalism. Let us now consider as an example a certain simple form of argument distilled from the recent anti-foundationalist literature.[5]

Doxastic ascent arguments

Several attacks on foundationalism turn on a sort of "doxastic ascent" argument that calls for closer scrutiny.[6] Here are two examples:

A.   A belief B is foundationally justified for S in virtue of having property F only if S is justified in believing (1) that most at least of his beliefs with property F are true, and (2) that B has property F. But this means that belief B is not foundational after all, and indeed that the very notion of (empirical) foundational belief is incoherent.

It is sometimes held, for example, that perceptual or observational beliefs are often justified through their origin in the exercise of one or more of our five senses in standard conditions of perception. The advocate of doxastic ascent would raise a vigorous protest, however, for in his view the mere fact of such sensory prompting is impotent to justify the belief prompted. Such prompting must be coupled with the further belief that one's senses work well in the circumstances, or the like. For we are dealing here with *knowledge*, which requires not blind faith but *reasoned* trust. But now surely the further belief about the reliability of one's

senses itself cannot rest on blind faith but requires its own backing of reasons, and we are off on the regress.

B.   A belief B of proposition P is foundationally justified for S only if S is justified in believing that there are no factors present that would cause him to make mistakes on the matter of the proposition P. But, again, this means that belief B is not foundational after all and indeed that the notion of (empirical) foundational belief is incoherent.

From the vantage point of formal foundationalism, neither of these arguments seems persuasive. In the first place, as we have seen, what makes a belief foundational (formally) is its having a property that is nonepistemic (not evaluative in the epistemic or cognitive mode), and does not involve inference from other beliefs, but guarantees, via a necessary principle, that the belief in question is justified. A belief B is made foundational by having some such nonepistemic property that yields its justification. Take my belief that I am in pain in a context where it is caused by my being in pain. The property that my belief then has, of being a self-attribution of pain caused by one's own pain is, let us suppose, a nonepistemic property that yields the justification of any belief that has it. So my belief that I am in pain is in that context foundationally justified. Along with my belief that I am in pain, however, there come other beliefs that are equally well justified, such as my belief that someone is in pain. Thus I am foundationally justified in believing that I am in pain only if I am justified in believing that someone is in pain. Those who object to foundationalism as in A or B above are hence mistaken in thinking that their premises would refute foundationalism. The fact is that they would not touch it. For a belief is no less foundationally justified for having its justification yoked to that of another closely related belief.

The advocate of arguments like A and B must apparently strengthen his premises. He must apparently claim that the beliefs whose justification is entailed by the foundationally justified status of belief B must in some sense function as a *necessary source* of the justification of B. And this would of course preclude giving B foundationally justified status. For if the *being justified* of those beliefs is an *essential* part of the source of the justification of B, then it is ruled out that there be a wholly *nonepistemic* source of B's justification.

That brings us to a second point about A and B, for it should now be clear that these cannot be selectively aimed at foundationalism. In particular, they seem neither more nor less valid objections to coherentism than to foundationalism, or so I will now argue about each of them in turn.

A′.   A belief X is justified for S in virtue of membership in a coherent set only if S is justified in believing (1) that most at least of his beliefs with the property of thus cohering are true, and (2) that X has that property.

Any coherentist who accepts A seems bound to accept A′. For what could he possibly appeal to as a relevant difference? But A′ is a quicksand of endless depth. (How is he justified in believing A′(1)? Partly through justified belief that it coheres? And what would justify *this*? And so on . . .)

B′.   A belief X is justified for S only if S is justified in believing that there are no factors present that would cause him to make mistakes on the subject matter of that belief.

Again, any coherentist who accepts B seems bound to accept B′. But this is just another road to the quicksand. (For S is justified in believing that there are no such factors only if . . . and so on.)

Why are such regresses vicious? The key is again, to my mind, the doctrine of supervenience. Such regresses are vicious because they would be logically incompatible with the supervenience of epistemic justification on such nonepistemic facts as the totality of a subject's beliefs, his cognitive and experiential history, and as many other nonepistemic facts as may seem at all relevant. The idea is that there is a set of such nonepistemic facts surrounding a justified belief such that no belief could possibly have been surrounded by those very facts without being justified. Advocates of A or B run afoul of such supervenience, since they are surely committed to the more general views derivable from either of A or B by deleting 'foundationally' from its first sentence. In each case the more general view would then preclude the possibility of supervenience, since it would entail that the source of justification *always* includes an *epistemic* component.

Coherentism and substantive foundationalism

a. The notions of coherentism and substantive foundationalism remain unexplicated. We have relied so far on our intuitive grasp of them. In this section we shall consider reasons for the view that substantive foundationalism is superior to coherentism. To assess these reasons, we need some more explicit account of the difference between the two.

By coherentism we shall mean any view according to which the ultimate sources of justification for any belief lie in relations among that belief and other beliefs of the subject: explanatory relations, perhaps, or relations of probability or logic.

According to substantive foundationalism, as it is to be understood here, there are ultimate sources of justification other than relations among beliefs. Traditionally these additional sources have pertained to the special content of the belief or its special relations to the subjective experience of the believer.

b. The view that justification is a matter of relations among beliefs is open to an objection from alternative coherent systems or detachment from reality, depending on one's perspective. From the latter perspective the body of beliefs is held constant and the surrounding world is allowed to vary, whereas from the former perspective it is the surrounding world that is held constant while the body of beliefs is allowed to vary. In either case, according to the coherentist, there could be no effect on the justification for any belief.

Let us sharpen the question before us as follows. Is there reason to think that there is at least one system B′, alternative to our actual system of beliefs B, such that B′ contains a belief X with the following properties:

(i)   in our present nonbelief circumstances we would not be justified in having belief X even if we accepted along with that belief (as our total system of beliefs) the entire belief system B′ in which it is embedded (no matter how acceptance of B′ were brought about); and

(ii) that is so despite the fact that belief X coheres within B′ at least as fully as does some actual justified belief of ours within our actual belief system B (where the justification of that actual justified belief is alleged by the coherentist to derive solely from its coherence within our actual body of beliefs B).

The coherentist is vulnerable to counterexamples of this sort right at the surface of his body of beliefs, where we find beliefs with minimal coherence, whose detachment and replacement with contrary beliefs would have little effect on the coherence of the body. Thus take my belief that I have a headache when I do have a splitting headache, and let us suppose that this *does* cohere within my present body of beliefs. (Thus I have no reason to doubt my present introspective beliefs, and so on. And if my belief does *not* cohere, so much the worse for coherentism, since my belief is surely justified.) Here then we have a perfectly justified or warranted belief. And yet such a belief may well have relevant relations of explanation, logic, or probability with at most a small set of other beliefs of mine at the time: say, that I am not free of headache, that I am in pain, that someone is in pain, and the like. If so, then an equally coherent alternative is not far to seek. Let everything remain constant, *including* the splitting headache, except for the following: replace the belief that I have a headache with the belief that I do *not* have a headache, the belief that I am in pain with the belief that I am *not* in pain, the belief that someone is in pain with the belief that someone is *not* in pain, and so on. I contend that my resulting hypothetical system of beliefs would cohere as fully as does my actual system of beliefs, and yet my hypothetical belief that I do *not* have a headache would not therefore be justified. What makes this difference concerning justification between my actual belief that I have a headache and the hypothetical belief that I am free of headache, each as coherent as the other within its own system, if not the actual splitting headache? But the headache is *not* itself a belief nor a relation among beliefs and is thus in no way constitutive of the internal coherence of my body of beliefs.

Some might be tempted to respond by alleging that one's belief about whether or not one has a headache is always *infallible*. But since we could devise similar examples for the various sensory modalities and propositional attitudes, the response given for the case of headache would have to be generalized. In effect, it would have to cover "peripheral" beliefs generally— beliefs at the periphery of one's body of beliefs, minimally coherent with the rest. These peripheral beliefs would all be said to be infallible. That is, again, a possible response, but it leads to a capitulation by the coherentist to the radical foundationalist on a crucial issue that has traditionally divided them: the infallibility of beliefs about one's own subjective states.

What is more, not all peripheral beliefs are about one's own subjective states. The direct realist is probably right that some beliefs about our surroundings are uninferred and yet justified. Consider my present belief that the table before me is oblong. This presumably coheres with such other beliefs of mine as that the table has the same shape as the piece of paper before me, which is oblong, and a different shape than the window frame here, which is square, and so on. So far as I can see, however, there is no insurmountable obstacle to replacing that whole set of coherent beliefs with an equally coherent set as follows: that the table before me is square, that the table has the same shape as the square window frame, and a different shape than the piece of paper, which is oblong, and so on. The important points are (a) that this replacement may be made without changing the rest of one's body of beliefs or any aspect of the world beyond, including one's present visual experience of something oblong, not square, as one looks at the table before one; and (b) that is so, in part, because of the fact (c) that the subject need not have any beliefs about his present sensory experience.

Some might be tempted to respond by alleging that one's present experience is *self-intimating*, i.e. always necessarily taken note of and reflected in one's beliefs. Thus if anyone has visual experience of something oblong, then he believes that he has such experience. But this would involve a further important concession by the coherentist to the radical foundationalist, who would have been granted two of his most cherished doctrines: the infallibility of introspective belief and the self-intimation of experience.

The foundationalist's dilemma

The antifoundationalist zeal of recent years has left several forms of foundationalism standing. These all share the conviction that a belief can be justified not only by its coherence within a comprehensive system but also by an appropriate combination of observational content and origin in the use of the senses in standard conditions. What follows presents a dilemma for any foundationalism based on any such idea.

a. We may surely suppose that beings with observational mechanisms radically unlike ours might also have knowledge of their environment. (That seems possible even if the radical difference in observational mechanisms precludes overlap in substantive concepts and beliefs.)

b. Let us suppose that there is such a being, for whom experience of type φ (of which we have no notion) has a role with respect to his beliefs of type φ analogous to the role that our visual experience has with respect to our visual beliefs. Thus we might have a schema such as the following:

Human	Extraterrestrial being
Visual experience	φ experience
Experience of something red	Experience of something F
Belief that there is something red before one	Belief that there is something F before one

c. It is often recognized that our visual experience intervenes in two ways with respect to our visual beliefs: as cause and as justification. But these are not wholly independent. Presumably, the justification of the belief that something here is red derives at least in part from the fact that it originates in a visual experience of something red that takes place in normal circumstances.

d. Analogously, the extraterrestrial belief that something here has the property of being F might be justified partly by the fact that it originates in a φ experience of something F that takes place in normal circumstances.

e. A simple question presents the foundationalist's dilemma: regarding the epistemic principle that underlies our justification for believing that something here is red on the basis of our visual experience of something red, is it proposed as a fundamental principle or as a derived generalization? Let us compare the famous Principle of Utility of value theory, according to which it is best for that to happen which, of all the possible alternatives in the circumstances, would bring with it into the world the greatest balance of pleasure over pain, joy over sorrow, happiness over unhappiness, content over discontent, or the like. Upon this fundamental principle one may then base various generalizations, rules of thumb, and maxims of public health, nutrition, legislation, etiquette, hygiene, and so on. But these are all then derived generalizations which rest for their validity on the fundamental principle. Similarly, one may also ask, with respect to the generalizations advanced by our foundationalist, whether these are proposed as fundamental principles or as derived maxims or the like. This sets him face to face with a dilemma, each of whose alternatives is problematic. If his proposals are meant to have the status of secondary or derived maxims, for instance, then it would be quite unphilosophical to stop there. Let us turn, therefore, to the other alternative.

f. On reflection it seems rather unlikely that epistemic principles for the justification of observational beliefs by their origin in sensory experience could have a status more fundamental than that of derived generalizations. For by granting such principles fundamental status we would open the door to a multitude of equally basic principles with no unifying factor. There would be some for vision, some for hearing, etc., without even mentioning the corresponding extraterrestrial principles.

g. It may appear that there is after all an idea, however, that unifies our multitude of principles. For they all involve sensory experience and sensible characteristics. But what is a sensible characteristic? Aristotle's answer appeals to examples: colors, shapes, sounds, and so on. Such a notion might enable us to unify per-

ceptual epistemic principles under some more fundamental principle such as the following:

> If σ is a sensible characteristic, then the belief that there is something with σ before one is (prima facie) justified if it is based on a visual experience of something with σ in conditions that are normal with respect to σ.

h. There are at least two difficulties with such a suggestion, however, and neither one can be brushed aside easily. First, it is not clear that we can have a viable notion of sensible characteristic on the basis of examples so diverse as colors, shapes, tones, odors, and so on. Second, the authority of such a principle apparently derives from contingent circumstances concerning the reliability of beliefs prompted by sensory experiences of certain sorts. According to the foundationalist, our visual beliefs are justified by their origin in our visual experience or the like. Would such beliefs be equally well justified in a world where beliefs with such an origin were nearly always false?

i. In addition, finally, even if we had a viable notion of such characteristics, it is not obvious that fundamental knowledge of reality would have to derive causally or otherwise from sensory experience of such characteristics. How could one impose reasonable limits on extraterrestrial mechanisms for noninferential acquisition of beliefs? Is it not possible that such mechanisms need not always function through sensory experience of any sort? Would such beings necessarily be denied any knowledge of their surroundings and indeed of any contingent spatio-temporal fact? Let us suppose them to possess a complex system of true beliefs concerning their surroundings, the structures below the surface of things, exact details of history and geography, all constituted by concepts none of which corresponds to any of our sensible characteristics. What then? Is it not possible that their basic beliefs should all concern fields of force, waves, mathematical structures, and numerical assignments to variables in several dimensions? This is no doubt an exotic notion, but even so it still seems conceivable. And if it is in fact possible, what then shall we say of the noninferential beliefs of such beings? Would we have to concede the existence of special epistemic principles that can validate their noninferential beliefs? Would it not be preferable to formulate more abstract principles that can cover both human and extraterrestrial foundations? If such more abstract principles are in fact accessible, then the less general principles that define the human foundations and those that define the extraterrestrial foundations are both derived principles whose validity depends on that of the more abstract principles. In this the human and extraterrestrial epistemic principles would resemble rules of good nutrition for an infant and an adult. The infant's rules would of course be quite unlike those valid for the adult. But both would still be based on a more fundamental principle that postulates the ends of well-being and good health. What more fundamental principles might support both human and extraterrestrial knowledge in the way that those concerning good health and well-being support rules of nutrition for both the infant and the adult?

Reliabilism: an ethics of moral virtues and an epistemology of intellectual virtues

In what sense is the doctor attending Frau Hitler justified in performing an action that brings with it far less value than one of its accessible alternatives? According to one promising idea, the key is to be found in the rules that he embodies through stable dispositions. His action is the result of certain stable virtues, and there are no equally virtuous alternate *dispositions* that, given his cognitive limitations, he might have embodied with equal or better total consequences, and that would have led him to

infanticide in the circumstances. The important move for our purpose is the stratification of justification. Primary justification attaches to virtues and other dispositions, to stable dispositions to act, through their greater contribution of value when compared with alternatives. Secondary justification attaches to particular acts in virtue of their source in virtues or other such justified dispositions.

The same strategy may also prove fruitful in epistemology. Here primary justification would apply to *intellectual* virtues, to stable dispositions for belief acquisition, through their greater contribution toward getting us to the truth. Secondary justification would then attach to particular beliefs in virtue of their source in intellectual virtues or other such justified dispositions.[7]

That raises parallel questions for ethics and epistemology. We need to consider more carefully the concept of a virtue and the distinction between moral and intellectual virtues. In epistemology, there is reason to think that the most useful and illuminating notion of intellectual virtue will prove broader than our tradition would suggest and must give due weight not only to the subject and his intrinsic nature but also to his environment and to his epistemic community. This is a large topic, however, to which I hope some of us will turn with more space, and insight, than I can now command.[8]

Summary

1   *Two assumptions:* (A1) that for a belief to constitute knowledge it must be (a) true and (b) justified; and (A2) that the justification relevant to whether or not one knows is a sort of epistemic or theoretical justification to be distinguished from its practical counterpart.

2   *Knowledge and criteria.* Particularism is distinguished from methodism: the first gives priority to particular examples of

knowledge over general methods of criteria, whereas the second reverses that order. The methodism of Descartes leads him to an elaborate dogmatism whereas that of Hume leads him to a very simple skepticism. The particularist is, of course, antiskeptical on principle.

3   *Two metaphors: the raft and the pyramid.* For the foundationalist every piece of knowledge stands at the apex of a pyramid that rests on stable and secure foundations whose stability and security does not derive from the upper stories or sections. For the coherentist a body of knowledge is a free-floating raft every plank of which helps directly or indirectly to keep all the others in place, and no plank of which would retain its status with no help from the others.

4   *A coherentist critique of foundationalism.* No mental state can provide a foundation for empirical knowledge. For if such a state is propositional, then it is fallible and hence no secure foundation. But if it is *not* propositional, then how can it possibly serve as a foundation for belief? How can one infer or justify anything on the basis of a state that, having no propositional content, must be logically dumb? An analogy with ethics suggests a reason to reject this dilemma. Other reasons are also advanced and discussed.

5   *The regress argument.* In defending his position, the foundationalist often attempts to rule out the very possibility of an infinite regress of justification (which leads him to the necessity for a foundation). Some of his arguments to that end are examined.

6   *The relation of justification and foundationalist strategy.* An alternative foundationalist strategy is exposed, one that does not require ruling out the possibility of an infinite regress of justification.

7   *Two levels of foundationalism.* Substantive foundationalism is distinguished from formal foundationalism, three grades of which are exposed: first, the supervenience of epistemic justification; second, its explicable supervenience; and, third, its supervenience explicable by means of a simple theory. There turns out to be a surprising kinship between coherentism and substantive foundationalism, both of which aim at a formal foundationalism of the highest grade, at a theory of the greatest simplicity that explains how epistemic justification supervenes on non-epistemic factors.

8   *Doxastic ascent arguments.* The distinction between formal and substantive foundationalism provides an unusual viewpoint on some recent attacks against foundationalism. We consider doxastic ascent arguments as an example.

9   *Coherentism and substantive foundationalism.* It is argued that substantive foundationalism is superior since coherentism is unable to account adequately for the epistemic status of beliefs at the "periphery" of a body of beliefs.

10   *The foundationalist's dilemma.* All foundationalism based on sense experience is subject to a fatal dilemma.

11   *Reliabilism.* An alternative to foundationalism of sense experience is sketched.

Notes

1   But Descartes's methodism was at most partial. James Van Cleve has supplied the materials for a convincing argument that the way out of the Cartesian circle is through a particularism of basic knowledge. (See James Van Cleve, "Foundationalism, Epistemic Principles, and the Cartesian Circle," *The Philosophical Review* 88 (1979): 55–91.) But this is, of course, compatible with methodism on inferred knowledge. Whether Descartes subscribed to such methodism is hard (perhaps impossible) to determine, since in the end he makes room for all the kinds of knowledge required by particularism. But his language when he introduces the method of

hyperbolic doubt, and the order in which he proceeds, suggest that he did subscribe to such methodism.

2 Cf. Laurence BonJour, "The Coherence Theory of Truth," *Philosophical Studies* 30 (1976): 281–312; and, especially, Michael Williams, *Groundless Belief* (New Haven, 1977); and L. BonJour, "Can Empirical Knowledge Have a Foundation?" *American Philosophical Quarterly* 15 (1978): 1–15.

3 Cf. Richard Foley, "Inferential Justification and the Infinite Regress," *American Philosophical Quarterly* 15 (1978): 311–16.

4 Cf. John Post, "Infinite Regress Arguments," *Philosophical Studies* 34 (1980).

5 The argument of this whole section is developed in greater detail in my paper "The Foundations of Foundationalism", *Nous* (1980).

6 For some examples of the influence of doxastic ascent arguments, see Wilfrid Sellars's writing in epistemology: e.g. "Empiricism and the Philosophy of Mind" in *Science, Perception, and Reality*, especially section VIII, and particularly p. 168. Also I. T. Oakley, "An Argument for Skepticism Concerning Justified Beliefs," *American Philosophical Quarterly* 13 (1976): 221–28; and BonJour, "Can Empirical Knowledge Have a Foundation?"

7 This puts in a more traditional perspective the contemporary effort to develop a "causal theory of knowing." From our viewpoint, this effort is better understood not as an attempt to *define* propositional knowledge but as an attempt to formulate fundamental principles of justification.

Cf. the work of D. Armstrong, *Belief, Truth and Knowledge* (London, 1973); and that of F. Dretske, A. Goldman, and M. Swain, whose relevant already published work is included in *Essays on Knowledge and Justification*, ed. G. Pappas and M. Swain (Ithaca and London, 1978). But the theory is still under development by Goldman and by Swain, who have reached general conclusions about it similar to those suggested here, though not necessarily—so far as I know—for the same reasons or in the same overall context.

8 I am indebted above all to Roderick Chisholm: for his writings and for innumerable discussions. The main ideas in the present paper were first presented in a seminar of 1976–77 at the University of Texas. I am grateful to Anthony Anderson, David and Jean Blumenfeld, Laurence BonJour, and Martin Perlmutter, who made that seminar a valuable stimulus. Subsequent criticism by my colleague James Van Cleve has also been valuable and stimulating.

PART SEVEN

What is the nature of the epistemic 'ought'?

INTRODUCTION TO PART SEVEN

Ram Neta and Duncan Pritchard

IF YOU ARE A WELL-EDUCATED American or European adult, then there are plenty of things that you ought to know. For instance, you ought to know that George W. Bush was president of the United States early in the twenty-first century, that France is not a monarchy, that Italy has many miles of Mediterranean coastline, that the euro is the currency most widely used in Europe, that Germany is a more populous nation that Switzerland, that the area of Russia is larger than that of Belgium and that millions of people were killed in each of the two world wars fought on European soil in the twentieth century. There are, of course, plenty of other facts that you might or might not know, but the facts that I've listed above are facts that you *ought* to know.

So there are some things that you ought to know. But there are also some propositions that you ought not believe. For instance, you ought not believe that the president of the United States is Gordon Brown, that the president of France is Benito Mussolini, that Italy is an island, that the shekel is the currency most widely used in Europe, that Switzerland is a more populous nation than Germany, that the area of Belgium is larger than that of Russia or that nobody was seriously hurt in World War I or World War II. These are all things that you ought not believe, at least not if you are a comfortable, well-educated American or European adult living today.

We have just stated some facts about what you ought to know, and some facts about what you ought not believe. But in addition to there being facts that you ought to know, and propositions that you ought not believe, there are also propositions that you ought to believe. For instance, if you are a normal human adult, then you ought to believe that you will die before you reach 120 years of age. But suppose that you end up living past 120 years of age. Does that mean that it was never true that you ought to have believed that you would die before you reached 120 years of age? Clearly not: given your evidence and your circumstances, you ought to have believed that you would die before reaching 120 years of age, even if that belief was false, and so you could not possibly have known that you would die before reaching 120 years of age.

So there are some things that you ought to know, some things that you ought to believe and some things that you ought not believe. Furthermore, there are some things of which you ought to be very confident, some things of which you ought to be somewhat less confident and some things of which you ought not to be confident at all. For instance, you ought to be very confident that it will snow somewhere in Canada this winter, you ought to be slightly less confident that it will snow in Montreal this winter and you ought not be at all confident that it will snow in Florida this winter (indeed, you ought to be rather confident that it will not snow in Florida this winter).

But what makes it the case that you *ought* to know something, or believe something, or not believe something, or be more or less confident in something? What makes these epistemic 'ought' claims true? The readings in this part are devoted to addressing one or another facet of this question.

The part begins with a popular 1877 essay, 'The Ethics of Belief' (Chapter 24), written by the English mathematician W. K. Clifford (1845–79). In this essay, Clifford argues for the startling thesis that 'it is wrong always, everywhere, and for anyone, to believe anything upon insufficient evidence'. When Clifford says that it is 'wrong' for us to do this, he is using the term 'wrong' in its moral sense: it is, Clifford argues, *a violation of our moral duty* to believe anything upon insufficient evidence. Thus, on Clifford's view, just as it is a violation of our moral duty to believe a man guilty of murder upon insufficient evidence, it is also a violation of our moral duty to believe the tenets of some religion upon insufficient evidence. This, of course, raises for Clifford the question of what evidence is sufficient, and under what conditions the testimony of others provides sufficient evidence for us to believe them. Much of Clifford's essay is devoted to addressing the latter question, and in particular to explaining why we may believe much of what modern science tells us, but not much of what religion tells us.

The influential American philosopher William James (1842–1910), one of the pioneers of the American school of philosophy known as 'pragmatism', replied to Clifford in his seminal essay 'The Will to Believe' (Chapter 25). James argued that it is not always wrong to believe something on the basis of insufficient evidence. Suppose, for example, that you have climbed up a mountain and have now reached a crevasse. You cannot climb back down the mountain because the terrain has become impassable. You have a choice: either jump over the crevasse, risking your life in so doing, or else remain stranded and likely die of prolonged exposure and dehydration. Between these two options, you reasonably prefer the former, since it provides your best chance for survival. But the likelihood of your successfully jumping over the crevasse depends upon your firmly believing that you can do so: if you do not believe that you can jump over the crevasse, then your attempt to do so will likely falter, and you will fall to your death. In circumstances such as this, James says, it is not wrong for you to believe that you are capable of successfully jumping over the crevasse, even if you lack evidence in support of this belief. More generally, according to James, whenever we are faced with a choice between various hypotheses where the choice is forced (i.e. the hypotheses are jointly logically exhaustive), living (i.e. each of the hypotheses is one that we could bring ourselves to believe), and momentous (i.e. it is of great practical consequence which hypothesis we believe, if any), it is permissible for us to believe one of the hypotheses that we take to be best for us to believe, whether or not it is supported by sufficient evidence. Thus, James concludes, it is *not* 'wrong always, everywhere, and for anyone, to believe anything upon insufficient evidence'.

Both Clifford and James assume that, once we assess the strength of someone's evidence for a belief, there remains a further, substantive question whether it is wrong for that person to hold that belief, and that the answer to this further question depends, at least in part, on how strongly the person's evidence supports that belief. In contrast, Roderick Chisholm's (1916–99) approach to the ethics of belief (Chapter 26) is to explain the strength of someone's evidence in support of a belief by appeal to (allegedly) primitive facts of the form *the proposition* p *is more worthy of person S's belief than is the proposition* q. Notice that, so long as we regard as primitive facts about which propositions are more worthy of someone's belief than which other propositions, it is open to us to say that the proposition that the mountain climber is capable of successfully jumping the crevasse is more worthy of her belief than its negation. But if we do this, then, by Chisholm's lights, we will be in a position to say that the mountain climber does have sufficient evidence to believe that she is capable of successfully jumping the crevasse! The strength of our evidence may thus – consistently with Chisholm's view – be understood to depend upon what we may permissibly believe, and not just vice versa.

Notice, however, that, despite their many differences of doctrine and approach, Clifford, James and Chisholm all agree on one point: the epistemic 'ought' facts that we are seeking to explain are facts about what is permissible, impermissible or obligatory. When someone ought not believe something, it is impermissible for her to believe it; when someone ought to believe something, it is permissible for her to believe it; when someone ought to be more confident of p than of q, it is impermissible for her to be no more confident of p than of q; and so on. In short, Clifford, James, and Chisholm all treat epistemic 'oughts' as *deontological* (viz. of or pertaining to *duties*). This is precisely the point on which William Alston (1921–) challenges all of them. As Alston argues in his article 'The Deontological Conception of Epistemic Justification' (Chapter 27), the epistemic appraisal of beliefs and of believers cannot be understood as the appraisal of their success or failure in fulfilling their duty, and that is because (1) we cannot have duties concerning matters beyond our direct control and (2) we cannot directly control our beliefs or credal states more generally. Thus, for Alston, epistemic appraisal cannot be understood deontologically.

Richard Fumerton (1949–) agrees that epistemic appraisal cannot be understood deontologically. But, in his article 'Epistemic Justification and Normativity' (Chapter 28), he argues that the property most centrally involved in epistemic appraisal – the property of epistemic justification – cannot be understood as 'normative' in *any* interesting sense of that philosophical term. Philosophers use the term 'normative' to characterize moral judgements, moral claims and moral properties (e.g. the property of being blameworthy), and to contrast them with, for instance, judgements about the mass of objects, claims about the mass of objects and the property of mass. But it is not entirely obvious what it is about moral judgements, claims and properties that makes them 'normative', and makes, say, judgements of mass, claims about mass and the property of mass non-normative. Fumerton considers various more or less plausible ways of understanding the difference between the normative and the non-normative, and argues that, on none of these ways of distinguishing the normative from the non-normative, do judgements concerning epistemic justification, claims concerning epistemic justification or the property of epistemic justification turn out to be normative in any interesting sense.

For example, Fumerton points out, when I say that a belief is unjustified, I am typically *criticising* that belief. But this cannot render my claim normative in any interesting sense, for it is also true, as Fumerton points out, that when I say that a car accelerates very slowly, I am typically criticising the car. Just as this latter fact has no tendency to show that the property of *accelerating very slowly* is a normative property in any interesting sense, so too, Fumerton claims, the former fact has no tendency to show that the property of *being epistemically justified* is a normative property in any interesting sense.

Whether or not Fumerton is right about this, we can still attempt to answer our original question concerning epistemic 'oughts', viz. what sorts of things make it the case that one ought to believe something, or ought not believe something, or ought to be highly confident of something, etc. A recently influential approach to this question is suggested, though not spelled out, in the last reading of this part, a selection from Edward Craig's (1942–) 1990 book *Knowledge and the State of Nature* (Chapter 29). What Craig is trying to do in that book is understand the nature of knowledge by appeal to a hypothesis about the point of having a concept of knowledge in circulation in society. Craig's hypothesis is this: the point of having a concept of knowledge is to enable us to flag approved sources of information on one or another topic. More precisely, the point of having locutions of the form 'S knows wh . . .' (e.g. 'knows when it's going to start raining', 'knows where the buffalo are sleeping', 'knows which direction the antelopes tend to run when you chase them', 'knows who will be doing the hunting tonight', 'knows why the bow and arrow tend to work for hunting rabbits but not for hunting armadillos', etc.) is to indicate to each other whom to consult on one or another question. Craig's book is devoted to showing that this hypothesis about the point of having the concept of knowledge sheds a great deal of light on the concept of knowledge, and on the nature of knowledge. But could a suitably generalised hypothesis concerning the point of having terms of epistemic appraisal also shed light on the nature of the properties ascribed in the course of epistemic appraisal? Might we gain some understanding of the nature of the epistemic 'oughts' to which we are subject by considering the point of the practice of making these 'ought' judgements or 'ought' claims? This question is a topic of much current research.

Study questions

1   Reconstruct Clifford's argument for his thesis that 'it is wrong always, everywhere, and for anyone, to believe anything upon insufficient evidence'. To precisely what point in this argument would James object? Would Chisholm accept this argument?

2   Do you agree with James that it is permissible for the mountain climber (in James's fictional example) to believe that she is capable of successfully jumping the crevasse? If not, then explain why not. If so, then explain just what it is about the mountain climber that makes it permissible for her to believe this.

3   The reading from Chisholm begins with Chisholm's defining the schematic and technical locution 'there is something that S perceives to be F'. Tracing out the long chains of definitions in the Chisholm article, explain precisely how Chisholm would define this locution. You may not include in your statement of the definition any expressions that Chisholm defines.

4   How does Alston argue against the deontological conception of epistemic justification? Do you think that his argument is sound? Why or why not?

5   How does Fumerton argue that epistemic justification is not in any interesting sense normative? Do you think that his argument is sound? Why or why not?

6   Can you think of a way to extend Craig's hypothesis concerning the point of having a concept of knowledge, so that it tells us about the point of having the whole practice of epistemic appraisal? Precisely what would such an extended hypothesis say? What might it tell us about the nature of the epistemic 'ought'?

Further reading

There is a useful discussion of deontological conceptions of justication at an introductory level in chapter 5 of Pritchard (2006). Adler (2002) is a recently influential monograph on the ethics of belief. Foley (1987) and Lehrer (1999) both contain accessible discussions of what makes it rational to believe something. There is also an instructive debate between Foley (2005) and Wolterstorff (2005) about whether justified belief is responsibly held.

References

Adler, Jonathan. (2002). *Belief's Own Ethics*, Cambridge, MA: MIT Press.

Foley, Richard. (1987). *The Theory of Epistemic Rationality*, Cambridge, MA: Harvard University Press.

—— (2005). 'Justified Belief as Responsible Belief', in M. Steup and E. Sosa, eds, *Contemporary Debates in Epistemology*, Malden, MA and Oxford: Blackwell..

Greco, J. and Sosa, E. (eds). (1999). *The Blackwell Guide to Epistemology*, Malden, MA and Oxford: Blackwell.

Lehrer, Keith. (1999). 'Rationality' in J. Greco and E. Sosa, eds, *The Blackwell Guide to Epistemology*, Malden, MA and Oxford: Blackwell.

Pritchard, Duncan. (2006). *What Is this Thing Called Knowledge?*, London: Routledge.

Steup, M. and Sosa, E., eds. (2005). *Contemporary Debates in Epistemology*, Malden, MA and Oxford: Blackwell.

Wolterstorff, Nicholas. 2005. 'Obligation, Entitlement, and Rationality', in M. Steup and E. Sosa, eds, *Contemporary Debates in Epistemology*, Malden, MA and Oxford: Blackwell.

Chapter 24

W. K. Clifford

THE ETHICS OF BELIEF

A shipowner was about to send to sea an emigrant ship. He knew that she was old, and not over-well built at the first; that she had seen many seas and climes, and often had needed repairs. Doubts had been suggested to him that possibly she was not seaworthy. These doubts preyed upon his mind and made him unhappy; he thought that perhaps he ought to have her thoroughly overhauled and refitted, even though this should put him to great expense. Before the ship sailed, however, he succeeded in overcoming these melancholy reflections. He said to himself that she had gone safely through so many voyages and weathered so many storms that it was idle to suppose she would not come safely home from this trip also. He would put his trust in Providence, which could hardly fail to protect all these unhappy families that were leaving their fatherland to seek for better times elsewhere. He would dismiss from his mind all ungenerous suspicions about the honesty of builders and contractors. In such ways he acquired a sincere and comfortable conviction that his vessel was thoroughly safe and seaworthy; he watched her departure with a light heart, and benevolent wishes for the success of the exiles in their strange new home that was to be; and he got his insurance money when she went down in midocean and told no tales.

What shall we say of him? Surely this, that he was verily guilty of the death of those men. It is admitted that he did sincerely believe in the soundness of his ship; but the sincerity of his conviction can in no wise help him, because *he had no right to believe on such evidence as was before him.* He had acquired his belief not by honestly earning it in patient investigation, but by stifling his doubts. And although in the end he may have felt so sure about it that he could not think otherwise, yet inasmuch as he had knowingly and willingly worked himself into that frame of mind, he must be held responsible for it.

Let us alter the case a little, and suppose that the ship was not unsound after all; that she made her voyage safely, and many others after it. Will that diminish the guilt of her owner? Not one jot. When an action is once done, it is right or wrong forever; no accidental failure of its good or evil fruits can possibly alter that. The man would not have been innocent, he would only have been not found out. The question of right or wrong has to do with the origin of his belief, not the matter of it; not what it was, but how he got it; not whether it turned out to be true or false, but whether he had a right to believe on such evidence as was before him.

There was once an island in which some of the inhabitants professed a religion teaching neither the doctrine of original sin nor that of eternal punishment. A suspicion got abroad that the professors of this religion had made use of unfair means to get their doctrines taught to children. They were accused of wresting the laws of their country in such a way as to remove

302 W. K. Clifford

children from the care of their natural and legal guardians; and even of stealing them away and keeping them concealed from their friends and relations. A certain number of men formed themselves into a society for the purpose of agitating the public about this matter. They published grave accusations against individual citizens of the highest position and character, and did all in their power to injure those citizens in the exercise of their professions. So great was the noise they made, that a Commission was appointed to investigate the facts; but after the Commission had carefully inquired into all the evidence that could be got, it appeared that the accused were innocent. Not only had they been accused on insufficient evidence, but the evidence of their innocence was such as the agitators might easily have obtained, if they had attempted a fair inquiry. After these disclosures the inhabitants of that country looked upon the members of the agitating society, not only as persons whose judgment was to be distrusted, but also as no longer to be counted honorable men. For although they had sincerely and conscientiously believed in the charges they had made, *yet they had no right to believe on such evidence as was before them.* Their sincere convictions, instead of being honestly earned by patient inquiring, were stolen by listening to the voice of prejudice and passion.

Let us vary this case also, and suppose, other things remaining as before, that a still more accurate investigation proved the accused to have been really guilty. Would this make any difference in the guilt of the accusers? Clearly not; the question is not whether their belief was true or false, but whether they entertained it on wrong grounds. They would no doubt say, "Now you see that we were right after all; next time perhaps you will believe us." And they might be believed, but they would not thereby become honorable men. They would not be innocent, they would only be not found out. Every one of them, if he chose to examine himself *in foro conscientiae,* would know that he had

acquired and nourished a belief, when he had no right to believe on such evidence as was before him; and therein he would know that he had done a wrong thing.

It may be said, however, that in both of these supposed cases it is not the belief which is judged to be wrong, but the action following upon it. The shipowner might say, "I am perfectly certain that my ship is sound, but still I feel it my duty to have her examined, before trusting the lives of so many people to her." And it might be said to the agitator, "However convinced you were of the justice of your cause and the truth of your convictions, you ought not to have made a public attack upon any man's character until you had examined the evidence on both sides with the utmost patience and care."

In the first place, let us admit that, so far as it goes, this view of the case is right and necessary; right, because even when a man's belief is so fixed that he cannot think otherwise, he still has a choice in regard to the action suggested by it, and so cannot escape the duty of investigating on the ground of the strength of his convictions; and necessary, because those who are not yet capable of controlling their feelings and thoughts must have a plain rule dealing with overt acts.

But this being premised as necessary, it becomes clear that it is not sufficient, and that our previous judgment is required to supplement it. For it is not possible so to sever the belief from the action it suggests as to condemn the one without condemning the other. No man holding a strong belief on one side of a question, or even wishing to hold a belief on one side, can investigate it with such fairness and completeness as if he were really in doubt and unbiased; so that the existence of a belief not founded on fair inquiry unfits a man for the performance of this necessary duty.

Nor is that truly a belief at all which has not some influence upon the actions of him who holds it. He who truly believes that which prompts him to an action has looked upon the action to lust after it, he has committed it already in his heart. If a belief is not realized immediately in open deeds, it is stored up for the guidance of the future. It goes to make a part of that aggregate of beliefs which is the link between sensation and action at every moment of all our lives, and which is so organized and compacted together that no part of it can be isolated from the rest, but every new addition modifies the structure of the whole. No real belief, however trifling and fragmentary it may seem, is ever truly insignificant; it prepares us to receive more of its like, confirms those which resembled it before, and weakens others; and so gradually it lays a stealthy train in our inmost thoughts, which may some day explode into overt action, and leave its stamp upon our character forever.

And no one man's belief is in any case a private matter which concerns himself alone. Our lives are guided by that general conception of the course of things which has been created by society for social purposes. Our words, our phrases, our forms and processes and modes of thought, are common property, fashioned and perfected from age to age; an heirloom which every succeeding generation inherits as a precious deposit and a sacred trust to be handed on to the next one, not unchanged but enlarged and purified, with some clear marks of its proper handiwork. Into this, for good or ill, is woven every belief of every man who has speech of his fellows. An awful privilege, and an awful responsibility, that we should help to create the world in which posterity will live.

In the two supposed cases which have been considered, it has been judged wrong to believe on insufficient evidence, or to nourish belief by suppressing doubts and avoiding investigation. The reason of this judgment is not far to seek: it is that in both these cases the belief held by one man was of great importance to other men. But for as much as no belief held by one man, however seemingly trivial the belief, and however obscure the believer, is ever actually insignificant or without its effect on the fate of mankind, we

have no choice but to extend our judgment to all cases of belief whatever. Belief, that sacred faculty which prompts the decisions of our will, and knits into harmonious working all the compacted energies of our being, is ours not for ourselves, but for humanity. It is rightly used on truths which have been established by long experience and waiting toil, and which have stood in the fierce light of free and fearless questioning. Then it helps to bind men together, and to strengthen and direct their common action. It is desecrated when given to unproved and unquestioned statements, for the solace and private pleasure of the believer; to add a tinsel splendor to the plain straight road of our life and display a bright mirage beyond it; or even to drown the common sorrows of our kind by a self-deception which allows them not only to cast down, but also to degrade us. Whoso would deserve well of his fellows in this matter will guard the purity of his belief with a very fanaticism of jealous care, lest at any time it should rest on an unworthy object, and catch a stain which can never be wiped away.

It is not only the leader of men, statesman, philosopher, or poet, that owes this bounden duty to mankind. Every rustic who delivers in the village alehouse his slow, infrequent sentences, may help to kill or keep alive the fatal superstitions which clog his race. Every hard-worked wife of an artisan may transmit to her children beliefs which shall knit society together, or rend it in pieces. No simplicity of mind, no obscurity of station, can escape the universal duty of questioning all that we believe.

It is true that this duty is a hard one, and the doubt which comes out of it is often a very bitter thing. It leaves us bare and powerless where we thought that we were safe and strong. To know all about anything is to know how to deal with it under all circumstances. We feel much happier and more secure when we think we know precisely what to do, no matter what happens, than when we have lost our way and do not know where to turn. And if we have supposed ourselves to know all about anything, and to be capable of doing what is fit in regard to it, we naturally do not like to find that we are really ignorant and powerless, that we have to begin again at the beginning, and try to learn what the thing is and how it is to be dealt with—if indeed anything can be learned about it. It is the sense of power attached to a sense of knowledge that makes men desirous of believing, and afraid of doubting.

This sense of power is the highest and best of pleasures when the belief on which it is founded is a true belief, and has been fairly earned by investigation. For then we may justly feel that it is common property, and holds good for others as well as for ourselves. Then we may be glad, not that I have learned secrets by which I am safer and stronger, but that *we men* have got mastery over more of the world; and we shall be strong, not for ourselves, but in the name of Man and in his strength. But if the belief has been accepted on insufficient evidence, the pleasure is a stolen one. Not only does it deceive ourselves by giving us a sense of power which we do not really possess, but it is sinful, because it is stolen in defiance of our duty to mankind. That duty is to guard ourselves from such beliefs as from a pestilence, which may shortly master our own body and then spread to the rest of the town. What would be thought of one who, for the sake of a sweet fruit, should deliberately run the risk of bringing a plague upon his family and his neighbors?

And, as in other such cases, it is not the risk only which has to be considered; for a bad action is always bad at the time when it is done, no matter what happens afterwards. Every time we let ourselves believe for unworthy reasons, we weaken our powers of self-control, of doubting, of judicially and fairly weighing evidence. We all suffer severely enough from the maintenance and support of false beliefs and the fatally wrong actions which they lead to, and the evil born when one such belief is entertained is great and wide. But a greater and wider evil arises when

the credulous character is maintained and supported, when a habit of believing for unworthy reasons is fostered and made permanent. If I steal money from any person, there may be no harm done by the mere transfer of possession; he may not feel the loss, or it may prevent him from using the money badly. But I cannot help doing this great wrong towards Man, that I make myself dishonest. What hurts society is not that it should lose its property, but that it should become a den of thieves; for then it must cease to be society. This is why we ought not to do evil that good may come; for at any rate this great evil has come, that we have done evil and are made wicked thereby. In like manner, if I let myself believe anything on insufficient evidence, there may be no great harm done by the mere belief; it may be true after all, or I may never have occasion to exhibit it in outward acts. But I cannot help doing this great wrong toward Man, that I make myself credulous. The danger to society is not merely that it should believe wrong things, though that is great enough; but that it should become credulous, and lose the habit of testing things and inquiring into them; for then it must sink back into savagery.

The harm which is done by credulity in a man is not confined to the fostering of a credulous character in others, and consequent support of false beliefs. Habitual want of care about what I believe leads to habitual want of care in others about the truth of what is told to me. Men speak the truth to one another when each reveres the truth in his own mind and in the other's mind; but how shall my friend revere the truth in my mind when I myself am careless about it, when I believe things because I want to believe them, and because they are comforting and pleasant? Will he not learn to cry, "Peace," to me, when there is no peace? By such a course I shall surround myself with a thick atmosphere of falsehood and fraud, and in that I must live. It may matter little to me, in my cloud-castle of sweet illusions and darling lies; but it matters much to Man that I have made my neighbors ready to deceive. The credulous man is father to the liar and the cheat; he lives in the bosom of this his family, and it is no marvel if he should become even as they are. So closely are our duties knit together, that whoso shall keep the whole law, and yet offend in one point, he is guilty of all.

To sum up: it *is wrong always, everywhere, and for anyone, to believe anything upon insufficient evidence.* If a man, holding a belief which he was taught in childhood or persuaded of afterwards, keeps down and pushes away any doubts which arise about it in his mind, purposely avoids the reading of books and the company of men that call in question or discuss it, and regards as impious those questions which cannot easily be asked without disturbing it—the life of that man is one long sin against mankind.

Chapter 25

William James

THE WILL TO BELIEVE

I

Let us give the name of hypothesis to anything that may be proposed to our belief; and just as the electricians speak of live and dead wires, let us speak of any hypothesis as either live or dead. A live hypothesis is one which appeals as a real possibility to him to whom it is proposed. If I ask you to believe in the Mahdi, the notion makes no electric connection with your nature—it refuses to scintillate with any credibility at all. As an hypothesis it is completely dead. To an Arab, however (even if he be not one of the Mahdi's followers), the hypothesis is among the mind's possibilities: It is alive. This shows that deadness and liveness in an hypothesis are not intrinsic properties, but relations to the individual thinker. They are measured by his willingness to act.

The maximum of liveness in an hypothesis means willingness to act irrevocably. Practically, that means belief; but there is some believing tendency wherever there is willingness to act at all.

Next, let us call the decision between two hypotheses an *option*. Options may be of several kinds. They may be, first, *living* or *dead*; secondly, *forced* or *avoidable*; thirdly, *momentous* or *trivial*; and for our purposes we may call an option a *genuine* option when it is of a forced, living, and momentous kind.

1   A living option is one in which both hypotheses are live ones. If I say to you: "Be a theosophist or be a Mohammedan," it is probably a dead option, because for you neither hypothesis is likely to be alive. But if I say: "Be an agnostic or be a Christian," it is otherwise: trained as you are, each hypothesis makes some appeal, however small, to your belief.

2   Next, if I say to you: "Choose between going out with your umbrella or without it," I do not offer you a genuine option, for it is not forced. You can easily avoid it by not going out at all. Similarly, if I say, "Either love me or hate me," "Either call my theory true or call it false," your option is avoidable. You may remain indifferent to me, neither loving nor hating, and you may decline to offer any judgment as to my theory. But if I say, "Either accept this truth or go without it," I put on you a forced option, for there is no standing place outside of the alternative. Every dilemma based on a complete logical disjunction, with no possibility of not choosing, is an option of this forced kind.

3   Finally, if I were Dr. Nansen and proposed to you to join my North Pole expedition, your option would be momentous; for this would probably be your singular opportunity, and your choice now would either exclude you from the North Pole

sort of immortality altogether or put at least the chance of it into your hands. He who refuses to embrace a unique opportunity loses the prize as surely as if he tried and failed. *Per contra*, the option is trivial when the opportunity is not unique, when the stake is insignificant, or when the decision is reversible if it later prove unwise. Such trivial options abound in the scientific life. A chemist finds an hypothesis live enough to spend a year in its verification: he believes in it to that extent. But if his experiments prove inconclusive either way, he is quit for his loss of time, no vital harm being done.

It will facilitate our discussion if we keep all these distinctions well in mind.

II

The next matter to consider is the actual psychology of human opinion. When we look at certain facts, it seems as if our passional and volitional nature lay at the root of all our convictions. When we look at others, it seems as if they could do nothing when the intellect had once said its say. Let us take the latter facts up first.

Does it not seem preposterous on the very face of it to talk of our opinions being modifiable at will? Can our will either help or hinder our intellect in its perceptions of truth? Can we, by just willing it, believe that Abraham Lincoln's existence is a myth, and that the portraits of him in *McClure's Magazine* are all of some one else? Can we, by any effort of our will, or by any strength of wish that it were true, believe ourselves well and about when we are roaring with rheumatism in bed, or feel certain that the sum of the two one-dollar bills in our pocket must be a hundred dollars? We can say any of these things, but we are absolutely impotent to believe them; and of just such things is the whole fabric of the truths that we do believe made up—

matters of fact, immediate or remote, as Hume said, and relations between ideas, which are either there or not there for us if we see them so, and which if not there cannot be put there by any action of our own.

In Pascal's *Thoughts* there is a celebrated passage known in literature as Pascal's wager. In it he tries to force us into Christianity by reasoning as if our concern with truth resembled our concern with the stakes in a game of chance. Translated freely his words are these: You must either believe or not believe that God is—which will you do? Your human reason cannot say. A game is going on between you and the nature of things which at the day of judgment will bring out either heads or tails. Weigh what your gains and your losses would be if you should stake all you have on heads, or God's existence: if you win in such case, you gain eternal beatitude; if you lose, you lose nothing at all. If there were an infinity of chances, and only one for God in this wager, still you ought to stake your all on God; for though you surely risk a finite loss by this procedure, any finite loss is reasonable, even a certain one is reasonable, if there is but the possibility of infinite gain. Go, then, and take holy water, and have masses said; belief will come and stupefy your scruples. . . . Why should you not? At bottom, what have you to lose?

You probably feel that when religious faith expresses itself thus, in the language of the gaming-table, it is put to its last trumps. Surely Pascal's own personal belief in masses and holy water had far other springs; and this celebrated page of his is but an argument for others, a last desperate snatch at a weapon against the hardness of the unbelieving heart. We feel that a faith in masses and holy water adopted wilfully after such a mechanical calculation would lack the inner soul of faith's reality; and if we were ourselves in the place of the Deity, we should probably take particular pleasure in cutting off believers of this pattern from their infinite reward. It is evident that unless there be some pre-existing tendency to believe in masses and holy water, the option offered to the will by Pascal is not a living option. Certainly no Turk ever took to masses and holy water on its account; and even to us Protestants these means of salvation seem such foregone impossibilities that Pascal's logic, invoked for them specifically, leaves us unmoved. As well might the Mahdi write to us, saying, "I am the Expected One whom God has created in his effulgence. You shall be infinitely happy if you confess me; otherwise you shall be cut off from the light of the sun. Weigh, then, your infinite gain if I am genuine against your finite sacrifice if I am not!" His logic would be that of Pascal; but he would vainly use it on us, for the hypothesis he offers us is dead. No tendency to act on it exists in us to any degree.

The talk of believing by our volition seems, then, from one point of view, simply silly. From another point of view it is worse than silly, it is vile. When one turns to the magnificent edifice of the physical sciences, and sees how it was reared; what thousands of disinterested moral lives of men lie buried in its mere foundations; what patience and postponement, what choking down of preference, what submission to the icy laws of outer fact are wrought into its very stones and mortar; how absolutely impersonal it stands in its vast augustness—then how besotted and contemptible seems every little sentimentalist who comes blowing his voluntary smoke-wreaths, and pretending to decide things from out of his private dream! Can we wonder if those bred in the rugged and manly school of science should feel like spewing such subjectivism out of their mouths? The whole system of loyalties which grow up in the schools of science go dead against its toleration; so that it is only natural that those who have caught the scientific fever should pass over to the opposite extreme, and write sometimes as if the incorruptibly truthful intellect ought positively to prefer bitterness and unacceptableness to the heart in its cup.

It fortifies my soul to know
That though I perish, Truth is so

sings Clough, while Huxley exclaims: "My only consolation lies in the reflection that, however bad our posterity may become, so far as they hold by the plain rule of not pretending to believe what they have no reason to believe, because it may be to their advantage so to pretend [the word 'pretend' is surely here redundant], they will not have reached the lowest depth of immorality." And that delicious *enfant terrible* Clifford writes: "Belief is desecrated when given to unproved and unquestioned statements for the solace and private pleasure of the believer. . . . Whoso would deserve well of his fellows in this matter will guard the purity of his belief with a very fanaticism of jealous care, lest at any time it should rest on an unworthy object, and catch a stain which can never be wiped away. . . . If [a] belief has been accepted on insufficient evidence [even though the belief be true, as Clifford on the same page explains] the pleasure is a stolen one. . . . It is sinful because it is stolen in defiance of our duty to mankind. That duty is to guard ourselves from such beliefs as from a pestilence which may shortly master our own body and then spread to the rest of the town. . . . It is wrong always, everywhere, and for every one, to believe anything upon insufficient evidence."

III

All this strikes one as healthy, even when expressed, as by Clifford, with somewhat too much of robustious pathos in the voice. Free will and simple wishing do seem, in the matter of our credences, to be only fifth wheels to the coach. Yet if any one should thereupon assume that intellectual insight is what remains after wish and will and sentimental preference have taken wing, or that pure reason is what then settles our opinions, he would fly quite as directly in the teeth of facts.

It is only our already dead hypotheses that our willing nature is unable to bring to life again. But what has made them dead for us is for the most part a previous action of our willing nature of an antagonistic kind. When I say "willing nature," I do not mean only such deliberate volitions as may have set up habits of belief that we cannot now escape from—I mean all such factors of belief as fear and hope, prejudice and passion, imitation and partisanship, the circum-pressure of our caste and set. As a matter of fact, we find ourselves believing, we hardly know how or why. Mr. Balfour gives the name of "authority" to all those influences, born of the intellectual climate, that make hypotheses possible or impossible for us, alive or dead. Here in this room, we all of us believe in molecules and the conservation of energy, in democracy and necessary progress, in Protestant Christianity and the duty of fighting for "the doctrine of the immortal Monroe," all for no reasons worthy of the name. We see into these matters with no more inner clearness, and probably with much less, than any disbeliever in them might possess. His unconventionality would probably have some grounds to show for its conclusions; but for us, not insight, but the *prestige* of the opinions, is what makes the spark shoot from them and light up our sleeping magazines of faith. Our reason is quite satisfied, in nine hundred and ninety-nine cases out of every thousand of us, if it can find a few arguments that will do to recite in case our credulity is criticized by some one else. Our faith is faith in some one else's faith, and in the greatest matters this is the most the case. . . .

Evidently, then our non-intellectual nature does influence our convictions. There are passional tendencies and volitions which run before and others which come after belief, and it is only the latter that are too late for the fair; and they are not too late when the previous passional work has been already in their own direction. Pascal's argument, instead of being powerless, then seems a regular clincher, and is the last stroke needed to make our faith in masses and holy water complete. The state of things is evidently far from simple; and pure insight and logic, whatever they might do ideally, are not the only things that really do produce our creeds.

IV

Our next duty, having recognized this mixed-up state of affairs, is to ask whether it be simply reprehensible and pathological, or whether, on the contrary, we must treat it as a normal element in making up our minds. The thesis I defend is, briefly stated, this: *Our passional nature not only lawfully may, but must, decide an option between propositions, whenever it is a genuine option that cannot by its nature be decided on intellectual grounds; for to say, under such circumstances, "Do not decide, but leave the question open," is itself a passional decision—just like deciding yes or no—and is attended with the same risk of losing the truth.* . . .

VII

One more point, small but important, and our preliminaries are done. There are two ways of looking at our duty in the matter of opinion—ways entirely different, and yet ways about whose difference the theory of knowledge seems hitherto to have shown very little concern. *We must know the truth; and we must avoid error*—these are our first and great commandments as would-be knowers; but they are not two ways of stating an identical commandment, they are two separable laws. Although it may indeed happen that when we believe the truth A, we escape as an incidental consequence from believing the falsehood B, it hardly ever happens that by merely disbelieving B we necessarily believe A. We may in escaping B fall into believing other falsehoods, C or D, just as bad as B; or we may escape B by not believing anything at all, not even A.

Believe truth! Shun error!—these, we see, are two materially different laws; and by choosing between them we may end by coloring differently our whole intellectual life. We may regard the chase for truth as paramount, and the avoidance of error as secondary; or we may, on the other hand, treat the avoidance of error as more imperative, and let truth take its chance. Clifford, in the instructive passage which I have quoted, exhorts us to the latter course. Believe nothing, he tells us, keep your mind in suspense forever, rather than by closing it on insufficient evidence incur the awful risk of believing lies. You, on the other hand, may think that the risk of being in error is a very small matter when compared with the blessings of real knowledge, and be ready to be duped many times in your investigation rather than postpone indefinitely the chance of guessing true. I myself find it impossible to go with Clifford. We must remember that these feelings of our duty about either truth or error are in any case only expressions of our passional life. Biologically considered, our minds are as ready to grind out falsehood as veracity, and he who says, "Better go without belief forever than believe a lie!" merely shows his own preponderant private horror of becoming a dupe. He may be critical of many of his desires and fears, but this fear he slavishly obeys. He cannot imagine any one questioning its binding force. For my own part, I have also a horror of being duped; but I can believe that worse things than being duped may happen to a man in this world: so Clifford's exhortation has to my ears a thoroughly fantastic sound. It is like a general informing his soldiers that it is better to keep out of battle forever than to risk a single wound. Not so are victories either over enemies or over nature gained. Our errors are surely not such awfully solemn things. In a world where we are so certain to incur them in spite of all our caution, a certain lightness of heart seems healthier than this excessive nervousness on their behalf. At any rate, it seems the fittest thing for the empiricist philosopher.

VIII

And now, after all this introduction, let us go straight at our question. I have said, and now repeat it, that not only as a matter of fact do we find our passional nature influencing us in our opinions, but that there are some options between opinions in which this influence must be regarded both as an inevitable and as a lawful determinant of our choice.

I fear here that some of you my hearers will begin to scent danger, and lend an inhospitable ear. Two first steps of passion you have indeed had to admit as necessary—we must think so as to avoid dupery, and we must think so as to gain truth; but the surest path to those ideal consummations, you will probably consider, is from now onwards to take no further passional step.

Well, of course, I agree as far as the facts will allow. Wherever the option between losing truth and gaining it is not momentous, we can throw the chance of *gaining truth* away, and at any rate save ourselves from any chance of *believing falsehood*, by not making up our minds at all till objective evidence has come. In scientific questions, this is almost always the case; and even in human affairs in general, the need of acting is seldom so urgent that a false belief to act on is better than no belief at all. Law courts, indeed, have to decide on the best evidence attainable for the moment, because a judge's duty is to make law as well as to ascertain it, and (as a learned judge once said to me) few cases are worth spending much time over: the great thing is to have them decided on *any* acceptable principle, and got out of the way. But in our dealings with objective nature we obviously are recorders, not makers, of the truth; and decisions for the mere sake of deciding promptly and getting on to the next business would be wholly out of place. Throughout the breadth of physical nature facts are what they are quite independently of us, and seldom is there any such hurry about them that the risks of being duped by believing a premature theory need be faced. The questions here are always trivial options, the hypotheses are hardly living (at any rate not living for us spectators), the choice between believing truth or falsehood is seldom forced. The attitude of skeptical balance is therefore the absolutely wise one if we would escape mistakes. What difference, indeed, does it make to most of us whether we have or have not a theory of the Röntgen rays, whether we believe or not in mind-stuff, or have a conviction about the causality of conscious states? It makes no difference. Such options are not forced on us. On every account it is better not to make them, but still keep weighing reasons *pro et contra* with an indifferent hand.

I speak, of course, here of the purely judging mind. For purposes of discovery such indifference is to be less highly recommended, and science would be far less advanced than she is if the passionate desires of individuals to get their own faiths confirmed had been kept out of the game. See, for example, the sagacity which Spencer and Weismann now display. On the other hand, if you want an absolute duffer in an investigation, you must, after all, take the man who has no interest whatever in its results: he is the warranted incapable, the positive fool. The most useful investigator, because the most sensitive observer, is always he whose eager interest in one side of the question is balanced by an equally keen nervousness lest he become deceived. Science has organized this nervousness into a regular *technique*, her so-called method of verification; and she has fallen so deeply in love with the method that one may even say she has ceased to care for truth by itself at all. It is only truth as technically verified that interests her. The truth of truths might come in merely affirmative form, and she would decline to touch it. Such truth as that, she might repeat with Clifford, would be stolen in defiance of her duty to mankind. Human passions, however, are stronger than technical rules. "*Le coeur a ses raisons,*" as Pascal says, "*que la raison ne connait pas,*" and however indifferent to all but the bare rules of

the game the umpire, the abstract intellect, may be, the concrete players who furnish him the materials to judge of are usually, each one of them, in love with some pet "live hypothesis" of his own. Let us agree, however, that wherever there is no forced option, the dispassionately judicial intellect with no pet hypothesis, saving us, as it does, from dupery at any rate, ought to be our ideal.

The question next arises: Are there not somewhere forced options in our speculative questions, and can we (as men who may be interested at least as much in positively gaining truth as in merely escaping dupery) always wait with impunity till the coercive evidence shall have arrived? It seems *a priori* improbable that the truth should be so nicely adjusted to our needs and powers as that. In the great boarding-house of nature, the cakes and the butter and the syrup seldom come out so even and leave the plates so clean. Indeed, we should view them with scientific suspicion if they did.

IX

Moral questions immediately present themselves as questions whose solution cannot wait for sensible proof. A moral question is a question not of what sensibly exists, but of what is good, or would be good if it did exist. Science can tell us what exists; but to compare the *worths*, both of what exists and of what does not exist, we must consult not science, but what Pascal calls our heart . . . .

Turn now from these wide questions of good to a certain class of questions of fact, questions concerning personal relations, states of mind between one man and another. *Do you like me or not?*—for example. Whether you do or not depends, in countless instances, on whether I meet you halfway, am willing to assume that you must like me, and show you trust and expectation. The previous faith on my part in your liking's existence is in such cases what makes your liking come. But if I stand aloof, and refuse to budge an inch until I have objective evidence, until you shall have done something apt, as the absolutists say, *ad extorquendum assensum meum*, ten to one your liking never comes. How many women's hearts are vanquished by the mere sanguine insistence of some man that they *must* love him! He will not consent to the hypothesis that they cannot. The desire for a certain kind of truth here brings about that special truth's existence; and so it is in innumerable cases of other sorts. . . . *And where faith in a fact can help create the fact*, that would be an insane logic which should say that faith running ahead of scientific evidence is the "lowest kind of immorality" into which a thinking being can fall. Yet such is the logic by which our scientific absolutists pretend to regulate our lives!

X

In truths dependent on our personal action, then, faith based on desire is certainly a lawful and possibly an indispensable thing.

But now, it will be said, these are all childish human cases, and have nothing to do with great cosmical matters, like the question of religious faith. Let us then pass on to that. Religions differ so much in their accidents that in discussing the religious question we must make it very generic and broad. What then do we now mean by the religious hypothesis? Science says things are; morality says some things are better than other things; and religion says essentially two things.

First, she says that the best things are the more eternal things, the overlapping things, the things in the universe that throw the last stone, so to speak, and say the final word. "Perfection is eternal"—this phrase of Charles Secrétan seems a good way of putting this first affirmation of religion, an affirmation which obviously cannot yet be verified scientifically at all.

The second affirmation of religion is that we are better off even now if we believe her first affirmation to be true.

Now, let us consider what the logical elements of this situation are *in case the religious hypothesis in both its branches be really true.* (Of course, we must admit that possibility at the outset. If we are to discuss the question at all, it must involve a living option. If for any of you religion be a hypothesis that cannot, by any living possibility, be true, then you need go no farther. I speak to the "saving remnant" alone.) So proceeding, we see, first, that religion offers itself as a *momentous* option. We are supposed to gain, even now, by our belief, and to lose by our non-belief, a certain vital good. Secondly, religion is a *forced* option, so far as that good goes. We cannot escape the issue by remaining skeptical and waiting for more light, because, although we do avoid error in that way *if religion be untrue*, we lose the good, *if it be true*, just as certainly as if we positively chose to disbelieve. It is as if a man should hesitate indefinitely to ask a certain woman to marry him because he was not perfectly sure that she would prove an angel after he brought her home. Would he not cut himself off from that particular angel-possibility as decisively as if he went and married some one else? Skepticism, then, is not avoidance of option; it is option of a certain particular kind of risk. *Better risk loss of truth than chance of error*—that is your faith-vetoer's exact position. He is actively playing his stake as much as the believer is; he is backing the field against the religious hypothesis, just as the believer is backing the religious hypothesis against the field. To preach skepticism to us as a duty until "sufficient evidence" for religion be found, is tantamount therefore to telling us, when in presence of the religious hypothesis, that to yield to our fear of its being error is wiser and better than to yield to our hope that it may be true. It is not intellect against all passions, then; it is only intellect with one passion laying down its law. And by what, forsooth, is the supreme wisdom of this passion warranted? Dupery for dupery, what proof is there that dupery through hope is so much worse than dupery through fear? I, for one, can see no proof; and I simply refuse obedience to the scientist's command to imitate his kind of option, in a case where my own stake is important enough to give me the right to choose my own form of risk. If religion be true and the evidence for it be still insufficient, I do not wish, by putting your extinguisher upon my nature (which feels to me as if it had after all some business in this matter), to forfeit my sole chance in life of getting upon the winning side—that chance depending, of course, on my willingness to run the risk of acting as if my passional need of taking the world religiously might be prophetic and right.

All this is on the supposition that it really may be prophetic and right, and that, even to us who are discussing the matter, religion is a live hypothesis which may be true. Now, to most of us religion comes in a still further way that makes a veto on our active faith even more illogical. The more perfect and more eternal aspect of the universe is represented in our religions as having personal form. The universe is no longer a mere It to us, but a *Thou*, if we are religious; and any relation that may be possible from person to person might be possible here. For instance, although in one sense we are passive portions of the universe, in another we show a curious autonomy, as if we were small active centers on our own account. We feel, too, as if the appeal of religion to us were made to our own active goodwill, as if evidence might be forever withheld from us unless we met the hypothesis halfway to take a trivial illustration: just as a man who in a company of gentlemen made no advances, asked a warrant for every concession, and believed no one's word without proof, would cut himself off by such churlishness from all the social rewards that a more trusting spirit would earn—so here, one who should shut himself up in snarling logicality and try to make the gods extort his recognition willy-nilly, or not get it at all, might cut himself off forever from his only opportunity of making the gods' acquaintance. This feeling, forced on us we know not whence that by obstinately believing that there are gods (although not to do so would be so easy both for our logic and our life) we are doing the universe the deepest service we can, seems part of the living essence of the religious hypothesis. If the hypothesis *were* true in all its parts, including this one, then pure intellectualism, with its veto on our making willing advances, would be an absurdity; and some participation of our sympathetic nature would be logically required. I therefore, for one, cannot see my way to accepting the agnostic rules for truth-seeking, or wilfully agree to keep my willing nature out of the game. I cannot do so for this plain reason, that *a rule of thinking which would absolutely prevent me from acknowledging certain kinds of truth if those kinds of truth were really there, would be an irrational rule.* That for me is the long and short of the formal logic of the situation, no matter what the kinds of truth might materially be.

I confess I do not see how this logic can be escaped. But sad experience makes me fear that some of you may still shrink from radically saying with me, *in abstracto*, that we have the right to believe at our own risk any hypothesis that is live enough to tempt our will. I suspect, however, that if this is so, it is because you have gone away from the abstract logical point of view altogether, and are thinking (perhaps without realizing it) of some particular religious hypothesis which for you is dead. The freedom to "believe what we will" you apply to the case of some patent superstition; and the faith you think of is the faith defined by the schoolboy when he said, "Faith is when you believe something that you know ain't true." I can only repeat that this is misapprehension. *In concreto*, the freedom to believe can only cover living options which the intellect of the individual cannot by itself resolve; and living options never seem absurdities to him who has them to consider. When I look at the religious question as it really puts itself to concrete men, and when I think of all the possibilities which both practically and theoretically it involves, then this command that we shall put a stopper on our heart, instincts, and courage, and *wait*—acting of course meanwhile more or less as if religion were not true—till doomsday, or till such time as our intellect and senses working together may have raked in evidence enough—this command, I say, seems to me the queerest idol ever manufactured in the philosophic cave. Were we scholastic absolutists, there might be more excuse. If we had an infallible intellect with its objective certitudes, we might feel ourselves disloyal to such a perfect organ of knowledge in not trusting to it exclusively, in not waiting for its releasing word. But if we are empiricists, if we believe that no bell in us tolls to let us know for certain when truth is in our grasp, then it seems a piece of idle fantasticality to preach so solemnly our duty of waiting for the bell. Indeed we *may* wait if we will—I hope you do not think that I am denying that—but if we do so, we do so at our peril as much as if we believed. In either case we *act*, taking our life in our hands. No one of us ought to issue vetoes to the other, nor should we bandy words of abuse. We ought, on the contrary, delicately and profoundly to respect one another's mental freedom: then only shall we bring about the intellectual republic; then only shall we have that spirit of inner tolerance without which all our outer tolerance is soulless, and which is empiricism's glory; then only shall we live and let live, in speculative as well as in practical things.

I began by a reference to Fitz-James Stephen; let me end by a quotation from him. "What do you think of yourself? What do you think of the world? . . . These are questions with which all must deal as it seems good to them. They are riddles of the Sphinx, and in some way or other we must deal with them. . . . In all important transactions of life we have to take a leap in the dark. . . . If we decide to leave the riddles unanswered, that is a choice; if we waver in our answer, that, too, is a choice: but whatever choice we make, we make it at our peril. If a man chooses to turn his back altogether on God and the future, no one can prevent him; no one can show beyond reasonable doubt that he is mistaken. If a man thinks otherwise and acts as he thinks, I do not see that any one can prove that he is mistaken. Each must act as he thinks best; and if he is wrong, so much the worse for him. We stand on a mountain pass in the midst of whirling snow and blinding mist, through which we get glimpses now and then of paths which may be deceptive. If we stand still we shall be frozen to death. If we take the wrong road we shall be dashed to pieces. We do not certainly know whether there is any right one. What must we do? 'Be strong and of a good courage.' Act for the best, hope for the best, and take what comes.

. . . If death ends all, we cannot meet death better."

Chapter 26

Roderick Chisholm

EPISTEMIC TERMS

1. If a man looks toward the roof and *sees* that his cat is there, he is not likely to *say*, "I have adequate evidence for the proposition or hypothesis that that is a cat," "I take that to be a cat," or "There is something which is appearing to me in a certain way." But, I suggest, if he does see that his cat is there, then he has adequate evidence for the proposition that a cat is there; moreover, there is something—his cat—which he *takes* to be his cat and which *is* appearing to him in a certain way. And I would suggest, more generally, that the locution "S perceives something to have such and such a characteristic," in one of its most important uses, may be defined as follows:

(1) "There is something that S *perceives* to be f" means: there is an x which is f and which appears in some way to S; S takes x to be f; and S has adequate evidence for the proposition that x is f.

By adding qualifications about sense organs, we could formulate similar definitions of important uses of "see" and of "hear."

Such definitions are not interesting or significant unless we can say what is meant by "appear," "take," and "adequate evidence" without using "see," "hear," or "perceive." I will begin, then, with "adequate evidence." In trying to understand this term, we will find ourselves involved in a number of philosophical problems.

2. "Adequate evidence"—like "acceptable," "unreasonable," "indifferent," "certain," "probable," and "improbable"—is a term we use in appraising the epistemic, or cognitive, worth of propositions, hypotheses, and beliefs. The statements in which we express such appraisal—for example, "We do not have adequate evidence for believing that acquired characteristics are inherited," "The astronomy of Ptolemy is unreasonable," and "In all probability, the accused is innocent"—are similar in significant respects to "Stealing is wicked," "We ought to forgive our enemies," and other statements expressing our ethical or moral appraisals. Many of the characteristics which philosophers and others have thought peculiar to ethical statements also hold of epistemic statements. And when we consider the application of "evident" and our other epistemic terms, we meet with problems very much like those traditionally associated with "right," "good," and "duty."

I shall propose definitions of several important epistemic terms. The definitions are intended to be adequate only to some of the epistemic uses of the terms defined. Many of the terms I shall define have other, nonepistemic uses I shall not mention. And there are many terms having important epistemic uses which I shall not attempt to define; the epistemic uses of such terms, I believe, can be defined by means of the epistemic vocabulary presented here.

The definitions make use of one undefined epistemic locution. This is the locution: "h is more worthy of S's belief than i," where "S" may be replaced by the name of a person and "h" and "i" by names of propositions, statements, or hypotheses. An alternative reading is "h is more acceptable than i for S." [. . .]

3. A proposition, statement, or hypothesis is *unreasonable* if it is less worthy of belief than is its denial or contradictory. Let us say, then:

(2) "It would be *unreasonable* for S to accept h" means that non-h is more worthy of S's belief than h.

If S *does* accept h, we may say, of course, that it *is* unreasonable of him to do so. When it is clear from the general context what subject S is intended, we may say, elliptically, that a proposition, statement, or hypothesis is unreasonable.

"Absurd" and "preposterous" are sometimes synonyms of "unreasonable" in its present sense. And the belief—or feeling—that a proposition is unreasonable may also be expressed by means of imperatives. If I say to you, "Don't count on seeing me before Thursday," I may mean that it would be unreasonable of you to believe that you will see me before Thursday.

Whenever it would be unreasonable for a man to accept a certain proposition, then he may be said to have *adequate evidence* for its contradictory. Our next definition is:

(3) "S has *adequate evidence* for h" means that it would be unreasonable for S to accept non-h.

When it is clear what subject S is intended, then we may speak elliptically, once again, and say that a proposition, statement, or hypothesis is *evident*. The expression "adequate evidence" as it is used in this definition should be thought of as a single term; I use it because it seems to be ordinarily used in such contexts. An alternative locution which I shall also use is "h is evident for S."

As examples of propositions which are evident, we could cite what a man knows or perceives to be true. But we are not defining "adequate evidence" in terms "know" or "perceive." In definition (1) we have defined "perceive" in terms of "adequate evidence." And in definition (6) we shall define "know" in terms of "adequate evidence." There are, moreover, propositions for which a man may have adequate evidence without knowing or perceiving them to be true. For there are times when, as we would ordinarily say, the available evidence may favor some proposition which is false; at such times, a false proposition is more worthy of one's belief than is a true proposition. Thus it may be true that a man is going to win a lottery and yet unreasonable for him to believe that he is. But once the drawings are announced, the belief may no longer be unreasonable.

The example indicates that our definitions should contain temporal references. For a proposition may be evident at one date and unreasonable at another. The phrase "at t" could be inserted in our definitions: a proposition would then be said to be evident *at a time t* provided only that its contradictory is unreasonable at t; and so on. But, for simplicity, I shall not make these temporal references explicit.

The *evident*, according to our definition, is more worthy of belief than is the unreasonable. But there is another sense of the phrase "worthy of belief" in which we can say, more simply, that the true is more worthy of belief than the false. If the evident, as I have suggested, is sometimes false, then there are hypotheses which, in the one sense, are more worthy of belief than are their contradictories but which, in the other, are less. This twofold sense of "worthy" is not peculiar to our epistemic terms, but holds of ethical terms generally. Following Richard Price, let us distinguish between the *absolute* and the *practical* senses of these terms.[1]

Using the ethical term "right" in its *absolute* sense, we may say that no one can ever know what actions are right; for no one can ever know what *all* of the consequences of any action will be. In this absolute sense of "right," perhaps it would have been right for someone to have killed Hitler and Stalin when they were infants; perhaps their parents acted (absolutely) wrongly in allowing them to live.[2] But in the *practical* sense of "right" such killings would *not* have been right. It was not possible, when Hitler and Stalin were infants, for anyone to foresee the harm they would do and, I think we may assume, there is no motive which would have justified putting them to death. If we try, as some philosophers do, to restrict "right" and "wrong" and other ethical terms to their absolute use, then other terms must take over their practical use. We might then say of the killings we have been discussing that, although they might have been right, they would hardly have been *praiseworthy*— or that, although they would not have been wrong, they would certainly have been *blameworthy*.

We cannot know, of any action, whether it is right or wrong in the absolute senses of these terms unless we know what all of its consequences are going to be. But, I believe, we can know, of any contemplated act of our own, whether it is right or wrong in the practical senses of these terms; we can know of any act we contemplate whether that act would be praiseworthy or blameworthy.

When it is said, then, that people ought to believe what is evident and that they ought not to believe what is unreasonable, "ought" has its practical use. But when it is said that they ought to believe what is true and that they ought not to believe what is false, "ought" has its absolute use.[3] Our locution "*h* is more worthy of belief than *i*" is to be taken in its practical sense. And all of the other epistemic terms to be used here are, similarly, to be taken in a practical and not in an absolute sense.

[. . .]

4. Let us say that a proposition, statement, or hypothesis is acceptable provided only that it is not unreasonable.

(4) "*h* is *acceptable* for S" means: it is false that it would be unreasonable for S to accept *h*.

In other words, if the contradictory of a proposition is not evident, then the proposition is acceptable. "Justifiable," "reasonable," or "credible" might be used in place of "acceptable" here; I have avoided them, however, because in their ordinary use in such contexts they are often taken as synonymous with "evident." The modal term "*possible*" is sometimes used as a synonym of "acceptable"; when a man says, "It is possible that we will have good news tomorrow," he may mean it is not unreasonable of us to believe that we will have good news tomorrow.

In his lecture "The Ethics of Belief," W. K. Clifford said, "It is wrong to believe upon insufficient evidence."[4] His ethics was somewhat more rigid than that suggested here, for he held that, for each of us, there is a large class of propositions concerning which we ought to withhold both assent and denial. But I have suggested, in effect, that a proposition should be treated as innocent until proven guilty. It is only when we have adequate evidence for the contradictory of a proposition that it is unreasonable for us to accept the proposition. We have adequate evidence for the proposition that Eisenhower was President in 1956; hence it is unreasonable for us to accept the proposition that he was *not* President in 1956. We do not now have adequate evidence for the proposition that a Republican will be President in 1975; Clifford would say, therefore, that we ought not to believe that a Republican will be President in 1975. I suggest that we *may* believe this, that the proposition is "acceptable" in the sense defined above.[5] But to say that we have a right to believe it is not to say that we have a right to bet our savings on it.

We may say that a hypothesis is acceptable for someone without implying that it is always reasonable for him to *act upon* it; indeed, we may say that he has *adequate evidence* for a hypothesis without implying that it is always reasonable for him to act upon it. And in saying that in a certain instance it may be reasonable for a man to act upon a hypothesis, we do not imply that the hypothesis is one for which he has adequate evidence. A man may have adequate evidence for believing he will win if he plays Russian roulette; he may also have adequate evidence for believing he will be paid $10 if he does win. But it would be foolish of him to play, despite the fact that, in so doing, he would be acting upon hypotheses for which he has adequate evidence. On the other hand, a swimmer may have adequate evidence for the hypothesis that he cannot swim ashore and yet be in a position wherein it would be unreasonable of him *not* to act upon it. And often, when we take precautionary measures— when we buy insurance, for example—we are justified in acting on hypotheses which are unreasonable and which we believe to be false. In deciding whether to act upon a hypothesis we must consider, not only the evidence that bears upon the hypothesis itself, but also the evidence that bears upon the "utility" or "moral gain" of acting upon it. We should try to decide, for example, what the value of acting upon the hypothesis would be if the hypothesis were true, what the "disvalue" of acting upon the hypothesis would be if the hypothesis were false, and we must try to compare these values and disvalues.[6] And we should also consider whether we ought to inquire further—whether we ought to seek out *additional* evidence. I have adequate evidence for the hypothesis that this is a piece of paper and in setting out to write I may be satisfied with the evidence at hand; but before betting my savings on the hypothesis I should make a more thorough investigation.

The question whether to *accept* a certain hypothesis—whether to *believe* it—is thus easier to answer than the question of whether to *act upon*

it.[7] In deciding whether to accept it, we need not consider the "utility" or "moral gain" that would result from acting upon it. And we need not consider whether we ought to make further inquiry and investigation.

If a proposition, statement, or hypothesis is acceptable but not evident, then its contradictory is also acceptable but not evident. Such a proposition might be called epistemically in-different. We may add, then, the following definition:

(5) "*h is indifferent* for S" means: (i) it is false that S has adequate evidence for h and (ii) it is also false that S has adequate evidence for non-h.

The hypothesis that it will rain in London a year from today is, for most of us, epistemically indifferent; we do not have adequate evidence either for it or for its contradictory. If a proposition or hypothesis is indifferent, its contradictory is also indifferent. An indifferent proposition is thus one which is neither evident nor unreasonable. According to Clifford, no proposition is epistemically indifferent. According to the "absolute skeptic," all propositions are epistemically indifferent.[8]

If we were to need the term "dubitable," meaning fit to be disbelieved, we could define "*h is dubitable* for S" as "non-h is acceptable for S." We could then say that an epistemically indif-ferent proposition is one that is both acceptable and dubitable.

5. Without attempting to formulate an exact logic of epistemic terms, let us note certain principles which have been assumed in the fore-going. The expressions "h is more worthy of S's belief than non-h" and "non-h is more worthy of S's belief than h" are contraries; they may both be false but they cannot both be true. (We should suppose that these expressions contain the tem-poral reference "at t.") Hence, for any hypothesis h and any subject S, either h is acceptable for S or

non-h is acceptable for S. This principle is not incompatible with saying that some hypotheses are epistemically indifferent; for, although it says, of any hypothesis and its contradictory, that at least one is acceptable, it does not preclude the possibility of both being acceptable.

In an important series of studies, G. H. von Wright has pointed out the logical analogy which holds between the *ethical* terms "wrong," "obligatory," "permitted," and "indifferent," respectively, and the *modal* terms "impossible," "necessary," "possible," and "contingent."[9] The analogy also holds between each of these sets of terms and our *epistemic* terms "unreasonable," "evident," "acceptable," and "indifferent." ("Dubitable" would correspond to terms "unrequired" and "unnecessary.") The assumptions discussed below have their analogues in ethics and in modal logic.

We should assume that the conjunction "h is acceptable for S and i is acceptable for S" does *not* imply "The conjunction of h and i is acceptable for S." The hypothesis that a certain object is a dog may be acceptable; the hypothesis that it is a stone may also be acceptable; but the hypothesis that it is both a dog and a stone is unreasonable. On the other hand, the conjunction "h is evident for S and i is evident for S" is equivalent to "The conjunction, h and i, is evident for S." If it is evident that the thief worked alone and also evident that he came at night, then it is evident that he worked alone and came at night. We should assume, further, that the disjunction "Either h is acceptable for S or i is acceptable for S" is equivalent to "The disjunction, h or i, is acceptable for S." But "The disjunction, h or i, is *evident* for S" is *not* equivalent to "Either h is evident for S or i is evident for S." It is now evident, for example, that the next man to be elected President of the United States will be either a Democrat or a Republican, but it is not now evident that he will be a Democrat and it is not now evident that he will be a Republican.

Note that we may form a logical square, whose upper right and left corners are, respec-

tively, "evident" and "unreasonable," and whose lower right and left corners are "acceptable" and "dubitable." For "h is evident" implies "h is acceptable" and contradicts "h is dubitable," and "h is unreasonable" implies "h is dubitable" and contradicts "h is acceptable."

I have been assuming that, if it is unreasonable for S to accept h, then S ought to *refrain* from accepting h. If we wish to avoid a rigid ethics of belief, we may confine our principles to what one ought to *refrain* from believing. In such a case, we may say that a man fulfills his epistemic obligations provided only that he doesn't believe what he ought not to believe. A more rigid ethics would be concerned, more positively, with what we *ought* to believe. It might tell us, for example, that, if a proposition is unreasonable and therefore one which ought *not* to be accepted, then its contradictory, which is evident, is a proposition which *ought* to be accepted. For our present purposes, it is not necessary to make a decision concerning these two types of ethics.[10]

An adequate epistemology would also include such principles as this: if it is evident that h implies i and if i is unreasonable, then h is unreasonable. It may be evident, for example, that if the Senator votes, he will vote against his party. If it is unreasonable to believe that he will vote against his party, then it is also unreasonable to believe that he will vote. But if, on the other hand, the hypothesis that he will vote is acceptable, then so, too, is the hypothesis that he will vote against his party.

There are other epistemic principles whose status is more difficult to determine. Suppose, for example, that h is evident, that h entails i, but that it is not evident that h entails i. Should we say, in such a case, that i is evident? R. B. Braithwaite, in *Scientific Explanation*, discusses similar questions in some detail, noting that the issues which they involve are very much like those involved in distinguishing between what we have called the "practical" and "absolute" senses of the ethical terms "right" and "duty."[11]

6. Let us now consider the epistemic uses of "know"—its uses in such statements as "He knows the earth to be round" and "The speaker knows that the hall is filled."

A number of authors have tried to reduce this epistemic sense of know—*knowing that*—to a kind of verbal *knowing how*. "Knowing that some fact is the case is to know how to tell the truth about matters of a certain kind."[12] Knowing that the earth is round, according to this conception, differs from knowing how to swim only in that a different kind of skill or aptness is involved, namely, "the capacity to state correctly what is the case."[13] If, by "the capacity to state correctly what is the case," we were to mean merely "the capacity to utter words truly describing what is the case," then this capacity, like the ability to swim, would be a kind of aptness of the body. But if we define "knowing that the earth is round" in terms of *this* capacity—the capacity to utter the sentence "The earth is round" (or some other sentence having the same meaning)—then we must say, of most of those people who believe that the earth is *flat*, that they *know* that it is round. For most of those people are capable of uttering the sentence "The earth is round." Hence a qualification must be introduced in the phrase "the capacity of uttering words truly describing what is the case" if this phrase is to provide us with an adequate definition of *knowing that*.

A definition of *knowing that* should be adequate, moreover, to the distinction between *knowing* and *believing truly*. If I now predict the winner on the basis of what the tea leaves say, then, even though my prediction may be true, I cannot now be said to *know* that it is true.

"Knowing that," I suggest, has at least two epistemic senses. In what follows, I shall confine "know" to the broader of these senses and use "certain" for the narrower sense. The following, then, will be our definition of "know":

(6) "S *knows* that h is true" means: (i) S accepts h; (ii) S has adequate evidence for h; and (iii) h is true.

If we wish to avoid the term "true," we may substitute this formulation:

"S knows that . . ." means: (i) S accepts the hypothesis (or proposition) that . . .; (ii) S has adequate evidence for the hypothesis (or proposition) that . . .; and (iii) . . . .

Or we may use the locution of definition (i) and speak of S knowing "that x is f."

The term "accepts" which appears in (6) has not been previously defined [. . .]. "Assumes" is an alternative: for "S accepts h" is replaceable by "S assumes that h is true"; and "S accepts the proposition or hypothesis that x is f" is replaceable by "S assumes that x is f."

If a man knows, say, that the hall has been painted, then, according to our definition, he accepts the hypothesis that it has been painted, he has adequate evidence for this hypothesis, and, finally, the hall *has* been painted. On the other hand, if he accepts the hypothesis, has adequate evidence for it, but does not know that it is true, then the hall has not been painted.

Should we say that, if S knows h to be true, then S *believes* that h is true? (It should be noted that *believing* a proposition is not the same as asserting, proclaiming, or announcing that one believes it. When we *assert* a proposition and when we *say* that we believe it, then, unless we are lying, we are *acting upon* the proposition. [. . .]) There is a sense of "believe," in its ordinary use, which is such that "S believes that h is true" entails "S does *not* know that h is true." If I *know* that La Paz is in Bolivia, I'm not likely to say, "I believe that La Paz is in Bolivia," for "I *believe* that La Paz is in Bolivia" suggests I don't know that it is. In this use, "S believes that h is true" means that S accepts h but does not know that h is true. Hence, if we interpret "believe" in this way, we cannot say that *knowing* entails *believing*. There is still another use of "believe" which is such that the expression "I believe"—an expression in the first person—entails "I know," or at least entails "I have adequate evidence." If a man says, "His policy, I believe, will not succeed," the parenthetical expression may be intended to express the claim to know or the claim to have adequate evidence that the policy will not succeed.[14]

But "believe" is also used to mean the same as "accept," in the sense in which "accept" is meant above, and in this use *knowing* does entail *believing*. I may believe that *x* is f, in this third sense of "believe," and yet not *say*, "I believe that *x* is f"; for, as we have noted, when "I believe" is used in this construction (in contrast with its parenthetical use) it is ordinarily intended to express doubt or hesitation. You may say of me, however, "He believes that *x* is f and, for all I know, he *knows* that *x* is f."

But even if there is a sense of "believe," or "accept," in which *knowing* entails *believing*, or *accepting*, we must not think of knowing as being, in any sense, a "species of" believing, or accepting. A man can be said to believe firmly, or reluctantly, or hesitatingly, but no one can be said to *know* firmly, or reluctantly, or hesitatingly. Professor Austin has noted that, although we may ask, "*How do you know?*" and "*Why do you believe?*" we may not ask, "*Why do you know?*" or "*How do you believe?*"[15] The relation of knowing to believing, in the present sense of "believe," is not that of falcon to bird or of airedale to dog; it is more like that of arriving to traveling. *Arriving* entails *traveling*—a man cannot arrive unless he has traveled—but arriving is not a species of traveling.[16]

When we exhort people epistemically, we say, not "You ought to *believe* h," but "You ought to *know* h." If I say to my friend, "You ought to know h," it is likely that I accept h and believe that he has adequate evidence for h; hence the only additional condition I'm exhorting him to meet is that of believing h. Or it may be that I claim to know h myself and am suggesting that he ought to make further inquiry or investigation (see Section 4 of the present chapter) and that when he does he will then have adequate evidence for h. Similar remarks hold of such statements as "You ought to have *known* h."

A second sense of "know" may be obtained by stipulating that the subject *know*, in the first sense, that he has adequate evidence. The statement "S knows that he has adequate evidence" raises important philosophical questions, comparable to certain controversial questions about ethics [. . .]. If, as many philosophers believe, there is reason to say that people cannot *know* what they ought to do, then there is also reason to say that people cannot know which of their beliefs are evident.

Still another sense of "know" may be obtained by stipulating that (ii), in definition (6), describe a *causal* condition of (i). Using "know" in this sense, we cannot say that a man knows a proposition to be true unless we can also say that he believes it *because* he has adequate evidence for it.

7. The term "certain," like "know," is used in many ways. Sometimes it is a synonym for the modal term "necessary"; sometimes one is said to be certain of a proposition only if one is unable to doubt it or if one accepts it with a "maximum degree of confidence"; and sometimes one is said to be certain only if one *knows* that one knows. But the sense of "certain" which is of most importance epistemically, I think, is this:

(7) "S is *certain* that h is true" means: (i) S knows that h is true and (ii) there is no hypothesis *i* such that *i* is more worthy of S's belief than h.

We could avoid "true," if we chose, in the manner suggested in connection with the definition of "know" above.

Sometimes the locution "S is certain" is used to mean merely that S *feels sure*. And in this use, of course, "S is certain" does not imply that S knows. I felt sure that my candidate would win the election, but since he did not, I could not have known that he would.

The present epistemic concept of *certainty* may

be illustrated by a quotation from Moritz Schlick. He does not use our epistemic terms, but he is telling us, in effect, that, although statements made by scientists may be evident, they are not certain and that there are other statements which, in contrast with those of the scientists, are certain:

> I do have trust in those good fellows, but that is only because I have always found them to be trustworthy whenever I was able to test their enunciations. I assure you most emphatically that I should *not* call the system of science true if I found its consequences incompatible with my own observations of nature, and the fact that it is adopted by the whole of mankind and taught in all the universities would make no impression on me. If all the scientists in the world told me that under certain experimental conditions I must see three black spots, and if under those conditions I saw only one spot, no power in the universe could induce me to think that the statement "there is now only one black spot in the field of vision" is false.[17]

This passage might be interpreted as saying that, at the present moment, there is no hypothesis, not even the best-confirmed hypotheses of science, which is more acceptable than the hypothesis that there is now only one black spot in the field of vision.

But we need not say, as Cardinal Newman did, that certitude is "indefectible" and permanent— that "whoever loses his conviction on a given point is thereby proved not to have been certain of it."[18] For definition (7), like our other definitions, should be thought of as containing a temporal reference. Even if a man in the position Schlick describes above is *now* certain of the proposition expressed by "There is only one black spot in the field of vision," a proposition about what is to be seen today, he will not be certain about today's black spots tomorrow. And it may well be that at some later date this

true proposition about today will become unreasonable.

We need not say that people are certain of all those propositions which they know to be true or which they perceive to be true. A man may know or perceive that there is smoke along the harbor without being certain—for there may be other propositions which, for him, are even more worthy of belief. In one of its many senses, "There *appears* to me to be smoke along the harbor," if it is true, expresses a proposition which, for any subject, no matter what he may be perceiving, is more acceptable than the proposition that there *is* smoke there. This point [. . .] is sometimes obscured by the other uses which "certain," "know," and "appear" happen to have in ordinary discourse.

It would be strange to say, "Not only do I *know* that that is true—I am *certain* of it." For one way of saying, "I am certain," in the present sense of the word, is to say, "I know," with emphasis.[19] Moreover, the negative expression "I am *not* certain that . . ." is often used to mean, not simply "It is false that I am certain that . . .," but, more strongly, "I do not believe, and am indeed inclined to doubt, that . . ." I may say, "I'm not certain I can attend the meeting," in order to convey my belief that I probably won't attend the meeting. But in saying above that *knowing* and *perceiving* do not imply *being certain*, I mean merely that there are some propositions which are even more worthy of our belief than many of those which we know or perceive to be true.

Notes

1 See Richard Price, *Review of the Principal Questions of Morals* (Oxford, 1948; first published in 1787), ch. viii. Compare H. A. Prichard's "Duty and Ignorance of Fact," reprinted in his *Moral Obligation* (Oxford, 1950), and W. D. Ross, *Foundations of Ethics* (London, 1939), ch. vii.

2 Compare Bertrand Russell, *Human Knowledge* (New York, 1948), pt. v, ch. vi.

3 There is a useful discussion of this distinction in R. B. Braithwaite, *Scientific Explanation* (Cambridge,

1953), pp. 279 ff. In *The Origin of the Knowledge of Right and Wrong* (London, 1902), sec. 23, Franz Brentano says in effect that we ought to believe only what is true. In a colloquium entitled "The Normative in the Descriptive," Konstantin Kolenda and Abraham Edel say we ought to believe only what is true, while Alan Ross Anderson, Max Black, and Irving Copi say there are times when we need not believe what is true (*Review of Metaphysics*, X [1956], pp. 106–121).

4   W. K. Clifford, *Lectures and Essays*, vol. II (London, 1879). It should be noted that our definitions, as they now stand, have this limitation: they do not enable us to formulate Clifford's position, for we cannot consistently say that a hypothesis and its contradictory are both unreasonable.

5   Compare this dialogue from Sheridan's *The Rivals*: "Absolute: 'Sure, Sir, this is not very reasonable, to summon my affection for a lady I know nothing of.' Sir Anthony: 'I am sure, Sir, 'tis more unreasonable in you to object to a lady you know nothing of' " (quoted by J. M. Keynes in *A Treatise on Probability* [London, 1921], p. 41).

6   These concepts are discussed with more exactness in writings on probability. See, for example, Rudolf Carnap, *Logical Foundations of Probability* (Chicago, 1950), pp. 226–279.

7   I suggest that the concept of *acting upon* a hypothesis must be defined by reference to *action*, *purpose*, and *belief* in some such way as this. "In acting A, S is *acting upon* h" means: in acting A, S is trying to produce E; and he is acting as he would act if, further, (i) he believed h and (ii) he believed that A will result in E if and only if h is true. I shall not discuss the concepts of *purpose* and *action* in this book.

8   See Sextus Empiricus, *Outlines of Pyrrhonism*, bk. I, especially pp. 9, 112, and 123 of vol. I of *Sextus Empiricus* (Loeb Classical Library, London, 1933).

9   Compare G. H. von Wright, *An Essay in Modal Logic* (Amsterdam, 1951); "Deontic Logic," *Mind*, LX (1951), pp. 1–13; and "On the Logic of Some Axiological and Epistemological Concepts," *Ajatus* (Helsinki), XVII (1952), pp. 213–234. Although von Wright does not discuss the epistemic concepts listed above, much of what I have said about the first four concepts is suggested by his work. In the *Ajatus* article, he introduces the epistemological concepts "falsified," "verified," "not-falsified," and "undecided." Compare Alan Ross Anderson,

The Formal Analysis of Normative Systems (Technical Report no. 2, Interaction Laboratory, Sociology Department, Yale University, 1956).

10   Some ought-statements—for example, "If you want to be happy, you ought to believe in God"—are concerned only with telling how to bring about certain ends, ends which can be described without ethical or epistemic terms. But ought-statements in contexts such as the above should not be interpreted in this way [. . .].

11   R. B. Braithwaite, *Scientific Explanation*, pp. 279 ff. Compare C. S. Peirce, *Collected Papers* (Cambridge, Mass., 1931), I, 311 ff.; C. I. Lewis, "Right Believing and Concluding," in *The Ground and Nature of the Right* (New York, 1955), ch. ii; and G. Polya, *Patterns of Plausible Inference* (Princeton, 1954), *passim*.

12   John Watling, "Inferences from the Known to the Unknown," *Proceedings of the Aristotelian Society*, LV (1954–1955), p. 58.

13   John Hartland-Swann, "The Logical Status of 'Knowing That,' " *Analysis*, XVI (1956), p. 114. [. . .]

14   Compare J. O. Urmson, "Parenthetical Verbs," *Mind*, vol. LXI (1952), reprinted in Antony Flew, ed., *Essays in Conceptual Analysis* (London, 1956).

15   J. L. Austin, "Other Minds," *Proceedings of the Aristotelian Society*, suppl. vol. XX (1946), reprinted in Antony Flew, ed., *Logic and Language*, 2nd ser. (Oxford, 1953).

16   Professor Gilbert Ryle has used this example in another connection [. . .].
[. . .]

17   Moritz Schlick, "Facts and Propositions," *Analysis*, II (1935), p. 70. Compare Norman Malcolm on "the strong sense of 'know,' " in "Knowledge and Belief," *Mind*, LXI (1952), pp. 178–189.

18   *The Grammar of Assent*, ch. vii.

19   A. D. Woozely contrasts this "certifying" or "guaranteeing" character of "I know that" with the tentativeness expressed by "I am certain," when "I am certain" means merely that I feel sure; see his *Theory of Knowledge* (London, 1949), pp. 187–189. Compare J. L. Austin, "Other Minds," *Proceedings of the Aristotelian Society*, suppl. vol. XX (1946), especially pp. 170–174, reprinted in Antony Flew, ed., *Logic and Language*, 2nd ser. In "Ordinary Language and Absolute Certainty," Paul Edwards points out ambiguities in uses of "certain" (*Philosophical Studies*, I [1950]).

Chapter 27

William Alston

THE DEONTOLOGICAL CONCEPTION OF EPISTEMIC JUSTIFICATION

The deontological conception

The terms "justified," "justification," and their cognates are most naturally understood in what we may term a "deontological" way, as having to do with obligation, permission, requirement, blame, and the like. We may think of *requirement*, *prohibition*, and *permission* as the basic deontological terms, with *obligation* and *duty* as species of requirement, and with *responsibility*, *blameworthiness*, *reproach*, *praiseworthiness*, *merit*, *being in the clear*, and the like as normative consequences of an agent's situation with respect to what is required, prohibited, or permitted. More specifically, when we consider the justification of *actions*, something on which we have a firmer grip than the justification of beliefs, it is clear that to be justified in having *done* something is for that action not to be in violation of any relevant rules, regulations, laws, obligations, duties, or counsels, the ones that govern actions of that sort. It is a matter of the action's being *permitted* by the relevant system of principles.[1] To say that the action was justified does not imply that it was required or obligatory, only that its negation was not required or obligatory. This holds true whether we are thinking of moral, legal, institutional, or prudential justification of actions. To say that Herman was (morally) justified in refusing to take time out from writing his book to join in a peace march is to say that the relevant moral principles do not

require him to march; it is not to say that he is morally obliged to stick to writing his book, though that may be true also. Likewise to say that Joan was legally justified in leaving the state is to say that her doing so contravened no law; it is not to say that any law required her to do so. Finally, consider my being justified in giving my epistemology class a take-home final rather than one to be taken in the classroom. Here we might be thinking of institutional justification, in which case the point would be that no regulations of my department, college, or university require a classroom final exam; but my being so justified does not imply that any regulations require a take-home exam. Or we might be thinking of pedagogical justification, in which case the point would be that sound pedagogical principles allow for a take-home exam for this kind of course, not that they require it; though, again, the latter might be true also.

The most natural way of construing the justification of beliefs is in parallel fashion. To say that S is justified in believing that p at time t is to say that the relevant rules or principles do not forbid S's believing that p at t. In believing that p at t, S is not in contravention of any relevant requirements. Again, it is not to say that S is required or obligated to believe that p at t, though that might also be true. With respect to beliefs we can again distinguish various modes of justification: moral, prudential, and epistemic. These may diverge. I may, for example, be morally justified in trusting my friend (believing that he is well intentioned toward me), and I may even be morally required to do so, even though, since all my evidence tends strongly against it, the belief is not epistemically justified. In this paper our concern is with epistemic justification. How is that distinguished from the other modes? The justification of anything, H, consists in H's being permitted by the relevant principles: epistemic, moral, or whatever. Thus the crucial question is: What distinguishes epistemic principles from moral principles? Well, the "epistemic point of view" is characterized by a concern with the twin goals of believing the true and not believing the false. To set this out properly we would have to go into the question of just how these goals are to be weighted relative to each other, and into a number of other thorny issues; but suffice it for now to say that epistemic principles for the assessment of belief will grade them in the light of these goals. Just how this is done depends on the conception of justification with which one is working. On a deontological conception of justification, the principles will forbid beliefs formed in such a way as to be likely to be false and either permit or require beliefs formed in such a way as to be likely to be true.[2] Thus on the deontological conception of the epistemic justification of belief that is as close as possible to the standard conception of the justification of action, to be justified in believing that p at t is for one's belief that p at t not to be in violation of any epistemic principles, principles that permit only those beliefs that are sufficiently likely to be true.[3] Let's say, for example, that beliefs in generalizations are permitted only if based on adequate inductive evidence, otherwise forbidden, and that a perceptual belief that p is permitted only if (a) it is formed on the basis of its perceptually seeming to one that p and (b) one does not have sufficient overriding reasons; otherwise it is forbidden. One will be justified in a belief of the specified sort if the relevant necessary conditions of permissibility are satisfied; otherwise the belief will be unjustified.

Since this is the natural way to use "justification", it is not surprising that it is the one most often formulated by those who seek to be explicit about their epistemic concepts. Perhaps the most eminent contemporary deontologist is Roderick Chisholm.[4] Because of the complexities of Chisholm's view, however, I shall take as my model deontologist Carl Ginet. He sets out the conception with admirable directness.

One is justified in being confident that p if and only if it is not the case that one ought not to be confident that p; one could not be justly reproached for being confident that p.[5]

Now this conception of epistemic justification is viable only if beliefs are sufficiently under voluntary control to render such concepts as requirement, permission, obligation, reproach, and blame applicable to them. By the time-honored principle that "Ought implies can," one can be obliged to do A only if one has an effective choice as to whether to do A.[6] It is equally obvious that it makes no sense to speak of S's being permitted or forbidden to do A if S lacks an effective choice as to whether to do A.[7] Therefore the most fundamental issue raised by a formulation like Ginet's is as to whether belief is under voluntary control. Only if it is can the question arise as to whether the epistemic justification of beliefs can be construed deontologically. As we shall see, there are various modes of voluntary control that have usually not been fully distinguished in the literature and that require separate treatment. I will be arguing in this paper that (a) we lack what I will call direct voluntary control over beliefs, (b) that we have only a rather weak degree of "long range" voluntary control over (only) some of our beliefs, and (c) that although our voluntary actions can influence our beliefs, the deontological notion of justification based on this indirect influence is not the sort of notion we need for the usual epistemological purposes to which the term "justification" is put.

The problem of voluntary control of belief

There are many locutions that encourage us to think of believing as subject to requirement, prohibition, and permission. We say "You shouldn't have supposed so readily that he wouldn't come through," "You have no right to assume that," "I had every right to think that she was honest," "I ought to have given him the benefit of the doubt," and "You shouldn't jump to conclusions." We also often seem to suggest the voluntary control of belief: "I finally decided that he was the man for the job," "Make up your mind; is it coreopsis or isn't it?", "I had to accept his testimony; I had no choice" (the suggestion being that in other cases one does have a choice). And philosophers frequently fall in with this, speaking of a subject's being in a situation in which he has to decide whether to accept, reject, or "withhold" a proposition.[8] All these turns of phrase, and many more, seem to imply that we frequently have the capacity to effectively decide or choose what we are to believe, and hence that we can be held responsible for the outcome of those decisions. It is natural to think of this capacity on the model of the maximally direct control we have over the motions of our limbs and other parts of our body, the voluntary movements of which constitute "basic actions," actions we perform "at will," just by an intention, volition, choice, or decision to do so, things we "just do," not "by" doing something else voluntarily. Let's call the kind of control we have over states of affairs we typically[9] bring about by basic actions, "basic voluntary[10] control." If we do have voluntary control of beliefs, we have the same sort of reason for supposing it to be basic control that we have for supposing ourselves to have basic control over the (typical) movements of our limbs, viz., that we are hard pressed to specify any voluntary action by doing which we get the limbs moved or the beliefs engendered. Hence it is not surprising that the basic voluntary control thesis has had dis-tinguished proponents throughout the history of philosophy, for example Augustine, Aquinas, Descartes, Kierkegaard, and Newman.[11] Though distinctly out of favor today, it still has its defenders.[12]

Before critically examining the thesis, we must make some distinctions that are important for our entire discussion. First, note that although the above discussion is solely in terms of belief, we need to range also over propo-sitional attitudes that are contrary to belief. Chisholm speaks in terms of a trichotomy of "believe," "reject," and "withhold" that p.[13] Since rejecting p is identified with believing some contrary of p, it brings in no new kind of propositional attitude; but withholding p, believing neither it nor any contrary, does. The basic point to be noted here is that one has control over a given type of state only if one also has control over some field of incompatible alternatives. To have control over believing that p is to have control over whether one believes that p or not, that is, over whether one believes that p or engenders instead some incompatible alternative.[14] The power to choose A at will *is* the power to determine at will whether it shall be A or (some form of) not-A. Therefore, to be strictly accurate we should say that our problem con-cerns voluntary control over propositional atti-tudes. Although in the sequel the formulation will often be in terms of belief, it should be understood as having this more general bearing.

Second, something needs to be said about the relation between the control of *actions* and of *states of affairs*. Thus far we have been oscillating freely between the two. Now a belief, in the psycho-logical sense that is being used here (as con-trasted with the abstract sense of that which is believed), is a more or less long-lived *state* of the psyche, a modification of the wiring that can influence various actions and reactions of the subject so long as it persists. And the same holds for other propositional attitudes. Thus in speaking of voluntary control of beliefs, we have been speaking of the control of states. But couldn't we just as well speak of the voluntary control of, and responsibility for, the action of bringing about such states: accepting, rejecting, or withholding a proposition, forming a belief, or refraining from believing?[15] The two loci of responsibility and control may seem strictly correlative, so that we can equally well focus on either. For one exercises voluntary control over a type of state, C, by voluntarily doing something to bring it about or inhibit it. And from the other side, every action can be thought of as the bringing about of a state of affairs. Whenever we are responsible for a state of affairs by virtue of having brought it about, we may just as well speak of being responsible for the action of bringing it about. There are the following reasons, however, for proceeding in terms of states.

First, in holding that beliefs are subject to deontological evaluation since under voluntary control, one need not restrict oneself to beliefs that were formed intentionally by a voluntary act. I can be blamed for believing that *p* in the absence of adequate evidence, even though the belief was formed quite automatically, not by voluntarily carrying out an intention to do so. Provided believing in general is under voluntary control, any belief can be assessed deontologically. It is enough that I could have adopted or withheld the proposition by a voluntary act, had I chosen to do so.

Another consideration that decisively favors the focus on states is that, as we shall see later, there is a way in which one can be responsible and blameworthy for a state of belief, or other state, even if one lacks the capacity to bring about such states intentionally.

The final preliminary note is this. Our issue does not concern free will or freedom of action, at least not in any sense in which that goes beyond one's action's being under the control of the will. On a "libertarian" conception of free will this is not sufficient; it is required in addition that both A and not-A be causally possible, given all the causal influences on the agent. And

other requirements may be imposed concerning agency. A libertarian will, no doubt, maintain that if deontological concepts are to apply to believings in the same way as to overt actions, then all of his conditions for freedom will have to apply to believings as well. In this essay, however, I shall only be concerned with the issue of whether believings are under voluntary control. If, as I shall argue, this condition is not satisfied for believings, that will be sufficient to show that they are not free in the libertarian sense as well.

Basic voluntary control

Let's turn now to a critical examination of the basic control thesis, the thesis that one can take up at will whatever propositional attitude one chooses. Those who have attacked this view are divided between those who hold that believing at will is logically impossible and those who hold that it is only psychologically impossible, a capacity that we in fact lack though one we conceivably could have had.[16] I cannot see any sufficient reasons for the stronger claim, and so I shall merely contend that we are not so constituted as to be able to take up propositional attitudes at will. My argument for this, if it can be called that, simply consists in asking you to consider whether you have any such powers. Can you, at this moment, start to believe that the United States is still a colony of Great Britain, just by deciding to do so? If you find it too incredible that you should be sufficiently motivated to try to believe this, suppose that someone offers you $500,000,000 to believe it, and you are much more interested in the money than in believing the truth. Could you do what it takes to get that reward? Remember that we are speaking about believing at will. No doubt, there are things you could do that would increase the probability of your coming to believe this, but that will be discussed later. Can you switch propositional attitudes toward that proposition just by deciding to do so? It seems clear to me that I have no such power. Volitions, decisions, or choosings don't hook up with anything in the way of propositional attitude inauguration, just as they don't hook up with the secretion of gastric juices or cell metabolism. There could conceivably be individual differences in this regard. Some people can move their ears at will, while most of us cannot. However, I very much doubt that any human beings are endowed with the power of taking on propositional attitudes at will. The temptation to suppose otherwise may stem from conflating that power with others that we undoubtedly do have but that are clearly distinct.[17] If I were to set out to bring myself into a state of belief that p, just by an act of will, I might assert that p with an expression of conviction, or dwell favorably on the idea that p, or imagine a sentence expressing p emblazoned in the heavens with an angelic chorus in the background intoning the Kyrie of Mozart's Coronation Mass. All this I can do at will, but none of this amounts to taking on a belief that p. It is all show, an elaborate pretence of believing. Having gone through all this, my doxastic attitudes will remain just as they were before; or if there is some change, it will be a result of these gyrations.

We should not suppose that our inability to believe at will is restricted to propositions that are obviously false. The inability also extends, at least, to those that are obviously true. A few pages back we made the point that voluntary control attaches to contrary pairs, or to more complex arrays of alternatives. If the sphere of my effective voluntary control does not extend both to A and to not-A, then it attaches to neither. If I don't have the power to choose between A and not-A, then we are without sufficient reason to say that I did A *at will*, rather than just doing A, accompanied by a volition. It is even more obvious, if possible, that responsibility, obligation, and their kindred attach to doing A only if the agent has an effective choice between doing and not doing A. If I would still have done A whatever I willed, chose, or preferred, I can hardly be blamed for doing it.

Thus, even if I willingly, or not unwillingly,

form, for instance, perceptual beliefs in the way I do, it by no means follows that I form those beliefs at will, or that I have voluntary control over such belief formation, or that I can be held responsible or blameworthy for doing so. It would have to be true that I have effective voluntary control over whether I do or do not believe that the tree has leaves on it when I see a tree with leaves on it just before me in broad daylight with my eyesight working perfectly. And it is perfectly clear that in this situation I have no power at all to refrain from that belief. And so with everything else that seems perfectly obvious to us. We have just as little voluntary control over ordinary beliefs formed by introspection, memory, and simple uncontroversial inferences.

The discussion to this point will suggest to the voluntarist that he can still make a stand on propositions that do not seem clearly true or false and hold that there one (often) has the capacity to adopt whatever propositional attitude one chooses. In religion, philosophy, and high level scientific matters it is often the case that, so far as one can see, the relevant arguments do not definitively settle the matter one way or the other. I engage in prolonged study of the mind–body problem or of the existence of God. I carefully examine arguments for and against various positions. It seems to me that none of the positions have decisively proved their case, even though there are weighty considerations that can be urged in support of each. There are serious difficulties with all the competing positions, though, so far as I can see, more than one contender is left in the field in each case. So what am I to do? I could just abandon the quest. But alternatively I could, so it seems, simply decide to adopt one of the positions and/or decide to reject one or more of the contenders. Is that not what I must do if I am to make any judgment on the matter? And isn't that what typically happens? I decide to embrace theism or epiphenomenalism, and forthwith it is embraced.

There are also practical situations in which we

are confronted with incompatible answers to a certain question, none of which we see to be clearly true or false. Here we often do not have the luxury of leaving the field; since we must act in one way rather than another, we are forced to form, and act on, some belief about the matter. It would be a good idea for me to plant these flowers today if and only if it will rain tomorrow. But it is not at all clear to me whether tomorrow will be rainy. I must either plant the flowers today or not, and it would surely be unwise to simply ignore the matter, thereby in effect acting uncritically on the assumption that it will not rain tomorrow. Hence the better part of wisdom would be to make some judgment on the matter, the best that I can. On a larger scale, a field commander in wartime is often faced with questions about the current disposition of enemy forces. But often the information at his disposal does not tell him just what that disposition is. In such a situation is it not clear that, weighing available indications as best he can, he simply decides to make a certain judgment on the matter and act on that? What else can he do?

Before responding to these claims I should point out that even if they were correct, it would still not follow that a deontological conception of justification is adequate for epistemology. For the voluntarist has already abandoned vast stretches of the territory. He has given up all propositions that seem clearly true or false, and these constitute the bulk of our beliefs. Controversial and difficult issues force themselves on our attention, especially if we are intellectuals, just because we spend so much of our time trying to resolve them. But if we survey the whole range of our cognitive operations, they will appear as a few straws floating on a vast sea of items about none of which we entertain the slightest doubt. Consider the vast number of perceptual beliefs we form about our environment as we move about in it throughout our waking hours, most of them short-lived and many of them unconscious. By comparison the controversial beliefs we have in religion, politics,

philosophy, and the conduct of our affairs are negligible in number, however significant they may be individually. Hence if only the uncertain beliefs are under voluntary control, that will not enable us to form a generally applicable deontological concept of epistemic justification.[18]

To return to our philosopher, gardener, and military commander, I would suggest that in each case the situation is better construed in some way other than as initiating a belief at will.[19] The most obvious suggestion is that although in these cases the supporting considerations are seen as less conclusive, here too the belief follows automatically, without intervention by the will, from the way things seem at the moment to the subject. In the cases of (subjective) certainty belief is determined by that sense of certainty, or, alternatively, by what leads to it, the sensory experience or whatever; in the cases of (subjective) uncertainty belief is still determined by what plays an analogous role, the sense that one alternative is more likely than the others, or by what leads to that. Thus when our philosopher or religious seeker "decides" to embrace theism or the identity theory, what has happened is that at that moment this position seems more likely to be true, seems to have weighter considerations in its favor, than any envisaged alternative. Hence S is, *at that moment*, no more able to accept atheism or epiphenomenalism instead, than he would be if theism or the identity theory seemed obviously and indubitably true. This can be verified by considering our capacities in a situation in which the above conditions are not satisfied; theism and atheism, or the various contenders on the mind–body issue, really seem equally likely to be true, equally well or ill supported. If that were strictly the case (and perhaps it seldom is), then could S adopt, for example, theism, just by choosing to do so? When I contemplate that possibility, it seems to me that I would be as little able to adopt theism at will as I would be if it seemed obviously true or obviously false. Here, like Buridan's ass, I am confronted with (subjectively) perfectly equivalent alternatives. If it were a choice between actions, such as that confronting the ass, I need not perish through indecision. I could arbitrarily make a choice, as we often do in a cafeteria line when two alternative salads look equally tempting. (Some people negotiate this more quickly than others.) But doxastic choice is another matter. How *could* I simply choose to believe one rather than the other when they seem exactly on a par with respect to the likelihood of truth, especially when that subjective probability is rather low? To do so would be to choose a belief in the face of the lack of any significant inclination to suppose it to be true. It seems clear to me that this is not within our power.[20]

The above account in terms of comparative subjective probability might be correct for all our cases, theoretical and practical. Thus the military commander might adopt the supposition about the disposition of enemy forces that seems to him at the moment best supported by the reports at his disposal. But I believe that there are cases, both theoretical and practical, in which the upshot is not triggered by some differential subjective probability of the alternatives. I have already argued that in those cases the upshot cannot be the formation of a belief, whether at will or otherwise. But then what? Here is one possibility. What S is doing is to resolve to act as if *p* is true, adopt it as a basis for action. This is often a correct description of situations like the military commander's. He may well have said to himself: "I don't know what the disposition of enemy forces is; I don't even have enough information to make an educated guess. But I have to proceed on some basis or other, so I'll just assume that it is H and make my plans accordingly." This is not to form the belief that the disposition is H; it is not to *accept* the proposition that the disposition is H, except as a basis for action. It would simply be incorrect to describe the commander as *believing* that the disposition of enemy forces is H, or having any other belief about the matter. He is simply pro-

ceeding on a certain assumption, concerning the truth of which he has no belief at all. One may also make an assumption for theoretical purposes, in order to see how it "pans out," in the hope that one will thereby obtain some additional reasons for supposing it to be true or false. Thus a scientist can adopt "as a working hypothesis" the proposition that the atomic nucleus is positively charged, draw various consequences from it, and seek to test those consequences. The scientist need not form the *belief* that the atomic nucleus is positively charged in order to carry out this operation; typically he would be doing this because he didn't know what to believe about the matter. Likewise a philosopher might take materialism as a working hypothesis to see how it works out in application to various problems. There may also be blends of the theoretical and the practical. One may adopt belief in God, or some more robust set of religious doctrines, as a guide to life, setting out to try to live in accordance with them, seeking to act and feel one's way into the religious community, in order to determine how the doctrines work out in the living of them, both in terms of how satisfactory and fulfilling a life they enable one to live and in terms of what evidence for or against them one acquires.

Where the "acceptance" of a proposition in the absence of a significant subjective probability is not the adoption of a working hypothesis, there are other alternatives. (1) S may be seeking, for whatever reason, to bring himself into a position of believing *p*; and S or others may confuse this activity, which can be undertaken voluntarily, with believing or judging the proposition to be true. (2) As noted earlier, S may assert that *p*, overtly or covertly, perhaps repeatedly and in a firm tone, and this, which can be done voluntarily, may be confused with a "judgment" that *p*, of the sort that inaugurates a state of belief. (3) S may align herself, objectively and/or subjectively, with some group that is committed to certain doctrines—a church, a political party, a movement, a group of thinkers—and this, which can be done voluntarily, may be confused with coming to believe those doctrines. I am convinced that the analysis of a wide variety of supposed cases of believing at will in the absence of significant subjective probability would reveal that in each case forming a belief that p has been confused with something else. Thus I think that there is a strong case for the proposition that no one ever acquires a belief at will. But even if I am wrong about that, the above considerations do at least show that it is of relatively rare occurrence, and that it certainly cannot be used as the basis for a generally applicable deontological concept of epistemic justification.

Nonbasic immediate voluntary control

The demise of basic control, however, is by no means the end of "voluntarism," as we may term the thesis that one has voluntary control of propositional attitudes. Many deontologists, after disavowing any commitment to what they usually call "direct voluntary control of belief" and what we have called "basic voluntary control," proceed to insist that beliefs are subject to what they term "indirect voluntary control."[21] All of them use the term "indirect control" in an undiscriminating fashion to cover any sort of control that is not "direct," that is, basic. As a result they fail to distinguish between the three sorts of nonbasic control I shall be distinguishing.[22] Some of their examples fit one of my three categories, some another. The ensuing discussion will show important differences between these three modes of control.

To get into this, let's first note that we take many familiar nonbasic overt actions to be voluntary (and their upshots to be under voluntary control) in a way that is sufficient for their being required, permitted, and prohibited. Consider opening a door, informing someone that p, and turning on a light. To succeed in any of these requires more than a volition on the part of the agent; in each case I must perform one or more bodily movements and these movements must have certain consequences, causal or conventional, in order that I can be said to have performed the nonbasic action in question. In order for it to be true that I opened a certain door, I must pull it, push it, kick it, or put some other part of my body into suitable contact with it (assuming that I lack powers of telekinesis), and this must result in the door's coming to be open. In order to inform H that p, I must produce various sounds, marks, or other perceptible products, and either these products must fall under linguistic rules in such a way as to constitute a vehicle for asserting that p (if we are thinking of informing as an illocutionary act), or H, upon perceiving these products, must be led to form the belief that p (if we are thinking of informing as a perlocutionary act). Hence actions like these are not immediately consequent on a volition and so are not strictly done "at will." Nevertheless I might be blamed for my failure to turn on the light when it was my obligation to do so. The point is that in many cases we take the extra conditions of success for granted. We suppose that if the agent will just voluntarily exert herself, the act will be done. Here we might say that the action, and its upshot, is under the "immediate voluntary control" of the agent (more strictly, *nonbasic* immediate voluntary control), even though more than an act of will is required of the agent. I call this "immediate"[23] control since the agent is able to carry out the intention "right away", in one uninterrupted intentional act, without having to return to the attempt a number of times after having been occupied with other matters.[24] I will use the term "direct control" for both basic and immediate control. It is clear that if beliefs were under one's immediate control, that would suffice to render them susceptible to deontological evaluation.

But are beliefs always, or ever, within our immediate voluntary control? Our discussion of this will be largely a rerun of the discussion of basic control, with some added twists. As in the earlier discussion we can first exempt most of our doxastic situations from serious consideration. With respect to almost all normal perceptual, introspective, and memory propositions, it is absurd to think that one has any such control over whether one accepts, rejects, or withholds the proposition. When I look out my window and see rain falling, water dripping off the leaves of trees, and cars passing by, I no more have immediate control over whether I accept those propositions than I have basic control. I form the belief that rain is falling willy-nilly. There is no way I can inhibit this belief. At least there is no way I can do so *on the spot*, in carrying out an uninterrupted intention to do so. How would I do so? What button would I push? I could try asserting the contrary in a confident tone of voice. I could rehearse some skeptical arguments. I could invoke the Vedantic doctrine of *maya*. I could grit my teeth and command myself to withhold the proposition. But unless I am a very unusual person, none of these will have the least effect. It seems clear that nothing any normal human being can do during the uninterrupted operation of an intention to reject the proposition that it is raining (in the above situation) will have any chance at all to succeed. And the same can be said for inferential beliefs in which it is quite clear to one that the conclusion is correct. Since cases in which it seems perfectly clear to the subject what is the case constitute an enormously large proportion (I would say almost all) of propositions that are either the object of a definite attitude or considered as a candidate for such, the considerations of this paragraph show that immediate voluntary control cannot be a basis for the application of deontological concepts to most of our propositional attitudes.

But what about situations in which it is not clear whether a proposition is true or false? This is where voluntarists tend to take their stand. After all, they say, that is what inquiry is for, to resolve matters when it is not clear what the

correct answer is. One certainly has voluntary control over whether to keep looking for evidence or reasons, and voluntary control over where to look, what steps to take, and so on. Since one has control over those matters, that amounts to what I have called immediate voluntary control over one's propositional attitudes.

If self-control is what is essential to activity, some of our beliefs, our believings, would seem to be acts. When a man deliberates and comes finally to a conclusion, his decision is as much within his control as is any other deed we attribute to him. If his conclusion was unreasonable, a conclusion he should not have accepted, we may plead with him: "But you needn't have supposed that so-and-so was true. Why didn't you take account of these other facts?" We assume that his decision is one he could have avoided and that, had he only chosen to do so, he could have made a more reasonable inference. Or, if his conclusion is not the result of a deliberate inference, we may say, "But if you had only stopped to think", implying that, had he chosen, he could have stopped to think. We suppose, as we do whenever we apply our ethical or moral predicates, that there was something else the agent could have done instead.[25]

To be sure, the mere fact that one often looks for evidence to decide an unresolved issue does not show that one has immediate control, or any other sort of control, over one's propositional attitudes. That also depends on the incidence of success in these enterprises. And sometimes one finds decisive evidence and sometimes one doesn't. But let's ignore this complexity and just consider whether there is a case for immediate control of propositional attitudes in the successful cases.

No, there is not, and primarily for the following reason. These claims ignore the difference between doing A in order to bring about E, for some definite E, and doing A so that some effect within a certain range will ensue. In order that the "looking for more evidence" phenomenon would show that we have immediate voluntary control over propositional attitudes in basically the way we do over the positions of doors and light switches, it would have to be the case that the search for evidence was undertaken with the intention of taking up a certain particular attitude toward a particular proposition. For only in that case would the outcome show that we have exercised voluntary control over *what* propositional attitude we take up. Suppose that I can't remember Al Kaline's lifetime batting average and I look it up in the baseball almanac. I read there the figure .320, and I thereby accept it. Does that demonstrate my voluntary control over my belief that Kaline's lifetime batting average was .320? Not at all. At most it shows that I have immediate voluntary control over whether I take up *some* propositional attitude toward *some* proposition ascribing a lifetime batting average to Kaline. This is not at all analogous to my exercising my capacity to get the door open whenever I choose to do so. Its nearest analogue in that area would be something like this. I am a servant and I am motivated to bring the door into whatever position my employer chooses. He has an elaborate electronic system that involves automatic control of many aspects of the household, including doors. Each morning he leaves detailed instructions on household operations in a computer. Doors can only be operated through the computer in accordance with his instructions. There is no way in which I can carry out an intention of my own to open or to close a door. All I can do is to actuate the relevant program and let things take their course. Since the employer's instructions will be carried out only if I actuate the program, I am responsible for the doors' assuming whatever position he specified, just as I was responsible for taking up some attitude or other toward some proposition within a given range. But I most emphatically am not respon-

sible for the front door's being open rather than closed, nor can I be said to have voluntary control over its specific position. Hence it would be idle to apply deontological concepts to me vis-à-vis the specific position of the door: to forbid me or require me to open it, or to blame or reproach me for its being open. I had no control over that; it was not subject to my will. And that's the way it is where the only voluntary control I have over my propositional attitudes is to enter onto an investigation that will eventuate in some propositional attitude or other, depending on what is uncovered. That would be no basis for holding me responsible for believing that *p* rather than rejecting or withholding it, no basis for requiring me or forbidding me to believe that *p*, or for reproaching me for doing so.

If Chisholm's claim is only that one can voluntarily put oneself in a position from which some doxastic attitude to *p* will be forthcoming (or perhaps that one can put oneself in a position such that a desirable doxastic attitude to *p* will be forthcoming), this capacity extends to all sorts of propositions, including those over which we obviously have no voluntary control. Consider propositions concerning what is visible. I have the power to open my eyes and look about me, thereby putting myself in a position, when conditions are favorable, to reliably form propositions about the visible environment. Again, with respect to past experiences I can "search my memory" for the details of my experiences of the middle of yesterday, thereby, usually, putting myself in an excellent position to reliably form beliefs about my experiences at that time. No one, I suppose, would take this to show that I have immediate voluntary control over what I believe about the visible environment or about my remembered experiences. And yet this is essentially the same sort of thing as the search for additional evidence, differing only in the type of belief-forming mechanism involved.

I suspect that deontologists like Chisholm secretly suppose that the additional evidence, rather than "automatically" determining the doxastic attitude, simply puts the subject in a position to make an informed choice of an attitude. That is, despite their official position, they really locate the voluntary control in the moment of attitude formation rather than in the preliminary investigation, thus in effect taking the direct voluntary control position. But then, faced with the crashing implausibility of that position, they think to save the application of deontological concepts by pushing the voluntary control back to the preliminary search for decisive considerations. It is, then, their secret, unacknowledged clinging to the basic control thesis that prevents them from seeing that voluntary control of the investigative phase has no tendency to ground the deontological treatment of propositional attitudes. I must confess that I have no real textual evidence for this speculation, and that I am attracted to it by the fact that it explains an otherwise puzzling failure of acute philosophers to see the irrelevance (to this issue) of our voluntary control over the conduct of inquiry.

Thus far I have been considering one way in which deontologists seek to defend a claim of immediate voluntary control over beliefs. We have seen that way to fail by irrelevance, since it has to do with voluntarily putting oneself in a position to form the most rational attitude, whatever that may be, rather than voluntarily taking up some specific attitude. However, there is no doubt but that people do sometimes set out to get themselves to believe that *p*, for some specific *p*. People try to convince themselves that X loves them, that Y will turn out all right, that the boss doesn't really have a negative attitude toward them, that the Red Sox will win the World Series, that materialism is true, or that God exists. Epistemologists don't like to cite such disreputable proceedings as a ground for the application of deontological concepts. To try to get oneself to believe that *p*, prior to being in a good position to tell whether *p* is true or not, is not a procedure to be commended from the epistemic standpoint. Nevertheless, these

undertakings have to be considered in a comprehensive survey of possible modes of voluntary control. Proceeding in that spirit, the point to note here is that such goings-on provide no support for a supposition of *immediate* voluntary control over belief. For such enterprises can be successfully carried out only as long-term projects. If I, not currently believing that X loves me, were to set out to bring about that belief in one fell swoop, that is, during a period of activity uninterruptedly guided by the intention to produce that belief, then, unless I am markedly abnormal psychologically, I am doomed to failure. We just don't work that way. Again, I wouldn't know what button to push. My only hope of success would lie in bringing various influences to bear upon myself and shielding myself from others, in the hope of thereby eventually moving myself from disbelief to belief. This might include dwelling on those encounters in which X had acted lovingly toward me, shutting out evidences of indifference or dislike, encouraging romantic fantasies, and so forth. Thus this sort of enterprise belongs, rather, to the category of *long-range voluntary control*, a topic to which we now turn.

Long-range voluntary control

We have seen that we cannot plausibly be credited with either sort of direct control over our propositional attitudes. Taking up such an attitude can be neither a basic action like raising one's arm nor a nonbasic action like flipping a switch. Hence the deontological treatment of belief can borrow no support from the applicability of deontological terms to actions like these. But the possibility still remains that we have more long-range voluntary control over belief. The considerations of the last paragraph encourage this supposition, at least for some cases. Before examining this possibility I will firm up the distinction between this type of control and the previous one.

In introducing the notion of "immediate control" I said that when one has this species of control over a type of state, C, one is able to bring about a C "right away, in one uninterrupted intentional act." When conditions are propitious, one can get a door open, get a light on, get one's shoes on, or tell Susie the mail has come, by doing various things under the direction of a single uninterrupted intention to bring about that state of affairs. One does not have to return to the attempt a number of times after having been occupied with other matters.[26] And since one is not ordinarily capable of keeping an intention in an active state for more than a relatively short period of time, the sorts of actions over which one has immediate control must be capable of execution within a short time after their inception.

Long-range control is simply the foil of immediate control. It is the capacity to bring about a state of affairs, C, by doing something (usually a number of different things) repeatedly over a considerable period of time, interrupted by activity directed to other goals. One has this sort of control, to a greater or lesser degree, over many things: one's weight, cholesterol concentration, blood pressure, and disposition; the actions of one's spouse or one's department. One can, with some hope of success, set out on a long-range project to reduce one's weight, improve one's disposition, or get one's spouse to be more friendly to the neighbors. The degree of control varies markedly among these examples. I have, within limits, complete control over my weight; only sufficient motivation is required to achieve and maintain a certain weight. My ability to change my disposition or to change behavior patterns in my spouse is much less. But all these cases, and many more, illustrate the point that one can have long-range control over many things over which one lacks direct control. I cannot markedly reduce my weight right away, by the uninterrupted carrying out of an intention to do so, for instance by taking a pill, running around the block, or saying "Abracadabra." But that doesn't nullify the fact that I have long-range control.

It does seem that we have some degree of long-range voluntary control over at least some of our beliefs. As just noted, people do set out on long-range projects to get themselves to believe a certain proposition, and sometimes they succeed in this. Devices employed include selective exposure to evidence, selective attention to supporting considerations, seeking the company of believers and avoiding nonbelievers, self-suggestion, and more bizarre methods like hypnotism. By such methods people sometimes induce themselves to believe in God, in materialism, in communism, in the proposition that they are loved by X, and so on. Why doesn't this constitute a kind of voluntary control that grounds deontological treatment?

Well, it would if, indeed, we do have sufficient control of this sort. Note that people could properly be held responsible for their attitudes toward propositions in a certain range only if those who set out to intentionally produce a certain attitude toward such a proposition, and made sufficient efforts, were frequently successful.[27] For only if we are generally successful in bringing about a goal, G, when we try hard enough to do so, do we have effective control over whether G obtains. And if I don't have effective control over G, I can hardly be held to blame for its nonoccurrence. Even if I had done everything I could to produce it, I would have had little chance of success; so how could I rightly be blamed for its absence? (I might be blamed for not trying to produce it or for not trying hard enough, but that is another matter.) This is a generally applicable principle, by no means restricted to the doxastic sphere. If I am so constituted that the most I can do with respect to my irritability is to make it somewhat less likely that it will exceed a certain (rather high) average threshold, I can hardly be blamed for being irritable.

It is very dubious that we have reliable long-range control over any of our beliefs, even in the most favorable cases, such as beliefs about religious and philosophical matters and about personal relationships. *Sometimes* people succeed in getting themselves to believe (disbelieve) something. But I doubt that the success rate is substantial. To my knowledge there are no statistics on this, but I would be very much surprised if attempts of this sort bore fruit in more than a very small proportion of the cases. In thinking about this, let's first set aside cases in which the attempt succeeds because the subject happens onto conclusive evidence that would have produced belief anyway without deliberate effort on his part to produce belief. These are irrelevant because the intention to believe that p played no effective role. Thus we are considering cases in which the subject is swimming against either a preponderance of contrary evidence or a lack of evidence either way. S is fighting very strong tendencies to believe when and only when something seems true to one. Some of these tendencies are probably innate and some engendered or reinforced by socialization; in any event they are deeply rooted and of great strength. To combat or circumvent them one must exercise considerable ingenuity in monitoring the input of information and in exposing oneself to nonrational influences. This is a tricky operation, requiring constant vigilance as well as considerable skill, and it would be very surprising if it were successful in a significant proportion of the cases. I am not suggesting that it is unusual for people to form and retain beliefs without adequate grounds, reasons, or justification. This is all too common. But in most such cases the proposition in question seems clearly true, however ill supported. The typical case of prejudice is not one in which S manages to believe something contrary to what seems to him to be the case or something concerning which he has no definite impression of truth or falsity. It is a case in which his socialization has led it to seem clearly true to him that, for example, blacks are innately inferior.

Thus a long-range control thesis does not provide much grounding for deontologism, even for the sorts of propositions people do sometimes try to get themselves to believe or disbelieve. Much less is there any such grounding for those propositions with respect to which people don't normally even try to manipulate their attitudes. We have already noted that most of our beliefs spring from doxastic tendencies that are too deeply rooted to permit of modification by deliberate effort. Most of the matters on which we form beliefs are such that the project of deliberately producing belief or disbelief is one that is never seriously envisaged, just because it is too obvious that there is no chance of success. Thus even if we were usually successful when we set out to produce a propositional attitude, the voluntary control thus manifested would not ground the application of deontological concepts to beliefs generally. So, once again, the most we could conceivably have (and I have argued that we do not in fact have even that) would fall short of a generally applicable deontological concept of justification.

Indirect voluntary influence: a different deontological conception of epistemic justification

Up to this point I have been examining the support for a deontological conception of epistemic justification provided by the treatment of propositional attitude formation on the model of intentional action. We have considered whether, or to what extent, it is in our power to carry out an intention to take up a certain propositional attitude, either at will (basic control), or while uninterruptedly guided by the intention to do so (immediate control), or as a complex long-term project (long-range control). We have seen that for most of our beliefs we have control of none of these sorts, and that for the others we have, at most, some spotty and unreliable control of the long-range sort. I conclude that we do *not* generally have the power to carry out an intention to take up a certain propositional attitude. Insofar as the conception of epistemic justification as *believing as one is permitted to* depends on that assumption, it must be rejected. The inauguration of propositional attitudes simply does not work like intentional action.

However, this is not necessarily the end of the line for the deontologist. He has another move. We can be held responsible for a state of affairs that results from our actions even if we did not produce that state of affairs intentionally, provided it is the case that something we did (didn't do) and should have not done (done) was a necessary condition (in the circumstances) of the realization of that state of affairs, that is to say, provided that state of affairs would not have obtained had we not done (done) something we should not have done (done). Suppose that, although I did not do anything with the intention of bringing about my cholesterol buildup, still I could have prevented it if I had done certain things I could and should have done, for instance reduce fat intake. In that case I could still be held responsible for the condition; it could be my fault. This is a way in which deontological concepts can be applied to me, with respect to a certain state of affairs, even though that state of affairs did not result from my carrying out an intention to produce it.

This suggests that even if propositional attitudes are not under our effective voluntary control, we might still be held responsible for them, provided we could and should have prevented them; provided there is something we could and should have done such that if we had done it we would not have had the attitude in question. If this is the case, it could provide a basis for the application of deontological concepts to propositional attitudes, and, perhaps, for a deontological concept of epistemic justification, one that bypasses the above critique. Let's use the term "indirect voluntary influence" for this kind of voluntary control, or, better, "voluntary impact," we may have on our beliefs.

It may be helpful to display in outline form the various modes of voluntary control we have distinguished.

(I)   Direct control
    (A) Basic control
    (B) Nonbasic immediate control
(II) Long-range control
(III) Indirect influence

Now it does seem that we have voluntary control over many things that influence belief. These can be divided into (1) activities that bring influences to bear, or withhold influences from, a particular situation involving a particular candidate, or a particular field of candidates, for belief, and (2) activities that affect our general belief-forming habits or tendencies.[28] There are many examples of (1). With respect to a particular issue, I have voluntary control over whether, and how long, I consider the matter, look for relevant evidence or reasons, reflect on a particular argument, seek input from other people, search my memory for analogous cases, and so on. Here we come back to the activities that people like Chisholm wrongly classify as the intentional inauguration of a propositional attitude. Although the fact that it is within my power to either look for further evidence or not does not show that I have voluntary control over what attitude I take toward p, it does show that I have voluntary control over influences on that attitude. The second category includes such activities as training myself to be more critical of gossip, instilling in myself a stronger disposition to reflect carefully before making a judgment on highly controversial matters, talking myself into being less (more) subservient to authority, and practicing greater sensitivity to the condition of other people. It is within my power to do things like this or not, and when I do them with sufficient assiduity I make some difference to my propositional attitude tendencies, and thus indirectly to the formation of such attitudes.[29]

Actually, there would be no harm in including in the first category attempts to bring about a certain specific attitude, and the successful carrying out of such an attempt when and if that occurs. For these too would be things over which we have voluntary control that influence our propositional attitudes. The point of stressing other things is that, since our earlier discussions have provided reason for thinking that such attempts are rarely successful, I want to emphasize the point that even if we are never successful in carrying out an intention to believe (reject, withhold) p, still there are many things over which we have voluntary control that do have a bearing on what propositional attitudes are engendered.

Thus it will sometimes be the case that had we performed (not performed) some voluntary actions A, B, . . ., we would have (not have) taken up some attitude we did not (did) take up. The only remaining question is as to whether deontological concepts apply to the sorts of activities we have been discussing. Is it ever the case that we ought or ought not to engage in some activity of searching for new evidence or refraining from doing so? Is it ever the case that we ought (ought not) to strive to make ourselves more (less) critical of gossip or more (less) sensitive to contrary evidence? Deontologists typically aver that we have *intellectual* obligations in such matters, obligations rooted in our basic intellectual obligation to seek the true and avoid the false, or, alternatively, rooted in our basic aim, need, or commitment to believe the true and avoid believing the false. Let's go along with our opponents on this point. I can do so with a clear conscience, since I am seeking to show that even if we admit this, and make the other concessions I have been making, a deontological conception of epistemic justification is not viable.

Thus it will sometimes be the case, when I believe that p, that I would not have done so had I done various things in the past that I could and should have done but failed to do. Suppose that I accept some idle gossip to the effect that Jim is trying to undermine Susie's position as chair of the department. It may be that had I been doing my duty by way of making myself more critical

of gossip, and by way of checking into this particular matter, I would not have formed that belief or would not have retained it for so long. In that case I could be held responsible for believing this in the same way as that in which I can be held responsible for my cholesterol buildup. I can be properly blamed for it, even though I did not intentionally bring it about.

Note that this application of deontological concepts to beliefs is a derivative one. What is primarily required, permitted, and forbidden are the voluntary activities we ranged in two categories, various sorts of activities that influence belief. Deontological concepts are applied to beliefs only because of some relation these attitudes have to those primary targets of permission, and the like. This asymmetrical relation of dependence attaches to all those cases in which one is responsible for a state of affairs without being responsible for an action of intentionally bringing it about.

Now let's consider just what deontological terms can be applied to beliefs in this derivative way and how this application is to be understood. Remember that we are taking requirement, prohibition, and permission to be the basic deontological concepts. When dealing with intentional actions, it is best to think first of general principles that lay down conditions under which an action of a certain sort is required, forbidden, or permitted, and then consider a particular action to have one of these statuses because it exemplifies some general principle. Thus if we take the forming of a belief to be an intentional action, we will envisage general principles that hold, for instance, that it is forbidden to believe that p in the absence of sufficient evidence. Then if I form a particular belief without sufficient grounds, that belief is forbidden, or, if you prefer, I have violated a prohibition in forming that belief. We can then apply other deontological terms like "responsible," "blame," and "praise" on this basis. If one intentionally does something that falls under a principle of one of the above sorts, one is responsible for what one has done. If in doing it one has violated a requirement or a prohibition, one can rightly be blamed for it. If one has not violated any requirement or prohibition, one is justified in doing it.

But on the present way of looking at the matter, we can have no principles laying down conditions under which a belief is required, forbidden, or permitted, just because we lack sufficient voluntary control over belief formation. What the relevant principles will require, and so forth, are activities that are designed to influence factors that, in turn, will influence belief formation.[30] Hence there is no basis for taking a particular belief to be required, prohibited, or forbidden. And so if we are to say, on the rationale given above, that one can be responsible and blameworthy for a belief, that will be the case even though the belief is not prohibited. If one is puzzled by this, the cure comes from realizing that responsibility and blame supervene on requirement, prohibition, and permission in two quite different ways. First, and most simply, one is to blame for doing something forbidden or for failing to do something required. But second, one is also to blame for the obtaining of some fact if that fact would not have obtained if one had not behaved in some manner for which one is to blame in the first sense, that is, for doing something forbidden or failing to do something required.

So far, in discussing indirect influence, we have seen that one can be to blame for a certain propositional attitude provided one wouldn't have that attitude had one not failed to conform to some intellectual requirement or prohibition. But this formulation must be refined. On reflection it turns out to be too broad. There are certain ways in which dereliction of duty can contribute to belief formation without rendering the subject blameworthy for forming that belief. Suppose that I fail to carry out my obligation to spend a certain period in training

myself to look for counterevidence. I use the time thus freed up to take a walk around the neighborhood. In the course of this stroll I see two dogs fighting, thereby acquiring the belief that they are fighting. There was a relevant intellectual obligation I didn't fulfill, which is such that if I had fulfilled it I wouldn't have acquired that belief. But if that is a perfectly normal perceptual belief, I am surely not to blame for having formed it.[31]

Here the dereliction of duty contributed to belief formation simply by facilitating access to the data. That is not the kind of contribution we had in mind. The sorts of cases we were thinking of were those most directly suggested by the two sorts of intellectual obligations we distinguished: (a) cases in which we acquire or retain the belief only because we are sheltered from adverse considerations in a way we wouldn't have been had we done what we should have done; (b) cases in which the belief was acquired by the activation of a habit we would not have possessed had we fulfilled our intellectual obligations. Thus we can avoid counterexamples like the above by the following reformulation:

> (I)   S is (intellectually) to blame for believing that p iff If S had fulfilled all her intellectual obligations, then S's belief forming habits would have changed, or S's access to relevant adverse considerations would have changed, in such a way that S would not have believed that p.

Another issue has to do with the "absoluteness" of the counterfactual involved in this formulation. (I) involves the flat requirement that S *would not have believed that p* under these conditions. But perhaps S is also blameworthy for believing that p if some weaker condition holds, for instance, that it would be much less likely that S would have believed that p had S fulfilled her intellectual obligations. Of course, the relation between this and (I) depends on one's account of counterfactuals. For present purposes we need not enter this forbidding swamp. I am shortly going to argue that the concept of epistemic justification that emerges from (I) is inadequate for epistemology, and that argument will not rest on taking the counterfactual to be stronger or weaker.

We can now move on to developing a deontological notion of epistemic justification that is based on the above. One point is obvious: when S is to blame for believing that p, that belief is not justified. But that will presumably cover only a tiny proportion of beliefs. What about the others?

One possibility would be to treat being justified as the mirror image of being unjustified. To justifiably believe that p, then, is for one's belief that p to be to one's credit. That is, one is justified in believing that p iff one wouldn't have believed that p unless one had fulfilled one's intellectual obligations in some way: by doing what is intellectually required of one or by refraining from doing what one is intellectually forbidden to do. This might seem to leave us with precious few justified beliefs. How many of our beliefs have intellectually dutiful deeds as an essential part of their ancestry? But before embracing that conclusion we should remember that part of the formulation that has to do with refraining from doing what is forbidden. The formulation does not imply that we are justified only where some positive act of duty is in the causal ancestry. One might argue that it is always open to us to engage in attempts to build up disreputable belief-forming tendencies, for example wishful thinking; and that often we wouldn't have the perfectly respectable beliefs we do have if we had engaged in that enterprise with sufficient vigor. But even so, it still remains that no such counterfactual would hold for beliefs that are beyond the reach of voluntary endeavors, like typical perceptual, memory, and introspective beliefs. No amount of striving after wishful thinking would dislodge most of these. Hence

they would fall outside the scope of justified belief on this construal.

There is a simple way to set up the justified–unjustified distinction on the basis of (I) without coming into so violent a conflict with our ordinary judgments. We can take any belief that is not unjustified by the above criterion to be justified. On this construal, "unjustified" would be the term that "wears the trousers" (Austin), and "justified" would simply be its negation. A belief is justified iff the subject is not intellectually to blame for holding it. This brings us back to the deontological conception of justification advocated by Ginet and others. Remember that we quoted Ginet as saying that one is justified provided that "one could not be justly reproached for being confident that p." The only difference is that whereas Ginet was thinking of blame as attaching to belief as something that is itself under voluntary control, we are thinking of it in the more complex, derivative way developed in this section.

Critique of this new conception

The upshot of the paper thus far is that the only viable deontological conception of justification is the one that identifies being justified in believing that p with not being intellectually to blame for believing that p, in a sense of "to blame for" explicated in (I). To put this into a canonical formula:

> (II)   S is justified in believing that p iff it is not the case that if S had fulfilled all her intellectual obligations, then S's belief-forming habits would have changed, or S's access to relevant adverse considerations would have changed, in such a way that S would not have believed that p.

What follows the iff is, of course, the denial of the account of being to blame for a belief given by (I). "Of course," since on this conception, being justified in believing that p is just not being to blame for believing that p.

In the remainder of the paper I shall present reasons for denying that (II) gives us a concept of justification that is what we are, or should be, looking for in epistemology. I shall point out ways in which one can be justified according to (II), and yet not justified in any way that is crucial for epistemological concerns; and, conversely, that one can be justified in an epistemologically crucial way and yet not deontologically justified, as spelled out by (II). But first a terminological disclaimer. My linguistic intuitions tell me that "justified" and its cognates are properly used only in a deontological sense. To be justified in doing or believing . . . something just is to not have violated any relevant rules, norms, or principles in so doing, believing. . . . If, as I believe, most epistemologists use "justified" for some quite different notion, they are speaking infelicitously. However, this way of talking is so firmly entrenched that I shall go along with it, albeit with an uneasy linguistic conscience.

If I am to argue that (II) does not amount to real epistemic justification, I must proceed on the basis of some assumption as to what epistemic justification really is. I have no time to argue for any such assumption at the tag end of this paper. Hence I shall argue the point separately for two different conceptions, one more externalist, the other more internalist. I shall devote most of the time to my favorite conception, which is basically externalist with an internalist twist. Let me begin by briefly explaining that.

Start from the idea of forming a belief in such a way as to be in a good position to get a true belief. Call this, if you like, a "strong position" conception of justification. One is justified in believing that p only if that belief that p was formed in such a way as to make it at least very likely that the belief is true, or, as is sometimes said, only if it was formed in a "truth-conducive" way.[32] Reliability theory is a natural

way of further developing the notion: the belief is justified only if it was formed in a *reliable* fashion, one that can generally be *relied* on to produce true beliefs. Note that there is no guarantee that the subject will be aware of the crucial aspects of the mode of formation, much less of the fact that that mode is truth conducive; that is what makes this conception externalist. My internalist twist consists in also requiring that the belief be based on a "ground" that the subject can be aware of fairly readily. This twist does not negate the externalism. I do not also require that the subject be aware, or have the capacity to become aware, that the ground is an adequate one or that the belief was formed in a reliable or a truth-conducive way. My internalist qualification will play no role in what follows. The argument will depend solely on the requirement that the ground be in fact an adequate one (sufficiently indicative of the truth of the belief). I mention my internalist twist only to point out that the ensuing argument against (II) does not depend on embracing the most extreme form of externalism.

The first point to mention about (II) is that the concept does not apply at all to subjects that lack sufficient sophistication, reflectiveness, or freedom to be subject to intellectual requirements, prohibitions, and the like. This includes lower animals and very young children as well as the mentally defective. But I don't want to stress this consideration, since it can be plausibly argued that the notion of epistemic justification has no significant application to such subjects either. If I went along with the popular view that justification is necessary for knowledge, I would resist this claim, for it is clear to me that lower animals and very young children often know what is going on in their environment. But since I am prepared to recognize knowledge without justification, I am free to acknowledge that the notion of epistemic justification gets a foothold only where subjects are capable of evaluating their own doxastic states and those of others and responding to those evaluations appropriately.

Hence the discussion will be restricted to normal adult humans, to whom deontological concepts are applicable.

Next I shall explore ways in which one may be deontologically justified in a belief without forming the belief in a truth-conducive way. But first, how we are to tell when one is free of blame in forming a belief? That depends on whether the belief stemmed, in the specified way, from any failure of obligations. But how are we to think of those obligations? I am not now asking about the content of our intellectual obligations. As for that, I shall simply draw on the illustrations given earlier. I am asking rather: how much is a person obliged to do along these lines in a particular situation? And the main point is that we must distinguish between "counsels of perfection" and what it is reasonable to expect of a person. With world enough and time we could require people to carry out an exhaustive investigation of each witness, search through all the relevant literature for considerations pertinent to each candidate for belief, check each calculation ten times, and so on. But we simply do not have time for all that. Even if we were exclusively devoted to the search for truth, we would not be able to do that for all the matters on which we need to form beliefs. And given that we have various other commitments and obligations, it is doubly impossible. Hence, abandoning counsels of perfection, let us say that one can properly be blamed for a belief only if that belief stems, in the specified way, from failures to do what could reasonably be expected of one; simply failing to do what would be ideally adequate is not enough.

[Elsewhere] I present two examples of subjects who are deontologically justified but in a poor position to get the truth. One is a case of cultural isolation. S has lived all his life in an isolated primitive community where everyone unhesitatingly accepts the traditions of the tribe as authoritative. These have to do with alleged events distant in time and space, about which S and his fellows have no chance to gather independent evidence. S has never encountered anyone who questions the traditions, and these traditions play a key role in the communal life of the tribe. Under these conditions it seems clear to me that S is in no way to blame for forming beliefs on the basis of the traditions. He has not failed to do anything he could reasonably be expected to do. His beliefs about, for example, the origins of the tribe stem from what, so far as he can see, are the best grounds one could have for such beliefs. And yet, let us suppose, the traditions have not been formed in such a way as to be a reliable indication of their own truth. S is deontologically justified, but he is not believing in a truth-conducive way.

The first half of this judgment has been challenged by Matthias Steup, who takes a hard line with my tribesman.

> No matter how grim the circumstances are, if an agent holds a belief contrary to evidence, it is within his power, given that he is a *rational* agent, to *reflect* upon his belief and thereby to find out that he had better withhold it, or even assent to its negation. Being a rational agent, I would say, involves the capacity to find out, with respect to any belief, whether or not it is being held on good grounds.[33]

Hence, contrary to my judgment, S is not free of intellectual blame and so is not deontologically justified.

I think that Steup is displaying an insensitivity to cultural differences. He supposes that there are standards recognized in all cultures that determine what is adequate evidence, or good enough grounds, for one or another kind of belief. That does not seem to me to be the case. There may very well be transcultural epistemic standards, such as consistency and reliability, but I see no reason to suppose that they are sufficient to settle all issues as to what counts as adequate reasons or grounds. On the contrary, the criteria for this vary significantly from one culture to another. The judgments of adequacy of grounds that are transmitted across generations will differ across cultures. Hence what can reasonably be expected of a subject with respect to, for instance, critical examination of beliefs and their bases will differ across cultures. We require adults in our culture to be critical of "tradition," but this is a relatively recent phenomenon, given the time humans have been on earth; it cannot be reasonably required of everyone in every society. Note that I am not saying that what *is* adequate evidence varies with the culture. I am no cultural relativist. On the contrary. My judgment that S's belief lacks adequate grounds was based on the supposition that there are objective standards for adequacy of grounds that hold whatever is accepted in one or another culture. But that is just the point. Deontological justification is sensitive to cultural differences because it depends on what can reasonably be expected of one, and that in turn depends on one's social inheritance and the influences to which one is exposed. But truth conducivity does not so depend. Hence they can diverge.

The other case I presented was a "cognitive deficiency" case. It concerned a college student who doesn't have what it takes to follow abstract philosophical exposition or reasoning. Having read parts of Book IV of Locke's *Essay*, he takes it that Locke's view is that everything is a matter of opinion. He is simply incapable of distinguishing between that view and Locke's view that one's knowledge is restricted to one's own ideas. There is nothing he could do, at least nothing that could reasonably be expected of him, given his other commitments and obligations, that would lead him to appreciate that difference. Hence he cannot be blamed for interpreting Locke as he does; he is doing the best he can. But surely this belief is outrageously ill grounded, based as it is on the student's dim-witted impressions of Locke.

Steup challenges this case by claiming that even if the student is incapable of attaining a better understanding of Locke, he could have done something that would have led him to

withhold acceptance of the interpretation in question, viz., ask himself "Do I understand Locke's *Essay* well enough to be justified in assenting to this interpretation?"[34] Now, as Steup intimates, I certainly don't want to depict the case in such a way that the student is incapable of asking himself this question. I do, however, want to construe it in such a way that asking the question would not lead him to withhold assent. The case I have in mind is one in which the student feels quite confident of his reading; this is definitely the way it strikes him, and he has no tendency to doubt it (at least not prior to seeing the grade he gets on the final exam). Certainly that scenario is a possible one, and it, too, illustrates the possibility of a gap between deontological justification and truth-conducive justification.

However, it may have been poor strategy to trot out this hapless student as one of only two cases, for it undoubtedly raises too many controversial issues. Moreover, it may give the impression that counterexamples based on cognitive deficiency are limited to such extreme and, we may hope, such unusual cases as this, whereas in fact they are all too common. We have such a case whenever one forms a belief, on poor grounds, on something beyond one's intellectual capacity; and this is surely a common occurrence. Just consider a person who forms the belief that socialism is contrary to Christianity, for the reasons that are often given for this view by the New Right, and who is intellectually incapable of figuring out how bad these reasons are.

However, cultural isolation and cognitive deficiency cases only scratch the surface. We have so far been considering cases that are either rather extreme in our culture or come from a very different culture. But there are other sorts of cases that are around us every day. I am thinking particularly of those in which we lack the time or resources to look into a matter in an epistemically ideal fashion. Consider the innumerable beliefs each of us forms on testimony or authority. Most of what we believe, beyond what we experience personally, comes from this source. Ideally we would check out each source to make sure that it is reliable before accepting the testimony. But who has time for that? We can do it in special cases where the matter is of particular importance, but no one could do it for even a small percentage of the items proferred by others for our belief. Nor is it a real option to withhold belief save where we do run a check. That would leave our doxastic structure so impoverished we would not be able to function in our society. Practically everything we believe about science, history, geography, and current affairs is taken on authority. Moreover, even if we had the time to check up on each authority, in most cases we lack the resources for making an informed judgment. For the same reason that I cannot engage in astrophysics on my own, I am in no position to determine who is a competent authority in the field, except by taking the word of other alleged authorities. Thus in most cases in which I uncritically accept testimony I have done as much as could reasonably be expected of me. And now let us consider those cases in which the authority is incompetent or the witness is unreliable. There we are forming a belief on an objectively unreliable basis, though deontologically justified in doing so. One could hardly deny that this happens significantly often.

This same pattern is found outside the sphere of testimony. Consider perception. Sometimes people's eyes deceive them because of physiological or psychological malfunctioning, or because of abnormalities in the environment (cleverly constructed imitations, unusual conditions of the medium, and the like). Should we check for such abnormalities each time we are on the verge of forming a perceptual belief? Obviously we have no time for this, even if our perceptual belief-forming mechanisms were sufficiently under voluntary control. Hence, except where there are definite indications that things are off, we will not have failed in our intellectual obligations if we simply form perceptual beliefs unself-consciously and uncritically; and hence we are deontologically justified in doing so. But now consider cases in which our visual impressions are misleading, even though we are not aware of any indications of this. There one is forming beliefs on an unreliable basis, though deontologically justified in doing so.

Next consider irresistible beliefs and belief tendencies. If it is strictly impossible for me to alter a certain belief or tendency, then I can hardly be expected to do so. But some of these irresistible beliefs may be formed in an unreliable fashion. The most obvious examples concern strong emotional attachments that are, in practice, unshakeable. For many people their religious, or irreligious, beliefs have this status, as do beliefs concerning one's country, one's close relations, or one's political party. Such beliefs are often not formed in a truth-conducive fashion. But the person cannot be blamed for having something she can't help having, and so we get our discrepancy once more.

Finally, consider timing problems. Suppose that I come to realize that it is incumbent on me to look more fully into matters relevant to basic religious issues: the existence of God, the conditions of salvation, the authority of Scriptures, and so on. I have deeply rooted beliefs on these matters; I am not going to throw them over just because I am reopening the questions, nor am I obliged to do so. And even if suspension of belief would be ideally required, it is not a real possibility for me until I see conclusive negative evidence. In any event, I enter onto my investigation. Let's say that the investigation reveals that my beliefs were ill founded all along. As soon as I see that, I cease to believe, either immediately or after some period of readjustment. But while the investigation is proceeding, something that might occupy many years, I am deontologically justified in continuing to hold the beliefs, for I am not obliged to give them up, even if I could, just because questions have been raised; and yet they are not held on truth-conducive grounds.

Again our discrepancy. And again it would seem that such cases are quite frequent.

This completes my case for the possibility, and the actuality, of deontological justification without truth-conducive justification. Even if I am mistaken about the possibility or actuality of some of the above cases, I can safely ignore the possibility that I am mistaken about all. We may take it that our deontological formula, (II), fails to capture what we are looking for in epistemology under the rubric of "justification," when we are looking for something in the neighborhood of "being in a favorable position in believing that p," favorable from the standpoint of the aim at believing the true and avoiding believing the false.

But we can have discrepancies in the opposite direction as well: believing on an adequately truth-conducive ground while not deontologically justified. This possibility will be realized where: (1) I form a belief that p on ground G; (2) G is in fact an adequate ground for that belief; (3) if I had reflected critically on this belief-forming proclivity, as I should have done, I would have found sufficient reasons to doubt its adequacy, and as a result this belief would not have been formed. Here is an example. Let's suppose that it is incumbent on me to look into the credentials of anyone on whose word I believe something of practical importance. An acquaintance, Broom, tells me that Robinson, whom we are considering for a position in my department, has just been made an offer by Princeton. The press of affairs and my instinctive confidence in Broom lead me to neglect my duty and accept Broom's report uncritically. If I had looked into the matter, I would have found strong evidence that Broom is untrustworthy in such matters. This evidence, however, would have been misleading, and in fact Broom is extremely scrupulous and reliable in reporting such things. Thus I formed the belief on an objectively adequate ground, but had I done my intellectual duty I would have mistrusted the ground and hence not formed the belief. I was

justified on truth-conducivity standards but not according to (II).

I have been seeking to show that the deontological conception of justification, the only one of that ilk we have found to be internally viable, fails to deliver what is expected of justification if those expectations include truth-conducivity. But not all contemporary epistemologists go along with this; in particular, the most extreme internalists do not. Not that they sever justification altogether from the aim at attaining the true and avoiding the false. They hold, to put it into my terms, that for a belief to be justified it is necessary, not that its ground be in fact such as to render it likely that the belief is true, but that the subject be justified in supposing this, that the belief appear to be truth-conducive "from the subject's own perspective on the world."[35] Although this kind of internalism is developed in various ways, by no means all of which exactly fit the formula given in the last sentence, we cannot go into all that in this paper. I shall work with the characterization just given.

I believe this view to be subject to an infinite regress of requirements of justification, and to other fatal difficulties. My present concern, however, is to point out divergencies between it and (II) and hence to show that the deontological conception runs afoul of both externalism and internalism. After the lengthy discussion just completed I can be briefer here. The general point is that even after one has done everything that is reasonably expected of one intellectually, it is by no means guaranteed that one is justified in supposing that the ground of one's belief is an adequate one. Let's glance at a few of the cases just presented in connection with my moderate externalism. First, the point with respect to irresistible beliefs is precisely the same. If a belief is irresistible, then no matter how intellectually virtuous I am, I will form that belief whether or not I am justified in supposing its ground to be an adequate one. Turning to resistible beliefs, let's note first that we often do not have time to look into whether the ground of the belief is an adequate one. In such cases (assuming the belief doesn't stem from some other failure to carry out intellectual obligations) one would be deontologically justified; but, assuming that a failure to consider the matter would prevent one from being justified in supposing one's ground to be adequate, one would not satisfy internalist requirements.[36] Again, consider another version of lack of cognitive powers. It seems plausible to suppose that many cognitive subjects are simply incapable of engaging in a rational consideration of whether the grounds of their beliefs (at least many sorts of beliefs, for instance those involving complex inductive grounds) are adequate ones. Even if they raise the question, they are not capable of coming to well-grounded conclusions. These people might have done everything that could reasonably be expected of them in an intellectual way, and yet, because of their inability to effectively submit the grounds of their beliefs to a critical assessment, would not be justified in supposing the ground of a certain belief to be sufficient. Again, deontological justification without internalist justification.

The internalist may reply that we have set our standards for higher level justification too high. It is only necessary that one *have* a justification for believing the ground of one's lower level belief to be an adequate one; and this does not require that one have actually formed any such higher level belief. That is, what should be required is that one be in possession of sufficient evidence for the proposition that the ground in question is adequate, whether or not one has actually made use of that evidence to support a belief in the adequacy of the ground. But we will still get divergencies. The irresistible beliefs will still pose problems. One can't be faulted for holding those beliefs, whether or not one is in possession of adequate evidence for a correlated higher level belief in adequacy. And again it seems that in cases of lack of time I could be deontologically justified in believing that p, whether or not I have sufficient evidence for supposing that ground of that belief to be adequate. Finally, in cases of

deficient cognitive powers one could not be faulted for failure of intellectual obligations in believing that p, even if one lacks evidence for the belief in the adequacy of grounds.

Moreover, here too we get the possibility of internalist justification without deontological justification. Consider one who is justified in supposing the ground of her belief that the hostages are in Iran to be an adequate one. That is, the information and general principles at her disposal indicate her evidence to be sufficient. She is internalistically justified in this belief about the hostages. Yet had she engaged in further investigation, as she should have done, her internal perspective would have been enlarged and corrected in such a way that she would no longer be justified in this higher level belief. Her total knowledge and justified belief would then have indicated that her evidence for this proposition is not sufficient. Here we have internalist justification without deontological justification.

Thus the deontological conception embodied in (II) matches an internalist conception of justification no better than it matches an externalist one. I conclude that there is nothing to be said for the deontological conception, the only one that is not vitiated by internal flaws, as a fundamental concept for epistemology. This is not to deny that it is an interesting and important concept. There are, no doubt, contexts in which it is highly relevant to consider whether a person has failed in any intellectual duty and what bearing this has on the fact that he now believes that p. We would want to consider this if, for example, we were engaged in training the person to be more intellectually responsible or to improve his belief-forming tendencies. But we have seen that these deontological issues are not central to the basic concerns of epistemology with truth and falsity, whether this is conceived externalistically as the formation of propositional attitudes in such a way as to maximize truth and minimize falsity, or internalistically as the formation of propositional attitudes in accordance with what is indicated by the subject's perspective as to the chances for maximizing truth and minimizing falsity. Deontological justification is not epistemic justification.

Conclusion

Let's draw the threads of this paper together. We have examined several forms of a deontological conception of epistemic justification in terms of freedom from blame in taking up a certain propositional attitude. All of these but one was seen to be untenable by reason of requiring a degree of control over our propositional attitudes that we do not enjoy. The only version that escapes this fate was seen to be not the sort of concept we need to play a central role in epistemology. Therefore, despite the connotations of the term, we are ill advised to think of epistemic justification in terms of freedom from blame for believing.[37]

Notes

1 Robert Audi has suggested that for me to have justifiably done A it is also necessary that I did it because it was permitted by the relevant system of principles (though this is not required, he says, for A's having been justified for me). This would be on the analogy of the distinction between S's being justified in believing that p, and the proposition that p's being justified for S. This may be right, but I am unable to go into the matter that fully here. The point I need for this paper is that permission, rather than requirement, by the relevant principles is necessary for the justification of action.

2 Principles having to do with the way a belief is formed is not the only possibility here. A deontologist might prefer to make the permissibility of a belief depend on what evidence or grounds the subject has for the belief, rather than on the grounds that were actually used as a basis in the formation of the belief. Again, she might prefer to make permissibility depend on whether the belief is formed in the right way or on the basis of an adequate ground, so far as the subject can tell, rather than on the actual chances of the belief's being true. Since these differences are not germane to the

issues of this paper, I have chosen to state the matter in terms of my position, according to which the actual adequacy of the basis on which a belief was formed is crucial for its justificatory status.

3 This formulation is itself subject to both internalist and externalist versions (in fact to several varieties of each), depending on whether the "likelihood" is objective or "within the subject's perspective." Moreover, as foreshadowed in the last sentence in the text, this version of a deontological conception is only the one that is closest to the usual concept of the justification of actions; in the course of this essay it will be found not to be viable and will be replaced by a deontological conception that is further from the action case.

4 See Roderick Chisholm, "Lewis' Ethics of Belief," in The Philosophy of C. I. Lewis, ed. P. A. Schilpp (La Salle, Ill.: Open Court, 1968); Theory of Knowledge, 2nd edn. (Englewood Cliffs, N.J.: Prentice-Hall, 1977); "A Version of Foundationalism," in The Foundations of Knowing (Minneapolis: University of Minnesota Press, 1982).

5 Carl Ginet, Knowledge, Perception, and Memory (Dordrecht: D. Reidel, 1975), p. 28. Other epistemologists who explicitly endorse a deontological conception are Laurence BonJour, The Structure of Empirical Knowledge (Cambridge: Harvard University Press, 1985), chap. 1; Paul Moser, Empirical Justification (Dordrecht: D. Reidel, 1985), chaps. 1, 4; Margery Naylor, "Epistemic Justification," American Philosophical Quarterly, 25, no. 1 (1988), 49–58; Alvin Plantinga, "Reason and Belief in God," in Faith and Rationality, ed. A. Plantinga and N. Wolterstorff (Notre Dame, Ind.: University of Notre Dame Press, 1983); Nicholas Wolterstorff, "Can Belief in God Be Rational If It Has No Foundations?," in ibid.; John Pollock, Contemporary Theories of Knowledge (Totowa, N.J.: Rowman & Littlefield, 1986), pp. 7–8. It should be noted that Plantinga makes it explicit that he would be just as happy with a conception in terms of "excellence" rather than in terms of freedom from blame. This indifference has since shifted to a definite preference for the latter. See his "Positive Epistemic Status and Proper Function," Philosophical Perspectives, 2 (1988). Alvin Goldman, though a reliabilist, also advocates a deontological conception in Epistemology and

Cognition (Cambridge: Harvard University Press, 1986), chap. 4.

6 Various exceptions to the principle have been noted recently. See, e.g., Michael Stocker, "'Ought' and 'Can'," *Australasian Journal of Philosophy*, 49, no. 3 (1971), 303–16. However, none of the exceptions involve kinds of actions that are not normally under voluntary control. Hence they have no tendency to show that one could be required or forbidden to believe while one generally lacks voluntary control over beliefs. The formulations in this paragraph should be taken as requiring that one normally has voluntary control over one's beliefs, not that one has voluntary control over a particular belief in a particular situation.

7 As we have pointed out, for an action or whatever to be justified in a deontological sense is for it to be *permitted*, rather than required. Thus it is the necessity of an effective choice for something to be *permitted* that is crucial here.

8 See, e.g., Chisholm, *Theory of Knowledge*, pp. 14–15.

9 This qualification is needed because things we can bring about by a basic action, e.g. a movement of one's arm, we *can* also bring about by doing something else, as when one lifts one arm by moving the other arm.

10 I will often omit the modifier "voluntary" in speaking of control. In this paper it is always to be tacitly understood.

11 Most of these people limit their voluntarism to cases in which it is not clear to the subject whether the belief is true or false. For an excellent account of the history of thought on this subject, with many specific references, see Louis Pojman, *Religious Belief and the Will* (London: Routledge & Kegan Paul, 1986).

12 See, e.g., Carl Ginet, "Contra Reliabilism," *The Monist*, 68, no. 2 (1985), and Jack Meiland, "What Ought We to Believe? The Ethics of Belief Revisited," *American Philosophical Quarterly*, 17 (1980). Neither of these maintains that belief is always under basic voluntary control.

13 *Theory of Knowledge*, chap. 1.

14 To be sure, one might lack the power to determine which of a number of incompatible alternatives is realized, but one could not have the power to choose A at will without also having the power to determine at will that some contrary of A (at least not-A) is realized.

15 I understand "accepting" a proposition as an activity that gives rise to a belief. Therefore, unlike Keith Lehrer, "The Gettier Problem and the Analysis of Knowledge" (in *Justification and Knowledge*, ed. G. S. Pappas [Dordrecht: D. Reidel, 1979]), and others, I am not using the term in such a sense that one could accept a proposition without believing it; though, of course, the belief engendered by an acceptance may be more or less long lived. I also recognize processes of belief formation that do not involve any activity of acceptance.

16 The best-known defense of the logical impossibility claim is by Bernard Williams, "Deciding to Believe," in *Problems of the Self* (Cambridge: Cambridge University Press, 1972). It has been criticized by, *inter alia*, Trudy Govier, "Belief, Values, and the Will," *Dialogue*, 15 (1976), and by Barbara Winters, "Believing at Will," *Journal of Philosophy*, 76 (1979).

17 It may also stem from misdiagnoses of a sort to be presented shortly.

18 Ginet disagrees. He holds that "we can interpret an ascription of unjustifiedness to a belief that the subject cannot help having as saying that, if the subject were able to help it, she ought not to hold the belief" (*Knowledge, Perception, and Memory*, p. 183). Thus we can extend a deontological concept of justification to irresistible beliefs by invoking a counterfactual. I have two comments to make on this move. (1) This renders epistemic justification quite different from the justification of action, where "justified" and other deontological terms are withheld from actions the subject couldn't help performing. (2) Insofar as we can make a judgment as to what would be permitted or forbidden were a certain range of involuntary states within our voluntary control, it will turn out that the deontological evaluation is simply a misleading way of making evaluations that could be stated more straightforwardly and more candidly in other terms. Suppose that we judge that if we had voluntary control over the secretion of gastric juices, then we ought to secrete them in such a way as to be maximally conducive to health and a feeling of well being; e.g. we should not secrete them so as to produce hyperacidity. But since gastric juices are not within our voluntary control, this would seem to be just a misleading way of saying that a certain pattern of secretion is

desirable or worthwhile. The deontological formulation is a wheel that moves nothing else in the machine.

19 Cf. Pojman, *Religious Belief and the Will*, chap. 13, for excellent diagnoses of putative cases of basic control of beliefs.

20 In maintaining that one cannot believe that *p* without its at least seeming to one that *p* is more probable than any envisaged alternative, I am not joining Richard Swinburne (*Faith and Reason* [Oxford: Clarendon Press, 1981], chap. 1) in supposing that to believe that *p* is just to take *p* to be more probable than some alternative(s).

21 See, e.g., Alvin Goldman, "The Internalist Conception of Justification," *Midwest Studies in Philosophy*, 5 (1980); Plantinga, "Reason and Belief in God"; Wolterstorff, "Can Belief in God Be Rational?"; Moser, *Empirical Justification*, chap. 4; Matthias Steup, "The Deontic Conception of Epistemic Justification," *Philosophical Studies*, 53, no. 1 (1988).

22 Even the extended treatment in Pojman, *Religious Belief and the Will*, fails to make any distinctions within "indirect control."

23 When the "nonbasic" qualifier is omitted, "immediate" is hardly a felicitous term for something that contrasts with basic control. Nevertheless, I shall, for the sake of concision, mostly speak in terms of "immediate control." The "nonbasic" qualifier is to be understood.

24 This notion of doing something "right away" will serve to distinguish the present form of direct control from the next.

25 Chisholm, "Lewis' Ethics of Belief," p. 224.

26 I should make it explicit that I do not suppose that an intention must be conscious, much less focally conscious, during all the time it is playing a role in guiding behavior.

27 I am not saying that S could be held responsible for taking attitude A toward *p* only if S himself had in fact been successful in intentionally bringing about that attitude. The requirement is rather that *p* be the sort of proposition toward which people generally are usually successful in bringing about a certain attitude when they try hard enough to do so. If the more stringent requirement were adopted, for actions generally, it would prevent us from holding S responsible for a purely habitual action where he could have successfully carried out an intention to refrain from that action if he had had such an intention. For in that case the action was not in fact the carrying out of a specific intention to perform it. Nevertheless, provided the agent could have inhibited the action had he formed an intention to do, we would feel justified in holding him responsible for it.

28 See Wolterstorff, "Can Belief in God Be Rational?," for an excellent discussion of these modes of influence.

29 Note that the activities in this second category are even further removed from the intentional formation of a certain belief than those in the first, which themselves are clearly distinct from any such thing. The activities in the first category are concerned with a small number of alternatives for attitude formation. Though the activities are not undertaken with the aim of taking up one particular attitude from this field, they are directed to seeking out influences that will resolve this indeterminancy in some way or other. The activities in the second group, however, are directed much more generally to our tendencies of attitude formation on a wide variety of topics and in a wide variety of situations. But the most important point is that in neither case do the activities in question involve the carrying out of an intention to take up a particular propositional attitude.

30 Thus the closest we get to the principle mentioned above would be something like: "One should do what one can to see to it that one is so disposed as to believe that *p* only when that belief is based on adequate evidence." Hence the power to do things that influence belief formation can be thought of as, *inter alia*, a higher level capacity to get ourselves into, or make it more likely that we will be in, a condition that would be required of us if we had sufficient voluntary control over belief.

31 I am indebted to Emily Robertson for calling this problem to my attention.

[...]

32 A more detailed account would look into the epistemic status of the belief at times subsequent to its formation as well. We must forego that in this brief discussion.

33 Steup, "The Deontic Conception of Epistemic Justification," p. 78.

34 Ibid., p. 80.

35 See, e.g., Richard Foley, *The Theory of Epistemic*

Rationality (Cambridge: Harvard University Press, 1987), esp. chaps. 1–3; BonJour, *The Structure of Empirical Knowledge*, chap. 1; Richard Fumerton, *Metaphysical and Epistemological Problems of Perception* (Dordrecht: D. Reidel, 1985), chap. 2; Keith Lehrer, "The Coherence Theory of Knowledge," *Philosophical Topics*, 14, no. 1 (1986).

[. . .]

36 Some epistemologists understand "S is justified in believing that *p*" to mean something like "If S were to believe that *p*, in S's present situation, that belief would be justified." On this understanding the above requirement does not hold. However, I have throughout the paper been understanding "S is justified in believing that *p*" as "S justifiably believes that *p*."

37 Thanks are due to Robert Audi and Jonathan Bennett for very useful comments on this paper. I have profited from discussions with Carl Ginet about these issues.

Chapter 28

Richard Fumerton

EPISTEMIC JUSTIFICATION AND NORMATIVITY

It is plausible to argue that the concept of epistemic justification is the most fundamental concept in epistemology. The so-called traditional account of knowledge takes justified belief to be a constituent of knowledge.[1] Furthermore, on many accounts of knowledge, the conditions for knowledge that go beyond having justified belief, for example the truth condition and conditions designed to "Gettier-proof" the analysis, seem to be less interesting to the philosopher seeking assurance of truth from the first-person perspective. There is a sense in which the best one can do through philosophical reflection is assure oneself that one has a justified belief—whether or not one has knowledge as well is a matter of "luck," is a matter of whether the world cooperates so as to reward justified belief with truth.

It is an understatement to suggest that there is no agreement among epistemologists as to how to analyze the concept of epistemic justification. But a surprising number of philosophers with radically different approaches to analyzing justified belief seem to agree that the concept of epistemic justification is in some sense a normative concept.[2] The issue is potentially significant because the alleged normativity of epistemic justification has been used to attack prominent analyses of justified belief. Ironically, many of these attacks have focused on externalism. The irony lies in the fact that the most prominent externalist, Alvin Goldman (1979 and 1986),

explicitly endorses the claim that the concept of epistemic justification is a normative concept and denies for that reason that he is proposing a meaning analysis of epistemic justification. Rather he proposes to identify the nonnormative (necessary and sufficient) conditions on which epistemic justification supervenes. But whether he was proposing a meaning analysis or identifying synthetic necessary and sufficient conditions for the application of concept, a number of his critics have complained that one can have a belief that results from an unreliable process, even though it would be quite inappropriate to blame the person for having the belief or criticize the person for the way in which the belief was formed.[3] If the concept of epistemic justification is genuinely normative, how can we describe such a belief as unjustified? How can we characterize the victims of demonic machination as having unjustified beliefs when such victims are believing precisely what they *should* believe given the available subjective evidence (evidence that is phenomenologically indistinguishable from the evidence you and I use to reach our conclusions about the physical world)?

The above objection may well confuse evaluation of a subject with evaluation of a subject's belief, but it may be enough to motivate a more-detailed examination of the question of whether and in what sense epistemic justification is usefully thought of as normative. In examining this question, we must get clear about what makes a concept or judgment normative.

Epistemic judgments and value terms

One might begin to suspect that a judgment is normative if it is equivalent in meaning to a conjunction of statements that include paradigmatically normative terms. This approach would seem to require that we give some characterization of what makes a term normative, but we might try to side-step this problem initially by simply listing some paradigmatic normative expressions and characterizing as derivatively normative other expressions whose meaning can be partially explicated using these. Our list of paradigm normative expressions might be long or short depending on whether we are reductionists with respect to the content of various sorts of normative judgments. Thus, if one is a consequentialist of some kind who thinks that all ethical judgments are ultimately judgments about the ways in which actions produce things of intrinsic value, one might get by with "intrinsically good/bad" as the fundamental normative terms—all other normative terms will be derivatively normative because an explication of their meaning will inevitably involve reference to intrinsic goodness/badness. But so as not to prejudice such issues, one might make the initial list relatively long and include such terms as "good," "ought," "should," "right," "permissible," "obligatory," and their opposites.

If we proceed in this fashion, it seems undeniable that the concept of epistemic justification looks suspiciously like a normative concept. As Plantinga (1992) has effectively reminded us, the etymology of the word "justification" certainly suggests that we are dealing with a value term. And epistemologists often seem quite comfortable interchanging questions about whether evidence E justifies one in believing P with questions about whether or not one *should* believe P on the basis of E. In what is

often taken to be one of the earliest statements of a justified true belief account of knowledge, Ayer (1956) described knowledge as true belief where one had the right to be sure. So again, the idea that the concept of justification is normative is at least prima facie plausible. But we must surely proceed more cautiously than this. While it may be all right to begin by listing paradigm normative expressions and characterizing judgments as normative whose meaning can be explicated (in part) through the use of these expressions, it doesn't require much reflection to convince us that expressions like "right" and "should" are importantly ambiguous. When we talk about whether someone should do X, we might be talking about what that person morally should do, prudentially should do, legally should do, should do given the rules of etiquette, should do given that the person has certain goals or ends, and so on. If we add to the mix judgments about what someone should *believe*, it seems that we must add to the list of "shoulds" the *epistemic* "should." If it makes sense to treat belief as something one can do (and be held responsible for), then it seems obvious that we must carefully distinguish our moral obligations with respect to what we should believe, what prudence dictates, and what it is epistemically rational to believe.[4] Thus it has been argued that a husband might have a special moral obligation to believe in his wife's innocence even in the face of rather strong evidence that she is guilty of infidelity. It might also be the prudent thing to do in the sense that his subjective goals or ends might be more effectively satisfied by trusting his wife. But at the same time it might be wildly irrational epistemically to believe in his wife's innocence.

There has been a great deal of literature attempting to cast doubt on the intelligibility of treating believing as an action, as something one chooses to do. One doesn't just decide to believe something the way one decides to go to the store. Many of our beliefs might seem to be forced on us in a way that makes inappropriate questions about whether we should have the beliefs in question.[5] At the same time, it is hard to deny that one can indirectly influence one's beliefs. If one concludes that one would be happier if one believed in an afterlife and that it would be advantageous to have such a belief, there are certainly things one can do that will increase the probability of bringing about the belief. In any event, I am not concerned in this essay with the question of whether it makes sense to talk about what a person ought to believe. I presuppose the intelligibility of such judgments but insist that we make the relevant distinctions between kinds of judgments we can make about what we ought to believe.

Ethical judgments as the paradigm of normativity

If we recognize the ambiguity inherent in judgments about what one ought to believe, then one must decide whether it is all or only some of these "oughts" that indicate the normativity of judgments that employ them. One approach is to begin by simply stipulating that the moral "ought" is the example of a normative expression, par excellence, and the question of whether the epistemic "ought" is normative rests on how close its meaning is to the moral "ought." But if this is the approach we take then to investigate the relevant similarities, we will still need to characterize what it is about *moral* judgments that makes *them* normative.

At this point, our investigation into the alleged normativity of epistemic judgments seems headed into a morass of issues involving metaethics. There is no agreement among ethical philosophers about what makes moral judgments distinctively normative, nor indeed what the relevant contrast is supposed to be between the normative and the nonnormative. For many, the relevant contrast is between *descriptive* judgments (concepts, terms) and *prescriptive* judgments (concepts, terms). According to many of the classic noncognitivists, the normativity of

ethical judgments consists specifically in the fact that their primary function is not to describe some state of affairs but rather to recommend or prescribe some specific action or action kind. The most straightforward version of this view is Hare's claim that moral judgments are grammatically disguised (universalizable) imperatives.[6] Frankly, I don't know of any prominent epistemologists who endorse the idea that epistemic judgments are normative and who explicitly intend thereby to contrast them with descriptive judgments that have a truth value.[7] We can put the conclusion conditionally. If moral judgments are disguised imperatives lacking truth value, and if one is a cognitivist with respect to epistemic judgments, then one must surely hesitate before reaching the conclusion that epistemic judgments are in some important sense normative.

Of course, not all ethical philosophers are noncognitivists. Indeed, noncognitivism is very much a product of twentieth-century philosophy. If one holds that there are genuine moral properties and that moral judgments typically describe their exemplification by things, people, or actions, what would the relevant contrast be between the way in which these judgments are normative and the way in which other descriptive claims are not normative? One can, of course, simply stipulate that a judgment is normative if and only if it refers directly or indirectly to these distinctively moral properties. But if we take this approach, then after we distinguish the epistemic "ought" from the moral "ought," there isn't even a prima facie reason to suppose that epistemic judgments are normative in this sense. If referring to moral properties is a necessary condition for a judgment's being normative and we reject any reduction, in part or in whole, of epistemic judgments to moral judgments, then we will have removed epistemic judgments from the class of normative judgments.

One can try to combine one's descriptivism in ethics with an acknowledgment of the claim that morality necessarily motivates rational people. And one could go on to describe the normative character of moral judgments as consisting precisely in this "pull" that moral judgments have. Just as one cannot recognize that one ought to take some action X without being "moved" to do X, so one cannot recognize that one epistemically ought to believe P without being at least moved to believe P. But it is precisely the acknowledgment of this special character that moral judgments are supposed to have that leads so many philosophers either to abandon descriptivism in ethics or combine it with some version of subjectivism. If moral judgments describe objective properties, it is more than a little difficult to see how the mere belief that something has the property can in itself necessarily motivate the person to pursue that thing.[8] If the connection is only contingent, then the claim that it exists might be philosophically unproblematic (though empirically suspect). I certainly have no interest in denying that when one decides that it is epistemically rational to believe P, one sometimes (or even usually) ends up believing P as a result, and if the existence of a propensity to believe what one judges epistemically rational to believe is all that is meant by claiming that epistemic judgments have normative force, I concede that they might well be normative in this sense (though again, the normative character of a judgment is now a matter for empirical investigation).

Normativity and rules

Without identifying normative judgments with prescriptive judgments, one might still suppose that Hare was on to something in his attempt to characterize what makes normative judgments special. A great many philosophers concerned with metaethics have sought to tie the meaning of ethical judgments to rules. Hare thought of those rules as universalizable imperatives, but one needn't go that far to embrace the conclusion that moral judgments always involve at

least implicit reference to rules. To judge that one ought to do X is to judge that the relevant rules of morality require one to do X. To judge that it is morally permissible that one do X is to judge that the relevant rules of morality do not prohibit one from doing X. And to judge that it would be wrong for one to do X is to judge that the relevant rules of morality do prohibit one from doing X. If we turn to judgments about what one is legally required, permitted, or prohibited from doing, one might suppose that there, too, the relevant concepts are to be defined by reference to rules, this time the rules of law. Legally prohibited actions are those the rules of law prohibit. Legally permitted actions are those the rules of law do not prohibit. Even etiquette has its "rules," and one can easily follow the model to define the relevant judgments concerning what one ought to do from the perspective of etiquette. Perhaps, then, we should view normative judgments as those that make implicit reference to rules that prescribe, permit, and prohibit certain actions or moves, and epistemic judgments might be viewed as paradigmatically normative because there are certain rules of inference that tell us when we must believe, are permitted to believe, or are prohibited from believing certain propositions, given that we believe certain others or are in certain non-doxastic states (in the case of noninferentially justified belief).

While the above might seem initially promising, it is clear that we must proceed more carefully lest we overlook important distinctions between the kinds of rules to which judgments might make implicit or explicit reference. In metaethics, there is again no consensus on whether the content of moral judgments does always involve reference to rules or, if they do, how we should understand those rules. It is useful, however, to distinguish two importantly different kinds of rules. Some rules, for example the rules that a rule utilitarian has in mind in analyzing the content of moral judgments, can themselves be thought of as propositions that have a truth value. Thus, according to some rule utilitarians, the relevant rules take the form: It is always (prima facie) right (wrong) to take some action of kind X. The statement of the rule will be true if a certain proposition describing the consequences of people following that rule compared to the consequences of their following alternative rules is true.[9] The rules of law, the rules of a game, or the rules of etiquette, might be better thought of as imperatives that are neither true nor false. Propositions describing particular actions as permissible or impermissible relative to the rules are true or false but are so because they report what the relevant rules prescribe and prohibit. One can, of course, take precisely the same approach with respect to moral judgments, but as I indicated, one certainly need not.

If epistemic judgments involve implicit reference to rules, how should we think of those rules? Again, one could be a noncognitivist with respect to the relevant rules. One could think that rules of nondeductive inference, for example, are imperatives that are neither true nor false. Individual epistemic judgments are either true or false but only because they report what the relevant epistemic rules require, permit, and prohibit. But I daresay most epistemologists would resist this suggestion. The relevant generalized rules of epistemology will take the form of propositions that assert that one is justified in believing certain propositions relative to one's justifiably believing certain others or relative to one's being in certain nondoxastic states. It doesn't hurt to characterize these propositions as rules, if one likes, but if the "rules" themselves have a truth value, then it is not clear to me that we have uncovered an interesting sense in which epistemic judgments are normative. Epistemic judgments are no more normative than judgments about lawful necessity and possibility are normative. Such judgments also implicitly involve reference to general propositions. To claim that it is lawfully possible that X is probably just to claim that the

conjunction of the laws of nature, L, is logically consistent with the proposition describing the occurrence of X. Events "obey" laws in the sense that we can usefully generalize over kinds of events that always occur. In the same sense, individual beliefs are justified or not in virtue of exemplifying certain general properties, where we think of the "rules" of epistemology as generalizations describing the kinds of conditions under which beliefs are justified.

Normativity and goals or ends

Richard Foley (1987) and others have suggested that we might profitably view the different "oughts" as species of a common genera. Crudely put, Foley's idea is that normative judgments all assess the efficacy of achieving goals or ends. In a sense, all normative judgments are species of judgments concerning practical rationality. There are different kinds of normative judgments concerning what we ought to do and what we ought to believe because there are different goals or ends that we are concerned to emphasize. Thus when we are talking about morally justified action (what we morally ought to do), the relevant goal might be something like producing moral goodness (avoiding evil), and the actions that we ought to perform are those that are conducive to the goal of producing the morally best world. When we are concerned with what prudence dictates, however, the relevant goals or ends to be considered expand, perhaps to include everything that is desired intrinsically, for example. On one (rather crude) view, what one prudentially ought to do is what maximizes satisfaction of one's desires. What one ought to do legally or what one is legally justified in doing is a function of the extent to which an action satisfies the goal of following the law. What one ought to do from the standpoint of etiquette is a function of following the goals or ends set down by the "experts" who worry about such things. So all one has to do to fit the epistemic "ought" into this framework (and thus classify usefully the kind of normativity epistemic judgments have) is delineate the relevant goals or ends that define what one epistemically ought to believe. And the obvious candidates are the dual goals of believing what is true and avoiding belief in what is false.

If Pascal were right about his famous wager, belief in God might be the path one *prudentially* ought to follow, focusing on such goals as avoiding pain and seeking comfort. If you have promised your parents to believe in God, if it is good to keep a promise, and if there are no other good or bad effects of such a belief to consider, it might follow that prima facie you *morally* ought to believe in the existence of God. But neither of these normative judgments is relevant to whether you *epistemically* ought to believe in the existence of God. The only consideration relevant to this normative judgment is the efficacy with which such a belief contributes to the goals of believing what is true and avoiding belief in what is false.

Now as plausible and potentially illuminating as this account might seem initially, it is, I think, fatally flawed. In the first place, it must be immediately qualified to accommodate certain obvious objections. Suppose, for example, that I am a scientist interested in getting a grant from a religious organization. Although I think that belief in the existence of God is manifestly irrational (from the epistemic perspective), I discover that this organization will give me the grant only if it concludes that I am religious. I further have reason to believe that I am such a terrible liar that unless I actually get myself to believe in the existence of God, they will discover that I am an atheist. Given all this *and my desire to pursue truth and avoid falsehood*, which I am convinced the grant will greatly enable me to satisfy, I may conclude that I ought to believe in the existence of God (or do what I can to bring it about that I believe in the existence of God). Yet, by hypothesis, this belief is one that I viewed as epistemically irrational. We cannot understand

epistemic rationality simply in terms of actions designed to satisfy the goals of believing what is true and avoiding belief in what is false.

How might one modify the account to circumvent this difficulty? Foley suggests restricting the relevant epistemic goal to that of *now* believing what is true and *now* avoiding belief in what is false.[10] Even this, however, will fall prey to a revised (albeit more farfetched) version of the objection presented above. Suppose, to make it simple, that belief is under one's voluntary control and that I know that there is an all-powerful being who will immediately cause me to believe massive falsehood *now* unless I accept the epistemically irrational conclusion that there are unicorns. It would seem that to accomplish the goal of believing what is true and avoiding belief in what is false *now*, I must again adopt an epistemically irrational belief.

The obvious solution at this point is to restrict the relevant goal that defines the epistemic "ought" to that of believing what is true now with respect to a given proposition. If I epistemically ought to believe that there is a God, the only relevant goal is that of believing what is true with respect to the question of whether there is or is not a God. If we say this, however, we must be very careful lest our account collapse the distinction between true belief and epistemically justified or rational belief. If we are actual consequence consequentialists[11] and we take what we ought to do or believe to be a function of the extent to which our actions and beliefs *actually* satisfy the relevant goals, then trivially we epistemically ought to believe in God when there is a God, and we epistemically ought not believe in God when there is no God. Foley suggests at this point that it is something about beliefs an agent has (or more precisely would have after a certain process of reflection) about the efficacy of achieving the epistemic goals that is relevant to evaluating what one epistemically ought to believe. But there is a much more natural way of explicating the relationship between epistemic goals and what a person ought to believe, just as there is a more natural way of explicating the relevant relation that holds between a person's moral goals and what a person morally ought to do and a person's prudential goals and what a person prudentially ought to do. The obvious move is to say simply that what a person ought to believe is a function of what that person is *justified* in believing would accomplish the goal of believing now what is true with respect to a given proposition. But that is, of course, a convoluted way of saying that what a person is justified in believing is what a person is justified in believing, an account entirely plausible but less than enlightening.

Notice too that on many standard consequentialist accounts of morality or practical rationality, it is also crucial to introduce *epistemic* concepts into the analyses of what one morally or prudentially ought to do. I have argued in some detail that the concepts of what one morally ought to do and what one rationally ought to do are extraordinarily ambiguous.[12] Although there are actual consequence consequentialist analyses of what one morally or rationally ought to do that find *occasional* expression in ordinary discourse, they are far from dominant.[13] Consider the sadist who kills for pleasure the pedestrian in the mall when that pedestrian (unbeknownst to the sadist) was a terrorist about to blow up the city. There is surely a clear *sense* in which the sadist did not behave as he morally ought to have behaved.[14] The conventional poker wisdom that one should not draw to fill an inside straight is not falsified by the fact that this person would have filled the straight and won a great deal of money. How can we acknowledge that a person did what he ought to have done even when the consequences are much worse than would have resulted from an alternative? How can we acknowledge that a person behaved as he should not have behaved even when the consequences are far better than would have resulted from some alternative? The answer seems obvious. We must recognize the relevance of the epistemic perspective of the agent.

To determine what someone (morally or prudentially) ought to have done, we must consider what that person was epistemically justified in believing the probable and possible consequences of the action to be. Indeed, I have argued that there are literally indefinitely many derivative concepts of morality and rationality that also take into account what a person was epistemically justified in believing about the morality or rationality of actions, given more fundamental concepts of morality and rationality.[15] But if the analysis of familiar concepts of what a person ought to do must take into account the epistemic situation of the agent, it is simply a mistake to try to assimilate the epistemic "ought" to the "ought" of morality or practical rationality. In fact, an understanding of the "oughts" of morality and practical rationality is *parasitic* on an understanding of rational or justified belief. It would be folly, needless to say, to try to understand fundamental epistemic concepts in terms of what the agent was epistemically justified in believing about the probable and possible consequences of having a certain belief. Even philosophers who do not mind "big" circles in their philosophical theories will get dizzy traveling the circumference of this one.

Normativity, praise, and criticism

So far the only sense in which we have acknowledged that epistemic judgments are normative is that they are sometimes expressed using an "ought." That "ought" has been shown not only to be distinct from other "oughts" used in the expression of paradigm value judgments, but it has been shown to be *fundamentally* different. Nevertheless, we have not yet exhausted attempts to explicate normativity in a way that allows us to fit both epistemic judgments and our paradigm normative moral judgments under the same umbrella. It is sometimes claimed that our epistemic judgments are normative in that they implicitly involve *praise* or *blame* and criticism.

Should we construe this as the relevant mark of normativity? Almost surely not. The problems with doing so are enormous. For one thing, however we define normativity, we want our paradigm of normative judgments, moral judgments, to fall under the concept. But it is far from clear what the relationship is between judging that someone did not do what he or she ought to have done and blaming or criticizing that person.

If you see a fire in the house next door and heroically attempt to save the people inside, I may conclude that you ought to have called the fire department instead of trying to solve the problem on your own. At the same time I might not *blame* you for failing to make the call. I might decide that under the circumstances it is perfectly natural for a person to panic and fail to do the rational thing. I might also think that you are just too stupid to figure out what you ought to do, and indeed, I might seldom blame you for the many idiotic things you do that you should not do. In short, there seems to be no conceptual connection between the evaluation of an agent's action and the praise or blame of the agent who acted that way. And if this seems right concerning the evaluation of what a person ought to have done, it seems even more obvious in the epistemic evaluation of a person's belief. Do we blame or criticize very stupid people for believing what they have no good epistemic reason to believe?[16] At the very least, logic does not require us to blame people for believing what it is epistemically irrational for them to believe.

It might be argued, however, that I am confusing the praise or blame of an agent with the positive evaluation or criticism of the agent's action or belief. "I am not criticizing you," someone might say, "I am criticizing what you did." And there surely does seem to be some sense in which when one's beliefs are called unjustified or irrational, one takes those *beliefs* to have been criticized. Shall we say that judgments about the epistemic justifiability or rationality of

a belief are normative in that they imply praise or criticism of the *belief* (as opposed to the subject who has that belief)?

This is not helpful for two reasons. First, the notion of implying praise or criticism is simply too vague. When I tell the store owner that the knife I bought is extremely dull, there is surely a sense in which I am criticizing the knife (or implying criticism). When after test driving the car, I complain that it accelerates very slowly and pulls to the left, I am in some sense criticizing the car. But does that make "dull," "accelerating slowly," and "pulling to the left" normative expressions? Surely not. But why? One answer might be that there is no *conceptual* connection between judging that something has these characteristics and criticism. I might have wanted a dull knife to minimize the possibility of accident, for example. Now is there any *conceptual* connection between judging of a belief that it is epistemically irrational and criticizing the belief? Can we not imagine societies in which one values a kind of irrationality much the way a few people value dull knives? Indeed, I can think of a few philosophical movements that for all the world seem to place a premium on the incoherence of belief systems. And if that suggestion seems a little snide, can we not at least find some subculture of poets who explicitly disdain the confines of epistemically rational belief systems, the pursuit of truth, and so on? I have already agreed, of course, that there is a sense of "ought" that is customarily used in describing beliefs that a person is justified or rational in holding. And one can claim that if a belief is judged to be irrational, it is being implicitly criticized as one that the subject ought not to have, but this will now take us full circle to the earlier problematic attempt to characterize the normativity of the epistemic "ought."

Conclusion

We have explored a number of different ways in which we might interpret the claim that epistemic judgments are normative. But after we have carefully distinguished the epistemic judgments we make about beliefs from the other ways in which we might evaluate beliefs, it is not clear to me that there is really any interesting sense in which epistemic judgments are normative. Indeed, it is not clear that we can really develop any philosophically interesting sense of normativity that does not itself presuppose highly controversial views. If any judgments are normative, it is ethical judgments, but unless some version of noncognitivism is true, ethical judgments describe some feature of the world in precisely the same sense in which other judgments describe some feature of the world. We explored the idea that the relevant feature of the world might be the existence of rules that lack a truth value, and that this might be the essence of their normativity, but we saw that a great many moral philosophers would deny that the relevant moral rules lack truth value, and an even greater number of epistemologists would resist the analogous suggestion that the relevant epistemic rules lack truth value. The idea that normative judgments all make implicit reference to goals or ends gave little comfort to the idea that epistemic judgments are normative, for on reflection, the way in which other normative judgments involve reference to goals or ends seems to presuppose a prior understanding of epistemic probability. It seems even more hopeless to claim that there is a conceptual connection between judgments about epistemic justification and praise and blame.

If the above is correct, then some epistemic internalists may be off target in their criticisms of externalism. As we noted at the beginning of the essay, many would argue that externalist epistemologies are implausible precisely because they fail to capture some alleged normativity of moral judgments. Although I believe there are fatal objections to the externalist's approach to understanding epistemic concepts, I'm not convinced that this is one of them.[17]

Notes

1 Butchvarov (1970) has argued, somewhat persuasively, that the "traditional" account of knowledge is remarkably hard to find in the history of philosophy.

2 Chisholm has flirted off and on with attempts to reduce epistemic concepts to normative concepts ever since he first toyed with the idea in Chisholm (1957). Goldman (1979 and 1986), Foley (1987), Sosa (1991), Kim (1988), Hookway (1994), Plantinga (1992 and 1993), and Steup (1988), among many others, have all stressed the normative dimension of epistemic concepts.

3 Goldman himself became so sensitive to this objection that he eventually introduced a second (nonreliabilist) conception of justification to accommodate it—see Goldman (1988). See also Foley (1985) for a clear presentation of the objection.

4 We could even imagine a society odd enough that it tries to legislate over matters of belief, thus creating legal obligations to believe and refrain from believing certain propositions.

5 See, for example, Alston (1988).

6 The emotivists Ayer and Stevenson also emphasize the "quasi-imperative" character of moral judgments. See Ayer (1952) and Stevenson (1944).

7 My colleague Laird Addis, whose area of specialization is not epistemology, would endorse the idea that epistemic judgments lack truth value, but as I say, he is surely the exception.

8 One of the fundamental objections to objectivism first raised by Hume (1988) and developed by many others, perhaps most vigorously by Mackie (1977).

9 This is, of course, a crude statement of rule utilitarianism. There are all kinds of subtle variations on the view designed to circumvent objections.

10 Foley (1987), 8.

11 For a detailed discussion of what constitutes actual consequence consequentialism and what differentiates it from other versions of consequentialism, see Fumerton (1990).

12 Fumerton (1990), chap. 4.

13 We do *sometimes* seem to tie our evaluation of an agent's action to the actual consequences of that action. The child playing catch in the living room

who breaks the picture window gets accused of a far greater wrongdoing than the child playing that same game of catch who makes a lucky stab at the ball deflecting it just before the window breaks. I'm inclined to think that appropriate philosophical reflection should lead one to reject an analysis of wrongdoing that makes it dependent on actual consequences, but in the end I'm content to argue that there are more interesting and fundamental concepts of what someone ought to do that must take into account epistemic perspective.

14   A sense that is still distinct from our evaluation of the moral character of the agent.

15   For a detailed discussion of these important derivative concepts of morality and rationality, see, again, Fumerton (1990), chap. 4, and Foley (1990).

16   For a useful critical evaluation of possible conceptual connections between epistemic evaluation and moral evaluation, see Alston (1988), Plantinga (1988), and Feldman (1988).

17   I owe special thanks to Matthias Steup. Through extensive e-mail correspondence, he helped me better understand many of these issues.

References

Alston, William. 1988. *The Deontological Conception of Epistemic Justification.* Vol. 2 of *Philosophical Perspectives,* edited by James Tomberlin. Atascadero, Calif.: Ridgeview.

Ayer, A. J. 1952. *Language, Truth, and Logic.* New York: Dover.

———. 1956. *The Problem of Knowledge.* Edinburgh, Scotland: Penguin.

Butchvarov, Panayot. 1970. *The Concept of Knowledge.* Evanston, Ill.: Northwestern University Press.

Chisholm, Roderick. 1957. *Perceiving: A Philosophical Study.* Ithaca, N.Y.: Cornell University Press.

Feldman, Richard. 1988. Epistemic Obligations. Vol. 2 of *Philosophical Perspectives,* edited by James Tomberlin. Atascadero, Calif.: Ridgeview.

Foley, Richard. 1985. What's Wrong with Reliabilism? *The Monist* 68 (April): 188–202.

———. 1987. *The Theory of Epistemic Rationality.* Cambridge, Mass.: Harvard University Press.

———. 1990. Fumerton's Puzzle. *Journal of Philosophical Research* 15: 109–13.

Fumerton, Richard. 1990. *Reason and Morality.* Ithaca, N.Y.: Cornell University Press.

Goldman, Alvin. 1979. What Is Justified Belief? In *Justification and Knowledge,* edited by George Pappas. Dordrecht, the Netherlands: Reidel.

———. 1986. *Epistemology and Cognition.* Cambridge, Mass.: Harvard University Press.

———. 1988. Strong and Weak Justification. Vol. 2 of *Philosophical Perspectives,* edited by James Tomberlin. Atascadero, Calif.: Ridgeview.

Hookway, Christopher. 1994. Cognitive Virtues and Epistemic Evaluations, *International Journal of Philosophical Studies* (2): 211–27.

Hume, David. 1888. *A Treatise of Human Nature.* Edited by L. A. Selby-Bigge. London: Oxford University Press.

Kim, Jaegwon. 1988. What Is "Naturalized Epistemology"? Vol. 2 of *Philosophical Perspectives,* edited by James Tomberlin. Atascadero, Calif.: Ridgeview.

Mackie, J. L. 1977. *Ethics: Inventing Right and Wrong.* New York: Penguin.

Plantinga, Alvin. 1988. Positive Epistemic Status and Proper Function. Vol. 2 of *Philosophical Perspectives,* edited by James Tomberlin. Atascadero, Calif.: Ridgeview.

———. 1992. Justification in the 20th Century. *Rationality in Epistemology.* Vol. 2 of *Philosophical Issues,* edited by Enrique Villanueva. Atascadero, Calif.: Ridgeview.

———. 1993. *Warrant: The Current Debate.* New York: Oxford University Press.

Sosa, Ernest. 1991. *Knowledge in Perspective.* Cambridge: Cambridge University Press.

Steup, Matthias. 1988. The Deontic Conception of Epistemic Justification, *Philosophical Studies* 58: 65–84.

Stevenson, C. L. 1944. *Ethics and Language.* New Haven: Yale University Press.

Chapter 29

Edward Craig

A CONTRACTARIAN CONCEPTION OF KNOWLEDGE

I

The standard approach to questions about the concept of knowledge has for some time consisted in attempts to analyse the everyday meaning of the word 'know' and its cognates. Such attempts have usually taken the form of a search for necessary and sufficient conditions which, when measured against our reactions to examples both real and imaginary, match our intuitive ascriptions and withholdings of the title of knowledge. We are to provide, if you like, an explicit intension to fit the intuitive extension.

One might wonder whether, if the idea is to analyse the concept of knowledge, this can really be the right programme. As well as intuitions about the extension of the concept, we seem also to have certain intuitions about its intension, that is to say intuitions about why certain cases do, and others do not, qualify as knowledge. Thus we may feel about a certain example, both that the subject does not have knowledge, and that he does not have it because the truth of his belief is accidental (for instance). The sceptic notoriously tries to show that the two do not mesh: our intuitions about the intension, the conditions of application of the concept, in fact determine a much smaller extension than that which our directly extensional intuitions mark out. If he is wrong, the point needs arguing; if he is right, the question arises: to which set of intuitions should

we give priority in order to arrive at the analysis of the 'everyday' concept? Either way, a good deal of work in epistemology and the theory of meaning (which in the light of history one can hardly expect to be uncontroversial) must be done or assumed just to reach the stage of saying that there is such a thing as the everyday concept of knowledge at all, let alone settle any question as to how one should proceed to analyse it. So if the standard approach runs into difficulties – and the work of the last twenty-five years makes it apparent that it does – it is surely worthwhile to try to think of another.

And there is another problem, though in this case it may be less a flaw in the approach itself than a defect in the attitude commonly taken towards it. Let us suppose, however optimistically, that the problem of the analysis of the everyday meaning of 'know' had both been shown to exist and subsequently solved, so that agreed necessary and sufficient conditions for the ascription of knowledge were now on the table. That would be a considerable technical achievement, and no doubt a long round of hearty applause would be in order, but I hope that philosophers would not regard it as a terminus, as many writers make one feel they would. I should like it to be seen as a prolegomenon to a further inquiry: why has a concept demarcated by those conditions enjoyed such widespread use? There seems to be no known language in which sentences using 'know' do not find a comfortable and colloquial equivalent. The implication is that it answers to some very general needs of human life and thought, and it would surely be interesting to know which and how. And the threat, of which some writers have seemed largely unaware, is that the more complex the analyses proffered in response to the flood of ingenious counterexamples (and some are very complex indeed), the harder that question will be to answer.

These two thoughts, that it will do no harm to have an alternative angle on the concept of knowledge that does not start from its supposed extension, and that its purpose should be at least as interesting as its analysis, together motivate an experiment. Instead of beginning with ordinary usage, we begin with an ordinary situation. We take some prima facie plausible hypothesis about what the concept of knowledge does for us, what its role in our life might be, and then ask what a concept having that role would be like, what conditions would govern its application. Such an investigation would still have an anchorage point in the everyday concept: should it reach a result quite different from the intuitive intension, or one that yielded an extension quite different from the intuitive extension, then, barring some special and especially plausible explanation of the mismatch, the original hypothesis about the role that the concept plays in our life would of course be the first casualty. For it is not the idea to construct an imaginary concept, but to illuminate the one we actually have, though it be vague or even inconsistent; and to illuminate it by showing that a concept with the hypothesised role would have characteristics closely resembling those that it exhibits itself. But should our intuitions prove indeterminate or elastic, this type of investigation might reveal constructive ways of stretching them, and the rationale behind the stretch. With luck it might also reveal the sources of the indeterminacy or elasticity which dogged the attempts to answer, or even to ask, the first familiar question.

It can at least be said for this way of creeping up on the concept of knowledge that we are asking a question that can reasonably be expected to have an answer. One doesn't have to commit oneself to a great deal of epistemology or semantic theory, as the standard approach evidently does, to presume that there is such a thing as the point of this concept, what it does for us, the role it plays in our lives. And if this is so, one way to find out must be to form some hypothesis about it, try to work out how a concept custom-designed for that role would look, and then see to what extent it matches our everyday practice with the concept of knowledge as actually found. We may then have to revise or supplement the hypothesis from which we began, but that will hardly be surprising, and certainly no cause for instant despair.

Whilst agreeing that we may expect the concept to serve some purpose, however, we might doubt whether the consideration of its purpose will necessarily lead to anything like an analysis, or to anything that can be measured against the intuitive extension. We might doubt, in fact, whether it will necessarily lead anywhere interesting at all. Every language, an objector might reason, has a word for water. And having that word has an important purpose, namely, to make it possible to talk about water, something which every community has an obvious need to be able to talk about. But no a priori thought about that purpose will bring us any closer to an analysis of the concept of water, even if the notion of an analysis be very generously interpreted. Couldn't it just be that knowledge, like water, is common and important stuff, and that the purpose of the concept is simply to enable us to think and talk about it?

Though I would be hard put to it to argue the point, I am fairly confident that this is mistaken. Knowledge is not a given phenomenon, but something that we delineate by operating with a concept which we create in answer to certain needs, or in pursuit of certain ideals. The concept of water, on the other hand, is determined by the nature of water itself and our experience of it.

But probably a better response here, at any rate a less dogmatic one, is 'the proof of the pudding': if some hypothetical but plausible purpose does issue in conditions of application showing a close fit to the intuitive extension of 'know', and does fit well with a variety of facts about the 'phenomenology' of the concept, then those who hold it to be mere coincidence may be requested to make a case for their attitude.

Another objection would be that the purpose, or purposes, of the concept of knowledge, though no doubt there are such things, are most unlikely to be anything so simple as the ones considered in this essay. The method presented here ties itself to purposes of a severely practical kind arising in what might be called a primitive situation. Suppose (and isn't it really more likely?) that the concept comes into existence in response to rather more sophisticated levels of consciousness?

With that I would initially have been inclined to agree, though I am not sure where the inclination comes from – there may just be an intellectual prejudice to the effect that everything must really be frightfully complex. Certainly there is one thing we shouldn't say in reply to this objection: that the concept under investigation is so widespread, so ancient, that it must have its origin in the most primitive requirements. What may well follow is that it must have its origin in primitive societies, but there is no guarantee whatever that primitive societies have only primitive requirements. Any society that has a well-developed language, sufficiently well developed for us to be able to say that it exercises a concept even approximately identifiable with our concept of knowledge, consists of creatures that have reached a considerable degree of mental complexity. Any number of different sorts of need may, for all we know to the contrary, follow in the wake of this complexity; so there is no a priori reason to think that we are tied by methodological principles to considering only needs of the very basic kind that I have actually tried to restrict myself to.

Again, the best response will be to treat our strategy as a hypothesis. If it doesn't work, doesn't issue in a concept having at least very close similarity to the concept we are 'explicating', then we shall have to modify the hypothesis and propose one involving rather more advanced features of human consciousness – but there is no reason to bring them in before the progress, or lack of progress, of the investigation makes it necessary to do so. To start off without them doesn't mean making the assumption that they will not in the end be needed; it is no more than good method to test the explanatory powers of the simple before resorting to the complex.

Something similar will apply to the question of what further 'needs' it will be legitimate to introduce, should that prove necessary. We shall be looking for features of human psychology which may plausibly be supposed to be possessed by all humans, preferably ones which there is some independent reason to suppose to be possessed by all humans. To illustrate the point with an example of one which cannot without qualms be thought of in this way, we might suggest the wish to explain, in some fashion, the behaviour of one's fellows, or the wish to understand them in a way which makes them the same sort of being as oneself. (It might be thought, and has been suggested to me, that this idea could help us to see the concept of knowledge as some sort of theoretical construct, useful for explaining why other members of our community behave as they do.) But just how widespread this concern with explanation is, in particular whether it is widespread enough to fit our present bill, is very hard to say – thinking in these terms might just be a reflection of our contemporary obsession with the methods of the natural sciences. For that reason alone – there may be others – it would not be advisable to allow ourselves such a starting point before we are sure that we have exhausted the potential of far less contentious claims about the human situation, like those which I have actually tried to exploit.

We should beware of an assumption which is easy to make, but which could prove restrictive or even worse: that when we render the final account of the concept which we have constructed, this account must go comfortably into the form of a list of conditions that are individually necessary and jointly sufficient for its correct application. The standard approach sets itself the problem in this form, but whether the most illuminating response to the request for specification of the concept of knowledge has to fit it ought to be regarded as an open question, especially if we are to approach it from this different angle. In fact, I shall shortly be arguing that in trying to fit our results to it we are more likely to switch the illumination off. On the other hand, one clear fact about this matter is that the concept does lend itself at least fairly well to treatment in the standard format; and that is one of the facts which an illuminating account of it ought to illuminate, whether or not it fits that format itself. And whilst we are about it we might aspire not just to illuminate that fact, but also to cast light on the appeal of the various particular analyses that have been advocated in the literature of the topic.

I have spoken so far as if there really were something which I have called the intuitive extension of the concept of knowledge, and that the problems lay in deciding whether or not it matches the intuitive intension, and what to do about it if it doesn't. But the difficulty may go one layer deeper: is it so clear that there is such a thing as the intuitive extension at all?

To say that there is might make things sound like this: we can describe cases in terms of the facts, the subject's beliefs, the subject's relation to the facts, his mental state, and so on. Then there will be, amongst speakers of English of a reasonable level of intelligence and education who can be persuaded to give the matter their undivided attention, unanimity as to which cases exemplify knowledge; the decision, in an individual case, will depend only on the features of the case as described, and will not vary from

umpire to umpire, nor with the same umpire from time to time. If that is what is implied it has to be said that it is very doubtful. There is at least some reason to think that our judgement varies with the circumstances in which we are invited to consider the case. If we come to believe that Fred has an identical twin who was in town that day, our decision that we knew that it was Fred catching the bus on the other side of the street may change. Our attitude to a lot of knowledge claims may change if we are asked to consider them with the thought of the Cartesian demon looming over us. And if it doesn't change, who is to say whether that is because we steadfastly hold to the proper application of 'know' in spite of the philosopher's attempts to deflect us, or rather because we obstinately refuse to pursue its proper application into these unaccustomed regions in spite of the philosopher's attempts to help us do so? Answers to questions like these are usually accompanied by sparks from the grinding of some philosophical axe; if we want to start from first principles we would do much better to record the fact that these 'sceptical' deliberations produce different reactions, often combined with a sense of puzzlement or irritation. Then we can take that fact as a part of the data about the life of the concept of knowledge and hope for an account which will allow us to assimilate it as it is, rather than begin by distorting it in the name of some supposedly well-defined 'extension' which the concept is arbitrarily alleged to have. Nor will we be tempted to pretend that we know where to draw a line between 'natural' and 'philosophical' consideration of knowledge-claims.

It seems, therefore, that we may be in the happy position of being able simultaneously to widen and strengthen the basis of the investigation. To widen it, because we can include amongst our *explananda* such facts as the various analyses of the concept of knowledge that philosophers have given, the fact that controversy about certain of their clauses seems difficult to resolve, the facts about the reactions to sceptical proposals like that of Descartes, and all this be it noted not instead of but as well as the 'extension' (or whatever can uncontroversially be found of it) on which the standard approach uniquely concentrates attention. And we can strengthen it, because these facts have more of the nature of an undoctored 'given' than those on which the standard approach fixates – even if it be true that all data are 'theory-laden', we have surely reduced the theoretical load.

The idea that it may be worth asking after the roots of the value of knowledge when investigating the concept has an ancient precedent. In Plato's *Meno*, Socrates wonders why we should be interested in anything beyond true belief: after all, if you believe that this is the road to Larissa, and want to go there, then acting on your belief will get you what you want just so long as it is true, so why ask any more of it? His answer is that true beliefs are even more valuable if they are stable, that is to say if we persist in holding them; and this means, so he continues, that it is advantageous to have good reasons, for then we will hold fast to the truth and not be easily lured away to falsehood.[1]

Plato's contribution here is far from negligible. But I shall not adopt it. Whether the stabilisation of true beliefs is important or not depends on which beliefs we are considering, and the circumstances of the agent – many beliefs are required for the guidance of single, 'one-off' actions under circumstances which will not recur, and once the particular occasion is past there is no obvious value at all in their persistence. (I might now need a true belief about the time; but that this belief should persist, so that tomorrow I will still know what the time was today, at the moment when I wanted to know it, may be of no interest to me whatever.) Apart from that, the possession of good reasons is not the only, nor necessarily the best, way to stabilise beliefs: effect of early upbringing, emotive ties or Humean psychological mechanisms may be just as good, and better. And apart from that again, we shall see that stability is not the only, and perhaps not even the chief, thing that we may want in a true belief.

Even if we confine ourselves to recent literature of the 'analytic' school the kind of approach I shall recommend is not without precedent. David Pears has suggested something of the kind:

> It often happens, as Aristotle saw, that understanding how a thing has developed from primitive beginnings helps us to understand it in its developed form. Certainly this is true of knowledge. In this case the primitive beginning is the ability to make a discriminating response to circumstances. In the early stages the response will be a piece of overt behaviour. Later, it may be internalised, and stored for future use.[2]

This point, which Pears did not go on to press, may well be useful, but its primary use is most likely to be that of shedding light on the concept of belief, and maybe, if we add the idea of the overt behaviour, when it arrives, being in some sense successful, that of true belief. It will not in itself bring us very close to the concept of knowledge as we have it, unless an adequate account of that concept turns out (somewhat against the early odds, most of us will feel) not to need, beyond true belief, any further apparatus. So we can't rest content with Pears' remarks, though we can, and should, take his hint.

I have elsewhere[3] referred to this project as the 'practical explication of knowledge'. The notion of an explication came into currency, I believe, through Carnap. To explicate a concept was not exactly to analyse it; it was to construct a new version of it satisfying certain standards, with the proviso that to count as a new version of that concept it had to emerge with many of its principal features intact. The procedure suggested here is analogous; but it is concerned with the practical rather than (as in Carnap) the theoretical aspect of the concept. Hence the title of the earlier paper. But let it not mislead:

Carnap's intentions were normative, the establishment of the concepts fit to form the rational basis of the unified science, whereas mine are the more purely theoretical ones of shedding light on the nature and origins of present practice. In that respect at least I shall follow the traditional approach.

Whilst speaking of precedents, we should notice that my project can claim membership of another tradition, one which spreads itself altogether wider than conceptual analysis, however widely that be conceived. I refer to the tradition of naturalism, in which thinkers see man, his behaviour and institutions, as natural facts to be understood as the (broadly speaking causal) outcome of other natural facts. What concepts we use, what linguistic practices are common amongst us, these are special cases of input to the more general naturalistic enterprise. Hume's treatment of the concept of causality is one. Another, in a quite different area, is Hobbes's account of political and legal institutions: they are more or less adequate attempts so to regulate the power-relationships between individuals as to avoid the otherwise inevitable 'war of every man against every man' and create stable circumstances in which humans, and human society, may flourish. Robert Nozick has written – and I think there is meant to be a note of criticism in the remark – that unlike political philosophy epistemology has not started from a consideration of the state of nature.[4] If that is true, and a defect, my project may be thought of as one way to supply the lack.

Hobbes believed, of course, that normative consequences were to be drawn: a particular kind of constitution ought to be adopted, and in this respect other state-of-nature theorists such as Locke, and more recently Nozick, have followed him. That is a different matter; whether it results from my deliberations that we in any sense ought to operate the concept of knowledge much as we do is a question I shall not address, for unlike Hobbes's theme it is not contentious. But it will, I believe, emerge that without it life,

whether or not brutish and nasty, would be a good deal more solitary, and almost certainly shorter. Some may also wish to ask a very different normative question: whether, if the concept of knowledge is to be developed or rendered more precise, this ought to be done in one way rather than another; clearly, there are parallels in political theory. Again, I shall not offer an opinion; in any case, unless we are told the purpose of such development we do well to have no opinion to offer.

In spite of such differences, these points suggest that one might view the whole of the following investigation in a different light: as an adaptation to the theory of knowledge of a procedure traditionally at home in ethics and politics. I began as if our theme were the analysis of the concept of knowledge: we were to apply a different method to the same topic. Somewhat less parochially, we may think of our starting point as state-of-nature theory: we are to apply similar methods to a different object: not political, but conceptual and linguistic institutions.

Finally, before we leave the job-description for the job itself, a third connection is to be noted. 'Evolutionary Epistemology', now widely so called, is a branch-arm of the prevailing stream of naturalism. It looks at our cognitive faculties as adaptive responses to changing circumstances and changing needs for information. My investigation is akin, though it differs in two respects. First, I am not concerned, except peripherally, with any particular sensory or inferential faculties, but with our concept of knowledge in general. Secondly, I shall not treat its development diachronically, and that is not just an omission: if what I shall say is along the right lines, the core of the concept of knowledge is an outcome of certain very general facts about the human situation; so general, indeed, that one cannot imagine their changing whilst anything we can still recognise as social life persists. Given those facts, and a modicum of self-conscious awareness, the concept will appear; and for the same reasons as caused it to appear, it will then stay. Our cognitive faculties may change, and if they do then what we know will change; but that, it will be seen, is not a reason to expect the concept of knowing to change as well.

II

Such is the programme; we can now begin its execution. Fortunately there is a firmly fixed point to start from. Human beings need true beliefs about their environment, beliefs that can serve to guide their actions to a successful outcome. That being so, they need sources of information that will lead them to believe truths. They have 'onboard' sources, eyes and ears, powers of reasoning, which give them a primary stock of beliefs. It will be highly advantageous to them if they can also tap the primary stocks of their fellows – the tiger that Fred can see and I can't may be after me and not Fred – that is to say, if they act as informants for each other. On any issue, some informants will be better than others, more likely to supply a true belief. (Fred, who is up a tree, is more likely to tell me the truth as to the whereabouts of the tiger than Mabel, who is in the cave.) So any community may be presumed to have an interest in evaluating sources of information; and in connection with that interest certain concepts will be in use. The hypothesis I wish to try out is that the concept of knowledge is one of them. To put it briefly and roughly, the concept of knowledge is used to flag approved sources of information.

I shall not for the moment be concerned with the evaluation of what I have called 'on-board' sources. In the ordinary way we simply take it that the beliefs they mediate are true. To find oneself in possession of a belief on the question whether p pre-empts inquiry; to take a self-conscious look at one's own apparatus with the doubt in mind that it may have delivered a falsehood calls for a considerable degree of sophistication. Our investigation ought to start from the position in which we as yet have no belief about

p, want a true belief about it one way or the other, and seek to get it from someone else. (I do not mean to suggest that it is ever in principle impossible for us to find out for ourselves; but in practice that will often be a hopelessly inefficient way of going about it.) Our interest in our own faculties as sound sources of information has a part to play, since under certain circumstances that interest becomes acute, for very good practical reasons; but it would not be good method to begin with it.

Consider then the position of someone seeking information on the point whether or not p. What does he want? In the first place, he wants an informant who will tell him the truth on that question. The informant, we may assume, will not in general tell him the truth unless he (the informant) holds a true belief about it. (Cases of people who, whilst not holding true beliefs, insincerely give 'information' which is in fact true, are rare; and informants who do that regularly are as good as non-existent.) So the inquirer wants an informant such that:

> Either p and he believes that p, or not-p and he believes that not-p.

This gives us a start on the analysis (or whatever we should at this stage call it) of the concept which characterises the source of information that the inquirer hopes to encounter. It is, obviously, very closely related to the first two clauses of the traditional definition of knowledge. I say 'closely related to' rather than 'identical with' only because there has been a change of perspective. The traditional analysis concentrates on the form 'X knows that p', whereas this approach directs us in the first instance to 'X knows whether p'. It is clear that the standard opening clause 'p is true' cannot feature in the analysis of the latter – we need something like the disjunctive formula given above.

The relevant part of the traditional analysis, true belief, is that which virtually all subsequent attempts to define knowledge have taken over.

But before we get into the contentious area of further conditions we should pause to ask: how strong a conviction is in question here, when we speak of the informant as believing that p? Some analyses speak of certainty at this point, some of being sure. But it has been argued that being certain, or sure, or confident, is not a necessary condition for knowledge, and Colin Radford[5] has gone further and claimed that the belief condition can be dropped altogether, since cases of knowledge of p can be found in which the subject actually believes, if anything, that not-p. Does our approach have anything to say on this score? It does, though what it offers is not a one-way-or-the-other decision; its contribution is not to divide the area into black and white but rather to make it comprehensible that this part of it should be grey.

In seeking information we are seeking to come by true beliefs; we do not want just to have truths enunciated in our presence, but we want to be brought to believe them, so that these beliefs, since they are beliefs (and not mere entertainings) can guide our actions – and guide them to success because they are true. We shall therefore want as an informant someone who has the following property:

> If he tells us that p, we shall thereupon believe that p.

Now because the confidence with which we believe things affects the way we announce them, and the way we announce them affects the likelihood that the audience will believe us, this may make it look as if there could be some minimum level of confidence necessary if the informant is to meet the inquirer's needs: for any lower level he will sound so hesitant that the inquirer will probably not come to believe what he says. To try to place a quantitative value on that level would be silly, but it is probably not too silly to describe it by using another vague term, and saying that if he is successfully to induce the belief that p in his audience, he had

better believe it himself. That would make it appear that the concept we are constructing will indeed include belief as one of the conditions for a good source of information.

But we are going too quickly – the matter is not so simple. Other things which we believe about the informant will also play a part in determining whether we believe what he tells us (or indeed, what is very much the same thing, whether we select him as an informant at all), and under certain circumstances they may well be overriding, so that we have little tendency to believe even a very confidently made claim, or are prepared to accept even a very diffident utterance. Very briefly, what I have in mind is that if the informant satisfies any condition which correlates well – as we believe – with telling the truth about p, he will be regarded as a good source. Confidence is only a special case of this, and not even one that we are always prepared to use. The point will become clearer later on, after the consideration of the further conditions – further to true belief, that is – which we shall want the informant to meet. For the moment we can best leave it at this: that since confidence is not essential to performance as a source, the constructed concept will concede some ground to those accounts of knowledge which play down the belief requirement. On the other hand, it will give no support to those which want to play it down to vanishing point. In the vast majority of cases a good informant will believe the information he gives, and will give it, what is more, precisely because he believes it – the counterexamples, though perfectly genuine, are freakish. One might add that on many matters, those who hold a belief at all nearly always hold a true one, so that in these types of case possession of a belief is itself a property which correlates well with being right. These are facts about our world which cannot be without influence on our concepts. So if our hypothesis is on the right track, it is neither surprising that so many take belief to be essential to knowledge, nor that some deny it, nor that many people's intuitions leave them in the lurch at this point.

Here we see starkly a major disadvantage of the approach which takes its sole target to be the listing of logically necessary and sufficient conditions. If it can be argued that belief is not a necessary condition for knowledge, then belief will make no appearance on the final balance sheet. There is no place on it where the conceptual accountant can present belief as a major component of the constellation of thoughts which go into the practice of operating with 'know' and its cognates. He can try to talk about it, just so long as the audience is prepared to listen to such periphera, as of something which very often accompanies knowledge. But when he is asked for the real outcome of the business, the analysis, anything not strictly a necessary condition simply vanishes without trace. Of all its deep centrality nothing whatever remains – it could be as incidental as the fact that nearly all knowers are less than 150 years old.

That greater flexibility in the description of concepts is required is hardly a new point. Wittgenstein famously wrote of family resemblance concepts, for which fixation on the format of necessary and sufficient conditions leads either to triviality or error. But we can also see, I think, why this greater flexibility is required, or at the least, why it is required in this case. We are asking not so much: when is the ascription of a certain concept correct, but rather, why is it applied? In freakish circumstances, a purpose may be achievable in unusual ways – factors which would usually frustrate it may, if other features of the situation are exceptional, do no damage, factors which are usually vital may, abnormally, be dispensable.

There is, however, an expository problem: how is this flexibility to be expressed? If we speak as if belief were not a component of knowledge we do it an injustice, if we say that it is then we risk being understood to say that it is a necessary condition. If, whenever the relation between believing and knowing crops up, we try

to present the situation as it actually is, long-winded clumsiness will engulf us. I can think of nothing better than to ask the reader for a change of gear: what may look like an attempt to state necessary conditions should rather be taken as part of the description of a prototypical case, a case from which speakers and their audiences will tolerate, in the right circumstances, varying degrees of deviation. How much deviation, and under what circumstances, ought to be related to the purpose behind the formation of the concept in question. The prototypical description enshrines the features that effect realisation of the purpose when things are going on as they nearly always do.

It is important to notice that 'the way things nearly always go on' enjoys special status in this context, not just numerical advantage. We must never forget that the inquirer's situation is a practical one: he must pick out the good informant, or decide whether to make use of a volunteered statement. Now freakish cases, in which for instance he would finish up with a true belief, though the informant offer him a falsehood, or offer him a truth without believing it, are not merely rare. It is also hard for the inquirer to detect that he is in the presence of such a case – which he must do, and do confidently, if he is to make use of it; if it is possible at all it will only be because he happens to be in possession of a good deal of collateral information. To try to make a practice of detecting freakish cases would mean incurring high costs in time and energy; and successful detection would scarcely ever offer any benefit which could not be had by finding a standard informant, or investigating for oneself. In practice, therefore, it must be the standard or prototypical case at which the inquirer's strategy is directed, so that one might almost say that for practical purposes what the concept amounts to is the essential description of the prototypical case.

The words 'almost' and 'for practical purposes' are not in that sentence for nothing, however. One thing a proper account of a conceptual practice ought to be able to explain is why prima facie counter-examples to a proposed definition have (at least prima facie) the feel of being such. What is it, for instance, that gives Radford's examples some purchase? Not every account of the concept of knowledge will automatically be able to answer that question. The present suggestion does so by reference to the hypothesised purpose underlying the practice. This purpose, in conjunction with a few platitudes about the way in which human inquirers operate, generates a set of descriptive conditions; what they describe is the prototypical case in which the purpose is standardly achieved. A speaker is not taught these conditions explicitly, any more than he is explicitly taught the purpose, but when a philosopher presents them to him as logically necessary and sufficient for knowledge he is not hard to convince – after all, they apply to all the cases that readily come to his mind, and it is perfectly understandable that they should. The exotic cases, on the other hand, in which he recognises the fulfilment of the familiar purpose in the absence of one of these conditions, pull him for that reason to acknowledge them as positive instances, though very unusual ones.

Is he to go along with the pull, or is he to resist it? The practice into which he has grown up cannot be expected to help him on that point. Why should it? It has no need to legislate for cases with highly unusual features, or rather highly unusual combinations of features. No need, and in a sense it has no way to do it either. It is precisely by being *everyday* practice that everyday practice manages to impress itself upon speakers and so stay what it is. How can it help in freakish, perhaps wholly imaginary, circumstances in which some of the familiar indicators fall one way, some another? And if it could, why bother? We can always resort to expressions like 'It's almost as if he knew'.

I cannot, of course, generate the slightest appearance of a counter-example to the sufficiency of an analysis of knowledge by postulating a human subject who will be 207 years old next birthday, whom I however allow to satisfy all the conditions of the proposed analysis – by no means every unusual case is felt to be undecidable. But nothing I have said implies that it should be. For that feeling to arise the unusual features of the situation must engage with the everyday practice so as to produce some contrary pressure – to make us feel that something that matters is lacking. Not every unfamiliar circumstance need have that effect.

Certain worries call for mention at this stage, just in case they are already beginning to worry the reader. First, it is not only persons, but also for instance books and video-cassettes, that can be sources of information; but although these are sometimes said to contain knowledge, as is also a library, they are not said to know anything. Why not, if the function of 'know' is to flag good sources of true belief? One might have replied that it is because they don't have beliefs, but what we have said in the earlier parts of this section seems to imply that the present line of thought will not satisfactorily explain why that should be a reason. So there is a problem here which needs attention. Secondly, someone who has a strong motive for concealing the truth may still be said to know it. But he is of very little value as a source of information, except in those infrequent situations where the inquirer is in a position to give him an even stronger motive for revealing it. (Luigi knows exactly where Mario's body is, and how it came to be there, but there is no point at all in turning to him for information on the subject.) Thirdly, someone who both knows the truth and is keen to reveal it may be useless to others because he has no credibility with them: the boy who cried 'Wolf!' so often that no-one would believe him when the wolf really came is a cautionary example, as is Matilda of Hillaire Belloc's *Cautionary Tales*. A gap threatens to open here between the constructed concept and the concept of knowledge as we operate it, a gap wide enough to suggest that the former is too different from the latter to throw any light on it. For the moment I would just ask that we take note of these difficulties. Reacting to them involves a complication of the picture that is best postponed, since the less complicated version still has a good deal more to yield.

Notes

1 Plato. 1956. *Meno*, trans. Guthrie. Penguin, 97ff.

2 Pears, D.F. 1972. *What Is Knowledge?* London: George Allen and Unwin.

3 Craig, Edward. 1987. 'The Practical Explication of Knowledge', *Proceedings of the Aristotelian Society* 87: 211–226.

4 Nozick, Robert. 1974. *Anarchy, State and Utopia.* Oxford: Basil Blackwell.

5 Radford, Colin. 1966. 'Knowledge – by Examples', *Analysis* 27: 1–11.

PART EIGHT

What are the sources of knowledge?

INTRODUCTION TO PART EIGHT

Ram Neta and Duncan Pritchard

THINK OF THE VARIOUS PROPOSITIONS that you know right now: that the sun will rise tomorrow; that Paris is the capital of France; that 2 + 2 = 4; that you are currently sitting reading the introduction to this part, and so on. Notice just how very varied these propositions are. One of them is about the future, one of them is about mathematics, one of them is a truth about geography and one of them is about your current experiences. Moreover, not only are these very different sorts of propositions but they are also propositions which, in all likelihood, you came to know in very different ways. In particular, the way that you know these four propositions is in all likelihood by, respectively, induction, testimony, reason and perception. We will take each source of knowledge in turn.

The topic of induction is the concern of the piece by Bertrand Russell (1872–1970) which is collected here (Chapter 30). Induction is a form of inference and the best way to understand what it involves is in contrast to non-inductive, or deductive, inference. In a deductive inference the premises entail the conclusion, in the sense that if the premises are true then the conclusion must be true. Here is an example of a deductive inference:

> *Sample deductive argument*
> Premise 1:   All men are mortal.
> Premise 2:   Socrates is a man.
> Conclusion: Socrates is mortal.

It ought to be clear that if the two premises of this argument are true, then the conclusion must be true also. That is, it is just not possible for all men to be mortal and for Socrates to be a man, and yet for Socrates not to be mortal.

An inductive inference, however, is different from a deductive inference in that the truth of the premises is compatible with the falsity of the conclusion. Here is an example of an inductive argument:

> *Sample inductive argument I*
> Premise 1:   It has been observed that the sun has risen every day for many, many years.
> Conclusion: The sun will rise tomorrow.

Although it is unlikely, it is at least *possible* that the sun will not rise tomorrow, and the fact that it has been observed to rise every day for many, many years does not alter this. Nevertheless, although the premises of inductive arguments do not entail the conclusion of that argument, it does seem that induction can be a legitimate form of inference and, indeed, lead us to knowledge. For doesn't the fact that the sun has risen every day for so long at least give one an excellent reason for thinking that it will rise tomorrow, a reason which suffices for me to know that it will rise tomorrow? If that's right, then induction can be a source of knowledge (inductive knowledge).

Unfortunately, there is a problem facing all inductive inferences, a problem that goes back to David Hume's (1711–76) writings on this topic, and which is expounded by Russell in the piece collected here. In essence, Hume argues that we have no non-circular justification for our inductive inferences, in that any justification we offer of our inductive inferences will itself appeal to induction. If that's right, then the mass of knowledge which, it seems, we gain every day through inductive inference is in jeopardy.

Your knowledge that Paris is the capital of France is unlikely to have been gained through inductive inference. Instead, it is most likely that you gained it on the basis of testimony, where this includes not just the spoken word of others but also the 'word' of others which appears in other forms, such as in books, documentaries and so forth. Just as a great deal of our knowledge is gained through induction, so an awful lot of our knowledge is gained via testimony, a point that Robert Audi (1941–) emphasises in his article on testimony which is reprinted in this part (Chapter 31). Indeed, in a wide range of cases, we have to rely on the word of others in order to be able to know certain truths, because there is no practical way in which we could find the relevant facts out ourselves. Take my knowledge that there are two planets closer to the sun than the Earth – namely, Venus and Mercury. Given how little I know about astronomy, I'm in no position to determine that this is the case all by myself; instead, I need to trust the word of others who do have the relevant expertise.

Given our dependence on testimony it is important that it is indeed able to provide us with knowledge. As with induction, however, there are some concerns about testimonial knowledge (or, at least, concerns that our testimonial knowledge is as widespread as we think it is). Interestingly, these concerns can also be traced back to worries raised by Hume. Essentially, the problem that Hume posed concerned whether the mere fact that someone is testifying to a certain proposition gives you any reason to believe that proposition. Think, for example, of someone you know telling you something – that, say, a certain film is to be screened on TV that night. Intuitively, one can on this basis come to know that this film is to be shown. But is the fact that your friend is testifying to this proposition in itself offering any epistemic support? After all, isn't the reason why you gain knowledge in this case more to do with the fact that you have independent grounds to trust your friend (e.g. you know from past experience that she is a reliable informant), you have independent grounds in any case to trust her in this instance (e.g. why would someone lie about something like this?) and you have independent grounds to believe the proposition testified to (e.g. you know from past experience that this is the sort of film that could well be screened on TV)? Hume's thought is thus that what is really providing the epistemic support in the case of testimony is not the testimony itself but rather independent grounds of this sort.

We can bring this issue into sharper relief by considering a case in which one has no independent grounds to back up the instance of testimony in question. Imagine, for example, someone who you've never met and have no prior knowledge of telling you something about a subject matter of which you are completely ignorant. Does the fact that this person is testifying to you give you any reason to believe the proposition in question? Clearly, it isn't obvious what to say in this case.

Those who think, like Hume, that testimony in itself does not provide any epistemic support are called *reductionists*, in that they think that the epistemic support that we have for our testimony-based beliefs is 'reducible' to independent epistemic support, such as the independent grounds that we have to trust our informants. In contrast, those who think that testimony can supply epistemic support all by itself are called *anti-reductionists*, because they hold that such epistemic support is not completely 'reducible' to other independent epistemic support. The challenge facing anti-reductionists is to explain how testimony can supply epistemic support all by itself. The challenge facing reductionists, in contrast, is to avoid scepticism about testimonial knowledge, since it seems to follow on this view that we have quite a lot less testimonial knowledge than we thought we had. After all, although there are certain cases in which we do have independent grounds in support of our testimony-based beliefs, there do seem to be an awful lot of testimony-based beliefs which we hold where such independent grounds are lacking.

Your belief that 2 + 2 = 4 may well have been initially gained through testimony, in that someone – a teacher, say – told you that this was the case. It is unlikely that the reason why you continue to hold it is because of this testimony, however. After all, this is the sort of proposition which one seems to be able to know just by reflecting on it. In fully understanding this proposition, does one not immediately recognise that it is true? This proposition thus seems to be part of a very special class of propositions which one can know just through the exercise of one's reason. Such propositions are called *a priori* propositions, and the knowledge that results when one comes to know an *a priori* proposition through the exercise of one's reason is called *a priori knowledge*. In contrast, those propositions which cannot be known through the exercise of reason and must instead be known through experience are called *a posteriori* propositions, and knowledge acquired in this way is called *a posteriori knowledge*. Your knowledge that Paris is the capital of France is *a posteriori* knowledge, since this is not the kind of proposition which one can come to know just by reflecting upon it; instead, one needs to investigate the world in some way (look up France in an atlas, for example).

Philosophers have long been very interested in *a priori* knowledge, partly because it seems that much (if not all) of our philosophical knowledge must be *a priori* knowledge (it is not knowledge that is gained via a worldly investigation, after all). A second reason why philosophers are interested in *a priori* knowledge concerns the fact that it seems to have a very special epistemic standing, in that, in paradigm cases of *a priori* knowledge at any rate, it seems that this is knowledge that one can personally vouchsafe. That is, it is knowledge that one can acquire all by oneself and which one can be completely certain of. (Compare *a priori* knowledge with testimonial knowledge on this score. Here one is essentially dependent upon the word of others and there is always room for doubt about a belief acquired in this fashion.) Still, even despite the central place that *a priori* knowledge occupies in philosophical inquiry, there are those who are sceptical about the existence of *a priori* knowledge. Some of the key issues surrounding the *a priori/a posteriori* distinction, including the grounds that some have offered for scepticism about the *a priori*, are considered in the piece by Roderick Chisholm which is reprinted in this part (Chapter 32).

Finally, we come to your knowledge that you are currently reading the introduction to this part. This is knowledge that is gained through your senses, and it is called *perceptual knowledge*. After all, your grounds for believing this arise out of what you can see before you, and your eyesight is one of your senses. Perceptual knowledge is the topic of the piece by William Alston reprinted in this part (Chapter 33).

Perceptual knowledge is perhaps the most direct kind of knowledge there is. For the most part, one does not need to do very much in order to gain perceptual knowledge. For example, one opens one's eyes in the morning and one thereby gains lots of knowledge about one's environment entirely spontaneously. (Compare the 'directness' of perceptual knowledge with the relative 'indirectness' of the types of knowledge – inductive knowledge, testimonial knowledge and *a priori* knowledge – that we have just considered.)

Our primary – if not sole – means of coming to have knowledge of the world around us is through perception. For while we could come to know truths about the world around us through, say, testimony (e.g. someone telling you that it is raining outside), ultimately there must be someone in the testimonial chain (i.e. if not your informant, then your informant's informant, etc.) who has gained this knowledge first-hand through perception. We can put this point by saying that while testimony is able to *preserve* knowledge, it cannot, unlike perception, *generate* new knowledge. This makes perception a very important source of knowledge indeed.

Study questions

1   What is inductive knowledge? In your own words, try to state the problem of induction.

2   What is testimonial knowledge? Does one always need independent grounds in order to accept an instance of testimony?

3   In your own words, try to describe the *a priori/a posteriori* distinction. Why might someone be suspicious of the idea of *a priori* knowledge? Would they be right to be suspicious?

4   In your own words, try to describe the four accounts of perceptual experience described by Alston (direct realism, the sense-datum theory, adverbial theory and the phenomenal quality view). Which of these views is preferable, do you think?

5   What does Alston mean when he describes Dretske's account of perceptual knowledge as 'externalist'? Do you find an externalist treatment of perceptual knowledge persuasive?

Further reading

An introductory discussion of the main sources of knowledge – including induction, memory, perception, testimony and reason – can be found in part II (chapters 7–10) of Pritchard (2006). There is a wealth of material freely available on the internet on the topics covered here. For a survey of research on the problem of induction, see Vickers (2006). For a survey of research on epistemological issues regarding testimony, see Adler (2006). For an overview of the *a priori/a posteriori* distinction, see Baehr (2006). For a survey of research on *a priori* justification and knowledge, see Casullo (2007). For a survey of research on epistemological issues regarding perception, see O'Brien (2004) and BonJour (2007). All of these sources contain guides for further reading.

References

Adler, J. (2006). 'Epistemological Problems of Testimony', *Stanford Encyclopaedia of Philosophy*, ed. E. Zalta, http://plato.stanford.edu/entries/testimony-episprob/.

Baehr, J. (2006). '*A Priori* and *A Posteriori*', *Internet Encyclopaedia of Philosophy*, eds J. Fieser and B. Dowden, http://www.iep.utm.edu/a/apriori.htm.

BonJour, L. (2007). 'Epistemological Problems of Perception', *Stanford Encyclopaedia of Philosophy*, ed. E. Zalta, http://plato.stanford.edu/entries/perception-episprob/.

Casullo, A. (2007). '*A Priori* Justification and Knowledge', *Stanford Encyclopaedia of Philosophy*, ed. E. Zalta, http://plato.stanford.edu/entries/apriori/.

O'Brien, D. (2004). 'Epistemological Problems of Perception', *Internet Encyclopaedia of Philosophy*, eds J. Fieser and B. Dowden, http://www.iep.utm.edu/e/epis-per.htm.

Pritchard, D. H. (2006). *What Is this Thing Called Knowledge?*, London: Routledge.

Vickers, J. (2006). 'The Problem of Induction', *Stanford Encyclopaedia of Philosophy*, ed. E. Zalta, http://plato.stanford.edu/entries/induction-problem/.

Chapter 30

Bertrand Russell

ON INDUCTION

In almost all our previous discussions we have been concerned in the attempt to get clear as to our data in the way of knowledge of existence. What things are there in the universe whose existence is known to us owing to our being acquainted with them? So far, our answer has been that we are acquainted with our sense-data, and, probably, with ourselves. These we know to exist. And past sense-data which are remembered are known to have existed in the past. This knowledge supplies our data.

But if we are to be able to draw inferences from these data – if we are to know of the existence of matter, of other people, of the past before our individual memory begins, or of the future, we must know general principles of some kind by means of which such inferences can be drawn. It must be known to us that the existence of some one sort of thing, A, is a sign of the existence of some other sort of thing, B, either at the same time as A or at some earlier or later time, as, for example, thunder is a sign of the earlier existence of lightning. If this were not known to us, we could never extend our knowledge beyond the sphere of our private experience; and this sphere, as we have seen, is exceedingly limited. The question we have now to consider is whether such an extension is possible, and if so, how it is effected.

Let us take as an illustration a matter about which none of us, in fact, feels the slightest doubt. We are all convinced that the sun will rise to-morrow. Why? Is this belief a mere blind outcome of past experience, or can it be justified as a reasonable belief? It is not easy to find a test by which to judge whether a belief of this kind is reasonable or not, but we can at least ascertain what sort of general beliefs would suffice, if true, to justify the judgement that the sun will rise to-morrow, and the many other similar judgements upon which our actions are based.

It is obvious that if we are asked why we believe that the sun will rise to-morrow, we shall naturally answer, 'Because it always has risen every day.' We have a firm belief that it will rise in the future, because it has risen in the past. If we are challenged as to why we believe that it will continue to rise as heretofore, we may appeal to the laws of motion: the earth, we shall say, is a freely rotating body, and such bodies do not cease to rotate unless something interferes from outside, and there is nothing outside to interfere with the earth between now and to-morrow. Of course it might be doubted whether we are quite certain that there is nothing outside to interfere, but this is not the interesting doubt. The interesting doubt is as to whether the laws of motion will remain in operation until to-morrow. If this doubt is raised, we find ourselves in the same position as when the doubt about the sunrise was first raised.

The *only* reason for believing that the laws of motion will remain in operation is that they have operated hitherto, so far as our knowledge of the past enables us to judge. It is true that we have a greater body of evidence from the past in favour of the laws of motion than we have in favour of the sunrise, because the sunrise is merely a particular case of fulfilment of the laws of motion, and there are countless other particular cases. But the real question is: do *any* number of cases of a law being fulfilled in the past afford evidence that it will be fulfilled in the future? If not, it becomes plain that we have no ground whatever for expecting the sun to rise tomorrow, or for expecting the bread we shall eat at our next meal not to poison us, or for any of the other scarcely conscious expectations that control our daily lives. It is to be observed that all such expectations are only *probable*; thus we have not to seek for a proof that they *must* be fulfilled, but only for some reason in favour of the view that they are *likely* to be fulfilled.

Now in dealing with this question we must, to begin with, make an important distinction, without which we should soon become involved in hopeless confusions. Experience has shown us that, hitherto, the frequent repetition of some uniform succession or coexistence has been a *cause* of our expecting the same succession or coexistence on the next occasion. Food that has a certain appearance generally has a certain taste, and it is a severe shock to our expectations when the familiar appearance is found to be associated with an unusual taste. Things which we see become associated, by habit, with certain tactile sensations which we expect if we touch them; one of the horrors of a ghost (in many ghost-stories) is that it fails to give us any sensations of touch. Uneducated people who go abroad for the first time are so surprised as to be incredulous when they find their native language not understood.

And this kind of association is not confined to men; in animals also it is very strong. A horse which has been often driven along a certain road resists the attempt to drive him in a different direction. Domestic animals expect food when they see the person who usually feeds them. We

know that all these rather crude expectations of uniformity are liable to be misleading. The man who has fed the chicken every day throughout its life at last wrings its neck instead, showing that more refined views as to the uniformity of nature would have been useful to the chicken.

But in spite of the misleadingness of such expectations, they nevertheless exist. The mere fact that something has happened a certain number of times causes animals and men to expect that it will happen again. Thus our instincts certainly cause us to believe that the sun will rise to-morrow, but we may be in no better a position than the chicken which unexpectedly has its neck wrung. We have therefore to distinguish the fact that past uniformities *cause* expectations as to the future, from the question whether there is any reasonable ground for giving weight to such expectations after the question of their validity has been raised.

The problem we have to discuss is whether there is any reason for believing in what is called 'the uniformity of nature'. The belief in the uniformity of nature is the belief that everything that has happened or will happen is an instance of some general law to which there are *no* exceptions. The crude expectations which we have been considering are all subject to exceptions, and therefore liable to disappoint those who entertain them. But science habitually assumes, at least as a working hypothesis, that general rules which have exceptions can be replaced by general rules which have no exceptions. 'Unsupported bodies in air fall' is a general rule to which balloons and aeroplanes are exceptions. But the laws of motion and the law of gravitation, which account for the fact that most bodies fall, also account for the fact that balloons and aeroplanes can rise; thus the laws of motion and the law of gravitation are not subject to these exceptions.

The belief that the sun will rise to-morrow might be falsified if the earth came suddenly into contact with a large body which destroyed its rotation; but the laws of motion and the law of gravitation would not be infringed by such an event. The business of science is to find uniformities, such as the laws of motion and the law of gravitation, to which, so far as our experience extends, there are no exceptions. In this search science has been remarkably successful, and it may be conceded that such uniformities have held hitherto. This brings us back to the question: have we any reason, assuming that they have always held in the past, to suppose that they will hold in the future?

It has been argued that we have reason to know that the future will resemble the past, because what was the future has constantly become the past, and has always been found to resemble the past, so that we really have experience of the future, namely of times which were formerly future, which we may call past futures. But such an argument really begs the very question at issue. We have experience of past futures, but not of future futures, and the question is: will future futures resemble past futures? This question is not to be answered by an argument which starts from past futures alone. We have therefore still to seek for some principle which shall enable us to know that the future will follow the same laws as the past.

The reference to the future in this question is not essential. The same question arises when we apply the laws that work in our experience to past things of which we have no experience – as, for example, in geology, or in theories as to the origin of the Solar System. The question we really have to ask is: 'When two things have been found to be often associated, and no instance is known of the one occurring without the other, does the occurrence of one of the two, in a fresh instance, give any good ground for expecting the other?' On our answer to this question must depend the validity of the whole of our expectations as to the future, the whole of the results obtained by induction, and in fact practically all the beliefs upon which our daily life is based.

It must be conceded, to begin with, that the fact that two things have been found often together and never apart does not, by itself, suffice to *prove* demonstratively that they will be found together in the next case we examine. The most we can hope is that the oftener things are found together, the more probable it becomes that they will be found together another time, and that, if they have been found together often enough, the probability will amount *almost* to certainty. It can never quite reach certainty, because we know that in spite of frequent repetitions there sometimes is a failure at the last, as in the case of the chicken whose neck is wrung. Thus probability is all we ought to seek.

It might be urged, as against the view we are advocating, that we know all natural phenomena to be subject to the reign of law, and that sometimes, on the basis of observation, we can see that only one law can possibly fit the facts of the case. Now to this view there are two answers. The first is that, even if *some* law which has no exceptions applies to our case, we can never, in practice, be sure that we have discovered that law and not one to which there are exceptions. The second is that the reign of law would seem to be itself only probable, and that our belief that it will hold in the future, or in unexamined cases in the past, is itself based upon the very principle we are examining.

The principle we are examining may be called the *principle of induction*, and its two parts may be stated as follows:

(a) When a thing of a certain sort A has been found to be associated with a thing of a certain other sort B, and has never been found dissociated from a thing of the sort B, the greater the number of cases in which A and B have been associated, the greater is the probability that they will be associated in a fresh case in which one of them is known to be present;

(b) Under the same circumstances, a sufficient number of cases of association will make the probability of a fresh association nearly a certainty, and will make it approach certainty without limit.

As just stated, the principle applies only to the verification of our expectation in a single fresh instance. But we want also to know that there is a probability in favour of the general law that things of the sort A are *always* associated with things of the sort B, provided a sufficient number of cases of association are known, and no cases of failure of association are known. The probability of the general law is obviously less than the probability of the particular case, since if the general law is true, the particular case must also be true, whereas the particular case may be true without the general law being true. Nevertheless the probability of the general law is increased by repetitions, just as the probability of the particular case is. We may therefore repeat the two parts of our principle as regards the general law, thus:

(a) The greater the number of cases in which a thing of the sort A has been found associated with a thing of the sort B, the more probable it is (if no cases of failure of association are known) that A is always associated with B;

(b) Under the same circumstances, a sufficient number of cases of the association of A with B will make it nearly certain that A is always associated with B, and will make this general law approach certainty without limit.

It should be noted that probability is always relative to certain data. In our case, the data are merely the known cases of coexistence of A and B. There may be other data, which *might* be taken into account, which would gravely alter the probability. For example, a man who had seen a great many white swans might argue, by our principle, that on the data it was *probable* that all swans were white, and this might be a perfectly sound argument. The argument is not disproved by the fact that some swans are black, because a

thing may very well happen in spite of the fact that some data render it improbable. In the case of the swans, a man might know that colour is a very variable characteristic in many species of animals, and that, therefore, an induction as to colour is peculiarly liable to error. But this knowledge would be a fresh datum, by no means proving that the probability relatively to our previous data had been wrongly estimated. The fact, therefore, that things often fail to fulfil our expectations is no evidence that our expectations will not *probably* be fulfilled in a given case or a given class of cases. Thus our inductive principle is at any rate not capable of being *disproved* by an appeal to experience.

The inductive principle, however, is equally incapable of being *proved* by an appeal to experience. Experience might conceivably confirm the inductive principle as regards the cases that have been already examined; but as regards unexamined cases, it is the inductive principle alone that can justify any inference from what has been examined to what has not been examined. All arguments which, on the basis of experience, argue as to the future or the unexperienced parts of the past or present, assume the inductive principle; hence we can never use experience to prove the inductive principle without begging the question. Thus we must either accept the inductive principle on the ground of its intrinsic evidence, or forgo all justification of our expectations about the future. If the principle is unsound, we have no reason to expect the sun to rise to-morrow, to expect bread to be more nourishing than a stone, or to expect that if we throw ourselves off the roof we shall fall. When we see what looks like our best friend approaching us, we shall have no reason to suppose that his body is not inhabited by the mind of our worst enemy or of some total stranger. All our conduct is based upon associations which have worked in the past, and which we therefore regard as likely to work in the future; and this likelihood is dependent for its validity upon the inductive principle.

The general principles of science, such as the belief in the reign of law, and the belief that every event must have a cause, are as completely dependent upon the inductive principle as are the beliefs of daily life. All such general principles are believed because mankind has found innumerable instances of their truth and no instances of their falsehood. But this affords no evidence for their truth in the future, unless the inductive principle is assumed.

Thus all knowledge which, on a basis of experience, tells us something about what is not experienced, is based upon a belief which experience can neither confirm nor confute, yet which, at least in its more concrete applications, appears to be as firmly rooted in us as many of the facts of experience. The existence and justification of such beliefs – for the inductive principle, as we shall see, is not the only example – raises some of the most difficult and most debated problems of philosophy. We will, in the next chapter, consider briefly what may be said to account for such knowledge, and what is its scope and its degree of certainty.

Chapter 31

Robert Audi

THE PLACE OF TESTIMONY IN THE FABRIC OF KNOWLEDGE AND JUSTIFICATION

Testimony is a pervasive and indispensable source of knowledge and justification, and it may be as significant for the theory of communication and the psychology of belief acquisition as it is for epistemology. It is a central concern of social epistemology, in which philosophers have shown increasing interest. But despite a small number of valuable discussions devoted to testimony in the past fifteen years,[1] it remains very much a secondary topic in epistemology. This treatment is neither adequate to its epistemological importance nor desirable from the point of view of a comprehensive account of knowledge and justification. An account of testimony can clarify both the social and the individual grounds of belief. It can also bring out major differences between two central epistemic concepts often too closely linked: knowledge and justification. I begin with a sketch of the nature and pervasiveness of testimony and proceed to explore its psychology, its epistemic status, and its place in human cognition.

Formal and informal testimony

The word "testimony" commonly evokes images of the courtroom, where someone sworn in testifies, offering information supposed to represent knowledge or belief. Often such testimony recounts what was witnessed firsthand, but testimony can be about something not witnessed, such as the implications of a scientific theory.[2] Formal testimony, however, is not the basic kind (if indeed there is a basic kind). Formal testimony differs from the informal kind in the conditions of its expression, but not necessarily in credibility. Testimony of the wide sort that concerns me—roughly, saying or affirming something in an apparent attempt to convey (correct) information—is what raises the question of how testimony is important for knowledge and justification.[3]

For the casual giving of information, say in telling someone where one was last night, "testimony" is a heavy term. We could speak of "informing," but this is too narrow, both in suggesting a prepared message (as in "Yesterday she informed me of her intention") and in (normally) implying its truth. We might regard all testimony as a kind of saying, but not all saying—even apart from what is said in fiction—is testimony. Someone who says, "Ah, what a magnificent tree!" is expressing a sense of its magnificence, but not giving testimony that it is magnificent.

As a broad rubric for the oral or written statements that concern us, I propose *attesting*. This covers both formally testifying that something is so and simply saying, in the relevant informational way, that it is so. It also captures the idea of saying something *to* someone. Testimony is always given to one or more persons (to oneself, perhaps, in the limiting case), but the audience may be hypothetical: a diarist describing atrocities for posterity may not know whether anyone will read the testimony. What we must understand is the role of testimony of all these kinds—roughly, of people's telling us things—in accounting for knowledge and justification. I want to begin with how testimony yields belief; its psychological role in cognition is both intrinsically interesting and epistemologically important.

The psychology of testimony

If we start by focusing on formal testimony, we might conclude that as a source of belief testimony is quite unlike perception in that testimony produces only inferential beliefs of what is said, whereas perception commonly produces non-inferential beliefs about what is perceived. The idea that beliefs based on testimony arise by inference from one or more premises is probably natural in relation to formal testimony. When I hear courtroom testimony, I appraise the witness, place the testimony in the context of the trial and my general knowledge, and accept what is said only if, from this broad perspective, it seems true. I do not just believe what I hear; I believe it only on the basis of certain premises, say that the witness seems sincere and that the testimony in question fits what I know about the case.[4]

In this inferentialist picture of testimony, it is apparently not as direct a source of belief as is perception: it yields belief only through both the testimony itself *and* one or more premises that support the proposition attested to or at least the attester's credibility. If that is so, testimony is also not as direct a source of knowledge or justification; for one would know, or be justified in believing, what is attested, only if one knows, or is at least justified in believing, one's premise(s). One could not know simply *from* testimony, but only from premises *about* it as well.[5]

Another, probably more plausible, account can also explain the psychological role of back-

ground beliefs. On this account, beliefs about the credibility of the attester and beliefs pertinent to the attested proposition play a mainly filtering role: they prevent our believing testimony that does not "pass," for instance because it seems insincere; but if no such difficulty strikes us, we "just believe" (non-inferentially) what is attested. These filtering beliefs are like a trap door that shuts only if triggered; its normal position is open, but it stays in readiness to block what should not enter.[6] The open position is a kind of *trust*. The absence or laxity of filtering beliefs yields credulity; excessively rigorous ones yield skepticism. It could turn out that the inferentialist and filtering belief accounts both apply, but in different circumstances (nor are beliefs the only psychological elements that can filter out certain attested propositions). The psychological possibilities here are too numerous to detail. It is enough to see that belief based on testimony need not be inferential, say grounded in a further belief that the attester has spoken plausibly.

In the case of informal testimony—the most common kind—the beliefs produced in the hearer are typically not inferential. When trusted friends speak to us on matters we do not think are beyond their competence, we normally just believe what they tell us. Indeed, if I am basically trusting of people's word, then normally, when someone tells me something, my belief system stands ready to be stocked; I hesitate only if (for instance) a would-be new belief conflicts with one or more beliefs already in my inventory.[7] If you look healthy and tell me you recently walked thirty miles, I may readily believe you, whereas in the absence of special evidence I would not believe someone claiming to have climbed Mt. Everest without rope. On my background beliefs, that feat is virtually impossible.

Just as it is misleading to build an account of the psychology of testimony from the formal cases, it is a mistake to take a momentary (synchronic) view of how testimony produces belief, even in the non-inferential cases. Our standing beliefs, and even our belief-forming processes, may change in the course of our receiving testimony; and a testimonially based belief may arise diachronically. Suppose I meet someone on a plane. She tells me that, at a conference, a speaker I know lost his temper. Initially, I suspend judgment about whether he did so. Such things are rare, and I do not know her. Then, as she describes the conference, other details begin to fit together and she confirms information I already have, such as who was there. Soon I am listening in an accepting attitude, forming beliefs of each thing she says. At the end, I find that I now believe that the speaker did lose his temper. Here my testimonially based belief is formed considerably later than my hearing the testimony it rests on.

Even when she first reported his losing his temper, I need not have inferred that (for instance) I should suspend judgment on this unlikely statement; suspended judgment (or simple non-belief) may be a non-inferential response to the constraints set by my independent beliefs. Moreover, her testimony is *neutralized*, but not *overridden*, by my antecedent beliefs and impressions: they prevent my believing what is attested to; they do not overturn a testimonially grounded belief I formed and then gave up, as where I discover it is inconsistent with apparent facts. As her narrative progresses, the constraints set by my independent beliefs relax; and, for each of her statements, I form beliefs both non-inferentially and even spontaneously, in the sense that any constraints that might have operated do not come in: her statements no longer have to pass through the gaze of my critical scrutiny, nor are any filtered out by whatever more nearly automatic checking the mind routinely does when people offer information.

The case also seems to show something beyond the point that testimony can produce belief after the fact. Perhaps the most difficult thing to explain here is why, at the end of her testimony, I believe the proposition that, at the beginning, was an object of suspended judgment. One hypothesis is an unconscious inference, say from the general credibility of her account to the conclusion that this proposition, as an essential part of it, is true. But this sort of inference does not seem adequate to the sometimes global character of the kind of belief formation in question. Perhaps some inferentialist account can satisfactorily explain the data, but there is no necessity to appeal to inference. The cognitive *influence* of standing beliefs, such as a newly formed belief that she is credible, need not proceed through an *inference* from any subset of them. There is a more moderate explanation of the formation of the belief, one that posits both fewer conscious events and, presumably, less expenditure of mental energy. Far from my having to consider one or more grounds for believing her in general or for accepting what she says, and even apart from my forming any belief about her competence on the topic of the attested proposition, her eventually appearing to me as a quite credible person can in some fairly direct way produce in me a general disposition to believe her. This disposition is strengthened as she speaks with an evident credibility, and at the end its strength overcomes the resistance to belief which was exercised earlier by my constraining beliefs. On the subject she is addressing, I have come to trust her.

There are other (related) possibilities; belief change can occur in many ways. Perhaps people (or some of us) have a credibility scale on which attesters acquire—usually without our conscious attention to the matter—a place that can change, also without our conscious attention. This is an interesting empirical hypothesis I cannot pursue, but all that is crucial is that we see how beliefs based on testimony (which might also be called testimonially grounded beliefs) can be constrained by other beliefs without being inferentially based on them, and how beliefs based on testimony can be formed later than the attestation that is their ultimate source. Perception, too, can produce belief after it begins or, with the help of memory, after it ceases. One may look at a distant shape a long time before believing that it is a tree stump and not a stroller who stopped to gaze at the sky. This same belief could also arise much later, from vividly recalling the image when one is queried as a witness of the scene. The connection in virtue of which a belief is based on a source need be neither direct nor simultaneous nor a result of inference.

Does the analogy with perception warrant concluding that testimony, like perception, is a basic source of belief, in the sense, roughly, that it can produce belief without the cooperation of another source of belief? Consider perception. If I see a painting, this can produce in me a belief that there is a painting before me, without my having a potentially belief-producing experience of any other sort, such as a separate consciousness of an image of a painting.[8] But I cannot form a testimonially based belief unless I *hear* (or otherwise perceive) the testimony. Perception is crucial for the formation of testimonially based beliefs in a way that no other belief source is crucial for the formation of perceptual beliefs.[9] Granted, perception does not produce belief without appropriate background conditions, nor does its being a basic source of belief imply that antecedent beliefs are irrelevant to the epistemic status of perceptual beliefs. If I firmly believe I am hallucinating the moon, then even if I actually see it I may withhold judgment on whether it is out. Although a basic source does not derive its generative power from another source, it is not completely independent of other sources or their outputs.[10]

Since testimonially based beliefs need not be inferential, and so need not be grounded on a belief that the attester is sincere (or even on a belief that someone is speaking to one), one may be puzzled by the point that testimony is not a basic source of belief. The puzzlement may arise from failing to appreciate that perception can be a basic requirement for the formation of belief grounded in testimony even if perceptual *belief* is not a requirement. To be sure, in order to

acquire, on the basis of testimony, a belief that the speaker lost his temper, I may have to be *disposed* to believe that someone said he did. But that seems to be only because I must perceive this being said, not because I must form the belief (or otherwise believe) that it was said, just as perception of a sentence in a convincing editorial can produce belief of what it says without one's forming the belief that the sentence says that. It is my perception of what is said, typically my hearing or reading it, that is required for formation of a testimonially based belief of the proposition attested to. Understanding and believing testimony that *p* when we hear that testimony may require that in some sense we *presuppose* the attester said that *p*—so that if (e.g.) we *disbelieve* the attester said that *p*, we will not believe *p* from the testimony. Moreover, there is no need to deny that the brain—or perhaps the mind at a subconscious level—does some kind of information processing, perhaps complex processing, not entailing belief formation. But I doubt that believing *p* on the basis of testimony requires believing that the attester said that *p*, any more than understanding a sentence which says that *p* requires believing that the sentence says that *p*.[11] Surely the testimonial acquisition of beliefs does not require the mind to keep double semantic books.

The main positive point here is that testimony can be a source of *basic beliefs*, in the minimal sense of beliefs not based on other beliefs (as opposed to the problematic sense of beliefs with a certain privileged epistemic status). This kind of belief can also be basic knowledge if it meets the conditions for non-inferential knowledge (and so is not based on premises).[12] It can certainly be basic for a person in the everyday sense of being central in the person's life. A major epistemological point that the case of testimony shows is that a basic belief—roughly, one basic in the order of one's beliefs—need not come from a basic source of belief—roughly, one basic in the order of cognitive sources. A testimonially based belief need not derive from other beliefs even though its formation depends on a non-testimonial source of beliefs—perception.

The epistemology of testimony

In the light of what has emerged about how testimony produces belief, we are in a good position to ask how testimony yields knowledge and justification and whether it ever yields basic knowledge or basic justification in the way perception and reflection, for instance, apparently do. The case of knowledge is in some respects easier to deal with than that of justification. Consider knowledge first.

If I do not know that the speaker lost his temper, you cannot come to know it on the basis of my attesting to it.[13] This is obvious if I am mistaken and he did not lose his temper. But suppose I make a lucky guess. Then I give you correct conjectured information, but you are also lucky to be correct and also do not know that he lost his temper. It is a fluke that I get it right; it is even more of a fluke that you get it right, since in your case there are, in addition to the chance of my making a mistake, the other liabilities you escape: of my having distorted the truth, of your having misheard me, of your adding a false detail to my testimony, and so forth. Imagine, on the other hand, that I do not guess at, but incautiously accept, the proposition that the speaker lost his temper, from someone I know often lies about others. Again, I lack knowledge that he lost his temper, even if this time the proposition is true; and again, others cannot know it on the basis of my testimony, which is now ill-grounded in another way. What I do not have, I cannot give.

Justification is different: even if I am not justified in believing that the speaker lost his temper, I can be credible in such a way that you *can* become justified in believing this on the basis of my attesting to it. Consider the two facets of testimonial credibility, the sincerity dimension, concerning the attester's honesty, and the competence dimension, concerning the attester's having experience or knowledge sufficient to make it at least likely that if the attester forms a belief that p, then p is true. Plainly, you can justifiedly regard me as credible on the topic of whether the speaker lost his temper if you have good reason to believe that I am honest, possess normal acuity and memory, and was reasonably attentive at the time.

This case shows, then, that whereas my testimony cannot give you testimonially grounded knowledge that p without my knowing that p, it can give you testimonially grounded justification for believing p without my having that justification—or any kind of justification—for believing p. This point subtly differs from a claim that may seem equivalent: that I cannot (testimonially) give you knowledge that p without knowing that p, yet I *can* (testimonially) give you justification for believing p without having any justification for believing p. This claim is at best misleading. In the case of my credible but false testimony that gives you justification for what I attest to, the main point is not that I give you justification for believing what I say—that the speaker lost his temper—without having that justification. Rather, the way I attest to the proposition, together with your background justification regarding me and the circumstances, gives you this justification, independently of whether I have it. This is not my giving you justification in the way one gives knowledge. Testimonially based knowledge is received by transmission and so depends on the attester's knowing that p. It is natural to say that in the first case you would gain knowledge *through* my testimony, whereas in the second you would gain justification *from* my testimony, but not through it.

Testimony that p can convey the attester's knowledge that p; it can *produce* in the hearer a justification for believing p; but it does not in itself convey the attester's justification for believing it. The attester need not even have such justification. This contrast helps to explain the original asymmetry: if I do not know that p, my testimony that p cannot transmit to you testimonially based knowledge that p; but even if I am not justified in believing p, my testimony can give you testimonially based justification for believing it, through providing the main materials for your becoming justified in believing it.[14]

The contrast between how testimony produces knowledge, and how it produces justification, in the recipient is reminiscent of a contrast applicable to memory. Just as we cannot know that p from memory unless we have come to know it in another way, say through perception, we cannot know that p on the basis of testimony unless the attester (or someone from whom the attester comes to know it) has come to know it (at least in part) in another way; whereas we can become justified in believing p through memory impressions whether or not p is true or known,[15] and we can become justified in believing p on the basis of testimony whether or not the attester has true belief or knowledge of it or even justification for it. Moreover, with testimonially based knowledge, as with memorial knowledge, there must apparently be at least one epistemically sound chain from the belief constituting that knowledge to a source of the knowledge in some other mode, such as perception; but with testimonially based justification, as with memorial justification, what seems essential is the present epistemic situation of the memorial subject or testimonial recipient, such as the contents of apparently memorial consciousness and the content and justifiedness of background beliefs. Memory and testimony can (in different ways) both generate justification; but they are not generative with respect to knowledge: characteristically, the former is preservative, the latter transmissive.[16]

There is another way justification and knowledge apparently differ in their relation to testimony. Suppose I am justified in believing p, but you have no justification of your own for believing p or for taking me to be credible on the

topic. To vary the conference example, imagine that in passing, and without giving evidence, I say that three speakers lost their tempers, and your background information neither disconfirms nor supports this claim or my credibility in the matter. Here justification follows your lights rather than mine: my would-be contribution to justifying you in believing p is undermined by your lack of justification for thinking my testimony is credible or for believing p on some other ground. Receptivity to justification sometimes requires already having some measure of it, say for believing the attester credible or for believing p or for both. (The justification might also be global if one may be justified in believing, in the absence of specific grounds for thinking otherwise, that serious testimony tends to be true.) Knowledge seems somewhat different on this score: to know something through my attesting to it in expression of my own knowledge, you do not have to know that I am credible; it is surely enough that you have some reason to believe I am and no reason to doubt it. I believe it is enough that you presuppose it and have no reason to doubt it. Surely you can know that it is nine o'clock, on the basis of my knowing this and telling it to you, even if you simply find me a normal-seeming person with a normal-looking watch and take me to be credible.[17] And why indeed must you meet any more than a negative condition: not having any reason to doubt my credibility? We are talking about a case where I know that it is nine o'clock, attest to this from my knowledge of it, and thereby produce your (true) belief that it is nine. These conditions seem normally sufficient for you to know that it is nine.

This conclusion seems plausible independently of any specific account of knowledge, but it is especially plausible from an externalist, reliabilist perspective.[18] The idea, in part, is that testimony can be (semantically embedded) evidence that plays an intermediary role in a reliable belief-producing process. It can do this whether or not the recipient forms beliefs supporting the attester's credibility, draws inferences about the competence of the attester or the likelihood of p, or has other positive grounds supporting credibility.

It is, to be sure, difficult to find cases of knowledge that p grounded in such a natural, reliable process but *not* accompanied by these or other grounds yielding justification for p. But consider this. I receive a letter in August in which, in an aside, Gisèle tells me she will attend a meeting in December. I believe her and (setting skepticism aside) can now know she will attend. In October I get another letter from her that does not mention the meeting. In late November I am asked if she will attend, and I say—from memory—that she will. Surely my testimony can enable my hearer to know that she will attend, even if I do not recall how I came to think this, say because I can now remember only her second letter. Still, I *remember* that she will be attending, which presumably implies that I know it. I might also have inductive grounds to think that if I seem to remember something like this, I know it; but I doubt that one *must* have such grounds. Perhaps I could even lack anything properly called a justification for my belief, yet (on the basis of my excellent memory) still know the proposition in question anyway.

A natural objection to this credible-unless-otherwise-indicated view of testimony as a ground for knowledge is that in our example one's evidence is so scanty that one would at best have only some reason to believe Gisèle will attend the meeting, or that it is nine o'clock. But is this true? Admittedly, that one has some reason to believe the proposition may be all one can *show* from one's evidence or from what one feels certain of. Still, surely I in fact do know that it is nine and that Gisèle will attend the meeting; and if I sincerely tell you she will, you can thereby know that she will. An epistemically sound chain connects your belief with her firsthand testimony. That appears to hold even where you simply have no reason to doubt my

credibility. One theory as to why it holds is that (some) testimony can serve as a kind of stand-in for our own perception, and sometimes we may as safely trust the word of others as our own senses. If testimony can never so serve—if it is never a reliable social intermediary between its recipient and the world it represents—then in scientific matters and even in cases where we rely less than that on others, we know far less than we commonly suppose.

If these points about testimony as a source of justification and knowledge are sound, at least two principles applicable to testimony emerge as plausible. Concerning knowledge, we might say that at least normally, a belief that p based on testimony thereby constitutes knowledge (i.e. counts as testimonially based knowledge) provided that the attester knows that p and the believer has no reason to doubt either p or the attester's credibility concerning it. From the point of view of reliabilism, one way to put the main idea here is to say that normally, reliable grounding of true beliefs is transmissible across testimony.[19] Regarding justification, we might say that at least normally, a belief based on testimony is thereby justified (i.e. counts as testimonially justified) provided the believer has overall justification for taking the attester to be credible regarding the proposition in question. *Having* this justification implies a capacity for inference, say about the attester's reliability, but not making an actual inference, conscious or unconscious. In any event, the first principle suggests that testimony serves—or can serve—as a ground of knowledge in an external way; the second principle suggests that it serves as a ground of justification only if the recipient has a measure of justification initially.[20] (Further support for this contrast and its implications for language-learning are pursued [on page 394].)

Whatever the exact conditions under which testimony grounds knowledge or justification, we have so far found no reason to doubt that under some conditions testimony can yield both knowledge and justified belief in its believing recipient. It appears, however, that it cannot be a basic source of knowledge, since one cannot know something on the basis of testimony unless the attester knows it. Testimony transmits knowledge but does not, as such, generate it. It may generate knowledge *incidentally*, as where, by saying in a surprised tone that it is four in the morning, I give a fellow insomniac knowledge that I am awake. This knowledge is grounded not on the testimony but on the mere hearing of it, and that kind of knowledge could as easily be conveyed by humming.

Testimony, like inference, can exist in indefinitely long chains. An attester might know that p on the basis of a third person's testimony that p, who might know it on the basis of a fourth person's testimony rather than from a generative source such as perception. How far back can this go? There is surely some limit or other in each situation, as opposed to an infinite regress, and there would be a limit even apart from the time required for receiving testimony, as we can see from noting a second respect in which testimony is not a basic source of knowledge. Surely if no one knew anything in a non-testimonial mode, no one would know anything on the basis of testimony. This is not to say that everything known (even in part) on the basis of testimony must be known by someone *entirely* on another basis. Consider a map cooperatively drawn by a team: each of the team knows some part of the charted territory firsthand, but none knows its overall shape except (largely) through the testimony of the others. Thus, although testimonial knowledge seems ultimately to depend on non-testimonial knowledge—say, knowledge grounded in perception or reflection—not everything testimonially known is also non-testimonially known. To enable others to know something by attesting to it, I must know it myself, and my knowledge must ultimately depend at least in part on non-testimonially based knowledge, such as knowledge grounded in seeing that the clock says nine; but working together we can provide testimony that takes knowledge beyond

what is discernible from any proper subset of our other sources.[21]

One might try to reinforce the view that testimonially based knowledge depends on other knowledge, as follows. Even if someone attests to p in my presence, I would have to *perceive* this and to know some supporting proposition, say, that someone has credibly said that p. Once the point is put this way, however, it quite evidently cannot stand unqualified. The required kind of perceiving does not entail forming a belief of this sort, perhaps not even the specific (partly) perceptual belief that someone said that p. The case shows, then, only that testimony is *operationally* dependent on perception, not that it is *inferentially* dependent on perceptual belief. It requires perceptual raw materials, but not believing any premises about those materials.[22]

If testimonially based knowledge and justification do not depend on premises that support the testimonially grounded belief—say premises confirming the credibility of the attester—this explains how such a belief can be basic. Testimony as a source of knowledge and justification need not be basic relative to other sources of knowledge and justification in order for beliefs grounded in testimony to be basic in the order of beliefs. That point, however, is different from the point made above—that the attester's knowledge that is the basis of the hearer's knowledge cannot ultimately be grounded wholly in testimony. Moreover, knowledge that is directly and wholly based on testimony for the recipient cannot be ultimately based wholly on testimony for the giver: the first would have no "right" to transfer it to the second, just as I would have no right to give someone what I had merely borrowed from someone else, who had merely borrowed it from a third person, and so on to infinity.

The point that testimonially grounded beliefs can be non-inferential and, in that way not dependent on premises, is important. But the operational dependence of testimony has both epistemological and conceptual significance. For if one did not have perceptual *grounds* for knowledge, or at least for justified belief, that someone has attested to p, one could not know p on the basis of the testimony. This is an epistemic dependence not paralleled in the case of perception.[23] It shows that even if testimonially based knowledge need not inferentially depend on *having* knowledge grounded in another mode, it does epistemically depend on having grounds, from another mode, grounds for knowledge in that other mode. Testimonially based knowledge thus depends on—and in this sense presupposes—the availability, or one might say the potential cooperation, of another source of knowledge, even if such knowledge does not require the actual operation of that source in yielding beliefs of the premises it stands ready to supply.

On this point, the case with justification is similar. I cannot acquire justification for believing something on the basis of testimony unless I have some degree of justification for believing that the attester is credible, as well as for certain other propositions, such as that I heard the testimony correctly. This justification cannot come entirely from testimony. Jane may assure me about Bert, but what if I have no justification for taking Jane to be credible? Other grounds of justification, such as perception or memory, must at least tacitly cooperate. But their cooperation can be justificational without being inferential: they need not produce in me beliefs of premises from which I infer that the attester is credible; they simply give me a justification for framing such premises if I need them.

It may help to describe one of my overall conclusions—that testimony is not a basic source of knowledge or justification—as reflecting a contrast between a central pattern in the psychology of testimony and a major aspect of its epistemology. Often, when we hear people attesting to various things, we just believe these things, non-inferentially and even unreservedly. But this natural psychological process yields knowledge and justification only when certain epistemic conditions are met: there must be

grounds, from another source, for knowledge and justification, even if there need be no knowledge or justified beliefs of the propositions warranted by these grounds. In the case of testimonially based knowledge, there must be knowledge, even if not necessarily justification, on the part of the attester, whereas in the case of testimonially based justification there must be justification, even if not knowledge, on the part of the recipient. The first requirement concerns the attester's epistemic situation with respect to the proposition attested to; the second concerns the recipient's epistemic situation with respect to the attester, or the proposition, or both.[24] Together, the requirements indicate how, although, psychologically speaking, testimony is a source of basic beliefs, it is not, epistemically speaking, a basic source of knowledge or justification.

The conceptual and developmental centrality of testimony

The epistemic dependence of testimony on other sources of belief must be squared with the plain fact that tiny children learn—and thereby acquire rudimentary knowledge—from what others tell them even before they are properly said to have grounds for knowledge or justification regarding the attester's credibility. Consider teaching color words. After a time, the child has learned that the sofa, say, is red. But the tiny child has no concept of credibility or other notions important in gaining justification from testimony and, initially, insufficient experience to be justified in believing its teachers are credible. On the view developed here, this point is quite compatible with the child's acquiring knowledge.

The first thing to note in explaining this compatibility is that there are at least two ways to learn from testimony: one can learn (in the sense of coming to know) the content attested to, and one can learn something shown by the testimony itself. The first case is *learning that*, i.e.

that something is so; the second is *learning of or about* something (and may extend to learning *how*). A tiny child learning the basic colors is not, primarily, learning *that* (say) the sofa is red, but, above all, becoming aware of redness as the color of the sofa. In introducing "red," the parent only incidentally attests to the proposition that the sofa is red, and the child can learn the main lesson without conceptualizing the sofa as such at all. The point is to pair "red" with an instance of what it stands for, in order to teach the child that word (or, say, what color red is). The former case—the propositional testimony—may result in propositional knowledge; we would thus have propositional learning. The parental introduction of vocabulary—ostensive testimony—may result in conceptual learning.

It is important to see that the success conditions for the introductory function of language apparently require that for the most part the attestations are at least approximately true. Normally, a child cannot learn "red" unless, in teaching the child English, a goodly proportion of the objects to which "red" is applied are red.[25] This does not of course show that most testimony is true, but it does imply that if communication is occurring when testimony is given, then one may reasonably assume that both attester and recipient have at some point benefited from a background in which a substantial proportion of attestations of a certain sort were true. This point in turn may provide *some* support for taking testimony to be normally credible, at least where the attester is communicating with the recipient.[26]

Commonly, belief and knowledge are acquired at the time concepts are initially understood. It is not self-evident, however, that conditions sufficient for conceptual learning imply propositional learning.[27] Testimony easily produces both together, but if it cannot produce the former without the latter, it apparently can produce the latter without the former. It is, however, difficult to say when a child begins to form beliefs, as opposed to mimicking its elders by saying things that in adults would express beliefs. Let us suppose both that it is very early in life and that many of the first beliefs—or, more likely, initial clusters of beliefs—formed are based on what adults tell the child is the case. Must this pose a problem for the epistemology of testimony suggested here? Again, it will help to consider knowledge and justification separately.

Very early in their lives we speak of babies and children as knowing things. One might object that such talk is simply projective: *we* would know in their situation if we behaved in the relevant way, so we say the child does. This line is defensible, but suppose for the sake of argument that by the time children begin to talk they do know certain things. We may surely speak of their learning—that the milk spills when tipped, that the stove is hot, and so on—and learning (in general) implies knowledge. At about the same time, children begin to learn things on the basis of testimony, for instance that steaming water is hot.

If, as seems a reasonable assumption, gaining testimonially based knowledge normally requires only having no reason to doubt the attester's credibility, then the view proposed above encounters no difficulty. If a tiny child perhaps *can* have no reason for doubt, at least the child has none; nor need there *be* any reason, since much testimony is highly credible. A stronger requirement might seem appropriate: that the child have (possibly in a preconceptual way) some ground for taking the speaker to be credible, for instance experiences repeatedly bearing out what the speaker says. Perhaps one could sketch, for such a correlational ground, conditions elementary enough to fit the rudimentary character of the child's knowledge. I doubt, however, that testimonially based knowledge requires such a ground.

With justification, it may be harder to deal with the case of tiny children. But notice that we do not use the vocabulary of justification, as compared with that of knowledge, for as conceptually undeveloped creatures. For a child to be justified in believing the sofa is red, the child would have to be capable not only of having a ground for believing this but, correspondingly, of failing to have one and believing this anyway, thereby being unjustified. Arguably, by the time we may properly speak of children in this two-sided way (which is perhaps soon after they can speak), they do have a sense of the track record of adults in giving them information that bears out in their experience. If parents say it is cold outside, it is; and so forth. Children do not, of course, use the notion of credibility; but they can understand related concepts, such as those needed for comprehending that Mommy is right about things and baby brother must be corrected. The more natural it is, and the less figurative it seems, to speak of growing children as acquiring justification based on testimony, the easier it is to find some elementary way in which they can satisfy the epistemic and justificational conditions set out above, such as making discriminations that enable them to assess what they are told and gaining some sense of the testimonial track record of those around them.

None of this is to say just when knowledge or justification enters the scene in human development, whether through testimony or through their more basic sources. These are questions largely for psychologists; a philosophical account of the epistemology of testimony need only leave room for plausible answers. The theory outlined here suggests that knowledge arises before justification. Testimonially based knowledge seems to be part of the cognitive foundation from which children acquire the evidence they need to achieve justification for accepting testimony. Perhaps this point is partly explained by the picture of conceptual learning I have sketched in describing ostensive testimony. In rough outline, the idea is this. In the natural developmental order of things, content goes from the outside in, justification from the inside out. Without the conceptualization that arises from the testimonial introduction of content, there would be no internal ground sufficiently

rich to nurture justification. Particularly in children, testimonially based knowledge arises inextricably bound up with conceptualization. This external epistemic success by some testimony is a precondition for the internal evidences that give a child justification for accepting other testimony.

The epistemic indispensability of testimony

The view that testimony is not a basic source of justification or knowledge is easily misunderstood. It does not imply that testimony is any less important in normal human life than a basic source. A source of knowledge and justification can be indispensable in life even if it is not basic. It may be that no normal human being would know anything apart from receiving testimony.[28] Suppose there is no innate knowledge and (though I want to leave this open) that one knows nothing before learning a language. Then, unless one could acquire linguistic competence without the help of others, they would be essential in one's coming to know anything at all. Moreover, if one tries to imagine what would be left if all the knowledge and beliefs one acquired on the basis of testimony were eliminated, it seems impossible to accomplish the sorting. Even beginning the task of putting aside what one knows in the indicated way suggests that one would at best be thrust back to a primitive stage of learning.

These and other points brought out above can help in appraising Hume's influential view of testimony as capable of grounding knowledge only on the basis of a kind of legitimation by other sources. The view can be applied to the overall practice of relying on testimony, to testimony by a particular group or individual, and to an individual attestation. In the first, global case a main question is whether we can construct a blanket justification for considering human testimony reliable. In the second, local case (some instances of which are more wide-ranging than others), some testimonially based beliefs may be presupposed in justifying one or more others. The same holds in the third, focal case, where a single belief is in question. Hume is a good point of departure for reflection on any of these justification problems. My concern here is mainly with the status of individual beliefs, but what follows will bear on wider justification problems as well. For Hume, any "assurance" grounded on testimony "is derived from no other principle than our observation of the veracity of human testimony, and of the usual conformity of facts to the reports of witnesses."[29] Leaving aside whether this claim implies that testimonially based beliefs must be inferential, is it true that for every proposition one justifiedly believes on the basis of testimony, one must have a justification from other sources?

I have already urged a negative answer to the counterpart question for knowledge, but justification may differ in this respect. Since these non-testimonial sources would include justified memory beliefs, they could contribute propositions originally based on testimony that is independent of the testimony needing support. Much of what is stored in our memories we have come to believe through testimony. On the assumption that what was testimonially learned and is memorially preserved can justify believing a proposition someone attests to, it may be that many people reach a point at which, for everything they justifiedly come to believe on the basis of testimony, they do have *some* degree of justification grounded independently of the testimony in question. Many of my beliefs about conditions under which testimony is credible, for instance, are preserved in my memory; thus, even if I have no evidence regarding p, I may, in the circumstances of an attestation, be justified in thinking the attester's saying it is some reason to believe it. Some of these memorially justified beliefs, however, depend for their justification on my previously being justified in believing something on the basis of testimony, as where I accept one person's testimony in checking on

another's. There may be, then, a kind of circularity in appealing to memorially justified beliefs originally justified on the basis of testimony, as support for other testimony.

It might be argued that since memory is a basic source of justification and since testimony itself is a source of non-inferential justification, there need be no vicious circularity. I find this claim plausible, though by no means obviously correct.[30] Consider a news program announcing an earthquake in Indonesia. On the basis of memory, I have a sense of the track record of the network and of the geological situation in Indonesia, a sense of how often errors of that kind are made, etc. Such a justification is far from conclusive, but it apparently need not be inadequate because of vicious circularity.

Might one go further than the modest project just described and fashion a global justification encompassing any of the entire set of beliefs that are testimonially based (or originally believed on the basis of testimony and retained in memory)? Could one even produce this global kind of justification for one's own testimonially based beliefs? Suppose one did not grant that some testimonially grounded beliefs can justify other such beliefs and tried to suspend judgment on all one's testimonially grounded beliefs (assuming such massive suspension of judgment is even possible). Surely this comprehensive justification project would fail.[31] It is doubtful that we can always avoid relying on testimony, at least indirectly, in appraising testimony. One's sense of an attester's track record, for instance, typically depends on what one believes from testimony, as where one news source serves as a check on another.

There seems to be no general procedure by which one can produce an overarching justification for the proposition that the whole set of our testimonially based beliefs (or even a major proportion of it) is justified. But there is no need to attempt that global project or even its local counterpart for a given individual, and the epistemology of testimony I have sketched implies, on this matter, at most that testimonially based beliefs that *are* justified be *individually* justifiable for the believer at least partly in terms of the "basic" (or other favored) sources of justification, such as perception and reflection.[32] With testimonially based knowledge, not even this seems required. The conditions by which knowledge is testimonially transmitted seem not to depend on justification in the same way: although testimony that p by someone who knows that p may be defeated by justified beliefs to the contrary, in the absence of such beliefs the recipient normally acquires knowledge even without having justification regarding the credibility of the attester. If this were not so, it would be at best difficult to explain how children learn language in the way they do.

Conclusion

Testimony is a pervasive and natural source of beliefs. Surely many of the beliefs it grounds are justified or constitute knowledge. They may even constitute basic knowledge or basic belief, both in the (moderate) sense that they are not grounded in premises and in the sense that they play a pivotal role in the life of the believer. We might thus say that testimonially based beliefs are psychologically, epistemically, and existentially basic. But they are epistemically basic only in the sense that they do not inferentially depend on knowledge or justified belief of prior premises. They are epistemically dependent, in a way perceptual beliefs are not, on one's having grounds for knowledge or justification, and they are psychologically dependent on one's having at least some non-propositional ground – such as hearing someone speak – in another, non-testimonial experiential mode. But this source-dependence does not make testimony premise-dependent. Testimony is a generative source of beliefs: it produces new ones other than through our simply building inferentially on those we already have. Testimony is not (except incidentally) a generative source of knowledge; it does not produce new knowledge independently of building on knowledge someone already has. And if I have been right, it is quite different as a source of knowledge, which it transmits, than as a source of justification, which it produces only in cooperation with justification the recipient already has. Once these points are appreciated, we can understand its essential role in concept acquisition and language learning. For if conceptual and linguistic knowledge could not be acquired in this elemental testimonial way, we would never have the cognitive materials necessary for justification. This primeval, elemental role, in turn, helps to explain why so much testimony must be regarded as credible. Its initial success in producing knowledge early in our lives may indeed be a condition for our intelligibly questioning that very success when we have learned to be skeptical.[33]

Notes

1   Among these are C. A. J. Coady, *Testimony* (Oxford: The Clarendon Press, 1992); B. K. Matilal and A. Chakrabarti, eds., *Knowing from Words* (Dordrecht: Kluwer, 1994); Fred Dretske, "A Cognitive Cul-de-Sac," *Mind* 81 (1982); Elizabeth Fricker, "The Epistemology of Testimony," *Proceedings of the Aristotelian Society* Supplementary Vol. 61 (1987) and "Against Gullibility," in Matilal and Chakrabarti; John Hardwig, "Epistemic Dependence," *Journal of Philosophy* LXXXII, 7 (1985); Ernest Sosa, "Testimony and Coherence," in his *Knowledge in Perspective* (Cambridge: Cambridge University Press, 1991); Alvin Plantinga, *Warrant and Proper Function* (Oxford: Oxford University Press, 1993); Mark Owen Webb, "Why I Know about as Much as You," *Journal of Philosophy* XC (1993) (in part a critique of Hardwig); and Jonathan E. Adler, "Testimony, Trust, Knowing," *The Journal of Philosophy* 91 (1994) (in part a critique of Webb).

2   For a wide-ranging, historically informative account of what constitutes testimony and of numerous epistemological problems surrounding it, see Coady, *op. cit.*

3 Perhaps "testimony" may apply where the speaker does not even seem to care about conveying information but is spontaneously describing witnessed past events in a detailed, connected fashion and accurately portrays them. Perhaps saying something may count as testimony so long as it is, in a certain way, appropriate to conveying information. We do not need a detailed analysis here, and the rough characterization suggested in the text begs no important questions.

4 Cf. Fricker's thesis in "Against Gullibility" that "a hearer should always engage in some assessment of the speaker for trustworthiness. To believe what is asserted without doing so is . . . gullibility" (p. 145); and her reference to "knowledge through testimony as inferential knowledge (in the sense that it must be backed by a substantial justification" (p. 156) though "monitoring for signs of untrustworthiness in a speaker is usually conducted at a non-conscious level" – p. 150). The view that testimony-based knowledge is inferential is not new – or confined to Western Philosophy: "Turning to the classical Indian side . . . The two well-entrenched philosophical traditions, the Vaisesika and the Buddhist, allow knowledge from words . . . but include it under inference." See B. K. Matilal, "Understanding, Knowing and Justification," in Matilal and Chakrabarti, op. cit., p. 359.

5 For knowledge and justified belief, I think the belief in question must be based, in a partly causal sense, on the relevant testimony. I defend this point for relevantly similar cases in "The Causal Structure of Indirect Justification," The Journal of Philosophy 80 (1983).

6 Reid spoke eloquently on this: "The wise author of nature hath implanted in the human mind a propensity to rely upon human testimony before we can give a reason for doing so. This, indeed, puts our judgment almost entirely in the hands of those who are about us in the first period of life." See the Essay on the Intellectual Powers of Man, in Thomas Reid's Inquiry and Essays, edited by Ronald Beanblossom and Keith Lehrer (Indianapolis: Hackett, 1983), p. 281.

7 I do not claim to have decisively established these (empirical) points about the structure of testimonially grounded belief, but they are psychologically plausible and are certainly consistent

with the concept of such belief. Supporting considerations are provided by Webb, op. cit.

8 Granted, I must have (and so must memorially retain) a concept of a painting; but this merely conceptual memorial state is not a potential source of belief (which is not to say it can play no causal role in belief-formation).

9 Three points may help here. First, telepathic or other strange receptions of testimony may, at least for our purposes, be construed as perceptual. Second, granting that one cannot form perceptual beliefs without having any additional beliefs needed to possess the concepts required to understand the perceptually believed proposition, this does not imply the kind of dependence on another belief source exhibited by that of testimony upon perception. Third, supposing perception cannot occur without some manifestations in consciousness (which is itself a source of beliefs) here consciousness is an element in perception in a way perception by an audience is plainly not an element in testimony. Testimony need not be received.

10 Similarly, a basic belief, such as one derived from testimony, can be credible apart from positive (e.g. inferential) dependence without being completely independent of other beliefs, say as potential defeaters. The relevant (and often neglected) distinction between positive and negative epistemic dependence is developed in my "Foundationalism, Epistemic Dependence, and Defeasibility," Synthese 55 (1983). That paper applies the distinction to the quite different view of epistemic dependence given by Hilary Kornblith in "Beyond Foundationalism and the Coherence Theory," The Journal of Philosophy 80 (1977), 597–611.

11 And, to be sure, no less requires it. To any who want to attribute a belief here, I would suggest that the reasons for doing this can be adequately accommodated by holding that there is a disposition to believe it (we could call it an implicit or presuppositional belief if we bear in mind its special character). My "Dispositional Beliefs and Dispositions to Believe," Nous 28, 4 (1994), defends this suggestion.

12 The relevant notion of basic knowledge is not a strong one; it is, e.g., unrestricted as to content and relativized to time, so that what is basic for a person at one time can be grounded in premises at

another, and it allows defeat by counterevidence, so that even basic knowledge can be unseated.

13   You might come to know it from something *about* my testimony: perhaps I give it nervously and you know the nervousness reveals my being shaken by the fit of temper, which I have since half forgotten and attest to conjecturally. This would be a case of belief merely *caused* by testimony but not *based* on it. One requirement for a belief's being based on testimony is the believer's holding the proposition because it was attested to, as opposed, e.g., to *how* it was attested to. Cf. Sosa, *op. cit.*, pp. 216–17. This point can be applied to an intermediate case, in which one knows that a speaker systematically distorts a certain topic, e.g. exaggerating the person's accomplishments. Then, like an accompanist reading in one key and playing in another, one can correct the error. This can yield not only knowledge based on something about testimony but knowledge semantically derived from testimony. Other cases in which testimony in some way produces knowledge not strictly based on it in the standard sense can be imagined from these examples, but I must leave them aside here.

14   The qualifier "testimonially based" is crucial: suppose I attest, in a baritone voice, that I have a baritone voice, but do not know this fact because I falsely believe I have a tenor voice; then you can come to know, *from* my testimony, but not on the basis of it (its content), the proposition to which I attest. The same point holds for justification in place of knowledge. One might also say that you come to know *through* my testimony in a weak sense of "through" not implying that the content of what I attest is crucial. Further, content, but not *my attesting it*, may be crucial: if I present an argument you know I barely understand, you can come to know its conclusion, not because I attest to it or the premises, but on the basis of your realizing, in the light of background knowledge, that they are true and entail it. This would be *knowledge based on the content of testimony* but not testimonially grounded knowledge.

15   I develop and defend this contrast in "Memorial Justification," *Philosophical Topics* 23 (1996).

16   I leave open whether knowledge transmitted by testimony can be as *well-grounded* as that of the attester (though I am inclined to doubt it can be). By contrast, so far as knowledge goes, "a testi-monial chain is no stronger than its weakest link," as Plantinga puts it (*op. cit.*, p. 84). He is speaking of warrant, roughly what makes true belief knowledge; and if the point holds there too, then justification differs from warrant on this score as it does from knowledge.

17   If this is so, it may show something else: on the assumption that you cannot know a proposition on the basis of premises you do not also know, this case would show that your testimonially based knowledge is not inferential, since the would-be credibility premise is not known.

18   For instance, of the kinds we find in Fred Dretske's *Knowledge and the Flow of Information* (Cambridge: MIT, 1981); Alvin I. Goldman's *Epistemology and Cognition* (Cambridge: Harvard University Press, 1986); and William P. Alston's *Epistemic Justification* (Ithaca: Cornell University Press, 1989), e.g. ch. 7.

19   The normality qualification is needed in part because of problems not peculiar to testimony, concerning what constitutes knowledge. For an indication of how difficult these can be in relation to testimony and other potential sources of knowledge, see Fred Dretske, "A Cognitive Cul-de-Sac," *Mind* 91 (1982), 109–11, and Coady's discussion of this paper, *op. cit.*, pp. 224–30. It should also be noted that what I call the *basis* of a belief does not include all the conditions necessary for it; but explicating this distinction is a major task that I cannot attempt here.

20   These principles are formulated cautiously: they allow, e.g. that abnormal circumstances may produce exceptions; that the testimonially based belief be inferential; that the resulting justification not be strong but only "adequate" for reasonable belief; that the subject have justification for or knowledge of *p* from some *other* source as well; that the recipient's justification regarding the attester's credibility be weak (though not defeated); and that the concept of justification be chiefly internal or chiefly external. The epistemic principle can be broadened by specifying that the recipient has no *overall* reason for doubt, but I leave that qualification open.

21   The map case is from Plantinga, *op. cit.*, p. 87. This differs from the case in Hardwig, *op. cit.*, in that whereas what any of the cartographers knows (largely) testimonially is equivalent to a *conjunction* of items each known non-testimonially by one or

more others, the cooperative scientific case is more complicated. Some coauthors may lack non-testimonial knowledge not only of a major conclusion but of both grounds for it and principles of reasoning by which they can be seen to support it. The special principles applying to these and other cases of mixed grounds are epistemologically important, but cannot be pursued here.

22 Here I differ from Fricker, who holds that the recipient must perceptually believe "that the speaker has made an assertion with a particular content . . . capable of being knowledge." See "The Epistemology of Testimony," cited in note 1, p. 70.

23 I grant that perceptual justification depends in a negative way on actual or possible justification from other sources (including other perceptual ones), since it may be defeated through their conflicting deliverances; but here the dependence is positive.

24 The epistemology of testimony suggested here may be more stringent than Reid's. For an interpretation and defense of the apparently Reidian view that testimonially grounded beliefs need not depend even for their justification on other sources of justification, see Webb, op. cit.

25 Strictly, they need only look red, as where white objects are flooded by red light. Arguably, one could even teach "red" by producing only hallucinations of the color.

26 The point can be connected with arguments such as some Donald Davidson gives to show that most of our beliefs must be true, but it does not imply that stronger conclusion. For discussion of this and other Davidsonian hypotheses, see Coady, op. cit., ch. 9. Cf. Fricker: "It is plausible that 'Make no unforced attributions of insincerity', and the parallel principle for false beliefs, are among the NIs [norms of interpretation]. But their being so does not ensure that the best interpreting description of an individual will show her as being mainly sincere, or as having mainly true beliefs . . . it is indeed a contingent empirical fact, not guaranteed by any concept-constituting norms . . . that, in some given linguistic community, nearly all apparently sincere utterances are so; and that the

speakers in the community nearly always have true beliefs . . . [though] there is an essentially vague lower bound on the possible incidence of insincerity" and of false belief ("Against Gullibility," pp. 152–3).

27 It is difficult to see how one could, through testimony, produce conceptual learning without producing some belief. Could a child become acquainted with what redness is in connection with being told the sofa is red, yet not acquire any belief, e.g. believing (de re) the sofa to be red?

28 One reason this point is restricted to normal human beings is that it seems possible for a human being to be created artificially, as a full-blown adult, in which case much knowledge of abstract propositions and perhaps of other sorts, such as knowledge of the perceptible external environment, can occur before any testimony is received.

29 An Enquiry Concerning Human Understanding, L. A. Selby-Bigge, ed. (Oxford: Oxford University Press, 1902), sect. 88.

30 For helpful discussion of how testimonially beliefs may be justified and their similarity on this score to memorial beliefs, see Sosa, op. cit., esp. pp. 218–22.

31 We would certainly not be able to appeal to any significant segment of scientific knowledge, for there we are heavily dependent on testimony, written and oral. A plausible case that this dependence is even greater than it seems is made by Hardwig, op. cit.

32 For supporting considerations favoring the possibility of the local justification and opposing that of a global one, see the papers cited by Fricker in note 1 and her "Telling and Trusting: Reductionism and Anti-Reductionism in the Epistemology of Testimony: C. A. J. Coady's Testimony: A Philosophical Study," Mind 104 (1995).

33 For helpful discussions of earlier versions I thank William Alston, Elizabeth Fricker, Hugh McCann, Lex Newman, Frederick Schauer, Walter Sinnott-Armstrong, Ernest Sosa, Mark Webb, and a lively audience at Syracuse University. I also benefited from a detailed report by an anonymous reader for APQ.

Chapter 32

Roderick Chisholm

THE *A PRIORI*

There are also two kinds of truths: those of reasoning and those of fact. The truths of reasoning are necessary, and their opposite is impossible. Those of fact, however, are contingent, and their opposite is possible. When a truth is necessary, we can find the reason by analysis, resolving the truth into simpler ideas and simpler truths until we reach those that are primary.

(Leibniz, *Monadology* 33)

There are propositions that are necessarily true and such that, once one understands them, one *sees* that they are true. Such propositions have traditionally been called *a priori*. Leibniz remarks, "You will find a hundred places in which the scholastic philosophers have said that these propositions are evident, from their terms, as soon as they are understood."[1]

If we say of an *a priori* proposition, that, "once you understand it then you see that it is true," then we must take the term "understand" in a somewhat rigid sense. You could not be said to "understand" a proposition, in the sense intended, unless you can grasp *what* it is for that proposition to be true. The properties or attributes that the proposition implies—those that would be instantiated if the proposition were true—must be properties or attributes that you can conceive or grasp. To "understand" a proposition, in the sense intended, it is not enough merely to be able to say what *sentence* in your language happens to express that proposition. The proposition must be one that you have contemplated and reflected upon.

One cannot *accept* a proposition, in the sense in which we have been using the word "accept," unless one also *understands* that proposition. We might say, therefore, that an *a priori* proposition is one such that, if you accept it, then it becomes certain for you. (For, if you accept it, then you understand it, and, as soon as you understand it, it becomes certain for you.) This account of the *a priori*, however, would be at once too broad and too narrow. It would be too broad in that it also applies to what is self-presenting, and what is self-presenting is not necessarily true. It would be too narrow in that it does not hold of all *a priori* propositions. We know some *a priori* propositions on the basis of others, and these propositions are not themselves such that, once they are understood, then they are certain.

Let us begin by trying to characterize more precisely those *a priori* propositions that are not known on the basis of any other *a priori* propositions.

Leibniz said that these propositions are "the first illuminations." He wrote, "The immediate awareness of our existence and of our thoughts furnishes us with the first *a posteriori* truths, or truths of fact, i.e., *the first experiences*, while identical propositions embody the first *a priori* truths, or truths of reason, i.e., *the first illuminations*. Neither admits of proof, and each may be called *immediate*."[2]

The traditional term for those *a priori* propositions which are "incapable of proof" is *axiom*. Thus Frege wrote, "Since the time of antiquity an axiom has been taken to be a thought whose truth is known without being susceptible by a logical chain of reasoning."[3] In *one* sense, of course, every true proposition *h* is capable of proof, for there will always be other true propositions from which we can derive *h* by means of some principle of logic. What did Leibniz and Frege mean, then, when they said that an axiom is "incapable of proof"?

The answer is suggested by Aristotle. An axiom, or "basic truth," he said, is a proposition "which has no other proposition prior to it"; there is no proposition which is "better known" than it is.[4] And what does "better known" mean? Perhaps this: of two propositions both of which are known by a subject S, one is better known than the other provided only that S is more justified in accepting the one than in accepting the other. Hence, if an axiomatic proposition is one such that no other proposition is better known than it is, then it is one that is certain. (It will be recalled that we characterized *certainty* by saying this: a proposition *h* is *certain* for a person S, provided that *h* is evident for S and provided that, for every proposition *i*, believing *h* is at least as justified for S as believing *i*.) Hence Aristotle said that an axiom is a "primary premise." Its ground does not lie in the fact that it is seen to follow from *other* propositions. Therefore we cannot prove such a proposition by making use of any premises that are "better known" than it is. (By "a proof," then, Aristotle, Leibniz, and Frege meant more than "a valid derivation from premises that are true.")

Let us now try to say what it is for a proposition to be an *axiom*:

D1   *h* is an axiom = Df   *h* is necessarily such (i) it is true and (ii) for every S, if S accepts *h*, then *h* is certain for S

The following propositions among countless others may be said to be *axioms* in our present sense of the term:

> If some men are Greeks, then some Greeks are men.
> If Jones is ill and Smith is away, then Jones is ill.
> The sum of 5 and 3 is 8.
> The product of 4 and 2 is 8.
> All squares are rectangles.

These propositions are axiomatic in the following sense for those people who *do* consider them:

D2   *h* is *axiomatic* for S = Df   (i) *h* is an axiom and (ii) S accepts *h*.

We have assumed that any conjunction of axioms is itself an axiom. But it does not follow from this assumption that any conjunction of propositions which are axiomatic for a subject S is itself axiomatic for S. If two propositions are axiomatic for S and if S does not accept their conjunction, then the conjunction is not axiomatic for S. (Failure to accept their conjunction need not be a sign that S is unreasonable. It may be a sign merely that the conjunction is too complex an object for S to grasp.)

Our knowledge of what is axiomatic is a subspecies of our *a priori* knowledge, that is to say, some of the things we know *a priori* are *not* axiomatic in the present sense. They are *a priori* but they are not what Aristotle called "primary premises."

What would be an example of a proposition that is *a priori* for S but not axiomatic for S? Consider the last two axioms on our list above, i.e.

> The sum of 5 and 3 is 8.
> The product of 4 and 2 is 8.

Let us suppose that their conjunction is also an axiom and that S accepts this conjunction; therefore the conjunction is axiomatic for S. Let us suppose further that the following proposition is axiomatic for S:

> If the sum of 5 and 3 is 8 and the product of 4 and 2 is 8, then the sum of 5 and 3 is the product of 4 and 2.

We will say that, if, in such a case, S accepts the proposition that the sum of 5 and 3 is the product of 4 and 2, then that proposition is *a priori* for S. Yet the proposition may not be one which is such that it is certain for anyone who accepts it. It may be that one can consider *that* proposition without thereby seeing that it is true.

There are various ways in which we might now attempt to characterize this broader concept of the *a priori*. We might say, for example, "You know a proposition *a priori* provided you accept it and provided it is implied by propositions that are axiomatic for you." But this would imply that *any* necessary proposition that you happen to accept is one that you know *a priori* to be true. (Any necessary proposition h is implied by any axiomatic proposition e. Indeed, any necessary proposition h is implied by *any*-proposition e— whether or not e is axiomatic and whether or not e is true or false. For if h is necessary, then it is necessarily true that, for any proposition e, either e is false or h is true. And to say, "e implies h," is to say it is necessarily true that either e is false or h is true.) *Some* of the necessary propositions that we accept may *not* be propositions that we know *a priori*. They may be such that, if we know them, we know them *a posteriori*—on the basis of authority. Or they may be such that we cannot be said to know them at all.

To capture the broader concept of the *a priori*, we might say that a proposition is known *a priori* provided it is axiomatic that the proposition follows from something that is axiomatic. Let us put the matter this way:

D3　h is known *a priori* by S = Df　There is an e such that (i) e is axiomatic for S, (ii) the proposition, e implies h, is axiomatic for S, and (iii) S accepts h

We may add that a person knows a proposition *a posteriori* if he knows the proposition but does not know it *a priori*.

We may assume that what is thus known *a priori* is evident. But the *a priori*, unlike the axiomatic, need not be certain. This accords with St. Thomas's observation that "those who have knowledge of the principles [i.e. the axioms] have a more certain knowledge than the knowledge which is through demonstration."[5]

Is this account too restrictive? What if S derives a proposition from a set of axioms, not by means of one or two simple steps, but as a result of a complex proof, involving a series of interrelated steps? If the proof is formally valid, then shouldn't we say that S knows the proposition *a priori*?

I think that the answer is no. Complex proofs or demonstrations, as John Locke pointed out, have a certain limitation. They take time. The result is that the "evident lustre" of the early steps may be lost by the time we reach the conclusion: "In long deductions, and the use of many proofs, the memory does not always so readily retain." Therefore, he said, demonstrative knowledge "is more imperfect than intuitive knowledge."[6]

Descartes also noted that memory is essential to demonstrative knowledge. He remarks in *Rules for the Direction of the Mind* that, if we can *remember* having deduced a certain conclusion step by step from a set of premises that are "known by intuition," then, even though we may not now recall each of the particular steps, we are justified in saying that the conclusion is "known by deduction."[7] But if, in the course of a demonstration, we must rely upon memory at various stages, thus using as premises contingent propositions about what we happen to remember, then, although we might be said to have "demonstrative knowledge" of our conclusion, in a somewhat broad sense of the expression "demonstrative knowledge," we cannot be said to have an *a priori* demonstration of the conclusion.

Of course, we may make mistakes in attempting to carry out a proof just as we may make mistakes in doing simple arithmetic. And one might well ask, How can this be, if the propositions we are concerned with are known *a priori*? Sometimes, as the quotation from Locke suggests, there has been a slip of memory. Perhaps we are mistaken about just *what* the propositions are that we proved at an earlier step—just as, in doing arithmetic, we may mistakenly think we have carried the 2 or we may pass over some figure having thought that we included it or we may inadvertently include something twice. And there are also occasions when we may just seem to get the *a priori* proposition wrong. In my haste I say to myself, "9 and 6 are 13," and then the result will come out wrong. But when I do this, I am not really considering the proposition that 9 and 6 are 13. I may just be considering the formula, "9 and 6 are 13," which sounds right at the time and not considering at all the proposition that that formula is used to express.

We have said what it is for a proposition to be known *a priori* by a given subject. But we should note, finally, that propositions are sometimes said to be *a priori* even though they may not be known by anyone at all. Thus Kant held that "mathematical propositions, strictly so called, are always judgments *a priori*."[8] In saying this, he did not mean to be saying merely that mathematical propositions are necessarily true; he was saying something about their epistemic status and something about the way in which they could be known. Yet he could not have been saying that all mathematical propositions are known or even believed, by someone or other, to be true for there are propositions of mathematics that no one knows to be true and there are propositions of mathematics that no one has ever even considered. What would it be, then, to say that a proposition might be *a priori* even though it has not been considered by anyone? I think the

answer can only be that the proposition is one that *could* be known *a priori*. In other words:

D4   h is *a priori* = Df   It is possible that there is someone for whom h is known *a priori*

This definition allows us to say that a proposition may be "objectively *a priori*"—"objectively" in that it is *a priori* whether or not anyone knows it *a priori*.

Our definitions are in the spirit of several familiar dicta concerning the *a priori*. Thus, we may say, as Kant did, that necessity is a mark of the *a priori*—provided we mean by this that, if a proposition is *a priori*, then it is necessary.[9] For our definitions assure us that whatever is *a priori* is necessarily true.

The definitions also enable us to say, as St. Thomas did, that these propositions are "manifest through themselves."[10] For an axiomatic proposition is one such that, once it is reflected upon or considered, then it is certain. What a given person knows *a priori* may not *itself* be such that, once it is considered, it is certain. But our definition enables us to say that, if a proposition is one that is *a priori* for you, then you can see that it follows from a proposition that is axiomatic.

Kant said that our *a priori* knowledge, like all other knowledge, "begins with experience" but that, unlike our *a posteriori* knowledge, it does not "arise out of experience."[11] *A priori* knowledge may be said to "begin with experience" in the following sense: there is no *a priori* knowledge until some proposition is in fact contemplated and understood. Moreover the acceptance of a proposition that is axiomatic is sufficient to make that proposition an axiom for whoever accepts it. But *a priori* knowledge does not "arise out of experience." For, if a proposition is axiomatic or *a priori* for us, then we have all the evidence we need to see that it is true. Understanding is enough; it is not necessary to make any further inquiry.

What Leibniz called "first truths *a posteriori*"

coincide with what we have called "the self-presenting." And his "first truths *a priori*" coincide with what we have called "the axiomatic."[12]

Analyzing the predicate out of the subject

The terms "analytic" and "synthetic" were introduced by Kant in order to contrast two types of *a priori* proposition. But Kant used the word "judgment" where we have been using "proposition."

An analytic judgment, according to Kant, is a judgment in which "the predicate adds nothing to the concept of the subject." If I judge that all squares are rectangles, then, in Kant's terminology, the concept of the subject of my judgment is the property of being square, and the concept of the predicate is the property of being rectangular. Kant uses the term "analytic," since, he says, the concept of the predicate helps to "break up the concept of the subject into those constituent concepts that have all along been thought in it."[13] Being square is the conjunctive property of being equilateral and rectangular; therefore the predicate of the judgment expressed by, "All squares are rectangular," may be said to "analyze out" what is contained in the subject. An analytic judgment, then, may be expressed in the form of an explicit redundancy, e.g. "Everything is such that if it is both equilateral and rectangular then it is rectangular." To deny such an explicit redundancy would be to affirm a *contradictio in adjecto*, for it would be to judge that there are things which both have and do not have a certain property—in the present instance, that there is something that both is and is not rectangular. Hence, Kant said that "the common principle of all analytic judgments is the law of contradiction."[14]

What did Kant mean when he said that, in an analytic judgment, the predicate may be "analyzed out" of the subject? Consider the sentence:

(1) All squares are rectangles.

What this sentence expresses may also be put as:

(2) Everything that is an equilateral thing and a rectangle is a rectangle.

Sentence (2) expresses a paradigm case of a proposition in which the predicate-concept (expressed by "a rectangle") may be said to be analyzed out of the subject-concept (expressed by "an equilateral thing and a rectangle"). The subject-concept is broken up into two constituent concepts, one of which is the same as the predicate concept.

The following sentence, which is logically equivalent to (2), does not express a proposition in which the predicate-concept may be said to be "analyzed out" of the subject concept:

(3) Everything that is a square and a rectangle is a rectangle.

In this case, the subject-concept (expressed by "a square and a rectangle") is not broken up into two "constituent concepts." The concept expressed by "square" includes that expressed by "rectangle." But in the earlier proposition (2), the concept expressed by "equilateral thing" does not include that expressed by "rectangle."

Let us now try to say precisely what Kant meant by saying that the predicate-concept of an analytic judgment may be "analyzed out" of the subject-concept.

Definition of analytic proposition

Kant's term "judgment" is ambiguous, for it may be taken to refer either (a) to the *act* of judging or (b) to that proposition which may be said to be the *object* of judging. Let us take the term in the second sense.

What, then, is an analytic proposition—in that sense of "analytic" that was singled out by Kant? To answer the question, let us recall our concept of *entailment*:

D5 The property of being F entails the property of being G = Df Believing something to be F includes believing something to be G

Property entailment may thus be distinguished from property implication:

D6 The property of being F implies the property of being G = Df The property of being F is necessarily such that if something exemplifies it then something exemplifies the property of being G

We have said that a property P *includes* a property Q provided only that P is necessarily such that whatever has it also has Q. We may now introduce an abbreviation:

D7 P is conceptually equivalent to Q = Df Whoever conceives P conceives Q, and conversely

And now we may say what an analytic proposition is:

D8 The proposition that all Fs are Gs is analytic = Df The property of being F is conceptually equivalent to a conjunction of two properties, P and Q, such that: (i) P does not imply Q, (ii) Q does not imply P, and (iii) the property of being G is conceptually equivalent to Q

The definiens may be said to tell us the sense in which, as Kant put it, the predicate of an analytic proposition may be "analyzed out" of the subject.

The following gives us the sense in which Kant understood "*synthetic proposition*":

D9 The proposition that all Fs are Gs is synthetic = Df The proposition that all Fs are Gs is not analytic

The synthetic *a priori*

Kant raised the question: Is there a synthetic *a priori*? In other words, are there synthetic propositions that can be known *a priori* to be true?

Unfortunately many contemporary philosophers who have discussed this question have taken "synthetic *a priori*" much more broadly than Kant took it and therefore much more broadly than the sense we have given above. They have taken "analytic proposition" to mean the same as "proposition that is not synthetic." In their use, such propositions as, "Either it is raining or it is not raining," and, "If all men are mortal and if Socrates is a man, then Socrates is mortal," are called "analytic." But in considering Kant's question, we will understand "analytic proposition" and "synthetic proposition" in the ways in which he understood these expressions.

The philosophical importance of the question is this: if a proposition can be shown to be analytic, to be such that the predicate can be analyzed out of the subject, then it is a kind of redundancy; it is relatively trivial and one may feel that it does not have any significant content. But this is not so of synthetic propositions. Hence, if there are synthetic propositions that can be known *a priori* to be true, then the kind of cognition that can be attributed to reason alone may be considerably more significant.

Let us consider, then, certain possible types of example of "the synthetic *a priori*," so conceived.

(1) One important candidate for the synthetic *a priori* is the knowledge that might be expressed either by saying, "Being square includes having a shape," or by saying, "Necessarily, everything that is square is a thing that has a shape." The sentence "Everything that is square is a thing that has a shape" recalls our paradigmatic "Everything that is square is a rectangle." In the case of the latter sentence, we were able to "analyze the predicate out of the subject": we replaced the subject term "square" with a conjunctive term, "equilateral thing and a rectangle," and were thus able to express our proposition in the form:

Everything that is an S and a P is a P.

where the predicate may be said to be "analyzed out of" the subject.

The problem is to fill the blank in:

Everything that is a _____ and a thing that has a shape is a thing that has a shape

in the appropriate way. But given our account of what it is to "analyze the predicate out of the subject," can we do this? I believe it is accurate to say that no one has ever *shown* how we can do this.

We might try filling the blank by, "either a square or a thing that does not have a shape," thus obtaining:

Everything that is (a) either a square or a thing that does not have a shape and (b) a thing that has a shape is a thing that has a shape.

But the property of being square is not conceptually equivalent to the property expressed by "either a square or a thing that does not have a shape." One could believe something to have the former property without believing it to have the latter. Therefore the proposed way of filling in the blank does not yield a proposition in which the predicate term may be said to be "analyzed out" of the subject.

Other possible ways of filling the blank seem to have the same result.

The proposition "Everything that is square has a shape" expresses what can be known *a priori* to be true. If we cannot find a way of showing that it is analytic (and, so far at least, we have not succeeded), then, it would seem, there is some presumption in favor of saying that it is synthetic *a priori*.

There are indefinitely many other sentences presenting essentially the same difficulties as "Everything that is square has a shape."

Examples are "Everything red is colored"; "Everyone who hears something in C-sharp minor hears a sound." The sentences express what is known *a priori*, but no one has been able to show that they are analytic.[15]

(2) What Leibniz called the "disparates" furnish us with a second candidate for the synthetic *a priori*. These are closely related to the example just considered, but they involve problems that are essentially different. An example of a sentence concerned with disparates would be our earlier "Being red excludes being blue," or, alternatively put, "Nothing that is red is blue."[16] Philosophers have devoted considerable ingenuity to trying to show that "Nothing that is red is blue" can be expressed as a sentence that is analytic, but so far as I have been able to determine, all of these attempts have been unsuccessful. Again, it is recommended that the reader try to reexpress "Nothing that is red is blue" in such a way that the predicate may be "analyzed out" of the subject in the sense we have described above.

(3) It has also been held, not without plausibility, that certain ethical sentences express what is synthetic *a priori*. Thus, Leibniz, writing on what he called the "supersensible element" in knowledge, said: "But to return to *necessary truths*, it is generally true that we know them only by this natural light, and not at all by the experience of the senses. For the senses can very well make known, in some sort, what is, but they cannot make known what *ought to be* or what could not be otherwise."[17] Or consider the sentence "All pleasures, as such are intrinsically good, or good in themselves, whenever and wherever they may occur." If this sentence expresses something that is known to be true, then what it expresses must be synthetic *a priori*. To avoid this conclusion, some philosophers deny that sentences about what is intrinsically good, or good in itself, *can* be known to be true.[18] An examination of this view would involve us, once again, in the problem of the criterion.

(4) Kant held that the propositions of arith-

metic are synthetic and *a priori*. In evaluating his view, we must, of course, understand "analytic" in the sense in which he intended it.

Does "2 + 1 = 3" express what Kant called an analytic proposition? If it does, the proposition is expressible in a way that satisfies D7, our definition of what it is for a proposition to be such that its predicate may be "analyzed out of" its subject.

Perhaps the most natural way of putting "2 + 1 = 3" in the form of "All S are P" (or of "For every *x*, if *x* is S, then *x* is P") is this:

> For every *x*, if *x* is a set of 2 sets which are such that (a) they have no members in common, (b) one of them has exactly 2 members, and (c) the other has exactly 1, then *x* has exactly 3 members

This statement is of the proper form, but it does not satisfy D8, our definition of the Kantian sense of "analytic proposition." The predicate-concept—expressed by "having exactly 3 members"—is not conceptually equivalent to any of the conjuncts of the subject-concept. Therefore this way of reading the *a priori* truth expressed by "2 + 1 = 3" is not analytic in Kant's sense of "analytic." Other ways of putting the proposition into the form of "All S are P" are equally unsatisfactory. There is reason to believe, therefore, that Kant is right in saying that such truths are synthetic *a priori*.

"Linguisticism"

It has been suggested that the sentences giving rise to the problem of the synthetic *a priori* are really "postulates about the meanings of words" and, therefore, that they do not express what is synthetic *a priori*. But if the suggestion is intended literally, then it would seem to betray the confusion between use and mention that we encountered earlier. A *postulate* about the meaning of the word "red," for example, or a sentence expressing such a postulate, would presumably

mention the word "red." It might read, "The word 'red' may be taken to refer to a certain color," or perhaps, "Let the word 'red' be taken to refer to a certain color." But, "Everything that is red is colored," although it uses the words "red" and "colored," does not mention them at all. It is not the case, therefore, that "Red is a color" refers only to words and the ways in which they are used.

A popular conception of the truths of reason is the view according to which they are essentially "linguistic." Many have said, for example, that the sentences formulating the truths of logic are "true in virtue of the rules of language" and, hence, that they are "true in virtue of the way in which we use words."[19] What could this possibly mean?

The two English *sentences* "Being round includes being square" and "Being rational and animal includes being animal" plausibly could be said to "owe their truth," in part, to the way in which we use words. If we used "being square" to refer to the property of being heavy and not to that of being square, then the first sentence (provided the other words in it had their present use) would be false instead of true. And if we used the word "and" to express the relation of disjunction instead of conjunction, then the second sentence (again, provided that the other words in it had their present use) would also be false instead of true. But as W. V. Quine has reminded us, "even so factual a sentence as 'Brutus killed Caesar' owes its truth not only to the killing but equally to our using the component words as we do."[20] Had "killed," for example, been given the use that "was survived by" happens to have, then, other things being the same, "Brutus killed Caesar" would be false instead of true.

It might be suggested, therefore, that the truths of logic and other truths of reason stand in this peculiar relationship to language: they are true "*solely* in virtue of the rules of our language" or *solely* in virtue of the ways in which we use words." But if we take the phrase "solely in virtue of" in the way in which it would naturally be taken, then the suggestion is obviously false.

To say of a sentence that it is true *solely* in virtue of the ways in which we use words or that it is true *solely* in virtue of the rules of our language, would be to say that the only condition that needs to obtain in order for the sentence to be true is that we use words in certain ways or that there be certain rules pertaining to the way in which words are to be used. But let us consider what conditions must obtain if the English sentence "Being round excludes being square" is to be true. One such condition is indicated by the following sentence, which we may call "T":

> The English sentence "Being square excludes being round" is true, if and only if, being square excludes being round.

Clearly, the final part of T, the part following the second "if," formulates a necessary condition for the truth of the English sentence "Being round excludes being square," but it refers to a relationship among properties and not to rules of language or ways in which we use words. Hence we cannot say that the *only* conditions that need to obtain in order for "Being round excludes being square" to be true is that we use words in certain ways or that there be certain rules pertaining to the ways in which words are to be used; and therefore, the sentence cannot be said to be true solely in virtue of the ways in which we use words.

There would seem to be no clear sense, therefore, in which the *a priori* truths of reason can be said to be primarily "linguistic."[21]

Notes

1   G. W. Leibniz, *New Essays Concerning Human Understanding*, translated and edited by Peter Remnant and Jonathan Bennett (New York: Cambridge University Press, 1982), Book IV, Ch. 7. Compare Alice Ambrose and Morris Lazerowitz, *Fundamentals of Symbolic Logic* (New York: Holt, Rinehart and Winston, Inc., 1962), p. 17. "A proposition is said to be true *a priori* if its truth can be ascertained by examination of the proposition alone or if it is deducible from propositions whose truth is so ascertained, and by examination of nothing else. Understanding the words used in expressing these propositions is sufficient for determining that they are true."

2   *New Essays Concerning Human Understanding*, Book IV, Ch. 9.

3   Gottlob Frege, *Kleine Schriften* (Hildesheim: Georg Olms Verlagsbuchhandlung, 1967), p. 262.

4   *Posterior Analytics*, Book I, Ch. 2.

5   Thomas Aquinas, *Exposition of the Posterior Analytics of Aristotle*, trans. Pierre Conway (Quebec: M. Doyon, 1952), Book II, Lecture 20, No. 4, (pp. 427–428).

6   *Essay Concerning Human Understanding*, Book IV, Chap. 2, Sec. 7.

7   See *The Philosophical Works of Descartes*, ed. E. S. Haldane and G. R. T. Ross, I (London: Cambridge University Press, 1934), p. 8. Some version of Descartes' principle should be an essential part of any theory of evidence. Compare Norman Malcolm's suggestion: "If a man previously had grounds for being sure that *p*, and now remembers that *p*, but does not remember what his grounds were," then he "*has* the same grounds he previously had." *Knowledge and Certainty* (Englewood Cliffs, NJ: Prentice-Hall, Inc., 1963), p. 230.

8   Immanuel Kant, *Critique of Pure Reason*, trans. Norman Kemp Smith (London: Macmillan and Co., Ltd., 1933), p. 52.

9   Compare *Critique of Pure Reason*, B4 (Kemp Smith edition, p. 44). But we should not assume that if a proposition is necessary and known to be true, then it is *a priori*.

10   *Exposition of the Posterior Analytics of Aristotle*, Book II, Lecture 20, No. 4 (pp. 427–428). Pierre Conway; Part I, Lecture 4, No. 10 (p. 26).

11   *Critique of Pure Reason*, B1 (Kemp Smith edition, p. 41).

12   Compare Franz Brentano, *The True and the Evident* (London: Routledge & Kegan Paul, 1966), p. 130ff.

13   *Critique of Pure Reason*, A7; Norman Kemp Smith edition, p. 48.

14   *Prolegomena to Any Future Metaphysics* (La Salle, IN: The Open Court Publishing Company, 1933), Sec. 2 (p. 15).

15 Compare C. H. Langford, "A Proof that Synthetic A Priori Propositions Exist," *Journal of Philosophy*, Vol. XLVI (1949), pp. 20–24.

16 Compare John Locke, *Essay Concerning Human Understanding*, Book IV, Chap. 1, Sec. 7; Franz Brentano, *Versuch über die Erkenntnis* (Leipzig: Felix Meiner, 1970), pp. 9–10.

17 Quoted from G. M. Duncan, ed., *The Philosophical Works of Leibniz* (New Haven, CT: The Tuttle, Morehouse & Taylor Company, 1908), p. 162.

18 Compare the discussion of this question in Chapters 5 and 6 in William Frankena, *Ethics*, Second Edition, Foundations of Philosophy Series (Englewood Cliffs, NJ: Prentice-Hall, Inc., 1973).

19 See Anthony Quinton, "The *A Priori* and the Analytic," in Robert Sleigh, ed., *Necessary Truth* (Englewood Cliffs, NJ: Prentice-Hall, Inc., 1972), pp. 89–109.

20 W. V. Quine, "Carnap and Logical Truth," *The Philosophy of Rudolf Carnap*, ed. P. A. Schilpp (La Salle, IL: Open Court Publishing Co., 1963), p. 386.

21 For further discussions of this question, see the selections in Paul K. Moser, ed., *A Priori Knowledge* (Oxford: Oxford University Press, 1987).

Chapter 33

William Alston

PERCEPTUAL KNOWLEDGE

I

This essay deals with epistemological issues concerning perception. These can be briefly indicated by the question: "How, if at all, is perception a source of knowledge or justified belief?" To keep a discussion of a very complex subject matter within prescribed bounds, I will mostly focus on the "justified belief" side of the above disjunction, bringing in questions about perceptual *knowledge* only when dealing with a position that is specially concerned with knowledge. There are some other housekeeping moves to be made before we can get under way.

(1) First a couple of points about epistemic justification. (a) Justification comes in degrees. I can be more or less justified in supposing that Yeltsin will resign the presidency, depending on the strength of my reasons for this. The epistemological literature mostly treats "justified" as an absolute term. Presumably this is because some minimal degree is being presupposed. I will follow this practice. (b) For most of our beliefs, including perceptual beliefs, what we typically identify as a justifier provides only *defeasible, prima facie* justification. Thus the way something looks to me *prima facie* justifies the belief that it is an elephant. That is, this belief will be justified, all things considered, provided there are no sufficient overriders of this *prima facie* justification, for example strong reasons that there could not be an elephant in this spot,

or reasons for thinking that my visual apparatus is malfunctioning. I will be thinking of *prima facie* justification in this essay.

(2) What sorts of beliefs are we to think of as candidates for being justified by perception? Perceptual beliefs, of course, i.e. beliefs that are given rise to by perception. But there is an important distinction between two sorts of beliefs that satisfy this condition.

A. Beliefs about what is putatively perceived—*The tree in front of me is a maple.*

B. Beliefs to the effect that one is perceiving something—*I see a maple tree* or *I see that this tree is a maple.*

It is beliefs of the A sort that are at the heart of the epistemology of perception, just because they constitute the most fundamental doxastic perceptual output—most fundamental in two ways. First, they are ontogenetically and phylogenetically most basic. Even the least sophisticated cognitive subjects—lower animals and very young infants who have no language—get information about the environment from perception. But it takes greater cognitive sophistication to form propositions to the effect that one is perceiving so-and-so. Second, it seems that the primary function of perception is to give the subject information about the environment, rather than information about the subject's perceptual activity and accomplishment. Hence this essay will deal with issues concerning how perception serves as a source of justification for beliefs about what is putatively perceived.

(3) Here, as elsewhere in epistemology, there is an important distinction between two enterprises. (a) We can raise the radical question as to whether we have any knowledge (justified belief) in the domain in question. This amounts to deciding how to react to a certain kind of skepticism. (b) Assuming that we do have knowledge (justified beliefs) of the relevant sort, we can try to understand that—determine what the conditions are under which one has knowledge (justified beliefs) in that domain, make such internal distinctions in the domain as seem called for, clarify the basic concepts involved in carrying out these tasks, and so on. In the history of epistemology (a) has bulked large. With perception in particular, many philosophers talk as if the concern with skepticism exhausts the subject. But, again in order to keep this essay within reasonable limits, I will forego grappling with skepticism [. . .] and focus on (b).

(4) Philosophers have been concerned both with the epistemology of perceptual belief and the nature of perception. Under the latter heading we can distinguish two main interrelated problems, (a) what it is to perceive an object (event, situation, state of affairs), and (b) what is the nature and structure of perceptual experience (consciousness). The positions taken on these issues, especially the second, have a crucial bearing on epistemological issues. It seems obvious this perceptual experience plays a major role in determining the epistemic status of beliefs based on it. But what kind of role it plays depends on what it is like. If we think of perceptual experience as purely internal, just a subjective state of the perceiver, its epistemic role *vis-à-vis* beliefs about the environment will be different from what it is if it involves some direct awareness of extramental reality. Again, if, as it is fashionable to think nowadays, perceptual experience is essentially propositionally struc-

tured, then it may be that it already contains perceptual beliefs of the sort we are concerned with here, in which case the experience is in need of epistemic support, instead of or as well as being an ultimate source thereof.

(5) It is obvious that one's general epistemological orientation has an important influence on one's epistemology of perception. This relevance will obtrude itself throughout the essay. But at this point I will set aside one branch of a major divide in epistemology, that over whether any belief can be justified otherwise than by its relation to other beliefs. Most of those who answer this question in the negative espouse some form of coherentism, the view that particular beliefs are justified or not by how they fit into some total system of belief, and how internally coherent that system is. A coherentist will have no use for the idea that perceptual beliefs can be justified by experience, whereas those who take a more "local" view of justification are free to allow this. This difference in general epistemology makes an enormous difference to the epistemology of perception. It seems to me incontestable that coherentism can't be the right way to approach perception. If I look out my window and see snow on the ground, and everything is working normally, then surely I am amply justified in believing there is snow on the ground, even if this does not fit coherently in my total belief system, and even if that system exhibits a very low degree of coherence. Hence I will exclude coherentist approaches from consideration.[1]

II

(6) Another preliminary point that needs more extensive consideration is the difference between the following questions. (1) How, if at all, are perceivers (sometimes) justified in their perceptual beliefs? (2) How, if at all, is it *possible* to justify perceptual beliefs? (1) is addressed to the (typical or frequent) situation of real-life perceivers. It tries to determine what, if anything, in

their actual situations renders their perceptual beliefs justified. (2) is a question about what considerations could be adduced to justify perceptual beliefs, whether or not this is something that perceivers typically, or ever, adduce or are aware of. Thus (2) could be answered by spelling out some elaborate philosophical argument that is so complex as to be available only to a select few. But (1) restricts itself to justificatory factors that are widely distributed, even though most perceivers might not be clearly aware of them or of their bearing. (2) is the enterprise often called "proving the existence of the external world."

One reason this distinction is important is that if we are not aware of it, as philosophers often are not, we will wind up arguing past each other. Thus Price, Broad, and others, object to a "causal theory of perception" that perceivers rarely if ever carry out a causal inference from perceptual experience to external cause when they form perceptual beliefs. But when Locke or Descartes or Russell or Lovejoy, or more recently Moser defend the epistemic credentials of perceptual beliefs by appealing to causal arguments, they are best read as engaging not in (1) but in (2).

As intimated above, even if (2) could be successfully carried out, it would leave (1) without a satisfactory answer, provided that the success depends on argumentation that few if any perceivers can be aware of. Nevertheless, (2) is not totally irrelevant to (1). Suppose we carry out (2) by showing that whenever one has a perceptual experience of a certain sort, a certain kind of fact obtains in the external world. That would show that having an experience of that sort confers a positive epistemic status (justification or knowledge) on a belief in that fact that stems from that experience. At least it would show this on an externalist account of justification or knowledge. We will look at some externalist accounts in section IV.

Partly because of this relevance, and partly for its intrinsic interest, it is worth glancing at some attempts to carry out (2). These are use-fully divided into a priori and empirical arguments. The former try to show that it is logically or conceptually impossible that perceptual beliefs should not often be true. An example is the claim that concepts of perceivable kinds and properties consist of "criteria" (Wittgenstein) or "justification conditions" (Pollock) in terms of sensory experience, so that it is conceptually necessary that when one is having a certain kind of sensory experience one is *prima facie* justified in supposing there is an object, or an object with a property, for which that experience is a justification condition.[2] Here I will concentrate on empirical arguments.

These typically proceed by assuming that it is unproblematic that perceivers have knowledge of the character of their own perceptual experiences. They then look for some way of making cogent inferences from that knowledge to the propositional contents of typical perceptual beliefs (for example, *there is a robin on my lawn*). But a survey of such arguments affords little ground for optimism about the prospect of success.[3] Look first at a very simple example. One might try to construct an enumerative induction from correlations of experience type and external fact. If experience of type *e* is conjoined in many cases with external putatively perceivable fact of type *f*, we can infer that they are generally correlated and hence be justified in inferring from an *e* to an *f*. But, as Hume and many others have noted, this runs into the difficulty that to get knowledge of particular instances of such pairings, we would already have to have perceptual knowledge of the external perceived objects, the very thing that is in question.

A somewhat more elaborate example is an argument to the best explanation. It is contended that there are various features of our experience that are best explained by the usual supposition that this experience has among its causes the physical objects we normally suppose ourselves to be perceiving in these experiences. Such considerations are found in the work of C.D. Broad.[4]

The features in question can be illustrated as follows.[5] (1) It often happens that whenever I look in a certain direction I undergo sensory experiences of pretty much the same sort. This can be explained by the supposition that there are physical things of the sort I believe myself to be perceiving that remain in that location and contribute to the production of similar experiences. And when I receive significantly different experiences from looking in that direction, this is plausibly explained in terms of physical changes in that location. (2) If I move from point a to point b my experiences undergo a characteristic continuous change that, again, is of roughly the same sort over a considerable period, and this is best explained by supposing that the objects I seem to be perceiving along the route remain relatively stable over the period of time in question. And again, when the sequence is different from what it had been, this can be plausibly explained by differences in the physical constituents along the route. Explanatory arguments like this are subject to two difficulties. (a) No one has ever succeeded in making a plausible case for the superiority of this "standard" explanation to its alternatives, like the self-generation of sensory experiences or their direct production by a Cartesian demon or a Berkeleian God. (b) More crucially, the patterns in experience cited as the explananda involve suppositions about the physical environment we could only know about through perception, thus introducing a circularity in the argument. In these cases those suppositions include my repeatedly looking in a certain (physical) direction, and my physically moving from one location to another. If we were to make the explanandum purely phenomenal, we would not be able to find patterns that it is plausible to explain in terms of the putatively perceived external objects, as I argue in The Reliability of Sense Perception.[6]

III

With these preliminaries out of the way I am ready to explore various ways in which philosophers have tried to understand the conditions of justification of perceptual belief. A good starting place is the intuitively plausible idea that when I form the visual belief that a robin is on my front lawn, that belief is justified, if at all, by my current visual experience. The experience, which, as we might say, is as if I am seeing a robin on the lawn, gives rise to the belief and thereby renders it justified. It is plausible to suppose that the experience has this epistemic efficacy because it consists in, or involves, a direct awareness of the robin and its position on the lawn. My visual experience justifies the belief because the latter is simply the conceptual encoding of the realities that are directly presented to my awareness in the visual experience. This is the so-called "naive" direct realism that is one of the perennial answers to our central question of how perceptual beliefs are justified. I shall be contending that it is, in essentials, the correct answer, though to make it adequate we will have to go some distance beyond this crude formulation.

We must distinguish two ways in which perceptual experience might be involved in the justification of perceptual beliefs. (a) The belief might be justified by the experience itself, or by the fact that the belief stems from the experience, as the last paragraph suggested. (b) The belief might be justified by the subject's knowledge (justified belief) that she has an experience of that kind. I have already hinted at reasons for rejecting (b) as an account of real-life justification of perceptual beliefs. For one thing, perceivers typically have no actual knowledge of the character of their experiences. Even if they could always acquire such knowledge by attending to the matter, they rarely so attend. Their attention is almost always fastened on the external (putatively) perceived scene, not the experience by virtue of which they perceive it.

Second, if they had such knowledge it would play that role by functioning as an adequate reason for the perceptual belief. And that in turn would require a successful inference from the fact that the experience is of a certain sort to the perceptual belief, or at least the possibility of such an inference. But, as I suggested above (but by no means proved), it looks as if no such inference is possible. Hence for this reason (b) cannot be successfully carried through.[7]

Before leaving this approach I should mention one consideration that has made (b) seem an attractive or even compelling prospect. Traditional foundationalism in epistemology (q.v.) has supposed that all knowledge (justified belief) must rest on foundations that are absolutely certain. It seems that if there are such foundations of empirical knowledge, they consist of one's knowledge of one's own conscious states. And so, on such a view, we must show that whatever empirical knowledge one has of other matters is derived from one's knowledge of one's own conscious states. But the difficulties that have attended attempts to develop this kind of foundationalism weaken any support it gives to (b).

Turning now to (a), before considering how, if at all, a perceptual belief might be justified by an experience on which it is based, we must consider the idea that even if that is part of the story it is not all of it, at least not always. It seems that other knowledge of the subject sometimes makes a contribution. I am looking for Bernice's house. I've been to her house a number of times and I recognize it by its appearance. If the look of the house is all that I go on, then my belief that this is Bernice's house is based solely on the character of the visual presentation. But is that so? For all I know, there are many other houses that look just like this, given the distance and angle and lighting with respect to which I am viewing it. It is reasonable to think that I am also taking into account my current location—that I am on a certain block of a certain street, or at least in a certain part of a certain town, whether I explicitly think about these matters or not. In that case my belief would be justified partly by the character of the visual presentation and partly by my knowledge of my current location.

Some philosophers think that all cases of perceptual recognition exhibit this mixed character. If so, the doxastic conditions will often have to be more hidden from the subject's awareness than the location beliefs in the above case. One candidate is what we might call "adequacy conditions." It might be thought that whenever I perceptually recognize x as P on the basis of a certain perceptual appearance, a belief that such an appearance is an adequate sign of P is also part of what justifies the belief. But the trouble with this is that it leads to an infinite regress. If for any basis, B_1, of a belief there is a further basis, B_2, which consists of a justified belief that B_1 is an adequate basis, then the same principle will apply to B_2, and so on ad infinitum. At some point we must take it as sufficient that the basis is adequate, without also requiring that the subject justifiably believe this. Another candidate for an omnipresent doxastic basis is the justified belief that one's perceptual apparatus is working normally. But one can recognize the relevance of this consideration without supposing that a justified belief in normality has to figure as part of the justification of the perceptual belief. One can hold, rather, that the experience suffices to justify *in the absence of any sufficient reasons to suspect abnormality*. That is, normality considerations can figure as possible overriders of *prima facie* justification, rather than as part of what confers *prima facie* justification.

If we can generalize from the disposal of these two candidates, we need not worry about the possibility that perceptual beliefs *always* draw their justification, at least in part, from other justified beliefs. Nevertheless, there is a strong case for the thesis that this is not infrequently the case, as my example of house identification indicates. Hence doxastic contributors to justification will figure in any comprehensive epistemology of perceptual belief. But in the space at my disposal here I will concentrate on the experiential contribution, which deserves to be called the heart of the matter, both because that is always involved and because it is distinctive of perceptual justification.

IV

When we begin to think about how to specify the conditions under which an experience provides support for a perceptual belief, two other oppositions in general epistemology become relevant. (In the ensuing discussion I will use "evidence" in a broad sense for anything that has the potentiality of increasing the justification of a belief, whether it is reasons, other things the subject knows or justifiably believes ("evidence" in a narrow sense), or experience.) First, there is the question whether it is sufficient for justification that one simply *has* evidence, or whether it is required that the belief is *based* on that evidence. Though a decision on this point will pervasively affect the shape an account of epistemic justification takes, it is not crucial for the present topic just because it is plausible to restrict perceptual beliefs to those *based on* perceptual experience, apart from questions about their justification. Hence there is little or no chance of a perceptual belief's not being based on experience that constitutes evidence for it.[8]

The second opposition is between internalism and externalism in epistemology [. . .]. These terms are used variously, but I will understand them here as follows. Internalism restricts factors bearing on epistemic status to those to which the subject has some high grade of cognitive access, typically specified as knowable just on reflection. While externalism, though not excluding such factors, does not enforce any such restriction. The most important divergence between these orientations concerns certain truth-conducive conditions which a subject cannot be expected to ascertain just on reflection. Two of these have been prominent in the epistemology of perception—reliability of belief

formation and the truth indicativeness of the experience on which the belief was based. Externalist accounts of the epistemology of perceptual beliefs can feature one or the other of these. I begin with an account of the latter sort by Fred Dretske.[9] This concerns knowledge specifically; Dretske deliberately ignores justification.

First, Dretske's epistemology of perceptual belief is based on a direct realism of object perception. He argues, successfully in my opinion, that at the heart of perception is an awareness of objects that does not involve belief (judgment) in any way. He calls this "non-epistemic seeing" and abbreviates it as "see$_n$".[10] Here are the conditions he lays down for a bit of visual knowledge ("S sees that b is P").

(i) b is P. (the truth condition)

(ii) S sees$_n$ b.

(iii) The conditions under which S sees$_n$ b are such that b would not look, L, the way it now looks to S, unless it was P.

(iv) S, believing the conditions are as described in (iii), takes b to be P.[11]

(Dretske explains that the belief that (iii) which he requires in condition (iv) can be more or less implicit.) What this account amounts to is that when I base a true belief that b is P on the way b looks, that belief counts as knowledge provided the look is an adequate indication of b's being P. And it is an adequate indication provided that b wouldn't look that way if it were not P. My visual belief that the tree is a maple, a belief based on the tree's looking a certain way, counts as knowledge provided that the tree wouldn't have looked that way (in these circumstances) if it weren't a maple.

This account is externalist, not only because of the truth condition (1), but, more distinctively, because the truth of the crucial counterfactual, (iii), is not the sort of thing one can ascertain just on reflection. And, like most externalists, Dretske, by condition (iv), requires that the belief be *based on* the relevant evidence in order that it achieve the positive epistemic status in question.

I find Dretske's view very attractive as an account of perceptual knowledge,[12] though, as I will bring out shortly, it, or rather suitable parts of it, is less promising as an account of justification. I will now say a few words about a *reliabilist* approach. The general idea of a reliabilist approach to knowledge or justification is that a belief gets one or another positive epistemic status by being formed in a way that is generally reliable, one that would yield mostly true beliefs in a suitably large and varied range of cases in conditions of the sort in which we typically find ourselves.[13] The relation of this to Dretske's "adequate indication" account depends on how this "way of being formed" is thought of. If we spell it out in terms of the way the belief is based on features of experience (way of looking), then it turns out to be another formulation of the same basic idea. For if the way of looking would not occur in those circumstances without the belief's being true, as Dretske requires, then forming the belief on the basis of that way of looking, in those circumstances, would be a reliable way of forming it. But if, with Goldman and many other reliabilists, we do not wish to restrict perceptual belief formation to any such formula, then the reliabilist approach would apply more widely. In any event, reliabilism is externalist for the same reason as Dretske's account: the general reliability of the mode of belief formation exemplified in this case is not something that one could be expected to ascertain just on reflection.

It is plausible to suppose that if we can handle Dretske's counterfactuals successfully, and if we can assign particular processes of belief formation to general "ways of forming beliefs" that can be assessed for reliability in epistemically useful ways, then either externalist approach identifies an important epistemically positive feature of beliefs, one that, together with truth, bids fair to be a sufficient condition of knowledge. The main dissatisfaction with such accounts is that they give us no hint as to how we tell whether their conditions are satisfied in a particular case. If we are interested not just in understanding the *concept* of perceptual knowledge but in finding out where we have it and where we do not, we are likely to feel let down. That is not to say that we have no capacity at all to determine when a Dretske-type counterfactual is true or when a way of forming a perceptual belief is of a reliable type. But it would obviously be desirable to have more of a general method for achieving this, and externalist epistemologists are not forthcoming on this point. They bend over backwards to make the (correct) point that knowing (being justified in believing) that b is P, on the basis of perception, does not require being able to know or show that one is. But being able to tell whether one is or not is obviously a cognitive desideratum. Moreover, if, as I argue in *The Reliability of Sense Perception*, we cannot construct a noncircular successful argument that what we ordinarily take as experiential bases of perceptual beliefs yield mostly true beliefs, this is a serious problem for externalists, for on their view one has perceptual knowledge only if the perceptual belief in question is based on experience in such a way as to generally yield true beliefs. It is worth noting that they seem mostly untroubled by this. Since they typically adopt the nonskeptical approach to epistemology in terms of which this essay is written, they feel warranted in assuming that our usual ways of forming perceptual (and other) beliefs are truth-conducive until we have reasons in particular cases to abandon that assumption.

V

There is a reason for holding that even if externalist accounts like these are adequate accounts of perceptual knowledge (not thought of in terms of justification), they are deficient as accounts of the justification of perceptual belief.[14] That is because there is an internalist constraint it is plausible to apply to justification but not to knowledge, viz., that in order for something to justify a belief the subject must have the capacity for some insight into its doing so. This is weaker than requiring a capacity to ascertain justificatory efficacy just by reflection. But it is sufficiently strong to rule out typical externalist accounts. It is clear that a case of perceptual belief formation can satisfy Dretske's conditions without the subject having any insight whatsoever into this. This is presumably the case with lower animals and small children, and may well be the case with many unsophisticated normal adult humans. I will now explore the ways in which the justification of perceptual beliefs might be construed from this kind of internalist perspective.

But first I should mention a recently prominent view that there is something fundamentally wrong-headed about the idea of a belief being justified by an experience. Davidson, after opining that "nothing can count as a reason for holding a belief except another belief," acknowledges that the only alternatives to this worth taking seriously attempt to ground beliefs on experience. But this won't do, he says. "The relation between a sensation and a belief cannot be logical, since sensations are not beliefs or other propositional attitudes. What then is the relation? . . . the relation is causal. Sensations cause some beliefs and in this sense are the basis or ground of those beliefs. But a causal explanation of a belief does not show that or why the belief is justified."[15] To be sure, Davidson offers this argument as a support for coherentism, and I have already excluded coherentism from consideration. Nevertheless, I want to say why I think that this argument doesn't do the job. In a word, it is much too heavy-handed. It question-beggingly assumes that only *logical* relations can carry justificatory force. Moreover it undiscriminatingly takes causation and justification to be mutually exclusive. But before swallowing this, we should reflect that there are causes and causes. Whether the kind of cause a visual experience is can

confer justification on the kind of effect a perceptual belief is depends on the details of what these causes and effects are like and further facts about their relationship. (Of *course*, the abstract fact that x causes y has no implications for justificatory efficacy.) That is, it depends on the outcome of the kind of exploration on which I am about to embark.

When we try to give an internalist account of the way perceptual experience confers justification on perceptual beliefs, we are forced to attend to the differences between ways of construing that experience. These differences do not make an important difference for externalist accounts, since those accounts do not trade on connections between the intrinsic character of experiences and the content of beliefs. So long as the experience wouldn't be formed in those circumstances without the belief's being true, or so long as the belief results from the experience in a way that is generally reliable, it doesn't matter how the experience is constituted. No doubt, we would have to attend to that if we tried to *explain* the truth of the counterfactual or to explain the reliability; but no such explanation has to enter into the externalist account of what it is to know (justifiably believe) something perceptually. But since the internalist enterprise requires us to find a way in which it can be apparent to the subject how the experience renders the belief justified, there seems to be no place to look for this except in some connection between the intrinsic character of one's perceptual consciousness and the content of the belief. And what connection there is depends on both ends of the link.

Turning then to the main alternatives for a characterization of the intrinsic nature of perceptual experience, I assume that even if that experience is by its very nature conceptually, propositionally, or judgmentally structured (none of which I accept), we are concerned here with that aspect of the experience that makes it distinctively perceptual, an aspect we are assuming to be non-conceptual, non-propositional.

Hence we can ignore the question of whether conceptualization is essentially involved. Proceeding on that basis, and painting the picture in broad strokes, we can discern four main accounts.

1   *Direct realism.* This takes perceptual consciousness to consist, most basically, in the fact that one or more objects *appear* to the subject *as so-and-so*, as (restricting ourselves to vision) round, bulgy, blue, jagged, etc. In other terms, they *present* themselves to the subject as so-and-so. This view takes perceptual consciousness to be irreducibly relational in character. And, where one is genuinely perceiving objects, situations, and events in the external environment, it takes the relation to have an external object as its other term. This distinguishes it from its rivals, all of whom take perceptual experience to be (intrinsically) purely intramental.

2   *The sense-datum theory.* This agrees with 1 in taking perceptual consciousness to consist in an awareness of objects, to have an "act–object" structure. But the objects in question are never the familiar denizens of the physical world, but are instead special, nonphysical objects of a markedly peculiar character. They have the special role of bearing the qualities that putatively external perceived objects sensorily appear to have.

3   *The adverbial theory.* Perceptual consciousness is simply a *way* of being conscious; it does not display any sort of "act–object" structure. Just as a mode of consciousness, it is not a cognition of objects of any kind.

4   *Phenomenal quality view.* This is a position that I think is rather widely held but has not received the systematic development of the first three. It agrees with 2 in taking perceptual experience to be a direct awareness of something "mental," something private, but it differs in construing these private objects as qualities of mental states, which you could term sensations, rather than as subsistent nonphysical particulars.[16]

Thus direct realism is distinguished from the other alternatives by insisting that perceptual consciousness is essentially, in itself, an *awareness of* objects, which are, in normal cases, *physical objects in the environment.* Unlike the other views, it does not regard perceptual experience, in normal cases, to be purely "inside the head."[17] When I take myself to be seeing a red apple, the direct realist will say that I am directly aware of something (an apple if things are going right) that looks red and apple-shaped to me. Sense-datum theory will say that I am directly aware of a red, apple-shaped sense datum that is a special nonphysical particular that exists only as a bearer of sensory qualia like color and shape. The phenomenal quality view will say that I am directly aware of sensory qualia of (some of my) current mental states, qualia like redness. And the adverbial theory will say that I am sensing in a red, apple-shaped *way* or *manner.*

To avoid misapprehension, let me make it clear that direct realism, as I construe it, does *not* hold that presented objects always are what they present themselves as. It is compatible with recognizing a considerable amount of misleading appearance. X can look like a cow when it is an automobile. A tower in the distance can look round when it is square. And so on. To be sure, if perceptual appearances were always or usually misleading, they would be of much less value epistemically than I take them to be. But that value does not require infallibility.

Reflecting on the bearing of these differences on perceptual epistemology, one can hardly avoid being struck by the apparent superiority of direct realism. On that view perceptual experience in itself involves, in normal cases, a cognitive relation with external objects that perceptual beliefs are about. Hence it seems obvious how an experience could be a source of knowledge (justified belief) about such objects. If the leaf looks yellow to me or the house visually presents two front windows, that is an obvious basis for supposing the leaf to be yellow or the house to have two front windows (a *prima facie*, defeasible basis of course). But with the other construals, according to which the experience involves no intrinsic cognitive connection with the external world, there is no such intuitive justificatory force. Perceptual experience is a purely subjective affair, and as such it wears on its face no (even apparent) information about the external environment. Why should we suppose that sensing in a certain way, or being aware of a nonphysical sense datum or a phenomenal quality of a mental state, should tell us anything about what there is in the immediate environment of the perceiver and about what that is like? Of course, there may be *externalist* connections of the sort envisaged by the counterfactual or reliabilist approaches. It may be that sensing in a certain way is a reliable indication of the presence of a maple tree, or that the way in which a certain sensing gives rise to a belief that a car is driving down the street is a reliable way. But we are currently exploring the possibility of a more internalist perceptual epistemology, according to which a perceptual belief is justified only if the perceiver has, or can have, some insight into how her experience provides justification for the belief about the external environment to which it gives rise. And the direct realist construal would seem to provide that in a way its alternatives do not. The supposition that a leaf's looking yellow supports the belief that that leaf is yellow is just as clear as the plausibility of the supposition that, by and large and in the absence of sufficient reasons to the contrary, perceived things are as they perceptually appear to be. Whereas on the other construals it is difficult to see how perceptual experience confers any such *prima facie* credibility. Later we will see that things are not so rosy for direct realism as this preliminary statement suggests. But for now I want to explore what

happens when advocates of the other views of perceptual experience address the epistemological problem. Since 4 has not been prominent in this literature, I will confine the discussion to the sense-datum and adverbial theorists.

My sample sense-datum theorists will be Broad, Price, Moore, Russell, and C. I. Lewis, while adverbial theory will be represented by Chisholm. The first point to note is that they all agree with me that there is a major problem in building an intuitively plausible bridge between perceptual experience, as they conceive it, and putatively perceived facts about the external environment. They all reject simple inductive arguments for general experience–external fact correlations, for reasons like those I gave in section II. But when it comes to attempting to show how experience provides a basis for beliefs about the physical world, they divide into two groups on the question of the proper construal of those beliefs. Some of them, including Broad, Moore, Price, and Chisholm are *realists* on this point. They accept the common-sense view that the physical world we take ourselves to perceive is of a radically different ontological nature from sensory experience itself and is what it is independently of our experience. *Phenomenalists* like C. I. Lewis and Russell (at a certain stage) advocate construing physical objects in terms of what sensory experiences a subject would have under certain conditions. To say that there is a plate on the table is to say something about what visual, tactual, and other experiences a percipient would have under certain conditions, *and that's all there is to it*. That's what there being a plate on the table consists in. Physical objects, to use a favorite term of Russell's, are "logical constructions" out of sense data (or sense experiences).[18]

Let's first look at how realist sense-datum theorists approach the epistemology of perceptual belief. Broad and Price, as we saw earlier, discuss various ways in which sense data are patterned, ways which suggest an explanation in terms of the influence of objects we suppose ourselves to perceive.[19] But they reject the claim that anything about the putatively perceived world can be established in this way. Broad goes so far as to say that if the "external world" hypothesis had a finite initial probability, its explanation of these facts would increase that probability, though he sees no grounds for such an initial probability. Price goes further than Broad in discerning the circularity involved in the argument, the ways in which the allegedly pure starting points are actually infected with all sorts of suppositions about the physical world, e.g. that the subject is or is not moving in a certain direction. They agree that one cannot successfully establish putatively perceived facts about the external world from premises concerning sense data or our experiences. And Chisholm, from the adverbial side, agrees with this.[20]

So what positive view do these philosophers have of the epistemic status of perceptual beliefs? The one favored by Price and Moore, and Chisholm part of the time, constitutes a sort of cop-out.[21] Having despaired of finding any reason for supposing that a certain kind of experience indicates the truth of a certain perceptual belief about the external world, they simply lay it down that perceptual beliefs are to be taken as *prima facie* credible just by virtue of being formed. They are, as we might say, *prima facie self-warranted* just by being perceptual beliefs. To quote Chisholm, "if he takes there to be a tree, then . . . this intentional attitude, this taking, tends to make it probable that the taking has an actual object."[22] And Price: "the existence of a particular visual or tactual sense-datum is prima facie evidence (1) for the existence of a material thing such that this sense-datum belongs to it, (2) for the possession by this thing of a front surface of a certain general sort."[23] I call this a "cop-out" because it abandons the attempt to find any kind of intelligible connection between the character of the experience and the content of the perceptual belief formed on its basis, such that this connection would enable us to understand how the experience can provide support

for the belief. This position is just as neutral with respect to the constitution of the experience as the externalist positions we surveyed earlier.

What basis, if any, is there for this *prima facie self-warrant* principle? Here attitudes vary. Chisholm sometimes takes it to be directly known a priori, sometimes to owe its status to the fact that it is part of a system of principles that best accommodates particular intuitive cognitions of particular cases of justification, sometimes to be the only way of escaping skepticism. Price, after surveying various alternatives, opts for the view that "perceptual consciousness is an *ultimate* form of consciousness not reducible to any other; and further, it is an *autonomous* or self-correcting form of consciousness." In other words, the principle needs no external support, even though it is not self-evident. It is clear that these theorists are settling for less than what they were hoping and aiming for initially, and finding ways to make do with what they have found.

As for phenomenalists, they are not faced with an ontological gap between experience and the physical world, but that does not mean that they are home free on the epistemological question. Even if there is nothing to physical things or facts other than what sense experiences would occur under certain conditions, we are still faced with the problem of how we know something about an unlimited number of such contingencies from a particular sense datum or sensation, or some limited number thereof. Phenomenalists generally claim that this is a matter of induction, a mode of inference that, even if not without its problems, is crucial in many other spheres of thought. They thus take themselves to have shown at least that there are no special epistemological problems about perception. But a more serious difficulty for their position concerns their phenomenalist account of physical objects. Chisholm showed, in a classic article, that one cannot begin to formulate a set of propositions concerning the conditions under which a subject S would have an experience of type E, a set that it is at all plausible to take as equivalent to a certain physical fact, without including physical facts in the antecedents of the conditional propositions.[74] Hence the project of reducing propositions about physical objects to propositions that are solely about experience cannot be carried through.

The difficulties that the likes of Price and Broad have with constructing a plausible view of how perceptual experience can justify beliefs about the external world depend, *inter alia*, on their taking epistemic justification to be essentially truth-conducive. This means that it is part of the concept of epistemic justification that if a belief is justified to a high degree, it thereby is likely to be true. As many epistemologists have persuasively argued, if we don't conceive epistemic justification in that way, why should we care so much whether our beliefs are justified?[25] It is combining this conviction with their sense-datum construal of perceptual experience and realism about physical objects that drives them to what I termed a "cop-out." But another reaction to the problem is to abandon truth-conducivity as a constraint on justification. This is what we find in Chisholm. He takes us to have an intuitive idea of a belief's being more or less justified, an idea that is conceptually independent of truth or probability of truth. He thinks that we know intuitively, a priori, in many cases that a given belief enjoys a certain degree of justification or not, and that we can inductively generalize from such cases to principles that lay down conditions for justification.[26] Thus, though he believes that having justified beliefs is the best way of getting the truth, he feels confident that he can tell when a belief is justified without showing that it is likely to be true.

Another way of divorcing justification from truth-conducivity is the Wittgensteinian idea that our concepts contain *criteria* of their correct application.

The fluctuation in grammar between criteria and symptoms makes it look as if there were nothing at all but symptoms. We say, for example: "Experience teaches that there is rain when the barometer falls, but it also teaches that there is rain when we have certain sensations of wet and cold, or such-and-such visual impressions." In defense of this one says that these sense-impressions can deceive us. But here one fails to reflect that the fact that the false appearance is precisely one of rain is founded on a definition.[27]

This idea has been developed by John Pollock in his view that the meaning of many of our concepts, including concepts of perceivable objects, is given by "justification conditions" rather than by "truth conditions."[28] Thus it is part of our concept of a bird that such-and-such visual experiences count as justifying the belief that what one sees is a bird. If this view can be successfully carried through, it obviously gives us an insight into how and why the kinds of experiences we ordinarily take to justify perceptual beliefs with a certain content really do so. There are problems with the approach. For example, it seems to require that we ascribe a concept of epistemic justification to all perceivers, at least all perceivers who have justified perceptual beliefs, and this seems questionable. But the main point I want to make in this context is that since the concept of justification has been cut loose from truth, by both Chisholm and Pollock, it runs up against the question of why we should be so concerned with how justified our beliefs are.

VI

So the sense-datum and adverbial views, which construe perceptual experience as purely intramental, run into difficulties in forging an account of the justification of perceptual beliefs by experience that gives us insight into how and why it works. I believe that the phenomenal qualities view, when combined with realism about the physical world and a truth-conducivity conception of justification, will run into similar problems. But before we award the palm to direct realism, we must surmount two obstacles.

First, we must confront the considerations that have seemed to most philosophers in the modern period to show conclusively that perceptual experience cannot essentially involve any cognitive relation to an extramental object. Here some historical background would be useful. An Aristotelian form of direct realism was dominant in the high Middle Ages, but it was widely abandoned at the beginning of the modern era because of its connection with Aristotelian physics. That physics took "secondary" qualities like color, and felt heat and cold, roughness and smoothness, to be objectively real and even, in some cases, physically efficacious. Thus the Aristotelians felt justified in supposing that when something looks red or feels cold, objective physical properties are presenting themselves to us perceptually.

But with the rise of the new mathematical physics, secondary qualities were banished from the physical world because they were not susceptible of mathematical treatment. And since nothing perceptually appears to us as solely bearing the "primary," mathematicizable properties like size, shape, and motion, thinkers rejected the view that we are directly aware of external physical reality in perception. Perceptual experience, being rife with secondary qualities, had to be construed as purely intramental, as, in the current jargon, an awareness of "ideas."

There are considerations independent of the shape of physical science that convince most current philosophers that perceptual experience does not consist of any cognitive relation to the extramental. The crucial point is that there are hallucinatory experiences in which the supposed external perceived object does not exist, and these are introspectively indistinguishable from veridical perception. Case studies of psychotics present examples aplenty. Such experiences have been taken to support a

stronger or weaker objection to direct realism. The stronger is that perceptual experience never includes a direct awareness of an existent external object. This is supposed to be shown by the intrinsic indistinguishability of hallucinations and the real thing. It need not be alleged that they are never phenomenally distinguishable; that is clearly false. It is enough that they sometimes are not. The argument is that since veridical perceptual experience is of just the same sort, experientially, as (some) hallucinations, then since the latter involves no awareness of an external object, neither does the former. Thus we are driven to some kind of purely subjective construal of all perceptual experience.

The Achilles heel of this argument is the supposition that the ontological constitution of an experience is completely displayed to introspection. Why suppose that? Why suppose that there are no differences in ontological structure that are not revealed to the subject's direct awareness? Why couldn't an experience in which something genuinely is presented to one be phenomenologically just like one in which nothing is? Once we ask these questions, we see that the above argument rests on groundless prejudices. If the demands of theory require it, we are free to take phenomenologically indistinguishable states of affairs as significantly different in ontology. Moreover, we need not confine ourselves to appeals to abstract possibilities. The persistent disputes about the constitution of perceptual experience are eloquent testimony to the point that our direct awareness of our experiences does not suffice to settle the question. If perceptual experience wears its ontological structure on its sleeve, how could many philosophers be confident that it consists of awareness of nonphysical sense data and many others be equally sure that it does not? The fine ontological structure of perceptual experience is a matter for theory, not one's normal awareness of one's own conscious states.

But even if hallucinations do not prove that

perceptual experience is never a direct awareness of external objects, they certainly prove that it isn't always that. And this is enough to show that direct realism, as so far presented, cannot be a comprehensive account of perceptual experience. We might take it as a correct account of veridical perceptual experience, but there are strong motivations for finding a single unified account. The best strategy for the direct realist would be to find some other kind of entity that is directly presenting itself to the subject's awareness as so-and-so when no physical object is available. In some cases this might be the air or the space in a certain area of the environment. But another alternative that would seem to cover all hallucinations (and dreams as well if they are to be ranged under perceptual experience) would be a particularly vivid mental image. This suggestion would not commend itself to materialists and many other contemporary philosophers as well. But there is, in fact, considerable psychological evidence that mental images are perceived in something like the way external objects are. We cannot pursue this issue here, beyond pointing to the necessity of some such development to enable direct realism to handle hallucinations.

More to the present purpose, the fact of hallucination complicates the application of direct realism to the question of how an experience can justify a perceptual belief. As I have been presenting this, a direct realist account of perceptual experience gives us real insight into how an experience can justify a perceptual belief in the following way. Since the experience just *is* a matter of an object, o, presenting itself to one's experience as P, that confers *prima facie* justification on the belief that o is P, on the enormously plausible principle that it is *prima facie* credible to suppose that things are as they experientially appear to be. But now we are forced to confront the fact that not all perceptual experiences *are* a matter of an object of the sort they seem to be perceptions of presenting itself as so-and-so. Suppose I have an hallucinatory experience of a computer that, so far as I can tell just by having the experience, is a case of a computer's visually presenting itself with the word "externalism" displayed on the screen? Does this experience provide *prima facie* justification for the belief that there is a computer in front of me with "externalism" displayed on the screen? On the one hand, it seems that I must hold that it does, so long as there is no way in which I can tell that I am not aware of a real computer. But then I must abandon the simple epistemological application of direct realism for which I have been commending it. Justification of perceptual beliefs by experience would no longer be confined to cases in which the object the belief is about directly appears to the subject as so-and-so. Indeed, it is beginning to look as if direct realism is in no better position than its rivals on this issue. For here too we are in the position of providing insight into how a purely intramental experience can confer justification on a belief about something extramental.

There are two positions direct realism can take on this issue, one more externalist and one more internalist. On the former, we stick to the original unqualified position. Perceptual experience justifies beliefs only about what the subject is thereby directly aware of. If in hallucinations it is visual images that appear so-and-so to the subject, it is the false belief that some image has sentences (really) appearing on its (real) screen that is *prima facie* justified by the experience. Since the subject has no direct cognitive access to the hallucinatory character of the experience, she doesn't realize that her belief is about a mental image; but that is what is more externalist about the position. On the latter, more fully internalist position, we limit our construal of the justifying experience to what is directly accessible to the subject. Since whether the experience is veridical or hallucinatory is not directly accessible, we limit the specification of the experiential justifier to what is neutral between those alternatives—something like *it is (experientially) just as if a computer is presenting itself to me* as having "externalist" on its screen. And what we can take to be *prima facie* justified by the experience is dictated by that description, viz., a belief that a real computer in front of her has "externalist" on its screen.[29] This *prima facie* justification will be overriden if the subject comes to know or justifiably believe that the experience is hallucinatory. Note that both of these positions are internalist in restricting the justifier, what does the justifying, to experiences that are directly accessible to the subject. They differ in that the former position takes the justification to accrue to a belief about what is actually appearing to the subject, while the latter takes it to accrue to a belief about what seems to the subject to be presenting itself to her.

Note that both positions enjoy the advantage I have attributed to the direct realist epistemology of perceptual belief. For they are both squarely based on the idea that X's appearing P to S provides *prima facie* justification for believing that X is P. The more externalist version preserves this idea unmodified, at the cost of leaving the subject unable to tell with certainty, from the inside, just what belief is so justified. The more internalist position extends the range of justifying experiences to include introspectively indistinguishable lookalikes, but their characterization is parasitic on the characterization of the real article. And so the original idea— that X's looking φ to S *prima facie* justifies S in supposing that X is φ—is still at the heart of the account.

Notes

1 For an interesting coherentist attempt to handle perceptual belief, see Laurence BonJour, *The Structure of Empirical Knowledge* (Cambridge, MA: Harvard University Press, 1985), ch. 6. For extensive criticism of coherentism, see John W. Bender, ed., *The Current State of the Coherence Theory* (Boston: Kluwer, 1989). [. . .]

2 I briefly discuss this argument at the end of section V.

3 For an extensive critique of both a priori and empirical arguments, see William Alston, *The Reliability of Sense Perception* (Ithaca: Cornell University Press, 1993).

4 C. D. Broad, *Scientific Thought* (London: Routledge & Kegan Paul, 1923), chs. 9 and 10, and *The Mind and Its Place in Nature* (London: Routledge & Kegan Paul, 1925), ch. 4.

5 Broad, *The Mind and Its Place in Nature*, pp. 196–8.

6 William Alston, *The Reliability of Sense Perception* (Ithaca: Cornell University Press, 1993).

7 At least his second reason holds on an internalist account of justification, on which the subject must have some insight into that and how a reason is adequate in order that the belief for which it is a reason be thereby justified. An externalist account of justification or knowledge is a different ball game, as I will note shortly. But even for externalism the first consideration, the typical absence of knowledge of the character of one's sensory experience, is applicable.

8 To be sure, even if a perceptual belief must be based on some experience, there may be experience that is fitted to be evidence for it on which it is not based. But that combination is not likely enough to warrant consideration.

9 Fred Dretske, *Seeing and Knowing* (London: Routledge & Kegan Paul, 1969).

10 Ibid., ch. 2.

11 Ibid., pp. 79–88.

12 There are problems, as usual, with the counterfactual involved. Dretske has insightful things to say about how to interpret it, but I can't go into that here.

13 See Alvin Goldman, "What Is Justified Belief?," *Journal of Philosophy*, 73 (1979), and *Epistemology and Cognition* (Cambridge, MA: Harvard University Press, 1986).

14 Needless to say, anyone who is thoroughly convinced that justification of belief is necessary for knowledge will not find any account of knowledge more attractive than a parallel account of justification, since she will hold that the former must go through the latter. It should also be noted that although Goldman takes reliability as what confers justification on beliefs, Dretske's account of perceptual knowledge spelled out above needs a bit of jimmying to turn it into an account of justification. (I), the truth requirement has to be dropped of course, and since (iii), as stated, implies that, it has

to be weakened, by making it a high probability claim, for example.

15 Donald Davidson, "A Coherence Theory of Truth and Knowledge," in Ernest LePore, ed., *Truth and Interpretation: Perspectives on the Philosophy of Donald Davidson* (Oxford: Blackwell, 1986), p. 310.

16 My colleague, Jonathan Bennett, has forced me (by rational argument, not threats) to acknowledge 4 as a serious alternative.

17 This, of course, raises the question of how direct realism treats complete hallucinations where no direct awareness of an external object is involved. I will come to that later.

18 See "The Ultimate Constituents of Matter" and "The Relations of Sense-Data to Physics," both in Bertrand Russell's *Our Knowledge of the External World as a Field for Scientific Method in Philosophy* (Chicago: Open Court, 1914). (Beginning in the 1920s Russell took an increasingly realist approach to the physical world.) For C. I. Lewis's phenomenalism, see his *An Analysis of Knowledge and Valuation* (La Salle, IL: Open Court, 1946), chs. 7–9.

19 Broad, *The Mind and Its Place in Nature*, ch. 4, and H. H. Price, *Perception* (London: Methuen, 1932), ch. 4.

20 Roderick Chisholm, *Theory of Knowledge* (Englewood Cliffs, NJ: Prentice-Hall, 3rd edn, 1989). Cf. G. E. Moore, *Philosophical Studies* (London: Routledge & Kegan Paul, 1922), chs. 2, 5, 7; and *Some Main Problems of Philosophy* (London: Allen & Unwin, 1953), chs. 2, 5, 7.

21 Broad seems content with the "would increase the initial probability if it had any" position hinted at above.

22 Chisholm, *Theory of Knowledge*, p. 47.

23 Price, *Perception*, p. 185.

24 Roderick Chisholm, "The Problem of Empiricism," *Journal of Philosophy* XLV (1948).

25 An incisive formulation of this argument is found in BonJour, *The Structure of Empirical Knowledge*, ch. 1.

26 Though the priority of particular cases is the dominant strand in his writings, he sometimes suggests, as noted earlier, that general principles of justification are directly known a priori.

27 Ludwig Wittgenstein, *Philosophical Investigations*, trans. G. E. M. Anscombe (Oxford: Blackwell, 1953), no. 354.

28 John Pollock, *Knowledge and Justification* (Princeton: Princeton University Press, 1974).

29 I would prefer not to say that she is justified in a singular belief about a particular object, because there is no object of the sort she believes herself to be directly aware of that is appearing to her in this case. Since there is a reference failure, no singular proposition forms that content of any belief of hers, and hence the question of whether a belief with such a content is justified, and if so how, does not arise. However, an existentially quantified belief, *there is a computer in front of me with "externalism" on its screen*, could still be *prima facie* justified.

PART NINE

What can we know?

INTRODUCTION TO PART NINE

Ram Neta and Duncan Pritchard

W E TEND TO SUPPOSE THAT WE KNOW a great deal about the world around us. Of course, there may be some things that we think we know which turn out not to have been known – think, for example, about some key thesis of contemporary scientific theory – but we tend to suppose that this fate couldn't befall *all* of the things that we think we know, or even most of them: we feel confident that we do in fact know many of these things, even if not all of them. There are philosophical arguments, however, which purport to show not just that we don't in fact know anything (anything of consequence at any rate), but also that knowledge is *impossible*. That is, according to these arguments it is not as if being cleverer or more observant (etc.) would make a difference to our knowledge, for no matter how clever or observant (etc.) we are we wouldn't know anything. Such arguments are called *sceptical arguments*, and the problem they pose is known as the problem of *scepticism*.

This problem comes in many different forms and dates right back to antiquity, to the very birth of philosophy. Indeed, just as soon as philosophers first began to discuss what knowledge was they were immediately confronted with the problem of showing that we are able to possess the knowledge that we think we possess. One particular kind of scepticism arises out of what seems to be an inevitable circularity in our thinking about knowledge. This problem is known as a *problem of the criterion*, and a relatively recent statement of this problem, due to Roderick Chisholm (1916–99), is collected here (Chapter 35).

The problem of the criterion concerns the question of how it is possible to determine what knowledge is. One might naturally think that the way to do this is simply to consider all the different cases of knowledge that one can think of and ask the question of what they all have in common that makes them instances of knowledge. The problem with this suggestion, however, is that if one is indeed able to pick out instances of knowledge then surely that must mean that one *already* knows what knowledge is – that is, one must already know what the distinguishing marks, or *criteria*, of knowledge are. In contrast, suppose that one doesn't assume that one already knows what the criteria for knowledge are. How then could one go about determining what knowledge is? We thus appear to be caught in a bind, unable to begin our investigation into the nature of knowledge.

We can roughly summarise this problem in terms of the following two claims:

(a)   I can only identify instances of knowledge provided I already know what the criteria for knowledge are.
(b)   I can only know what the criteria for knowledge are provided I am already able to identify instances of knowledge.

We thus seem to be trapped inside a very small set of unpleasant options. I must either assume that I know what the criteria for knowledge are in order to identify instances of knowledge, or else I must assume that I can identify instances of knowledge in order to determine what the criteria for knowledge are. Either way, the dubious nature of the assumption in question appears to call into question the legitimacy of the epistemological project of defining knowledge.

Chisholm argues that if we want to avoid scepticism, then we need to be willing to groundlessly assume either (1) that we are able to identify instances of knowledge independently of having any prior grip on what the criteria of knowledge are or (2) that we are able to determine what the criteria for knowledge are independently of having any prior ability to identify instances of knowledge. Chisholm calls views which endorse the first option *particularist* and views which endorse the second option *methodist*. He argues that the former option is preferable to the latter, on account of the fact that the latter view tends to assume an implausible rationalism – i.e. that simply through reflection we are able to determine what the criteria of knowledge are. Still, even Chisholm accepts that both positions are highly problematic.

Even supposing that we can respond to the problem of the criterion, and so determine what knowledge is, we still face the other sceptical problem of showing that such knowledge is even possible. Although sceptical problems can trace their source back to antiquity, the variety of scepticism that has been the chief focus of contemporary epistemological theorising is due to the French philosopher René Descartes (1596–1650), and a selection of his writings on this topic is collected here (Chapter 36).

It is worth emphasising that Descartes himself is not a sceptic. The problem of scepticism plays for him a *methodological* role, in that he is using this problem in order to evaluate and motivate a particular theory of knowledge, one which he thinks is immune to the sceptical doubts that he articulates. Descartes lived during a time when many of the received doctrines of the day – such as regarding whether the earth orbits the sun rather than vice versa – were found to be false. Moreover, a lot of the change in scientific thinking was due to a new scientific methodology which, rather than simply accepting the received teaching of the church, aimed to discover truths for itself via experiment and observation. What Descartes was interested in was whether he could offer a new methodology for epistemology which would parallel the new scientific methodology, and the sceptical problem was key to this enterprise.

What Descartes did was employ what he called a 'method of doubt' which involved doubting everything that he thought could be doubted. In doing so, he thought that he would be able to discern those beliefs of his which were beyond doubt and which could thus serve as a solid foundation for the rest of our beliefs. The core foundation that he came across was that of his belief in his own existence, for he noticed that one could not coherently doubt that one existed, since in doubting it one thereby *proves* that one exists (hence his famous remark, 'I think, therefore I am').

Interestingly, however, although Descartes only used his sceptical method of doubt in order to arrive at a new theory of knowledge, many were more impressed by the scepticism that he proposed than by the theory of knowledge that he put forward in the light of that problem and which he thought was immune to scepticism. In particular, in order to pursue his method of doubt Descartes offered various *sceptical hypotheses* and many have found the sceptical problems posed by these hypotheses to be extremely hard to solve. Sceptical hypotheses are scenarios which are indistinguishable from normal life but in which one is radically deceived. Descartes offered two very famous examples of sceptical hypotheses.

The first is the hypothesis that one might currently be dreaming. After all, dreams can be very vivid and when they are they are indistinguishable from waking life. But given that that's the case, how does one know that one is not dreaming right now? It is not as if, for example, one could just pinch oneself and see if one wakes up, since how would one know that one is not simply dreaming that one is pinching oneself? Moreover, if one were dreaming right now, then one wouldn't know many of the things that one thinks one knows. It seems to follow, then, that we can't be sure that we do know all the things that we think we know because we can't rule out the sceptical hypothesis that we are currently dreaming. (A vivid example of the kind of sceptical problem that can be raised by the possibility that one might now be dreaming, due to Jorge Luis Borges (1899–1986), is collected in the readings for this part (Chapter 34)).

The second sceptical hypothesis that Descartes introduced and which has been very influential in contemporary epistemology is that of the evil demon. Descartes imagined that there was some being with similar powers to a God but who used those powers to deceive us. In particular, the demon's goal is to ensure that as many of our beliefs are false as is possible. The point is not whether such a demon actually exists; the point is that such a demon *could* exist, and if s/he did we wouldn't know very much. Moreover, as with the sceptical hypothesis that one could be dreaming, it seems that there is nothing that one could do to rule out such a possibility. What, after all, would you do to ensure that you were not being deceived in this way? Given that we cannot rule out this possibility, and given that we would know very little if this hypothesis were to obtain, it seems to follow that we don't know very much, or so the sceptic claims. An influential discussion of Descartes' evil demon hypothesis (otherwise known as the 'evil genius' hypothesis), which is due to O. K. Bouwsma (1898–1978), is collected here (Chapter 37).

Some have responded to the sceptical problem by arguing that, contrary to first appearances, we do know that sceptical hypotheses are false. The British philosopher G. E. Moore (1873–1958) falls into this category, and a sample of his writing is contained here (Chapter 38). In particular, Moore belongs to a 'commonsense' tradition in philosophy which wants to privilege commonsense thinking over the conclusions of philosophical arguments. Moore's particular concern in this paper is with the sceptical hypothesis involving dreaming. While Moore grants to the sceptic that if one is in fact dreaming, then one does not know very much (one does not know that one is at present standing up, for instance, to use his example), he argues that this is a consideration which cuts both ways. This is because he claims that if one does know that one is at present standing up – and Moore argues that one is in a position to know this – then it follows that one is in a position to know that one is not dreaming after all, *contra* the sceptic. At the very least, argues Moore, one's argument that one knows that one is at present standing and therefore one knows that one is not dreaming is at least as good as the sceptic's contrary argument that one does not know that one is not dreaming and so one does not know that one is standing up.

A very different kind of argument in favour of scepticism is offered by Peter Unger (1942–) in his paper contained in this part (Chapter 39). Unger proceeds by claiming that 'knowledge' is what he calls an 'absolute' term. What is crucial to absolute terms is that, strictly speaking, they only apply if an absolute standard is met. An example that Unger offers in this respect is that of 'flat'. To say that, for example, a table is *quite* flat is, it seems, to say that it is not, strictly speaking, flat at all, but rather contains some imperfections on its surface. Indeed, were we to say that the table was flat and were someone to insist that it wasn't, we would understand perfectly what they meant and, indeed, regard their opposing statement as true. More generally, it seems that while in normal contexts we judge surfaces to be flat, we also implicitly recognise that, strictly speaking, nothing is really flat, since there is no such thing as a frictionless plane. Such judgements, then, are, strictly speaking, false.

Unger argues that the same goes for 'knowledge'. There are two stages to his argument. The first is to claim that knowledge entails certainty. It makes no sense, argues Unger, to say that one knows a particular proposition and yet one is uncertain of it. The second claim that Unger makes is that 'certain' is itself an absolute adjective, in that, strictly speaking, to be certain is to be absolutely certain. Just as to say that a table is quite flat is to thereby concede that, strictly speaking, it isn't really flat at all, so (argues Unger) to concede that one is only quite certain of a proposition is thereby to concede that, strictly speaking, one isn't really certain of this proposition at all. It follows from the conjunction of these two claims that, strictly speaking, in order to possess knowledge that a particular proposition is true, one must be appropriately absolutely certain of the proposition in question. But there are very few propositions, if any, towards which the appropriate attitude would be one of absolute certainty, and so Unger concludes that we don't really know anything (anything much at any rate).

The final selection in this part (Chapter 40), due to David Lewis (1941–2001), could be regarded as responding, in part at least, to the problem that Unger poses, and thereby to the more general sceptical problem that traces its source back to Descartes. It is central to Unger's view that while we unhesitatingly attribute knowledge to ourselves and one another in normal conversational contexts, we also recognise, once we reflect on the matter, that such judgements are, strictly speaking, false (just as we recognise once we reflect on the matter that our everyday judgements of flatness are also, strictly speaking, false). In contrast to this 'infallibilist' account of 'knowledge', Lewis instead proposes a contextualist reading. On this view, in different conversational contexts different standards for what counts as 'knowledge' apply, and so while it might be true in one conversational context to say that an agent 'knows', that very same judgement might be false in another conversational context where the standards are higher. Moreover, Lewis argues that reflecting on sceptical hypotheses might be one way in which the standards for 'knowledge' could get raised.

In order to see what Lewis has in mind here, think again about our 'flat' judgements. Just as we might treat 'knows' as a context-sensitive term, so we might be tempted to take the same line as regards 'flat'. On this view, it is not that we are speaking falsely when we say things are flat in ordinary contexts, but rather that the standards for flatness are just very low in normal contexts. Crucially, however, the standards for flatness can be raised, and so in a different conversational context the very same judgement that such-and-such is flat may no longer be treated as true. The idea is that the same might apply to 'knows'. In normal conversational contexts, we speak truly in saying that we know much of what we think we know. In sceptical conversational contexts, however, contexts in which we consider sceptical hypotheses, the standards for 'knows' get implicitly raised and so it is then no longer true to say that we know many of the propositions which we (ordinarily) think we know.

The key advantage to such an approach is that it can explain the attraction of scepticism while nonetheless resisting the sceptical conclusion. After all, in conversational contexts in which we are considering the sceptical problem, the sceptical conclusion that we know very little is *true*. But this fact is entirely consistent with the anti-sceptical claim that when we attribute knowledge to each other and to ourselves in normal conversational contexts we also speak truly.

Study questions

1   Try to state in your own words what the problem of the criterion is, and how the particularist and the methodist respond to that problem. Is either view plausible as a response to this problem, do you think?

2   What is a sceptical hypothesis? What is the sceptical problem posed by the dreaming sceptical hypothesis? What is the problem posed by the evil demon sceptical hypothesis? How, if at all, do they pose different sceptical problems?

3   Is Moore right to say that the argument 'I know that I am standing up, and therefore I know that I am not dreaming' is at least as good as the sceptic's 'You don't know that you're not dreaming, and therefore you don't know that you are standing up'? Assuming he is right, does this observation suffice to resolve the sceptical problem posed by the dreaming sceptical hypothesis, do you think?

4   What does Unger mean by saying that 'knows' is an 'absolute' term? Explain how this claim leads to the sceptical problem that Unger develops.

5   Describe Lewis' contextualist account of 'knows'. What does Lewis mean when he says that on this view knowledge is 'elusive'?

Further reading

For an accessible discussion of the sceptical problem which is targeted at the general reader, see Pritchard (2006: chapter 12). For two general overviews of the contemporary literature on the problem of scepticism, see Pritchard (2002b) and Klein (2005), both of which are freely available on the internet and contain useful lists of further readings. A more sophisticated version of the Pritchard article is Pritchard (2002a). For further discussion of the contextualist response to the problem of scepticism, see Black (2006) and Rysiew (2007), both of which are freely available on the internet and contain useful lists of further readings. There are a number of anthologies on scepticism. Of these, two stand out: DeRose and Warfield (1999) is an excellent selection of the contemporary literature on scepticism, while Landesman and Meeks (2003) presents a more historical overview of the literature on this problem.

References

Black, T. (2006). 'Contextualism in Epistemology', *Internet Encyclopaedia of Philosophy*, eds J. Fieser and B. Dowden, http://www.iep.utm.edu/c/contextu.htm.

DeRose, K., and Warfield, T. (eds). (1999). *Skepticism: A Contemporary Reader*, Oxford: Oxford University Press.

Klein, P. (2005). 'Skepticism', *Stanford Encyclopaedia of Philosophy*, ed. E. Zalta, http://plato.stanford.edu/entries/skepticism/.

Landesman, C. and Meeks, R. (eds). (2003). *Philosophical Skepticism*, Oxford: Blackwell.

Pritchard, D. H. (2002a). 'Recent Work on Radical Skepticism', *American Philosophical Quarterly* 39: 215–57.

—— (2002b). 'Scepticism, Contemporary', *Internet Encyclopaedia of Philosophy*, eds J. Fieser and B. Dowden, http://www.iep.utm.edu/s/skepcont.htm.

—— (2006). *What Is this Thing Called Knowledge?*, London: Routledge.

Rysiew, P. (2007). 'Epistemic Contextualism', *Stanford Encyclopaedia of Philosophy*, ed. E. Zalta, http://plato.stanford.edu/entries/contextualism-epistemology/.

Chapter 34

Jorge Luis Borges

THE CIRCULAR RUINS

No one saw him disembark in the unanimous night, no one saw the bamboo canoe sink into the sacred mud, but in a few days there was no one who did not know that the taciturn man came from the South and that his home had been one of those numberless villages upstream in the deeply cleft side of the mountain, where the Zend language has not been contaminated by Greek and where leprosy is infrequent. What is certain is that the grey man kissed the mud, climbed up the bank with pushing aside (probably, without feeling) the blades which were lacerating his flesh, and crawled, nauseated and bloodstained, up to the circular enclosure crowned with a stone tiger or horse, which sometimes was the color of flame and now was that of ashes. This circle was a temple which had been devoured by ancient fires, profaned by the miasmal jungle, and whose god no longer received the homage of men. The stranger stretched himself out beneath the pedestal. He was awakened by the sun high overhead. He was not astonished to find that his wounds had healed; he closed his pallid eyes and slept, not through weakness of flesh but through determination of will. He knew that this temple was the place required for his invincible intent; he knew that the incessant trees had not succeeded in strangling the ruins of another propitious temple downstream which had once belonged to gods now burned and dead; he knew that his immediate obligation was to dream. Toward midnight he was awakened by the inconsolable shriek of a bird. Tracks of bare feet, some figs and a jug warned him that the men of the region had been spying respectfully on his sleep, soliciting his protection or afraid of his magic. He felt a chill of fear, and sought out a sepulchral niche in the dilapidated wall where he concealed himself among unfamiliar leaves.

The purpose which guided him was not impossible, though supernatural. He wanted to dream a man; he wanted to dream him in minute entirety and impose him on reality. This magic project had exhausted the entire expanse of his mind; if someone had asked him his name or to relate some event of his former life, he would not have been able to give an answer. This uninhabited, ruined temple suited him, for in it is contained a minimum of visible world; the proximity of the workmen also suited him, for they took it upon themselves to provide for his frugal needs. The rice and fruit they brought him were nourishment enough for his body, which was consecrated to the sole task of sleeping and dreaming.

At first, his dreams were chaotic; then in a short while they became dialectic in nature. The stranger dreamed that he was in the center of a circular amphitheater which was more or less the burnt temple; clouds of taciturn students filled the tiers of seats; the faces of the farthest ones hung at a distance of many centuries and as high as the stars, but their features were completely precise. The man lectured his pupils on anatomy, cosmography, and magic: the faces listened anxiously and tried to answer understandingly, as if they guessed the importance of that examination which would redeem one of them from his condition of empty illusion and interpolate him into the real world. Asleep or awake, the man thought over the answers of his phantoms, did not allow himself to be deceived by imposters, and in certain perplexities he sensed a growing intelligence. He was seeking a soul worthy of participating in the universe.

After nine or ten nights he understood with a certain bitterness that he could expect nothing from those pupils who accepted his doctrine passively, but that he could expect something from those who occasionally dared to oppose him. The former group, although worthy of love and affection, could not ascend to the level of individuals; the latter pre-existed to a slightly greater degree. One afternoon (now afternoons were also given over to sleep, now he was only awake for a couple hours at daybreak) he dismissed the vast illusory student body for good and kept only one pupil. He was a taciturn, sallow boy, at times intractable, and whose sharp features resembled of those of his dreamer. The brusque elimination of his fellow students did not disconcert him for long; after a few private lessons, his progress was enough to astound the teacher. Nevertheless, a catastrophe took place. One day, the man emerged from his sleep as if from a viscous desert, looked at the useless afternoon light which he immediately confused with the dawn, and understood that he had not dreamed. All that night and all day long, the intolerable lucidity of insomnia fell upon him. He tried exploring the forest, to lose his strength; among the hemlock he barely succeeded in experiencing several short snatches of sleep, veined with fleeting, rudimentary visions that were useless. He tried to assemble the student body but scarcely had he articulated a few brief words of exhortation when it became deformed and was then erased. In his almost perpetual vigil, tears of anger burned his old eyes.

He understood that modeling the incoherent and vertiginous matter of which dreams are composed was the most difficult task that a man could undertake, even though he should penetrate all the enigmas of a superior and inferior order; much more difficult than weaving a rope out of sand or coining the faceless wind. He swore he would forget the enormous hallucination which had thrown him off at first, and he sought another method of work. Before putting it into execution, he spent a month recovering his strength, which had been squandered by his delirium. He abandoned all premeditation of dreaming and almost immediately succeeded in sleeping a reasonable part of each day. The few times that he had dreams during this period, he paid no attention to them. Before resuming his task, he waited until the moon's disk was perfect. Then, in the afternoon, he purified himself in the waters of the river, worshiped the planetary gods, pronounced the prescribed syllables of a mighty name, and went to sleep. He dreamed almost immediately, with his heart throbbing.

He dreamed that it was warm, secret, about the size of a clenched fist, and of a garnet color within the penumbra of a human body as yet without face or sex; during fourteen lucid nights he dreamed of it with meticulous love. Every night he perceived it more clearly. He did not touch it; he only permitted himself to witness it, to observe it, and occasionally to rectify it with a glance. He perceived it and lived it from all angles and distances. On the fourteenth night he lightly touched the pulmonary artery with his index finger, then the whole heart, outside and inside. He was satisfied with the examination. He deliberately did not dream for a night; he took up the heart again, invoked the name of a planet, and undertook the vision of another of the principle organs. Within a year he had come to the skeleton and the eyelids. The innumerable hair was perhaps the most difficult task. He dreamed an entire man—a young man, but who did not sit up or talk, who was unable to open his eyes. Night after night, the man dreamed him asleep.

In the Gnostic cosmosgonies, demiurges fashion a red Adam who cannot stand; as clumsy, crude and elemental as this Adam of dust was the Adam of dreams forged by the wizard's nights. One afternoon, the man almost destroyed his entire work, but then changed his mind. (It would have been better had he destroyed it.) When he had exhausted all supplications to the deities of earth, he threw himself at the feet of the effigy which was perhaps a tiger or perhaps a colt and implored its unknown help. That evening, at twilight, he dreamed of the statue. He dreamed it was alive, tremulous: it was not an atrocious bastard of a tiger and a colt, but at the same time these two firey creatures and also a bull, a rose, and a storm. This multiple god revealed to him that his earthly name was Fire, and that in this circular temple (and in others like it) people had once made sacrifices to him and worshiped him, and that he would magically animate the dreamed phantom, in such a way that all creatures, except Fire itself and the dreamer, would believe to be a man of flesh and blood. He commanded that once this man had been instructed in all the rites, he should be sent to the other ruined temple whose pyramids were still standing downstream, so that some voice would glorify him in that deserted edifice. In the dream of the man that dreamed, the dreamed one awoke.

The wizard carried out the orders he had been given. He devoted a certain length of time (which finally proved to be two years) to instructing him in the mysteries of the universe and the cult of fire. Secretly, he was pained at the idea of being separated from him. On the pretext of pedagogical necessity, each day he increased the number of hours dedicated to dreaming. He also remade the right shoulder, which was somewhat defective. At times, he was disturbed by the impression that all this had

already happened . . . In general, his days were happy; when he closed his eyes, he thought: Now I will be with my son. Or, more rarely: The son I have engendered is waiting for me and will not exist if I do not go to him.

Gradually, he began accustoming him to reality. Once he ordered him to place a flag on a faraway peak. The next day the flag was fluttering on the peak. He tried other analogous experiments, each time more audacious. With a certain bitterness, he understood that his son was ready to be born—and perhaps impatient. That night he kissed him for the first time and sent him off to the other temple whose remains were turning white downstream, across many miles of inextricable jungle and marshes. Before doing this (and so that his son should never know that he was a phantom, so that he should think himself a man like any other) he destroyed in him all memory of his years of apprenticeship.

His victory and peace became blurred with boredom. In the twilight times of dusk and dawn, he would prostrate himself before the stone figure, perhaps imagining his unreal son carrying out identical rites in other circular ruins downstream; at night he no longer dreamed, or dreamed as any man does. His perceptions of the sounds and forms of the universe became somewhat pallid: his absent son was being nourished by this diminution of his soul. The purpose of his life had been fulfilled; the man remained in a kind of ecstasy. After a certain time, which some chronicles prefer to compute in years and others in decades, two oarsmen awoke him at midnight; he could not see their faces, but they spoke to him of a charmed man in a temple of the North, capable of walking on fire without burning himself. The wizard suddenly remembered the words of the god. He remembered that of all the creatures that people the earth, Fire was the only one who knew his son to be a phantom. This memory, which at first calmed him, ended by tormenting him. He feared lest his son should meditate on this abnormal privilege and by some means find out he was a mere simulacrum. Not to be a man, to be a projection of another man's dreams—what an incomparable humiliation, what madness! Any father is interested in the sons he has procreated (or permitted) out of the mere confusion of happiness; it was natural that the wizard should fear for the future of that son whom he had thought out entrail by entrail, feature by feature, in a thousand and one secret nights.

His misgivings ended abruptly, but not without certain forewarnings. First (after a long drought) a remote cloud, as light as a bird, appeared on a hill; then, toward the South, the sky took on the rose color of leopard's gums; then came clouds of smoke which rusted the metal of the nights; afterwards came the panic-stricken flight of wild animals. For what had happened many centuries before was repeating itself. The ruins of the sanctuary of the god of Fire were destroyed by fire. In a dawn without birds, the wizard saw the concentric fire licking the walls. For a moment, he thought of taking refuge in the water, but then he understood that death was coming to crown his old age and absolve him from his labors. He walked toward the sheets of flame. They did not bite his flesh, they caressed him and flooded him without heat or combustion. With relief, with humiliation, with terror, he understood that he also was an illusion, that someone else was dreaming him.

Chapter 35

Roderick Chisholm

THE PROBLEM OF THE CRITERION

1

"The problem of the criterion" seems to me to be one of the most important and one of the most difficult of all the problems of philosophy. I am tempted to say that one has not begun to philosophize until one has faced this problem and has recognized how unappealing, in the end, each of the possible solutions is . . .

2

What is the problem, then? It is the ancient problem of "the dialectus"—the problem of "the wheel" or "the vicious circle." It was put very neatly by Montaigne in his *Essays*. So let us begin by para-paraphrasing his formulation of the puzzle. To know whether things really are as they seem to be, we must have a *procedure* for distinguishing appearances that are true from appearances that are false. But to know whether our procedure is a good procedure, we have to know whether it really *succeeds* in distinguishing appearances that are true from appearances that are false. And we cannot know whether it does really succeed unless we already know which appearances are *true* and which ones are *false*. And so we are caught in a circle.

Let us try to see how one gets into a situation of this sort.

The puzzles begin to form when you ask yourself, "What can I really know about the world?" We all are acquainted with people who think they know a lot more than in fact they do know. I'm thinking of fanatics, bigots, mystics, various types of dogmatists. And we have all heard of people who claim at least to know a lot less than what in fact they do know. I'm thinking of those people who call themselves "skeptics" and who like to say that people cannot know what the world is really like. People tend to become skeptics, temporarily, after reading books on popular science: the authors tell us we cannot know what things are like really (but they make use of a vast amount of knowledge, or a vast amount of what is claimed to be knowledge, to support this skeptical conclusion). And as we know, people tend to become dogmatists, temporarily, as a result of the effects of alcohol, or drugs, or religious and emotional experiences. Then they claim to have an inside view of the world and they think they have a deep kind of knowledge giving them a key to the entire workings of the universe.

If you have a healthy common sense, you will feel that something is wrong with both of these extremes and that the truth is somewhere in the middle: we can know far more than the skeptic says we can know and far less than the dogmatist or the mystic says that he can know. But how are we to decide these things?

3

How do we decide, in any particular case, whether we have a genuine item of knowledge? Most of us are ready to confess that our beliefs far transcend what we really know. There are things we believe that we don't in fact know. And we can say of many of these things that we know that we don't know them. I believe that Mrs. Jones is honest, say, but I don't know it, and I know that I don't know it. There are other things that we don't know, but they are such that we don't know that we don't know them. Last week, say, I thought I knew that Mr. Smith was honest, but he turned out to be a thief. I didn't know that he was a thief, and, moreover, I didn't know that I didn't know that he was a thief; I thought I knew that he was honest. And so the problem is: How are we to distinguish the real cases of knowledge from what only seem to be cases of knowledge? Or, as I put it before, how are we to decide in any particular case whether we have genuine items of knowledge?

What would be a satisfactory solution to our problem? Let me quote in detail what Cardinal Mercier says:

> If there is any knowledge which bears the mark of truth, if the intellect does have a way of distinguishing the true and the false, in short, if there is a criterion of truth, then this criterion should satisfy three conditions: it should be *internal*, *objective*, and *immediate*.
>
> It should be *internal*. No reason or rule of truth that is provided by an *external authority* can serve as an ultimate criterion. For the reflective doubts that are essential to criteriology can and should be applied to this authority itself. The mind cannot attain to certainty until it has found *within itself* a sufficient reason for adhering to the testimony of such an authority.
>
> The criterion should be *objective*. The ultimate reason for believing cannot be a merely *subjective* state of the thinking subject.

> A man is aware that he can reflect upon his psychological states in order to control them. Knowing that he has this ability, he does not, so long as he has not made use of it, have the right to be sure. The ultimate ground of certitude cannot consist in a subjective feeling. It can be found only in that which, objectively, produces this feeling and is adequate to reason.
>
> Finally, the criterion must be *immediate*. To be sure, a certain conviction may rest upon many different reasons some of which are subordinate to others. But if we are to avoid an infinite regress, then we must find a ground of assent that presupposes no other. We must find an *immediate* criterion of certitude.

Is there a criterion of truth that satisfies these three conditions? If so, what is it?

4

To see how perplexing our problem is, let us consider a figure that Descartes had suggested. . . . Descartes' figure comes to this.

Let us suppose that you have a pile of apples and you want to sort out the good ones from the bad ones. You want to put the good ones in a pile by themselves and throw the bad ones away. This is a useful thing to do, obviously, because the bad apples tend to infect the good ones and then the good ones become bad, too. Descartes thought our beliefs were like this. The bad ones tend to infect the good ones, so we should look them over very carefully, throw out the bad ones if we can, and then—or so Descartes hoped—we would be left with just a stock of good beliefs on which we could rely completely. But how are we to do the sorting? If we are to sort out the good ones from the bad ones, then, of course, we must have a way of recognizing the good ones. Or at least we must have a way of recognizing the bad ones. And—again, of course—you and I do have a way of recognizing good apples and also of recognizing bad ones. The good ones have their own special feel, look, and taste, and so do the bad ones.

But when we turn from apples to beliefs, the matter is quite different. In the case of the apples, we have a method—a criterion—for distinguishing the good ones from the bad ones. But in the case of the beliefs, we do not have a method or a criterion for distinguishing the good ones from the bad ones. Or, at least, we don't have one yet. The question we started with was: How *are* we to tell the good ones from the bad ones? In other words, we were asking: What is the proper method for deciding which are the good beliefs and which are the bad ones—which beliefs are genuine cases of knowledge and which beliefs are not?

And now, you see, we are on the wheel. First, we want to find out which are the good beliefs and which are the bad ones. To find this out we have to have some way—some method—of deciding which are the good ones and which are the bad ones. But there are good and bad methods—good and bad ways—of sorting out the good beliefs from the bad ones. And so we now have a new problem: How are we to decide which are the good methods and which are the bad ones?

If we could fix on a good method for distinguishing between good and bad methods, we might be all set. But this, of course, just moves the problem to a different level. How are we to distinguish between good methods for choosing a good method? If we continue in this way, of course, we are led to an infinite regress and we will never have the answer to our original question.

What do we do in fact? We do know that there are fairly reliable ways of sorting out good beliefs from bad ones. Most people will tell you, for example, that if you follow the procedures of science and of common sense—if you tend carefully to your observations and if you make use of the canons of logic, induction, and the theory of probability—you will be following the best possible procedure for making sure that you will have more good beliefs than bad ones. This is doubtless true. But how do we know that it is? How do we know that the procedures of science, reason, and common sense are the best methods that we have?

If we do know this, it is because we know that these procedures work. It is because we know that these procedures do in fact enable us to distinguish the good beliefs from the bad ones. We say "See—these methods turn out good beliefs." But *how* do we know that they do? It can only be that we already know how to tell the difference between the good beliefs and the bad ones.

And now you can see where the skeptic comes in. He'll say this: "You said you wanted to sort out the good beliefs from the bad ones. Then to do this, you apply the canons of science, common sense, and reason. And now, in answer to the question, 'How do you know that that's the right way to do it?', you say 'Why, I can see that the ones it picks out are the good ones and the ones it leaves behind are the bad ones.' But if you can *see* which ones are the good ones and which ones are the bad ones, why do you think you need a general method for sorting them out?"

5

We can formulate some of the philosophical issues that are involved here by distinguishing two pairs of questions. These are:

A   "*What* do we know? What is the *extent* of our knowledge?"

B   "How are we to decide *whether* we know? What are the *criteria* of knowledge?"

If you happen to know the answers to the first of these pairs of questions, you may have some hope of being able to answer the second. Thus, if you happen to know which are the good apples and which are the bad ones, then maybe you could explain to some other person how he could go about deciding whether or not he has a good apple or a bad one. But if you don't know the answer to the first of these pairs of questions—if you don't know what things you know or how far your knowledge extends—it is difficult to see how you could possibly figure out an answer to the second.

On the other hand, if, somehow, you already know the answers to the second of these pairs of questions, then you may have some hope of being able to answer the first. Thus, if you happen to have a good set of directions for telling whether apples are good or bad, then maybe you can go about finding a good one—assuming, of course, that there are some good apples to be found. But if you don't know the answer to the second of these pairs of questions—if you don't know how to go about deciding whether or not you know, if you don't know what the criteria of knowing are—it is difficult to see how you could possibly figure out an answer to the first.

And so we can formulate the position of the *skeptic* on these matters. He will say: "You cannot answer question A until you have answered question B. And you cannot answer question B until you have answered question A. Therefore you cannot answer either question. You cannot know what, if anything, you know, and there is no possible way for you to decide in any particular case." Is there any reply to this?

6

Broadly speaking, there are at least two other possible views. So we may choose among three possibilities.

There are people—philosophers—who think that they do have an answer to B and that, given their answer to B, they can then figure out their answer to A. And there are other people—other philosophers—who have it the other way around: they think that they have an answer to A and that, given their answer to A, they can then figure out the answer to B.

There don't seem to be any generally accepted names for these two different philosophical positions. (Perhaps this is just as well. There are more than enough names, as it is, for possible philosophical views.) I suggest, for the moment, we use the expressions "methodists" and "particularists." By "methodists," I mean, not the followers of John Wesley's version of Christianity, but those who think they have an answer to B, and who then, in terms of it, work out their answer to A. By "particularists" I mean those who have it the other way around.

7

Thus John Locke was a methodist—in our present, rather special sense of the term. He was able to arrive—somehow—at an answer to B. He said, in effect: "The way you decide whether or not a belief is a good belief—that is to say, the way you decide whether a belief is likely to be a genuine case of knowledge—is to see whether it is derived from sense experience, to see, for example, whether it bears certain relations to your sensations." Just what these relations to our sensations might be is a matter we may leave open, for present purposes. The point is: Locke felt that if a belief is to be credible, it must bear certain relations to the believer's sensations—but he never told us *how* he happened to arrive at this conclusion. This, of course, is the view that has come to be known as "empiricism." David Hume followed Locke in this empiricism and said that empiricism gives us an effective criterion for distinguishing the good apples from the bad ones. You can take this criterion to the library, he said. Suppose you find a book in which the author makes assertions that do not conform to the empirical criterion. Hume said: "Commit it to the flames: for it can contain nothing but sophistry and illusion."

8

Empiricism, then, was a form of what I have called "methodism." The empiricist—like other types of methodist—begins with a criterion and then he uses it to throw out the bad apples. There are two objections, I would say, to empiricism. The first—which applies to every form of methodism (in our present sense of the word)—is that the criterion is very broad and far-reaching and at the same time completely arbitrary. How can one *begin* with a broad generalization? It seems especially odd that the empiricist—who wants to proceed cautiously, step by step, from experience—begins with such a generalization. He leaves us completely in the dark so far as concerns what *reasons* he may have for adopting this particular criterion rather than some other. The second objection applies to empiricism in particular. When we apply the empirical criterion—at least, as it was developed by Hume, as well as by many of those in the nineteenth and twentieth centuries who have called themselves "empiricists"—we seem to throw out, not only the bad apples but the good ones as well, and we are left, in effect, with just a few parings or skins with no meat behind them. Thus Hume virtually conceded that, if you are going to be empiricist, the only matters of fact that you can really know about pertain to the existence of sensations. " 'Tis vain," he said, "to ask whether there be body." He meant you cannot know whether any physical things exist—whether there are trees, or houses, or bodies, much less whether there are atoms or other such microscopic particles. All you can know is that there are and have been certain sensations. You cannot know whether there is any you who experiences those sensations— much less whether any other people exist who experience sensations. And I think, if he had been consistent in his empiricism, he would also have said you cannot really be sure whether there have been any sensations in the past; you can know only that certain sensations exist here and now.

9

The great Scottish philosopher Thomas Reid reflected on all this in the eighteenth century. He was serious about philosophy and man's place in the world. He finds Hume saying things implying that we can know only of the existence of certain sensations here and now. One can imagine him saying: "Good Lord! What kind of nonsense is this?" What he did say, among other things, was this: "A traveller of good judgment may mistake his way, and be unawares led into a wrong track; and while the road is fair before him, he may go on without suspicion and be followed by others but, when it ends in a coal pit, it requires no great judgment to know that he hath gone wrong, nor perhaps to find out what misled him."

Thus Reid, as I interpret him, was not an empiricist; nor was he, more generally, what I have called a "methodist." He was a "particularist." That is to say, he thought that he had an answer to question A, and in terms of the answer to question A, he then worked out kind of an answer to question B. An even better example of a "particularist" is the great twentieth century English philosopher G. E. Moore.

Suppose, for a moment, you were tempted to go along with Hume and say, "The only thing about the world I can really know is that there are now sensations of a certain sort. There's a sensation of a man, there's the sound of a voice, and there's a feeling of bewilderment or bore- dom. But that's all I can really know about." What would Reid say? I can imagine him saying something like this: "Well, you can talk that way if you want to. But you know very well that it isn't true. You know that you are there, that you have a body of such and such a sort and that other people are here, too. And you know about this building and where you were this morning and all kinds of other things as well." G. E. Moore would raise his hand at this point and say: "I know very well this is a hand, and so do you. If you come across some philosophical theory that implies that you and I cannot know that this is a hand, then so much the worse for the theory." I think that Reid and Moore are right, myself, and I'm inclined to think that the "methodists" are wrong.

Going back to our questions A and B, we may summarize the three possible views as follows: there is skepticism (you cannot answer either question without presupposing an answer to the other, and therefore the questions cannot be answered at all); there is "methodism" (you begin with an answer to B); and there is "particularism" (you begin with an answer to A). I suggest that the third possibility is the most reasonable.

10

I would say—and many reputable philosophers would disagree with me—that, to find out whether you know such a thing as that this is a hand, you don't have to apply any test or criterion. Spinoza has it right. "In order to know," he said, "there is no need to know that we know, much less to know that we know that we know."

This is part of the answer, it seems to me, to the puzzle about the diallelus. There are many things that, quite obviously, we do know to be true. If I report to you the things I now see and hear and feel—or, if you prefer, the things I now think I see and hear and feel—the chances are that my report will be correct; I will be telling you something I know. And so, too, if you report the things that you think you now see and hear and feel. To be sure, there are hallucinations and illusions. People often think they see or hear or feel things that in fact they do not see or hear or feel. But from this fact—that our senses do sometimes deceive us—it hardly follows that your senses and mine are deceiving you and me right now. One may say similar things about what we remember.

Having these good apples before us, we can look them over and formulate certain criteria of goodness. Consider the senses, for example. One important criterion—one epistemological principle—was formulated by St. Augustine. It is more reasonable, he said, to trust the senses than to distrust them. Even though there have been illusions and hallucinations, the wise thing, when everything seems all right, is to accept the testimony of the senses. I say "when everything seems all right." If on a particular occasion something about *that* particular occasion makes you suspect that particular report of the senses, if, say, you seem to remember having been drugged or hypnotized, or brainwashed, then perhaps you should have some doubts about what you think you see, or hear, or feel, or smell. But if nothing about this particular occasion leads you to suspect what the senses report on this particular occasion, then the wise thing is to take such a report at its face value. In short the senses should be regarded as innocent until there is some positive reason, on some particular occasion, for thinking that they are guilty on that particular occasion.

One might say the same thing of memory. If, on any occasion, you think you remember that such-and-such an event occurred, then the wise thing is to assume that that particular event did occur—unless something special about this particular occasion leads you to suspect your memory.

We have then a kind of answer to the puzzle about the diallelus. We start with particular cases of knowledge and then from those we generalize and formulate criteria of goodness—criteria telling us what it is for a belief to be epistemologically respectable. Let us now try to sketch somewhat more precisely this approach to the problem of the criterion.

11

The theory of evidence, like ethics and the theory of value, presupposes an objective right and wrong. To explicate the requisite senses of "right" and "wrong," we need the concept of right *preference*—or, more exactly, the concept of one state of mind being *preferable*, epistemically, to another. One state of mind may be *better*, epistemically, than another. This concept of epistemic preferability is what Cardinal Mercier called an *objective* concept. It is one thing to say, objectively, that one state of mind is *to be preferred* to another. It is quite another thing to say, subjectively, that one state of mind is in fact preferred to another—that someone or other happens to prefer the one state of mind to the other. If a state of mind A is to be preferred to a state of mind B, if it is, as I would like to say, intrinsically preferable to B, then anyone who prefers B to A is *mistaken* in his preference.

Given this concept of epistemic preferability, we can readily explicate the basic concepts of the theory of evidence. We could say, for example, that a proposition *p* is *beyond reasonable doubt* t provided only that believing *p* is then epistemically preferable for S to withholding *p*—where by "withholding *p*" we mean the state of neither accepting *p* nor its negation. It is evident to me, for example, that many people are here. This means it is epistemically preferable for me to believe that many people are here than for me neither to believe nor to disbelieve that many are people here.

A proposition is *evident* for a person if it is beyond reasonable doubt for that person and is such that his including it among the propositions upon which he bases his decisions is preferable to his not so including it. A proposition is *acceptable* if withholding it is *not* preferable to believing it. And a proposition is *unacceptable* if withholding it is preferable to believing it.

Again, some propositions are not beyond reasonable doubt but they may be said to have *some presumption in their favor*. I suppose that the proposition that each of us will be alive an hour from now is one that has some presumption in its favor. We could say that a proposition is of this sort provided only that believing the proposition

is epistemically preferable to believing its negation.

Moving in the other direction in the epistemic hierarchy, we could say that a proposition is *certain*, absolutely certain, for a given subject at a given time, if that proposition is then evident to that subject and if there is no other proposition that is such that believing that other proposition is then epistemically preferable for him to believing the given proposition. It is certain for me, I would say, that there seem to be many people here and that 7 and 5 are 12. If this is so, then each of the two propositions is evident to me and there are no other propositions that are such that it would be even better, epistemically, if I were to believe those other propositions.

This concept of epistemic preferability can be axiomatized and made the basis of a system of epistemic logic exhibiting the relations among these and other concepts of the theory of evidence. For present purposes, let us simply note how they may be applied in our approach to the problem of the criterion.

12

Let us begin with the most difficult of the concepts to which we have just referred—that of a proposition being *certain* for a man at a given time. Can we formulate *criteria* of such certainty? I think we can.

Leibniz had said that there are two kinds of immediately evident proposition—the "first truths of fact" and the "first truths of reason." Let us consider each of these in turn.

Among the "first truths of fact," for any man at any given time, I would say, are various propositions about his own state of mind at that time—his thinking certain thoughts, his entertaining certain beliefs, his being in a certain sensory or emotional state. These propositions all pertain to certain states of the man that may be said to manifest or present themselves to him at that time. We could use Meinong's term and say that certain states are "self-presenting," where this concept might be marked off in the following way.

A man's being in a certain state is *self-presenting* to him at a given time provided only that (i) he is in that state at that time and (ii) it is necessarily true that if he is in that state at that time then it is evident to him that he is in that state at that time.

The states of mind just referred to are of this character. Wishing, say, that one were on the moon is a state that is such that a man cannot be in that state without it being evident to him that he is in that state. And so, too, for thinking certain thoughts and having certain sensory or emotional experiences. These states present themselves and are, so to speak, marks of their own evidence. They cannot occur unless it is evident that they occur. I think they are properly called the "first truths of fact." Thus St. Thomas could say that "the intellect knows that it possesses the truth by reflecting on itself."

Perceiving external things and remembering are not states that present themselves. But thinking that one perceives (or seeming to perceive) and thinking that one remembers (or seeming to remember) *are* states of mind that present themselves. And in presenting themselves they may, at least under certain favorable conditions, present something else as well.

Coffey quotes Hobbes as saying that "the inn of evidence has no sign-board." I would prefer saying that these self-presenting states are sign-boards—of the inn of indirect evidence. But these sign-boards need no further sign-boards in order to be presented, for they present themselves.

13

What of the first truths of reason? These are the propositions that some philosophers have called "a priori" and that Leibniz, following Locke, referred to as "maxims" or "axioms." These propositions are all necessary and have a further characteristic that Leibniz described in this way: "You will find in a hundred places that

the Scholastics have said that these propositions are evident, *ex terminis*, as soon as the terms are understood, so that they were persuaded that the force of conviction was grounded in the nature of the terms, i.e. in connection of their ideas." Thus St. Thomas referred to propositions that are "manifest through themselves."

An axiom, one might say, is a necessary proposition such that one cannot understand it without thereby knowing that it is true. Since one cannot know a proposition unless it is evident and one believes it, and since one cannot believe a proposition unless one understands it, we might characterize these first truths of reason in the following way:

A proposition is *axiomatic* for a given subject at a given time provided only that (i) the proposition is one that is necessarily true and (ii) it is also necessarily true that if the person then believes that proposition, the proposition is then evident to him.

We might now characterize the *a priori* somewhat more broadly by saying that a proposition is a priori for a given subject at a given time provided that one or the other of these two things is true: either (i) the proposition is one that is axiomatic for that subject at that time, or else (ii) the proposition is one such that it is evident to the man at that time that the proposition is entailed by a set of propositions that are axiomatic for him at that time.

In characterizing the "first truths of fact" and the "first truths of reason," I have used the expression "evident." But I think it is clear that such truths are not only evident but also certain. And they may be said to be *directly*, or *immediately*, evident.

What, then, of the indirectly evident?

14

I have suggested in rather general terms above what we might say about memory and the senses. These ostensible sources of knowledge are to be treated as innocent until there is positive ground for thinking them guilty. I will not attempt to develop a theory of the indirectly evident at this point. But I will note at least the kind of principle to which we might appeal in developing such a theory.

We could *begin* by considering the following two principles, M and P; M referring to memory, and P referring to perception or the senses.

> M   For any subject S, if it is evident to S that she seems to remember that *a* was F, then it is beyond reasonable doubt for S that *a* was F.
>
> P   For any subject S, if it is evident to S that she thinks she perceives that *a* is F, then it is evident to S that *a* is F.

"She seems to remember" and "she thinks she perceives" here refer to certain self-presenting states that, in the figure I used above, could be said to serve as sign-boards for the inn of indirect evidence.

But principles M and P, as they stand, are much too latitudinarian. We will find that it is necessary to make qualifications and add more and more conditions. Some of these will refer to the subject's sensory state; some will refer to certain of her other beliefs; and some will refer to the relations of confirmation and mutual support. To set them forth in adequate detail would require a complete epistemology.

So far as our problem of the criterion is concerned, the essential thing to note is this. In formulating such principles we will simply proceed as Aristotle did when he formulated his rules for the syllogism. As "particularists" in our approach to the problem of the criterion, we will fit our rules to the cases—to the apples we know to be good and to the apples we know to be bad. Knowing what we do about ourselves and the world, we have at our disposal certain instances that our rules or principles should countenance, and certain other instances that our rules or

principles should rule out or forbid. And, as rational beings, we assume that by investigating these instances we can formulate criteria that any instance must satisfy if it is to be countenanced and we can formulate other criteria that any instance must satisfy if it is to be ruled out or forbidden.

If we proceed in this way we will have satisfied Cardinal Mercier's criteria for a theory of evidence or, as he called it, a theory of certitude. He said that any criterion, or any adequate set of criteria, should be internal, objective, and immediate. The type of criteria I have referred to are certainly *internal*, in his sense of the term. We have not appealed to any external authority as constituting the ultimate test of evidence. (Thus we haven't appealed to "science" or to "the scientists of our culture circle" as constituting the touchstone of what we know.) I would say that our criteria are *objective*. We have formulated them in terms of the concept of epistemic preferability—where the location "p is epistemically preferable to q for S" is taken to refer to an objective relation that obtains independently of the actual preferences of any particular subject. The criteria that we formulate, if they are adequate, will be principles that are necessarily true. And they are also *immediate*. Each of them is such that, if it is applicable at any particular time, then the fact that it is then applicable is capable of being directly evident to that particular subject at that particular time.

15

But in all of this I have presupposed the approach I have called "particularism." The "methodist" and the "skeptic" will tell us that we have started in the wrong place. If now we try to reason with them, then, I am afraid, we will be back on the wheel.

What few philosophers have had the courage to recognize is this: we can deal with the problem only by begging the question. It seems to me that, if we do recognize this fact, as we should, then it is unseemly for us to try to pretend that it isn't so.

One may object: "Doesn't this mean, then, that the skeptic is right after all?" I would answer: "Not at all. His view is only one of the three possibilities and in itself has no more to recommend it than the others do. And in favor of our approach there is the fact that we *do* know many things, after all."

Chapter 36

René Descartes

MEDITATION ONE

Of the things which may be brought within the sphere of the doubtful

It is now some years since I detected how many were the false beliefs that I had from my earliest youth admitted as true, and how doubtful was everything I had since constructed on this basis; and from that time I was convinced that I must once for all seriously undertake to rid myself of all the opinions which I had formerly accepted, and commence to build anew from the foundation, if I wanted to establish any firm and permanent structure in the sciences. But as this enterprise appeared to be a very great one, I waited until I had attained an age so mature that I could not hope that at any later date I should be better fitted to execute my design. This reason caused me to delay so long that I should feel that I was doing wrong were I to occupy in deliberation the time that yet remains to me for action. Today, then, since very opportunely for the plan I have in view I have delivered my mind from every care [and am happily agitated by no passions] and since I have procured for myself an assured leisure in a peaceable retirement, I shall at last seriously and freely address myself to the general upheaval of all my former opinions.

Now for this object it is not necessary that I should show that all of these are false—I shall perhaps never arrive at this end. But inasmuch as reason already persuades me that I ought no less carefully to withhold my assent from matters which are not entirely certain and indubitable than from those which appear to me manifestly to be false, if I am able to find in each one some reason to doubt, this will suffice to justify my rejecting the whole. And for that end it will not be requisite that I should examine each in particular, which would be an endless undertaking; for owing to the fact that the destruction of the foundations of necessity brings with it the downfall of the rest of the edifice, I shall only in the first place attack those principles upon which all my former opinions rested.

All that up to the present time I have accepted as most true and certain I have learned either from the senses or through the senses; but it is sometimes proved to me that these senses are deceptive, and it is wiser not to trust entirely to any thing by which we have once been deceived.

But it may be that although the senses sometimes deceive us concerning things which are hardly perceptible, or very far away, there are yet many others to be met with as to which we cannot reasonably have any doubt, although we recognize them by their means. For example, there is the fact that I am here, seated by the fire, attired in a dressing gown, having this paper in my hands and other similar matters. And how could I deny that these hands and this body are mine, were it not perhaps that I compare myself to certain persons, devoid of sense, whose cerebella are so troubled and clouded by the violent vapors of black bile, that they constantly assure us that they think they are kings when they are really quite poor, or that they are clothed in purple when they are really without covering, or who imagine that they have an earthenware head or are nothing but pumpkins or are made of glass. But they are mad, and I should not be any the less insane were I to follow examples so extravagant.

At the same time I must remember that I am a man, and that consequently I am in the habit of sleeping, and in my dreams representing to myself the same things or sometimes even less probable things, than do those who are insane in their waking moments. How often has it happened to me that in the night I dreamt that I found myself in this particular place, that I was dressed and seated near the fire, whilst in reality I was lying undressed in bed! At this moment it does indeed seem to me that it is with eyes awake that I am looking at this paper; that this head which I move is not asleep, that it is deliberately and of set purpose that I extend my hand and perceive it; what happens in sleep does not appear so clear nor so distinct as does all this. But in thinking over this I remind myself that on many occasions I have in sleep been deceived by similar illusions, and in dwelling carefully on this reflection I see so manifestly that there are no certain indications by which we may clearly distinguish wakefulness from sleep that I am lost in astonishment. And my astonishment is such that it is almost capable of persuading me that I now dream.

Now let us assume that we are asleep and that all these particulars, e.g. that we open our eyes, shake our head, extend our hands, and so on, are but false delusions; and let us reflect that possibly neither our hands nor our whole body are such as they appear to us to be. At the same time we must at least confess that the things which are represented to us in sleep are like painted representations which can only have been formed as the counterparts of something real and true, and that in this way those general things at least, i.e.

eyes, a head, hands, and a whole body, are not imaginary things, but things really existent. For, as a matter of fact, painters, even when they study with the greatest skill to represent sirens and satyrs by forms the most strange and extraordinary, cannot give them natures which are entirely new, but merely make a certain medley of the members of different animals; or if their imagination is extravagant enough to invent something so novel that nothing similar has ever before been seen, and that then their work represents a thing purely fictitious and absolutely false, it is certain all the same that the colors of which this is composed are necessarily real. And for the same reason, although these general things, to wit, [a body], eyes, a head, hands, and such like, may be imaginary, we are bound at the same time to confess that there are at least some other objects yet more simple and more universal, which are real and true; and of these just in the same way as with certain real colors, all these images of things which dwell in our thoughts, whether true and real or false and fantastic, are formed.

To such a class of things pertains corporeal nature in general, and its extension, the figure of extended things, their quantity or magnitude and number, as also the place in which they are, the time which measures their duration, and so on.

That is possibly why our reasoning is not unjust when we conclude from this that Physics, Astronomy, Medicine, and all other sciences which have as their end the consideration of composite things, are very dubious and uncertain; but that Arithmetic, Geometry, and other sciences of that kind which only treat of things that are very simple and very general, without taking great trouble to ascertain whether they are actually existent or not, contain some measure of certainty and an element of the indubitable. For whether I am awake or asleep, two and three together always form five, and the square can never have more than four sides, and it does not seem possible that truths so clear and apparent can be suspected of any falsity [or uncertainty].

Nevertheless I have long had fixed in my mind the belief that an all-powerful God existed by whom I have been created such as I am. But how do I know that He has not brought it to pass that there is no earth, no heaven, no extended body, no magnitude, no place, and that nevertheless [I possess the perceptions of all these things and that] they seem to me to exist just exactly as I now see them? And, besides, as I sometimes imagine that others deceive themselves in the things which they think they know best, how do I know that I am not deceived every time that I add two and three, or count the sides of a square, or judge of things yet simpler, if anything simpler can be imagined? But possibly God has not desired that I should be thus deceived, for He is said to be supremely good. If, however, it is contrary to His goodness to have made me such that I constantly deceive myself, it would also appear to be contrary to His goodness to permit me to be sometimes deceived, and nevertheless I cannot doubt that He does permit this.

There may indeed be those who would prefer to deny the existence of a God so powerful, rather than believe that all other things are uncertain. But let us not oppose them for the present, and grant that all that is here said of a God is a fable; nevertheless in whatever way they suppose that I have arrived at the state of being that I have reached—whether they attribute it to fate or to accident, or make out that it is by a continual succession of antecedents, or by some other method—since to err and deceive oneself is a defect, it is clear that the greater will be the probability of my being so imperfect as to deceive myself ever, as is the Author to whom they assign my origin the less powerful. To these reasons I have certainly nothing to reply, but at the end I feel constrained to confess that there is nothing in all that I formerly believed to be true, of which I cannot in some measure doubt, and that not merely through want of thought

or through levity, but for reasons which are very powerful and maturely considered; so that henceforth I ought not the less carefully to refrain from giving credence to these opinions than to that which is manifestly false, if I desire to arrive at any certainty [in the sciences].

But it is not sufficient to have made these remarks; we must also be careful to keep them in mind. For these ancient and commonly held opinions still revert frequently to my mind, long and familiar custom having given them the right to occupy my mind against my inclination and rendered them almost masters of my belief; nor will I ever lose the habit of deferring to them or of placing my confidence in them, so long as I consider them as they really are, i.e. opinions in some measure doubtful, as I have just shown, and at the same time highly probable, so that there is much more reason to believe in than to deny them. That is why I consider that I shall not be acting amiss, if, taking of set purpose a contrary belief, I allow myself to be deceived, and for a certain time pretend that all these opinions are entirely false and imaginary, until at last, having thus balanced my former prejudices with my latter [so that they cannot divert my opinions more to one side than to the other], my judgement will no longer be dominated by bad usage or turned away from the right knowledge of the truth. For I am assured that there can be neither peril nor error in this course, and that I cannot at present yield too much to distrust, since I am not considering the question of action, but only of knowledge.

I shall then suppose, not that God who is supremely good and the fountain of truth, but some evil genius not less powerful than deceitful, has employed his whole energies in deceiving me; I shall consider that the heavens, the earth, colors, figures, sound, and all other external things are nought but the illusions and dreams of which this genius has availed himself in order to lay traps for my credulity; I shall consider myself as having no hands, no eyes, no flesh, no blood, nor any senses, yet falsely believing myself to possess all these things; I shall remain obstinately attached to this idea, and if by this means it is not in my power to arrive at the knowledge of any truth, I may at least do what is in my power [i.e. suspend my judgement], and with firm purpose avoid giving credence to any false thing, or being imposed upon by this arch deceiver, however powerful and deceptive he may be. But this task is a laborious one, and insensibly a certain lassitude leads me into the course of my ordinary life. And just as a captive who in sleep enjoys an imaginary liberty, when he begins to suspect that his liberty is but a dream, fears to awaken, and conspires with these agreeable illusions that the deception may be prolonged, so insensibly of my own accord I fall back into my former opinions, and I dread awakening from this slumber, lest the laborious wakefulness which would follow the tranquility of this repose should have to be spent not in daylight, but in the excessive darkness of the difficulties which have just been discussed.

Chapter 37

O. K. Bouwsma

DESCARTES' EVIL GENIUS

There was once an evil genius who promised the mother of us all that if she ate of the fruit of the tree, she would be like God, knowing good and evil. He promised knowledge. She did eat and she learned, but she was disappointed, for to know good and evil and not to be God is awful. Many an Eve later, there was rumor of another evil genius. This evil genius promised no good, promised no knowledge. He made a boast, a boast so wild and so deep and so dark that those who heard it cringed in hearing it. And what was that boast? Well, that apart from a few, four or five, clear and distinct ideas, he could deceive any son of Adam about anything. So he boasted. And with some result? Some indeed! Men going about in the brightest noonday would look and exclaim: "How obscure!" and if some careless merchant counting his apples was heard to say: "Two and three are five," a hearer of the boast would rub his eyes and run away. This evil genius still whispers, thundering, among the leaves of books, frightening people, whispering: "I can. Maybe I will. Maybe so, maybe not." The tantalizer! In what follows I should like to examine the boast of this evil genius.

I am referring, of course, to that evil genius of whom Descartes writes:

I shall then suppose, not that God who is supremely good and the fountain of truth, but some evil genius not less powerful than deceitful, has employed his whole energies in deceiving me; I shall consider that the heavens, the earth, the colors, figures, sound, and all other external things are nought but illusions and dreams of which this evil genius has availed himself, in order to lay traps for my credulity; I shall consider myself as having no hands, no eyes, no flesh, no blood, nor any senses, yet falsely believing myself to possess all these things.[1]

This then is the evil genius whom I have represented as boasting that he can deceive us about all these things. I intend now to examine this boast, and to understand how this deceiving and being deceived are to take place. I expect to discover that the evil genius may very well deceive us, but that if we are wary, we need not be deceived. He will deceive us, if he does, by bathing the word "illusion" in a fog. This then will be the word to keep our minds on. In order to accomplish all this, I intend to describe the evil genius carrying out his boast in two adventures. The first of these I shall consider a thoroughly transparent case of deception. The word "illusion" will find a clear and familiar application. Nevertheless in this instance the evil genius will not have exhausted "his whole energies in deceiving us." Hence we must aim to imagine a further trial of the boast, in which the "whole energies" of the evil genius are exhausted. In this instance I intend to show that the evil genius is himself befuddled, and that if we too exhaust some of our energies in sleuthing after the peculiarities in his diction, then we need not be deceived either.

Let us imagine the evil genius then at his ease meditating that very bad is good enough for him, and that he would let bad enough alone. All the old pseudos, pseudo names and pseudo statements, are doing very well. But today it was different. He took no delight in common lies, everyday fibs, little ones, old ones. He wanted something new and something big. He scratched his genius; he uncovered an idea. And he scribbled on the inside of his tattered halo, "Tomorrow, I will deceive," and he smiled, and his words were thin and like fine wire. "Tomorrow I will change everything, every-thing, everything. I will change flowers, human beings, trees, hills, sky, the sun, and everything else into paper. Paper alone I will not change. There will be paper flowers, paper human beings, paper trees. And human beings will be deceived. They will think that there are flowers, human beings, and trees, and there will be nothing but paper. It will be gigantic. And it ought to work. After all men have been deceived with much less trouble. There was a sailor, a Baptist I believe, who said that all was water. And there was no more water then than there is now. And there was a pool-hall keeper who said that all was billiard balls. That's a long time ago of course, a long time before they opened one, and listening, heard that it was full of the sound of a trumpet. My prospects are good. I'll try it."

And the evil genius followed his own direc-tions and did according to his words. And this is what happened.

Imagine a young man, Tom, bright today as he was yesterday, approaching a table where yesterday he had seen a bowl of flowers. Today it suddenly strikes him that they are not flowers. He stares at them troubled, looks away, and looks again. Are they flowers? He shakes his head. He chuckles to himself. "Huh! that's funny. Is this a trick? Yesterday there certainly were flowers in that bowl." He sniffs suspiciously, hopefully, but smells nothing. His nose gives no assurance. He thinks of the birds that flew down to peck at the grapes in the picture and of the mare that whinnied at the likeness of Alexander's horse. Illusions! The picture oozed no juice, and the likeness was still. He walked slowly to the bowl of flowers. He looked, and he sniffed, and he raised his hand. He stroked a petal lightly, lover of flowers, and he drew back. He could scarcely believe his fingers. They were not flowers. They were paper.

As he stands, perplexed, Milly, friend and dear, enters the room. Seeing him occupied with the flowers, she is about to take up the bowl and offer them to him, when once again he is overcome with feelings of strangeness. She looks just like a great big doll. He looks more closely, closely as he dares, seeing this may be Milly after all. Milly, are you Milly?—that wouldn't do. Her mouth clicks as she opens it, speaking, and it shuts precisely. Her forehead shines, and he shudders at the thought of Mme Tussaud's. Her hair is plaited, evenly, perfectly, like Milly's but as she raises one hand to guard its order, touching it, preening, it whispers like a news-paper. Her teeth are white as a genteel monthly. Her gums are pink, and there is a clapper in her mouth. He thinks of mama dolls, and of the rub-ber doll he used to pinch; it had a misplaced navel right in the pit of the back, that whistled. Galatea in paper! Illusions!

He notes all these details, flash by flash by flash. He reaches for a chair to steady himself and just in time. She approaches with the bowl of flowers, and, as the bowl is extended towards him, her arms jerk. The suppleness, the smooth-ness, the roundness of life is gone. Twitches of a smile mislight up her face. He extends his hand to take up the bowl and his own arms jerk as hers did before. He takes the bowl, and as he does so sees his hand. It is pale, fresh, snowy. Trembling, he drops the bowl, but it does not break, and the water does not run. What a mockery!

He rushes to the window, hoping to see the real world. The scene is like a theater-set. Even the pane in the window is drawn very thin, like cellophane. In the distance are the forms of men walking about and tossing trees and houses and boulders and hills upon the thin cross section of a truck that echoes only echoes of chugs as it moves. He looks into the sky upward, and it is low. There is a patch straight above him, and one seam is loose. The sun shines out of the blue like a drop of German silver. He reaches out with his pale hand, crackling the cellophane, and his hand touches the sky. The sky shakes and tiny bits of it fall, flaking his white hand with confetti.

Make-believe!

He retreats, crinkling, creaking, hiding his sight. As he moves he misquotes a line of poetry: "Those are perils that were his eyes," and he mutters, "Hypocritical pulp!" He goes on: "I see that the heavens, the earth, colors, figures, sound, and all other external things, flowers, Milly, trees and rocks and hills are paper, paper laid as traps for my credulity. Paper flowers, paper Milly, paper sky!" Then he paused, and in sudden fright he asked, "And what about me?" He reaches to his lip and with two fingers tears the skin and peels off a strip of newsprint. He looks at it closely, grim. "I shall consider myself as having no hands, no eyes, no flesh, no blood, or any senses." He lids his paper eyes and stands dejected. Suddenly he is cheered. He exclaims: "*Cogito me papyrum esse, ergo sum.*" He has triumphed over paperdom.

I have indulged in this phantasy in order to illustrate the sort of situation which Descartes' words might be expected to describe. The evil genius attempts to deceive. He tries to mislead Tom into thinking what is not. Tom is to think that these are flowers, that this is the Milly that was, that those are trees, hills, the heavens, etc. And he does this by creating illusions, that is, by making something that looks like flowers, artificial flowers; by making something that looks like and sounds like and moves like Milly, an artificial Milly. An illusion is something that looks like or sounds like, so much like, some-

thing else that you either mistake it for something else, or you can easily understand how someone might come to do this. So when the evil genius creates illusions intending to deceive he makes things which might quite easily be mistaken for what they are not. Now in the phantasy as I discovered it Tom is not deceived. He does experience the illusion, however. The intention of this is not to cast any reflection upon the deceptive powers of the evil genius. With such refinements in the paper art as we now know, the evil genius might very well have been less unsuccessful. And that in spite of his rumored lament: "And I made her of the best paper!" No, that Tom is not deceived, that he detects the illusion, is introduced in order to remind ourselves how illusions are detected. That the paper flowers are illusory is revealed by the recognition that they are paper. As soon as Tom realizes that though they look like flowers but are paper, he is acquainted with, sees through the illusion, and is not deceived. What is required, of course, is that he know the difference between flowers and paper, and that when presented with one or the other he can tell the difference. The attempt of the evil genius also presupposes this. What he intends is that though Tom knows this difference, the paper will look so much like flowers that Tom will not notice the respect in which the paper is different from the flowers. And even though Tom had actually been deceived and had not recognized the illusion, the evil genius himself must have been aware of the difference, for this is involved in his design. This is crucial, as we shall see when we come to consider the second adventure of the evil genius.

As you will remember I have represented the foregoing as an illustration of the sort of situation which Descartes' words might be expected to describe. Now, however, I think that this is misleading. For though I have described a situation in which there are many things, nearly all of which are calculated to serve as illusions, this question may still arise. Would this paper world still be properly described as a world of illusions? If Tom says: "These are flowers," or "These look like flowers" (uncertainly), then the illusion is operative. But if Tom says: "These are paper," then the illusion has been destroyed. Descartes uses the words: "And all other external things are nought but illusions." This means that the situation which Descartes has in mind is such that if Tom says: "These are flowers," he will be wrong, but he will be wrong also if he says: "These are paper," and it won't matter what sentence of that type he uses. If he says: "These are rock"—or cotton or cloud or wood—he is wrong by the plan. He will be right only if he says: "These are illusions." But the project is to keep him from recognizing the illusions. This means that the illusions are to be brought about not by anything so crude as paper or even cloud. They must be made of the stuff that dreams are made of.

Now let us consider this second adventure.

The design then is this. The evil genius is to create a world of illusions. There are to be no flowers, no Milly, no paper. There is to be nothing at all, but Tom is every moment to go on mistaking nothing for something, nothing at all for flowers, nothing at all for Milly, etc. This is, of course, quite different from mistaking paper for flowers, paper for Milly. And yet all is to be arranged in such a way that Tom will go on just as we now do, and just as Tom did before the paper age, to see, hear, smell the world. He will love the flowers, he will kiss Milly, he will blink at the sun. So he thinks. And in thinking about these things he will talk and argue just as we do. But all the time he will be mistaken. There are no flowers, there is no kiss, there is no sun. Illusions all. This then is the end at which the evil genius aims.

How now is the evil genius to attain this end? Well, it is clear that a part of what he aims at will be realized if he destroys everything. Then there will be no flowers, and if Tom thinks that there are flowers he will be wrong. There will be no face that is Milly's and no tumbled beauty on her head, and if Tom thinks that there is Milly's face

and Milly's hair, he will be wrong. It is necessary then to see to it that there are none of these things. So the evil genius, having failed with paper, destroys even all paper. Now there is nothing to see, nothing to hear, nothing to smell, etc. But this is not enough to deceive. For though Tom sees nothing, and neither hears nor smells anything, he may also think that he sees nothing. He must also be misled into thinking that he does see something, that there are flowers and Milly, and hands, eyes, flesh, blood, and all other senses. Accordingly the evil genius restores to Tom his old life. Even the memory of that paper day is blotted out, not a scrap remains. Witless Tom lives on, thinking, hoping, loving as he used to, unwitted by the great destroyer. All that seems so solid, so touchable to seeming hands, so biteable to apparent teeth, is so flimsy that were the evil genius to poke his index at it, it would curl away save for one tiny trace, the smirch of that index. So once more the evil genius has done according to his word.

And now let us examine the result.

I should like first of all to describe a passage of Tom's life. Tom is all alone, but he doesn't know it. What an opportunity for methodologico-metaphysico-solipsimo! I intend, in any case, to disregard the niceties of his being so alone and to borrow his own words, with the warning that the evil genius smiles as he reads them. Tom writes:

Today, as usual, I came into the room and there was the bowl of flowers on the table. I went up to them, caressed them, and smelled over them. I thank God for flowers! There's nothing so real to me as flowers. Here the genuine essence of the world's substance, at its gayest and most hilarious speaks to me. It seems unworthy even to think of them as erect, and waving on pillars of sap. Sap! Sap!

There was more in the same vein, which we need not bother to record. I might say that the evil genius was a bit amused, snickered in fact, as he read the words "so real," "essence," "substance," etc., but later he frowned and seemed puzzled. Tom went on to describe how Milly came into the room, and how glad he was to see her. They talked about the flowers. Later he walked to the window and watched the gardener clearing a space a short distance away. The sun was shining, but there were a few heavy clouds. He raised the window, extended his hand and four large drops of rain wetted his hand. He returned to the room and quoted to Milly a song from *The Tempest*. He got all the words right, and was well pleased with himself. There was more he wrote, but this is enough to show how quite normal everything seems. And, too, how successful the evil genius is.

And the evil genius said to himself, not quite in solipsimo, "Not so, not so, not at all so."

The evil genius was, however, all too human. Admiring himself but unadmired, he yearned for admiration. To deceive but to be unsuspected is too little glory. The evil genius set about then to plant the seeds of suspicion. But how to do this? Clearly there was no suggestive paper to tempt Tom's confidence. There was nothing but Tom's mind, a stream of seemings and of words to make the seemings seem no seemings. The evil genius must have words with Tom and must engage the same seemings with him. To have words with Tom is to have the words together, to use them in the same way, and to engage the same seemings is to see and to hear and to point to the same. And so the evil genius, free spirit, entered in at the door of Tom's pineal gland and lodged there. He floated in the humors that flow, glandwise and sensewise, everywhere being as much one with Tom as difference will allow. He looked out of the same eyes, and when Tom pointed with his finger, the evil genius said "This" and meant what Tom, hearing, also meant, seeing. Each heard with the same ear what the other heard. For every sniffing of the one nose there were two identical smells, and there were two tactualities for every touch. If Tom had had a toothache, together they would

have pulled the same face. The twinsomeness of two monads finds here the limit of identity. Nevertheless there was otherness looking out of those eyes as we shall see.

It seems then that on the next day, the evil genius "going to and fro" in Tom's mind and "walking up and down in it," Tom once again, as his custom was, entered the room where the flowers stood on the table. He stopped, looked admiringly, and in a caressing voice said: "Flowers! Flowers!" And he lingered. The evil genius, more subtle "than all the beasts of the field," whispered "Flowers? Flowers?" For the first time Tom has an intimation of company, of some intimate partner in perception. Momentarily he is checked. He looks again at the flowers. "Flowers? Why, of course, flowers." Together they look out of the same eyes. Again the evil genius whispers, "Flowers?" The seed of suspicion is to be the question. But Tom now raises the flowers nearer to his eyes almost violently as though his eyes were not his own. He is, however, not perturbed. The evil genius only shakes their head. "Did you ever hear of illusions?" says he.

Tom, still surprisingly good-natured, responds: "But you saw them, didn't you? Surely you can see through my eyes. Come, let us bury my nose deep in these blossoms, and take one long breath together. Then tell whether you can recognize these as flowers."

So they dunked the one nose. But the evil genius said "Huh!" as much as to say: What has all this seeming and smelling to do with it? Still he explained nothing. And Tom remained as confident of the flowers as he had been at the first. The little seeds of doubt, "Flowers? Flowers?" and again "Flowers?" and "Illusions?" and now this stick in the spokes, "Huh!" made Tom uneasy. He went on: "Oh, so you are one of these seers that has to touch everything. You're a tangibilite. Very well, here's my hand, let's finger these flowers. Careful! They're tender."

The evil genius was amused. He smiled inwardly and rippled in a shallow humor. To be taken for a materialist! As though the grand illusionist was not a spirit! Nevertheless, he realized that though deception is easy where the lies are big enough (where had he heard that before?), a few scattered, questioning words are not enough to make guile grow. He was tempted to make a statement, and he did. He said, "Your flowers are nothing but illusions."

"My flowers illusions?" exclaimed Tom, and he took up the bowl and placed it before a mirror. "See," said he, "here are the flowers and here, in the mirror, is an illusion. There's a difference surely. And you with my eyes, my nose, and my fingers can tell what that difference is. Pollen on your fingers touching the illusion? Send Milly the flowers in the mirror? Set a bee to suck honey out of this glass? You know all this as well as I do. I can tell flowers from illusions, and my flowers, as you now plainly see, are not illusions."

The evil genius was now sorely tried. He had his make-believe, but he also had his pride. Would he now risk the make-believe to save his pride? Would he explain? He explained.

"Tom," he said, "notice. The flowers in the mirror look like flowers, but they only look like flowers. We agree about that. The flowers before the mirror also look like flowers. But they, you say, are flowers because they also smell like flowers and they feel like flowers, as though they would be any more flowers because they also like flowers multiply. Imagine a mirror such that it reflected not only the looks of flowers, but also their fragrance and their petal surfaces, and then you smelled and touched, and the flowers before the mirror would be just like the flowers in the mirror. Then you could see immediately that the flowers before the mirror are illusions just as those in the mirror are illusions. As it is now, it is clear that the flowers in the mirror are thin illusions, and the flowers before the mirror are thick. Thick illusions are the best for deception. And they may be as thick as you like. From them you may gather pollen, send them to Milly, and foolish bees may sleep in them."

But Tom was not asleep. "I see that what you mean by thin illusions is what I mean by illusions, and what you mean by thick illusions is what I mean by flowers. So when you say that my flowers are your thick illusions this doesn't bother me. And as for your mirror that mirrors all layers of your thick illusions, I shouldn't call that a mirror at all. It's a duplicator, and much more useful than a mirror, provided you can control it. But I do suppose that when you speak of thick illusions you do mean that thick illusions are related to something you call flowers in much the same way that the thin illusions are related to the thick ones. Is that true?"

The evil genius was now diction-deep in explanations and went on. "In the first place let me assure you that these are not flowers. I destroyed all flowers. There are no flowers at all. There are only thin and thick illusions of flowers. I can see your flowers in the mirror, and I can smell and touch the flowers before the mirror. What I cannot smell and touch, having seen as in the mirror, is not even thick illusion. But if I cannot also *cerpicio* what I see, smell, touch, etc., what I have then seen is not anything real. *Esse est cerpici.* I just now tried to *cerpicio* your flowers, but there was nothing there. Man is after all a four- or five- or six-sense creature and you cannot expect much from so little."

Tom rubbed his eyes and his ears tingled with an eighteenth-century disturbance. Then he stared at the flowers. "I see," he said, "that this added sense of yours has done wickedly with our language. You do not mean by illusion what we mean, and neither do you mean by flowers what we mean. As for *cerpicio* I wouldn't be surprised if you'd made up that word just to puzzle us. In any case what you destroyed is what, according to you, you used to *cerpicio*. So there is nothing for you to *cerpicio* any more. But there still are what we mean by flowers. If your intention was to deceive, you must learn the language of those you are to deceive. I should say that you are like the doctor who prescribes for his patients what is so bad for himself and is then surprised at the health of his patients." And he pinned a flower near their nose.

The evil genius, discomfited, rode off on a corpuscle. He had failed. He took to an artery, made haste to the pineal exit, and was gone. Then "sun by sun" he fell. And he regretted his mischief.

I have tried in this essay to understand the boast of the evil genius. His boast was that he could deceive, deceive about "the heavens, the earth, the colors, figures, sound, and all other external things." In order to do this I have tried to bring clearly to mind what deception and such deceiving would be like. Such deception involves illusions and such deceiving involves the creation of illusions. Accordingly I have tried to imagine the evil genius engaged in the practice of deception, busy in the creation of illusions. In the first adventure everything is plain. The evil genius employs paper, paper making believe it's many other things. The effort to deceive, ingenuity in deception, being deceived by paper, detecting the illusion — all these are clearly understood. It is the second adventure, however, which is more crucial. For in this instance it is assumed that the illusion is of such a kind that no seeing, no touching, no smelling, are relevant to detecting the illusion. Nevertheless the evil genius sees, touches, smells, and does detect the illusion. He made the illusion; so, of course, he must know it. How then does he know it? The evil genius has a sense denied to men. He senses the flower-in-itself, Milly-in-herself, etc. So he creates illusions made up of what can be seen, heard, smelled, etc., illusions all because when seeing, hearing, and smelling have seen, heard, and smelled all, the special sense senses nothing. So what poor human beings sense is the illusion of what only the evil genius can sense. This is formidable. Nevertheless, once again everything is clear. If we admit the special sense, then we can readily see how it is that the evil genius should have been so confident. He has certainly created his own illusions, though he has not himself been deceived. But neither has anyone else been deceived. For human beings do not use the word "illusion" by relation to a sense with which only the evil genius is blessed.

I said that the evil genius had not been deceived, and it is true that he has not been deceived by his own illusions. Nevertheless he was deceived in boasting that he could deceive, for his confidence in this is based upon an ignorance of the difference between our uses of the words, "heavens," "earth," "flowers," "Milly," and "illusions" of these things, and his own uses of these words. For though there certainly is an analogy between our own uses and his, the difference is quite sufficient to explain his failure at grand deception. We can also understand how easily Tom might have been taken in. The dog over the water dropped his meaty bone for a picture on the water. Tom, however, dropped nothing at all. But the word "illusion" is a trap.

I began this essay uneasily, looking at my hands and saying "no hands," blinking my eyes and saying "no eyes." Everything I saw seemed to me like something Cheshire, a piece of cheese, for instance, appearing and disappearing in the leaves of the tree. Poor kitty! And now? Well . . .

Note

1 *Philosophical Works of Descartes*, I, 147.

Chapter 38

G. E. Moore

CERTAINTY

Suppose I say: 'I know for certain that I am standing up; it is absolutely certain that I am; there is not the smallest chance that I am not.' Many philosophers would say: 'You are wrong: you do not know that you are standing up; it is *not* absolutely certain that you are; there is *some* chance, though perhaps only a very small one, that you are not.' And one argument which has been used as an argument in favour of saying this, is an argument in the course of which the philosopher who used it would assert: 'You do not know for certain that you are not dreaming; it is not absolutely certain that you are not; there is *some* chance, though perhaps only a very small one, that you are.' And from this, that I do not know for certain that I am not dreaming, it is supposed to follow that I do not know for certain that I am standing up. It is argued: If it is not certain that you are not dreaming, then it is not certain that you are standing up. And that if I don't know that I'm not dreaming, I also don't know that I'm not sitting down, I don't feel at all inclined to dispute. From the hypothesis that I am dreaming, it would, I think, certainly follow that I don't *know* that I am standing up; though I have never seen the matter argued, and though it is not at all clear to me how it is to be proved that it would follow. But, on the other hand, from the hypothesis that I am dreaming, it certainly would not follow that I am *not* standing up; for it is certainly logically possible that a man should be fast asleep and dreaming, while he is standing

up and not lying down. It is therefore logically possible that I should both be standing up and also at the same time dreaming that I am; just as the story, about a well-known Duke of Devonshire, that he once dreamt that he was speaking in the House of Lords and, when he woke up, found that he *was* speaking in the House of Lords, is certainly logically possible. And if, as is commonly assumed, when I am dreaming that I am standing up it may also be correct to say that I am *thinking* that I am standing up, then it follows that the hypothesis that I am now dreaming is quite consistent with the hypothesis that I am both thinking that I am standing up and also actually standing up. And hence, if as seems to me to be certainly the case and as this argument assumes, from the hypothesis that I am now dreaming it *would* follow that I don't know that I am standing up, there follows a point which is of great importance with regard to our use of the word 'knowledge,' and therefore also of the word 'certainty' – a point which has been made quite conclusively more than once by Russell, namely that from the conjunction of the two facts that a man thinks that a given proposition *p* is true, and that *p* is in fact true, it does *not* follow that the man in question *knows* that *p* is true: in order that I may be justified in saying that I know that I am standing up, something more is required than the mere conjunction of the two facts that I both think I am and actually am – as Russell has expressed it, true belief is not identical with knowledge; and I think we may further add that even from the conjunction of the two facts that I feel certain that I am and that I actually am it would not follow that I know that I am, nor therefore that it is certain that I am. As regards the argument drawn from the fact that a man who dreams that he is standing up and happens at the moment actually to be standing up will nevertheless not *know* that he is standing up, it should indeed be noted that from the fact that a man is dreaming that he is standing up, it certainly does not *follow* that he *thinks* he is standing up; since it does sometimes happen in a dream that we *think* that it is a dream, and a man who thought this certainly might, although he was dreaming that he was standing up, yet *think* that he was not, although he could not *know* that he was not. It is not therefore the case, as might be hastily assumed, that, if I dream that I am standing up at a time when I am in fact lying down, I am necessarily *deceived*: I should be deceived only if I thought I was standing when I wasn't; and I may dream that I am, without thinking that I am. It certainly does, however, often happen that we do dream that so-and-so is the case, without at the time thinking that we are only dreaming; and in such cases, I think we may perhaps be said to *think* that what we dream is the case is the case, and to be deceived if it is not the case; and therefore also, in such cases, if what we dream to be the case happens also to *be* the case, we may be said to be thinking truly that it is the case, although we certainly do not *know* that it is.

I agree, therefore, with that part of this argument which asserts that if I don't know now that I'm not dreaming, it follows that I don't know that I am standing up, even if I both actually am and think that I am. But this first part of the argument is a consideration which cuts both ways. For, if it is true, it follows that it is also true that if I *do* know that I am standing up, then I do know that I am not dreaming. I can therefore just as well argue: since I do know that I'm standing up, it follows that I do know that I'm not dreaming; as my opponent can argue: since you don't know

that you're not dreaming, it follows that you don't know that you're standing up. The one argument is just as good as the other, unless my opponent can give better reasons for asserting that I don't know that I'm not dreaming, than I can give for asserting that I do know that I am standing up.

What reasons can be given for saying that I don't know for certain that I'm not at this moment dreaming?

I do not think that I have ever seen clearly stated any argument which is supposed to show this. But I am going to try to state, as clearly as I can, the premisses and the reasonings from them, which I think have led so many philosophers to suppose that I really cannot now know for certain that I am not dreaming.

I said, you may remember, in talking of the seven assertions with which I opened this lecture, that I had 'the evidence of my senses' for them, though I also said that I didn't think this was the only evidence I had for them, nor that this by itself was necessarily conclusive evidence. Now if I had *then* 'the evidence of my senses' in favour of the proposition that I was standing up, I certainly have *now* the evidence of my senses in favour of the proposition that I *am* standing up, even though this may not be all the evidence that I have, and may not be conclusive. But have I, in fact, the evidence of my senses *at all* in favour of this proposition? One thing seems to me to be quite clear about our use of this phrase, namely, that, if a man at a given time is only dreaming that he is standing up, then it follows that he has *not* at that time the evidence of his senses in favour of that proposition: to say 'Jones last night was *only* dreaming that he was standing up, and yet all the time he had the evidence of his senses that he was' is to say something self-contradictory. But those philosophers who say it is possible that I am now dreaming, certainly mean to say also that it is possible that I am *only dreaming* that I am standing up; and this view, we now see, entails that it is possible that I have *not* the evidence of my senses that I am. If, therefore, they are right, it follows that it is not certain even that I have the evidence of my senses that I am; it follows that it is not certain that I have *the evidence of my senses* for anything at all. If, therefore, I were to say now, that I certainly have the evidence of my senses in favour of the proposition that I am standing up, even if it's not certain that I am standing up, I should be begging the very question now at issue. For if it is not certain that I am not dreaming, it is not certain that I even have the evidence of my senses that I am standing up.

But, now, even if it is not certain that I have at this moment the evidence of my senses for anything at all, it is quite certain that I *either* have the evidence of my senses that I am standing up *or* have an experience which is *very like* having the evidence of my senses that I am standing up. If I am dreaming, this experience consists in having dream-images which are at least very like the sensations I should be having if I were awake and had the sensations, the having of which would constitute 'having the evidence of my senses' that I am standing up. Let us use the expression 'sensory experience', in such a way that this experience which I certainly am having will be a 'sensory experience', whether or not it merely consists in the having of dream-images. If we use the expression 'sensory experience' in this way, we can say, I think, that, if it is not certain that I am not dreaming now, then it is not certain that *all* the sensory experiences I am now having are not mere dream-images.

What then are the premisses and the reasonings which would lead so many philosophers to think that all the sensory exeperiences I am having now *may* be mere dream-images – that I do not know for certain that they are not?

So far as I can see, one premiss which they would certainly use would be this: 'Some at least of the sensory experiences which you are having now are similar in important respects to dream-images which actually have occurred in dreams.' This seems a very harmless premiss, and I am quite willing to admit that it is true. But I think

there is a very serious objection to the procedure of using it as a premiss in favour of the derived conclusion. For a philosopher who does use it as a premiss, is, I think, in fact *implying*, though he does not expressly say, that he himself knows it to be true. He is *implying* therefore that he himself knows that dreams have occurred. And, of course, I think he would be right. All the philosophers I have ever met or heard of certainly did know that dreams have occurred: we all know that dreams *have* occurred. But can he consistently combine this proposition that he knows that dreams have occurred, with his conclusion that he does not know that he is not dreaming? Can anybody possibly know that dreams have occurred, if, at the time, he does not himself know that he is not dreaming? If he *is* dreaming, it may be that he is only dreaming that dreams have occurred; and if he does not know that he is not dreaming, can he possibly know that he is *not* only dreaming that dreams have occurred? Can he possibly know therefore that dreams *have* occurred? I do not think that he can; and therefore I think that anyone who uses this premiss and also asserts the conclusion that nobody ever knows that he is not dreaming, is guilty of an inconsistency. By using this premiss he implies that he himself knows that dreams have occurred; while, if his conclusion is true, it follows that he himself does not know that he is not dreaming, and therefore does not know that he is not only dreaming that dreams have occurred.

However, I admit that the premiss is true. Let us now try to see by what sort of reasoning it might be thought that we could get from it to the conclusion.

I do not see how we can get forward in that direction at all, unless we first take the following huge step, unless we say, namely: since there have been dream-images similar in important respects to some of the sensory experiences I am now having, it is logically possible that there should be dream-images *exactly like all* the sensory experiences I am now having, and logically possible, therefore, that all the sensory experiences I am now having *are* mere dream-images. And it might be thought that the validity of this step could be supported to some extent by appeal to matters of fact, though only, of course, at the cost of the same sort of inconsistency which I have just pointed out. It might be said, for instance, that some people have had dream-images which were *exactly like* sensory experiences which they had when they were awake, and that therefore it must be logically possible to have a dream-image exactly like a sensory experience which is *not* a dream-image. And then it may be said: If it is logically possible for some dream-images to be exactly like sensory experiences which are not dream-images, surely it must be logically possible for *all* the dream-images occurring in a dream at a given time to be exactly like sensory experiences which are not dream-images, and logically possible also for all the sensory experiences which a man has at a given time when he is awake to be exactly like all the dream-images which he himself or another man had in a dream at another time.

Now I cannot see my way to deny that it is logically possible that all the sensory experiences I am having now should be mere dream-images. And if this is logically possible, and if further the sensory experiences I am having now were the only experiences I am having, I do not see how I could possibly know for certain that I am not dreaming.

But the conjunction of my memories of the immediate past with these sensory experiences *may* be sufficient to enable me to know that I am not dreaming. I say it *may* be. But what if our sceptical philosopher says: It is *not* sufficient; and offers as an argument to prove that it is not, this: It is logically possible *both* that you should be having all the sensory experiences you are having, and also that you should be remembering what you do remember, and *yet* should be dreaming. If this *is* logically possible, then I don't see how to deny that I cannot possibly know for certain that I am not dreaming: I do not see that I possibly could. But can any reason be given for saying that it *is* logically possible? So far as I know nobody ever has, and I don't know how anybody ever could. And so long as this is not done my argument, 'I know that I am standing up, and therefore I know that I am not dreaming,' remains at least as good as his, 'You don't know that you are not dreaming, and therefore don't know that you are standing up.' And I don't think I've ever seen an argument expressly directed to show that it is not.

One final point should be made clear. It is certainly logically possible that I *should have* been dreaming now; I *might* have been dreaming now; and therefore the proposition that I *am* dreaming now is not self-contradictory. But what I am in doubt of is whether it is logically possible that I should *both* be having all the sensory experiences and the memories that I have and *yet* be dreaming. The conjunction of the proposition that I have these sense experiences and memories with the proposition that I am dreaming does seem to me to be very likely self-contradictory.

Chapter 39

Peter Unger

AN ARGUMENT FOR SKEPTICISM

I mean to offer a positive argument for skepticism about knowledge; I do not mean just to raise some doubts, however general, about statements to the effect that people know. The argument to be offered has as its conclusion the universal form of the skeptical thesis, that is, the proposition that nobody ever knows *anything* to be so. If this argument is sound, as I am inclined to think, then it will follow in particular that nobody ever knows anything about the past or future or even the present, about others or even about himself, about external objects or even about his own experiences, about complicated contingencies or even the simplest mathematical necessities. This, then, is an argument for an extremely strong and sweeping conclusion indeed.

The opposite of skepticism is often called dogmatism. In these terms, dogmatism is the view that certain things are known to be so. The stronger the form of dogmatism, the more sorts of things would be claimed to be known and, so, the weaker the form of skepticism which might still be allowed to hold. Thus, one might be a dogmatist about the past but a skeptic about the future in the sense that one might hold that we know a fair amount about the past but know nothing of the future. But typical arguments to the effect that we know things about the past do not *look* dogmatic in any usual sense. And, arguments to the effect that we know nothing of the future do not in any standard sense look

particularly undogmatic; they do not *look* particularly indicative of an open-minded approach to things. Going by the typical arguments, then, the label "dogmatist" is unfairly prejudicial and there is no force in the claim that skepticism is to be preferred because the alternative is dogmatism. Unlike such typical arguments, the argument I mean to offer gives substance to the claim that the alternative to skepticism is a view which sanctions a dogmatic attitude. In that one may well not appreciate that this is indeed skepticism's only alternative, one might, perhaps, innocently believe that one knows things without being dogmatic in the process. But once the implications of that belief are brought out, as my argument means to do, the persistence in such a belief may itself be considered dogmatic. Of course, I do not want to be dogmatic in asserting any of this and, indeed, confess to only a moderate amount of confidence in what I have to offer. But as I am inclined to think it true, I offer it in a spirit which I hope may be taken as quite undogmatic and open-minded.

A preliminary statement of the argument

I begin by giving a statement of the argument which, while correct in all essentials, does not account for certain complications. On this statement, the argument is exceedingly simple and straightforward. It has but two premises and each of them makes no exceptions whatsoever. The first of these is the proposition:

(1) If someone *knows* something to be so, then it is all right for the person to be absolutely *certain* that it is so.

For example, if it is true that Knute *knows* that there was a general called "Napoleon," then it is (perfectly) all right for him to be absolutely *certain* that there was. And, if Rene really *knows* that he exists, then it is (perfectly) all right for Rene to be absolutely certain that he does.

Our second and final premise, then, is this categorical proposition:

(2) It is never all right for anyone to be absolutely *certain* that anything is so.

According to this premise, it is not all right for Knute to be absolutely certain that there was a general called "Napoleon," nor is it even all right for Rene to be absolutely certain that he exists. No matter what their situations, these people should not have this "attitude of absolute certainty." When one understands what is involved in having this attitude, or in being absolutely certain of something, one will presumably understand why it is never all right to be absolutely certain.

These two premises together entail our conclusion of universal skepticism:

(3) Nobody ever *knows* that anything is so.

In particular, Knute does not really *know* that there was a general called "Napoleon," nor does Rene really *know* that he exists.

The first premise: the idea that if one knows it is all right for one to be certain

We often have the idea that someone is certain of something but he shouldn't be. Perhaps from his expressive behavior, perhaps from something else, we *take* it that he is certain of something—whether or not he really is certain of it. We ask him, if we are so inclined, "How can you be *certain* of that?" In asking this question, we manage to imply that it might not be all right for him to be certain and imply, further, that this is because he might not really *know* the thing. If the man could show us that he does know, then we should withdraw the question and, perhaps, even apologize for implying what we did by raising it. But, then, how do we manage to imply so much just by asking this question in the first place? Neither "know" nor any cognate expression ever crosses our lips in the asking. We are able to imply so much, I suggest, because we all accept the idea that, at least generally, if one does know something then it is all right for one to be certain of it—but if one doesn't then it isn't. This suggests that there is some analytic connection between knowing, on the one hand, and on the other, its being all right to be certain.

The very particular idea that knowing *entails* its being all right to be certain is suggested, further, by the fact that knowing entails, at least, that one *is* certain. That this is a fact is made quite plain by the inconsistency expressed by sentences like "He really *knew* that it was raining, but he *wasn't* absolutely *certain* that it was." Such a sentence can express no truth: if he wasn't certain, then he didn't know. We get further confirmation here from considering transitivity. The sentences "He was *sad that* it was raining, but he *didn't know* it was" and "He was really *sad that* it was raining, but he *wasn't* absolutely *certain* it was" are likewise inconsistent. Their inconsistency means an entailment from being sad that to knowing, in the first case, and to being certain in the second. This can be best explained, it would seem, by an entailment from knowing to being certain. The entailment from knowing to being certain is convincingly clinched, I think, by appreciating the equivalence between someone's knowing something and his knowing it for certain, or with absolute certainty. To be sure, we may describe cases which we would more naturally react to with the words "He knew it" than "He knew it for certain": Consider a man who, looking for his cuff links, unerringly went to the very spot they were while doubts went through his mind. Did he know that they were in that spot? But our readiness to say he knew might only indicate loose usage of those words by us, while we are more strict in our use when the word "certain" enters the picture. That this is much the more plausible hypothesis than thinking there to be an inequivalence here is evidenced by the inconsistency of the relevant sentences: "He *knew* it, but he *didn't* know it for certain," "He really *knew* it, but he *didn't* know it with *absolute certainty*," "He knew it was there, but he didn't *really* know it," and so on. No truth can be found in these words no matter when they might be uttered. Even if they are put forth at the end of stories like that of the cuff-link finder, where we are inclined at first to say he knows, we realize that they must express what is false. Accordingly, we are forced to be unswayed by our tendency to loose usage and to admit the equivalence between knowing with absolute certainty and just plain knowing to be so. Admitting this equivalence, we can be quite confident that knowing does indeed entail being absolutely certain.

Now, it cannot be too strongly emphasized that everything I said is meant to be compatible with the sense which the ordinary word "know" actually has. Indeed, it fairly relies on this word's having only one ("strong") sense as it occurs in sentences of the forms "S knows that *p*" and "S knows about X." Some philosophers have suggested "weak" senses of "know" in which it does not even have an entailment to absolute certainty.[1] But though there is some reason to suppose that "know" has different meanings in "John knows that Jim is his friend" and "John knows Jim,"[2] there appears no reason at all to suppose that "knows" may mean different things as it occurs in the former sentence. Indeed, reason seems to favor the opposite view. If a

genuine ambiguous sentence has a meaning on which it is inconsistent, there will generally be one also on which it is consistent. Once the latter meaning is pointed out, this difference is appreciated and felt to be quite striking. Thus, the sentence "John really *types* many things, but he produces symbols *only orally*" has an obvious meaning on which it is inconsistent. But, it may be pointed out that "types" has another sense, which it shares (roughly) with "classifies." Once this is pointed out, the consistent meaning is appreciated, and the effect is a striking one. No similar phenomenon is ever found with the sentence "John really *knows* that he types things, but he *isn't* absolutely *certain* that he does." There may be many *ad hoc* explanations of this fact. But the only plausible explanation is, I think, that "know" doesn't have a weak sense with no entailment to absolute certainty.[3]

To deny our first premise, then, is to do violence to the meaning of "know" and to our concept of knowledge. If our argument is to be stopped, it must be with the consideration of the second premise. In any case, it is with that premise that the *substantive* claim of the argument is made: It is not only mere questions of logical relations with which we must now contend. Accordingly, we now come to the largest and most important part of our discussion.

What attitude is involved in one's being absolutely certain?

I will now, at last, begin to argue for the idea that to be absolutely certain of something is, owing to a certain feature of personal certainty, to be *dogmatic* in the matter of whether that thing is so. It is because of this dogmatic feature that there is always *something* wrong with being absolutely certain. In other words, it is because of this feature that our second premise, (2), is correct. My argument for the idea that this feature ensures this dogmatism falls naturally into two parts. The first part, which will occupy us in this present section, is aimed at specifying the feature. Thus, we will argue here that one's being absolutely certain of something involves one in having a certain severely negative *attitude* in the matter of whether that thing is so: the attitude that *no* new information, evidence or experience which one might ever have will be seriously considered by one to be *at all* relevant to *any possible* change in one's thinking in the matter. The second part is aimed at showing this attitude to be wrongly dogmatic even in matters which may appear to be quite simple and certain. That more normative segment will be reserved for the section immediately to follow.

That such an absolutely severe attitude should be essential to one's knowing is hardly novel with me. Indeed, philosophers who are quite plainly anti-skeptical proclaim just this attitude as essential to one's knowing. Thus Norman Malcolm thinks himself to know that there is an ink-bottle before him, and describes what he takes to be implicit in this knowledge of his:

> Not only do I not *have* to admit that (those) extraordinary occurrences would be evidence that there is no ink-bottle here; the fact is that I *do not* admit it. There is nothing whatever that could happen in the next moment that would by me be called *evidence* that there is not an ink-bottle here now. No future experience or investigation could prove to me that I am mistaken . . .
>
> It will appear to some that I have adopted an *unreasonable* attitude towards that statement. There is, however, nothing unreasonable about it.
>
> In saying that I should regard nothing as evidence that there is no ink-bottle here now, I am not *predicting* what I should do if various astonishing things happened. . . .
>
> That assertion describes my *present* attitude towards the statement that here is an ink-bottle.[4]

Now, Malcolm, it is true, aligns himself with the idea that there are two (or more) senses of "know" to be found in sentences like "John *knows* that there is an ink-bottle before him." The idea is neither correct nor essential to his position in those passages. We have already argued, in section 2 [of the original publication], that this idea is not correct. That this incorrect idea is not essential to the main thrust of his quoted remarks is, I think, equally clear. For he allows that there is at least *a* sense of "know" where knowing entails one's having the extreme attitude they characterize. Presumably, that sense, at least, is just the sense where knowing entails being absolutely certain, and the extreme attitude is just the one which is necessarily involved in absolute certainty. In that such philosophers think that when one knows the attitude of certainty is not only present but quite all right, their thinking that the attitude is to be characterized in such severe negative terms is some indirect evidence for thinking so. An attitude which is so *severely* negative as this might well *not* be one which is very often justified. However, even if one wants to avoid skepticism, a concern for the truth about this attitude makes a severe characterization of it quite unavoidable.

The attitude of certainty concerns *any* sequence of experience or events which could consistently be presented to a sentient subject, without its description prejudging the issue on which it might supposedly bear. Thus, one is certain that there is an ink-bottle before one only if one's attitude is this: Insofar as I care about being right about whether an ink-bottle is or was before me, no matter how things may seem to appear, *I will not count* as contrary evidence even such extraordinary sequences as these:

> when I next reach for this ink-bottle my hand should seem to pass *through* it and I should not feel the contact of any object . . . in the next moment the ink-bottle will suddenly vanish from sight . . . I should find myself under a tree in the garden with no ink-bottle about . . . one or more persons should enter this room and declare that they see no ink-bottle

on this desk . . . a photograph taken now of the top of the desk should clearly show all of the objects on it except the ink-bottle.[5]

Now, however (nearly) certain one may be that some or all of these sequences will not occur, that is of course not the same thing as being (at all) certain that there is an ink-bottle before one. But, though there are many differences between the two, perhaps the one which should most clearly be focused on is this: If one is really certain of the ink-bottle, and not just of other things however related, then one's attitude is that *even if one should* seem to find oneself in *a* contrary garden, one *would disregard* this experience as irrelevant to the question of whether, at the time in question, there is or was an ink-bottle before one. One might resist this characterization, but then, I think, one would lose one's proper focus on what it is of which one is certain.

Here is a line of resistance to our characterization of being certain. Suppose, in contrast, one's attitudes were these: If strange things seemed to happen, then perhaps I would change my mind, I just might. But, I am absolutely certain that no strange things will ever happen to speak against there being an ink-bottle. Might not these attitudes be those of a man who was *absolutely* certain that *there is an ink-bottle before him?* Might not he be certain of the ink-bottle, not in or by having a completely exclusionary attitude on that matter itself but, rather, indirectly, so to speak, in or by having just such an attitude toward the possibility of apparently contrary appearances?[6]

This suggestion, this line of resistance, is an interesting one, but it is neither correct nor of any use even if it were correct. First, let us notice that *at least almost* invariably when one is even very close to being absolutely certain of something, one is not nearly so certain that no contrary appearances will turn up. For example, you may be quite sure that I am married. But, you will not be quite so sure that no appearances to the contrary might show up: I may be married

but say to you "No, I'm not really married. Mary and I don't believe in such institutions. We only sent out announcements to see the effect— and it's easier to have most people believe that we are." I might, at a certain point, say these things to you and get a few other people to say apparently confirmatory things. All of this, and some more if need be, should and would, I think, incline you to be at least a bit less certain that I am married. Thus, at least with things where one is *quite* certain, the matter seems to be quite the *opposite* of what was suggested: One will not be so certain that nothing strangely contradictory will turn up—but one will be inclined to reject any such thing even if it does turn up. We may plausibly project that things work quite the same in situations where someone is absolutely certain (if there really are any such).[7]

Let us now take something of which you are as certain as anything, say, that one and one are two. Suppose that you are very sure that your favorite mathematician will never say something false to you about any simple sum. Imagine that he, or God, tells you and insists that one and one are three, and not two. If your attitude is that he is still to be trusted or, at least, that you would no longer be quite so sure of the sum, then you are not absolutely certain that one and one are two. If you think you *are absolutely certain* of this sum, then, I submit, you should think also that your attitude will be to reject entirely the message from the mathematician or God. In this simple arithmetical matter, you are to give it, perhaps unlike other messages from the same source, no weight at all in your thinking. It seems, then, that this line of resistance is not faithful to the idea of being certain of a particular thing. But would it be of any use in countering skepticism, or the skeptic's charge of dogmatism, even if it were right?

It seems to me that it is at least as dogmatic to have the position that it is absolutely certain that nothing will ever even appear to speak against one's position as to have the attitude that any such appearances which might show up should be entirely rejected. What about appearances to the effect that some contrary appearances, their precise nature left open as yet, are likely to show up in the future? If one is absolutely certain that the latter sort of appearances won't ever show up, one would, presumably, have the attitude of rejecting entirely the indication of the former appearances. One's attitude of rejection gets pushed farther back from the matter itself. Perhaps, on our line of resistance, this may go on indefinitely. But each retreat, and the consequent new place for rejection, only makes a man look more and more obvious in his dogmatism and unreasonableness about the whole affair. Even going back no farther than the second level, so to speak, only a quite foolhardy man would, it seems to me, reject out of hand any suggestion that some things might be brought forth to speak against his position. If anything, it is better for him to allow that they may and to be ready to reject them. So, even if our line of resistance had presented us with a case of being certain, the "indirect" way of being certain would hardly help us to avoid the skeptical charge. That is quite surely no way for being perfectly certain to be perfectly all right.

It is important to stress very hard that a clause like "I should regard nothing as evidence that there is no ink-bottle now" must be regarded as the expression of a man's *current attitude*, and not as any prediction of what he will do under certain future circumstances.[8] Thus, one may allow that a sentence like the following is indeed consistent: "He is absolutely *certain* that there are automobiles, but he *may* change his mind should certain evidence come up." That is because even if his present attitude is that he will not, things may not happen in accordance with his attitude. For example, things might happen to him which *cause* him to become uncertain. Or, his attitude might just evaporate, so to speak, the new evidence then affecting him in the unwanted way; and so on. Such conditions as these give us a consistent interpretation for the

foregoing sentence, even if not a very ordinary one. A sentence which will always express an inconsistency, on the other hand, is obtained once we make sure that our severely negative clause is embedded so that it is clear that the man's current attitude is the point. Thus, in contrast with the foregoing, it is always inconsistent to say, "He is absolutely *certain* that there are automobiles, but *his attitude* is that he *may* change his mind should certain evidence come up." A proper assessment of the direct linguistic evidence supports the idea that the attitude of certainty is thus absolutely severe.

This direct linguistic evidence cannot be enough to satisfy one that being certain, or the attitude in knowing, demands so much as we claim. And, it is not enough to add the indirect evidence from anti-skeptical authors. What we want is to fit a severe characterization of this attitude into some more general account of things. Toward this end, I now recall my account of absolute terms.[9] On this account, *absolute adjectives* like "flat," "useless" and "certain" purport to denote a limiting state or situation to which things may approximate more or less closely. Thus, in the case of these adjectives, the modifier "absolutely," as well as "completely" and "perfectly," is redundant apart from points of emphasis. Now, various locutions with "certain" may appear to indicate matters of degree. But they will always admit of a paraphrase where this appearance is dispelled in favor of a more explicit reference to an *absolute limit*: "That's pretty certain" goes into "That's pretty *close to being absolutely* certain"; "He is more certain of this than of that" goes into "He is *absolutely* certain of this but not of that or else he is *closer to being absolutely* certain of this than of that," and so on. None of this is peculiar to "certain"; with locutions containing other absolute adjectives. Thus, these sentences seem to denote matters of degree, but their paraphrases dispel the illusory appearance: "That's the flattest (most useless) thing I've ever seen" goes into "That's the only *absolutely* flat (useless) thing I've ever seen or else that's *closer to being absolutely* flat (useless) than anything else I've seen." In light of these paraphrases, we may repose some confidence in the following formula as saying what it is for something to be *x* where that is the same as being absolutely *x*: Something or someone is *x* (flat, useless, certain, etc.) just in case nothing *could possibly* ever be more *x*, or *x*-er, than that thing or person is right now. It is in this strict sense, then, that being certain, and *a fortiori* being absolutely certain, is being at an absolute limit. Now, absolute adjectives typically have contrasting terms which are *relative adjectives*: "certain" has "confident"' and "doubtful," "flat" has "bumpy" and "curved," "useless" has "useful" and "serviceable," and so on. Because matters of degree *are* concerned, there is nothing which is deceptive about the locutions with *these* terms: The sentence "He is pretty confident" does not go into the apparently senseless "He is pretty close to being absolutely confident"; nor does "That is very useful" go into "That is very close to being absolutely useful." These relative terms really do denote matters of degree and not any state or situation which is an absolute limit. If something is bumpy, it is *not* true that nothing could possibly be more bumpy or bumpier. And if someone is confident of something, it does not follow that no one could ever be more confident. Now, a necessary condition for the correct application of an absolute adjective is, at least generally, that certain things denoted by relative adjectives be entirely absent. Thus, it is a necessary condition of something's being flat that it be *not at all* bumpy, that is, that bumpiness not be present even in the least degree. Also, it is a necessary condition of being flat that the thing be *not at all* curved, or that curvature or curvedness not be present at all. We might expect the same sort of thing to hold in the case of someone's being certain of something, and indeed it does: If someone is certain of something, then that thing is *not at all* doubtful so far as he is concerned, that is, doubt or doubtfulness is not present at all in that man with respect to that

thing. I have already argued this before, but there are other things which must also be entirely absent if a man is to be certain, though their absence may be included, I suggest, in the absence of all doubt.

One thing which must be entirely absent, and which is, I think, implicit in the absence of all doubt, is this: any *openness* on the part of the man to consider new experience or information as seriously relevant to the truth or falsity of the thing. In other words, if S is certain that p, then it follows that S is *not at all* open to consider any new experience or information as relevant to his thinking in the matter of whether p.

Why is there always something wrong with having this absolute attitude?

At the beginning of his brilliant paper, "Certainty," G. E. Moore, perhaps the most influential opponent of skepticism in this century, makes some assertions and, as he points out, does so in a very positive and definite way. In just this way, he says, for example, that he had clothes on and was not absolutely naked. Moore goes on to note that although he did not expressly *say* of the things which he asserted that he *knew* them to be true, he implied as much by asserting them in the way he did. His words are these:

> I *implied* . . . that I myself knew for certain, in each case, that what I asserted to be the case was, at the time I asserted it, in fact the case. And I do not think that I can be justly accused of dogmatism or over-confidence for having asserted these things positively in the way that I did. In the case of some kinds of assertions, and under some circumstances, a man can be justly accused of dogmatism for asserting something positively. But in the case of assertions such as I made, made under the circumstances under which I made them, the charge would be absurd.[10]

I think that we may take it that, according to

Moore, the reason he could not so be accused is that he was *not* dogmatic here. And the reason for that is that he *knew* these things, e.g. that he was not naked, so that he was *justified* in being absolutely *certain* of them. And, so, in those innocuous circumstances of speech, he was justified in acting out of, or in accord with, his position or attitude of personal certainty. Moore was saying, in effect, that one could have this by now familiarly characterized attitude without any pain of being at all dogmatic in the matter: That no new experience or information will have any effect at all on one's thinking in the matter at hand, in this case, in the matter of whether at the then present time one is absolutely naked or not. Moore's position here is, then, quite of a piece with Malcolm's thought that it is *not at all unreasonable* of him to allow nothing to count as contrary evidence in the matter of whether an ink-bottle is before him. But Moore's point is more particular than Malcolm's, for he notes the *particular way* in which one who is certain might be thought to be unreasonable, or not justified, in his attitude: He might be thought to be such *in that* he is *dogmatic* in the matter. Moore similarly foreshadows, while focusing more clearly on the form of the opposite view, Hintikka's implication that in many matters one is *justified* in disregarding any further information: In situations where one knows, Moore says or implies, one is not at all dogmatic in having just such an absolutely negative position or attitude. It seems, then, that Moore was more sensitive than these other authors to the possibility that *dogmatism* might (almost) always be charged of one who was absolutely certain, even when he might rather plausibly claim to know. Now, it strikes me as oddly unfortunate, in a way, that others who actually spelled out what was involved in being certain, were not so sensitive to this particular charge. For it is, I think, precisely the feature they spell out which makes the charge of dogmatism live and convincing. By the same token, however, it is to Moore's credit that, without articulating the key idea, he was able to sense

the charge of *dogmatism* as a particular threat to his position, perhaps as the key one. Indeed, in the three full sentences I quoted, he refers to this charge as many times. We may put the substantial question, then, in these words: Was Moore referring to a charge of some real substance, or was he right in contending that (because he knew) there was really nothing to be feared?

We may now, I think, more fairly assess the question of whether in cases where one is absolutely certain, supposing there are any such, one's attitude is dogmatic at least in some degree. In such a case, there may be no relevant inconsistency, there being no disparity between one's tenacity and willingness to risk and infer. And, it may well be that no one will ever disagree with one, or even be much less certain of the thing. For, when one is absolutely certain, as we are supposing, the matter is likely to be clear-cut. But, even if nothing rubs the wrong way, from within oneself or without, one's attitude in the matter is this: I will not allow *anything at all* to count as evidence against my present view in the matter. The case being clear-cut, this attitude will cause one no trouble nor bring any challenge. But, what is one to think of it anyway, even if no penalty or embarrassment is liable ever to occur? I think that any reflection at all makes it pretty plain that, no matter how certain things may seem, *this* attitude is always dogmatic and one who has it will always be open to that charge even if circumstances mean that he will never be exposed to it.

Now, in order to see more clearly why, even in the apparently most clear-cut and certain matters, there is something wrong with letting nothing count against one's being right, it will *help* to describe some sequences of experience. I do *not* think that such an appreciation of detail is really necessary to gaining conviction that the attitude of certainty is always dogmatic and, providing there are no other considerations in its favor, to be foregone in favor of a more open-minded position. One must favor such an attitude in any case, no matter how certain something seems and no matter how little one is able to imagine what experiences there might be which, should they ever occur, one had best consider seriously and not just disregard. This is the right view in the matter however poor our own imaginations might be. But, the strength of habits to the contrary being so great, it will be a big help if we can succeed in imagining sequences of experience which seem to cry out for serious thought. Even in the cases of things which at first seem quite certain, then, and beyond any possibility of questioning at all, I will strive to be of service by imagining experiences. These described experiences should help one grasp firmly the idea that the attitude of certainty is always dogmatic.

Helpful experiences for rejecting the attitude of certainty

In quoting Malcolm's meditations on himself and his ink-bottle, we looked at some sequences of experiences which, if they occurred, might rightly be considered to have some weight and, accordingly, result in one's not being quite so certain as before that there is or was an ink-bottle before one. Malcolm says he wouldn't take those experiences as relevant here, that that is his attitude and that all of that is perfectly all right. I would disagree. But, in any event, it seems that one can easily imagine experiences which are more telling in this regard. And, also, with only more difficulty, one can imagine others which are easily more telling.

In respect of the matter of that ink-bottle, there are, it seems to me, all sorts of possible experiences which might cast some doubt. For example, one may be approached by government officials who seem to demonstrate that the object on one's desk is a container of a material to poison the water supply, which somehow found its way out of government hands and into one's home. It was disguised to look like an ink-bottle, but it is seen to have many small structural

features essential to such a container of poison but which no ink-bottles have. One might well think, then, that though this object holds ink it is not an ink-bottle but, rather, is something else. Perhaps, then, there never was *an ink-bottle* before one, but only some such other object. It seems, at any rate, that such an experience as this should not be disregarded out of hand no matter what one eventually should come to think about whether an ink-bottle was before one. An attitude which would thus disregard it seems, then, to be a dogmatic one.

The experience just described is, I suppose, less than completely convincing. And, even if it is admitted that the experience does have some weight, it seems easy enough to retreat to other statements which are not thus susceptible to experimental challenge. For example, one may be, instead, absolutely certain that there is before one something which looks like an ink-bottle, or that there is something with a circular top, or whatever the favored things turn out to be. Though the sort of experience just imagined might go against one's being certain that *an ink-bottle* is before one, such a sequence of experience will not go against one's certainty about many other things: that there are automobiles, that there have been automobiles for quite some time now, and that one is not now absolutely naked. To get a more completely convincing case about one ink-bottle, and to begin to get a convincing case for these less susceptible things, one's imagination must work more radically. Descartes was quite well aware of the problem when he imagined his evil demon. We may do well to follow suit, though in a more modern and scientific vein.[11]

I begin to imagine a more radical sequence of experience by supposing myself to experience a voice, coming from no definite location, which tells me this, in no uncertain terms: All the experiences I am having, including that of the voice, are artificially induced. Indeed, this has been going on for all of my conscious life and it will continue to do so. The voice tells me of various experiences I have had, some of which I had myself forgotten almost entirely. It then says that scientists accomplish all of this with me; it seems to tell me what they are like, what I am really like and, in great detail, how they manage to bring about these effects in me. To make its case most convincing, the voice says what experiences I will next have, and next after that and, then, after that. First, I will seem to fly off the face of the earth to a planet where the inhabitants worship me because I have only one mouth. After that, I am to come back to earth and seem to find that I have been elected Secretary-Treasurer of the International Brotherhood of Electricians. Finally, if that is not preposterous enough, I will seem to open up my body and find myself stuffed with fried shrimps, even unto the inner reaches of my thighs. Miraculously enough, I experience just these to happen. The experiences are not as in a dream but indistinguishable from what I call the most ordinary waking experiences—except, of course, for the extraordinary content. Nor does this predicted sequence seem to take place in a flash, or in any very brief interval. To mirror what I take as reality, it seems to take a couple of months. After a convincing talk with the voice at the end of this experiential journey, I am left in a blue homogenous field of visual experience, feeling little but wonder, to think over whether an ink-bottle was ever before me, whether there are now or ever were any automobiles, and so on. Of course, the voice has told me that none of these things ever were, and told me why I thought otherwise. What am I to think now?

My attitude toward these imagined experiences is that if they should occur I would be at least somewhat less certain than I now am about these matters. I would be at least somewhat unconfident, even, that I was not naked at the time in question. This is my present attitude. If things would not develop in accord with it, that would be something I can now only hope will not happen. Moreover, I think it pretty plain that this is the attitude which I ought to have and

that anyone who held an opposite one would have a dogmatic attitude in these matters. That is, if one's attitude is that these experiences will not be counted as having any weight at all, one would be dogmatic in these matters.

Now, some people might have the attitude that if these experiences occurred one should think himself to be quite mad or, at least, to have had his capacity for judgment impaired in some damaging way.[12] My own attitude is more open than this. But it should be pointed out that even this attitude of prospective self-defeat is quite compatible with that of lessening one's confidence. One's total attitude, that is, might be that if the imagined experiences really came to pass one would both be less certain that there ever were automobiles and also be inclined to think that one must have become quite mad. All that I am claiming or need to claim is that one ought to have at least the first part of this total attitude or, more precisely, that one ought not to have the opposite attitude that any such experiences will be completely disregarded.

Helpful experiences for the hardest cases

In respect of almost any matter, the possibility of certain imagined sequences of experience makes quite a convincing case that one ought not, on pain of dogmatism, have the attitude of absolute certainty. There are, however, two sorts of matters where something more must be said to explain how such experience might help us to appreciate the wrongness of this severe attitude. I treat them in turn, proceeding from the less to the more difficult.

The first and lesser difficulty concerns certain sorts of matters about the past. The most famous of these, due to Russell,[13] is the matter of whether the world sprang into existence five minutes ago. But the matter of whether oneself has existed for more than a brief moment will pose the problem more clearly so far as sequences of convincing experiences are concerned. The problem may be put like this: If any sequence of experience is to be convincing, it must itself endure for much more than a brief moment. Even in advance of any experiences which might look to show that one has been in existence only for a brief moment, one can and ought to appreciate this fact about the conditions of convincing. Therefore, it is in any case quite all right to have the attitude that no possible experience will be counted as convincing evidence for the claim that one has existed only for a brief moment. Rather, one may disregard any new experience which purports to be to this effect.

The difficulty with this reasoning is that it doesn't take into account how new experiences might make us view time differently. If our voice told us new things about time, we might not be able to disregard it without ourselves being dogmatic. Suppose that the voice says that one has been brought into existence only a brief moment ago complete with an accurate understanding of how long temporal intervals are. But one is also provided, the voice says, with an appealing consistent web of ostensible memories: to believe that one has experienced the things it seems to one that one has will be, then, only to believe what is false. Now, the recent experiences one indeed has had are, according to the voice, part of a sequence which has gone on only for a brief moment, a billionth of a second, to be quite precise. And, this includes these very messages that even now are coming to one. Though it seems to one that the experiences have been going on for some months, one has in fact been alive for only a brief moment and, indeed, the world of concrete things, including the source of the voice, has existed for less than a minute. In response to these vocal claims one might put forward some relativistic theory of time on which the claims would make no sense and, at any rate, on which they could not possibly be true. But, that would only be to adduce some theory. And, if there is anything scientific about science it is that one

should never be too certain of any theory, no matter how beautiful, comprehensive and powerful it may seem. So it seems that, no matter how one might wish to reply, one would do well to allow some influence for such a sequence of experience as the one just imagined. One should have the attitude, at least, that should it occur one will be not quite *so* certain, as one otherwise might be, that one has been alive for more than a brief moment.

The greatest difficulty in finding possible experience a help in abandoning the attitude of certainty comes, I think, in matters where we think that the only possible error must be a "purely verbal" one. This occurs, I take it, with matters of "immediate experience," e.g. with whether one is now experiencing phenomenal blueness or pain. And, it occurs with the "simplest matters of logical necessity," e.g. with whether two is the sum of one and one. Perhaps the most famous case, due to Descartes, is that concerning one's own present moment thinking and existence, e.g. whether one now exists. Now, some philosophers have found it quite an article of faith to suppose that there might be anything to answer to the word "I." They would think, I suppose, that what one ought to be sure of is that *something* now exists, leaving it quite open, what that thing might be. Even if it is true that in such matters as these, any error must be purely verbal, why shouldn't the possibility of just such an error make the attitude of absolute certainty dogmatic in these very matters? I have never heard anything to convince me of the opposite. It is said that what one believes or is certain of are propositions or, at least, some things that are too abstract to have uncertainty over words interfere with their status. Let us agree at the outset that we understand such attempts to downgrade the effect that words might have. But, nevertheless, ought not the following story about possible experience cause at least some very small doubts to enter one's mind? Again, we have our voice. After going through the sequence of experiences I described before, the voice tells me that I become easily confused about the meanings of certain terms. It says that on occasions, and now is one of them, I confuse the meaning of "exist," a word which means, roughly, "to continue on in the face of obstacles," with the meaning of "persist," a word which, roughly, shares a meaning with the verb "to be." Consequently, in philosophizing, I often say to myself "I exist" and "It seems certain to me that I *exist* now." And, I then seem to remember that I have never thought otherwise. But, in fact, of course, I am quite a changeable fellow, and so I rarely if ever *exist*. It is true that I *persist*, as everyone does, and I *should* say *this* when I do that philosophizing. No doubt, I will soon change once again and say and think, rightly, that what I do is persist. This will then seem certain to me, which is better than its seeming certain to me that what I do is exist, since at least the former is something which is *true*. But, it would be far better still if *neither* ever even *seemed* to be absolutely certain. At the very least, the voice concludes, I ought never to *be* certain of these things, no matter how tempting that might be. This is especially true in my case because I am so changeable and, as a consequence, so often and so easily confused.

I have no doubt that many would want to protest to this voice. Some might say that the matter of whether the words "I exist now" express a truth and that of whether I exist now are two utterly different matters. Now, it is very true that these matters are very different. But, why should that lead anyone to protest what I am saying? What I am saying is just that under certain conditions of experience one ought to become less certain than before that one indeed *exists*, that one thing one does is exist. Indeed, one may be in just such an experiential situation even while being quite confident that the words "I exist now" do indeed express a truth. We may suppose, after all, that the voice tells one that one *does* continue on in the face of obstacles, and so one ought to be confident that one exists, as well as that one persists. Now, it *may* be that there is something deeply wrong with any of these vocal

suggestions and, so, that one ought never to allow any to affect one's beliefs or attitudes even in the most minimal way. But I can't see how anyone can be absolutely certain that this is so. And, suppose that the *voice itself* went through all those matters with you and told you to rest assured that such verbal confusions can get you, and are now getting you, into error here. In that one might experience even this, so far as I can see, one's attitude in any of these matters ought not to be that of absolute certainty. Thus, one ought not, really, be absolutely certain that one now exists, or that something exists, or that one now feels pain, or whatever. Of course, the source of uncertainty we have just uncovered is present in matters which are not so apparently certain or simple. Thus, we may now appreciate a bit more fully why it is at least a bit dogmatic to be certain that there is an ink-bottle before one, that there ever are any automobiles, or that one has existed for more than a brief moment.

As I said earlier, these imagined sequences of experience are only meant to be a help in coming to the idea that being certain involves being dogmatic. Their role is to exemplify some situations where this feature of dogmatism might be brought out. I hope that the sequences I have described have been thus revealing and, so, convincing. But that they be so is hardly essential to making good our claim. For even if the particular experience one is able to imagine does not seem to jeopardize some statement which seems quite certain, one shouldn't be *sure* that there isn't any such sequence—possibly, even one which a human imagination just can't grasp in advance. And, even if there is no sequence of *experience* which ought to make one less certain, *mightn't* there be some other factor information about which ought to give one pause? Perhaps, there are some currently obscure conceptual truths about the nature of thought and reason, which show how any thinking at all is parasitic on the possibility of error in the case. No matter how comfortable one feels in his philosophy and his view of the world, I can't see how he might properly be *certain* that there is no way that he could possibly be wrong. He cannot properly be certain that he has given a complete accounting of every sort of experience, evidence and information which might possibly exist. For this reason, if for no other, it will be dogmatic of him ever to have the attitude that he will disregard *any* new experience, evidence and information which run counter to what he holds.

This is our case, then, that being certain involves being dogmatic and, so, that there is always at least *something* wrong with being certain. As we noticed, whatever is wrong with this dogmatism may be overridden by other considerations, considerations which are not properly epistemological ones. But, the fact that there is always some dogmatism, whether overridden or not, means that nobody ever knows anything about anything. In this sense, then, dogmatism is the opposite of skepticism, and the necessary presence of dogmatism means that skepticism is really true.

Notes

1 For example, see Norman Malcolm, "Knowledge and Belief," in *Knowledge and Certainty* (Englewood Cliffs, New Jersey, 1963), pp. 62ff; and Jaakko Hintikka, *Knowledge and Belief* (Ithaca, New York, 1962), pp. 18ff.

2 For example, Spanish uses the verb *"saber"* to translate the first of these sentences and *"conocer"* to translate the second, and so for various other languages. This evidence is both indirect and inconclusive, but it is *some* evidence anyway.

3 Perhaps philosophers who seem to see more senses than I do are using "sense" in a different sense. Or, perhaps more likely, they are inventing a new sense for "sense," so as to use the word to make important distinctions about the meaning of our expressions. But, without being impertinent, I can only request to see some reason for supposing that, even in such a new sense of "sense," our verb "know" has two senses.

4 Malcolm, "Knowledge and Belief," pp. 67–8.

5 Ibid., p. 67. The introductory clause "Insofar as I care about being right about . . ." is left out by Malcolm. I think it may be necessary for ruling out certain counterexamples concerning untoward motivations. As it plays no important part in our argument, however, I will leave it out from now on.

6 Some such line of resistance was suggested to me by Gilbert Harman and also by Michael Lockwood.

7 I owe to Saul Kripke the idea that these observations are important to consider for such matters.

8 In a footnote on p. 68 of "Knowledge and Belief," Malcolm says that he doesn't think the word "attitude" is very satisfactory. He would rather put things, he says there, in terms of some conditional statements about what he would say or think right now if or when he imagines things now as happening. But, actually, this latter suggestion is much the poorer and, indeed, Malcolm's choice of the word "attitude" is quite apt and satisfactory.

9 Peter Unger, "A Defense of Skepticism," *The Philosophical Review*, vol. LXXX, no. 2 (April 1971), sections II–IV. In a later issue of this journal, James Cargite replied to the skeptical suggestions in that paper of mine: "In Reply to a Defense of Skepticism," *The Philosophical Review*, vol. LXXXI, no. 2 (April 1972). Perhaps the present paper may be taken as deepening the debate between myself and this critic in a way that would not be possible in a brief and direct rejoinder on my part.

10 Moore, "Certainty," *Philosophical Papers* (New York: Collier Books, 1962), ch. 4.

11 For a rather different but quite congenial description of unsettling experiences, see Edward Erwin's "The Confirmation Machine," in *Boston Studies in the Philosophy of Science*, vol. VIII, ed. Roger C. Buck and Robert S. Cohen.

12 Malcolm suggests this sort of view in his lecture "Memory and The Past," *Knowledge and Certainty*, p. 201. He considers it in a somewhat different context, being most concerned there with the proposition that the earth has existed for no more than five minutes. I will treat such propositions as that in the section following this one. My thoughts on this view owe something to conversation with Michael Slote.

13 Bertrand Russell, *The Analysis of Mind* (New York: The Macmillan Company, 1921), pp. 159–60.

Chapter 40

David Lewis

ELUSIVE KNOWLEDGE

We know a lot. I know what food penguins eat. I know that phones used to ring, but nowadays squeal, when someone calls up. I know that Essendon won the 1993 Grand Final. I know that here is a hand, and here is another.

We have all sorts of everyday knowledge, and we have it in abundance. To doubt that would be absurd. At any rate, to doubt it in any serious and lasting way would be absurd; and even philosophical and temporary doubt, under the influence of argument, is more than a little peculiar. It is a Moorean fact that we know a lot. It is one of those things that we know better than we know the premises of any philosophical argument to the contrary.

Besides knowing a lot that is everyday and trite, I myself think that we know a lot that is interesting and esoteric and controversial. We know a lot about things unseen: tiny particles and pervasive fields, not to mention one another's underwear. Sometimes we even know what an author meant by his writings. But on these questions, let us agree to disagree peacefully with the champions of 'post-knowledgeism'. The most trite and ordinary parts of our knowledge will be problem enough.

For no sooner do we engage in epistemology – the systematic philosophical examination of knowledge – than we meet a compelling argument that we know next to nothing. The sceptical argument is nothing new or fancy. It is just this: it seems as if knowledge must be by definition infallible. If you claim that S knows that P, and yet you grant that S cannot eliminate a certain possibility in which not-P, it certainly seems as if you have granted that S does not after all know that P. To speak of fallible knowledge, of knowledge despite uneliminated possibilities of error, just *sounds* contradictory.

Blind Freddy can see where this will lead. Let your paranoid fantasies rip – CIA plots, hallucinogens in the tap water, conspiracies to deceive, old Nick himself – and soon you find that uneliminated possibilities of error are everywhere. Those possibilities of error are far-fetched, of course, but possibilities all the same. They bite into even our most everyday knowledge. We never have infallible knowledge.

Never – well, hardly ever. Some say we have infallible knowledge of a few simple, axiomatic necessary truths; and of our own present experience. They say that I simply cannot be wrong that a part of a part of something is itself a part of that thing; or that it seems to me now (as I sit here at the keyboard) exactly as if I am hearing clicking noises on top of a steady whirring. Some say so. Others deny it. No matter; let it be granted, at least for the sake of the argument. It is not nearly enough. If we have only that much infallible knowledge, yet knowledge is by definition infallible, then we have very little knowledge indeed – not the abundant everyday knowledge we thought we had. That is still absurd.

So we know a lot; knowledge must be infallible; yet we have fallible knowledge or none (or next to none). We are caught between the rock of fallibilism and the whirlpool of scepticism. Both are mad!

Yet fallibilism is the less intrusive madness. It demands less frequent corrections of what we want to say. So, if forced to choose, I choose fallibilism. (And so say all of us.) We can get used to it, and some of us have done. No joy there – we know that people can get used to the most crazy philosophical sayings imaginable. If you are a contented fallibilist, I implore you to be honest, be naive, hear it afresh. 'He knows, yet he has not eliminated all possibilities of error.' Even if you've numbed your ears, doesn't this overt, explicit fallibilism *still* sound wrong?

Better fallibilism than scepticism; but it would be better still to dodge the choice. I think we can. We will be alarmingly close to the rock, and also alarmingly close to the whirlpool, but if we steer with care, we can – just barely – escape them both.

Maybe epistemology is the culprit. Maybe this extraordinary pastime robs us of our knowledge. Maybe we do know a lot in daily life; but maybe when we look hard at our knowledge, it goes away. But only when we look at it harder than the sane ever do in daily life; only when we let our paranoid fantasies rip. That is when we are forced to admit that there always are uneliminated possibilities of error, so that we have fallible knowledge or none.

Much that we say is context-dependent, in simple ways or subtle ways. Simple: 'it's evening' is truly said when, and only when, it is said in the evening. Subtle: it could well be true, and not just by luck, that Essendon played rottenly, the Easybeats played brilliantly, yet Essendon won. Different contexts evoke different standards of evaluation. Talking about the Easybeats we

apply lax standards, else we could scarcely distinguish their better days from their worse ones. In talking about Essendon, no such laxity is required. Essendon won because play that is rotten by demanding standards suffices to beat play that is brilliant by lax standards.

Maybe ascriptions of knowledge are subtly context-dependent, and maybe epistemology is a context that makes them go false. Then epistemology would be an investigation that destroys its own subject matter. If so, the sceptical argument might be flawless, when we engage in epistemology – and only then![1]

If you start from the ancient idea that justification is the mark that distinguishes knowledge from mere opinion (even true opinion), then you well might conclude that ascriptions of knowledge are context-dependent because standards for adequate justification are context-dependent. As follows: opinion, even if true, deserves the name of knowledge only if it is adequately supported by reasons; to deserve that name in the especially demanding context of epistemology, the arguments from supporting reasons must be especially watertight; but the special standards of justification that this special context demands never can be met (well, hardly ever). In the strict context of epistemology we know nothing, yet in laxer contexts we know a lot.

But I myself cannot subscribe to this account of the context-dependence of knowledge, because I question its starting point. I don't agree that the mark of knowledge is justification.[2] First, because justification is not sufficient: your true opinion that you will lose the lottery isn't knowledge, whatever the odds. Suppose you know that it is a fair lottery with one winning ticket and many losing tickets, and you know how many losing tickets there are. The greater the number of losing tickets, the better is your justification for believing you will lose. Yet there is no number great enough to transform your fallible opinion into knowledge – after all, you just might win. No justification is good enough – or none short of a watertight deductive argument, and all but the sceptics will agree that this is too much to demand.[3]

Second, because justification is not always necessary. What (non-circular) argument supports our reliance on perception, on memory, and on testimony?[4] And yet we do gain knowledge by these means. And sometimes, far from having supporting arguments, we don't even know how we know. We once had evidence, drew conclusions, and thereby gained knowledge; now we have forgotten our reasons, yet still we retain our knowledge. Or we know the name that goes with the face, or the sex of the chicken, by relying on subtle visual cues, without knowing what those cues may be.

The link between knowledge and justification must be broken. But if we break that link, then it is not – or not entirely, or not exactly – by raising the standards of justification that epistemology destroys knowledge. I need some different story.

To that end, I propose to take the infallibility of knowledge as my starting point.[5] Must infallibilist epistemology end in scepticism? Not quite. Wait and see. Anyway, here is the definition. Subject S *knows* proposition P iff P holds in every possibility left uneliminated by S's evidence; equivalently, iff S's evidence eliminates every possibility in which not-P.

The definition is short, the commentary upon it is longer. In the first place, there is the proposition, P. What I choose to call 'propositions' are individuated coarsely, by necessary equivalence. For instance, there is only one necessary proposition. It holds in every possibility; hence in every possibility left uneliminated by S's evidence, no matter who S may be and no matter what his evidence may be. So the necessary proposition is known always and everywhere. Yet this known proposition may go unrecognised when presented in impenetrable linguistic disguise, say as the proposition that every even number is the sum of two primes. Likewise, the known proposition that I have two

hands may go unrecognised when presented as the proposition that the number of my hands is the least number n such that every even number is the sum of n primes. (Or if you doubt the necessary existence of numbers, switch to an example involving equivalence by logic alone.) These problems of disguise shall not concern us here. Our topic is modal, not hyperintensional, epistemology.[6]

Next, there are the possibilities. We needn't enter here into the question whether these are concrete, abstract constructions, or abstract simples. Further, we needn't decide whether they must always be maximally specific possibilities, or whether they need only be specific enough for the purpose at hand. A possibility will be specific enough if it cannot be split into sub-cases in such a way that anything we have said about possibilities, or anything we are going to say before we are done, applies to some sub-cases and not to others. For instance, it should never happen that proposition P holds in some but not all sub-cases; or that some but not all sub-cases are eliminated by S's evidence.

But we do need to stipulate that they are not just possibilities as to how the whole world is; they also include possibilities as to which part of the world is oneself, and as to when it now is. We need these possibilities *de se et nunc* because the propositions that may be known include propositions *de se et nunc*.[7] Not only do I know that there are hands in this world somewhere and somewhen. I know that *I* have hands, or anyway I have them *now*. Such propositions aren't just made true or made false by the whole world once and for all. They are true for some of us and not for others, or true at some times and not others, or both.

Further, we cannot limit ourselves to 'real' possibilities that conform to the actual laws of nature, and maybe also to actual past history. For propositions about laws and history are contingent, and may or may not be known.

Neither can we limit ourselves to 'epistemic' possibilities for S – possibilities that S does not know not to obtain. That would drain our definition of content. Assume only that knowledge is closed under strict implication. (We shall consider the merits of this assumption later.) Remember that we are not distinguishing between equivalent propositions. Then knowledge of a conjunction is equivalent to knowledge of every conjunct. P is the conjunction of all propositions not-W, where W is a possibility in which not-P. That suffices to yield an equivalence: S knows that P iff, for every possibility W in which not-P, S knows that not-W. Contraposing and cancelling a double negation: iff every possibility which S does not know not to obtain is one in which P. For short: iff P holds throughout S's epistemic possibilities. Yet to get this far, we need no substantive definition of knowledge at all! To turn this into a substantive definition, in fact the very definition we gave before, we need to say one more thing: S's epistemic possibilities are just those possibilities that are uneliminated by S's evidence.

So, next, we need to say what it means for a possibility to be eliminated or not. Here I say that the uneliminated possibilities are those in which the subject's entire perceptual experience and memory are just as they actually are. There is one possibility that actually obtains (for the subject and at the time in question); call it *actuality*. Then a possibility W is *uneliminated* iff the subject's perceptual experience and memory in W exactly match his perceptual experience and memory in actuality. (If you want to include other alleged forms of basic evidence, such as the evidence of our extrasensory faculties, or an innate disposition to believe in God, be my guest. If they exist, they should be included. If not, no harm done if we have included them conditionally.)

Note well that we do not need the 'pure sense-datum language' and the 'incorrigible protocol statements' that for so long bedevilled foundationalist epistemology. It matters not at all whether there are words to capture the subject's perceptual and memory evidence, nothing more

and nothing less. If there are such words, it matters not at all whether the subject can hit upon them. The given does not consist of basic axioms to serve as premises in subsequent arguments. Rather, it consists of a match between possibilities.

When perceptual experience E (or memory) eliminates a possibility W, that is not because the propositional content of the experience conflicts with W. (Not even if it is the narrow content.) The propositional content of our experience could, after all, be false. Rather, it is the existence of the experience that conflicts with W: W is a possibility in which the subject is not having experience E. Else we would need to tell some fishy story of how the experience has some sort of infallible, ineffable, purely phenomenal propositional content ... Who needs that? Let E have propositional content P. Suppose even − something I take to be an open question − that E is, in some sense, fully characterized by P. Then I say that E eliminates W iff W is a possibility in which the subject's experience or memory has content different from P. I do *not* say that E eliminates W iff W is a possibility in which P is false.

Maybe not every kind of sense perception yields experience; maybe, for instance, the kinaesthetic sense yields not its own distinctive sort of sense-experience but only spontaneous judgements about the position of one's limbs. If this is true, then the thing to say is that kinaesthetic evidence eliminates all possibilities except those that exactly resemble actuality with respect to the subject's spontaneous kinaesthetic judgements. In saying this, we would treat kinaesthetic evidence more on the model of memory than on the model of more typical senses.

Finally, we must attend to the word 'every'. What does it mean to say that every possibility in which not-P is eliminated? An idiom of quantification, like 'every', is normally restricted to some limited domain. If I say that every glass is empty, so it's time for another round, doubtless

I and my audience are ignoring most of all the glasses there are in the whole wide world throughout all of time. They are outside the domain. They are irrelevant to the truth of what was said.

Likewise, if I say that every uneliminated possibility is one in which P, or words to that effect, I am doubtless ignoring some of all the uneliminated alternative possibilities that there are. They are outside the domain, they are irrelevant to the truth of what was said.

But, of course, I am not entitled to ignore just any possibility I please. Else true ascriptions of knowledge, whether to myself or to others, would be cheap indeed. I may properly ignore some uneliminated possibilities; I may not properly ignore others. Our definition of knowledge requires a *sotto voce* proviso. S *knows* that P iff S's evidence eliminates every possibility in which not-P – Psst! – except for those possibilities that we are properly ignoring.

Unger suggests an instructive parallel.[8] Just as P is known iff there are no uneliminated possibilities of error, so likewise a surface is flat iff there are no bumps on it. We must add the proviso: Psst! – except for those bumps that we are properly ignoring. Else we will conclude, absurdly, that nothing is flat. (Simplify by ignoring departures from flatness that consist of gentle curvature.)

We can restate the definition. Say that we *pre-suppose* proposition Q iff we ignore all possibilities in which not-Q. To close the circle: we *ignore* just those possibilities that falsify our presuppositions. *Proper* presupposition corresponds, of course, to proper ignoring. Then S knows that P iff S's evidence eliminates every possibility in which not-P – Psst! – except for those possibilities that conflict with our proper presuppositions.[9]

The rest of (modal) epistemology examines the *sotto voce* proviso. It asks: what may we properly presuppose in our ascriptions of knowledge? Which of all the uneliminated alternative possibilities may not properly be ignored?

Which ones are the 'relevant alternatives'? – relevant, that is, to what the subject does and doesn't know?[10] In reply, we can list several rules.[11] We begin with three prohibitions: rules to tell us what possibilities we may not properly ignore.

First, there is the *Rule of Actuality*. The possibility that actually obtains is never properly ignored; actuality is always a relevant alternative; nothing false may properly be presupposed. It follows that only what is true is known, wherefore we did not have to include truth in our definition of knowledge. The rule is 'externalist' – the subject himself may not be able to tell what is properly ignored. In judging which of his ignorings are proper, hence what he knows, we judge his success in knowing – not how well he tried.

When the Rule of Actuality tells us that actuality may never be properly ignored, we can ask: *whose* actuality? Ours, when we ascribe knowledge or ignorance to others? Or the subject's? In simple cases, the question is silly. (In fact, it sounds like the sort of pernicious nonsense we would expect from someone who mixes up what is true with what is believed.) There is just one actual world, we the ascribers live in that world, the subject lives there too, so the subject's actuality is the same as ours.

But there are other cases, less simple, in which the question makes perfect sense and needs an answer. Someone may or may not know who he is; someone may or may not know what time it is. Therefore I insisted that the propositions that may be known must include propositions *de se et nunc*; and likewise that the possibilities that may be eliminated or ignored must include possibilities *de se et nunc*. Now we have a good sense in which the subject's actuality may be different from ours. I ask today what Fred knew yesterday. In particular, did he then know who he was? Did he know what day it was? Fred's actuality is the possibility *de se et nunc* of being Fred on September 19th at such-and-such possible world; whereas my actuality is the possibility *de se et nunc* of being David on September 20th at such-and-such world. So far as the world goes, there is no difference: Fred and I are worldmates, his actual world is the same as mine. But when we build subject and time into the possibilities *de se et nunc*, then his actuality yesterday does indeed differ from mine today.

What is more, we sometimes have occasion to ascribe knowledge to those who are off at other possible worlds. I didn't read the newspaper yesterday. What would I have known if I had read it? More than I do in fact know. (More and less: I do in fact know that I left the newspaper unread, but if I had read it, I would not have known that I had left it unread.) I-who-did-not-read-the-newspaper am here at this world, ascribing knowledge and ignorance. The subject to whom I am ascribing that knowledge and ignorance, namely I-as-I-would-have-been-if-I-had-read-the-newspaper, is at a different world. The worlds differ in respect at least of a reading of the newspaper. Thus the ascriber's actual world is not the same as the subject's. (I myself think that the ascriber and the subject are two different people: the subject is the ascriber's otherworldly counterpart. But even if you think the subject and the ascriber are the same identical person, you must still grant that this person's actuality *qua* subject differs from his actuality *qua* ascriber.)

Or suppose we ask modal questions about the subject: what must he have known, what might he have known? Again we are considering the subject as he is not here, but off at other possible worlds. Likewise if we ask questions about knowledge of knowledge: what does he (or what do we) know that he knows?

So the question 'whose actuality?' is not a silly question after all. And when the question matters, as it does in the cases just considered, the right answer is that it is the subject's actuality, not the ascriber's, that never can be properly ignored.

Next, there is the *Rule of Belief*. A possibility that the subject believes to obtain is not properly ignored, whether or not he is right to so believe. Neither is one that he ought to believe to obtain – one that evidence and arguments justify him in believing – whether or not he does so believe.

That is rough. Since belief admits of degree, and since some possibilities are more specific than others, we ought to reformulate the rule in terms of degree of belief, compared to a standard set by the unspecificity of the possibility in question. A possibility may not be properly ignored if the subject gives it, or ought to give it, a degree of belief that is sufficiently high, and high not just because the possibility in question is unspecific.

How high is 'sufficiently high'? That may depend on how much is at stake. When error would be especially disastrous, few possibilities may be properly ignored. Then even quite a low degree of belief may be 'sufficiently high' to bring the Rule of Belief into play. The jurors know that the accused is guilty only if his guilt has been proved beyond reasonable doubt.[12]

Yet even when the stakes are high, some possibilities still may be properly ignored. Disastrous though it would be to convict an innocent man, still the jurors may properly ignore the possibility that it was the dog, marvellously well-trained, that fired the fatal shot. And, unless they are ignoring other alternatives more relevant than that, they may rightly be said to know that the accused is guilty as charged. Yet if there had been reason to give the dog hypothesis a slightly less negligible degree of belief – if the world's greatest dog-trainer had been the victim's mortal enemy – then the alternative would be relevant after all.

This is the only place where belief and justification enter my story. As already noted, I allow justified true belief without knowledge, as in the case of your belief that you will lose the lottery. I allow knowledge without justification, in the cases of face recognition and chicken sexing. I even allow knowledge without belief, as in the case of the timid student who knows the answer but has no confidence that he has it right, and so does not believe what he knows.[13] Therefore any proposed converse to the Rule of Belief should be rejected. A possibility that the subject does not believe to a sufficient degree, and ought not to believe to a sufficient degree, may nevertheless be a relevant alternative and not properly ignored.

Next, there is the *Rule of Resemblance*. Suppose one possibility saliently resembles another. Then if one of them may not be properly ignored, neither may the other. (Or rather, we should say that if one of them may not properly be ignored *in virtue of rules other than this rule*, then neither may the other. Else nothing could be properly ignored; because enough little steps of resemblance can take us from anywhere to anywhere.) Or suppose one possibility saliently resembles two or more others, one in one respect and another in another, and suppose that each of these may not properly be ignored (in virtue of rules other than this rule). Then these resemblances may have an additive effect, doing more together than any one of them would separately.

We must apply the Rule of Resemblance with care. Actuality is a possibility uneliminated by the subject's evidence. Any other possibility *W* that is likewise uneliminated by the subject's evidence thereby resembles actuality in one salient respect: namely, in respect of the subject's evidence. That will be so even if *W* is in other respects very dissimilar to actuality – even if, for instance, it is a possibility in which the subject is radically deceived by a demon. Plainly, we dare not apply the Rules of Actuality and Resemblance to conclude that any such *W* is a relevant alternative – that would be capitulation to scepticism. The Rule of Resemblance was never meant to apply to this resemblance! We seem to have an *ad hoc* exception to the Rule, though one that makes good sense in view of the function of attributions of knowledge. What would be better, though, would be to find a way to

reformulate the Rule so as to get the needed exception without *ad hocery*. I do not know how to do this.

It is the Rule of Resemblance that explains why you do not know that you will lose the lottery, no matter what the odds are against you and no matter how sure you should therefore be that you will lose. For every ticket, there is the possibility that it will win. These possibilities are saliently similar to one another: so either every one of them may be properly ignored, or else none may. But one of them may not properly be ignored: the one that actually obtains.

The Rule of Resemblance also is the rule that solves the Gettier problems: other cases of justified true belief that are not knowledge.[14]

1   I think that Nogot owns a Ford, because I have seen him driving one; but unbeknownst to me he does not own the Ford he drives, or any other Ford. Unbeknownst to me, Havit does own a Ford, though I have no reason to think so because he never drives it, and in fact I have often seen him taking the tram. My justified true belief is that one of the two owns a Ford. But I do not know it; I am right by accident. Diagnosis: I do not know, because I have not eliminated the possibility that Nogot drives a Ford he does not own whereas Havit neither drives nor owns a car. This possibility may not properly be ignored. Because, first, actuality may not properly be ignored; and, second, this possibility saliently resembles actuality. It resembles actuality perfectly so far as Nogot is concerned; and it resembles actuality well so far as Havit is concerned, since it matches actuality both with respect to Havit's carless habits and with respect to the general correlation between carless habits and carlessness. In addition, this possibility saliently resembles a third possibility: one in which Nogot drives a Ford he owns while Havit neither drives

nor owns a car. This third possibility may not properly be ignored, because of the degree to which it is believed. This time, the resemblance is perfect so far as Havit is concerned, rather good so far as Nogot is concerned.

2　The stopped clock is right twice a day. It says 4:39, as it has done for weeks. I look at it at 4:39; by luck I pick up a true belief. I have ignored the uneliminated possibility that I looked at it at 4:22 while it was stopped saying 4:39. That possibility was not properly ignored. It resembles actuality perfectly so far as the stopped clock goes.

3　Unbeknownst to me, I am travelling in the land of the bogus barns; but my eye falls on one of the few real ones. I don't know that I am seeing a barn, because I may not properly ignore the possibility that I am seeing yet another of the abundant bogus barns. This possibility saliently resembles actuality in respect of the abundance of bogus barns, and the scarcity of real ones, hereabouts.

4　Donald is in San Francisco, just as I have every reason to think he is. But, bent on deception, he is writing me letters and having them posted to me by his accomplice in Italy. If I had seen the phoney letters, with their Italian stamps and postmarks, I would have concluded that Donald was in Italy. Luckily, I have not yet seen any of them. I ignore the uneliminated possibility that Donald has gone to Italy and is sending me letters from there. But this possibility is not properly ignored, because it resembles actuality both with respect to the fact that the letters are coming to me from Italy and with respect to the fact that those letters come, ultimately, from Donald. So I don't know that Donald is in San Francisco.

Next, there is the *Rule of Reliability*. This time, we have a presumptive rule about what *may* be

properly ignored; and it is by means of this rule that we capture what is right about causal or reliabilist theories of knowing. Consider processes whereby information is transmitted to us: perception, memory, and testimony. These processes are fairly reliable.[15] Within limits, we are entitled to take them for granted. We may properly presuppose that they work without a glitch in the case under consideration. Defeasibly – *very* defeasibly! – a possibility in which they fail may properly be ignored.

My visual experience, for instance, depends causally on the scene before my eyes, and what I believe about the scene before my eyes depends in turn on my visual experience. Each dependence covers a wide and varied range of alternatives.[16] Of course, it is possible to hallucinate – even to hallucinate in such a way that all my perceptual experience and memory would be just as they actually are. That possibility never can be eliminated. But it can be ignored. And if it is properly ignored – as it mostly is – then vision gives me knowledge. Sometimes, though, the possibility of hallucination is not properly ignored; for sometimes we really do hallucinate. The Rule of Reliability may be defeated by the Rule of Actuality. Or it may be defeated by the Rules of Actuality and of Resemblance working together, in a Gettier problem: if I am not hallucinating, but unbeknownst to me I live in a world where people mostly do hallucinate and I myself have only narrowly escaped, then the uneliminated possibility of hallucination is too close to actuality to be properly ignored.

We do not, of course, presuppose that nowhere ever is there a failure of, say, vision. The general presupposition that vision is reliable consists, rather, of a standing disposition to presuppose, concerning whatever particular case may be under consideration, that we have no failure in that case.

In similar fashion, we have two permissive *Rules of Method*. We are entitled to presuppose – again, very defeasibly – that a sample is representative;

and that the best explanation of our evidence is the true explanation. That is, we are entitled properly to ignore possible failures in these two standard methods of non-deductive inference. Again, the general rule consists of a standing disposition to presuppose reliability in whatever particular case may come before us.

Yet another permissive rule is the *Rule of Conservatism*. Suppose that those around us normally do ignore certain possibilities, and it is common knowledge that they do. (They do, they expect each other to, they expect each other to expect each other to, . . .) Then – again, very defeasibly! – these generally ignored possibilities may properly be ignored. We are permitted, defeasibly, to adopt the usual and mutually expected presuppositions of those around us.

(It is unclear whether we need all four of these permissive rules. Some might be subsumed under others. Perhaps our habits of treating samples as representative, and of inferring to the best explanation, might count as normally reliable processes of transmission of information. Or perhaps we might subsume the Rule of Reliability under the Rule of Conservatism, on the ground that the reliable processes whereby we gain knowledge are familiar, are generally relied upon, and so are generally presupposed to be normally reliable. Then the only extra work done by the Rule of Reliability would be to cover less familiar – and merely hypothetical? – reliable processes, such as processes that relied on extrasensory faculties. Likewise, *mutatis mutandis*, we might subsume the Rules of Method under the Rule of Conservatism. Or we might instead think to subsume the Rule of Conservatism under the Rule of Reliability, on the ground that what is generally presupposed tends for the most part to be true, and the reliable processes whereby this is so are covered already by the Rule of Reliability. Better redundancy than incompleteness, though. So, leaving the question of redundancy open, I list all four rules.)

Our final rule is the *Rule of Attention*. But it is more

a triviality than a rule. When we say that a possibility is properly ignored, we mean exactly that; we do not mean that it *could have been* properly ignored. Accordingly, a possibility not ignored at all is *ipso facto* not properly ignored. What is and what is not being ignored is a feature of the particular conversational context. No matter how far-fetched a certain possibility may be, no matter how properly we might have ignored it in some other context, if in *this* context we are not in fact ignoring it but attending to it, then for us now it is a relevant alternative. It is in the contextually determined domain. If it is an uneliminated possibility in which not-P, then it will do as a counter-example to the claim that P holds in every possibility left uneliminated by S's evidence. That is, it will do as a counter-example to the claim that S knows that P.

Do some epistemology. Let your fantasies rip. Find uneliminated possibilities of error everywhere. Now that you are attending to them, just as I told you to, you are no longer ignoring them, properly or otherwise. So you have landed in a context with an enormously rich domain of potential counter-examples to ascriptions of knowledge. In such an extraordinary context, with such a rich domain, it never can happen (well, hardly ever) that an ascription of knowledge is true. Not an ascription of knowledge to yourself (either to your present self or to your earlier self, untainted by epistemology); and not an ascription of knowledge to others. That is how epistemology destroys knowledge. But it does so only temporarily. The pastime of epistemology does not plunge us forevermore into its special context. We can still do a lot of proper ignoring, a lot of knowing, and a lot of true ascribing of knowledge to ourselves and others, the rest of the time.

What is epistemology all about? The epistemology we've just been doing, at any rate, soon became an investigation of the ignoring of possibilities. But to investigate the ignoring of them was *ipso facto* not to ignore them. Unless this investigation of ours was an altogether atypical sample of epistemology, it will be inevitable that epistemology must destroy knowledge. That is how knowledge is elusive. Examine it, and straightaway it vanishes.

Is resistance useless? If you bring some hitherto ignored possibility to our attention, then straightaway we are not ignoring it at all, so *a fortiori* we are not properly ignoring it. How can this alteration of our conversational state be undone? If you are persistent, perhaps it cannot be undone – at least not so long as you are around. Even if we go off and play backgammon, and afterward start our conversation afresh, you might turn up and call our attention to it all over again.

But maybe you called attention to the hitherto ignored possibility by mistake. You only suggested that we ought to suspect the butler because you mistakenly thought him to have a criminal record. Now that you know he does not – that was the *previous* butler – you wish you had not mentioned him at all. You knows as well as we do that continued attention to the possibility you brought up impedes our shared conversational purposes. Indeed, it may be common knowledge between you and us that we would all prefer it if this possibility could be dismissed from our attention. In that case we might quickly strike a tacit agreement to speak just as if we were ignoring it; and after just a little of that, doubtless it really would be ignored.

Sometimes our conversational pruposes are not altogether shared, and it is a matter of conflict whether attention to some far-fetched possibility would advance them or impede them. What if some far-fetched possibility is called to our attention not by a sceptical philosopher, but by counsel for the defence? We of the jury may wish to ignore it, and wish it had not been mentioned. If we ignored it now, we would bend the rules of cooperative conversation; but we may have good reason to do exactly that. (After all, what matters most to us as jurors is not whether we can truly be said to know; what

really matters is what we should believe to what degree, and whether or not we should vote to convict.) We would ignore the far-fetched possibility if we could – but can we? Perhaps at first our attempted ignoring would be make-believe ignoring, or self-deceptive ignoring; later, perhaps, it might ripen into genuine ignoring. But in the meantime, do we know? There may be no definite answer. We are bending the rules, and our practices of context-dependent attributions of knowledge were made for contexts with the rules unbent.

If you are still a contented fallibilist, despite my plea to hear the sceptical argument afresh, you will probably be discontented with the Rule of Attention. You will begrudge the sceptic even his very temporary victory. You will claim the right to resist his argument not only in everyday contexts, but even in those peculiar contexts in which he (or some other epistemologist) busily calls your attention to far-fetched possibilities of error. Further, you will claim the right to resist without having to bend any rules of cooperative conversation. I said that the Rule of Attention was a triviality: that which is not ignored at all is not properly ignored. But the Rule was trivial only because of how I had already chosen to state the *sotto voce* proviso. So you, the contented fallibilist, will think it ought to have been stated differently. Thus, perhaps: 'Psst! – except for those possibilities we *could* properly have ignored'. And then you will insist that those far-fetched possibilities of error that we attend to at the behest of the sceptic are nevertheless possibilities we could properly have ignored. You will say that no amount of attention can, by itself, turn them into relevant alternatives.

If you say this, we have reached a standoff. I started with a puzzle: how can it be, when his conclusion is so silly, that the sceptic's argument is so irresistible? My Rule of Attention, and the version of the proviso that made that Rule trivial, were built to explain how the sceptic manages to sway us – why his argument seems irresistible, however temporarily. If you continue to find it eminently resistible in all contexts, you have no need of any such explanation. We just disagree about the explanandum phenomenon.

I say S knows that P iff P holds in every possibility left uneliminated by S's evidence – Psst! – except for those possibilities that *we* are properly ignoring. 'We' means: the speaker and hearers of a given context; that is, those of us who are discussing S's knowledge together. It is our ignorings, not S's own ignorings, that matter to what we can truly say about S's knowledge. When we are talking about our own knowledge or ignorance, as epistemologists so often do, this is a distinction without a difference. But what if we are talking about someone else?

Suppose we are detectives; the crucial question for our solution of the crime is whether S already *knew*, when he bought the gun, that he was vulnerable to blackmail. We conclude that he did. *We* ignore various far-fetched possibilities as hard-headed detectives should. But S does not ignore them. S is by profession a sceptical epistemologist. He never ignores much of anything. If it is our own ignorings that matter to the truth of our conclusion, we may well be right that S already knew. But if it is S's ignorings that matter, then we are wrong, because S never knew much of anything. I say we may well be right; so it is our own ignorings that matter, not S's.

But suppose instead that we are epistemologists considering what S knows. If we are well-informed about S (or if we are considering a well-enough specified hypothetical case), then if S attends to a certain possibility, we attend to S's attending to it. But to attend to S's attending to it is *ipso facto* to attend to it ourselves. In that case, unlike the case of the detectives, the possibilities we are properly ignoring must be among the possibilities that S himself ignores. We may ignore fewer possibilities than S does, but not more.

Even if S himself is neither sceptical nor an epistemologist, he may yet be clever at thinking up far-fetched possibilities that are uneliminated by his evidence. Then again, we well-informed epistemologists who ask what S knows will have to attend to the possibilities that S thinks up. Even if S's idle cleverness does not lead S himself to draw sceptical conclusions, it nevertheless limits the knowledge that we can truly ascribe to him when attentive to his state of mind. More simply: his cleverness limits his knowledge. He would have known more, had he been less imaginative.[17]

Do I claim you can know P just by presupposing it?! Do I claim you can know that a possibility W does not obtain just by ignoring it? Is that not what my analysis implies, provided that the presupposing and the ignoring are proper? Well, yes. And yet I do not claim it. Or rather, I do not claim it for any specified P or W. I have to grant, in general, that knowledge just by presupposing and ignoring *is* knowledge; but it is an *especially* elusive sort of knowledge, and consequently it is an unclaimable sort of knowledge. You do not even have to practise epistemology to make it vanish. Simply *mentioning* any particular case of this knowledge, aloud or even in silent thought, is a way to attend to the hitherto ignored possibility, and thereby render it no longer ignored, and thereby create a context in which it is no longer true to ascribe the knowledge in question to yourself or others. So, just as we should think, presuppositions alone are not a basis on which to *claim* knowledge.

In general, when S knows that P some of the possibilities in which not-P are eliminated by S's evidence and others of them are properly ignored. There are some that can be eliminated, but cannot properly be ignored. For instance, when I look around the study without seeing Possum the cat, I thereby eliminate various possibilities in which Possum is in the study; but had those possibilities not been eliminated, they could not properly have been ignored. And there are other possibilities that never can be eliminated, but can properly be ignored. For instance, the possibility that Possum is on the desk but has been made invisible by a deceiving demon falls normally into this class (though not when I attend to it in the special context of epistemology).

There is a third class: not-P possibilities that might either be eliminated or ignored. Take the far-fetched possibility that Possum has somehow managed to get into a closed drawer of the desk – maybe he jumped in when it was open, then I closed it without noticing him. That possibility could be eliminated by opening the drawer and making a thorough examination. But if uneliminated, it may nevertheless be ignored, and in many contexts that ignoring would be proper. If I look all around the study, but without checking the closed drawers of the desk, I may truly be said to know that Possum is not in the study – or at any rate, there are many contexts in which that may truly be said. But if I did check all the closed drawers, then I would know *better* that Possum is not in the study. My knowledge would be better in the second case because it would rest more on the elimination of not-P possibilities, less on the ignoring of them.[18,19]

Better knowledge is more stable knowledge: it stands more chance of surviving a shift of attention in which we begin to attend to some of the possibilities formerly ignored. If, in our new shifted context, we ask what knowledge we may truly ascribe to our earlier selves, we may find that only the better knowledge of our earlier selves still deserves the name. And yet, if our former ignorings were proper at the time, even the worse knowledge of our earlier selves could truly have been called knowledge in the former context.

Never – well, hardly ever – does our knowledge rest entirely on elimination and not at all on ignoring. So hardly ever is it quite as good as we might wish. To that extent, the lesson of scepticism is right – and right permanently, not just in the temporary and special context of epistemology.[20]

What is it all for? Why have a notion of knowledge that works in the way I described? (Not a compulsory question. Enough to observe that we do have it.) But I venture the guess that it is one of the messy short-cuts – like satisficing, like having indeterminate degrees of belief – that we resort to because we are not smart enough to live up to really high, perfectly Bayesian, standards of rationality. You cannot maintain a record of exactly which possibilities you have eliminated so far, much as you might like to. It is easier to keep track of which possibilities you have eliminated if you – Psst! – ignore many of all the possibilities there are. And besides, it is easier to list some of the propositions that are true in *all* the uneliminated, unignored possibilities than it is to find propositions that are true in *all and only* the uneliminated, unignored possibilities.

If you doubt that the word 'know' bears any real load in science or in metaphysics, I partly agree. The serious business of science has to do not with knowledge *per se*; but rather, with the elimination of possibilities through the evidence of perception, memory, etc., and with the changes that one's belief system would (or might or should) undergo under the impact of such eliminations. Ascriptions of knowledge to yourself or others are a very sloppy way of conveying very incomplete information about the elimination of possibilities. It is as if you had said:

> The possibilites eliminated, whatever else they may also include, at least include all the not-P possibilities; or anyway, all of those except for some we are presumably prepared to ignore just at the moment.

The only excuse for giving information about what really matters in such a sloppy way is that at least it is easy and quick! But it *is* easy and quick; whereas giving full and precise information about which possibilities have been eliminated seems to be extremely difficult, as witness the futile search for a 'pure observation language'. If I am right about how ascriptions of knowledge work, they are a handy but humble approximation. They may yet be indispensable in practice, in the same way that other handy and humble approximations are.

If we analyse knowledge as a modality, as we have done, we cannot escape the conclusion that knowledge is closed under (strict) implication.[21] Dretske has denied that knowledge is closed under implication; further, he has diagnosed closure as the fallacy that drives arguments for scepticism. As follows: the proposition that I have hands implies that I am not a handless being, and *a fortiori* that I am not a handless being deceived by a demon into thinking that I have hands. So, by the closure principle, the proposition that I know I have hands implies that I know that I am not handless and deceived. But I don't know that I am not handless and deceived – for how can I eliminate that possibility? So, by *modus tollens*, I don't know that I have hands. Dretske's advice is to resist scepticism by denying closure. He says that although having hands *does* imply not being handless and deceived, yet knowing that I have hands *does not* imply knowing that I am not handless and deceived. I do know the former, I do not know the latter.

What Dretske says is close to right, but not quite. Knowledge *is* closed under implication. Knowing that I have hands *does* imply knowing that I am not handless and deceived. Implication preserves truth – that is, it preserves truth in any given, fixed context. But if we switch contexts midway, all bets are off. I say (1) pigs fly; (2) what I just said had fewer than three syllables (true); (3) what I just said had fewer than four syllables (false). So 'less than three' does not imply 'less than four'? No! The context switched midway, the semantic value of the context-dependent phrase 'what I just said' switched with it. Likewise in the sceptical argument the context switched midway, and the semantic value of the context-dependent word 'know'

switched with it. The premise 'I know that I have hands' was true in its everyday context, where the possibility of deceiving demons was properly ignored. The mention of that very possibility switched the context midway. The conclusion 'I know that I am not handless and deceived' was false in its context, because that was a context in which the possibility of deceiving demons was being mentioned, hence was not being ignored, hence was not being properly ignored. Dretske gets the phenomenon right, and I think he gets the diagnosis of scepticism right; it is just that he misclassifies what he sees. He thinks it is a phenomenon of logic, when really it is a phenomenon of pragmatics. Closure, rightly understood, survives the test. If we evaluate the conclusion for truth not with respect to the context in which it was uttered, but instead with respect to the different context in which the premise was uttered, then truth is preserved. And if, *per impossibile*, the conclusion could have been said in the same unchanged context as the premise, truth would have been preserved.

A problem due to Saul Kripke turns upon the closure of knowledge under implication. P implies that any evidence against P is misleading. So, by closure, whenever you know that P, you know that any evidence against P is misleading. And if you know that evidence is misleading, you should pay it no heed. Whenever we know – and we know a lot, remember – we should not heed any evidence tending to suggest that we are wrong. But that is absurd. Shall we dodge the conclusion by denying closure? I think not. Again, I diagnose a change of context. At first, it was stipulated that S knew, whence it followed that S was properly ignoring all possibilities of error. But as the story continues, it turns out that there is evidence on offer that points to some particular possibility of error. Then, by the Rule of Attention, that possibility is no longer properly ignored, either by S himself or by we who are telling the story of S. The advent of that evidence destroys S's knowledge, and thereby destroys S's licence to ignore the evidence lest he be misled.

There is another reason, different from Dretske's, why we might doubt closure. Suppose two or more premises jointly imply a conclusion. Might not someone who is compartmentalized in his thinking – as we all are? – know each of the premises but fail to bring them together in a single compartment? Then might he not fail to know the conclusion? Yes; and I would not like to plead idealization-of-rationality as an excuse for ignoring such cases. But I suggest that we might take not the whole compartmentalized thinker, but rather each of his several overlapping compartments, as our 'subjects'. That would be the obvious remedy if his compartmentalization amounted to a case of multiple personality disorder; but maybe it is right for milder cases as well.[22]

A compartmentalized thinker who indulges in epistemology can destroy his knowledge, yet retain it as well. Imagine two epistemologists on a bushwalk. As they walk, they talk. They mention all manner of far-fetched possibilities of error. By attending to these normally ignored possibilities they destroy the knowledge they normally possess. Yet all the while they know where they are and where they are going! How so? The compartment in charge of philosophical talk attends to far-fetched possibilities of error. The compartment in charge of navigation does not. One compartment loses its knowledge, the other retains its knowledge. And what does the entire compartmentalized thinker know? Not an altogether felicitous question. But if we need an answer, I suppose the best thing to say is that S knows that P iff any one of S's compartments knows that P. Then we can say what we would offhand want to say: yes, our philosophical bushwalkers still know their whereabouts.

Context-dependence is not limited to the ignoring and non-ignoring of far-fetched possibilities. Here is another case. Pity poor Bill! He squanders all his spare cash on the pokies, the races and the lottery. He will be a wage slave all his days. We know he will never be rich. But if he wins the lottery (if he wins big), then he will be rich. Contrapositively: his never being rich, plus other things we know, imply that he will lose. So, by closure, if we know that he will never be rich, we know that he will lose. But when we discussed the case before, we concluded that we cannot know that he will lose. All the possibilities in which Bill loses and someone else wins saliently resemble the possibility in which Bill wins and the others lose; one of those possibilities is actual; so by the Rules of Actuality and of Resemblance, we may not properly ignore the possibility that Bill wins. But there is a loophole: the resemblance was required to be salient. Salience, as well as ignoring, may vary between contexts. Before, when I was explaining how the Rule of Resemblance applied to lotteries, I saw to it that the resemblance between the many possibilities associated with the many tickets was sufficiently salient. But this time, when we were busy pitying poor Bill for his habits and not for his luck, the resemblance of the many possibilities was not so salient. At that point, the possibility of Bill's winning was properly ignored; so then it was true to say that we knew he would never be rich. Afterward I switched the context. I mentioned the possibility that Bill might win, wherefore that possibility was no longer properly ignored. (Maybe there were two separate reasons why it was no longer properly ignored, because maybe I also made the resemblance between the many possibilities more salient.) It was true at first that we knew that Bill would never be rich. And at that point it was also true that we knew he would lose – but that was only true so long as it remained unsaid! (And maybe unthought as well.) Later, after the change in context, it was no longer true that we knew he would lose. At that point, it was also no longer true that we knew he would never be rich.

But wait. Don't you smell a rat? Haven't I, by my own lights, been saying what cannot be said?

(Or whistled either.) If the story I told was true, how have I managed to tell it? In trendyspeak, is there not a problem of reflexivity? Does not my story deconstruct itself?

I said: S knows that P iff S's evidence eliminates every possibility in which not-P – Psst! – except for those possibilities that we are properly ignoring. That 'psst' marks an attempt to do the impossible – to mention that which remains unmentioned. I am sure you managed to make believe that I had succeeded. But I could not have done.

And I said that when we do epistemology, and we attend to the proper ignoring of possibilities, we make knowledge vanish. First we do know, then we do not. But I had been doing epistemology when I said that. The uneliminated possibilities were not being ignored – not just then. So by what right did I say even that we used to know?[23]

In trying to thread a course between the rock of fallibilism and the whirlpool of scepticism, it may well seem as if I have fallen victim to both at once. For do I not say that there are all those uneliminated possibilities of error? Yet do I not claim that we know a lot? Yet do I not claim that knowledge is, by definition, infallible knowledge?

I did claim all three things. But not all at once! Or if I did claim them all at once, that was an expository shortcut, to be taken with a pinch of salt. To get my message across, I bent the rules. If I tried to whistle what cannot be said, what of it? I relied on the cardinal principle of pragmatics, which overrides every one of the rules I mentioned: interpret the message to make it make sense – to make it consistent, and sensible to say.

When you have context-dependence, ineffability can be trite and unmysterious. Hush! [moment of silence] I might have liked to say, just then, 'All of us are silent'. It was true. But I could not have said it truly, or whistled it either. For by saying it aloud, or by whistling, I would have rendered it false.

I could have said my say fair and square, bending no rules. It would have been tiresome, but it could have been done. The secret would have been to resort to 'semantic ascent'. I could have taken great care to distinguish between (1) the language I use when I talk about knowledge, or whatever, and (2) the second language that I use to talk about the semantic and pragmatic workings of the first language. If you want to hear my story told that way, you probably know enough to do the job for yourself. If you can, then my informal presentation has been good enough.

Acknowledgements

Thanks to many for valuable discussions of this material. Thanks above all to Peter Unger; and to Stewart Cohen, Michael Devitt, Alan Hajek, Stephen Hetherington, Denis Robinson, Ernest Sosa, Robert Stalnaker, Jonathan Vogel, and a referee for [the original] Journal. Thanks also to the Boyce Gibson Memorial Library and to Ormond College.

Notes

1 The suggestion that ascriptions of knowledge go false in the context of epistemology is to be found in Stroud 1989 and in Hetherington 1992. Neither of them tells the story just as I do; however, it may be that their versions do not conflict with mine.

2 Unless, like some, we simply define 'justification' as 'whatever it takes to turn true opinion into knowledge' regardless of whether what it takes turns out to involve argument from supporting reasons.

3 The problem of the lottery was introduced in Kyburg 1961, and in Hempel 1962. It has been much discussed since, as a problem both about knowledge and about our everyday, nonquantitative concept of belief.

4 The case of testimony is less discussed than the others; but see Coady 1992, pp. 79–129.

5 I follow Unger 1975. But I shall not let him lead me into scepticism.

6 See Stalnaker 1984. pp. 59–99.

7 See Lewis 1979a; and Chisholm 1979.

8 Unger 1975, chap. II. I discuss the case, and briefly foreshadow the present paper, in Lewis 1979b, esp. pp. 353–355.

9 See Stalnaker 1973 and 1974. See also Lewis 1979b.

The definition restated in terms of presupposition resembles the treatment of knowledge in Ferguson 1980.

10 See Dretske 1970 and 1981; Goldman 1976; Stine 1976; and Cohen 1988.

11 Some of them, but only some, taken from the authors just cited.

12 Instead of complicating the Rule of Belief as I have just done, I might equivalently have introduced a separate Rule of High Stakes saying that when error would be especially disastrous, few possibilities are properly ignored.

13 Woozley 1953; Radford 1966.

14 See Gettier 1963. Diagnoses have varied widely. The four examples below come from: (1) Lehrer and Paxson 1969; (2) Russell 1948, p. 154; (3) Goldman 1976; (4) Harman 1973, p. 143.

Though the lottery problem is another case of justified true belief without knowledge, it is not normally counted among the Gettier problems. It is interesting to find that it yields to the same remedy.

15 See Goldman 1967; Armstrong 1973.

16 See Lewis 1980. John Bigelow has proposed to model knowledge-delivering processes generally on those found in vision.

17 See Elgin 1988. The 'efficacy' takes many forms; some to do with knowledge (under various rival analyses), some to do with justified belief. See also Williams 1991, on the instability of knowledge under reflection.

18 Mixed cases are possible: Fred properly ignores the possibility W_1 which Ted eliminates; however, Ted properly ignores the possibility W_2 which Fred eliminates. Ted has looked in all the desk drawers but not the file drawers, whereas Fred has checked the file drawers but not the desk. Fred's knowledge that Possum is not in the study is better in one way, Ted's is better in another.

19 To say truly that X is known, I must be properly ignoring any uneliminated possibilities in which not-X; whereas to say truly that Y is better known than X, I must be attending to some such possibilities. So I cannot say both in a single context. If I say 'X is known, but Y is better known', the context changes in mid-sentence: some previously ignored possibilities must stop being ignored. That can happen easily. Saying it the other way around 'Y is better known than X, but even X is known' is harder, because we must suddenly start to ignore previously unignored possibilities. That cannot be done, really; but we could bend the rules and make believe we have done it, and no doubt we would be understood well enough. Saying 'X is flat, but Y is flatter' (that is, 'X has no bumps at all, but Y has even fewer or smaller bumps') is a parallel case. And again, 'Y is flatter, but even X is flat' sounds clearly worse – but not altogether hopeless.

20 Thanks here to Stephen Hetherington. While his own views about better and worse knowledge are situated within an analysis of knowledge quite unlike mine, they withstand transplantation.

21 A proof-theoretic version of this closure principle is common to all 'normal' modal logics: if the logic validates an inference from zero or more premises to a conclusion, then also it validates the inference obtained by prefixing the necessity operator to each premise and to the conclusion. Further, this rule is all we need to take us from classical sentential logic to the least normal modal logic. See Chellas 1980, p. 114.

22 See Stalnaker 1984, pp. 79–99.

23 Worse still: by what right can I even say that we used to be in a position to say truly that we knew? Then, we were in a context where we properly ignored certain uneliminated possibilities of error. Now, we are in a context where we no longer ignore them. If *now* I comment retrospectively upon the truth of what was said *then*, which context governs: the context now or the context then? I doubt there is a general answer, apart from the usual principle that we should interpret what is said so as to make the message make sense.

References

Armstrong, D. M. 1973. *Belief, Truth and Knowledge*, Cambridge: Cambridge University Press.

Chisholm, R. M. 1979. 'The Indirect Reflexive', in C. Diamond and J. Teichman (eds) *Intention and*

Intentionality: Essays in Honour of G. E. M. Anscombe, Brighton: Harvester.

Coady, C. A. J. 1992. Testimony: A Philosophical Study, Oxford: Clarendon Press.

Cohen, S. 1988. 'How to be a Fallibilist', Philosophical Perspectives 2: 91–123.

Dretske, F. 1970. 'Epistemic Operators', Journal of Philosophy 67: 1007–23.

Dretske, F. 1981. Knowledge and the Flow of Information, Oxford: Blackwell.

Elgin, C. 1988. 'The Epistemic Efficacy of Stupidity', Synthese 74: 297–311.

Ferguson, K. S. 1980. Philosophical Scepticism. Cornell University doctoral dissertation.

Gettier, E. 1963. 'Is Justified True Belief Knowledge?', Analysis 23: 121–3.

Goldman, A. 1967. 'A Causal Theory of Knowing', Journal of Philosophy 64: 357–72.

Goldman, A. 1976. 'Discrimination and Perceptual Knowledge', Journal of Philosophy 73: 771–91.

Harman, G. 1973. Thought, Princeton, NJ: Princeton University Press.

Hempel, C. G. 1962. 'Deductive-Nomological vs. Statistical Explanation', in H. Feigl and G. Maxwell (eds) Minnesota Studies in the Philosophy of Science, vol. 2, Minneapolis: University of Minnesota Press.

Hetherington, S. 1992. 'Lacking Knowledge and Justification by Theorizing about Them', lecture given at the University of New South Wales, August.

K. Lehrer and T. Paxson 1969. 'Knowledge: Undefeated Justified True Belief', Journal of Philosophy 66: 225–37.

Kyburg, H. E. 1961. Probability and the Logic of Rational Belief, Middletown, CT: Wesleyan University Press.

Lewis, D. 1979a. 'Attitudes De Dicto and De Se', The Philosophical Review 88: 513–43.

Lewis, D. 1979b. 'Scorekeeping in a Language Game', Journal of Philosophical Logic 8: 339–59.

Lewis, D. K. 1980. 'Veridical Hallucination and Prosthetic Vision', Australasian Journal of Philosophy 58: 239–49.

Radford, C. 1966. 'Knowledge - By Examples', Analysis 27: 1–11.

Russell, B. 1948. Human Knowledge: Its Scope and Its Limits, London: George Allen & Unwin.

Stalnaker, R. 1973. 'Presuppositions', Journal of Philosophical Logic 2: 447–57.

Stalnaker, R. 1974. 'Pragmatic Presupposition', in M. Munitz and P. Unger (eds) Semantics and Philosophy, New York: New York University Press.

Stalnaker, R. 1984. Inquiry, Cambridge, MA: MIT Press.

Stine, G. 1976. 'Skepticism, Relevant Alternatives, and Deductive Closure', Philosophical Studies 29: 249–61.

Stroud, B. 1989. 'Understanding Human Knowledge in General', in (ed.) M. Clay and K. Lehrer, Knowledge and Scepticism, Boulder, CO: Westview.

Unger, P. 1975. Ignorance: A Case for Skepticism, Oxford: Oxford University Press.

Williams, M. 1991. Unnatural Doubts: Epistemological Realism and the Basis of Scepticism, Oxford: Blackwell.

Woozley, A. D. 1953. 'Knowing and Not Knowing', Proceedings of the Aristotelian Society 53: 151–72.

PART TEN

Is knowledge in the eye of the beholder?

INTRODUCTION TO PART TEN
Ram Neta and Duncan Pritchard

IN THE PREVIOUS PART we examined scepticism about the *extent* of our knowledge; whether we know as much as we think we do. There is a different way of being sceptical about knowledge, however, which doesn't concern the extent of our knowledge but rather its *objectivity*. Here the sceptical challenge is posed by *relativism* which, in its strongest forms at least, argues that our knowledge is not objective at all.

It is important to understand just how radical this view is. After all, while we might regard some truths as subjective (e.g. truths about which flavour of ice cream tastes best), we do not normally suppose that there are many truths which are subjective in this same way. In particular, we do not normally regard known truths about the world around us as subjective. Take, for example, my knowledge that the Earth orbits the sun rather than vice versa. One would naturally regard this knowledge as knowledge of something that is objectively true; what makes it true has to do with how the heavens above us operate and has nothing to do with us. So, for example, it cannot be the case that it is true for some people that the Earth (currently) orbits the sun and yet false for others. That the Earth orbits the sun is simply a fact, and it is a fact independently of what anyone may think about it, or whether anyone happens to know about it.

The readings for this part open with Luigi Pirandello's (1867–1936) famous play, 'Right You Are (If You Think You Are)' (Chapter 41), which gives a vivid dramatic expression to some of the ideas behind relativism. We then move on to Peter Winch's (1926–97) famous paper, 'Understanding a Primitive Society' (Chapter 42). In a broadly Wittgensteinian spirit, Winch's concern in this paper is to argue that the best way to avoid misunderstanding a primitive society – or, for that matter, any society which appears substantively different from our own in terms of its beliefs and practices – is to understand it as employing its own logic, and standards of judgement and reasoning, rather than to approach it through our own standards of judgement and reasoning. This way of thinking about other societies seems to imply relativism because it does not distinguish correct from incorrect standards of judgement and reasoning. In support of this theoretical approach, Winch draws on the work of the anthropologist E. E. Evans-Pritchard, who produced a seminal study of the Azande, a traditional people who inhabit Africa's Nile–Congo divide and who appear to have some very different beliefs and customs from our own.

Our next reading comes from the American philosopher Paul Boghossian (1957–), who examines the implications of the famous 'Sokal hoax' (Chapter 43). This is a hoax that was perpetrated by a theoretical physicist, Alan Sokal (1955–), on the journal *Social Text*. This journal was held to be at the forefront of a form of relativism which has been particularly prominent in intellectual circles since the late twentieth century (albeit, it is worth noting, not in mainstream English-speaking philosophy departments), known as *postmodernism*. Central to the postmodernist perspective is a relativistic disdain for so-called 'meta-narratives', which are objective descriptions of reality. What was so dramatic about this article was that it was riddled with inaccuracies, some of which were obviously false, but was accepted for publication anyway. (Worse, as Boghossian notes early on in his article, the special issue of the journal that this article appeared in was explicitly devoted to rebutting the charge that critiques of science from the perspective of cultural studies are riddled with incompetence.)

Boghossian draws three conclusions from this hoax. The first is that it demonstrates the extent to which the relativism that is at the core of postmodernism has (as he would put it) infected intellectual life. The second is that such an acceptance of relativism inevitably results in a shoddy level of scholarship, as the publication of this article indicates. Finally, Boghossian also tries to rebut the potential counter-charge that his criticism of postmodernism is politically motivated by arguing that a commitment to postmodernism does not further the ends of a progressive political programme but in fact positively undermines them.

The final piece collected in this part is by Michael Williams (1947–) (Chapter 44), and explores the extent to which the kind of epistemology that is suggested by some of the later writings of Ludwig Wittgenstein (1889–1951) really does lend support to relativism as many suppose. The reason why these writings are thought to imply relativism is because they embody a kind of epistemological contextualism. Contextualism of this sort holds that whether one's belief is justified will depend on which context one is in, where what determines one's context is the 'hinge propositions' (as Wittgenstein calls them) or 'methodological necessities' (as Williams calls them) of that context. These are the propositions which cannot be called into question in that context, but rather serve as the 'fixed epistemic points' of that context relative to which all epistemic evaluation takes place. Crucially, since all justification is context dependent, and since these hinge propositions are the fixed epistemic points of that context relative to which all epistemic evaluation takes place, such propositions are not themselves justified in that context. The result is that not only is all justification context dependent on this view, but it is also relative to the acceptance of propositions which are fundamental to that context and yet which themselves lack epistemic support in that very context. Many see in this conception of epistemic justification a licence for relativism.

Against this prevailing view of epistemological contextualism, however, Williams argues that the sense of epistemic objectivity that is being denied here is unduly strong and not remotely plausible on closer inspection. In particular, it leads, he argues, to an implausible epistemological view which he terms 'epistemological realism'. It is thus a form of epistemic objectivity that one ought not to subscribe to in the first place. Moreover, Williams argues that once this implausible form of epistemic objectivity is denied, then the impetus towards relativism – and hence away from a weaker, more plausible conception of epistemic objectivity – is undermined. According to Williams, then, Wittgensteinian contextualism thus not only is not a form of relativism but is in fact the *cure* for relativism.

Study questions

1   In your own words, try to describe the methodology that Winch sets out for understanding a primitive society. How, if at all, might this methodology lead to relativism?

2   What conclusions, if any, should we draw from the Sokal hoax? In particular, describe and critically assess the conclusions that Boghossian draws from this hoax.

3   Boghossian claims that postmodernist ideas do not further the ends of a progressive political programme, but in fact undermine them. Why does he claim this? Is he right?

4   In your own words, try to describe the form of epistemological contextualism put forward by Williams. Why might such a view be thought to lead to relativism?

5   Critically evaluate Williams' claim that his version of epistemological contextualism not only does not lead to relativism but in fact removes much of the theoretical impetus towards relativistic ideas.

Further reading

For an accessible introduction to some of the issues regarding relativism, see Pritchard (2006: chapter 13). For an excellent and comprehensive overview of the issues regarding relativism, which is freely available on the internet, see Swoyer (2003). See also Westacott (2006). Both of these articles contain details of relevant further readings. Boghossian (2006) is a book-length treatment of relativism which builds on his article contained here, and which is aimed at the general reader. See also Blackburn (2006), Lynch (2004) and O'Grady (2002).

References

Blackburn, S. (2006). *Truth: A Guide for the Perplexed*, London: Penguin.

Boghossian, P. (2006). *Fear of Knowledge: Against Relativism and Constructivism*, Oxford: Oxford University Press.

Lynch, M. P. (2004). *True to Life: Why Truth Matters*, Cambridge, MA: MIT Press.

O'Grady, P. (2002). *Relativism*, Chesham: Acumen.

Pritchard, D. H. (2006). *What Is this Thing Called Knowledge?*, London: Routledge.

Swoyer, C. (2003). 'Relativism', *Stanford Encyclopaedia of Philosophy*, ed. E. Zalta, http://plato.stanford.edu/entries/relativism/.

Westacott, E. (2006). 'Cognitive Relativism', *Internet Encyclopaedia of Philosophy*, eds J. Fieser and B. Dowden, http://www.iep.utm.edu/c/cog-rel.htm.

Chapter 41

Luigi Pirandello

RIGHT YOU ARE (IF YOU THINK YOU ARE)

Act one

COUNCILLOR AGAZZI's *drawing room.* LAMBERTO LAUDISI *is pacing the room, nervously. He has a quiet elegance and a very quick wit. He constantly sips a glass of wine.* AMALIA AGAZZI *and her daughter* DINA *are watching him.* AMALIA *is self-important and overly aware of her husband's position in society. Her manner makes it quite clear that she believes she could not only supplant but outdo him on any given occasion.* DINA *has a vibrant, youthful charm that compensates for her tendency to know better than anyone else, especially her parents.*

LAUDISI: Let me get this straight – he's gone to the Mayor??

AMALIA: For God's sake, Lamberto, it *is* one of his underlings!

LAUDISI: In his office, not at home. This is none of his business.

DINA: But the man has rented a flat for his mother-in-law right here in our building; in fact, the flat next door.

LAUDISI: Excuse me – is that illegal? Are you actually telling me you're upset because the mother-in-law of one of your husband's subordinates only lives next door to you but – shock! horror! – hasn't paid her respects?

AMALIA: It's the opposite. Dina and I decided to pay our respects to *her.* And we were not invited in.

LAUDISI: And *that's* what your husband is reporting to the Mayor? What does he want him to do – chuck her into prison?

AMALIA: Don't be absurd. We simply want justice. One doesn't leave two ladies standing in front of a door as if they were . . .

DINA: Hitching posts.

LAUDISI: But don't people have the right to behave how they choose in their own home?

AMALIA: *We* were the ones who wished to be courteous, who wanted to welcome a stranger . . .

DINA: I can see that look in your eye, I know exactly what you're thinking: we were only being courteous because we were so curious – right?

LAUDISI: Umm . . .

DINA: Well, why not? Isn't that natural?

LAUDISI: Yes, when you haven't anything better to do.

DINA: Look – imagine that you are standing here—

LAUDISI: I *am* standing here.

DINA: Imagine it, anyway. You're standing here, minding your own business, and then I walk in and place something on a table in front of you . . .

LAUDISI: What?

DINA: Shoes.

LAUDISI: Shoes?

DINA: The cook's shoes.

LAUDISI: *Why* the cook's shoes?

DINA: Ah! Got you! You're *curious,* aren't you? You see – it's natural.

LAUDISI: Clever. But you put the cook's shoes on the table purposely to arouse my curiosity, so I would be certain to ask why. Fine. Now prove to me that this Signor Ponza – the man your father is branding a criminal – brought his mother-in-law to live next door to you *on purpose*.

DINA: Well, perhaps not on purpose. But, Uncle, you can't deny the man is very, well . . . extravagant, extravagant enough to have the whole town talking. Look – he moves to this town. He rents another flat on the top floor of a gloomy old house on the other side of town next to the market. Have you seen that building?

LAUDISI: I imagine you have.

DINA: Of course. Mother and I both. Not just us. The whole town's had a look. It has a very dark courtyard – it's spooky, like the bottom of a well – and there's a balcony on the top floor which is surrounded by an iron railing and there are baskets hanging from the railing on ropes—

LAUDISI (*mock horror*): My God! Baskets! (*Pause.*) So what?

DINA: His wife is in that flat! He's shut her away!

AMALIA: And meanwhile he's put his mother-in-law next to us!

LAUDISI: In a beautiful flat in the centre of town. That's rather sweet.

AMALIA: He forces her to live apart from her daughter.

LAUDISI: How do you know that? Perhaps it's the mother-in-law's choice. Perhaps she wanted some space—

AMALIA: Space?! At her age!

DINA: Don't be daft. It's him. Everyone knows it's him.

AMALIA: Obviously, when a girl marries she'll leave her mother's home and live with her husband, even if it is in another town. But if the mother, poor thing, can't bear to be apart from her daughter, and follows her to that other town, where they are, in fact, both strangers, don't you think it odd that instead of being invited into her daughter's household, she is forced to live on the other side of town?

LAUDISI: Perhaps she and her daughter, or more likely, she and her son-in-law, simply don't like each other.

AMALIA: Hardly. They're always together.

LAUDISI: Mother and daughter?

DINA: Mother and son-in-law. That's why everyone's talking.

AMALIA: He comes every evening to keep her company.

DINA: And at least once or twice a day.

LAUDISI: Ah! They're lovers!

AMALIA: Oh please! She's an old lady.

LAUDISI: Stranger things have happened.

AMALIA: And he never brings her daughter. He never, never brings his wife to see her mother.

LAUDISI: Perhaps the old woman's ill.

DINA: She's not. She leaves the house . . .

AMALIA: And goes . . .

DINA: Across town . . .

AMALIA: Every day . . .

DINA: To see her daughter . . .

AMALIA: But she's forbidden to go upstairs . . .

DINA: She can only talk to her . . .

AMALIA: From the courtyard.

DINA: She goes into the courtyard and pulls the string of a basket, which rings a bell in the flat, and then her daughter comes on to the balcony, and the mother talks to her, from the courtyard, and she can't even see her daughter because the sun is in her eyes . . .

The BUTLER *enters.*

BUTLER: Signora.

AMALIA: Who is it?

BUTLER: Signor and Signora Sirelli with another lady.

AMALIA (*makes a face*): Oh my. Well – show them in.

SIRELLI *and* SIGNORA SIRELLI *and* SIGNORA CINI *enter.* SIGNORA SIRELLI *is overdressed, unable to hide her provincial taste. She radiates curiosity, as well as a public distaste for her husband.*

SIRELLI *has pretensions to elegance, exemplified by his squeaky, overly polished shoes.* SIGNORA CINI *is a classic passive-aggressive, invariably ready to stick the knife in.*

AMALIA (*to* SIGNORA SIRELLI): My dear . . .

SIGNORA SIRELLI: I've taken the liberty of bringing my friend, Signora Cini, who has been longing to meet you.

AMALIA: How sweet. Lovely to meet you. Please – make yourself comfortable. (*Introducing* DINA *and* LAUDISI.) May I introduce my daughter, Dina, and my brother, Lamberto Laudisi.

SIRELLI (*shakes hands with* LAUDISI, *then to the others*): Signora, Signorina.

SIGNORA SIRELLI: I said to my husband we must go to the source.

AMALIA: Source?

SIGNORA SIRELLI: We're starved for news.

AMALIA: What news?

SIGNORA SIRELLI: About the clerk. The new clerk at your husband's office.

SIGNORA CINI: Yes . . . is it all right to say this? . . . We're very curious . . .

AMALIA: But we don't know anything.

SIRELLI (*to his wife*): What did I tell you! They don't know as much as I do. (*To the others.*) Are you aware of the reason – the reason that poor mother can't go into her daughter's home?

AMALIA: We were just discussing it.

LAUDISI: I think you're all barking!

DINA: Because the son-in-law forbids it.

SIGNORA CINI: Oh dear . . . I think . . . Am I permitted to say this? . . . *It's more than that* . . .

SIRELLI: I've been told, on the highest authority, and I might add, in strict confidence, that he keeps her prisoner.

AMALIA: The mother-in-law?

SIRELLI: No, the wife.

SIGNORA SIRELLI: The wife! The wife!

SIGNORA CINI: Oh dear . . . I think what they say is . . . under lock and key . . .

DINA: Ah, you see, Uncle. You've been trying to justify his actions.

SIRELLI: What? You've defended this monster?

LAUDISI: I haven't defended anyone. I just find

your curiosity grotesque, not least because it serves no purpose.

SIRELLI: No purpose?!

LAUDISI: Useless, actually.

SIGNORA CINI: Oh dear . . . it's just that . . . you see . . . *we want to know.* . .

LAUDISI: Know *what*? What on earth can we ever know about anybody else? Do you think we know, really know, who other people are, or what they are, or what they do, or why?

SIGNORA SIRELLI: But you can find out little things, little bits of information . . .

LAUDISI: Actually, Signora, you can't be starved for information, as your husband is so obviously well informed . . .

SIRELLI: Now hold on . . .

SIGNORA SIRELLI (*to* AMALIA): And that's my tragedy, you see – my husband always says he knows everything, but I end up in the dark.

SIRELLI: Are you surprised? You never believe a word I say. You always insist that my information can't be true and you proceed to believe the exact opposite.

SIGNORA SIRELLI: Because you tell me ludicrous things.

LAUDISI (*laughs*): May I answer your husband for you? My dear man, how can you expect your wife to be happy with the information you give her if you are only able to report matters as they seem to be *to you*?

SIGNORA SIRELLI: Exactly. He talks nonsense.

LAUDISI: Permit me to disagree. Your husband tells you exactly what he sees.

SIGNORA SIRELLI: But he's never right.

SIRELLI: I'm always right!

LAUDISI: Now please, my friends, calm down. He *is* right. But, of course, he is wrong. May I explain? (*Walks to the centre of the room.*) Look. Look at me. Standing here. Do you see me?

SIRELLI: Of course.

LAUDISI: No, no, don't jump to conclusions. Come here, please . . .

SIRELLI *is perplexed and unwilling to participate.*

SIRELLI: Why should I?

SIGNORA SIRELLI: For God's sake, go over there. (*Pushes her husband towards* LAUDISI.)

LAUDISI: So. Do you see me? Take a closer look. Touch me.

SIRELLI *hesitates.*

SIGNORA SIRELLI: Touch him!

SIRELLI *gingerly touches* LAUDISI.

LAUDISI: Bravo! Now – are you certain you are touching the person you see?

SIRELLI: Yes . . .

LAUDISI: Without a doubt, he? Now – please – return to your seat.

SIRELLI *stands motionless, astonished and confused.*

SIGNORA SIRELLI: Don't stand there like a zombie. Sit down.

LAUDISI (*to* SIGNORA SIRELLI, *as her husband returns to his seat*): Now please, Signora Sirelli, if you wouldn't mind coming here. No – better still. I'll come to you. (*Kneels before her.*) I assume you see me – here – in front of you. Lift your hand, please. Touch me. (*As she places a hand on his shoulder, he leans forward and kisses it.*) What a lovely little hand . . .

SIRELLI: Now just a minute . . .

LAUDISI: Ignore him. Are you certain you have touched the person you see? Have you any doubts? Whatever you do, don't tell your husband who you have touched, or my sister, or niece, or this lady here . . .

SIGNORA CINI: Signora Cini.

LAUDISI: If you say so. Don't tell them who you touched. They will agree with you on the surface; you have, after all, touched Lamberto Laudisi, have you not? – But deep down they will think you are wrong. Because you see one Lamberto Laudisi, your husband sees another, my sister another still, my niece also, and this lady . . .

SIGNORA CINI: Signora Cini.

LAUDISI: If you insist. And you are, each of you, correct. I am whatever Lamberto Laudisi you choose to see.

SIGNORA SIRELLI: Do you mean you appear differently to each one of us?

LAUDISI: But of course I do. Don't you?

SIGNORA SIRELLI: Oh no, no . . . I'm always the same.

LAUDISI: And I am as well – to me. And I could easily say to you that you must see me as I see myself. But don't you think that would be presumptuous?

SIRELLI: What does all this mumbo-jumbo have to do with anything?

LAUDISI: Well, you're all so anxious who other people are, to insist that things are exactly this way or that way . . .

SIGNORA SIRELLI: Are you saying we can never know?

SIGNORA CINI: If I'm allowed to comment . . . I think that would be terrible . . . never to know . . .

LAUDISI: But why is it terrible? All I'm trying to say is we must respect other people's perceptions even if they are opposite to our own.

SIGNORA SIRELLI: I think I'm going to ignore you. For the sake of my sanity.

LAUDISI: Please, continue your conversation. Keep talking about Signora Frola and her son-in-law Signor Ponza. I'm all ears.

AMALIA: Wouldn't you like to take a nap or something?

DINA: Or read a newspaper? In another room.

LAUDISI: Oh no. I quite like it here. All this gossip. But I'll be quiet if you wish. Not a peep. Pay me no heed. Although I might laugh every so often. But if I laugh too loud, just ignore me.

SIGNORA SIRELLI (*to* AMALIA): Now tell us, my dear, isn't your husband Signor Ponza's superior?

AMALIA (*suddenly amused, looks at* LAUDISI): Oh yes, but in his office, not at home.

SIGNORA SIRELLI: But aren't you curious about this mother-in-law? Haven't you tried to see her?

DINA: Oh yes. We've tried twice.

SIGNORA CINI: Oh dear . . . does this mean . . . you have spoken to her??

DINA: We were not received.

SIRELLI/SIGNORA SIRELLI/SIGNORA CINI: Not received!/Oh no!/Why?

DINA: We went this morning.

AMALIA: We waited at least fifteen minutes. At her door. No one opened the door. We weren't even able to leave a card. We tried again this afternoon. And (*catches her breath*) . . . he came to the door.

SIGNORA SIRELLI: Oh my dear! You saw his face! Isn't his face *evil*?! Frightening! It's upset the entire town, that face. And I hear he always wears black. In fact, they all do; the mother-in-law as well, and the wife, the daughter . . .

SIRELLI: What are you going on about? You've never seen the daughter. No one has seen the daughter. Although it wouldn't surprise me if she did wear black. After all, they come from one of those villages in Marsica . . .

AMALIA: Which were evidently destroyed . . .

SIRELLI: Completely – wiped out – by an earthquake . . .

DINA: And supposedly all their relatives were killed . . .

SIGNORA CINI: But . . . please . . . you were about to tell us . . . *he opened the door* . . .

AMALIA: Yes. And I was terrified. I mean – as you say – *that face*! I was speechless, and then, finally, I summoned my courage and said we had come to call on his mother in-law. And he said . . .

SIGNORA SIRELLI: Yes?

AMALIA: Nothing.

SIRELLI/SIGNORA SIRELLI: Nothing??

AMALIA: Not even thank you. Nothing.

DINA: Well, he did bow.

AMALIA: But only slightly. Ever so slightly. With his head.

DINA: But his *eyes*! We could see into his eyes. They were the eyes of a *demon*!

SIGNORA CINI: But . . . but . . . did he not say anything??

DINA: Oh yes. Finally. He was embarrassed. Wasn't he?

AMALIA: No. Confused. He said . . .

SIGNORA SIRELLI: Yes?

AMALIA: That his mother-in-law wasn't well . . .

SIGNORA SIRELLI: Oh!

AMALIA: And then he thanked us for enquiring . . . and then . . .

SIGNORA CINI: And then?

AMALIA: He just stood there. Waiting for us to leave.

DINA: It was humiliating.

AMALIA: My husband was furious when he found out. He thought it a criminal lack of courtesy, so he's reporting it to the Mayor, demanding an apology.

DINA: Oh, thank God! Daddy's back.

COUNCILLOR AGAZZI *enters, rather ill-natured and authoritarian.*

AGAZZI: Sirelli, what a pleasant surprise . . . (*Bows to the others and shakes hands with* SIGNORA SIRELLI.) Signora.

AMALIA (*presenting* SIGNORA CINI): Darling, this is Signora Citti.

SIGNORA CINI: Cini.

AGAZZI: Lovely to meet you. Well – I have news. The old lady is on her way.

SIGNORA SIRELLI (*bursting with excitement*): Signora Frola? Coming here?

AGAZZI: Of course. This is a very serious matter. I wasn't about to allow my wife and daughter to be insulted . . .

SIRELLI: Of course not. We were just saying that.

AGAZZI: I thought it was important that the Mayor be informed of the rumours surrounding this gentleman . . .

SIRELLI: Good. Good.

SIGNORA CINI: Oh dear . . . if I may say . . .

AMALIA: He's keeping them both prisoner!

DINA: Actually, we don't know about the mother-in-law.

SIGNORA SIRELLI: We know about the wife.

SIRELLI: And the Mayor? . . .

AGAZZI: Distressed, of course . . .

SIRELLI: Good.

AGAZZI: He had already heard some of the stories, so now he will have to investigate and discover the truth for himself.

LAUDISI *bursts out laughing.*

LAUDISI: Oh, sorry.

AMALIA: Just what we needed.

AGAZZI: Why is your brother laughing?

LAUDISI: Don't mind me.

SIGNORA SIRELLI: Because he says it's not possible to know the truth.

The BUTLER *enters.*

BUTLER: Signora Frola has arrived.

SIRELLI: She's here!

AGAZZI: Not possible, my dear Lamberto? We'll see about that.

AMALIA: Shall we ask her in?

AGAZZI: Please – everybody sit down. Try to look casual. All right? Sit down. (*To the* BUTLER.) Show her in.

The BUTLER *leaves and returns with* SIGNORA FROLA. *Everyone stands up.* SIGNORA FROLA *is a pleasant woman, modest and friendly. Her eyes seem sad, but they are offset by a constant smile.* AMALIA *steps forward and holds out her hand.*

AMALIA: Signora Frola, please come in. May I introduce my husband, my daughter, my brother, and my friends Signor and Signora Sirelli and their friend Signora . . .

CINI: Cini! Cini!

AMALIA: Please, have a seat.

SIGNORA FROLA: I must apologise. I've been remiss. I'm so sorry. I believe you were kind enough to visit me earlier today, whereas it is I – I – who should have been the first to call.

AMALIA: Oh, does it matter who's first? Not amongst neighbours. My daughter and I were merely concerned that, as you were a stranger in our town, you might have needed . . . something . . .

SIGNORA FROLA: Thank you . . . you're very kind . . .

SIGNORA SIRELLI: Are you alone in our town then?

SIGNORA FROLA: Alone? No. I have a married daughter, who moved here rather recently.

SIRELLI: Ah yes – her husband is a clerk at the municipal building, isn't he? Signor Ponza, I think.

SIGNORA FROLA: Oh yes. Yes he is. (*To* AGAZZI) He works for you. I hope you haven't been upset by his behaviour.

AGAZZI: Well, frankly, Signora, I've been a bit . . . disconcerted . . .

SIGNORA FROLA: Oh, I understand, of course I understand. But please, you must try to comprehend his situation. He is – we are – all of us – still in a state of shock . . .

AMALIA: Oh, my dear. Of course. You've had a terrible tragedy. (*To the others*) The earthquake.

SIGNORA SIRELLI: How horrible. Did you lose anyone close? . . .

SIGNORA FROLA: Close? Oh yes. (*Pause*) Our relatives. (*Pause*) All of them, Signora. Our village no longer exists.

SIRELLI: I think news did reach us . . .

SIGNORA FROLA: I lost my sister and her only daughter. But my son-in-law, my poor son-in-law suffered far more: he lost his mother, two brothers and their wives, and their children . . .

DINA: All wiped away?

SIGNORA FROLA: Yes. As you say. Wiped away. (*Pause*) It's not easy to recover.

AMALIA: Of course not.

SIGNORA SIRELLI: I think it would drive me mad.

SIGNORA FROLA: Well, perhaps not mad. But certainly forgetful. And at times, I fear – impolite – without ever intending to be, my dear sir.

AGAZZI: I completely understand . . .

AMALIA: My daughter and I had heard about this disaster and that's exactly why we wanted to call on you.

SIGNORA SIRELLI: Why, of course, they thought you might be lonely. Although, Signora, as you do have a daughter here in town, after such a traumatic event, wouldn't . . . well . . . wouldn't you want to be together, instead of . . .

SIGNORA FROLA: Being on my own?

SIRELLI: Yes. Exactly. It seems odd.

SIGNORA FROLA: Of course. Of course it does. (*Pause*) But don't you feel that when a daughter or son first marries it's important for the parent to leave them be – for a bit, certainly, to give them breathing space?

LAUDISI: Yes! That's extremely wise. They are, after all, starting a new life . . .

SIGNORA SIRELLI: But is it necessary to totally exclude one's parents? . . .

LAUDISI: Sorry, did I say *exclude*? Look, if I understand this lady properly, she realises that her daughter must not remain as closely tied to her as she was before, because she is now embarked on a life of her own . . .

SIGNORA FROLA (*gratefully*): Oh yes, thank you. That's exactly what I wanted to say.

SIGNORA CINI: But . . . may I ask . . . does your . . . does your . . . does your daughter come to visit you?

SIGNORA FROLA (*uncomfortable*): Ah. Yes. Yes. Of course we do see each other.

SIRELLI: But I'm told your daughter never leaves her house.

SIGNORA CINI: Perhaps they have . . . children to look after . . .

SIGNORA FROLA: No. No children. I'm afraid there may never be children now. They have been married seven years. She is, of course, occupied with home-making, as it were. (*Smiles sadly*) In the type of small country town that we come from, the town that is now 'wiped away', we women were quite used to staying indoors.

AGAZZI: But surely, one would make an exception – to visit a mother . . .

AMALIA: But I'm certain you visit her . . .

SIGNORA FROLA: Oh yes, of course. I go there once or twice a day.

DINA: But your daughter lives on the fifth floor, doesn't she? Do you have to climb all those stairs every day?

SIGNORA FROLA: No, no. I never go up. You're quite right – the stairs . . . it would be difficult. I stand in the courtyard and my daughter looks out on her balcony over the courtyard, and we see each other, and we talk.

SIGNORA SIRELLI: Is that all? You never touch?

DINA: I must say, as a daughter, I would not expect my mother to climb ninety or one hundred steps a day to see me; but, on the other hand, I couldn't bear only to see her in the distance. I mean, how would we embrace?

SIGNORA FROLA: Embrace? Yes. You're right. Well . . . it *is* complicated. But I don't want you to misjudge my daughter or to misunderstand how considerate she is of me. Or I of her. I can assure you that no matter what my age, ninety or one hundred steps would not prevent me from rushing to my daughter and clasping her to my breast.

SIGNORA SIRELLI: Well then! As we suspected. There's another reason.

AMALIA (*to* LAUDISI): You see, there is a reason.

SIRELLI: Your son-in-law, perhaps.

SIGNORA FROLA: Oh no – please – do not mistrust my son-in-law. He is a very good man. I cannot begin to describe *how* good he is. He is tender and kind to me. How can I possibly make you understand the love he has for my daughter? It would have been impossible to find a better husband for her.

SIRELLI: Then *what is the problem?*

SIGNORA CINI: Oh dear . . . isn't he the reason? . . .

AGAZZI: So then he doesn't forbid his wife to call on you – or prevent you from having physical contact with your daughter?

SIGNORA FROLA: Of course not. I never meant to suggest that he has forbidden us anything. On no – the contrary. It's us. It's my daughter and me. We are the ones who have set the rules. It is entirely our decision. But a decision reached in consideration for him.

AGAZZI: I'm lost.

SIGNORA FROLA: It's very difficult to explain. Or understand. I recognise that. It concerns . . . well . . . his nature. But if you do understand, I promise you will sympathise. Obviously, this is done at enormous cost to both my daughter and myself . . .

AGAZZI: I don't grasp what you're talking about. Which leaves me . . . confused . . . and suspicious . . .

SIGNORA FROLA: Suspicious? Oh no – certainly not suspicious of my poor son-in-law – oh, please don't say that.

AGAZZI: Don't be upset. I simply meant that it's natural to suspect certain things . . .

SIGNORA FROLA: But why? My daughter and I are in complete agreement. And we are happy. We are both very, very happy.

SIGNORA SIRELLI: It's jealousy, isn't it?

SIGNORA FROLA: Jealousy?

SIGNORA SIRELLI: He's jealous.

SIGNORA FROLA: Well, that's not exactly the word. You can't really say jealous when it involves a mother, can you? Oh, I don't know. It's so much more complicated. You see, he wants her heart, my daughter's heart, his wife's heart, for himself, completely. So completely that even the love my daughter has for her mother – which, of course, he finds natural and admirable – even that must pass through him in order to reach me. Do you understand?

AGAZZI: Not exactly. What you're saying sounds very cruel.

SIGNORA FROLA: Oh no, please don't say that. He's not cruel. Not at all. But he's . . . as if under a spell, you see. A spell or an illness – it's one or the other. He has – what can I call it? – a condition, a condition of love. He is overwhelmed by love. And the force of this love has created a circle – a magic circle – that surrounds his wife – and she cannot leave it, nor can anyone else enter it.

DINA: Not even her mother?

SIRELLI: This is extraordinarily selfish.

SIGNORA FROLA: Selfish? Yes, perhaps. But a selfishness that gives everything, offers everything, every ounce of his being, to the woman he loves. If I broke into this world, if I disrupted this magic circle which my daughter so happily lives in, would I be the selfish one? No, I must respect it – and leave it be. And take comfort in her happiness. And remember I do see and speak to her. I put a letter in a basket, after all, and she pulls it up. And she, in turn, sends a letter down to me. So we chat and

gossip and laugh – in our letters. It's enough, you see. It's enough. And now I am quite used to the routine; it's become perfectly natural to me. I don't mind. I no longer suffer.

AGAZZI: Well – I suppose if you are happy . . .

SIGNORA FROLA: Yes. I am. Because my son-in-law is a good man. A kind man. I suppose we all have our little weaknesses, but it's not difficult to accept a weakness based on love. (Holds her hand out to AMALIA.) I really must leave. (Bows to the others, then turns to AGAZZI.) I hope you have forgiven me.

AGAZZI: You mustn't give it another thought. We are so grateful for your visit.

SIGNORA FROLA: Please, don't get up . . . I'll see myself out . . .

AMALIA: Nonsense, my dear. I'll see you out . . .

AMALIA *takes* SIGNORA FROLA *to the door, then returns.*

SIRELLI: Good God! What a story!

AGAZZI: Indeed. It begs as many questions as it answers.

SIGNORA SIRELLI: Can you imagine the pain she must feel? . . .

DINA: And the daughter as well . . .

SIGNORA CINI: I heard . . . oh my . . . tears in her voice . . .

AMALIA: I did as well. When she said she would climb one hundred steps in order to hold her daughter . . .

LAUDISI: What I found intriguing was her determination to protect her son-in-law from any kind of suspicion.

SIGNORA SIRELLI: She wasn't really able to excuse him.

LAUDISI: What is there to excuse? We've heard no violence or cruelty.

The BUTLER *enters.*

BUTLER: Sir, it's Signor Ponza. He asked if you will receive him.

SIGNORA SIRELLI: Oh my God! It's him!

AGAZZI: He wishes to speak to me?

BUTLER: Yes, sir.

SIGNORA SIRELLI: Oh please, you must, you must. I'm petrified to look at the man, but how can we not grab the opportunity?

AMALIA: But what on earth can he want?

AGAZZI: Let's find out. Please – we must all sit down. Try to look casual. (*To the* BUTLER.) Show him in.

The BUTLER *bows and goes out. A pause and then* SIGNOR PONZA *enters. He is dressed in black. He clenches and unclenches his fists and speaks with effort; a hint of violence underneath. From time to time he wipes perspiration from his face with a black-bordered handkerchief. His eyes are hard and unhappy.*

AGAZZI: Come in, Ponza. (*Introducing him*) This is my new clerk, Signor Ponza: my wife, my daughter, my brother-in-law, our friends the Sirellis, and their friend . . . I'm so sorry, I've forgotten . . .

CINI (*defeated; mumbles*): Cini.

AGAZZI: Please sit down.

SIGNOR PONZA: Thank you. I'll only take a moment of your time.

AGAZZI: Would you prefer to speak to me in private?

SIGNOR PONZA: No . . . no . . . it's important that I speak to everyone, so I can clear the air and explain . . . certain things.

AGAZZI: You're referring to your mother-in-law's visit?

SIGNOR PONZA: Indeed. First, I must tell you that Signora Frola would have called much earlier, before your wife and daughter were kind enough to call on her, but I prevented her doing so. I am utterly opposed to her paying or receiving visits.

AGAZZI: May I ask why?

PONZA (*becoming more nervous despite his efforts at self-control*): Well, she will have talked to you about her daughter, won't she? She will have said that I forbid her to see my wife or to come upstairs to my flat.

AGAZZI: No. Not at all. She spoke of you lovingly.

DINA: She said only the sweetest things about you.

AGAZZI: She said she refrains from going inside your wife's home out of consideration for your feelings, although I confess I was a bit confused about the nature of those feelings . . .

SIGNORA SIRELLI: Actually, if you want the truth . . .

AGAZZI: We did think your behaviour cruel.

PONZA: That's exactly why I have come here. I knew you had to be confused. I'm afraid the poor woman is in a pitiable state. But then, so am I, because I am forced to reveal . . . explain . . . certain things I would rather were left unsaid. (*Stops and looks at everyone, then speaks slowly, with great emphasis.*) Signora Frola is insane.

ALL (*startled*): Insane??!!

PONZA: She's been insane for four years.

AGAZZI: How is that possible?

PONZA: She seems perfectly normal, I grant you, but trust me, she's mad. Her madness is contained in her belief – her genuine belief – that I don't wish her to see her daughter. (*Pause*) Her daughter! *What* daughter? Her daughter is dead!

ALL: Dead?

PONZA: She died four years ago. I was devastated, of course, but she – the poor woman – lost her mind.

SIRELLI: But your wife . . .

PONZA: I had to go on living. I married my present wife two years ago. She is my second wife.

AMALIA: And Signora Frola thinks she's her daughter?

PONZA: Yes. She was confined to an asylum when her daughter died; her grief was that overwhelming. It was assumed she would never recover. And then one day from her window she saw me on the street with my second wife and she thought she was looking at her daughter, she imagined her daughter was alive, and she smiled, and then laughed, and suddenly she was released from an almost catatonic state into a kind of exultation. Later, she grew calmer and was allowed to leave the institution. She is now, in her way, quite happy, for she believes her daughter is not dead, and she has convinced herself that I want the woman totally, obsessively, for myself and thus do not allow her to see her. In a sense, she is cured, in that she now has a *presentable* madness. If you speak to her she seems quite sane.

AGAZZI: Yes, she does.

SIGNORA SIRELLI: She says she is happy.

PONZA: And she is. And I think she cares about me. I try to help her, although at a considerable sacrifice. I have to maintain two homes and oblige my wife, who thankfully is extremely compassionate, to sustain the illusion. So my wife comes to the window and talks to her and sends her notes. But I can only be generous up to a point. I cannot ask my wife to live with a madwoman who think she's her mother. My wife *has* a mother and I can assure you one is enough. As kind as my wife is, she cannot allow a stranger to embrace her and call her daughter. But it means my wife is afraid to leave our flat. She is trapped. It is a dreadful situation.

AMALIA: Oh – the poor woman.

SIGNORA SIRELLI: So, it's your wife's choice not to leave? . . .

PONZA: Now I hope you understand why I did not wish Signora Frola to call on you.

AGAZZI: I understand. Everything is suddenly very clear.

PONZA: A person with that kind of affliction should keep a very low profile, but as my mother-in-law has made a visit to you, I have no choice but to offer you this full explanation. After all, I occupy a respectable post, and it would be terrible if the town believed a public official was behaving reprehensively. That is, preventing an unfortunate mother from seeing her child. Needless to say, I am deeply embarrassed by all of this. (*To ladies*) I apologise for having to relate such a distressing story. (*Pause*) I had no choice. (*Bows*) Councillor. Gentlemen.

PONZA *leaves.*

CINI: Such a nice man!

AMALIA: So she's mad!

SIGNORA SIRELLI: Poor thing.

DINA: She thinks Signor Ponza is her son-in-law when actually he *was* her son-in-law, so I suppose technically, he still is, although his wife is not the daughter who once was his wife . . . oh God!

SIGNORA CINI: Who could have imagined . . .

AMALIA: There was something in her tone of voice . . .

LAUDISI: That made you suspect?

AMALIA: Not exactly . . . but she seemed unsure of herself . . . she wasn't always able to find the right words . . .

SIGNORA SIRELLI: How could she? She's on another bus!

SIRELLI: Well, yes, but I must admit, not mad enough to be without reason – I mean, she had some very clever and original excuses for her son-in-law's behaviour.

AGAZZI: Which proves she's deranged. She had made excuses, but they were fanciful.

AMALIA: Actually, she would say one thing and then change her story. The pieces didn't fit together.

AGAZZI (*to* SIRELLI): Do you really imagine a sane woman could accept that bizarre fairy tale of unconditional love, and agree to the conditions imposed on her?

SIRELLI: Accepting those conditions might have been a rational response. I'm not sure . . . it doesn't all fit . . . (*To* LAUDISI) How about you? What do you have to say about this?

LAUDISI: Me? I'm not saying a word.

The BUTLER *enters.*

BUTLER: Signora Frola is here again.

AMALIA: Oh my God! Again! We'll never be rid of her.

SIGNORA SIRELLI: Especially as she's unbalanced . . .

SIGNORA CINI: But . . . this is so . . . I mean . . . I can't wait to hear what she says next . . .

SIRELLI: I'm curious myself. I'm not convinced she's insane.

DINA: Don't be afraid, Mamma. She's harmless.

AGAZZI: Well, we can't *not* see her. Let's hear her

out. But please – everyone – sit down. And, for God's sake, try to act casual. (*To* BUTLER) Show her in.

The BUTLER *leaves.*

AMALIA (*to the others*): I need your help. I don't know what to say to her.

(SIGNORA FROLA *enters again.* AMALIA, *somewhat frightened, goes gingerly to her. The others look on, astonished.*)

SIGNORA FROLA: May I . . .

AMALIA: Oh, please . . . Signora Frola . . . please . . . come in. Look . . . look at us . . . still here . . .

SIGNORA FROLA (*with a sad smile*): Yes. Staring at me as if I were mad.

AMALIA: No, what makes you think that?

SIGNORA FROLA: If only I had remained rude. If only I had left you standing on the sidewalk as I did the first time you called. I never imagined you would return again on the same day. That forced me to visit you here, which has had exactly the consequences I had foreseen.

AMALIA: But we're delighted to see you again.

SIRELLI: I think Signora Frola is upset and we don't know why. We must let her tell us.

SIGNORA FROLA: Hasn't my son-in-law just left this room?

AGAZZI: Yes. But he was here on office matters.

SIGNORA FROLA: Thank you. Thank you for lying. You want to soothe my nerves.

AGAZZI: No, no, I promise you, I'm telling the truth.

SIGNORA FROLA: What kind of state was he in? Was he calm? Did he speak calmly?

AGAZZI: Oh yes . . . yes . . . very calm. Wasn't he? . . .

AGAZZI *looks to the others; they nod in agreement.*

ALL: Yes . . . Calm . . .

SIGNORA FROLA: I know you are trying to reassure me. But it's I who wish to reassure you.

SIGNORA SIRELLI: But it isn't necessary . . .

AGAZZI: Office matters. He spoke about office matters.

ALL: Yes . . . Office matters . . .

SIGNORA FROLA: But it's obvious from the way you're looking at me . . . I know what you're thinking . . . When I was here before I did try to answer your questions, often very painful questions, but I was sometimes at a loss, and I gave explanations that, I must admit, stretched credulity. But how could I tell you the truth? Or, equally, how could I tell you, as he surely did, that my daughter has been dead for four years but that I believe that she is still alive and still married to him which is why he won't allow me to see her? In other words – that I am certifiably insane.

AGAZZI (*startled by her sincerity*): I don't understand . . .

SIGNORA FROLA: He did tell you that, didn't he? You mustn't spare my feelings.

SIRELLI (*watching her closely*): He did say that . . . yes . . .

SIGNORA FROLA: I knew it. And it upsets him – to have to tell that story about me. Somehow – somehow – we are able to work our way through it, but only if we continue to live exactly as we do at the present. Do you understand? The problem is we're attracting attention; we've become the focus of a great deal of gossip. But really what matters is that he's an excellent employee – isn't that true? Meticulous. Honourable; I'm sure you've seen that already.

AGAZZI: Well . . .

SIGNORA FROLA: He certainly seems to be efficient. I know he is good at his work; all of his employers have praised him. I don't understand why there is so much interest in his family life, in a private misfortune that he has, I must repeat, overcome, but which, if revealed, would do him professional harm.

AGAZZI: You mustn't worry. No one wishes to harm him.

SIGNORA FROLA: But how can I not worry, especially when I see that he's been forced to tell you this ludicrous tale. Asking you to believe that my daughter is dead. And that I am mad. That the woman he lives with is his second wife. But he has to tell you that. He has no choice. It's the only way he can remain . . . balanced. But he knows it's not true, and when forced to repeat it he becomes agitated. Surely you noticed.

AGAZZI: He was a bit excited . . .

SIGNORA SIRELLI: So then you're not mad — he is!

SIRELLI: See! (*Triumphantly*) Just what I said.

AGAZZI: But is *that* possible?

AMALIA: He seemed perfectly sane to me.

Everyone is now very agitated.

SIGNORA FROLA: No! No! Why would you think him mad? It is only this one little matter that is any sort of problem. Everything else is perfectly normal. Would I leave my daughter alone with a madman? Of course not. And surely you can tell from his behaviour in the office that he's perfectly rational.

AGAZZI: Then, Signora, you must explain to us what on earth is going on. Did your son-in-law come to us and deliberately lie?

SIGNORA FROLA: I'll try to explain. But you must have compassion for him.

AGAZZI: So then — you're trying to tell us that your daughter is not dead.

SIGNORA FROLA: Dead? Heaven forbid!

AGAZZI (*irritated*): So then *he* is crazy.

SIGNORA FROLA: No . . . no . . .

SIRELLI: But he has to be.

SIGNORA FROLA: No! Listen to me, please. He is not mad. You have seen him yourselves; surely you observed his strength; his physical strength — he is very robust. When he married he was caught in a storm, a tornado, a veritable hurricane of love. No, more than love — *desire*. Desire so strong, so physically overbearing it threatened to destroy my daughter, who was rather . . . delicate. I trust you take my meaning. She stopped eating. She had a complete breakdown. The doctors advised a rest cure, as indeed did all our relatives, those who have tragically perished

in the earthquake. She was placed into a sanatorium. Well, you can imagine what effect this had on him. His monumental passion had no outlet. He fell into a morbid depression. He was convinced that his wife was dead. He went into mourning. He dressed in black. Nothing could convince him that she was alive, only . . . away. Finally, my daughter recovered. She was beautiful and healthy once again. She returned to his house. He refused to acknowledge her. He looked at her and said, 'No . . . no . . . this is not my wife. My wife is dead.' Then he would look at her again and his eyes seemed to recognise her, but the moment passed, and again he said, 'No . . . no . . . this is not she.' There was only one thing for us to do. We had to pretend that my daughter was indeed another woman. We pretended to have a second wedding. He thinks she is his second wife. And he is gentler with her now. But she is not his second wife. She is his first.

SIGNORA SIRELLI: That explains why he says —

SIGNORA FROLA: What he says and what he thinks are possibly quite different. He may not really believe this charade. Deep in his heart, he may know the truth. But he mustn't say it out loud. He must persuade everyone that she is his second wife. That is the only way he can feel safe. For he is afraid she will be taken away again. (*Smiles*) And so he keeps her to himself. And for himself. Do you see? He worships her. And my daughter has grown to need his love. She is finally . . . content. (*Rises*) I must leave. If he finds I'm not at home, he'll work himself up into even more of a state. (*Sighs*) This deception takes a lot of patience. My daughter must pretend she is someone else and I have to pretend that I am mad. But what choice do we have? As long as he's happy. Please, don't get up. I know the way out. Good afternoon.

She bows and smiles and hurries out. The others stand, stunned and astonished. They look at each other. Silence. LAUDISI cuts a path through them.

LAUDISI: Cat got your tongue? (*Pause*) Well, don't look at me. You wanted the truth. (*Starts to laugh. Then – to audience*) Truth!

He continues to laugh.

Act two

COUNCILLOR AGGAZI's *study.* AGAZZI *is talking on the telephone.* LAUDISI *and* SIRELLI *are looking at him expectantly;* LAUDISI *again sipping a drink.*

AGAZZI: Yes? . . . What then? . . . (*Pause*) I think you had better snap to it . . . (*Pause*) It's unacceptable. Surely you can . . . (*Pause*) I see . . . (*Pause*) Then you have to try again. (*Lays the receiver down.*)

SIRELLI (*anxiously*): Well?

AGAZZI: Nothing.

SIRELLI: Nothing can be found?

AGAZZI: They're trying. There are several policemen on the case. But evidently the earthquake destroyed everything; all the archives and records, even the town hall itself . . .

SIRELLI: But surely they can interview a survivor.

AGAZZI: There aren't any. And if there were, they've disappeared.

SIRELLI: You mean we have to believe one or the other, without having any evidence . . .?

AGAZZI: I'm afraid so.

LAUDISI: Well, my advice would be . . . to believe them both.

AGAZZI: And how do we do that?

SIRELLI: When one says black and the other white?

LAUDISI: Oh. Sorry. Well, then don't believe either of them.

SIRELLI: Very funny. One of them must be telling the truth, even if we aren't able to come up with facts.

LAUDISI: Facts! Oh please! What can you learn from *facts*?

AGAZZI: We would learn a great deal if we had the daughter's death certificate, for example – that's assuming it's Signora Frola who's the loopy one; unfortunately, we can't find birth or death certificates or anything in between; if

one were to turn up, it would be clear proof that the son-in-law is telling the truth.

SIRELLI: If we had a death certificate, could you deny that was clear evidence?

LAUDISI: Me? I'm quite careful not to deny anything as possible; that's my point. You're the ones who need records, archives, certificates . . . I find them utterly useless, because for me the truth lies not in documents but in the minds of those two people, which I have no way of penetrating. Aside from the few clues they may choose to hand out.

SIRELLI: But they both say the other is mad. So one of them must be. That is inescapable. But which one?

AGAZZI: Exactly.

LAUDISI: Actually, that isn't quite true; they don't both say it. Ponza does claim his mother-in-law is insane, but she doesn't suggest that he is. She only reports that he was a bit unsettled by an excess of passion, but that now he is quite healthy and happy.

SIRELLI: So then you believe her account, as I think I do.

AGAZZI: If you accept her story, everything makes sense.

LAUDISI: It does indeed. Of course, it also makes perfect sense if you accept *his* story.

SIRELLI: What are you saying now? That neither one is crazy. Sorry – one of them must be.

LAUDISI: Ah. So which one? You don't know. No one knows. And it isn't because the evidence has been destroyed by an earthquake in a village; there's been an earthquake inside their heads as well; the documents have been swept away inside their own souls. Don't you understand that? She has created for him, or he for her, whichever, a fantasy that is utterly indistinguishable from reality, although, of course, it might be the other way round, and they live with this fantasy or this reality in complete harmony. And no document can destroy this fantasy slash reality, because it is the very air they breathe. Oh yes, a document might be of use to *you*, it would satisfy your foolish curiosity. But you can't find one, can you? So you're stuck in some purgatory, watching fantasy and reality dancing together, rather gracefully in fact, and suddenly you can't tell the difference between them.

AGAZZI: Is that philosophy? I despise philosophy. One of them is lying, and I'll prove it.

SIRELLI: We should bring them together, don't you think? A confrontation. That's the only way to discover the truth.

LAUDISI: Fine. As long as I'm allowed to laugh.

AGAZZI: Be my guest. But we'll see which of us laughs last. Let's stop wasting time. (*Goes to door and calls.*) Amalia, Signora, come in – please.

AMALIA, DINA *and* SIGNORA SIRELLI *enter.*

SIGNORA SIRELLI (*wagging her finger flirtatiously at* LAUDISI): Still here, are you?

SIRELLI: He's insufferable.

SIGNORA SIRELLI: But aren't you consumed by the mystery, the way we are? You must be. It's driving me mad. I haven't been able to sleep.

AGAZZI: Ignore him.

LAUDISI: Yes, that's rather good advice. Ignore me. You'll sleep easier.

AGAZZI: All right. I have a plan. The ladies will call on Signora Frola.

AMALIA: But she won't receive us.

AGAZZI: Of course she will.

DINA: It's actually our duty to return her visit.

AMALIA: But he won't allow her to receive calls.

SIRELLI: That was before you met her.

SIGNORA SIRELLI: It's probably a relief for her to be able to talk to us about her daughter.

AGAZZI: Well, let's not make our minds up yet. Now here is the plan . . . (*Looks at the clock.*) Make it a short visit. About ten minutes.

SIRELLI (*to his wife*): So don't yap on and on . . .

SIGNORA SIRELLI: What do you mean??

DINA (*stepping in, to prevent a row*): Ten minutes. I'll time it.

AGAZZI: I'm going to my office; I'll be back in fifteen minutes.

SIRELLI: And what shall I do?

AGAZZI (*to the ladies*): Then make an excuse and somehow convince Signora Frola to return here with you.

AMALIA: What kind of excuse?

AGAZZI: You'll think of something. Women are good at excuses. Dina and Signora Sirelli will help you. When you return, go into the drawing room . . . (*Opens a door.*) I'll leave this door open. It must not be closed under any circumstances. That way we will be able to hear you talking from this room. I'm going to leave these papers on the desk; these are documents that require Ponza's attention. I'll say I've forgotten them and ask him to return home with me to fetch them. Then—

SIRELLI: Excuse me, but what do I do?

AGAZZI: Ah. At five past eleven, when I am here with him, and the ladies are in the drawing room, you must call, supposedly to take your wife home. I'll make sure the butler shows you in here, and then I have an excuse to invite the women in.

LAUDISI: Aha! They will be face to face. The truth will out!

DINA: But, Uncle, if we have them both in the same room . . .

AGAZZI: Don't answer him; he's just trying to get a rise out of you. OK. Let's do it. Off you go.

SIGNORA SIRELLI: Yes, let's. (*To* LAUDISI) I'm not going to say goodbye to you.

LAUDISI: Oh dear, I'll have to say goodbye to myself. (*Shakes his own hand.*) Cheerio, Lamberto, old chap. Lovely seeing you.

AMALIA, DINA *and* SIGNORA SIRELLI *leave.*

AGAZZI: Right. We're off as well.

SIRELLI: Yes. (*Bows to* LAUDISI) Signor.

LAUDISI (*with mock graciousness*): Fare thee well.

AGAZZI *and* SIRELLI *leave.*

LAUDISI *walks around the study and then stands in front of a mirror. He talks to his image.*

LAUDISI: Well, well, well – look at you. (*Winks.*) So which one of us is mad? (*Lifts his hand and points at his image.*) Am I pointing at you or are you pointing at me? Am I you? Or are you me? Whichever – we know each other quite well, don't we? The trouble is I see you quite differently than others see you. But then you're an illusion, aren't you? You're glass. Well, perhaps. Perhaps I'm the illusion. Perhaps I'm glass. Somewhere inside – glass. Reflecting myself. Or not. These people are quite blind, you know, they can't see the illusion within themselves. The ghost inside our souls. They chase after other people's ghosts but they can't see their own. Oh well. (*Bows to his image.*) It's nice to have had this little chat.

The BUTLER *enters, astonished to find* LAUDISI *talking to himself.*

BUTLER: Signor . . .

LAUDISI: Oh?

BUTLER: Two ladies are here.

LAUDISI: Do they want to see me?

BUTLER: I told them the others were out but that you were in.

LAUDISI: But am I?

BUTLER: Are you what?

LAUDISI: In.

BUTLER: Pardon?

LAUDISI: Is it really me that's here or the person they think is me.

BUTLER (*sighs – he's played these games before*): I don't know, sir.

LAUDISI: Do you think I'm me?

BUTLER: Don't know, Signor.

LAUDISI: Then who are you talking to?

BUTLER: To you, Signor.

LAUDISI: But am I the same person those ladies wish to see?

BUTLER: I believe they wish to see the brother of Signora Agazzi, Signor.

LAUDISI: Oh dear. Then I believe that *is* me. Why didn't you say so? Show them in.

The BUTLER *ushers* SIGNORA CINI *and* SIGNORA NENNI *in. The latter is even more anxious than her friend.*

SIGNORA CINI: Oh dear . . . may I come in?

LAUDISI: But of course, my dear lady.

SIGNORA CINI: I'm told Signora Agazzi is not at home. I brought my friend Signora Nenni . . .

LAUDISI: Who—?

SIGNORA CINI: Nenni. My friend. She was dying to meet . . .

LAUDISI: Signora Frola.

SIGNORA CINI: Oh no . . . goodness, no . . . dying to meet your sister.

LAUDISI: My sister is suddenly very popular. She'll be back soon. Meanwhile, please sit down . . .

The two women sit on a settee; he sits between them.

LAUDISI: Ah, this is nice. Very cosy, eh? Signora Sirelli is with my sister, you know. Everything is meticulously planned. It's going to be very dramatic. You've come just in time.

SIGNORA CINI: Oh dear . . . have we? . . . But what for?

LAUDISI (*mysteriously*): The confrontation! It's a wonderful idea! I'm so excited, I can barely contain myself.

SIGNORA CINI: So am I . . . So am I . . . *What confrontation?*

LAUDISI: Them! The two of them! I have goosebumps, don't you? He's going to come into this room—

SIGNORA CINI: He? Signor Ponza? . . .

LAUDISI: And she will be in the other room . . .

SIGNORA CINI: She? Signora Frola? . . .

LAUDISI: Bravo! You've worked it out! Ponza and Frola! Together again! Well – nearly together. It's brilliantly arranged. One will meet the other, here, in this room, and all of us will finally find out . . .

SIGNORA CINI: Find out?

LAUDISI: The truth!

SIGNORA CINI (*unbearably excited*): The truth!

LAUDISI: Of course, we already know the truth. This meeting will merely provide the necessary evidence.

SIGNORA CINI: You already know . . . you know . . . you know which of the two is . . .

LAUDISI: Of course. Don't you?

SIGNORA CINI: Well, yes . . .

LAUDISI: Which one then?

SIGNORA CINI: Oh dear . . . well . . . of course . . . it has to be . . . (*Forcing herself to guess.*) Him.

LAUDISI: Signora, you take my breath away. You've known all along. Yes. It is him.

SIGNORA CINI (*giggles*): Of course . . . yes . . . naturally . . .

SIGNORA NENNI (*hisses*): I told you!

SIGNORA CINI: But . . . did you discover . . . proof?

LAUDISI (*motions them closer to him*): You mustn't say a word. This is between us. The police found a certificate . . .

SIGNORA CINI: Certificate? . . .

LAUDISI: Of marriage.

SIGNORA CINI: Which marriage?

LAUDISI: His second marriage.

SIGNORA CINI: Second?

LAUDISI: Yes.

SIGNORA CINI: Then he's telling the truth.

SIGNORA NENNI (*shattered*): And she is the mad one.

LAUDISI: Yes, it would seem so.

SIGNORA CINI: But you said he was the one . . .

LAUDISI: It is, of course, quite possible that the certificate is a fake. A forgery! Perhaps instigated by his friends to confirm his delusion . . .

SIGNORA CINI: You mean . . . the certificate . . . is worthless . . .

LAUDISI: Do you think so?

SIGNORA CINI: You just said . . .

LAUDISI: Well, then I see your point. That certificate is worth as much as you choose. It has whatever value you wish to invest in it. Rather like the letters Signora Frola claims she receives every day from her daughter. You know – the letters in the baskets. They exist, don't they?

SIGNORA CINI: Well, yes, I'm sure . . .

LAUDISI: Then surely they have value. Surely they must be proof of something. But then Ponza might come along and suggest that they are false, written purposely to pamper Signora Frola's fantasy . . .

SIGNORA CINI: But then you can't be certain of anything.

LAUDISI: What a cynical thing to say. Not certain! I'm shocked! Come on: how many days are there in the week?

SIGNORA CINI: Seven.

LAUDISI: Exactly. Monday, Tuesday, Wednesday . . .

SIGNORA CINI (*invited to continue*): Thursday, Friday, Saturday . . .

LAUDISI: And Sunday! You see. And how many months are there in the year?

SIGNORA NENNI: January, February . . .

SIGNORA CINI: You're making fun of us, aren't you? . . . I think . . . can I say . . . that you're very cruel . . .

DINA *runs in.*

DINA: Uncle, would you . . . (*Stops when she sees* SIGNORA CINI.) Oh, Signora, I didn't realise you were here . . .

SIGNORA CINI: Yes, I've brought Signora Nenni.

LAUDISI: Who is dying to meet Signora Frola.

SIGNORA NENNI: I never said that.

SIGNORA CINI: He's trying to confuse us . . . it's as if a train enters a station . . . and then switches from one track to another . . .

DINA (*smiles at her uncle*): And then crashes. Pay him no heed. We haven't listened to him in years. I'll tell Mamma you're here. Actually, Uncle, you shouldn't be such a smarty-pants. Signora Frola is the sweetest little old lady, honestly. She's so gentle. And clean. You should see her house. Immaculate. Little white covers on the furniture. She showed us the letters her daughter wrote . . .

SIGNORA NENNI: Oh no! The letters are forgeries!

DINA: What?

SIGNORA NENNI: Signor Laudisi was talking about them—

DINA: Who cares what *he* says? He hasn't read them. (*To* LAUDISI) Really, Uncle! Forgeries!

LAUDISI: I didn't quite say that.

DINA: Do you think a mother doesn't know her own daughter's handwriting and turn of phrase? Yesterday's letter is particularly touching . . . (*Hears voices in the drawing room.*) They've arrived. (*Looks into the drawing room.*)

SIGNORA CINI: Arrived? With her? With Signora Frola?

DINA: Come with me. We all should be in the drawing room. Is it eleven o'clock yet?

AMALIA *enters, agitated.*

AMALIA: There's no need to go on with this! I need no further proof.

DINA: Nor I. A confrontation is pointless.

AMALIA (*greeting* SIGNORA CINI): Oh my dear . . . what a pleasant surprise . . .

SIGNORA CINI: Signora Nenni, who has come with me to . . .

AMALIA: Of course. A pleasure, Signora. (*Pause*) He's the one. There is no doubt.

SIGNORA CINI: Oh dear . . . are you sure . . . it's him, then? . . .

DINA: We must warn Father. We shouldn't be playing a trick on the poor lady . . .

AMALIA: We never should have brought her here. I feel that I'm betraying her.

LAUDISI: Oh yes. What a horrible, horrible thing to do. Especially as it is now becoming quite clear that it is she, after all, who is mad.

AMALIA: What? What are you talking about?

LAUDISI: It's her! It's her!

AMALIA: Oh no. Don't say that.

DINA: We're convinced the opposite is true.

LAUDISI: Exactly. And I'm convinced that it is she, because you're so certain it's not.

DINA: Let's go into the drawing room. He does this on purpose.

AMALIA: Yes. Please, ladies, come with me . . .

AMALIA *leaves with* SIGNORA CINI *and* SIGNORA NENNI. DINA *starts to follow.*

LAUDISI: Dina!

DINA (*turns back*): I'm not listening.

LAUDISI: If you don't wish to play a trick on the old lady, then don't. Shut the door to the drawing room.

DINA: Papa insisted we leave it open. If he finds the door closed, he'll be furious. Come into the drawing room and listen to Signora Frola.

LAUDISI: All right. But I'll close the door behind me.

DINA: Before you listen to her?

LAUDISI: I don't need to listen to her. I am con-

vinced your father also thinks that further proof is unnecessary.

DINA: Really?

LAUDISI: Naturally. He has been talking, after all, to Ponza. I'm certain he now thinks that *she's* the mad one. (*Walks towards the next room.*) So I'll shut the door. All right?

DINA (*shouts*): No! (*Regains her composure*) If you think that, it's better then to leave it open, isn't it?

LAUDISI *laughs.*

DINA: I'm only thinking of Papa.

LAUDISI: And I'm sure he'll only be thinking of you. Well then – the door stays open.

A piano is heard from the drawing room – an old melancholy tune from Nina, Mad With Love by Paisiello.

DINA: It's her! She's playing!

LAUDISI: The old lady?

DINA: Yes. She mentioned this tune. She said that years ago her daughter used to play this tune for her. It was her favourite.

They walk into the drawing room.

Pause.

The piano continues to be heard.

AGAZZI *and* PONZA *enter.* PONZA *hears the music and is acutely distressed.*

AGAZZI: Please – after you.

AGAZZI *walks to his desk and pretends to look for papers.*

AGAZZI: I'm certain I left them here. (*Laughs.*) It must be age – I've become forgetful. Please – have a seat.

PONZA *remains standing, his attention focused on the drawing room and the sound of the piano.*

AGAZZI: Ah! Found them. (*Gathers papers up and shows them to* PONZA.) Quite an old case, a lot of complications, impossible to decide what's true. (*Turns and looks towards the drawing room, seemingly annoyed by the piano.*) How odd! Music in the morning. (*Turns back.*) I can't imagine who's playing. (*Walks towards the drawing room, looks through the door and feigns astonishment as he sees* SIGNORA FROLA.) Good grief!

PONZA: It's her, isn't it? It's her!

AGAZZI: Why, yes, your mother-in-law. She's quite accomplished.

PONZA: I don't understand. Why is she here? Why is she playing the piano?

AGAZZI: There's never any harm in a little music.

PONZA: But not that song! It's the one her daughter used to play.

AGAZZI: Oh, I see. It brings back painful memories.

PONZA: Memories? For both of us. But in her fragile condition . . .

AGAZZI (*trying to pacify him*): I'm certain it's all right . . .

PONZA: . . . she has to be left in peace. Don't you understand? *She must not see people!* I'm the only one who knows how to handle her. You may be causing her considerable harm.

AGAZZI: I'm sure you're exaggerating. My wife and daughter are extremely sensitive, they won't—

He stops suddenly as the music in the drawing room stops, followed by a round of applause.

AGAZZI: Ah, you see! She's made a few fans.

Conversation is heard clearly from the drawing room.

DINA (*off*): You play beautifully, Signora.

SIGNORA FROLA (*off*): Me? Oh no. Not nearly as well as my Lina. You must hear her play.

PONZA (*trembling*): Did you hear that? Her Lina!

AGAZZI: Her daughter's name, I assume.

PONZA: But she said you must hear her play. In the present tense.

Again, from inside the drawing room:

SIGNORA FROLA: But then she doesn't play her piano any more. Not in the present circumstances. She misses it terribly.

AGAZZI: This is exactly as you described it. She believes her daughter is still alive.

PONZA: But to hear it spoken . . . out loud . . . it's too cruel . . . she is describing . . . the piano . . . that belonged to my wife . . . my wife, who is dead; her daughter, who is dead . . .

SIRELLI appears at the door. AGAZZI motions to him to come in.

AGAZZI: Ah, Sirelli. Please ask the ladies in.

SIRELLI calls the ladies.

PONZA: In here? No, no, you mustn't. I beg you . . .

The ladies, at a signal from SIRELLI, enter as does LAUDISI. SIGNORA FROLA sees her trembling son-in-law and is terrified.

PONZA: You! Why are you here?

SIGNORA FROLA: Please don't be upset . . . I came here because . . .

PONZA: Because you want to cause more trouble. What have you been telling them?

SIGNORA FROLA: Nothing. I promise you. Nothing.

PONZA: What do you mean 'Nothing'? I heard what you said. This gentleman heard as well. (*Indicates AGAZZI.*) You said, 'You must hear her play.' How on earth can they hear her play? I don't want to say this to you, but you leave me no choice . . . Your daughter has been dead for four years.

SIGNORA FROLA: Yes, of course. I know, I know. Please, don't be upset . . .

PONZA: Do you think they can hear a ghost? How can they hear her play if she's dead?

SIGNORA FROLA: But I said she can't play her piano any more. I meant, of course, as she is dead . . .

PONZA: Why are you talking about her old piano then?

SIGNORA FROLA: I wasn't. I was playing the piano in the other room, and it brought back certain memories . . .

PONZA: I destroyed it. I chopped it into pieces. When she died. You know that. So that the new one would never touch it. Not that the new one plays. She doesn't know how.

SIGNORA FROLA: No, of course. She doesn't know how to play.

PONZA: And what was she called? What was your daughter called? Answer me? Lina, wasn't it? Her name was Lina! Now tell us what the new one is called. Come on. I want to hear you say it. What is her name?

SIGNORA FROLA: Julia! Her name is Julia! Your second wife's name is Julia.

PONZA: Julia, not Lina?

SIGNORA FROLA: No, not Lina. Julia.

PONZA: You winked!

SIGNORA FROLA: Winked?

PONZA: I saw you. You winked your eye. When you said Julia . . .

SIGNORA FROLA: I didn't . . .

PONZA: I saw you. It was a signal. You want them to think you're humouring me. You're trying to destroy me, aren't you? You want to make these people believe I'm keeping your daughter captive, that I'm keeping her for myself (*sobs*), but how can I possibly do that, if *your daughter is dead* . . .

SIGNORA FROLA (*goes to him, tenderly*): No, no . . . my dear . . . I never said that . . . I never made them think . . . please, you must calm down . . . I promise you everything will be all right . . . (*Beseeching the others*) I never said that, did I?

AMALIA: No, she never said that.

DINA: She always said she was dead.

SIGNORA FROLA: There. You see. I always said she was dead. Always. It's all right. Everything will be all right. I said she was dead. And that you were good to me. (*To the others*) Didn't I? Tell him, please. I would never harm you. Never.

PONZA: But you go to other people's homes and purposely search out a piano and then play your daughter's melodies on them and then you say here, these are the melodies Lina played . . .

SIGNORA FROLA: No . . . you don't understand . . . I was trying . . .

PONZA: Trying what? How could you? How could you play the same song your daughter played? . . . She's gone . . . she gone . . .

SIGNORA FROLA: I know. I know. (*Also begins to weep.*) I'm so sorry . . . I'll never do it again . . . Please, you must forgive me . . .

PONZA: Get out of here! Get out of my sight!

SIGNORA FROLA: Yes . . . yes . . . I'm going . . . I'm going . . . God help me . . .

She looks beseechingly at the others, and then backs away, silently urging them to have pity on her son-in-law. She leaves in tears.

The others regard PONZA *with pity and trepidation. But the moment his mother-in-law has left, his composure changes, and he becomes calm and composed.*

PONZA: I am so sorry. Please, please forgive me for this little charade. This play-acting. But I'm afraid I had no choice; it was the only way to undo the harm that you had caused. Your intentions, of course, were pure, but—

AGAZZI: What are you talking about?

PONZA: I had to maintain her delusion. Don't you see?

AGAZZI: I don't understand. She thinks that you think—

PONZA: She thinks that I am mad. If I am mad, then her daughter is alive. So if I tell her the truth, then I mustn't do it quietly, I must shout it as if I were crazy. If I remind her that I have remarried, as indeed I have, it must, nonetheless, sound like the ravings of a lunatic. I must ensure that the truth always sounds untrue. Now you must excuse me. I must go to her.

He leaves. The others stand in astonished silence.

LAUDISI (*coming forward*): Well, thank God! Now we know the truth.

He bursts out laughing.

Act three

LAUDISI *is lying on an easy chair, reading, drink still in hand. Voices are heard offstage. The* BUTLER *appears, leading on a* POLICE INSPECTOR.

BUTLER: This way, please. I'll let the Councillor know you're here.

LAUDISI: Ah! Inspector! (*To* BUTLER) One minute, please. (*To* INSPECTOR, *a rather gloomy official.*) Is there news?

INSPECTOR: A bit, yes.

LAUDISI: Excellent. (*To* BUTLER) It's all right. I'll fetch my brother-in-law myself.

The BUTLER *bows and withdraws.*

LAUDISI: My, my, my, you're a bit of a miracle worker, Inspector. You may have single-handedly saved this town.

INSPECTOR: Well, I only . . .

LAUDISI: Don't be modest. Do you hear them in the next room? Loud, aren't they? It's because they're agitated. So – tell me your news.

INSPECTOR: We've traced someone . . .

LAUDISI: Ah! You have an eagle eye, I can see that. Someone from Ponza's town, I assume? . . .

INSPECTOR: Yes, but . . .

LAUDISI: Someone who knows . . .

INSPECTOR: A little bit.

LAUDISI: Little bit?

INSPECTOR: A few facts . . .

LAUDISI: Excellent, excellent. What are they?

INSPECTOR: I have this . . . (He holds out a sheet of paper to LAUDISI.)

LAUDISI: Give it here.

He hands the sheet to LAUDISI, who starts to read it, occasionally exclaiming, first an eager 'Ah' then 'Eh' and then finally 'Oh' in disappointment.

LAUDISI: But this is meaningless.

INSPECTOR: It's all we could find.

LAUDISI: But it remains as confusing as ever. (Looks at the INSPECTOR, then makes a hasty decision.) Would you like to be a genuine hero, Inspector? Would you like to render a great service to this town?

INSPECTOR: What kind of service?

LAUDISI: Tear this sheet of paper up. Throw it away. Then take another sheet and write down something definite.

INSPECTOR: Definite?

LAUDISI: Yes. Make up some information. You've managed to trace one witness. Good. Put words into his mouth. For God's sake, Inspector, this town will never get a night's sleep if you don't. They're all breaking into rashes and cold sores. Half of the town council are suffering from constipation. Only you can relieve their bowels.

INSPECTOR: I don't see how I—

LAUDISI: Give them a truth. Any old truth. It doesn't matter. And it certainly doesn't have to be true. As long as it masquerades as a fact.

INSPECTOR (indignant): You want me to lie?!

LAUDISI (thrilled): Yes! Of course!

INSPECTOR: How can you dare suggest such a thing. Lie!!?? I'm a policeman, for God's sake.

LAUDISI (defeated): Indeed.

INSPECTOR (heads towards the door): Shall I announce myself?

LAUDISI (wearily): No, no. I'll do it.

LAUDISI walks into the other room. The voices in the other room become louder. LAUDISI is heard announcing, 'The Inspector is here. He has news.' There are delighted cries and applause. The INSPECTOR flinches, sensing their anticipation.

LAUDISI returns, followed by AGAZZI, AMALIA, DINA, SIRELLI, SIGNORAS SIRELLI, CINI and NENNI, and many other TOWNSPEOPLE, some of whom emerge from the audience. In fact, the room seems to be surrounded by the entire town.

AGAZZI (hands extended): I knew I could trust you, Inspector. I knew you'd come up with the goods.

TOWNSPEOPLE: Thank God . . . We can't wait to hear . . . Which one is it? . . .

INSPECTOR: No, I'm afraid I'm . . .

AGAZZI: Please – ladies and gentlemen, silence! Let the gentleman speak.

INSPECTOR: Well, yes, you see. I've worked very hard, we all have, but I heard Signor Laudisi say to you . . .

AGAZZI: That you've brought us news. Well – go on then.

SIRELLI: And please, be very precise.

LAUDISI: He's been able to track someone down, you see. From Ponza's home town. Someone who knows the facts.

TOWNSPEOPLE: At last . . . Finally . . . Tell us . . .

The INSPECTOR shrugs and hands the paper to AGAZZI.

INSPECTOR: See for yourself, then.

AGAZZI (opens the sheet, as the crowd surrounds him): Let's have a look at it . . .

INSPECTOR (approaching LAUDISI): You've behaved disgracefully . . .

LAUDISI (loudly): Give the Councillor a chance to read the document.

AGAZZI: Yes – please. Let me have some breathing space. I must examine this carefully.

A silence, broken by LAUDISI.

LAUDISI: Of course, I've already read it.

TOWNSPEOPLE (*leave* AGAZZI *and run to* LAUDISI): Then what does it say? . . . Tell us . . .

LAUDISI: It doesn't mince words. It gives very definite information. It says that a neighbour of Signor Ponza has testified that . . . Signora Frola was once in a sanatorium.

TOWNSPEOPLE (*disappointed*): Oh!

SIGNORA SIRELLI: Signora Frola!

DINA: Are you certain?

AGAZZI (*who has, meanwhile, read the sheet*): Absolute nonsense! It says nothing of the sort!

LAUDISI: It says exactly that. It says the lady was in a sanatorium.

AGAZZI: Yes, it does. But which lady? The mother or the daughter?

TOWNSPEOPLE: Ah!

LAUDISI: Obviously it means the mother.

SIRELLI: No. It must be the daughter.

SIGNORA SIRELLI: Signora Frola told us her daughter had been in a sanatorium . . .

AMALIA: Yes. When she was taken away from her husband . . .

AGAZZI: And furthermore, this witness isn't even from their town. He was just passing through and he's merely repeating gossip and in fact he's not even certain the gossip was exactly as he remembers.

LAUDISI: Ah! So you're certain that Signora Frola's story is accurate?

SIRELLI: Yes.

LAUDISI: Then what's the problem? She's telling the truth. Full stop. So there is no mystery. And everyone can go home.

SIRELLI: The problem is the Mayor. The Mayor believes Ponza.

INSPECTOR: Yes, that's true. He told me that this morning . . .

AGAZZI: Because he's never talked with the old lady.

SIGNORA SIRELLI: He's only spoken to Ponza.

SIRELLI: But the Mayor isn't the only one who believes Ponza . . .

FIRST GENTLEMAN: Ponza's telling the truth! It happened to my wife's cousin. Her daughter

died as well. And she went insane as well. Exactly the same story.

SECOND GENTLEMAN: Except in that case the son-in-law remained a widower, whereas this Ponza has a woman living in his house.

LAUDISI: Ah! That's it! That's how we solve the riddle. (*Slaps the* SECOND GENTLEMAN *on the back.*) Well done.

SECOND GENTLEMAN: Er . . . What did I say?

LAUDISI: What did you say? What *didn't* you say! (*To* AGAZZI) Is the Mayor coming to see you?

AGAZZI: Yes, shortly. Why?

LAUDISI: It's utterly pointless for him to come and speak to Signora Frola. Right now he believes in her son-in-law. He isn't confused at all. If he speaks to her, he'll be as ga-ga as everyone else. He'll have no idea who's telling the truth. But there is something the Mayor can do instead. Something that might solve everything. And only he can do it.

TOWNSPEOPLE: What is it? . . .

LAUDISI: Didn't you hear what this gentleman said. 'A woman living in his house.' The wife!

SIRELLI: The wife! You mean – ask the wife?

DINA: But she's not allowed to leave . . .

SIRELLI: The Mayor can demand that she comes here.

AMALIA: She is the only one who knows the truth.

SIGNORA SIRELLI: But she'll say what her husband wants her to say.

LAUDISI: Only if she's interviewed in front of him.

AGAZZI: Then she must have a private conversation with the Mayor. Of course! It's so simple. What do you think, Inspector?

INSPECTOR: It's worth a try.

AGAZZI: It's the only answer. We must let the Mayor know before he arrives here. Will you speak to him, Inspector?

INSPECTOR: Yes. Right away. (*Bows and leaves.*)

SIGNORA SIRELLI (*to* LAUDISI): Well, well! Aren't you the clever one!

DINA (*smiles*): Well, you finally earned your keep . . .

LAUDISI (*holds up his glass*): A toast to me – then?

AGAZZI: I don't know why I didn't think of it.

SIRELLI: No reason to. We've never seen her, after all.

LAUDISI *shrugs and drinks his own toast, and then suddenly struck by* SIRELLI's *last statement:*

LAUDISI: Of course, we have no idea if she really exists.

AMALIA: Lamberto! Enough!

SIRELLI: You mean you doubt that *she's* real.

LAUDISI: Well, you just said that no one has ever seen her . . .

DINA (*exasperated*): Uncle!! (*Pause*) The old lady sees her. Every day.

SIGNORA SIRELLI: So does he. The son-in-law.

LAUDISI: Perhaps what they see is a ghost.

TOWNSPEOPLE: A ghost?!

AGAZZI: Laudisi! This is intolerable!

LAUDISI: Don't interrupt me; I'm on a roll. If Signora Frola is right, the lady is then the ghost of the second wife. Or if Ponza is right, she's the ghost of the daughter. This ghost is very real to both of them, but the question is, is it only a ghost, or is there a real person, a real woman behind the ghost, in other words, does she exist for herself? Perhaps not.

AMALIA: If I understood a word of what you just said, I'd have myself sectioned.

SIGNORA CINI: Oh no . . . we learned . . . my dear . . . not to listen . . .

SIGNORA NENNI: Still, ghosts are frightening . . .

SIRELLI: She's not a ghost. She's flesh and blood.

AGAZZI: But you're the one who suggested that she talk to the Mayor.

LAUDISI: Oh. Did I? Yes, of course . . . That was me. And a very good idea it is too. Assuming of course there really is a woman in that flat; well, there may be a woman, but not an ordinary woman, that I can assure you; not an ordinary woman.

SIGNORA SIRELLI: And what does *that* mean?

The INSPECTOR *returns.*

INSPECTOR: The Mayor is here.

AGAZZI: Here? Already?

INSPECTOR: I met him on the street, on his way to this house. He was with Ponza.

SIRELLI: Ponza?

AGAZZI: No, that's impossible. Ponza will take him to meet the mother-in-law. Look – don't let him go next door. Tell him I must see him immediately. See if you can separate him from Ponza.

INSPECTOR: Yes, of course.

The INSPECTOR *leaves.*

AGAZZI: I think we must have a private conversation. If you don't mind. Amalia, please take our guests into the next room . . .

SIGNORA SIRELLI: But make sure he understands that the wife is our only chance of knowing . . .

AGAZZI: Yes, yes. I know what to say. Please.

AMALIA (*to the others*): If you'll follow me . . . (*Leads the others into the next room.*)

AGAZZI: Sirelli, you stay. You too, Lamberto.

LAUDISI: Really? Me?

AGAZZI: If you promise to shut up.

LAUDISI: You won't even know I'm here.

The INSPECTOR *leads the* MAYOR *in. The* MAYOR *is rather affable.*

MAYOR: Ah, my dear friends . . . (*Shakes their hands.*)

AGAZZI: Forgive me for asking you to come here first.

MAYOR: I always intended to drop by. Now, Sirelli, I hear you're one of the people most intrigued by all this gossip.

SIRELLI: No more than anyone else.

AGAZZI: That's quite true. *Everyone* is in a state.

MAYOR: I don't understand why.

AGAZZI: Because we've been witness to certain dramas . . . as the mother-in-law happens to live next door.

SIRELLI: So you haven't met her yet?

MAYOR: I was on my way to do so. (*To* AGAZZI) I intended to meet her here, as you wished, but Signor Ponza implored me to see her in her own house, which, I must say, impressed me; he would hardly ask me to do that if he wasn't absolutely certain such a visit would confirm his story.

AGAZZI: Well, yes, but you see, when she's in front of him, the poor woman . . .

SIRELLI: Says just what he wants her to say. Which is proof that she's not mad.

MAYOR: But isn't that because he tries to make her believe he's the mad one. He told me all about it. It's the only way for the poor woman to maintain her fantasy. I have to say, it must be torture for that poor man . . .

SIRELLI: Unless she is making him believe that she believes her daughter is dead, so he never has to worry about his wife being taken from him again. If that's the case, it's the old woman who is living through hell . . .

MAYOR: Well, I have no doubt where the truth lies. And seemingly, neither do you. We simply believe in opposite truths. How about you, Laudisi?

LAUDISI (*makes terrible noises as if his mouth has been taped*): Mmmmm . . . mmmmm . . .

AGAZZI: Oh, stop it. If the Mayor asks you a question, you must reply. But try for a straight answer for once. (*To the* MAYOR) He's spent the last two days trying to exacerbate our confusion.

LAUDISI: On the contrary, I've been doing my best to clarify the situation.

SIRELLI: Clarify? He's just told us a ghost lives in Ponza's house.

MAYOR (*laughs*): What? A ghost? Oh – jolly good.

LAUDISI: The truth is it was my idea to invite you here.

MAYOR: Oh, I see. Because you think I should talk to the mother-in-law??

LAUDISI: Good God, no. You should believe Signor Ponza and leave it at that.

MAYOR: Ah, so you agree that Signor Ponza is—

LAUDISI: No. I also wish everyone simply believed Signora Frola.

AGAZZI: Do you see what I mean about him?

MAYOR (*to* LAUDISI): Explain yourself, please.

LAUDISI: You must believe what they *both* say.

SIRELLI: But they both say the opposite.

MAYOR: So then what do we do?

AGAZZI: Let's not take sides. Let's not say he's right or she's right. There's only one way to settle this matter.

MAYOR: Which is?

AGAZZI: You have to exercise your authority and obtain a statement from the wife.

MAYOR: From Signora Ponza?

SIRELLI: But only if you see her in private; not in front of her husband.

AGAZZI: That's the only way she'll tell the truth.

MAYOR: Yes. I understand. Good idea. And it should please Ponza. He wants us to believe he's telling the truth. I think he'll be delighted by this solution. And certainly it will put the town's mind at rest. Inspector – would you mind going next door and calling Signor Ponza. Ask him to drop in here for a moment.

INSPECTOR: Yes, sir.

He leaves.

AGAZZI: If only he agrees.

MAYOR: Of course he'll agree. We'll have this cleared up in fifteen minutes. In front of your very eyes.

AGAZZI: Here? In my house?

MAYOR: Well, certainly. If you don't see and hear for yourselves you'd never believe it.

AGAZZI: Good heavens. We would take your word for it.

SIRELLI: Of course we would.

MAYOR (*laughs*): I don't think so. You're aware that I already believe Ponza, so you'd always suspect that I'd manipulated the outcome to flatter his story. I think it's best that everybody hears. Where is your wife?

AGAZZI: In the next room.

MAYOR (*looks into the next room*): Good God! It's Standing Room Only. Half the town is there.

The INSPECTOR *returns, followed by* PONZA.

INSPECTOR: I've brought Signor Ponza.

MAYOR: Thank you, Inspector. Ponza, old man, please come in.

PONZA *bows.*

AGAZZI: Please have a seat.

PONZA *bows again and sits.*

MAYOR: I believe you've met everyone here. I wanted to see you, Ponza, to tell you that my friends here and I . . . (*Stops himself, seeing* PONZA's *apparent agitation.*) Is there something you wish to say?

PONZA: Yes, Your Honour. I'd like to request an immediate transfer.

MAYOR: Why? Just a few moments ago you seemed delighted to be in this town . . .

PONZA: No, no, I'm persecuted here.

MAYOR: 'Persecuted'? That's a heavy word.

AGAZZI: Were you alluding to me, by any chance?

PONZA: To everyone! The entire town! I have to leave. I cannot tolerate this morbid fascination with my private life, which is bound to end in tragedy, undoing all the sacrifices I've made for the sake of my poor mother-in-law, who I love as if she were my own mother. Yesterday, in this room, I was forced to treat her in a cruel and hurtful fashion. I've just been to see her in her flat; she's in a dreadful state, depressed and disorientated . . .

AGAZZI: But this is why we are so confused. When she is with us she always speaks calmly. She seems very self-possessed. The only person who ever seems agitated or disorientated is you.

PONZA: Because you have no idea what your meddling is doing to me.

MAYOR: Now come on . . . let's calm down . . . You're talking to me now, remember? And you know that I trust you, don't you? And have enormous compassion for your position.

PONZA: Yes, you have. I'm so sorry. You've been good to me.

MAYOR: Now – you said you care about Signora Frola as if she were your own mother. As it happens, my friends here are also fond of her and concerned for her. That's precisely why they are so anxious about her situation.

PONZA: But they're killing her! I keep trying to explain this to them . . .

MAYOR: I think a little patience is in order. We just need some clarity, that's all. And it's actually quite easy to achieve. These people do doubt you, that's true, and there's nothing I can do to lift those doubts; you, on the other hand, have a very simple way of dispelling all this confusion.

PONZA: There's nothing I can do to make them believe me.

AGAZZI: Actually, when you first came here, after your mother-in-law's first visit, we believed you, we all believed you. But then, of course, the lady came back . . .

MAYOR: And when she spoke, they believed her. And so it goes, round and round, an emotional carousel. The answer is not to listen to either you or your mother-in-law any more. As you are certain that you are telling the truth – and, incidentally, I am as well – you can surely have no objection if your story is confirmed by the only person, other than the two of you, who is privy to the facts.

PONZA: Who is that?

MAYOR: Your wife, of course.

PONZA: My wife!! (*Angry.*) No! Never!

MAYOR: Why not?

PONZA: Do I have to parade my wife in front of those people who refuse to believe a word I say?

MAYOR: It's for me. Not for them.

PONZA: I beg you, not my wife. We must leave her out of this. You must have faith in my word.

MAYOR: Well, it's rather difficult, when you place so many obstacles in your path.

AGAZZI: Remember, he tried to prevent his mother-in-law coming here, even though it meant a supreme discourtesy to my wife and daughter.

PONZA: What do you want of me? What exactly do you want of me? Isn't it enough that you torment me and my mother-in-law? Do you want to do the same to my wife? I will not allow her to be put through this hell. I have no intention of throwing her to the wolves. She shall not leave her house! (*To the* MAYOR) I am satisfied that you believe me. As for the rest, I am requesting a transfer to another town.

MAYOR (*angered*): Just hold on. You're wearing my patience very thin. I won't have you speak to the Councillor that way, and certainly not to me, who has, until this moment, shown you profound respect. I must admit your obstinacy is giving me second thoughts; what I have requested is purely in your own interest, and I see no logic in your refusal.

PONZA: Are you saying I have no choice?

MAYOR: Damn it; *this is for your own good*. I could, of course, order you to comply.

PONZA: I see. (*Pause*) Then indeed yes . . . no choice. Very well. I shall bring my wife here. It will put an end to the matter. But I must have a guarantee that the old lady will not see her.

MAYOR: That's difficult. She does live next door.

AGAZZI: If it helps, we could visit her, as a distraction . . .

PONZA: No. No more of your games. They always end in disaster.

MAYOR: If you prefer, you can bring her to my office.

PONZA: No. I want to get it over with. It might as well be here. Once I've brought her here, I'll slip next door and keep watch over the old woman. And you can talk to my wife. *And it will be done.*

PONZA *leaves, in a fury.*

MAYOR: I must admit I wasn't expecting such a reaction.

AGAZZI: He'll tell his wife exactly what she must say.

MAYOR: Don't worry. I'll question her myself. But he's never been this way before, not with me . . . I suppose he's just traumatised by the idea of bringing his wife here.

SIRELLI: Releasing her from captivity.

MAYOR: That's a heavy assumption. Anyhow, imprisoning your wife doesn't mean you're mad.

SIRELLI: What then?

MAYOR: Just jealous, perhaps.

SIRELLI: He doesn't even have a servant. The wife has to do all the housework by herself.

AGAZZI: And he does all the shopping himself, every morning.

MAYOR: Oh, I know. He told me. He has perfectly logical reasons. He's trying to save money. Remember, he maintains two households.

SIRELLI: But you're asking us to believe that a second wife would agree to such a burden for the sake of a woman who is, after all, a complete stranger to her?

AGAZZI: It is a bit much.

MAYOR: Yes, difficult to believe . . .

LAUDISI: Assuming, of course, that she were an *ordinary* second wife.

AGAZZI: Forgive me. I forgot. She's a ghost.

Confused voices are heard in the other room.

AGAZZI: What's that racket?

AMALIA *rushes in, hugely agitated.*

AMALIA: It's Signora Frola! She's here!

AGAZZI: Oh dear God. Who asked her . . . ?

AMALIA: Nobody asked her. She just showed up . . .

MAYOR: This isn't the time. Send her away.

AMALIA: I can't really . . .

AGAZZI: Get rid of her, for God's sake. She mustn't be in this house. If Ponza sees her here, he'll think it's a trap.

SIGNORA FROLA *enters, trembling and crying, holding a handkerchief in her hand. She is surrounded by most of the town.*

SIGNORA FROLA (*to* AGAZZI, *indicating crowd*): Please, Signor, I beg you, you must tell them to leave us alone.

AGAZZI: Signora, you must leave. You cannot stay here.

SIGNORA FROLA: Why? Why not? (*To* AMALIA) Please . . . I'm begging you . . .

AMALIA: This isn't a good time . . . The Mayor is here . . .

SIGNORA FROLA: Oh, but that's good. The Mayor. I want to talk to him.

MAYOR: Signora, I'm so sorry. I am unable to see you now. I'll arrange a meeting with you later. But at the moment it is imperative that you leave.

SIGNORA FROLA: Oh, I will leave. I will. I promise you. Today. I will leave for good.

AGAZZI: There's no need for that. Just return next door to your flat. Just for an hour or so. As a favour to us. Then you can talk to the Mayor.

SIGNORA FROLA: But why? What is the problem?

AGAZZI: Your son-in-law is about to return. Now do you understand?

SIGNORA FROLA: Oh. Oh, I see. Well, then I will have to go. Of course. I'll go at once. I only wanted to ask you to stop it. To stop this. All of this. I know you wish to help me, but you are causing me so much pain. I'll have no choice but to leave this town, to leave right now, today, if it means he will be left in peace. I don't understand what you want. Why do you need to see him again? Why is he coming here again?

MAYOR: It's nothing to worry about, I assure you. Now – please go.

AMALIA: Do as we ask – please.

SIGNORA FROLA: But you will force me to leave behind my only pleasure, my only comfort – the chance to see my daughter every day, if only from a distance.

MAYOR: We only want you to leave this room, not the town. You will still be able to see her. Please don't worry.

SIGNORA FROLA: But it's him I'm worried about. Him! I came here to implore you on his behalf . . .

MAYOR: You needn't worry about him. You have my word. We have made arrangements to draw this affair to a close –

SIGNORA FROLA: How can you do that? It's obvious that everyone in this room hates him.

MAYOR: That isn't true. I am myself quite fond of him. And I have his interests at heart. Trust me.

SIGNORA FROLA: Is that true? Do you really understand? . . .

MAYOR: Yes, I believe I do understand.

SIGNORA FROLA: Oh, thank God. I have tried over and over to explain it to these people; that

he had a problem, which he has overcome, which is now in the past, and we must let it go . . .

MAYOR: Yes, I do understand that . . .

SIGNORA FROLA: We have been happy living this way. Until we arrived in this town. My daughter is happy as well. So you must see that they leave him alone . . . because if they don't, then I really will have no choice but to leave . . . and I will never see her again, not even from a distance. Please, I beg you . . . *make them leave him alone!*

Suddenly – movement in the crowd. Exclamations. People looking towards the door.

TOWNSPEOPLE: It's her! . . . She's here! . . .

SIGNORA FROLA (puzzled): What is it? What is happening?

The crowd moves aside as SIGNORA PONZA *enters. She is a simple woman, dressed in mourning.*

SIGNORA FROLA (screams with joy): Oh! Lina! Lina! Lina!

She runs to the younger woman and throws her arms around her, with the passion and thirst of a mother who has been unable to embrace her daughter for many years. But suddenly PONZA's *voice can be heard from the next room.*

PONZA: Julia! Julia! Julia!

SIGNORA PONZA, *at the sound of her husband's voice, stiffens in the arms of* SIGNORA FROLA.

PONZA *runs into the room and, seeing his mother-in-law desperately clinging to his wife, cries out in a fury to the* MAYOR, AGAZZI *and the assembled* TOWNSPEOPLE.

PONZA: I knew it! I knew it! I allowed myself to trust you once again, and this is how you've repaid me.

SIGNORA PONZA (solemnly turns her veiled head to PONZA and SIGNORA FROLA): It's all right. You needn't be afraid any more. You can leave me now.

PONZA: Yes. (Pause) Yes. (To SIGNORA FROLA, lovingly) We must go.

SIGNORA FROLA *moves away from* SIGNORA PONZA. *Trembling, she turns to* PONZA, *and with great humility, repeats his words.*

SIGNORA FROLA: Yes. We must go. Come, my dearest . . . we must go . . .

SIGNORA FROLA *and* PONZA *reach out and place their arms round each other. They are both crying, but the sounds of their weeping differ. They whisper affectionate words to each other, and caress each other, as they move towards the door. They seem to be two creatures from a totally different planet. And suddenly, they are gone.*

Silence.

The TOWNSPEOPLE, *utterly astonished and strangely moved, turn back to* SIGNORA PONZA. *She stares at them with sadness and dignity.*

SIGNORA PONZA: What more do you want of me? We have all suffered so much. Don't you see that? You must have *compassion* – for only that, and love, and *silence* can bring salvation.

MAYOR: We have the deepest compassion, Signora. But we need to hear from you . . .

SIGNORA PONZA: Please don't ask me . . .

AMALIA: We simply want to know . . .

SIGNORA PONZA: There has been so much unhappiness . . .

AGAZZI: We would like you to tell . . .

SIGNORA PONZA (*speaking slowly and deliberately*): What? The truth? Is that what you want from me? The truth. Very well then. The truth is this, simply this. I am the daughter of Signora Frola.

TOWNSPEOPLE (*sighing in relie*): Ah!

SIGNORA PONZA: . . . And the second wife of Signor Ponza.

TOWNSPEOPLE (*shocked and disappointed*): Oh! But how? . . .

SIGNORA PONZA: But I am, within myself, neither. I am no one at all.

MAYOR: That's not possible. You must be one or the other.

SIGNORA PONZA: Must I be? I think not. (*Pause*) I am whoever you believe me to be.

She looks at them for a moment and then leaves.

Silence.

LAUDISI: There you have it, my friends. Truth has spoken. (*He looks at the others.*) Are you satisfied?

He starts to laugh.

Chapter 42

Peter Winch

UNDERSTANDING A PRIMITIVE SOCIETY

This essay will pursue further some questions raised in my book *The Idea of a Social Science*.[1] That book was a general discussion of what is involved in the understanding of human social life. I shall here be concerned more specifically with certain issues connected with social anthropology. In the first part I raise certain difficulties about Professor E. E. Evans-Pritchard's approach in his classic *Witchcraft, Oracles and Magic among the Azande*.[2] In the second part, I attempt to refute some criticisms recently made by Mr. Alasdair MacIntyre of Evans-Pritchard and myself, to criticize in their turn MacIntyre's positive remarks, and to offer some further reflections of my own on the concept of learning from the study of a primitive society.

I. The reality of magic

Like many other primitive people, the African Azande hold beliefs that we cannot possibly share and engage in practices which it is peculiarly difficult for us to comprehend. They believe that certain of their members are witches, exercising a malignant occult influence on the lives of their fellow. They engage in rites to counteract witchcraft; they consult oracles and use magic medicines to protect themselves from harm.

An anthropologist studying such a people wishes to make those beliefs and practices intelligible to himself and his readers. This means presenting an account of them that will somehow satisfy the criteria of rationality demanded by the culture to which he and his readers belong: a culture whose conception of rationality is deeply affected by the achievements and methods of the sciences, and one which treats such things as a belief in magic or the practice of consulting oracles as almost a paradigm of the irrational. The strains inherent in this situation are very likely to lead the anthropologist to adopt the following posture: *We* know that Zande beliefs in the influence of witchcraft, the efficacy of magic medicines, the role of oracles in revealing what is going on and what is going to happen, are mistaken, illusory. Scientific methods of investigation have shown conclusively that there are no relations of cause and effect such as are implied by these beliefs and practices. All we can do then is to show how such a system of mistaken beliefs and inefficacious practices can maintain itself in the face of objections that seem to us so obvious.[3]

Now although Evans-Pritchard goes a very great deal further than most of his predecessors in trying to present the sense of the institutions he is discussing as it presents itself to the Azande themselves, still, the last paragraph does, I believe, pretty fairly describe the attitude he himself took at the time of writing this book. There is more than one remark to the effect that "obviously there are no witches"; and he writes of the difficulty he found, during his field work with the Azande, in shaking off the "unreason" on which Zande life is based and returning to a clear view of how things really are. This attitude is not an unsophisticated one but is based on a philosophical position ably developed in a series of papers published in the 1930s in the unhappily rather inaccessible *Bulletin of the Faculty of Arts* of the University of Egypt. Arguing against Lévy-Bruhl, Evans-Pritchard here rejects the idea that the scientific understanding of causes and effects which leads us to reject magical ideas is evidence of any superior intelligence on our part. Our scientific approach, he points out, is as much a function of our culture as is the magical approach of the "savage" a function of his.

The fact that we attribute rain to meteorological causes alone while savages believe that Gods or ghosts or magic can influence the rainfall is no evidence that our brains function differently from their brains. It does not show that we "think more logically" than savages, at least not if this expression suggests some kind of hereditary psychic superiority. It is no sign of superior intelligence on my part that I attribute rain to physical causes. I did not come to this conclusion myself by observation and inference and have, in fact, little knowledge of the meteorological processes that lead to rain. I merely accept what everybody else in my society accepts, namely that rain is due to natural causes. This particular idea formed part of my culture long before I was born into it and little more was required of me than sufficient linguistic ability to learn it. Likewise a savage who believes that under suitable natural and ritual conditions the rainfall can be influenced by use of appropriate magic is not on account of this belief to be considered of inferior intelligence. He did not build up this belief from his own observations and inferences but adopted it in the same way as he adopted the rest of his cultural heritage, namely, by being born into it. He and I are both thinking in patterns of thought provided for us by the societies in which we live.

It would be absurd to say that the savage is thinking mystically and that we are thinking scientifically about rainfall. In either case like mental processes are involved and, moreover, the content of thought is similarly derived. But we can say that the social content of our thought about rainfall is scientific, is in accord with objective facts, whereas the social content of savage thought about rainfall is unscientific since it is not in accord with reality and may also be mystical where it assumes the existence of supra-sensible forces.[4]

In a subsequent article on Pareto, Evans-Pritchard distinguishes between "logical" and "scientific."

Scientific notions are those which accord with objective reality both with regard to the validity of their premises and to the inferences drawn from their propositions. . . . Logical notions are those in which according to the rules of thought inferences would be true were the premises true, the truth of the premises being irrelevant. . . .

A pot has broken during firing. This is probably due to grit. Let us examine the pot and see if this is the cause. That is logical and scientific thought. Sickness is due to witchcraft. A man is sick. Let us consult the oracles to discover who is the witch responsible. That is logical and unscientific thought.[5]

I think that Evans-Pritchard is right in a great deal of what he says here, but wrong, and crucially wrong, in his attempt to characterize the scientific in terms of that which is "in accord with objective reality." Despite differences of emphasis and phraseology, Evans-Pritchard is in fact hereby put into the same metaphysical camp as Pareto: for both of them the conception of "reality" must be regarded as intelligible and applicable *outside* the context of scientific reasoning itself, since it is that to which scientific notions do, and unscientific notions do not, have a relation. Evans-Pritchard, although he emphasizes that a member of scientific culture has a different conception of reality from that of a Zande believer in magic, wants to go beyond merely registering this fact and making the differences explicit, and to say, finally, that the scientific conception agrees with what reality actually is like, whereas the magical conception does not.

It would be easy, at this point, to say simply that the difficulty arises from the use of the unwieldy and misleadingly comprehensive expression "agreement with reality"; and in a sense this is true. But we should not lose sight of the fact that the idea that men's ideas and beliefs must be checkable by reference to something independent—some reality—is an important one. To abandon it is to plunge straight into an extreme Protagorean relativism, with all the paradoxes that involves. On the other hand great care is certainly necessary in fixing the precise role that this conception of the independently real does play in men's thought. There are two related points that I should like to make about it at this stage.

In the first place we should notice that the check of the independently real is not peculiar to science. The trouble is that the fascination science has for us makes it easy for us to adopt its scientific form as a paradigm against which to measure the intellectual respectability of other modes of discourse. Consider what God says to Job out of the whirlwind: "Who is this that darkeneth counsel by words without knowledge? . . . Where wast thou when I laid the foundations of the earth? declare, if thou hast understanding. Who hath laid the measures thereof, if thou knowest? or who hath stretched the line upon it. . . . Shall he that contendeth with the Almighty instruct him? he that reproveth God, let him answer it." Job is taken to task for having gone astray by having lost sight of

the reality of God; this does not, of course, mean that Job has made any sort of theoretical mistake, which could be put right, perhaps, by means of an experiment.[6] God's reality is certainly independent of what any man may care to think, but what that reality amounts to can only be seen from the religious tradition in which the concept of God is used, and this use is very unlike the use of scientific concepts, say of theoretical entities. The point is that it is within the religious use of language that the conception of God's reality has its place, though, I repeat, this does not mean that it is at the mercy of what anyone cares to say; if this were so, God would have no reality.

My second point follows from the first. Reality is not what gives language sense. What is real and what is unreal shows itself in the sense that language has. Further, both the distinction between the real and the unreal and the concept of agreement with reality themselves belong to our language. I will not say that they are concepts of the language like any other, since it is clear that they occupy a commanding, and in a sense a limiting, position there. We can imagine a language with no concept of, say, wetness, but hardly one in which there is no way of distinguishing the real from the unreal. Nevertheless we could not in fact distinguish the real from the unreal without understanding the way this distinction operates in the language. If then we wish to understand the significance of these concepts, we must examine the use they actually do have—in the language.

Evans-Pritchard, on the contrary, is trying to work with a conception of reality which is *not* determined by its actual use in language. He wants something against which that use can itself be appraised. But this is not possible; and no more possible in the case of scientific discourse than it is in any other. We may ask whether a particular scientific hypothesis agrees with reality and test this by observation and experiment. Given the experimental methods, and the established use of the theoretical terms entering into the hypothesis, then the question whether it holds or not is settled by reference to something independent of what I, or anybody else, care to think. But the general nature of the data revealed by the experiment can only be specified in terms of criteria built into the methods of experiment exployed and these, in turn, make sense only to someone who is conversant with the kind of scientific activity within which they are employed. A scientific illiterate, asked to describe the results of an experiment which he "observes" in an advanced physics laboratory, could not do so in terms relevant to the hypothesis being tested; and it is really only in such terms that we can sensibly speak of the "results of the experiment" at all. What Evans-Pritchard wants to be able to say is that the criteria applied in scientific experimentation constitute a true link between our ideas and an independent reality, whereas those characteristic of other systems of thought—in particular, magical methods of thought—do not. It is evident that the expressions "true link" and "independent reality" in the previous sentence cannot themselves be explained by reference to the scientific universe of discourse, as this would beg the question. We have then to ask how, by reference to what established universe of discourse, the use of those expressions is to be explained; and it is clear that Evans-Pritchard has not answered this question.

Two questions arise out of what I have been saying. First, is it in fact the case that a primitive system of magic, like that of the Azande, constitutes a coherent universe of discourse like science, in terms of which an intelligible conception of reality and clear ways of deciding what beliefs are and are not in agreement with this reality can be discerned? Second, what are we to make of the possibility of understanding primitive social institutions, like Zande magic, if the situation is as I have outlined? I do not claim to be able to give a satisfactory answer to the second question. It raises some very important and fundamental issues about the nature of

human social life, which require conceptions different from, and harder to elucidate, than those I have hitherto introduced. I shall offer some tentative remarks about these issues in the second part of this essay. At present I shall address myself to the first question.

It ought to be remarked here that an affirmative answer to my first question would not commit me to accepting as rational all beliefs couched in magical concepts or all procedures practiced in the name of such beliefs. This is no more necessary than is the corresponding proposition that all procedures "justified" in the name of science are immune from rational criticism. A remark of Collingwood's is apposite here:

> Savages are no more exempt from human folly than civilized men, and are no doubt equally liable to the error of thinking that they, or the persons they regard as their superiors, can do what in fact cannot be done. But this error is not the essence of magic; it is a perversion of magic. And we should be careful how we attribute it to the people we call savages, who will one day rise up and testify against us.[7]

It is important to distinguish a system of magical beliefs and practices like that of the Azande, which is one of the principal foundations of their whole social life and, on the other hand, magical beliefs that might be held, and magical rites that might be practiced, by persons belonging to our own culture. These have to be understood rather differently. Evans-Pritchard is himself alluding to the difference in the following passage: "When a Zande speaks of witchcraft he does not speak of it as we speak of the weird witchcraft of our own history. Witchcraft is to him a commonplace happening and he seldom passes a day without mentioning it. . . . To us witchcraft is something which haunted and disgusted our credulous forefathers. But the Zande expects to come across witchcraft at any time of the day or night. He would be just as surprised if he were not brought into daily contact with it as we would be if confronted by its appearance. To him there is nothing miraculous about it."[8]

The difference is not merely one of degree of familiarity, however, although, perhaps, even this has more importance than might at first appear. Concepts of witchcraft and magic in our culture, at least since the advent of Christianity, have been parasitic on, and a perversion of, other orthodox concepts, both religious and, increasingly, scientific. To take an obvious example, you could not understand what was involved in conducting a Black Mass, unless you were familiar with the conduct of a proper Mass and, therefore, with the whole complex of religious ideas from which the Mass draws its sense. Neither would you understand the relation between these without taking account of the fact that the Black practices are rejected as *irrational* (in the sense proper to religion) in the system of beliefs on which these practices are thus parasitic. Perhaps a similar relation holds between the contemporary practice of astrology and astronomy and technology. It is impossible to keep a discussion of the rationality of Black Magic or of astrology within the bounds of concepts peculiar to them; they have an essential reference to something outside themselves. The position is like that which Socrates, in Plato's *Gorgias*, showed to be true of the Sophists' conception of rhetoric: namely, that it is parasitic on rational discourse in such a way that its irrational character can be shown in terms of this dependence. Hence, when we speak of such practices as "superstitious," "illusory," "irrational," we have the weight of our culture behind us; and this is not just a matter of being on the side of the big battalions, because those beliefs and practices belong to, and derive such sense as they seem to have, from that same culture. This enables us to show that the sense is only apparent, in terms which are culturally relevant.

It is evident that our relation to Zande magic is quite different. If we wish to understand it, we must seek a foothold elsewhere. And while there may well be room for the use of such critical expressions as "superstition" and "irrationality," the kind of rationality with which such terms might be used to point a contrast remains to be elucidated. The remarks I shall make in Part II will have a more positive bearing on this issue. In the rest of this part, I shall develop in more detail my criticisms of Evans-Pritchard's approach to the Azande.

Early in this book he defines certain categories in terms of which his descriptions of Zande customs are couched.

> MYSTICAL NOTIONS ... are patterns of thought that attribute to phenomena supra-sensible qualities which, or part of which, are not derived from observation or cannot be logically inferred from it, *and which they do not possess.*[9] COMMON-SENSE NOTIONS ... attribute to phenomena only what men observe in them or what can logically be inferred from observation. So long as a notion does not assert something which has not been observed, it is not classed as mystical even though it is mistaken on account of incomplete observation.... SCIENTIFIC NOTIONS. Science has developed out of common-sense but is far more methodical and has better techniques of observation and reasoning. Common sense uses experience and rules of thumb. Science uses experiment and rules of Logic. ... *Our body of scientific knowledge and Logic are the sole arbiters of what are mystical, common sense, and scientific notions.* Their judgments are never absolute. RITUAL BEHAVIOUR. Any behaviour that is accounted for by mystical notions. *There is no objective nexus* between the behaviour and the event it is intended to cause. Such behaviour is usually intelligible to us only when we know the mystical notions associated with it. EMPIRICAL BEHAVIOUR. Any behaviour that is accounted for by common-sense notions.[10]

It will be seen from the phrases which I have italicized that Evans-Pritchard is doing more here than just defining certain terms for his own use. Certain metaphysical claims are embodied in the definitions: identical in substance with the claims embodied in Pareto's way of distinguishing between "logical" and "non-logical" conduct.[11] There is a very clear implication that those who use mystical notions and perform ritual behavior are making some sort of mistake, detectable with the aid of science and logic. I shall now examine more closely some of the institutions described by Evans-Pritchard to determine how far his claims are justified.

Witchcraft is a power possessed by certain individuals to harm other individuals by "mystical" means. Its basis is an inherited organic condition, "witchcraft-substance" and it does not involve any special magical ritual or medicine. It is constantly appealed to by Azande when they are afflicted by misfortune, not so as to exclude explanation in terms of natural causes, which Azande are perfectly able to offer themselves within the limits of their not inconsiderable natural knowledge, but so as to supplement such explanations. "Witchcraft explains why[12] events are harmful to man and not how[12] they happen. A Zande perceives how they happen just as we do. He does not see a witch charge a man, but an elephant. He does not see a witch push over the granary, but termites gnawing away its supports. He does not see a psychical flame igniting thatch, but an ordinary lighted bundle of straw. His perception of how events occur is as clear as our own."[13]

The most important way of detecting the influence of witchcraft and of identifying witches is by the revelations of oracles, of which in turn the most important is the "poison oracle." This name, though convenient, is significantly misleading insofar as, according to Evans-Pritchard, Azande do not have our concept of a poison and do not think of, or behave toward, *benge*—the substance administered in the consultation of the oracle—as we do of and toward poisons. The gathering, preparation, and administering of *benge* are hedged with ritual and strict taboos. At an oracular consultation *benge* is administered to a fowl, while a question is asked in a form permitting a yes or no answer. The fowl's death or survival is specified beforehand as giving the answer "yes" or "no." The answer is then checked by administering *benge* to another fowl and asking the question the other way round. "Is Prince Ndoruma responsible for placing bad medicines in the roof of my hut? The fowl DIES giving the answer 'Yes.' . . . Did the oracle speak truly when it said that Ndoruma was responsible? The fowl SURVIVES giving the answer 'Yes'." The poison oracle is all-pervasive in Zande life and all steps of any importance in a person's life are settled by reference to it.

A Zande would be utterly lost and bewildered without his oracle. The mainstay of his life would be lacking. It is rather as if an engineer, in our society, were to be asked to build a bridge without mathematical calculation, or a military commander to mount an extensive co-ordinated attack without the use of clocks. These analogies are mine, but a reader may well think that they beg the question at issue. For, he may argue, the Zande practice of consulting the oracle, unlike my technological and military examples, is completely unintelligible and rests on an obvious illusion. I shall now consider this objection.

First I must emphasize that I have so far done little more than note the *fact*, conclusively established by Evans-Pritchard, that the Azande *do* in fact conduct their affairs to their own satisfaction in this way and are at a loss when forced to abandon the practice—when, for instance, they fall into the hands of European courts. It is worth remarking too that Evans-Pritchard himself ran his household in the same way during his field researches and says: "I found this as satisfactory a way of running my home and affairs as any other I know of."

Further, I would ask in my turn: *to whom* is the practice alleged to be unintelligible? Certainly it is difficult for us to understand what the Azande are about when they consult their oracles; but it might seem just as incredible to them that the engineer's motions with his slide rule could have any connection with the stability of his bridge. But this riposte of course misses the intention behind the objection, which was not directed to the question whether anyone in fact understands, or claims to understand, what is going on, but rather whether what is going on actually does make sense: i.e. in itself. And it may seem obvious that Zande beliefs in witchcraft and oracles cannot make any sense, however satisfied the Azande may be with them.

What criteria have we for saying that something does, or does not, make sense? A partial answer is that a set of beliefs and practices cannot make sense insofar as they involve contradictions. Now it appears that contradictions are bound to arise in at least two ways in the consultation of the oracle. On the one hand two oracular pronouncements may contradict each other; and on the other hand a self-consistent oracular pronouncement may be contradicted by future experience. I shall examine each of these apparent possibilities in turn.

Of course, it does happen often that the oracle first says "yes" and then "no" to the same question. This does not convince a Zande of the futility of the whole operation of consulting oracles: obviously, it cannot, since otherwise the practice could hardly have developed and maintained itself at all. Various explanations may be offered, whose possibility, it is important to notice, is built into the whole network of Zande beliefs and may, therefore, be regarded as belonging to the concept of an oracle. It may be said, for instance, that bad *benge* is being used; that the operator of the oracle is ritually unclean; that the oracle is being itself influenced by witchcraft or sorcery; or it may be that the oracle is showing that the question cannot be answered straightforwardly in its present form, as with

"Have you stopped beating your wife yet?" There are various ways in which the behavior of the fowl under the influence of *benge* may be ingeniously interpreted by those wise in the ways of the poison oracle. We might compare this situation perhaps with the interpretation of dreams.

In the other type of case: where an internally consistent oracular revelation is apparently contradicted by subsequent experience, the situation may be dealt with in a similar way, by references to the influence of witchcraft, ritual uncleanliness, and so on. But there is another important consideration we must take into account here too. The chief function of oracles is to reveal the presence of "mystical" forces—I use Evans-Pritchard's term without committing myself to his denial that such forces really exist. Now though there are indeed ways of determining whether or not mystical forces are operating, these ways do not correspond to what we understand by "empirical" confirmation or refutation. This indeed is a tautology, since such differences in "confirmatory" procedures are the main criteria for classifying something as a mystical force in the first place. Here we have one reason why the possibilities of "refutation by experience" are very much fewer than might at first sight be supposed.

There is also another closely connected reason. The spirit in which oracles are consulted is very unlike that in which a scientist makes experiments. Oracular revelations are not treated as hypotheses and, since their sense derives from the way they are treated in their context, they therefore *are not* hypotheses. They are not a matter of intellectual interest but the main way in which Azande decide how they should act. If the oracle reveals that a proposed course of action is fraught with mystical dangers from witchcraft or sorcery, that course of action will not be carried out; and then the question of refutation or confirmation just does not arise. We might say that the revelation has the logical status of an unfulfilled hypothetical, were it not that the context in which this logical term is generally used may again suggest a misleadingly close analogy with scientific hypotheses.

I do not think that Evans-Pritchard would have disagreed with what I have said so far. Indeed, the following comment is on very similar lines:

> Azande observe the action of the poison oracle as we observe it, but their observations are always subordinated to their beliefs and are incorporated into their beliefs and made to explain them and justify them. Let the reader consider any argument that would utterly demolish all Zande claims for the power of the oracle. If it were translated into Zande modes of thought it would serve to support their entire structure of belief. For their mystical notions are eminently coherent, being interrelated by a network of logical ties, and are so ordered that they never too crudely contradict sensory experience but, instead, experience seems to justify them. The Zande is immersed in a sea of mystical notions, and if he speaks about his poison oracle he must speak in a mystical idiom.[14]

To locate the point at which the important philosophical issue does arise, I shall offer a parody, composed by changing round one or two expressions in the foregoing quotation.

> Europeans observe the action of the poison oracle just as Azande observe it, but their observations are always subordinated to their beliefs and are incorporated into their beliefs and made to explain them and justify them. Let a Zande consider any argument that would utterly refute all European scepticism about the power of the oracle. If it were translated into European modes of thought it would serve to support their entire structure of belief. For their scientific notions are eminently coherent, being interrelated by a network of logical ties, and are so ordered that they never too crudely contradict mystical

experience but, instead, experience seems to justify them. The European is immersed in a sea of scientific notions, and if he speaks about the Zande poison oracle he must speak in a scientific idiom.

Perhaps this too would be acceptable to Evans-Pritchard. But it is clear from other remarks in the book to which I have alluded, that at the time of writing it he would have wished to add: and the European is right and the Zande wrong. This addition I regard as illegitimate and my reasons for so thinking take us to the heart of the matter.

It may be illuminating at this point to compare the disagreement between Evans-Pritchard and me to that between the Wittgenstein of the *Philosophical Investigations* and his earlier *alter ego* of the *Tractatus Logico-Philosophicus*. In the *Tractatus* Wittgenstein sought "the general form of propositions": what made propositions possible. He said that this general form is: "This is how things are"; the proposition was an articulated model, consisting of elements standing in a definite relation to each other. The proposition was true when there existed a corresponding arrangement of elements in reality. The proposition was capable of saying something because of the identity of structure, of logical form, in the proposition and in reality.

By the time Wittgenstein composed the *Investigations* he had come to reject the whole idea that there must be a general form of propositions. He emphasized the indefinite number of different uses that language may have and tried to show that these different uses neither need, nor in fact do, all have something in common, in the sense intended in the *Tractatus*. He also tried to show that what counts as "agreement or disagreement with reality" takes on as many different forms as there are different uses of language and cannot, therefore, be taken as given *prior* to the detailed investigation of the use that is in question.

The *Tractatus* contains a remark strikingly like something that Evans-Pritchard says.

The limits of my language mean the limits of my world. Logic fills the world: the limits of the world are also its limits. We cannot therefore say in logic: This and this there is in the world, and that there is not.

For that would apparently presuppose that we exclude certain possibilities, and this cannot be the case since otherwise logic must get outside the limits of the world: that is, if it could consider these limits from the other side also.[15]

Evans-Pritchard discusses the phenomena of belief and skepticism, as they appear in Zande life. There is certainly widespread skepticism about certain things, for instance, about some of the powers claimed by witchdoctors or about the efficacy of certain magic medicines. But, he points out, such skepticism does not begin to overturn the mystical way of thinking, since it is necessarily expressed in terms belonging to that way of thinking.

In this web of belief every strand depends on every other strand, and a Zande cannot get outside its meshes because this is the only world he knows. The web is not an external structure in which he is enclosed. It is the texture of his thought and he cannot think that his thought is wrong.[16]

Wittgenstein and Evans-Pritchard are concerned here with much the same problem, though the difference in the directions from which they approach it is important too. Wittgenstein, at the time of the *Tractatus*, spoke of "language," as if all language is fundamentally of the same kind and must have the same kind of "relation to reality"; but Evans-Pritchard is confronted by two languages which he recognizes as fundamentally different in kind, such that much of what may be expressed in the one has no possible counterpart in the other. One might, therefore, have expected this to lead to a position closer to that of the *Philosophical Investigations* than to

that of the *Tractatus*. Evans-Pritchard is not content with elucidating the differences in the two concepts of reality involved; he wants to go further and say: our concept of reality is the correct one, the Azande are mistaken. But the difficulty is to see what "correct" and "mistaken" can mean in this context.

Let me return to the subject of contradictions. I have already noted that many contradictions we might expect to appear in fact do not in the context of Zande thought, where provision is made for avoiding them. But there are some situations of which this does not seem to be true, where what appear to us as obvious contradictions are left where they are, apparently unresolved. Perhaps this may be the foothold we are looking for, from which we can appraise the "correctness" of the Zande system.[17]

Consider Zande notions about the inheritance of witchcraft. I have spoken so far only of the role of oracles in establishing whether or not someone is a witch. But there is a further and, as we might think, more "direct" method of doing this, namely by post-mortem examination of a suspect's intestines for "witchcraft-substance." This may be arranged by his family after his death in an attempt to clear the family name of the imputation of witchcraft. Evans-Pritchard remarks: "to our minds it appears evident that if a man is proven a witch the whole of his clan are *ipso facto* witches, since the Zande clan is a group of persons related biologically to one another through the male line. Azande see the sense of this argument but they do not accept its conclusions, and it would involve the whole notion of witchcraft in contradiction were they to do so."[18] Contradiction would presumably arise because a few positive results of post-mortem examinations, scattered among all the clans, would very soon prove that everybody was a witch, and a few negative results, scattered among the same clans, would prove that nobody was a witch. Though, in particular situations, individual Azande may avoid personal implications arising out of the presence of witchcraft-substance in deceased relatives, by imputations of bastardy and similar devices, this would not be enough to save the generally contradictory situation I have sketched. Evans-Pritchard comments: "Azande do not perceive the contradiction as we perceive it because they have no theoretical interest in the subject, and those situations in which they express their belief in witchcraft do not force the problem upon them."[19]

It might now appear as though we had clear grounds for speaking of the superior rationality of European over Zande thought, insofar as the latter involves a contradiction which it makes no attempt to remove and does not even recognize: one, however, which is recognizable as such in the context of European ways of thinking. But does Zande thought on this matter really involve a contradiction? It appears from Evans-Pritchard's account that Azande do not press their ways of thinking about witches to a point at which they would be involved in contradictions.

Someone may now want to say that the irrationality of the Azande in relation to witchcraft shows itself in the fact that they do not press their thought about it "to its logical conclusion." To appraise this point we must consider whether the conclusion we are trying to force on them is indeed a logical one; or perhaps better, whether someone who does press this conclusion is being more rational than the Azande, who do not. Some light is thrown on this question by Wittgenstein's discussion of a game,

such that whoever begins can always win by a particular simple trick. But this has not been realized—so it is a game. Now someone draws our attention to it—and it stops being a game.

What turn can I give this, to make it clear to myself?—For I want to say: "and it stops being a game"—not: "and now we see that it wasn't a game."

That means, I want to say, it can also be taken like this: the other man did not *draw our* attention to anything; he taught us a different game in place of our own. But how can the new game have made the old one obsolete? We now see something different, and can no longer naively go on playing.

On the one hand the game consisted in our actions (our play) on the board; and these actions I could perform as well now as before. But on the other hand it was essential to the game that I blindly tried to win; and now I can no longer do that.[20]

There are obviously considerable analogies between Wittgenstein's example and the situation we are considering. But there is an equally important difference. Both Wittgenstein's games: the old one without the trick that enables the starter to win and the new one with the trick, are in an important sense on the same level. They are both *games*, in the form of a contest where the aim of a player is to beat his opponent by the exercise of skill. The new trick makes this situation impossible and this is why it makes the old game obsolete. To be sure, the situation could be saved in a way by introducing a new rule, forbidding the use by the starter of the trick which would ensure his victory. But our intellectual habits are such as to make us unhappy about the artificiality of such a device, rather as logicians have been unhappy about the introduction of a Theory of Types as a device for avoiding Russell's paradoxes. It is noteworthy in my last quotation from Evans-Pritchard, however, that the Azande, when the possibility of this contradiction about the inheritance of witchcraft is pointed out to them, do *not* then come to regard their old beliefs about witchcraft as obsolete. "They have no theoretical interest in the subject." This suggests strongly that the context from which the suggestion about the contradiction is made, the context of our scientific culture, is not on the same level as the context in which the beliefs about witchcraft operate. Zande notions of witchcraft do not constitute a theoretical system in terms of which Azande try to gain a quasi-scientific understanding of the world.[21] This in its turn suggests that it is the European, obsessed with pressing Zande thought where it would not naturally go—to a contradiction—who is guilty of misunderstanding, not the Zande. The European is in fact committing a category-mistake.

Something else is also suggested by this discussion: the forms in which rationality expresses itself in the culture of a human society cannot be elucidated *simply* in terms of the logical coherence of the rules according to which activities are carried out in that society. For, as we have seen, there comes a point where we are not even in a position to determine what is and what is not coherent in such a context of rules, without raising questions about the point which following those rules has in the society. No doubt it was a realization of this fact which led Evans-Pritchard to appeal to a residual "correspondence with reality" in distinguishing between "mystical" and "scientific" notions. The conception of reality is indeed indispensable to any understanding of the point of a way of life. But it is not a conception which can be explicated as Evans-Pritchard tries to explicate it, in terms of what science reveals to be the case; for a form of the conception of reality must already be presupposed before we can make any sense of the expression "what science reveals to be the case."

II. Our standards and theirs

In Part I, I attempted, by analyzing a particular case, to criticize by implication a particular view of how we can understand a primitive institution. In this Part I shall have two aims. First, I shall examine in a more formal way a general philosophical argument, which attempts to show that the approach I have been criticizing is in principle the right one. This argument has been advanced by Mr. Alasdair MacIntyre in two places: (a) in a paper entitled *Is Understanding Religion Compatible with Believing?* read to the Sesqui-

centennial Seminar of the Princeton Theological Seminar in 1962.[22] (b) In a contribution to *Philosophy, Politics and Society (Second Series)*,[23] entitled *A Mistake about Causality in Social Science*. Next, I shall make some slightly more positive suggestions about how to overcome the difficulty from which I started: how to make intelligible in our terms institutions belonging to a primitive culture, whose standards of rationality and intelligibility are apparently quite at odds with our own.

The relation between MacIntyre, Evans-Pritchard, and myself is a complicated one. MacIntyre takes Evans-Pritchard's later book, *Nuer Religion*, as an application of a point of view like mine in *The Idea of a Social Science*; he regards it as an object lesson in the absurd results to which such a position leads, when applied in practice. My own criticisms of Evans-Pritchard, on the other hand, have come from precisely the opposite direction. I have tried to show that Evans-Pritchard did not at the time of writing *The Azande* agree with me *enough*; that he did not take seriously enough the idea that the concepts used by primitive peoples can only be interpreted in the context of the way of life of those peoples. Thus I have in effect argued that Evans-Pritchard's account of the Azande is unsatisfactory precisely to the extent that he agrees with MacIntyre and not me.

The best point at which to start considering MacIntyre's position is that at which he agrees with me—in emphasizing the importance of possibilities of *description* for the concept of human action. An agent's action "is identified fundamentally as what it is by the description under which he deems it to fall." Since, further, descriptions must be intelligible to other people, an action "must fall under some description which is socially recognizable as the description of an action."[24] "To identify the limits of social action in a given period," therefore, "is to identify the stock of descriptions current in that age."[25] MacIntyre correctly points out that descriptions do not exist in isolation, but occur "as constituents of beliefs, speculations and projects." As these in turn "are continually criticized, modified, rejected, or improved, the stock of descriptions changes. The changes in human action are thus intimately linked to the thread of rational criticism in human history."

This notion of rational criticism, MacIntyre points out, requires the notion of choice between alternatives, to explain which "is a matter of making clear what the agent's criterion was and why he made use of this criterion rather than another and to explain why the use of this criterion appears rational to those who invoke it."[26] Hence "in explaining the rules and conventions to which action in a given social order conform (sic) we cannot omit reference to the rationality or otherwise of those rules and conventions." Further, "the beginning of an explanation of why certain criteria are taken to be rational in some societies is that they *are* rational. And since this has to enter into our explanation we cannot explain social behaviour independently of our own norms of rationality."

I turn now to criticism of this argument. Consider first MacIntyre's account of changes in an existing "stock" of available descriptions of actions. How does a candidate for inclusion *qualify* for admission to the stock? Unless there are limits, all MacIntyre's talk about possibilities of description circumscribing possibilities of action becomes nugatory, for there would be nothing to stop anybody inventing some arbitrary verbal expression, applying it to some arbitrary bodily movement, and thus adding that expression to the stock of available descriptions. But of course the new description must be an *intelligible* one. Certainly, its intelligibility cannot be decided by whether or not it belongs to an *existing* stock of descriptions, since this would rule out precisely what is being discussed: the addition of *new* descriptions to the stock. "What can intelligibly be said" is not equivalent to "what has been intelligibly said," or it would never be possible to say anything new. *Mutatis mutandis* it would never be possible to *do* anything

new. Nevertheless the intelligibility of anything new said or done does depend in a certain way on what already has been said or done and understood. The crux of this problem lies in how we are to understand that "in a certain way."

In *Is Understanding Religion Compatible with Believing?* MacIntyre asserts that the development through criticism of the standards of intelligibility current in a society is ruled out by my earlier account (in *The Idea of a Social Science*) of the origin in social institutions themselves of such standards. I shall not now repeat my earlier argument, but simply point out that I did, in various passages,[27] emphasize the *open* character of the "rules" which I spoke of in connection with social institutions: i.e. the fact that in changing social situations, reasoned decisions have to be made about what is to count as "going on in the same way." MacIntyre's failure to come to terms with this point creates difficulties for him precisely analogous to those which he mistakenly attributes to my account.

It is a corollary of his argument up to this point, as well as being intrinsically evident, that a new description of action must be intelligible to the members of the society in which it is introduced. On my view the point is that what determines this is the further development of rules and principles already implicit in the previous ways of acting and talking. To be emphasized are not the actual members of any "stock" of descriptions; but the *grammar* which they express. It is through this that we understand their structure and sense, their mutual relations, and the sense of new ways of talking and acting that may be introduced. These new ways of talking and acting may very well at the same time involve modifications in the grammar, but we can only speak thus if the new grammar is (to its users) intelligibly related to the old.

But what of the intelligibility of such changes to observers from another society with a different culture and different standards of intelligibility? MacIntyre urges that such observers must make clear "what the agent's criterion was and why he made use of this criterion rather than another and why the use of this criterion appears rational to those who invoke it." Since what is at issue is the precise relation between the concepts of rationality current in these different societies it is obviously of first importance to be clear about *whose* concept of rationality is being alluded to in this quotation. It seems that it must be that which is current in the society in which the criterion is invoked. Something can appear rational to someone only in terms of *his* understanding of what is and is not rational. If *our* concept of rationality is a different one from his, then it makes no sense to say that anything either does or does not appear rational to *him* in *our* sense.

When MacIntyre goes on to say that the observer "cannot omit reference to the rationality or otherwise of those rules and conventions" followed by the alien agent, whose concept of rationality is now in question: ours or the agent's? Since the observer must be understood now as addressing himself to members of his own society, it seems that the reference must here be to the concept of rationality current in the observer's society. Thus there is a *non sequitur* in the movement from the first to the second of the passages just quoted.

MacIntyre's thought here and in what immediately follows, seems to be this. The explanation of why, in Society S, certain actions are taken to be rational, has got to be an explanation for *us*; so it must be in terms of concepts intelligible to us. If then, in the explanation, we say that in fact those criteria *are* rational, we must be using the word "*rational*" in *our* sense. For this explanation would require that we had previously carried out an independent investigation into the actual rationality or otherwise of those criteria, and we could do this only in terms of an understood concept of rationality—*our* understood concept of rationality. The explanation would run: members of Society S have seen to be the case something that we know to be the

case. If "what is seen to be the case" is common to us and them, it must be referred to under the same concept for each of us.

But obviously this explanation is not open to us. For we start from the position that standards of rationality in different societies do not always coincide; from the possibility, therefore, that the standards of rationality current in S are different from our own. So we cannot assume that it will make sense to speak of members of S as discovering something which we have also discovered; such discovery presupposes initial conceptual agreement.

Part of the trouble lies in MacIntyre's use of the expression "the rationality of criteria," which he does not explain. In the present context to speak thus is to cloak the real problem, since what we are concerned with are differences in *criteria of rationality*. MacIntyre seems to be saying that certain standards are taken as criteria of rationality because they *are* criteria of rationality. But whose?

There are similar confusions in MacIntyre's other paper: *Is Understanding Religion Compatible with Believing?* There he argues that when we detect an internal incoherence in the standards of intelligibility current in an alien society and try to show why this does not appear, or is made tolerable to that society's members, "we have already invoked our standards." In what sense is this true? Insofar as *we* "detect" and "show" something, obviously we do so in a sense intelligible to us; so we are limited by what *counts* (for us) as "detecting," "showing" something. Further, it may well be that the interest in showing and detecting such things is peculiar to our society—that we are doing something in which members of the studied society exhibit no interest, because the institutions in which such an interest could develop are lacking. Perhaps too the pursuit of that interest in our society has led to the development of techniques of inquiry and modes of argument which again are not to be found in the life of the studied society. But it cannot be guaranteed in advance that the methods and techniques we have used in the past—e.g. in elucidating the logical structure of arguments in our own language and culture—are going to be equally fruitful in this new context. They will perhaps need to be extended and modified. No doubt, if they are to have a logical relation to our previous forms of investigation, the new techniques will have to be recognizably continuous with previously used ones. But they must also so extend our conception of intelligibility as to make it possible for us to see what intelligibility amounts to in the life of the society we are investigating.

The task MacIntyre says we must undertake is to make intelligible (a) (to us) why it is that members of S think that certain of their practices are intelligible (b) (to them), when in fact they are not. I have introduced differentiating letters into my two uses of "intelligible," to mark the complexity that MacIntyre's way of stating the position does not bring out: the fact that we are dealing with two different senses of the word "intelligible." The relation between these is precisely the question at issue. MacIntyre's task is not like that of making intelligible a natural phenomenon, where we are limited only by what counts as intelligibility for us. We must somehow bring S's conception of intelligibility (b) into (intelligible!) relation with our own conception of intelligibility (a). That is, we have to create a new unity for the concept of intelligibility, having a certain relation to our old one and perhaps requiring a considerable realignment of our categories. We are not seeking a state in which things will appear to us just as they do to members of S, and perhaps such a state is unattainable anyway. But we *are* seeking a way of looking at things which goes beyond our previous way in that it has in some way taken account of and incorporated the other way that members of S have of looking at things. Seriously to study another way of life is necessarily to seek to extend our own—not simply to bring the other way within the already existing boundaries of our own, because the point about the latter in

their present form, is that they *ex hypothesi* exclude that other.

There is a dimension to the notions of rationality and intelligibility which may make it easier to grasp the possibility of such an extension. I do not think that MacIntyre takes sufficient account of this dimension and, indeed, the way he talks about "norms of rationality" obscures it. Rationality is not just a concept in a language like any other; it is this too, for, like any other concept it must be circumscribed by an established use: a use, that is, established in the language. But I think it is not a concept which a language may, as a matter of fact, have and equally well may not have, as is, for instance, the concept of politeness. It is a concept necessary to the existence of any language: to say of a society that it has a language[28] is also to say that it has a concept of rationality. There need not perhaps be any *word* functioning in its language as "rational" does in ours, but at least there must be features of its members' use of language analogous to those features of our use of language which are connected with our use of the word "rational." Where there is language it must make a difference what is said and this is only possible where the saying of one thing rules out, on pain of failure to communicate, the saying of something else. So in one sense MacIntyre is right in saying that we have already invoked our concept of rationality in saying of a collection of people that they constitute a society with a language: in the sense, namely, that we imply formal analogies between their behavior and that behavior in our society which we refer to in distinguishing between rationality and irrationality. This, however, is so far to say nothing about what in particular constitutes rational behavior in that society; that would require more particular knowledge about the norms they appeal to in living their lives. In other words, it is not so much a matter of invoking "our own norms of rationality" as of invoking our notion of rationality in speaking of their behavior in terms of "conformity to norms." But how precisely this notion is to be applied to them will depend on our reading of their conformity to norms—what counts for them as conformity and what does not.

Earlier I criticized MacIntyre's conception of a "stock of available descriptions." Similar criticisms apply to his talk about "our norms of rationality," if these norms are taken as forming some finite set. Certainly we learn to think, speak, and act rationally through being trained to adhere to particular norms. But having learned to speak, etc., rationally does not *consist* in having been trained to follow those norms; to suppose that would be to overlook the importance of the phrase "and so on" in any description of what someone who follows norms does. We must, if you like, be open to new possibilities of what could be invoked and accepted under the rubric of "rationality"—possibilities which are perhaps suggested and limited by what we have hitherto so accepted, but not uniquely determined thereby.

This point can be applied to the possibilities of our grasping forms of rationality different from ours in an alien culture. First, as I have indicated, these possibilities are limited by certain formal requirements centering round the demand for consistency. But these formal requirements tell us nothing about what in particular is to *count* as consistency, just as the rules of the propositional calculus limit, but do not themselves determine, what are to be proper values of p, q, etc. We can only determine this by investigating the wider context of the life in which the activities in question are carried on. This investigation will take us beyond merely specifying the rules governing the carrying out of those activities. For, as MacIntyre quite rightly says, to note that certain rules are followed is so far to say nothing about the *point* of the rules; it is not even to decide whether or not they have a point at all.

MacIntyre's recipe for deciding this is that "in bringing out this feature of the case one shows also whether the use of this concept is or is not a possible one for people who have the standards of intelligibility in speech and action which we have."[29] It is important to notice that his argument, contrary to what he supposes, does not in fact show that our *own* standards of rationality occupy a peculiarly central position. The appearance to the contrary is an optical illusion engendered by the fact that MacIntyre's case has been advanced in the English language and in the context of twentieth-century European culture. But a formally similar argument could be advanced in *any* language containing concepts playing a similar role in that language to those of "intelligibility" and "rationality" in ours. This shows that, so far from overcoming relativism, as he claims, MacIntyre himself falls into an extreme form of it. He disguises this from himself by committing the very error of which, wrongly as I have tried to show, he accuses me: the error of overlooking the fact that "criteria and concepts have a history." While he emphasizes this point when he is dealing with the concepts and criteria governing action in particular social contexts, he forgets it when he comes to talk of the *criticism* of such criteria. Do not the criteria appealed to in the criticism of existing institutions equally have a history? And in whose society do they have that history? MacIntyre's implicit answer is that it is in ours; but if we are to speak of difficulties and incoherencies appearing and being detected in the way certain practices have hitherto been carried on in a society, surely this can only be understood in connection with problems arising in the carrying on of the activity. Outside that context we could not begin to grasp what was problematical.

Let me return to the Azande and consider something which MacIntyre says about them, intended to support the position I am criticizing.

The Azande believe that the performance of certain rites in due form affects their common welfare; this belief cannot in fact be refuted. For they also believe that if the rites are ineffective it is because someone present at them had evil thoughts. Since this is always possible, there is never a year when it is unavoidable for them to admit that the rites were duly performed, but they did not thrive. Now the belief of the Azande is not unfalsifiable in principle (we know perfectly well what would falsify it—the conjunction of the rite, no evil thoughts and disasters). But in fact it cannot be falsified. Does this belief stand in need of rational criticism? And if so by what standards? It seems to me that one could only hold the belief of the Azande rational *in the absence* of any practice of science and technology in which criteria of effectiveness, ineffectiveness and kindred notions had been built up. But to say this is to recognize the appropriateness of scientific criteria of judgment from our standpoint. The Azande do not intend their belief either as a piece of science or as a piece of non-science. They do not possess these categories. It is only *post eventum*, in the light of later and more sophisticated understanding that their belief and concepts can be classified and evaluated at all.[30]

Now in one sense classification and evaluation of Zande beliefs and concepts does require "a more sophisticated understanding" than is found in Zande culture; for the sort of classification and evaluation that are here in question are sophisticated philosophical activities. But this is not to say that Zande forms of life are to be classified and evaluated in the way MacIntyre asserts: in terms of certain specific forms of life to be found in our culture, according as they do or do not measure up to what is required within these. MacIntyre confuses the sophistication of the interest in classification with the sophistication of the concepts employed in our classificatory work. It is of interest to us to understand how Zande magic is related to science; the concept of such a comparison is a very sophisticated one; but this does not mean that we have to see the unsophisticated Zande practice in the light of more sophisticated practices in our own culture, like science—as perhaps a more primitive form of it. MacIntyre criticizes, justly, Sir James Frazer for having imposed the image of his own culture on more primitive ones; but that is exactly what MacIntyre himself is doing here. It is extremely difficult for a sophisticated member of a sophisticated society to grasp a very simple and primitive form of life: in a way he must jettison his sophistication, a process which is itself perhaps the ultimate in sophistication. Or, rather, the distinction between sophistication and simplicity becomes unhelpful at this point.

It may be true, as MacIntyre says, that the Azande do not have the categories of science and non-science. But Evans-Pritchard's account shows that they do have a fairly clear working distinction between the technical and the magical. It is neither here nor there that individual Azande may sometimes confuse the categories, for such confusions may take place in any culture. A much more important fact to emphasize is that *we* do not initially have a category that looks at all like the Zande category of magic. Since it is we who want to understand the Zande category, it appears that the onus is on us to extend our understanding so as to make room for the Zande category, rather than to insist on seeing it in terms of our own ready-made distinction between science and non-science. Certainly the sort of understanding we seek requires that we see the Zande category in relation to our own already understood categories. But this neither means that it is right to "evaluate" magic in terms of criteria belonging to those other categories; nor does it give any clue as to which of our existing categories of thought will provide the best point of reference from which we can understand the point of the Zande practices.

MacIntyre has no difficulty in showing that if the rites which the Azande perform in connection with their harvests are "classified and evaluated" by reference to the criteria and standards of science or technology, then they are subject to serious criticism. He thinks that the Zande "belief" is a sort of *hypothesis* like, e.g., an Englishman's belief that all the heavy rain we have been having is due to atomic explosions.[31] MacIntyre believes that he is applying as it were a neutral concept of "*A* affecting *B*," equally applicable to Zande magic and western science. In fact, however, he is applying the concept with which *he* is familiar, one which draws its significance from its use in scientific and technological contexts. There is no reason to suppose that the Zande magical concept of "*A* affecting *B*" has anything like the same significance. On the contrary, since the Azande do, in the course of their practical affairs, apply something very like our technical concept—though perhaps in a more primitive form—and since their attitude to and thought about their magical rites are quite different from those concerning their technological measures, there is every reason to think that their concept of magical "influence" is quite different. This may be easier to accept if it is remembered that, even in our own culture, the concept of causal influence is by no means monolithic: when we speak, for example, of "what made Jones get married," we are not saying the same kind of thing as when we speak of "what made the aeroplane crash"; I do not mean simply that the events of which we speak are different in kind but that the relation between the events is different also. It should not then be difficult to accept that in a society with quite different institutions and ways of life from our own, there may be concepts of "causal influence" which behave even more differently.

But I do not want to say that we are quite powerless to find ways of thinking in our own society that will help us to see the Zande institution in a clearer light. I only think that the direction in which we should look is quite different from what MacIntyre suggests. Clearly the nature of Zande life is such that it is of very great importance to them that their crops should thrive. Clearly too they take all kinds of practical

"technological" steps, within their capabilities, to ensure that they *do* thrive. But that is no reason to see their magical rites as a further, misguided such step. A man's sense of the importance of something to him shows itself in all sorts of ways: not merely in precautions to safeguard that thing. He may want to come to terms with its importance to him in quite a different way: to contemplate it, to gain some sense of his life in relation to it. He may wish thereby, in a certain sense, to *free* himself from dependence on it. I do not mean by making sure that it does not let him down, because the point is that, *whatever* he does, he may still be let down. The important thing is that he should understand *that* and come to terms with it. Of course, merely to understand that is not to come to terms with it, though perhaps it is a necessary condition for so doing, for a man may equally well be transfixed and terrorized by the contemplation of such a possibility. He must see that he can still go on even if he is let down by what is vitally important to him; and he must so order his life that he still *can* go on in such circumstances. I stress once again that I do not mean this in the sense of becoming "technologically independent," because from the present point of view technological independence is yet another form of dependence. Technology destroys some dependencies but always creates new ones, which may be fiercer—because harder to understand—than the old. This should be particularly apparent to us.[32]

In Judaeo-Christian cultures the conception of "If it be Thy Will," as developed in the story of Job, is clearly central to the matter I am discussing. Because this conception is central to Christian prayers of supplication, they may be regarded from one point of view as freeing the believer from dependence on what he is supplicating for.[33] Prayers cannot play this role if they are regarded as a means of influencing the outcome for in that case the one who prays is still dependent on the outcome. He frees himself from this by acknowledging his complete dependence on God; and this is totally unlike any dependence on the outcome precisely because God is eternal and the outcome contingent.

I do not say that Zande magical rites are at all like Christian prayers of supplication in the positive attitude to contingencies which they express. What I do suggest is that they are alike in that they do, or may, express an attitude to contingencies; one, that is, which involves recognition that one's life is subject to contingencies, rather than an attempt to control these. To characterize this attitude more specifically one should note how Zande rites emphasize the importance of certain fundamental features of their life which MacIntyre ignores. MacIntyre concentrates implicitly on the relation of the rites to consumption, but of course they are also fundamental to social relations and this seems to be emphasized in Zande notions of witchcraft. We have a drama of resentments, evil-doing, revenge, expiation, in which there are ways of dealing (symbolically) with misfortunes and their disruptive effect on a man's relations with his fellows, with ways in which life can go on despite such disruptions.

How is my treatment of this example related to the general criticisms I was making of MacIntyre's account of what it is for us to see the point of the rules and conventions followed in an alien form of life? MacIntyre speaks as though our own rules and conventions are somehow a paradigm of what it is for rules and conventions to have a point, so that the only problem that arises is in accounting for the point of the rules and conventions in some other society. But in fact, of course, the problem is the same in relation to our own society as it is in relation to any other; no more than anyone else's are our rules and conventions immune from the danger of being or becoming pointless. So an account of this matter cannot be given simply in terms of any set of rules and conventions at all: our own or anyone else's; it requires us to consider the relation of a set of rules and conventions to something else. In my discussion of Zande

magical rites just now what I tried to relate the magical rites to was a sense of the significance of human life. This notion is, I think, indispensable to any account of what is involved in understanding and learning from an alien culture; I must now try to say more about it.

In a discussion of Wittgenstein's philosophical use of language games[34] Mr. Rush Rhees points out that to try to account for the meaningfulness of language solely in terms of isolated language games is to omit the important fact that ways of speaking are not insulated from each other in mutually exclusive systems of rules. What can be said in one context by the use of a certain expression depends for its sense on the uses of that expression in other contexts (different language games). Language games are played by men who have lives to live—lives involving a wide variety of different interests, which have all kinds of different bearings on each other. Because of this, what a man says or does may make a difference not merely to the performance of the activity upon which he is at present engaged, but to his life and to the lives of other people. Whether a man sees point in what he is doing will then depend on whether he is able to see any unity in his multifarious interests, activities, and relations with other men; what sort of sense he sees in his life will depend on the nature of this unity. The ability to see this sort of sense in life depends not merely on the individual concerned, though this is not to say it does not depend on him at all; it depends also on the possibilities for making such sense which the culture in which he lives does, or does not, provide.

What we may learn by studying other cultures are not merely possibilities of different ways of doing things, other techniques. More importantly we may learn different possibilities of making sense of human life, different ideas about the possible importance that the carrying out of certain activities may take on for a man, trying to contemplate the sense of his life as a whole. This dimension of the matter is precisely what MacIntyre misses in his treatment of Zande magic: he can see in it only a (misguided) technique for producing consumer goods. But a Zande's crops are not just potential objects of consumption: the life he lives, his relations with his fellows, his chances for acting decently or doing evil, may all spring from his relation to his crops. Magical rites constitute a form of expression in which these possibilities and dangers may be contemplated and reflected on—and perhaps also thereby transformed and deepened. The difficulty we find in understanding this is not merely its remoteness from science, but an aspect of the general difficulty we find, illustrated by MacIntyre's procedure, of thinking about such matters at all except in terms of "efficiency of production"—production, that is, for consumption. This again is a symptom of what Marx called the "alienation" characteristic of man in industrial society, though Marx's own confusions about the relations between production and consumption are further symptoms of that same alienation. Our blindness to the point of primitive modes of life is a corollary of the pointlessness of much of our own life.

I have now explicitly linked my discussion of the "point" of a system of conventions with conceptions of good and evil. My aim is not to engage in moralizing, but to suggest that the concept of *learning from* which is involved in the study of other cultures is closely linked with the concept of *wisdom*. We are confronted not just with different techniques, but with new possibilities of good and evil, in relation to which men may come to terms with life. An investigation into this dimension of a society may indeed require a quite detailed inquiry into alternative techniques (e.g. of production), but an inquiry conducted for the light it throws on those possibilities of good and evil. A very good example of the kind of thing I mean is Simone Weil's analysis of the techniques of modern factory production in *Oppression and Liberty*, which is not a contribution to business management, but part of an inquiry into the peculiar form which the evil of oppression takes in our culture.

In saying this, however, I may seem merely to have lifted to a new level the difficulty raised by MacIntyre of how to relate our own conceptions of rationality to those of other societies. Here the difficulty concerns the relation between our own conceptions of good and evil and those of other societies. A full investigation would thus require a discussion of ethical relativism at this point. I have tried to show some of the limitations of relativism in an earlier paper.[35] I shall close the present essay with some remarks which are supplementary to that.

I wish to point out that the very conception of human life involves certain fundamental notions—which I shall call "limiting notions"—which have an obvious ethical dimension, and which indeed in a sense determine the "ethical space," within which the possibilities of good and evil in human life can be exercised. The notions which I shall discuss very briefly here correspond closely to those which Vico made the foundation of his idea of natural law, on which he thought the possibility of understanding human history rested: birth, death, sexual relations. Their significance here is that they are inescapably involved in the life of all known human societies in a way which gives us a clue where to look, if we are puzzled about the point of an alien system of institutions. The specific forms which these concepts take, the particular institutions in which they are expressed, vary very considerably from one society to another; but their central position within a society's institutions is and must be a constant factor. In trying to understand the life of an alien society, then, it will be of the utmost importance to be clear about the way in which these notions enter into it. The actual practice of social anthropologists bears this out, although I do not know how many of them would attach the same kind of importance to them as I do.

I speak of a "limit" here because these notions, along no doubt with others, give shape to what we understand by "human life"; and because a concern with questions posed in terms of them seems to me constitutive of what we understand by the "morality" of a society. In saying this, I am of course disagreeing with those moral philosophers who have made attitudes of approval and disapproval, or something similar, fundamental in ethics, and who have held that the *objects* of such attitudes were conceptually irrelevant to the conception of morality. On that view, there might be a society where the sorts of attitude taken up in our society to questions about relations between the sexes were reserved, say, for questions about the length people wear their hair, and *vice versa*. This seems to me incoherent. In the first place, there would be a confusion in *calling* a concern of that sort a "moral" concern, however passionately felt. The story of Samson in the Old Testament confirms rather than refutes this point, for the interdict on the cutting of Samson's hair is, of course, connected there with much else: and pre-eminently, it should be noted, with questions about sexual relations. But secondly, if that is thought to be merely verbal quibbling, I will say that it does not seem to me a merely conventional matter that T. S. Eliot's trinity of "birth, copulation and death" happen to be such deep objects of human concern. I do not mean just that they are made such by fundamental psychological and sociological forces, though that is no doubt true. But I want to say further that the very notion of human life is limited by these conceptions.

Unlike beasts, men do not merely live but also have a conception of life. This is not something that is simply added to their life; rather, it changes the very sense which the word "life" has, when applied to men. It is no longer equivalent to "animate existence." When we are speaking of the life of man, we can ask questions about what is the right way to live, what things are most important in life, whether life has any significance, and if so what.

To have a conception of life is also to have a conception of death. But just as the "life" that is

here in question is not the same as animate existence, so the "death" that is here in question is not the same as the end of animate existence. My conception of the death of an animal is of an event that will take place in the world; perhaps I shall observe it—and my life will go on. But when I speak of "my death," I am not speaking of a future event in my life;[36] I am not even speaking of an event in anyone else's life. I am speaking of the cessation of my world. That is also a cessation of my ability to do good or evil. It is not just that *as a matter of fact* I shall no longer be able to do good or evil after I am dead; the point is that my very *concept* of what it is to be able to do good or evil is deeply bound up with my concept of my life as ending in death. If ethics is a concern with the right way to live, then clearly the nature of this concern must be deeply affected by the concept of life as ending in death. One's attitude to one's life is at the same time an attitude to one's death.

This point is very well illustrated in an anthropological datum which MacIntyre confesses himself unable to make any sense of.

According to Spencer and Gillen some aborigines carry about a stick or stone which is treated *as* if it is or embodies the soul of the individual who carries it. If the stick or stone is lost, the individual anoints himself as the dead are anointed. Does the concept of "carrying one's soul about with one" make sense? Of course we can redescribe what the aborigines are doing and transform it into sense, and perhaps Spencer and Gillen (and Durkheim who follows them) misdescribe what occurs. But if their reports are not erroneous, we confront a blank wall here, so far as meaning is concerned, although it is easy to give the rules for the use of the concept.[37]

MacIntyre does not say why he regards the concept of carrying one's soul about with one in a stick "thoroughly incoherent." He is presumably influenced by the fact that it would be hard to make sense of an action like this if performed by a twentieth-century Englishman or American; and by the fact that the soul is not a material object like a piece of paper and cannot, therefore, be carried about in a stick as a piece of paper might be. But it does not seem to me so hard to see sense in the practice, even from the little we are told about it here. Consider that a lover in our society may carry about a picture or lock of hair of the beloved; that this may symbolize for him his relation to the beloved and may, indeed, change the relation in all sorts of ways: for example, strengthening it or perverting it. Suppose that when the lover loses the locket he feels guilty and asks his beloved for her forgiveness: there might be a parallel here to the aboriginal's practice of anointing himself when he "loses his soul." And is there necessarily anything irrational about either of these practices? Why should the lover not regard his carelessness in losing the locket as a sort of betrayal of the beloved? Remember how husbands and wives may feel about the loss of a wedding ring. The aborigine is clearly expressing a concern with his life as a whole in this practice; the anointing shows the close connection between such a concern and contemplation of death. Perhaps it is precisely this practice which makes such a concern possible for him, as religious sacraments make certain sorts of concern possible. The point is that a concern with one's life as a whole, involving as it does the limiting conception of one's death, if it is to be expressed *within* a person's life, can necessarily only be expressed quasi-sacramentally. The form of the concern shows itself in the form of the sacrament.

The sense in which I spoke also of sex as a "limiting concept" again has to do with the concept of a human life. The life of a man is a man's life and the life of a woman is a woman's life: the masculinity or the femininity are not just *components* in the life, they are its *mode*. Adapting Wittgenstein's remark about death, I might say that my masculinity is not an experience in the world, but my way of experiencing the world. Now the concepts of masculinity and femininity obviously require each other. A man is a man in relation to women; and a woman is a woman in relation to men.[38] Thus the form taken by man's relation to women is of quite fundamental importance for the significance he can attach to his own life. The vulgar identification of morality with sexual morality certainly *is* vulgar; but it is a vulgarization of an important truth.

The limiting character of the concept of birth is obviously related to the points I have sketched regarding death and sex. On the one hand, my birth is no more an event in my life than is my death; and through my birth ethical limits are set for my life quite independently of my will: I am, from the outset, in specific relations to other people, from which obligations spring which cannot but be ethically fundamental.[39] On the other hand, the concept of birth is fundamentally linked to that of relations between the sexes. This remains true, however much or little may be known in a society about the contribution of males and females to procreation; for it remains true that man is born of woman, not of man. This, then, adds a new dimension to the ethical institutions in which relations between the sexes are expressed.

I have tried to do no more, in these last brief remarks, than to focus attention in a certain direction. I have wanted to indicate that forms of these limiting concepts will necessarily be an important feature of any human society and that conceptions of good and evil in human life will necessarily be connected with such concepts. In any attempt to understand the life of another society, therefore, an investigation of the forms taken by such concepts—their role in the life of the society—must always take a central place and provide a basis on which understanding may be built.

Now since the world of nations has been made by men, let us see in what institutions men agree and always have agreed. For these institutions will be able to give us the universal and eternal principles (such as every science must have) on which all nations were founded and still preserve themselves.

We observe that all nations, barbarous as well as civilized, though separately founded because remote from each other in time and space, keep these three human customs: all have some religion, all contract solemn marriages, all bury their dead. And in no nation, however savage and crude, are any human actions performed with more elaborate ceremonies and more sacred solemnity than the rites of religion, marriage and burial. For by the axiom that "uniform ideas, born among peoples unknown to each other, must have a common ground of truth," it must have been dictated to all nations that from these institutions humanity began among them all, and therefore they must be most devoutly guarded by them all, so that the world should not again become a bestial wilderness. For this reason we have taken these three eternal and universal customs as the first principles of this Science.[40]

Notes

1 London and New York (Routledge & Kegan Paul; Humanities Press), 1958.

2 Oxford (Oxford University Press), 1937.

3 At this point the anthropologist is very likely to start speaking of the "social function" of the institution under examination. There are many important questions that should be raised about functional explanations and their relations to the issues discussed in this essay; but these questions cannot be pursued further here.

4 E. E. Evans-Pritchard, "Lévy-Bruhl's Theory of Primitive Mentality," *Bulletin of the Faculty of Arts*, University of Egypt, 1934.

5 "Science and Sentiment," *Bulletin of the Faculty of Arts*, ibid., 1935.

6 Indeed, one way of expressing the point of the story of Job is to say that in it Job is shown as going astray by being induced to make the reality and goodness of God contingent on what happens.

7 R. G. Collingwood, *Principles of Art* (Oxford, Oxford University Press, Galaxy Books, 1958), p. 67.

8 *Witchcraft, Oracles and Magic among the Azande*, p. 64.

9 The italics are mine throughout this quotation.

10 *Op. cit.*, p. 12.

11 For further criticism of Pareto see Peter Winch, *The Idea of a Social Science*, pp. 95–111.

12 Evans-Pritchard's italics.

13 *Op. cit.*, p. 72.

14 Ibid., p. 319.

15 Wittgenstein, *Tractatus Logico-Philosophicus*, paras. 5.6–5.61.

16 Evans-Pritchard, *op. cit.*, p. 194.

17 I shall discuss this point in a more general way in Part II.

18 Ibid., p. 24.

19 Ibid., p. 25.

20 L. Wittgenstein, *Remarks on the Foundations of Mathematics*, Pt. II, § 77. Wittgenstein's whole discussion of "contradiction" in mathematics is directly relevant to the point I am discussing.

21 Notice that I have *not* said that Azande conceptions of witchcraft have nothing to do with understanding the world at all. The point is that a different form of the concept of understanding is involved here.

22 To be published along with other papers, by the Macmillan Company.

23 Edited by Peter Laslett and W. G. Runciman (Oxford, Basil Blackwell, 1962).

24 Ibid., p. 58.

25 Ibid., p. 60.

26 Ibid., p. 61.

27 Pp. 57–65; 91–94; 121–123.

28 I shall not discuss here what justifies us in saying this in the first place.

29 *Is Understanding Religion Compatible with Believing?*

30 Ibid.

31 In what follows I have been helped indirectly, but greatly, by some unpublished notes made by Wittgenstein on Frazer, which Mr. Rush Rhees was kind enough to show me; and also by various scattered remarks on folklore in *The Notebooks of Simone Weil* (London, Routledge & Kegan Paul, 1963).

32 The point is beautifully developed by Simone Weil in her essay on "The Analysis of Oppression" in *Oppression and Liberty* (London, Routledge & Kegan Paul, 1958).

33 I have been helped to see this point by a hitherto unpublished essay on the concept of prayer by Mr. D. Z. Phillips.

34 Rush Rhees, "Wittgenstein's Builders," *Proceedings of the Aristotelian Society*, vol. 20 (1960), pp. 171–186.

35 Peter Winch, "Nature and Convention," *Proceedings of the Aristotelian Society*, vol. 20 (1960), pp. 231–252.

36 Cf. Wittgenstein, *Tractatus Logico-Philosophicus*, 6.431–6.4311.

37 *Is Understanding Religion Compatible with Believing?*

38 These relations, however, are not simple converses. See Georg Simmel, "Das Relative und das Absolute im Geschlechter-Problem" in *Philosophische Kultur* (Leipzig, Werner Klinkhardt, 1911).

39 For this reason, among others, I think A. I. Melden is wrong to say that parent–child obligations and rights have nothing directly to do with physical genealogy. Cf. Melden, *Right and Right Conduct* (Oxford, Basil Blackwell, 1959).

40 Giambattista Vico, *The New Science*, §§ 332–333.

Chapter 43

Paul Boghossian

WHAT THE SOKAL HOAX OUGHT TO TEACH US

The pernicious consequences and internal contradictions of 'postmodernist' relativism

In the autumn of 1994, New York University theoretical physicist, Alan Sokal, submitted an essay to *Social Text*, the leading journal in the field of cultural studies. Entitled 'Transgressing the Boundaries: Toward a Transformative Hermeneutics of Quantum Gravity', it purported to be a scholarly article about the 'postmodern' philosophical and political implications of twentieth century physical theories. However, as the author himself later revealed in the journal *Lingua Franca*, his essay was merely a farrago of deliberately concocted solecisms, howlers and non-sequiturs, stitched together so as to look good and to flatter the ideological preconceptions of the editors. After review by five members of *Social Text*'s editorial board, Sokal's parody was accepted for publication as a serious piece of scholarship. It appeared in April 1996, in a special double issue of the journal devoted to rebutting the charge that cultural studies critiques of science tend to be riddled with incompetence.

Sokal's hoax is fast acquiring the status of a classic *succès de scandale*, with extensive press coverage in the United States and to a growing extent in Europe and Latin America. In the United States, over twenty public forums devoted to the topic have either taken place or are scheduled, including packed sessions at Princeton, Duke, the University of Michigan, and New York University. But what exactly should it be taken to show?

I believe it shows three important things. First, that dubiously coherent relativistic views about the concepts of truth and evidence really have gained wide acceptance within the contemporary academy, just as it has often seemed. Second, that this has had precisely the sorts of pernicious consequence for standards of scholarship and intellectual responsibility that one would expect it to have. Finally, that neither of the preceding two claims need reflect a particular political point of view, least of all a conservative one.

It's impossible to do justice to the egregiousness of Sokal's essay without quoting it more or less in its entirety; what follows is a tiny sampling. Sokal starts off by establishing his postmodernist credentials: he derides scientists for continuing to cling to the 'dogma imposed by the long post-Enlightenment hegemony over the Western intellectual outlook', that there exists an external world, whose properties are independent of human beings, and that human beings can obtain reliable, if imperfect and tentative knowledge of these properties 'by hewing to the "objective" procedures and epistemological strictures prescribed by the (so-called) scientific method'. He asserts that this 'dogma' has already been thoroughly undermined by the theories of general relativity and quantum mechanics, and that physical reality has been shown to be 'at bottom a social and linguistic construct'. In support of this he adduces nothing more than a couple of pronouncements from physicists Niels Bohr and Werner Heisenberg, pronouncements that have been shown to be naive by sophisticated discussions in the philosophy of science over the past fifty years.

Sokal then picks up steam, moving to his central thesis that recent developments within quantum gravity – an emerging and still-speculative physical theory – go much further, substantiating not only postmodern denials of the objectivity of truth, but also the beginnings of a kind of physics that would be truly 'liberatory', of genuine service to progressive political causes. Here his 'reasoning' becomes truly venturesome, as he contrives to generate political and cultural conclusions from the physics of the very, very small. His inferences are mediated by nothing more than a hazy patchwork of puns (especially on the words 'linear' and 'discontinuous'), strained analogies, bald assertions and what can only be described as *non-sequiturs* of numbing grossness (to use a phrase that Peter Strawson applied to the far less deserving Immanuel Kant). For example, he moves immediately from Bohr's observation that in quantum mechanics 'a complete elucidation of one and the same object may require diverse points of view' to:

> In such a situation, how can a self-perpetuating secular priesthood of credentialed 'scientists' purport to maintain a monopoly on the production of scientific knowledge? The content and methodology of postmodern science thus provide powerful intellectual support for the progressive political project, understood in its broadest sense: the transgressing of boundaries, the breaking down of barriers, the radical democratization of all aspects of social, economic, political and cultural life.

He concludes by calling for the development of a correspondingly emancipated mathematics, one that, by not being based on standard (Zermelo–Fraenkel) set theory, would no longer constrain the progressive and postmodern ambitions of emerging physical science.

As if all this weren't enough, *en passant*, Sokal peppers his piece with as many smaller bits of transparent nonsense as could be made to fit on any given page. Some of these are of a purely mathematical or scientific nature – that the well-known geometrical constant pi is a variable, that complex number theory, which dates from the nineteenth century and is taught to schoolchildren, is a new and speculative branch of mathematical physics, that the crackpot New Age fantasy of a 'morphogenetic field' constitutes a leading theory of quantum gravity. Others have to do with the alleged philosophical or political implications of basic science – that quantum field theory confirms Lacan's psychoanalytic speculations about the nature of the neurotic subject, that fuzzy logic is better suited to leftist political causes than classical logic, that Bell's theorem, a technical result in the foundations of quantum mechanics, supports a claimed linkage between quantum theory and 'industrial discipline in the early bourgeois epoch'. Throughout, Sokal quotes liberally and approvingly from the writings of leading postmodern theorists, including several editors of *Social Text*, passages that are often breathtaking in their combination of self-confidence and absurdity.

Commentators have made much of the scientific, mathematical and philosophical illiteracy that an acceptance of Sokal's ingeniously contrived gibberish would appear to betray. But talk about illiteracy elides an important distinction between two different explanations of what might have led the editors to decide to publish Sokal's piece. One is that, although they understood perfectly well what the various sentences of his article actually mean, they found them plausible, whereas he, along with practically everybody else, doesn't. This might brand them as kooky, but wouldn't impugn their motives. The other hypothesis is that they actually had very little idea what many of the sentences mean, and so were not in a position to evaluate them for plausibility in the first place. The plausibility, or even the intelligibility, of Sokal's arguments just didn't enter into their deliberations.

I think it's very clear, and very important, that it's the second hypothesis that's true. To see why consider, by way of example, the following passage from Sokal's essay:

> Just as liberal feminists are frequently content with a minimal agenda of legal and social equality for women and are 'pro-choice,' so liberal (and even some socialist) mathematicians are often content to work within the hegemonic Zermelo–Fraenkel framework (which, reflecting its nineteenth-century origins, already incorporates the axiom of equality) supplemented only by the axiom of choice. But this framework is grossly insufficient for a liberatory mathematics, as was proven long ago by Cohen 1966.

It's very hard to believe that an editor who knew what the various ingredient terms actually mean would not have raised an eyebrow at this passage. For the axiom of equality in set theory simply provides a definition of when it is that two sets are the same set, namely, when they have the same members; obviously, this has nothing to do with liberalism, or, indeed, with a political philosophy of any stripe. Similarly, the axiom of choice simply says that, given any collection of mutually exclusive sets, there is always a set consisting of exactly one member from each of those sets. Again, this clearly has nothing to do with the issue of choice in the abortion debate. But even if one were somehow able to see one's way clear − I can't − to explaining this first quoted sentence in terms of the postmodern love for puns and wordplay, what would explain the subsequent sentence? Paul Cohen's 1966 proves that the question whether or not there is a number between two other particular (transfinite cardinal) numbers isn't settled by the axioms of

Zermelo–Fraenkel set theory. How could this conceivably count as a proof that Zermelo–Fraenkel set theory is inadequate for the purposes of a 'liberatory mathematics', whatever precisely that is supposed to be? Wouldn't any editor who knew what Paul Cohen had actually proved in 1966 have required just a little more by way of explanation here, in order to make the connection just a bit more perspicuous?

Since one could cite dozens of similar passages − Sokal goes out of his way to leave telltale clues as to his true intent − the conclusion is inescapable that the editors of *Social Text* didn't know what many of the sentences in Sokal's essay actually meant; and that they just didn't care. How could a group of scholars, editing what is supposed to be the leading journal in a given field, allow themselves such a sublime indifference to the content, truth and plausibility of a scholarly submission accepted for publication?

By way of explanation, coeditors Andrew Ross and Bruce Robbins have said that as 'a non-refereed journal of political opinion and cultural analysis produced by an editorial collective' *Social Text* has always seen itself in the '"little magazine" tradition of the independent left as much as in the academic domain'. But it's hard to see this as an adequate explanation; presumably, even a journal of political opinion should care whether what it publishes is intelligible.

What Ross and Co. should have said, it seems to me, is that *Social Text* is a political magazine in a deeper and more radical sense: under appropriate circumstances, it is prepared to let agreement with its ideological orientation trump every other criterion for publication, including something as basic as sheer intelligibility. The prospect of being able to display in their pages a natural scientist − a physicist, no less − throwing the full weight of his authority behind their cause was compelling enough for them to overlook the fact that they didn't have much of a clue exactly what sort of support they were being offered. And this, it seems to me, is what's at the heart of the issue raised by Sokal's hoax: not the mere existence of incompetence within the academy, but rather that specific form of it that arises from allowing ideological criteria to displace standards of scholarship so completely that not even considerations of intelligibility are seen as relevant to an argument's acceptability. How, given the recent and sorry history of ideologically motivated conceptions of knowledge – Lysenkoism in Stalin's Soviet Union, for example, or Nazi critiques of 'Jewish science' – could it again have become acceptable to behave in this way?

The complete historical answer is a long story, but there can be little doubt that one of its crucial components is the brush-fire spread, within vast sectors of the humanities and social sciences, of the cluster of simple-minded relativistic views about truth and evidence that are commonly identified as 'postmodernist'. These views license, and on the most popular versions insist upon, the substitution of political and ideological criteria for the historically more familiar assessment in terms of truth, evidence and argument.

Most philosophers accept the claim that there is no such thing as a totally disinterested inquirer, one who approaches his or her topic utterly devoid of any prior assumptions, values or biases. Postmodernism goes well beyond this historicist observation, as feminist scholar Linda Nicholson explains (without necessarily endorsing):

> The traditional historicist claim that all inquiry is inevitably influenced by the values of the inquirer provides a very weak counter to the norm of objectivity: [T]he more radical move in the postmodern turn was to claim that the very criteria demarcating the true and the false, as well as such related distinctions as science and myth or fact and superstition, were internal to the traditions of modernity and could not be legitimized outside of those traditions. Moreover, it was argued that the

very development and use of such criteria, as well as their extension to ever wider domains, had to be described as representing the growth and development of 'specific regimes of power.'

(From the 'Introduction' to her anthology *Feminism and Postmodernism*)

As Nicholson sees, historicism, however broadly understood, doesn't entail that there is no such thing as objective truth. To concede that no one ever believes something *solely* because it's true is not to deny that anything is objectively true. Furthermore, the concession that no inquirer or inquiry is fully bias-free doesn't entail that they can't be more or less bias-free, or that their biases can't be more or less damaging. To concede that the truth is never the only thing that someone is tracking isn't to deny that some people or methods are better than others at staying on its track.

Historicism leaves intact, then, both the claim that one's aim should be to arrive at conclusions that are objectively true and justified, independently of any particular perspective, and that science is the best idea that anyone has had about how to satisfy that aim. Postmodernism, in seeking to demote science from the privileged epistemic position it has come to occupy, and thereby to blur the distinction between it and 'other ways of knowing' – myth and superstition, for example – needs to go much further than historicism, all the way to the denial that objective truth is a coherent aim that inquiry may have. Indeed, according to postmodernism, the very development and use of the rhetoric of objectivity, far from embodying a serious metaphysics and epistemology of truth and evidence, represents a mere play for power, a way of silencing these 'other ways of knowing'. It follows, given this standpoint, that the struggle against the rhetoric of objectivity isn't primarily an intellectual matter, but a political one: the rhetoric needs to be defeated, rather than just refuted. Against this backdrop, it becomes very easy to explain the behaviour of the editors of *Social Text*.

Although it may be hard to understand how anyone could actually hold views as extreme as these, their ubiquity these days is a distressingly familiar fact. A front-page article in the *New York Times* of 22 October 1996 provided a recent illustration. The article concerned the conflict between two views of where Native American populations originated – the scientific archeological account, and the account offered by some Native American creation myths. According to the former extensively confirmed view, humans first entered the Americas from Asia, crossing the Bering Strait over 10,000 years ago. By contrast, some Native American creation accounts hold that native peoples have lived in the Americas ever since their ancestors first emerged onto the surface of the earth from a subterranean world of spirits. The *Times* noted that many archeologists, torn between their commitment to scientific method and their appreciation for native culture, 'have been driven close to a postmodern relativism in which science is just one more belief system'. Roger Anyon, a British archeologist who has worked for the Zuni people, was quoted as saying: 'Science is just one of many ways of knowing the world. [The Zunis' world view is] just as valid as the archeological viewpoint of what prehistory is about.'

How are we to make sense of this? (Sokal himself mentioned this example at a recent public forum in New York and was taken to task by Andrew Ross for putting Native Americans 'on trial'. But this issue isn't about Native American views; it's about postmodernism.) The claim that the Zuni myth can be 'just as valid' as the archeological theory can be read in one of three different ways, between which postmodern theorists tend not to distinguish sufficiently: as a claim about truth, as a claim about justification, or as a claim about purpose. As we shall see, however, none of these claims is even remotely plausible.

Interpreted as a claim about truth, the sugges-tion would be that the Zuni and archeological views are equally true. On the face of it, though, this is impossible, since they contradict each other. One says, or implies, that the first humans in the Americas came from Asia; the other says, or implies, that they did not, that they came from somewhere else, a subterranean world of spirits. How could a claim and its denial both be true? If I say that the earth is flat, and you say that it's round, how could we both be right?

Postmodernists like to respond to this sort of point by saying that both claims can be true because both are true relative to some perspec-tive or other, and there can be no question of truth outside of perspectives. Thus, according to the Zuni perspective, the first humans in the Americas came from a subterranean world; and according to the Western scientific perspective, the first humans came from Asia. Since both are true according to some perspective or other, both are true.

But to say that some claim is true according to some perspective sounds simply like a fancy way of saying that someone, or some group, believes it. The crucial question concerns what we are to say when what I believe – what's true according to my perspective – conflicts with what you believe – with what's true according to your perspective? The one thing not to say, it seems to me, on pain of utter unintelligibility, is that both claims are true.

This should be obvious, but can also be seen by applying the view to itself. For consider: If a claim and its opposite can be equally true provided that there is some perspective relative to which each is true, then, since there is a perspective – realism – relative to which it's true that a claim and its opposite cannot both be true, postmodernism would have to admit that it itself is just as true as its opposite, realism. But postmodernism cannot afford to admit that: presumably, its whole point is that realism is false. Thus, we see that the very statement of postmodernism, construed as a view about truth, undermines itself: facts about truth independent of particular perspectives are presupposed by the view itself.

How does it fare when considered as a claim about evidence or justification? So construed, the suggestion comes to the claim that the Zuni story and the archeological theory are equally justified, given the available evidence. Now, in contrast with the case of truth, it is not incoherent for a claim and its negation to be equally justified, for instance, in cases where there is very little evidence for either side. But, prima facie, anyway, this isn't the sort of case that's at issue, for according to the available evidence, the archeological theory is far better confirmed than the Zuni myth.

To get the desired relativistic result, a postmodernist would have to claim that the two views are equally justified *given their respective rules of evidence*, and add that there is no objective fact of the matter which set of rules is to be preferred. Given this relativization of justification to the rules of evidence characteristic of a given perspective, the archeological theory would be justified relative to the rules of evidence of Western science, and the Zuni story would be justified relative to the rules of evidence employed by the relevant tradition of myth-making. Furthermore, since there are no perspective-independent rules of evidence that could adjudicate between these two sets of rules, both claims would be equally justified and there could be no choosing between them.

Once again, however, there is a problem not merely with plausibility, but with self-refutation. For suppose we grant that every rule of evidence is as good as any other. Then any claim could be made to count as justified simply by formulating an appropriate rule of evidence relative to which it is justified. Indeed, it would follow that we could justify the claim that not every rule of evidence is as good as any other, thereby forcing the postmodernist to concede that his views about truth and justification are

just as justified as his opponent's. Presumably, however, the postmodernist needs to hold that his views are better than his opponent's; otherwise what's to recommend them? On the other hand, if some rules of evidence can be said to be better than others, then there must be perspective-independent facts about what makes them better and a thoroughgoing relativism about justification is false.

It is sometimes suggested that the intended sense in which the Zuni myth is 'just as valid' has nothing to do with truth or justification, but rather with the different purposes that the myth subserves, in contrast with those of science. According to this line of thought, science aims to give a descriptively accurate account of reality, whereas the Zuni myth belongs to the realm of religious practice and the constitution of cultural identity. It is to be regarded as having symbolic, emotional and ritual purposes other than the mere description of reality. And as such, it may serve those purposes very well – better, perhaps, than the archeologist's account.

The trouble with this as a reading of 'just as valid' is not so much that it's false, but that it's irrelevant to the issue at hand: even if it were granted, it couldn't help advance the cause of postmodernism. For if the Zuni myth isn't taken to compete with the archeological theory, as a descriptively accurate account of prehistory, its existence has no prospect of casting any doubt on the objectivity of the account delivered by science. If I say that the earth is flat, and you make no assertion at all, but instead tell me an interesting story, that has no potential for raising deep issues about the objectivity of what either of us said or did.

Is there, perhaps, a weaker thesis that, while being more defensible than these simple-minded relativisms, would nevertheless yield an anti-objectivist result? It's hard to see what such a thesis would be. Stanley Fish, for example, in seeking to discredit Sokal's characterization of postmodernism, offers the following (Opinion piece, *The New York Times*):

What sociologists of science say is that of course the world is real and independent of our observations but that accounts of the world are produced by observers and are therefore relative to their capacities, education and training, etc. It is not the world or its properties but the vocabularies in whose terms we know them that are socially constructed.

The rest of Fish's discussion leaves it thoroughly unclear exactly what he thinks this observation shows; but claims similar to his are often presented by others as constituting yet another basis for arguing against the objectivity of science. The resultant arguments are unconvincing.

It goes without saying that the *vocabularies* with which we seek to know the world are socially constructed and that they therefore reflect various contingent aspects of our capacities, limitations and interests. But it doesn't follow that those vocabularies are therefore incapable of meeting the standards of adequacy relevant to the expression and discovery of objective truths.

We may illustrate why by using Fish's own example. There is no doubt that the game of baseball as we have it, with its particular conceptions of what counts as a 'strike' and what counts as a 'ball', reflects various contingent facts about us as physical and social creatures. 'Strike' and 'ball' are socially constructed concepts, if anything is. However, once these concepts have been defined – once the strike zone has been specified – there are then perfectly objective facts about what counts as a strike and what counts as a ball. (The fact that the umpire is the court of last appeal doesn't mean that he can't make mistakes.)

Similarly, our choice of one conceptual scheme rather than another, for the purposes of doing science, probably reflects various contingent facts about our capacities and limitations, so that a thinker with different capacities and limitations, a Martian for example, might find it natural to employ a different scheme. This does nothing to show that our conceptual scheme is incapable of expressing objective truths. Realism is not committed to there being only one vocabulary in which objective truths might be expressed; all it's committed to is the weaker claim that, once a vocabulary is specified, it will then be an objective matter whether or not assertions couched in that vocabulary are true or false.

We are left with two puzzles. Given what the basic tenets of postmodernism are, how did they ever come to be identified with a progressive political outlook? And given how transparently refutable they are, how did they ever come to gain such widespread acceptance?

In the United States, postmodernism is closely linked to the movement known as multiculturalism, broadly conceived as the project of giving proper credit to the contributions of cultures and communities whose achievements have been historically neglected or undervalued. In this connection, it has come to appeal to certain progressive sensibilities because it supplies the philosophical resources with which to prevent anyone from accusing oppressed cultures of holding false or unjustified views.

Even on purely political grounds, however, it is difficult to understand how this could have come to seem a good way to conceive of multiculturalism. For if the powerful can't criticize the oppressed, because the central epistemological categories are inexorably tied to particular perspectives, it also follows that the oppressed can't criticize the powerful. The only remedy, so far as I can see, for what threatens to be a strongly conservative upshot, is to accept an overt double standard: allow a questionable idea to be criticized if it is held by those in a position of power – Christian creationism, for example – but not if it is held by those whom the powerful oppress – Zuni creationism, for example. Familiar as this stratagem has recently become, how can it possibly appeal to anyone with the slightest degree of intellectual integrity; and how can it fail to seem anything other than deeply offensive to the progressive sensibilities whose cause it is supposed to further?

As for the second question, regarding wide-spread acceptance, the short answer is that questions about truth, meaning and objectivity are among the most difficult and thorny questions that philosophy confronts and so are very easily mishandled. A longer answer would involve explaining why analytic philosophy, the dominant tradition of philosophy in the English-speaking world, wasn't able to exert a more effective corrective influence. After all, analytic philosophy is primarily known for its detailed and subtle discussion of concepts in the philosophy of language and the theory of knowl-edge, the very concepts that postmodernism so badly misunderstands. Isn't it reasonable to expect it to have had a greater impact on the philosophical explorations of its intellectual neighbors? And if it hasn't, can that be because its reputation for insularity is at least partly

deserved? Because philosophy concerns the most general categories of knowledge, categories that apply to any compartment of inquiry, it is inevitable that other disciplines will reflect on philosophical problems and develop philo-sophical positions. Analytic philosophy has a special responsibility to ensure that its insights on matters of broad intellectual interest are available widely, to more than a narrow class of insiders.

Whatever the correct explanation for the current malaise, Alan Sokal's hoax has served as a flashpoint for what has been a gathering storm of protest against the collapse in standards of scholarship and intellectual responsibility that vast sectors of the humanities and social sciences are currently afflicted with. Significantly, some of the most biting commentary has come from distinguished voices on the left, showing that when it comes to transgressions as basic as these, political alliances afford no protection. Anyone still inclined to doubt the seriousness of the problem has only to read Sokal's parody.

Chapter 44

Michael Williams

WHY (WITTGENSTEINIAN) CONTEXTUALISM IS NOT RELATIVISM[1]

[...]

1. I have long defended a conception of justification that, following David Annis, I call "contextualist."[2] Central to this conception—which in my version owes a good deal to Wittgenstein—is the idea that standards of justification are subject to significant circumstantial variation, hence in some sense neither "absolute" nor "invariant." Now everyone agrees that justification is in some respects relative to circumstances: for example, whether I am justified in accepting a hypothesis can depend on the evidence at my disposal. But according to some critics, my version of contextualism goes farther than that: by implying that epistemic standards are "less than fully objective," it amounts to a kind of epistemic relativism.[3] But while I agree that, in a sense, justification is not "absolute," I deny that this contextualist view amounts to epistemic relativism. On the contrary, contextualism is the cure for all skeptical temptations, relativism included. Or rather, it is the cure for all skeptical temptations *that ought to matter to us*.

My argument will proceed in four stages. First I shall explain what I understand by epistemic relativism. Then, glancing back at classical foundationalism, I shall isolate a notion of absolute justification, teasing out the conception of objective epistemic standards that it implies. With this notion of absolute justification in hand, and drawing on Wittgenstein's notes in On Certainty (Wittgenstein 1969)[4] I shall sketch the contextualist alternative, highlighting the ways in which it departs from the foundationalist's "absolute" and "objective" conception. Finally, I shall argue that my denial that justification is "absolute" or "objective," in the senses indicated, entails no objectionably relativistic consequences. Rather, what is often taken for relativism, on the part of writers like Wittgenstein or myself, is really something else: not pessimism about objective knowledge but a certain skepticism about the pretensions of traditional epistemology.

2. I am going to take epistemic relativism to be relativism about (epistemic) justification.[5] So even when, for variety of expression, I speak of knowledge, my primary interest will be in justification. Further, though relativism can take individualist forms ("justified for me"), the cultural version is what seems to be popular today. Accordingly, I shall be primarily concerned with epistemic relativism as a form of cultural relativism, though what I have to say goes for epistemic relativism in all its forms.

Using the phrase "epistemic system" in a very broad sense to refer to the assemblage of principles and procedures that a given society or culture (allegedly) relies on, explicitly or implicitly, in distinguishing justified from unjustified beliefs, we can characterize epistemic relativism in terms of three theses:

System-dependence. A belief's epistemic status (as justified or not) is not an intrinsic property but depends on the believer's epistemic system. This is a logical (or semantic or perhaps metaphysical) claim. It is a claim about what we mean, or ought to mean, when we say that a belief is justified.

System-variability. Epistemic systems vary from culture to culture or within single cultures from one historical epoch to another. This is an empirical claim.

System-equality. No epistemic system is superior to another. This is a normative claim.

Clearly, epistemic relativism is a notably skeptical doctrine. Indeed, if we really came to think that our own epistemic system was not better than any alternatives, it is not clear that we could continue to think of our beliefs as justified *even by our own lights.* Relativism has a tendency to collapse into skepticism.

Examples of cultural variation in epistemic procedures are not hard to come up with. Many cultures have consulted oracles to foretell the future; we don't. Some cultures take tribal myths and traditions, or literal readings of sacred texts, to be the last word on the origins of the tribe and even the world; we tend to approach such issues scientifically. But although such examples lend color to the idea of epistemic relativism, at bottom relativism is not an empirical thesis. The relativist's crucial normative claim cannot be established simply by pointing to differences of opinion, even if the differences concern how to form one's opinions. The fundamental argument for epistemic relativism is a variant of one of the oldest forms of skeptical argument: the *diallelos* or "wheel." The argument aims to show that epistemic systems cannot be defended in a non-circular way.

Fundamental argument for epistemic relativism. In determining whether a belief—any belief— is justified, we always rely, implicitly or explicitly, on an epistemic system: some standards or procedures that separate justified from unjustified convictions. But what about the claims embodied in the system itself: are they justifiable? In answering this question, we inevitably apply our own epistemic system. So, assuming that our system is coherent and does not undermine itself, the best that we can hope for is a justification that is epistemically circular, employing our epistemic system in support of itself. Since this procedure can be followed by anyone, whatever his epistemic system, all such systems, provided they are coherent, are equally defensible (or indefensible).

Variations on this theme are common in the writings of Sextus Empiricus. As a particular application of one of the Five Modes of Agrippa—the Mode of Circularity—the wheel is intimately connected with what we think of as the regress problem. Tracing the connections illuminates how the argument for relativism treats epistemic systems.

Suppose that someone (call him "the claimant") makes a claim, P, in such a way that he represents himself as knowing P to be true: a challenger can ask him *how* he knows. After all, we might think, if someone represents himself as knowing something, rather than *merely* believing it, he invites the question, which therefore cannot reasonably be refused. However, if the claimant accepts the challenge, he must give his reason for believing that P, citing evidence for P or other grounds for supposing P to be true. In so doing, he enters a new claim, Q, and the question will arise as to whether Q is something that he knows (or justifiably believes). But since anything he says in support of Q may itself be challenged, requiring a further supporting claim, we seem to have opened up a vicious regress of reasons for reasons for reasons, and so on without end.

In practical terms, the danger of getting trapped in an infinite regress is remote. When challenged to justify a claim, we all run out of things to say *very quickly*. In some cases, this may lead the claimant to wonder whether the belief expressed by his claim is as well founded as he supposed. But if he continues to think of it as well founded, this will be because in giving backup for backup, etc., he eventually comes upon some claim, B, that he takes himself to *just know* to be true. Maybe, in some cases, his initial claim strikes him this way, so that he refuses to respond even to the first challenge. But at whatever point, if the claimant simply refuses to respond to a challenge, the challenger (now revealed as the skeptic) will say that the claimant is just *making an assumption*.

In all likelihood, since the claimant thinks that the belief expressed by his initial claim is justified, he will repudiate the charge of making a mere assumption. Granted, he may say, he cannot give *specific reasons* for thinking B to be true. But he can still defend B's epistemic credentials by saying something like "I can see that B" or "I remember vividly that B" or "I read that B only this morning" or that "Everyone knows that B" or "It stands to reason that B." That is, he will cite some relevant *source of knowledge* (or justified belief): perception, memory, expert opinion, the *consensus gentium*, or elementary logical insight. Such a source, he implies, is authoritative: information derived from it is definitely *to be trusted*. In this way, the claimant reveals his commitment to a *source principle*.

To treat a source as authoritative is to take it to be reliable, or at least not wildly unreliable. What justifies this? Some sources may be derivative: I may be able to justify relying on them by citing evidence that is itself legitimated by more fundamental sources. Perhaps I have found that following Ordnance Survey maps is a very good way of getting around Britain, from which I conclude that such maps are a highly reliable source of information. But obviously this can't go on for ever. At some point—and again, almost certainly rather quickly—I am going to get down to one or more *fundamental* source. But by definition, once we get down to fundamental

sources, there is nowhere else to go. Accordingly, *fundamental sources can be validated only by employing them*: i.e. circularly. So if different cultures recognize different epistemic systems, in the sense of different sets of fundamental source principles, there is no way to argue that one system is superior to another. This is how we find ourselves on the wheel. The argument can be given a relativist spin or a skeptical spin. It is the same argument either way. At bottom, it exploits *Agrippa's Trilemma*, the thought that any attempt to justify a belief must end in one of three unsatisfactory ways: a vicious regress, a brute assumption, or circular reasoning.

3. The problem of justification is to halt the regress without getting stuck on the wheel. By far the most popular approach to this problem has been to develop some foundational theory of justification. But traditional foundationalism has another motive: to articulate the fundamental epistemic framework within which all significant disputes can, in principle, be rationally resolved. Foundationalism connects the *problem of justification* with what we can call the *problem of method*. This connection will prove worth looking into.

Foundational theories of justification postulate basic beliefs. Different kinds of basic beliefs correspond to different source principles. Non-basic beliefs depend for their justification on the evidence provided by basic beliefs, so foundational theories also recognize a range of distribution principles, which transmit positive epistemic status from basic to non-basic beliefs.

By definition, basic beliefs do not depend for their justification on further evidence. It is natural to think that there must be *something* to this thought. There must be some distinction between inferential and non-inferential justification: for example, between *concluding* that something is so and *seeing* that it is. However, there is a lot more to traditional foundationalism than respect for this commonsense distinction.[6] Foundationalists hold that certain beliefs (or perhaps some more primitive cognitive states or episodes, such as perceptual experiences) constitute *ultimate* sources of justification. On this approach, beliefs will not be truly basic unless they are justified independently of whatever else we happen to believe, if anything. Basic beliefs must therefore constitute an autonomous class or stratum of justified beliefs. This *independence condition* is a serious constraint on how we think about justification (and indeed much else besides). For example, suppose that we could not have any beliefs *at all*, unless we had lots of other beliefs. If this were so, though we might have beliefs that were in some sense non-inferential, those beliefs would not be basic. The independence condition excludes semantic as well as epistemic holism.

Today, many philosophers are *externalists* about justification. They hold that beliefs count as justified if they are *in fact* the products of some reliable process (i.e. a process that tends to produce a preponderance of true beliefs). To be justified, beliefs need not be known or even believed to be such products. For externalists, I can know things without knowing that I know them: animal knowledge is generally thought to be like this. By tracing justification to the fact of reliability, externalism offers a way off the wheel. However, traditional foundationalism respects internalist intuitions. Every traditional foundationalist accepts at least the following constraint:

> *Weak Internalism.* If for all you know (or have reason to believe) your epistemic system is wildly unreliable, then relying on that system to form or evaluate beliefs does not yield beliefs that are justified.

Combining weak internalism with the independence condition further constrains basic beliefs: not only must such beliefs not presuppose any further beliefs, they must not depend for their credibility on *general empirical facts*. Obviously, basic beliefs can't derive their credibility

from *beliefs* about reliability: that would make them inferential. But weak internalism also precludes their deriving their credibility straight from the reliability-facts themselves.

According to traditional foundationalism, then, basic beliefs are *intrinsically* credible. They don't depend for their credibility on anything. Their credibility is *absolute*. Some forms of foundationalism are *strong*, insisting that basic beliefs are indubitable or incorrigible. This is absolute justification in its most uncompromising form. Other forms of foundationalism are modest: while always *prima facie* justified, basic beliefs can sometimes be rejected down the line (though never wholesale). But whether the credibility of basic beliefs is total or only *prima facie*, it is always *intrinsic*. This is the idea of absolute justification that I reject.

The idea of intrinsic credibility is problematic. If it cannot be clarified, foundationalism's escape from the regress is a case of explanation *obscurum per obscurius*. Further, it seems obvious that most of our beliefs are not intrinsically credible. Basic beliefs must be beliefs of some very special kind. How are such kinds to be identified? Now it may seem that explaining intrinsic credibility—identifying the sources of basic beliefs—threatens to put the foundationalist back on the wheel. Though the matter is delicate, it can be argued that this need not be so. Basic beliefs are not credible because they belong to certain kinds. Rather, the character of the kinds is determined—thus the source of intrinsic credibility identified—by examining examples of beliefs that clearly have the right kind of epistemic status. In Chisholm's terms, a foundationalist can be a *methodological particularist*, though his aim, as a theorist, remains to characterize basic beliefs in a general way.[7]

The traditional approach has been to identify basic beliefs by their subject matter. For example, it has often been noted that I cannot be mistaken about perceptual appearances. Suppose that it seems to me that there is something red in front of me: I may be mistaken in thinking that there really is something red there (I may be hallucin-ating), but I cannot be mistaken about how things seem to be. Things can seem to be other than they are, but can't seem to seem other than they seem: the "seems" operator doesn't iterate. It has often been concluded that such seemings are "self-presenting states": knowable by their mere presence to the mind and thus suitable objects of basic beliefs. Thinking along these lines, traditional foundationalists sort beliefs into fundamental epistemic kinds, according to certain broad features of their content. These kinds are thought to stand in a hierarchy accord-ing to relations of epistemic priority. At the foundation are the basic beliefs, which are prior to all other beliefs. Next are beliefs that are directly inferentially dependent on basic beliefs. Above them come whatever beliefs are inferen-tially dependent on beliefs at the second level, and so on. For example, it might be held that beliefs concerning natural laws depend on beliefs about particular events in the external world, which in turn depend on basic experien-tial beliefs. Here is another aspect in which foundational justification is absolute. Not only are there basic beliefs, there is an invariant order of epistemic priority between fundamental epistemic kinds.

The conception of absolute justification we have been exploring goes with a comparably demanding idea of what it is for epistemic standards to be "objective." Consider a natural kind: acids, say. We can state a non-trivial criterion for acidity, a principle that we can use for sorting chemical compounds into acids and non-acids. Now contrast acids with things that happen on a Tuesday.[8] Obviously, there is no non-trivial criterion for determining the kind of thing that happens on a Tuesday. There is no kind of thing that happens on a Tuesday: things that happen on a Tuesday are a mere aggregate, not a natural kind. Now, as we have seen, traditional foundationalism treats the class of justified beliefs as theoretically tractable. So for foundationalists, justified beliefs are more

like acids than like things that happen on a Wednesday. It is the nature of a basic belief to be intrinsically credible, as it is the nature of an acid to be a proton donor. Other beliefs are naturally non-basic: they owe any credibility they have to evidence provided by beliefs that are naturally epistemically prior to them. Beliefs fall into natural epistemological kinds, ordered by nat-ural relations of epistemological priority: what Descartes called "the order of reasons."

The domain of epistemic facts that traditional epistemologists have purported to investigate is supposed to be not only theorizable but also autonomous. For example, intrinsic credibility, as traditionally understood, entails that the epistemic status of basic beliefs owes nothing to empirical facts. Thus it has traditionally been held that there is a basic observational vocabu-lary—composed of terms suitable for capturing our ultimate evidence—that is invariant, thus not subject to revision in the light of empirical developments. I sometimes call the idea that (ultimately) standards of justification reflect an autonomous domain of epistemic facts "epistemological realism." Contextualism says that epistemological realism is false. If this is what it is to reject "full objectivity" with respect to epistemic standards, then full objectivity should be rejected.

Although problematic, traditional founda-tionalism has its attractions. Its strong in-variantism—its postulation of a base level of intrinsically credible beliefs, formulated in basic observational vocabulary and lying at the base of a definite hierarchy of epistemic kinds—promises a "permanent neutral matrix" for the rational resolution of all significant disputes. The solution to the problem of justification also solves the problem of method. If we deny that there is such a matrix, it looks as though we may be opening the door to epistemic relativism. But as I shall argue, this is not so.

4. Contextualism is a radical alternative to trad-itional foundationalism. There are two main

lines of defense for the contextualist view: that it stays much closer to ordinary epistemic practice; and that alternatives serve only to generate unnecessary skeptical puzzles, such as epistemic relativism. Since, in my view, skepticism and traditional epistemology are two sides of the same coin, a good way to develop contextualism is diagnostically: by identifying certain presuppositions of skeptical argumentation and seeing what happens if they are denied.

Let us go back to the regress of justification. The skeptic assumes that epistemic challenges are indefinitely iterable. Behind this is the assumption of a fundamental epistemic claimant–challenger asymmetry.

> *Claimant–challenger asymmetry.* Whenever knowledge is claimed, the burden of justification lies with the claimant. If I represent myself as knowing that P, I invite you to ask me how I know. There is nothing you have to do, or no way that things have to be, in order for you to have the right to enter a challenge.

This principle reflects a particular model of epistemic justification, in which justification depends on positive authorization. Whenever a belief or claim is justified, there is some statable *positive property* in virtue of which it is justified. All the skeptic wants is to be told what it is: a reasonable request, given the model.

Behind the positive authorization requirement lies the assumption of epistemological realism. To see this, we need only remind ourselves that the *general* threat of a trilemma—regress, assumption, or circular reasoning—is entirely theoretical. In practice, though some conversations get stuck in a rut, others don't. You may be skeptical of some claim I advance. But when I explain my reasons for advancing it, you may find them acceptable and convincing. However, the skeptic will say that such a resolution is *merely dialectical*: even if a series of claims and challenges ends in agreement, there is still the question of why either of us is justified in holding to the claims we agree on. The skeptic—who might as well be the traditional epistemologist—wants to get at the underlying epistemological facts. And his assumption is that these owe nothing to agreement. Quite the opposite: when justified, agreement owes everything to them.

Although it may seem plausible at first, the principle of claimant–challenger asymmetry will be false if challenges are themselves subject to justificatory constraints, so that challenges that fail to respect them are not legitimate. And if challenges are not always legitimate, there need not always be some positive property on which a claim's positive epistemic status supervenes. Maybe it is justified because, in the circumstances, there is nothing to be said *against* it. Globally, justification will not conform to a positive authorization model but will exhibit what Robert Brandom calls a "default and challenge structure."[9] Positive authorization will be an essentially *local* phenomenon. Contextualism accepts this structure. But it adds that the factors influencing default justification are contextually sensitive. I will briefly discuss four kinds of factor that can place propositions at least temporarily beyond question, or which limit how they can be questioned. They are semantic, methodological, dialectical, and economic. I will then say something about the place of source principles in the contextualist picture.

Beginning with semantic factors, to be legitimate a challenge must at least be intelligible. This is not automatic. I take it for granted that two plus three equals five. It would be ridiculous for someone to say, "I see what you mean, but why do you say that?" Anyone who thinks that a challenge is in place here does not see what I mean. Of course, traditional foundationalists have often thought of basic beliefs for which understanding and truth are closely linked. However, for the contextualist, this sort of immunity from challenge is not the special prerogative of any particular kind of judgment.

Rather, there is a general connection between meaning, truth and immunity from epistemic challenge in that our getting lots of things right—and agreeing about them—is a condition of our having any thoughts at all. This is a central theme in Wittgenstein:

> 79. That I am a man and not a woman can be verified, but if I were to say that I am a woman, and then tried to explain the error by saying I hadn't checked the statement, the explanation would not be accepted.
> 80. The truth of my statements is the test of my understanding of these statements.
> 81. That is to say: if I make certain false statements, it becomes uncertain whether I understand them.
> 156. In order to make a mistake, a man must already judge in conformity with mankind.

Nor does the point apply only to *standing certainties*. In the right circumstances, simple perceptual judgments are comparably insulated from doubt in that, if someone expressed reservations, we would have no idea what he was getting at. Thus Wittgenstein:

> 17. Suppose now I say "I'm incapable of being wrong about this: that is a book" while I point to an object. What would a mistake here be like? And have I any clear idea of it?
> 155. In certain circumstances a man cannot make a mistake. ("Can" is used here logically, and the proposition does not mean that a man cannot say anything false in those circumstances.) . . .

There are circumstances in which giving voice to particular falsehoods would be evidence of some kind of mental disturbance, thus not a case of expressing an unjustified belief. It would not be an appropriate occasion for asking, "Why do you say that?"

The reference to circumstances brings a dimension of contextual variability to concepts like "mistake" and "legitimate challenge." Given the right setting, judgments that would not normally be questionable might become so. Suppose that I am in an antique shop, specializing in smoking paraphernalia, where there are not only books about tobacco but also cigarette boxes that look like books. In this situation, my pointing to a "book" could legitimately be challenged. But in other cases not so: for example, when I am holding the book, riffling the pages, etc. Similarly, in the right circumstances, facts that it would not normally be appropriate to check—indeed, where seeming to "check" would be a bizarre parody of investigation—can be looked into. That I have two legs is as certain as anything gets to be. But if I were caught up in a bombing outrage, I might find myself looking nervously toward my lower extremities.

Now it may look as though the conception of justification we are working towards is a kind of foundationalism, though with shifting rather than fixed foundations. However, it is important to be clear just how different the conception is from that enshrined in traditional foundationalism. In particular, we must be absolutely clear that the kind of certainty that is connected with the impossibility of mistake—or with the unintelligibility of epistemic challenges—does not allow us to define the epistemic kinds that are the hallmark of traditional foundationalism. First, as Wittgenstein is quick to insist, the boundary between certainties and hypotheses is not a sharp one:

> 52. [The] situation is . . . not the same for a proposition like "At this distance from the sun there is a planet" and "Here is a hand" (namely my own hand). The second can't be called a hypothesis. But there isn't a sharp boundary between them.

Second, whether tokens of the same judgment-type are intelligibly questionable can vary with circumstances in ways that cannot be reduced to rule. If we try to formulate rules or criteria, we will find ourselves using phrases like "normal circumstances," and it is far from obvious that we can determine, in any general way, what circumstances count as "normal." Wittgenstein claims (plausibly) that we can't and that it wouldn't do us any good if we could.

25. One may be wrong even about "there being a hand there." Only in particular circumstances is it impossible—"even in a calculation one can be wrong—only in certain circumstances one can't."
26. But can it be seen from a *rule* what circumstances logically exclude a mistake in the employment of rules of calculation?

What use is a rule to us here? Mightn't we (in turn) go wrong in applying it?
27. If, however, one wanted to give something like a rule here, then it would contain the expression "in normal circumstances." And we recognize normal circumstances but cannot precisely describe them. At most, we can describe a range of abnormal ones.

Circumstances are normal provided they are not "funny" in some way or other; but although we can typically recognize when circumstances are normal—and thus know what can and cannot appropriately be questioned—we cannot state a criterion of normality. But Wittgenstein adds the important *caveat* that, even if we could state a criterion, our epistemic situation would not be improved. Contextually embedded certainties are *already* as certain as any propositions could be. We would only seek rules if we were already in thrall to the skeptical demand for authorization by epistemic principles, which is the very model we are trying to undermine. So the claim that a certain kind of epistemological understanding is off-limits—not because we can't get at the epistemic facts, but because justification doesn't work like that—is no cause for alarm. Contextualism suggests that we don't *need* that kind of understanding in the first place.

Challenges that are potentially intelligible need not always be immediately so. Thus the correct response to an epistemic challenge can often be: "What's the problem: where do you think I might be going wrong?" One reason that this is often an appropriate first move is that you can't respond appropriately to a challenge without determining precisely what you need to respond to. It is not generally sufficient for a challenger to reply, "I don't have anything particular in mind, but no one's infallible."

Even when intelligible, challenges are not always legitimate. They can be far-fetched or utterly groundless. The logical possibility of a certain kind of error is not generally sufficient for a legitimate challenge. Often one needs some reason to think that the possibility is live: that there is some reasonable probability of its having been realized. Challenges can also fail to be legitimate by being irrelevant to current concerns. So another potent source of epistemic entitlement is *direction of inquiry*. What we are looking into is a function of what we are leaving alone. This is true even in mundane matters. But it is particularly interesting as an aspect of more formal varieties of investigation. Wittgenstein makes a lot of this:

341. ... the questions that we raise and our doubts depend on the fact that some propositions are exempt from doubt, are as it were like hinges on which those turn.
342. That is to say, it belongs to the logic of our scientific investigations that certain things are indeed not doubted.
343. But it isn't that the situation is like this: We just can't investigate everything, and for this reason we are forced to rest content with assumption. If I want the door to turn, the hinges must stay put.

I call such presuppositions, which give particular forms of inquiry their characteristic shape and direction, *disciplinary constraints* or *methodological necessities*. Wittgenstein again:

163. We check the story of Napoleon, but not whether all reports about him are based on sense-deception, forgery and the like. For whenever we test anything, we are already presupposing something that is not tested. Now am I to say that the experiment which perhaps I make in order to test the truth of a proposition presupposes the truth of the proposition that the apparatus I believe I see is really there (and the like)?

Methodological necessities are standing presuppositions such that questioning them would lead one to question the competence of the form of inquiry they enable. In this way, they determine the *disciplinary meta-context* for such practices as historical research.

Presuppositions of this kind are not mere assumptions. For even though they make more detailed kinds of justification possible, they are not beyond evidence. First, though they may begin life as postulates, perhaps never even articulated, if inquiries that proceed on their basis throw up significant results, such methodological necessities acquire a measure of indirect validation. Second, they can be questioned and revised. The motive for questioning may be internally generated; our inquiries get into difficulties. Or challenges may come from outside, as when physical methods give us new ways of dating or authenticating historical artifacts and documents. However, radical questioning can involve a change of subject. This is especially relevant to skeptical questioning. Raising general doubts about the usability of documentary and other historical evidence would not be an especially rigorous approach to historical research, any more than entertaining skeptical doubts about the reality of the external world would be an exceptionally careful way of conducting experiments in physics. Rather, to bring up such issues changes the subject from history, or physics, to (a certain kind of) epistemology (which, as we are discovering, has disciplinary presuppositions of its own).

Here we must make a concession: practices like doing historical research are culturally variable, contingent developments. Wittgenstein insists on this.

85. [W]hat goes into someone's knowing . . . history, say? He must know what it means to say: the earth has already existed for such and such a length of time. For not any intelligent adult must know that. We see men building a house and demolishing houses, and are led to ask: "How long has this house been here?" But how does one come on the idea of asking this about a mountain, for example?

The presuppositions of historical thinking are not common knowledge. They do not automatically fall out of everyday experiences. There is a leap from asking about the age of a house to asking about the age of the earth. Whether this raises the specter of relativism is a question I shall return to. For the time being, I want to stress yet again contextualism's theoretical modesty. While we can point to the importance of methodological necessities in generating default entitlements, by virtue of enabling definite forms of inquiry, there is a good deal of indeterminacy as to which propositions have that status. While we can't do history at all if we are *a priori* distrustful of all potential evidence, the reliability of many of our sources is itself often a perfectly reasonable topic of investigation. In any case, "hinge" propositions are not confined to epistemological presuppositions. In physics, the question of whether a certain surprising experimental result might be accounted for by divine intervention doesn't arise at all: an appeal to the supernatural just doesn't count as a physical explanation. But commitments like this are not set in stone. Partisans of a rigorously mechanical conception of nature were distrustful of Newton's theory of gravitation: it smacked of a reversion to occult powers and stellar "influences," just the sort of supernaturalism that science should dispense with. But the insistence on rigorously mechanical explanations of physical processes proved to be a straitjacket and was abandoned, largely because of the success of Newton's more flexible approach. There is no sharp boundary between methodological propositions and propositions within a method; and even the vague boundary is one that propositions can cross. Here we encounter a further instance of limits to epistemological theorizing.

Contextually determined entitlements are also affected by dialectical factors: for example, the state of discussion at a given time. I said that challenges sometimes need legitimation. But sometimes they don't. Even with semantic and disciplinary constraints in place, a claim or belief may face standing objections that need to be dealt with. Or new problems may arise, as new evidence comes in or old evidence is impugned. Theoretical innovations, too, can affect the range of hypotheses that we can even take seriously. This means that the epistemic status of a belief can change with developments in the dialectical environment, developments that are in principle unpredictable—another limit to epistemological understanding.

Justification also has a pragmatic dimension. For one thing, epistemic standards are affected by *economic* considerations, which can vary from context to context. I am justified in accepting a hypothesis if I have sufficient evidence: but how much is enough? When is it legitimate to demand more? Here we must remember that information isn't free: it has to be gathered, which imposes costs, including opportunity costs. (We all have better things to do than conduct investigations.) If I need to make a decision, if the cost of error is low, and if the cost of gathering further information is high, I may be justified in accepting a proposition on relatively weak evidence. But if the costs of error are high, much more rigorous standards may be in order. Once more, it is doubtful how far any of this can be reduced to rule. Economic factors are not generally thought of as epistemic. But they are

relevant to rational conduct: including rational epistemic conduct. Descartes's idea of "pure inquiry"—where only epistemic factors are in play—is a fantasy.

There is one further topic that calls for some comment. If we follow Wittgenstein and stress the primacy of *particular certainties*, we may wonder whether general epistemic beliefs concerning the reliability of various information-sources are of any importance at all. As we have seen, such commitments will number among the methodological necessities of various specialized forms of inquiry. But is there any role for generic source-principles asserting the reliability of perception, say, or memory? Not only does Wittgenstein have little to say on this topic—a lacuna in his thinking—he shows signs of questioning whether generic reliability-knowledge is important at all. Thus:

> 34. If someone is taught to calculate, is he also taught that he can rely on a calculation of his teacher's? But these explanations must after all sometimes come to an end. Will he also be taught that he can trust his senses—since he is indeed told in many cases that in such and such a special case you cannot trust them?
>   Rule and exception.

Now we already know that the extent to which judgments can be challenged is heavily restricted by intelligibility constraints. If you don't get lots of things right, you won't have any beliefs at all. Calculating correctly, in elementary cases, is a possession-condition for numerical concepts; a reliable recognitional capacity is a possession-condition for a concept in its observational use, though these are enabling conditions, rather than things that could be straightforwardly appealed to in ordinary contexts of justification. However, if this is all we say, we are left with a version of externalism, albeit with a semantic spin. This will make contextualism implausible to those who think—as I do—that internalist intuitions cannot simply be dismissed.

Contextualists can say more. If we think that justification conforms to a default and challenge structure, we must hold that knowing how we can mis-perceive our situation is an essential ingredient in knowing how perceptually based beliefs can legitimately be challenged, and what we have to do to meet such challenges. Indeed, we can think of this as itself an essential ingredient in the mastery of the observational use of concepts. In this way, contextualism incorporates weak internalism. It also shows why much of the force of the rule derives from the exceptions: the exceptions do the essential conceptual-epistemic work. Knowledge of our reliability—particularly knowledge of its limits—can be essential, even though such knowledge does not always serve to authorize particular performances.

A further motive for countenancing basic observational (or experiential) beliefs is that we want observational evidence to carry special weight. Here is a second asymmetry principle: observation–theory asymmetry. Ultimately, theory should be answerable to observation in a way that observation is not answerable to theory. Reliability-knowledge is the key to meeting this requirement. Well-entrenched beliefs about the reliability of basic information-sources increase the epistemic weight of beliefs arising from them. We can't ride rough-shod over the evidence derived from such sources without calling into question what we have already found to be essential reliability-presuppositions. But it does not follow from this that beliefs deriving from such sources are always implicitly *justified* by reliability-commitments.

While much more could be said on this topic, I hope that I have said enough to explain how reliability-knowledge concerning basic information-sources can be epistemically vital, without that knowledge functioning to ground *ultimate* source-principles. On the view I am suggesting, questions about the reliability of sources cannot be decided independently of substantive knowledge about ourselves and the world. Reliability-principles, with respect to such information sources as observation, are fact-dependent; and the facts in question are not "purely epistemological." There are questions about *what* is observable. These can be world-directed, in that they concern whether there is anything to be observed. An example would be whether "true" motions are observable, a question that divided Galileo and his Aristotelian critics and that cannot be decided independently of physics. But questions about what is observable can also be observer-directed. People with special training (birdwatchers, say) can spot at a glance things that non-specialists have to identify by consciously applying simpler criteria (checking size, markings, etc. and consulting a field guide). Further, there are questions about how reliable observation is with respect to particular things and circumstances. Naturally, there can be individual variation here: think of the "personal equation" for astronomers, which takes account of differences in reaction time. Our knowledge of the extent and reliability of observation is indefinitely refinable.

Let me sum up the crucial features of the contextualist conception of justification just sketched.

(i) The skeptic's assumption of claimant–challenger asymmetry is false. Claimants and challengers are both subject to justificatory burdens. Who has it depends on contextually variable factors. This point alone derails the traditional threat of an infinite regress of justification.

(ii) Justification, in the sense of "being justified," does not always require positive authorization. One can be justified in accepting a proposition if there is no serious reason not to accept it: one does not have to be able to justify it. This is not to say that, in claiming knowledge or justified belief, one has *no* burden of justification. The point is rather that one does not acquire such a burden *merely* by taking oneself to be justified. Rather, one must know how to recognize and to respond to legitimate challenges *when they arise*. Accordingly, justification, in the special form of giving reasons, takes place at the margins. It is an essentially local undertaking.

(iii) Factors that *explain* why it is that we are often entitled to hold particular beliefs need not be factors that justify or even could justify your holding those beliefs: certainly not to a determined skeptic. The explanation for why beliefs of a certain kind tend to be true may be no more certain than the beliefs in question, and may well be less so.

(iv) "Epistemic systems" involve much more than generic source and distribution principles. Standing certainties and contextually fixed commitments encompass not just general epistemic principles, or beliefs validated by them, but a wide array of particular, factual commitments. "We use judgments as principles of judgment."[10]

(v) There are indeed generic sources of justified beliefs—observation, memory, and so on—and it is important that they be reliable. Indeed, it is important that we know something about their reliability, thus satisfying Weak Internalism. But the role of reliability-knowledge in our epistemic economy is not always that of authorizing particular beliefs.

(vi) Generic source-principles are not *ultimate* but rather empirical and open to revision. Moreover, they are essentially incomplete. We learn their limits in particular cases: mirages, funny lighting, and so on. There is no recipe for identifying in advance all the error-possibilities we may eventually need to allow for.

(vii) There is no fixed observational vocabulary, adequate to resolve all significant questions, of the sort envisaged by traditional foundationalism. Nor is there an invariant, content-related order of epistemic priority. What is properly used to test what varies with our interests, the dialectical environment and our real-world circumstances. There are no fundamental epistemic kinds.

(viii) The massive background of beliefs, recognitional capacities, investigational procedures, etc., which is required for playing the game of justification must be acquired through education and training. Even then, what we can personally discover or verify is extremely limited. Most justification depends on deference. Knowledge is an essentially social achievement. This implies that what is taken to be common knowledge is culturally variable.

(ix) Epistemic justification is not theoretically tractable. We can describe, in a general way, the factors that determine our epistemic entitlements. However, we cannot do so in a way that permits the formulation of general rules or criteria for effectively sorting out justified from unjustified beliefs. "Justified" lies somewhere between "acidic" and "happens on Tuesday." Contextualism about knowledge and justification is more descriptive (phenomenological, in Heidegger's sense) than it is theoretical. But although it rejects what I call "epistemological realism," in another sense of "realistic" it is much more realistic than traditional foundationalism. Contextualism takes its cue from epistemic practices as we find them, rather than from a purely theoretical threat of skepticism.

(x) What makes contextualism's dismissal of "ultimate" principles and theoretical tractability innocuous is its *comprehensive fallibilism*. Epistemic systems are as open to correction as anything else.

5. It should be clear that contextualism does not encourage epistemic relativism. Epistemic relativism depends on the idea that ultimate source

principles cannot be justified in a non-circular way. The main thrust of contextualism is to deny that justification depends on such principles in anything like the simple way that the skeptical-relativist argument requires. "Epistemic systems" are more complex, variable and fact-dependent than the fundamental relativist argument supposes. Neither is justification as straightforwardly system-dependent as the relativist imagines. (For the contextualist, these points are really the same point, differently stated.) So while the relativist suggests that an epistemic system (composed of source and distribution principles) either undermines itself, and is thus incoherent, or offers only question-begging self-support, the contextualist replies that the dilemma is false. Self-support (of the kind envisaged) is not needed, and self-undermining is not incoherence but the occasion for revising our epistemic procedures or standards.

This said, contextualism is easily misunderstood in ways that encourage the charge of relativism.

One mistake is to rigidify the idea of context. For example, Robert Fogelin objects to contextualism that I may concede that a person is justified in reaching a certain conclusion, given the "epistemic framework" he is operating in, but deny that he is justified *simpliciter*. For example, I may object to his framework: perhaps he is using astrological tables.[11] But no contextualist denies this. As we have seen, epistemic procedures are as open to challenge as anything else. Methodological presuppositions do not create hermetically sealed disciplines. On the contrary, results from one discipline can influence work in another. The evaluation and authentication of historical documents profits from the development of carbon-dating. Indeed, Fogelin's own example—astrology—makes the point. What undermined belief in astrology was not so much empirical problems arising within the framework—failed predictions can always be explained away, at least to the satisfaction of true believers—but a new conception of the physical universe, which made the astrologer's geocentric world of stellar and planetary influences hard even to take seriously. Belief in witchcraft suffered a similar fate: a mechanical world just seemed to have no place for it. Of course, the physical ideas that turned astrology and witchcraft into superstitions were themselves open to refinement and even fundamentally revised or abandoned. But this is the open-endedness of inquiry, not the traditional regress of justification. To sum up, justificatory frameworks (if we are to use this language at all)—precisely because of their factual commitments—are essentially penetrable. They can be discredited from without as well as from within. Fogelin's criticism misses the point that contextualists not only can but must be as fallibilist about epistemic frameworks as they are about beliefs in general. For contextualists, there is no sharp line between epistemic and factual commitments, and so no clear boundary between methodological propositions and propositions within a method. Fogelin's criticism equates the contextualist's revisable methodological presuppositions with the relativist's ultimate principles.

A second source of misplaced charges of relativism is the recognition, on the part of contextualists, that what is taken to be common knowledge is to some extent culturally variable. For semantic reasons, human beings can never *wholly* lack common ground, or even common epistemic procedures. But while we all use our eyes and ears and share discriminative capacities, not everything that we would take to be common knowledge is something that every rational person would be bound to accept. Since we use judgments as principles of judgment, and since our epistemic beliefs (about the reliability of various sources of information) are heavily fact-committed, if we assign either kind of element in the epistemic systems of different groups to the culturally variable segment of supposed "common knowledge," we seem to concede the cultural relativity of epistemic systems.

I do not think that we do. It is one thing to admit that, in any given situation, there may be limits to our *powers of argument* or persuasion. It is something else entirely to assert that all ways of viewing the world are equally valid, or that all epistemic procedures are equally reliable. No route leads from the first claim to the second.

Foundationalists have tended to think otherwise. According to traditional foundationalism, all justification depends on fundamental source and distribution principles that are constitutive of our human epistemic condition. So given sufficient time and good will, anyone can rationally be convinced of anything that is itself rationally justifiable. For a contextualist, this is one of foundationalism's great illusions. What we can argue for depends on rich commitments about the world around us. This means that individuals and groups can vary widely in their epistemic resources. Accordingly, whether you can convince another person by argument depends on how much common ground there is between you. However, these limitations are contingent and variable: they do not reflect imprisonment in permanently incommensurable world-views.

Wittgenstein is sensitive to this point. Writing before space-flight, and thinking of Moore's assurance that he knows that neither he nor anyone else has ever been very far from the surface of the Earth, Wittgenstein wonders:

106. Suppose some adult had told a child that he had been on the moon. The child tells me the story, and I say it was only a joke, the man hadn't been on the moon; no one has ever been on the moon; the moon is a long way off and it is impossible to climb up there or fly there.—If the child now insists, saying perhaps there is a way of getting there which I don't know, etc. what reply could I make to him? What reply could I make to the adults of a tribe who believe that people sometimes go to the moon (perhaps that is how they inter-pret their dreams), and who indeed grant that there are no ordinary means of climbing up to it or flying there?—But a child will not ordinarily stick to such a belief and will soon be convinced by what we tell him seriously.

This prompts a question from Wittgenstein's interlocutor:

108. "But is there then no objective truth? Isn't it true, or false, that someone has been on the moon?" If we are thinking within our system, then it is certain that no one has ever been on the moon. Not merely is nothing of the sort ever reported to us by reasonable people, but our whole system of physics forbids us to believe it. For this demands answers to the questions "How did he overcome the force of gravity?" "How could he live without an atmosphere?" and a thousand others which could not be answered. But suppose that instead of all these answers we met the reply "We don't know how one gets to the moon, but those who get there know at once that they are there; and even you can't explain everything." We should feel ourselves intellectually very distant from someone who said this.

For us, physics is a potent source of standing objections to the claims of the moon-visitors. The presence of such objections is a prominent feature of the dialectical environment. If people simply refuse to recognize the force of such questions—turning aside specific challenges with a bland, all-purpose epistemic response ("Even you don't know everything"), there is no arguing with them. This is a fact of life. But it imposes no obligation to accept equal validity. Wittgenstein again:

286. What we believe depends on what we learn. We all believe that it isn't possible to get to the moon; but there might be people who believe that it is possible and that it sometimes

happens. We say: these people do not know a lot that we know. And, let them be never so sure of their belief—they are wrong and we know it.

If we compare our system of knowledge with theirs then theirs is evidently the poorer one by far.

But to get them to see this, or even to appreciate the force of our doubts, we should have to teach them physics—*teach*, not argue with them—which means that they would have to be willing to learn. They might not be, in which case we would be stuck. This is what Wittgenstein is getting at when he asks:

608. Is it wrong for me to be guided in my actions by the propositions of physics? Am I to say I have no good ground for doing so? Isn't this precisely what we call a "good ground"?
609. Supposing we met people who did not regard that as a telling reason. Now, how do we imagine this? Instead of the physicist they consult an oracle (and for that reason we consider them primitive). Is it wrong for them to consult an oracle and be guided by it?—If we call this "wrong" aren't we using our language-game as a base from which to *combat* theirs?
612. I said I would "combat" the other man—but wouldn't I give him *reasons*? Certainly; but how far do they go? At the end of reasons comes *persuasion*. (Think what happens when missionaries convert natives.)

If the persuasion works, and they learn some physics, they will probably stop believing that they go to the moon, or that they should consult oracles, without the need to be convinced by particular arguments (as Europeans lost their beliefs in astrology and witchcraft in the light of the Scientific Revolution). If we can't get them to listen, they will remain in their ignorant state.

While this may sound like cultural arrogance, the point in question should be uncontroversial. Switching for the moment from cultural to subjective relativism, would it show anything about the tenability of some arcane piece of theoretical physics that its proponents couldn't convince *me* to accept it? Of course not. Still, the objection will now be lodged "Ignorant according to whom?" Or "Who are you to say?" Contextualism may seem to invite such questions. Tellingly, a critic might note, Wittgenstein only observes that we will *say* that we know a lot that they don't; he doesn't say that we would be *definitely right*. That's true, but I don't think that Wittgenstein's reticence has anything to do with relativism. What it reflects is something that contextualists are committed to, namely, not expecting too much from epistemology. We can describe the language game, but we cannot provide it with the kind of "external" endorsement that makes our beliefs more secure than they are anyway. The best reasons for trusting physics come from physics itself. They don't get better for having a philosopher's *imprimatur*.

The point is worth pursuing. Here is another pregnant passage from Wittgenstein:

599. [O]ne could describe the certainty of the proposition that water boils at circa 100°C. That isn't e.g. a proposition I have once heard . . . I made the experiment myself at school. The proposition is a very elementary one in our textbooks, which are to be trusted in matters like this because . . .—Now one can offer counter-examples to all this, which show that human beings have held this or that to be certain which later, according to our opinion, proved false. But the argument is worthless. To say: in the end we can only adduce such grounds as *we* hold to be grounds, is to say nothing at all.

I believe that at the bottom of this is a misunderstanding of the nature of our language-games.

The argument under review is that, since we have gone wrong in the past, we have no reason to suppose that we are any better placed now. A relativist could make this the basis of an equal validity claim: we can only offer such grounds as we hold to be grounds; and anyone else can do as much. But the argument amounts to an attempt to move from fallibilism (I might be wrong) to skepticism (I am not entitled to suppose that I am right). The argument is fallacious and will seem in order only if one is already willing to concede the principle of claimant–challenger asymmetry. With that principle in place, the mere possibility of error places the burden of justification on the claimant. Any attempt to discharge it will eventually run into commitments that not all groups share (grounds that *we* hold to be grounds), at which point the skeptic remarks that one dogma is as good as another. But that is not how justification works or even could work. Default-justified beliefs are neither *mere* assumptions nor dogmatic commitments: many are revisable. With enough stage-setting, perhaps all are. Detached from the skeptic's contentious presuppositions, all the argument for epistemic relativism comes to is that in inquiring, arguing, justifying, etc., we work with whatever beliefs and techniques we currently have on hand; and to say that really is to say nothing at all. It is like saying you are always where you happen to be.

We have worked our way back to our recurrent theme: the limits (and limited utility) of epistemological theorizing. Contextualists think that we simply have to live with a modest level of epistemic self-understanding. They also think that the sort of modest understanding that the subject matter allows shows that there is no passage from a general understanding of epistemic justification to a method for resolving disputes. As a rule, when people's beliefs differ profoundly, there is no guarantee that there will be neutral epistemic principles adequate for determining who is right and who is wrong. To be sure, human beings can never lack altogether for common ground. However—and this is hardly surprising—the issues that divide them most seriously are those that common knowledge does not easily resolve. This doesn't mean that such questions cannot in principle be decided. It does not even mean that they cannot be decided to the satisfaction of all parties. Where common ground does not exist, we can look for it. Or perhaps we will stumble across it while looking for something else. Who knows? Only relativists think of different groups as locked into different, fundamental epistemic systems. But resolving deep differences of opinion depends on ingenuity and luck: epistemology cannot offer guarantees. So while, unlike relativists, contextualists don't make equal validity claims, they don't say that all disputes are in principle rationally resolvable either. They think that resolvability is a contingent matter. We never know what we might find out, or think up, such that parties to even the most intractable dispute suddenly see matters in a new light.[12] Thus whereas traditional foundationalism sees the problem of justification as the key to the problem of method, contextualism suggests that they should be decoupled or, rather, that there is no such thing as method; there are only methods, which change with our understanding of the world and ourselves.

Notes

1   An earlier version of this paper was presented at a Symposium on Epistemic Relativism, APA Central Division meeting 2006. My co-symposiast was Paul Boghossian.

2   Annis (1978). The name may be unfortunate, since "contextualism" is now widely used to designate a different (though not entirely unrelated) epistemological view concerning the truth conditions for attributions of knowledge. My kind of contextualism is sometimes called "issue contextualism" to distinguish it from contextualism of the other kind. But lacking a better name, I am going to continue to call my view "contextual-

ism." Readers can take "issue" as understood. For a brief statement of my view, see Williams (1999). For more detailed treatments, see Williams (1996, 2001).

3 In Kim and Sosa (2000), selections from *Unnatural Doubts* (Williams 1996) appear in the section "Epistemological Relativism."

4 Quotations in the text are identified by paragraph number.

5 This doesn't beg any questions, since I am placing no undue restrictions on the factors that may be relevant to justification. In particular, I am not suggesting that justification always involves having reasons or being able to produce evidence. Justification is a matter of positive epistemic status, whatever that is and however it is acquired. Since knowledge is by definition an epistemically positive state, knowing implies being justified. This terminological convention is compatible with pure externalism. I focus on justification for two reasons: to avoid getting entangled in Gettierology and (knowledge being factive) to avoid as far as possible discussing relativism with respect to truth.

6 For more on foundationalism, particularly the idea of basic beliefs, see my exchange with James Pryor in Steup and Sosa (2005, ch. 7).

7 Chisholm (1982). See, for example, ch. 5.

8 The example is Jerry Fodor's, but I cannot recall where he gives it.

9 Brandom (1995, ch. 4).

10 Wittgenstein (1969, para.124).

11 Fogelin (1994, pp. 95–8).

12 Paul Boghossian takes Richard Rorty to task for suggesting that there was no way of saying that, in condemning Galileo, Cardinal Bellarmine was "unscientific" in taking scriptural texts to be relevant to the acceptability of the Copernican system. First, I think that Boghossian is a bit hard on Bellarmine. Bellarmine did not object to Galileo's teaching the Copernican hypothesis as a hypothesis: the objection was to his teaching it as a truth. He did not think that scriptural evidence trumped scientific evidence: on the contrary, he held that God has given us Reason as a way of coming to understand the world around us, so that if Reason led decisively to the conclusion that the Earth was in motion (which was the crux of the dispute), scripture would have to be re-interpreted. But

being acutely concerned with the authority of the Church, he held that the verdict of Reason had to be truly decisive. Quite rightly, he thought that Galileo had failed to make his case. Galileo had no dynamical theory that would make sense of the motion of the Earth. His argument from the tides was inconsistent with his own principle of relativity. The telescopic evidence settled nothing, for even if the Ptolemaic system had to be abandoned, there was still the Tychonic alternative, which reserved the Earth at rest. Neither Bellarmine nor Galileo could have forseen the Newtonian synthesis, which led the Church to change its position. Indeed, Galileo was unsympathetic to ideas that turned out to be crucial to getting the Copernican system to work. Most notably, he remained under the spell of the naturalness of circular motion. He seems never to have appreciated Kepler and did not take seriously the possibility of elliptical orbits. He also tried to account for the apparent straight-line descent of a heavy object dropped from a tower by postulating something like a principle of *circular* inertia. (I say "something like" because it is not clear how general the principle is supposed to be. Galileo certainly knew that, if I twirl a weight on the end of a string and let go of the string, the weight flies off at a tangent and does not continue going round and round. It seems that the Earth is still playing an important role in fixing what motions are "natural.") Considering the Galileo case, Rorty writes:

> the conclusion I wish to draw is that the "grid" which emerged in the later seventeenth and eighteenth centuries was not there to be appealed to in the early seventeenth century, at the time that Galileo was on trial. No conceivable epistemology, no study of the nature of human knowledge, could have "discovered" it before it was hammered out. The notion of what it was to be scientific was in the process of being formed. If one endorses the values—or perhaps the ranking of competing values—common to Galileo and Kant, then indeed Bellarmine was being "unscientific." But of course, almost all of us . . . are happy to endorse them.

> (Rorty 1979, 330)

Boghossian thinks that Rorty is advocating relativism. I don't. So while I find things to criticize in this passage, they aren't the same things. First, Bellarmine was well aware that his reluctance to re-interpret scripture to suit every fashionable speculation on the part of some natural philosopher was guided by more than narrowly "scientific" considerations. Second, as indicated above, I think that Bellarmine was right in thinking that Galileo's scientific arguments were less compelling than Galileo liked to suppose. Third, I don't think that what settled the dispute was a new set, or ranking, of epistemic values (or standards): that sounds way too like a criterial conception of justification to me; and this is the very conception that encourages relativism. But all that said, Rorty has a good point about epistemology. What eventually vindicated Galileo were developments in physics, thus neither highly general considerations about the nature of human knowledge nor a new set of "values." After all, the Church reconciled itself to Copernicanism, without changing its views on either Reason or Scripture. For Rorty's discussion of Galileo, see Rorty (1979, ch. 7). For Boghossian's discussion of Rorty (and also Wittgenstein), see Boghossian (2006, ch. 5). He attacks their alleged relativism in ch. 6.

References

Annis, David. 1978. "A Contextualist Theory of Epistemic Justification." *American Philosophical Quarterly* 15: 213–219.

Boghossian, Paul. 2006. *Fear of Knowledge*. Oxford: Oxford University Press.

Brandom, Robert. 1995. *Making It Explicit*. Cambridge, MA: Harvard University Press.

Chisholm, Roderick. 1982. *The Foundations of Knowing*. Minneapolis: University of Minnesota Press.

Fogelin, Robert. 1994. *Pyrrhonian Reflections on Knowledge and Justification*. Oxford: Oxford University Press.

Kim, Jaegwon and Ernest Sosa. 2000. *Epistemology: An Anthology*. Oxford: Blackwell.

Rorty, Richard. 1979. *Philosophy and the Mirror of Nature*. Princeton: Princeton University Press.

Steup, Matthias and Ernest Sosa. 2005. *Contemporary Debates in Epistemology*. Oxford: Blackwell.

Williams, Michael. 1996. *Unnatural Doubts*. Princeton: Princeton University Press.

Williams, Michael. 1999. "Skepticism." Pp. 35–69 in *A Companion to Epistemology*, ed. John Greco and Ernest Sosa, Oxford: Blackwell.

Williams, Michael. 2001. *Problems of Knowledge*. Oxford: Oxford University Press.

Wittgenstein, Ludwig. 1969. *On Certainty*, trans. Denis Paul and G. E. M. Anscombe. New York: Harper.

Index

Related titles from Routledge

What is this thing called Knowledge?

Duncan Pritchard

What is Knowledge? Where does it come from? Can we know anything at all?

This lucid and engaging introduction grapples with these central questions in the theory of knowledge, offering a clear, non-partisan view of the main themes of epistemology including recent developments such as virtue epistemology and contextualism.

Duncan Pritchard discusses both traditional issues and contemporary ideas in thirteen easily digestible sections which include:

- the value of knowledge
- the structure of knowledge
- virtues and faculties
- perception
- testimony and memory
- induction
- scepticism.

What is this thing called Knowledge? contains many helpful student-friendly features. Each chapter concludes with a useful summary of the main ideas discussed, study questions, annotated further reading, and a guide to web resources. Text-boxes provide bite-sized summaries of key concepts and major philosophers, and clear and interesting examples are used throughout, whilst a helpful glossary explains important terms. This is an ideal first textbook in the theory of knowledge for undergraduates taking a first course in philosophy.

ISBN 13 hbk 978–0–415–38797–2
ISBN 13 pbk 978–0–415–38798–9

Available at all good bookshops
For ordering and further information please visit:
www.routledge.com

Related titles from Routledge

What is this thing called Metaphysics?

Brian Garrett

Why is there something rather than nothing? Does god exist? Who am I?

Metaphysics is concerned with ourselves and reality, and the most fundamental questions regarding existence. This clear and accessible introduction covers the central topics in Metaphysics in a concise but comprehensive way.

Brian Garrett discusses the crucial concepts in a highly readable manner, easing the reader in with a look at paradoxes that aptly illustrate some important philosophical problems. He then goes on to address key areas of metaphysics:

- existence and modality
- causation
- God
- time
- universals
- personal identity
- truth.

What is this thing called Metaphysics? contains many helpful student-friendly features. Each chapter concludes with a useful summary of the main ideas discussed, a glossary of important terms, study questions, annotated further reading, and a guide to web resources. Text-boxes provide bite-sized summaries of key concepts and major philosophers, and clear and interesting examples are used throughout.

ISBN 13 hbk 978–0–415–39391–1
ISBN 13 pbk 978–0–415–39392–8

Related titles from Routledge

Epistemology 2nd edition

Robert Audi

'No less than one would expect from a first-rate epistemologist who is also a master expositor: lucid, comprehensive, well-structured, and excellently informed both by the tradition and by recent developments. A superb introduction.'

Ernest Sosa, Brown University

'A state-of-the-art introduction to epistemology by one of the leading figures in the field.'

William Alston, Syracuse University

'Impressively up-to-date.'

Dr T.J. Diffey, University of Sussex

'An excellent book. It is comprehensive in scope and very systematically organised. Its most impressive quality is the balance it achieves between argumentative complexity and simplicity of exposition.'

Philosophical Books

Epistemology, or the theory of knowledge, is concerned with how we know what we do, what justifies us in believing what we do, and what standards of evidence we should use in seeking truths about the world and human experience. This comprehensive book introduces the concepts and theories central for understanding knowledge. It aims to reach students who have already done an introductory philosophy course.

This revised edition builds on the topics covered by the hugely successful and widely read first edition. It includes new material on subjects such as virtue epistemology, feminist epistemology and social epistemology. The chapter on moral, scientific and religious knowledge has also been expanded and revised. Robert Audi's style is exceptionally clear and highly accessible for anyone coming to the subject for the first time.

ISBN 13 hbk 978–0–415–28108–9
ISBN 13 pbk 978–0–415–28109–6

Available at all good bookshops
For ordering and further information please visit:

www.routledge.com

Made in the USA
Las Vegas, NV
03 January 2023

64852847R10334